1986

KARL JASPERS

BASIC PHILOSOPHICAL
WRITINGS

KARL JASPERS

BASIC PHILOSOPHICAL WRITINGS

— SELECTIONS —

Edited, translated, with
introductions by

EDITH EHRLICH
LEONARD H. EHRLICH
GEORGE B. PEPPER

OHIO UNIVERSITY PRESS
ATHENS, OHIO
LONDON

Library of Congress Cataloging-in-Publication Data

Jaspers, Karl, 1883-1969.

   Karl Jaspers : basic philosophical writings.

   Bibliography: p.

   1. Philosophy—Addresses, essays, lectures.   I. Ehrlich, Edith.
II. Ehrlich, Leonard H.   III. Pepper, George B.   IV. Title.
B3279.J32E5   1986   193   85-25945
ISBN 0-8214-0712-0
ISBN 0-8214-0713-9 (pbk.)

KARL JASPERS

1883–1969

In 1983 several international societies and congresses ran special programs commemorating the centenary of Jaspers's birth and acknowledging his important contribution to philosophy. The editors want their efforts in preparing this book to be taken as their contribution to this commemoration and acknowledgment.

Contents

Part Four

WHAT IS TRUTH?

Part Five

PHILOSOPHY:

DISTINCTIONS AND RELATIONS

Part Six

TESTIMONY OF COMMUNICATION

Part Seven

ENCOUNTERS WITH LIMIT SITUATIONS

BIBLIOGRAPHY

Preface

WHY THIS BOOK?—Jaspers is one of the most original and potentially one of the most seminal thinkers of the twentieth century. His thinking is rich in ideas, far-ranging in its explorations, complex in structure, varied in application, and vast in scope. It is distributed over many publications which vary in size and content. With a few significant exceptions, the majority of Jaspers's most important works are available in English translation. However, it is precisely the size and complexity of Jaspers's output which tend to make Jaspers inaccessible even though a succession of secondary literature on Jaspers has helped in advancing scholarship and arousing interest in Jaspers. Therefore it has long been felt by colleagues on both sides of the Atlantic that the corpus of translations and of books on Jaspers had to be supplemented by a guided introduction to the scope and content of Jaspers's writings. This, then, is the reason for this book.

THE SCOPE AND LIMITS OF THIS BOOK—The present book is not the first compilation of selected writings by Jaspers. It was preceded by *La mia filosofia* (1945), edited by Renato de Rosa and Norberto Bobbio, and *Karl Jaspers: Was ist Philosophie?* (1975), edited by Hans Saner. However, this book is the first one that endeavors, by means of a systematic organization of selected excerpts from various writings, to give the interested reader an insight into the wide scope of Jaspers's philosophical achievement. An attempt to present such selections from the work of a thinker as productive and far-ranging as Jaspers runs risks and makes compromises. The main risk consists in presenting, in Jaspers's own words, what is not Jaspers but an interpretive construction on the part of the editors: the excerpts are, after all, taken out of their contexts and placed within a topical matrix that, no matter how strongly suggested by the author, is forced on him. (De Rosa/Bobbio and Saner avoided this risk by including in their respective editions only self-integral essays and short works and by refraining from arranging them in accordance with substantive topics.) The main compromise was imposed by the limits of space: out of all the material that we judged to be the most desirable we had to choose what to include and what to leave out, fully aware of good reasons for making a different choice. Thus, even though inclusions and omissions as well as the structure by which the selections have been organized may occasion criticism, it was the editors' aim to convey a reasonably accurate presentation of the content and movement of Jaspers's philosophizing to the kinds of readers whom we hope this book will find:

One is the relatively uninformed reader, whether academic or layman, who is interested in becoming acquainted with Jaspers directly without (or prior

to) wading through the mass of available translations and secondary literature. Another is the student, undergraduate or graduate, whose introduction
to and outlook on Jaspers may decisively depend on this book. A third kind of
reader is the teacher who, in teaching Jaspers, may wish to use the guidance
which a plausibly designed Jaspers-Reader would provide. And finally, there
is the informed and critical reader who may wish to gain a new perspective on
Jaspers through the interpretation that is unavoidably implicit in a book of
selections.

The editors will consider this collection of readings to be a success if it
motivates the reader to give the writings of Jaspers, individually and collectively, the attention they deserve.

TRANSLATING JASPERS—In the translations and emendations the editors have aimed at achieving the greatest fidelity possible both to the thought
and to the language of Karl Jaspers in order that he emerge as the human
being paradigmatic of his philosophy. It is erroneous to believe—or to
expect—that thoughts leading us to the very brink of what is thinkable can be
expressed and understood without considerable effort. Jaspers is not easy
reading, neither in German nor in English. Masterful as was his command of
the language and committed as he was to expressing his thoughts in the most
precise and limpid terms, he would never have sacrificed, in his writings or in
conversation, the breadth and depth of what he meant to say to facile and
hence more easily understood formulations. Thus, if, in translating Jaspers,
one were to attempt to make him more accessible by cosmetic surgery, one
would land in doubtful interpretation, approximation and, ultimately, misunderstanding. This would do injustice to the author and especially to the readers who would lose out on mastering one of the original and liberating minds
of the twentieth century. Therefore faithfulness to Jaspers's expression has
controlled the translation effort even when more felicitous constructions
would seem desirable.

THE ORGANIZATION OF THIS BOOK—The seventy-four selections
included are organized systematically in seven parts as well as consecutively
numbered, as can be seen in the Table of Contents. Each selection, as well as
each part and subpart, is preceded by an editors' introduction which provides a
guide to the import of the selection and a reference to sources. About forty
percent of the book appears here in translation for the first time, in particular
the essay on greatness in philosophy (selection 30), the writings on periechontology (16–27), most of the subpart on truth (35–42), the sections on
Heidegger, Arendt and Gertrud Jaspers, and all of Part VII. One-third of the
book is selected from *Von der Wahrheit*, which has not appeared in English
translation. Most of the selections from previous translations have been retranslated, the rest have been emended by the editors, primarily for the sake of
consistency in style, tone, interpretation and expression.

Acknowledgments

The editors express their appreciation for permissions to reprint selections from Jaspers's works in original or in emended translation, graciously extended by the following persons and publishing houses: Hans Saner (Basel) as the successor to the rights to all works by Karl Jaspers published by R. Piper & Co. Verlag (Munich, Zurich); Springer Verlag (Berlin, Heidelberg, New York); The University of Chicago Press; Regnery Gateway, Inc. (Chicago); University of Pennsylvania Press; Doubleday & Company Inc. (New York). Acknowledgment for permission is also to be found in the editors' introduction to each selection in the form of a reference to the source of the selection and, where appropriate, to its previous published translation.

Our colleague Richard Wisser (Mainz) has taken extraordinary interest in the project and has given unstintingly of his time and effort without which the editors' work would not have reached fruition. The editors take pleasure in recording their appreciation of his contribution.

The advice and encouragement of many other colleagues proved to be indispensable and are deeply appreciated. We would like to note our debt to Paul Arthur Schilpp (Southern Illinois), John R. Silber (Boston), Charles F. Wallraff (Arizona), Oswald O. Schrag (Fisk), James Collins (St. Louis), Sebastian Samay (St. Vincent), Elisabeth Young-Bruehl (Wesleyan), the late Richard F. Grabau, Jeanne Hersch (Geneva), Hans Saner (Basel), Adolf Lichtigfeld (Johannesburg), and Jaspers's nephew, the late Enno Dugend. A noteworthy by-product of our contact with colleagues regarding this book was the establishment, in 1980, of the Jaspers Society of North America.

The University of Massachusetts/Amherst and Iona College provided clerical and other support services, as well as released time from teaching duties for work on this project. Particular recognition is extended to Susan Holden, Lilyann Porter, Margaret Nash and Donald Schneier for their contributions in preparing the manuscript.

Lester Embree (Duquesne) is to be credited for the initiative he took in having this volume included in the Series in Continental Thought.

Leonard H. Ehrlich,	Edith Ehrlich,	George B. Pepper,
University of Massachusetts	Hadley, Massachusetts	Iona College
at Amherst		

February 23, 1983

Part One

THE OPEN HORIZON

EDITOR'S INTRODUCTION TO PART ONE:

What is the origin and aim of human existence? What is Truth—the truth that binds me to my fellow humans, the truth that grounds knowledge and its pursuit, the truth that justifies my living and action? The search for clear answers to such questions constitutes philosophical activity for Jaspers. Inasmuch as these questions arise at the limits of what can be known with scientific objectivity and certainty, philosophy is an activity more fundamental than scientific cognition. It is, however, only with a clear understanding of the limits of scientific cognition that these questions can be appropriately raised for philosophy. Only then can philosophy seek forms of clarity that are fitting for the questions it faces.

But what systematic clarity is appropriate to philosophy? Unlike science, philosophical thought is not tied to a publicly discernible and definable subject matter, to the constraint of intersubjectively repeatable research-procedures with their apparatus of presuppositions, rules of evidence, methods of validation, and to a progressively changing corpus of results. On the other hand, again unlike science, the truth concerning a philosophical question does not depend on the method of establishing it any more than on who believes it and whether and how it is testified to. Moreover, the next person or a tradition other than one's own may have an answer to a philosophical question different and even incompatible with one's own. This other answer may be a matter of indifference until it poses a threat or a challenge to oneself. Thus in addition to the sort of philosophical questions mentioned, at first we must ask how philosophy is possible at all, and what the meaning of philosophical truth is.

What is necessary, then, for philosophical thought to be carried out, and for thinkers to meet, is to clear the space in which such thought can take place and move freely. At the same time, in our attainment of a dimension where thought can move freely from the discipline of one vision of truth to another, we need not and must not fail to see that significant thought requires specific disciplines, even as we need not and must not fail in our loyalty to our own vision of truth. According to Jaspers, philosophical activity in a full and proper sense is and has always been carried out in such a dimension of freely moving thought. For him the attainment of this dimension is a distinct and decisive step, and fundamental for philosophical thought. Jaspers regards it as a pivotal task of his philosophy to undertake the step of attaining this "open horizon" deliberately, and to carry out his thinking within it. Accordingly the first part of this Jaspers-Reader consists of excerpts that elucidate this step. Jaspers speaks of it as the "basic philosophic operation." With reference to this operation Wisser, a writer on Jaspers, speaks of him as having "thought himself free."

Jaspers's "basic philosophic operation" had its antecedents in his earlier work as a scientist and in the influence which Kant had on his thinking. All this is reflected in the following selections. The first set of selections, under the title "Origins in Scientific Research," show how what in his most mature philosophy was worked out as the "basic philosophic operation" was effectively operative in the scientific work he previously did in psychopathology. The second set, "Philosophical Foundations," presents Jaspers's explicit elaboration of the basic philosophic operation.

I

Origins in Scientific Research

Selection 1

AN AUTOBIOGRAPHICAL ACCOUNT

EDITORS:

In the following selection Jaspers gives an autobiographical account of how he came to work out and apply his idea of methodological pluralism. In his youth he pursued a career in psychopathology because he thought this to be the only branch of medicine in which his debilitating, chronic illness would allow him a full career: the "drawbacks of my position" which he mentions at the beginning of the selection refer to his illness. He describes here the diversity and the confusion of methodological dogmatism which he perceived as prevailing in psychiatry at the beginning of the twentieth century. With his philosophical bent Jaspers set to defining the nature, the reach, and the use of different approaches to psychological reality, and to promote some order among them. In the process he also adapted and introduced into psychological research Husserl's phenomenology and Dilthey's methodology; the latter Jaspers called *Verstehen*. The foundation that made this movement possible from one to another defined mode of methodical research is expressed by Jaspers in the proposition that "man is always more than he knows, and can know, about himself."

The selection is taken from the "Philosophical Memoir" which Jaspers originally contributed to *The Library of Living Philosophers,* Vol. IX, *Karl Jaspers,* edited by Paul Arthur Schilpp. The Memoir was retranslated by E.B. Ashton for Jaspers's *Philosophy and the World: Selected Essays and Lectures.* This excerpt is a slightly emended version of pp. 206–214 of the latter edition.

TEXT:

Even without the regular daily practice of an assistant, I had access to the entire experience of a psychiatrist. . . . The drawbacks of my position turned into advantages. I could see and explore everything without being limited in time by routine duties. . . .

The common intellectual basis of the hospital was Kraepelin's psychiatry, with modifications leading to a stock of concepts and views which no individual could claim to have originated. A prevailing idea, for instance, was the polarity of the two broad spheres of dementia praecox (later called schizophrenia) and the manic-depressive disorders. . . .

In the psychiatry of those days—about 1910—somatic medicine was still in control. Freud's influence was limited to small groups. Psychological efforts were considered subjective, futile, and unscientific, with the sole exception of the psychological tests which Kraepelin had introduced. . . .

Stagnation of scientific research and treatment was widely felt in German psychiatric hospitals. The great institutions for the insane kept growing more hygienic and imposing. The lives of these unfortunates, unchangeable in essence, were managed for them. . . .

In view of their own infinitesimal knowledge and skill, intelligent but intellectually sterile psychiatrists took refuge in skepticism and in the elegantly phrased hauteur of men of the world.

In Nissl's hospital, too, therapy was unambitious. At bottom, we were therapeutically hopeless but kind. . . . In dealing with the patients we were humane without pathos, cheerful and tolerant. "Psychiatric lenity" was deemed a matter of course, not only toward the patients but in life. . . .

All this I found when I came. Fascinated by each fact and method, I tried to absorb everything. . . . Often the same thing was said in other words, usually vague ones. Several schools had terminologies of their own. They seemed to be speaking different languages, and the divergencies extended to the jargon of each individual hospital. There seemed to be no common scientific psychiatry uniting all the workers in the field. At our regular staff meetings and demonstrations I sometimes felt we were constantly starting all over.

One cause of this intellectual jumble seemed to me to lie in the nature of the case. For the subject matter of psychiatry was man, not just his body—or indeed his body least of all, but his soul, his personality, his self. I read not only Griesinger's somatic dogma—that mental diseases were diseases of the brain—but Schüle's thesis that mental diseases were diseases of the personality. Our subject was also that of the *Geisteswissenschaften*. They had developed the same concepts, only far more subtly and distinctly. One day we were taking down utterances made in states of confusion or paranoid talk, and I told Nissl, "We must learn from the philologists." I started looking for what philosophy and psychology might have to offer us.

It was in this situation, in 1911, that Wilmanns and the publisher Ferdinand Springer asked me to write a "General Psychopathology." . . . Taken aback at first, I soon felt inspired or reckless enough to put at least the facts in order, and to boost my methodical consciousness as best I could. I felt supported by the spirit of the hospital and by our common stock of knowledge. In this circle it was really not difficult to write on general psychopathology. The task was long overdue. And I was commissioned to undertake it.

My own studies and reflections on what was being said and done in psychiatry had shown me ways that were new at the time. The impulses for two main steps came from philosophers.

As a method I adopted and retained Husserl's phenomenology—which he initially called "descriptive psychology"—discarding only its refinement to essence perception. It turned out to be possible and fruitful to describe the inner experiences of the sick as phenomena of consciousness. By the patient's own self-description, not only hallucinations but delusive experiences, modes of ego-consciousness and types of emotion could be defined well enough for positive recognition in other cases. Phenomenology became a research method.

The other influence was Dilthey's call for a psychology that would be "descriptive and analytical" rather than theoretically explicative. I accepted the challenge, termed the matter "the psychology of *Verstehen*," and worked out the procedures—long known in practice, and actually used by Freud in a manner peculiar to him—which let us comprehend the genetic links of the psyche, the motivations and relationships of meaning, as distinguished from immediately experienced phenomena. For these procedures I was seeking a methodical justification and a systematic arrangement. Along with the description of facts, an abundance of known but unorganized psychological rudiments seemed to me to be falling into place.

I am not going into . . . other methodological clarifications of matters of actual knowledge. One thing I should like to point out, however. In each area I fought what was mere talk without real knowledge, notably the "theories" which played so large a part in the psychiatrists' language. I showed that the psychological theories, even though drawn up in analogy to those of natural science, were never the same in kind. There could never be, in their case, a progressively evolving knowledge of some basic process governing all psychological phenomena. . . . Common research could not yield any discovery of proof or disproof in experience, in the ceaseless quest of counter-indications. For on this road there were, in fact, only metaphors—not implausible, perhaps, but possible in various ways, never quite right, never subject to radical proof. It was a mistake to look upon them as underlying realities. Yet what I tried to find in all thinking—eventually even in this theoretical thinking— was the element of positive value to science. My *Psychopathology* gave a systematic picture of the theories as means of describing analogically what would otherwise remain beyond our cognitive horizon. What mattered was to survey the possible images without succumbing to any of them. The theories chiefly prevailing at the time were those of Wernicke and Freud, both since forgotten. Even among psychoanalysts, the theory of Freud is today considered largely dated and no longer generally applicable.

Time and again, by one way or another, men thought they had found methods to comprehend man as a whole—in his constitution, in his character, in his type of body structure, in the clinical entity. These ways bore fruit in limited measure, but the supposed entirety always proved to be an entirety within the one comprehensive, never to be objectivized entirety of being human, never this entirety itself. For man as a whole lies beyond any comprehensible objectivation. He cannot be completed—not as a being for himself nor as an object of cognition for the scientist, not as an object of knowledge. He remains open, so to speak. Man is always more than he knows, and can know, of himself.

The scientific impulse for a full systematic treatment was to compile all these points of view. The goal was the conceptual clarification of what is known in psychopathology, how it is known, and what is not known. The basic idea of the critique was to realize the ways in which an explorable object manifests itself. This type of questioning came naturally to me at an early age. Asked about the structure of the spinal cord in my pre-clinical medical examination, I replied by citing the investigative methods and the several results of their use. The anatomist (Merkel of Göttingen) was surprised and praised me—which surprised me in turn.

A systematic treatment required that no . . . fundamentally distinct methodical approach, even if yielding only a minimum of knowledge, be omitted. Every approach to reality was to be made conscious, and thus to be kept open. But each one also was to be elucidated according to its presuppositions and its limits.

From the outset, therefore, I opposed schools insofar as they excluded anything, and went along with any as long as they evinced something real. A maximum of scientific openmindedness should be attempted in the field of psychopathology.

The principle of my book was, and remained, to unfold and organize knowledge along the lines of the methods used in obtaining it—to understand the act of cognition, and thereby to clarify the material.

Yet this meant at the same time that methodological inquiries were irrelevant unless the methods led to factual knowledge. As the old saying goes: poolside talk of swimming gets you nowhere; you have to jump into the water. My goal, therefore, was to keep my *Psychopathology* free of logical disquisitions in the abstract; they would be presented only if their meaning could be demonstrated in perceivable material of cognition. No method has value except by some real content—that is to say, by what it will let us observe. The basic empirical attitude of my book demanded that intuitability and factuality remain the conditions for acknowledging something to be psychopathological knowledge, yet the heterogeneousness of the factual was to be given its due. Facts and opinions do not lie on one level; they show themselves as essentially different, rather, by the variety of ways to approach them. My readers were not just to learn the subject matter; they were to learn to consider how, and within what limits, this subject matter might be deemed a matter of fact.

This principle of methodological reflection and arrangement seemed the more important since the object of psychiatry is man. What sets man apart from all things in the world is the fact that he as a whole can no more become an object than the world as a whole. When we know him, we know something about him rather than himself. Every total cognition of man turns out to be deceptive and comes into being by elevating one way of looking at things to the status of the only way, by elevating one method to the status of the universal method.

Our deliverance from a supposed total awareness lies in the principle of ascertaining the way of cognition by the consciousness of the specific method used. For the physician, the point is to keep his humanity by never losing his sense of the infinity of every single human being. This alone can safeguard the respect which a humane physician must have for every individual, even if insane. To the mind of a physician and scientist, no man is beyond saving. No scientific means will ever let us close the books, so to speak, on a human being. Like every person, every patient is unfathomable. Knowledge will never advance so far that the hidden secret of the personality can no longer be sensed at least as a possibility, as reflected in strange remnants.

Selection 2

PLURALISTIC METHODOLOGY

EDITORS:
The first edition of Jaspers's *General Psychopathology* appeared in 1913, when he was thirty years old. After 1921, when he became a full-time philosopher, Jaspers's only major effort in his former field was the complete revision of that work in 1941–42, during the eight-year period when the Nazi regime had forced him into retirement. The following selection is taken from the Introduction to this last edition, in which only a few passages from the original edition have been retained. Here Jaspers shows that it is the scientist's job is to be open to all fruitful methods as he delves into his subject matter. It is not the scientist's job to restrict significant research to one or only some methods, as if he had the key to reality. For Jaspers, methodical research and

the advocacy of a view of reality do not mix; scientific cognition does not mix with ontology. In this way the exposition of an orderly methodological pluralism within psychology leads to the philosophical question: what does it mean to say that human cognition is methodical in nature? The two main points Jaspers develops here in answer to this question are: First, all our knowledge is perspectival in character. Even our empirical study of "wholes," such as the "whole" of being human, or "wholes" of the individual, the personality, etc., is perspectival in accordance with the method of approach which is used. Thus, as we go from one method to another we are changing perspective and also expanding our view. Second, methodical cognition and the movement from one method to another imply a horizon of knowable reality that encompasses any one methodical perspective as well as the combination of all of them. The development of his methodological pluralism leads, then, to what Jaspers calls (as we shall see later in this part) the "basic philosophic operation."

Jaspers's last revision of the *General Psychopathology* has gone through several editions and is still in print. Even though some of the concrete empirical research of the book may be outdated, it is unique in rejecting those schools of psychology which aspire to exclusive system-building, while incorporating in a methodologically clear and orderly way the research these various schools are able to produce; in this sense the book continues to be valuable as a teacher of scientific thought. The last revision of the *General Psychopathology* was translated by J. Honig and Marian W. Hamilton. The following selection consists of excerpts from pages 20 to 40 of the original *Allgemeine Psychopathologie*. The translation is provided by the editors; the equivalent passages in the Honig and Hamilton translation appear on pages 22 to 47. It is in this selection that the phrase "the open horizon" occurs which we have chosen as the title for Part One.

TEXT:

In studying the works of others as well as in our own research we must always ask: what are the facts? what am I being shown? what are the findings one starts out from or arrives at? how are the facts being interpreted, how much is added speculation? what must I experience in order to follow the meaning of a line of thought?—Faced with experientially impoverished ideas one must ask if they are to be rejected as being empty. We must demand that the ideas make new findings possible or put given findings before us in a more meaningful way or connect them more profitably. We should not be forced to waste time with empty, torturous ideas and imaginary constructs. Here we are helped by methodological reflection and clarity. They enable us to grasp deliberately and with certainty what is essential. They teach us to see differences between empirical research on the one hand and pointless activity, indifferent repetition, and unstructured verbiage on the other.

Progress in the cognition of facts carries with it progress in method. Often, but by no means always, one is aware of one's method. Not all great advances in knowledge are accompanied, from the outset, by methodological self-awareness. Such self-awareness, however, purifies and safeguards what has in fact been achieved.

The object of methodical research is always a selected object. It is not the whole of reality but something particular, a certain aspect or perspective, and not an event in its totality.

We are confronted at every turn by the question how far one can be methodically successful in extracting a definite actuality out of the endless confusing flood of actualities and to present it clearly, in constructing models, finding measurable data, bringing out curves, schemata and images, in short to create the configurations in which actuality can be comprehended and arranged. The discovery of a new way of making facts comprehensible so that others can also recognize them is always the beginning of further research.

Technical methods of inquiry—experiments, measurements, statistical compilations—often present to the examiner accidental observations on the patient for the sake of which these procedures turn out to be useful and are impressive in their own right, while their specifically intended purpose yields little. Intelligence testing leads to situations where one can observe interesting behavior on the part of the patient that would not otherwise be caught in the objective testing situation. Anatomical measurement makes us go deeply into the structure of the body, makes us observe it in all possible ways; the quantitative element becomes unimportant in this process. Thus we arrive at a wrong evaluation of the method if its objective purpose is confused with what is brought to light in the course of its application. . . .

Concrete Methods: Data-arrangement and Research

In the actual process of cognition we make use of several methods at the same time. As we reflect upon them scientifically, we divide them, and with them the basic kinds of cognition contained in them. We have chosen a division into three major groups: (1) the arrangement of *individual facts*; (2) the inquiry into the *connections*; (3) the grasping of *wholes*.

1. The Arrangement of Individual Facts

Individual facts emerge out of the flow of psychic reality. The innumerable individual facts arrange themselves into several groups that are fundamentally different from each other according to our method of arrangement.

(a) The first step toward a scientific grasp of the psychic consists in the separation, delimitation, differentiation, and description of specific *inwardly experienced* [erlebte] *phenomena.* By virtue of their being experienced these phenomena are clearly presented and normatively designated by means of familiar expressions. In this manner we describe the kinds of illusions, hallucinations, compulsive behavior, the different modes of one's awareness of being a person, drives, etc. Here we are not yet dealing with the origin of phenomena, with the emergence from each other of psychic phenomena, or with the theories of underlying causes; rather we are concerned here purely with the actually experienced. The presentation of psychic experiences and states, their delimitation and determination for the purpose of always designating the same thing with the same term, is the task of *phenomenology.*

(b) What is brought out in phenomenology we know only indirectly from descriptions, by patients, of their states which we then understand analogously to our own modes of inward experience. These phenomena are called *subjective* in distinction from *objective* phenomena whose existence is ostensible. We observe objective phenomena in several ways fundamentally different from each other: as attendant physical phenomena, e.g., pulse rate during excitement, or dilation of pupils during fear; as expression, e.g., cheerful or sad facial expressions; as performance, e.g., feats of memory, or work output; as actions, behavior; as linguistic and artistic productions. All these objective phenomena serve to answer the question, what are the basic types of objective psychic fact? . . . .

2. *Inquiry into Connections* (Verstehen *and Explanation*)

Phenomenology presents us with a series of fragments broken out of a person's actual inward experience. The psychology of performance, of somatic events, of expression, the actions and the world of the sick and the creations of their minds show us each time different kinds of data. The question now arises how all these various data are to be related? In some cases we understand directly *how one psychic event emerges evidentially from another.* But this sort of understanding is possible only in deliberate confrontation of the psyche as psyche. In this way we understand the anger of someone attacked, . . . or how decisions and aćts spring from certain motives. In phenomenology, where we are faced with individual qualities and with conditions which, in isolation, are regarded as constant, our understanding is *static.* But here we grasp psychic perturbation, motion, connection, the emergence of one thing from another. Here we understand *genetically* (*Verstehen*-psychology). But we understand in such genetic connections not only the subjectively experienced phenomena but all that is observed statically at first, so also psychic reality discerned directly in expressions, further the achievements and creations, the actions and the worlds of the patient. . . .

However, genetic *Verstehen* (also called psychological explanation and justifiably contrasted with real explanation as being essentially different from

it) soon arrives at certain limits, especially in psychopathology. A psychic
event can emerge as something new in a manner quite incomprehensible to
us. Also, one psychic event may follow another psychic event in a way incomprehensible to us. Such events follow each other, they do not arise one from
the other. Examples of such incomprehensible temporal sequences are developmental stages of the normal psyche, and the phases and periods of the
abnormal. The facts of psychic life in its temporal sequentiality simply cannot
be understood by means of genetic *Verstehen* alone. They must be *explained
causally* as objects of the natural sciences which are seen—in contrast to those
of psychopathology—not "from the inside" but merely "from the outside". . . .

Thus "*Verstehen*" and "explanation" each have fixed meanings that will
become clearer in the course of study as the instances increase in number. . . .
The possibility of systematic study and clear-eyed research in psychopathology depends on insight into the fundamental distinction between static *Verstehen* and external sensuous perception, between genetic *Verstehen* and causal explanation. We are faced here with completely different, basic sources of
knowledge.

3. Grasp of Wholes

All research differentiates, separates, takes as its object something specific
and individual and searches in it for the general. But that out of which the
specific is taken is actually a whole. Knowledge of the specific is erroneous if
we lose sight of the whole in which and through which it exists. This whole,
however, becomes our object not directly but by way of the specific, and it
further becomes this object not as itself but as a schema of its essence. The
whole itself remains idea.

Categorical generalizations can be made about the whole, such as the following: the whole is prior to its parts; the whole is not the sum of its parts but
more, it is an independent source; it is a configuration [*Gestalt*]. Therefore
the whole cannot be comprehended from its elements; the whole in its totality
can persist even if parts of it are lost or altered. It is not possible to derive the
whole from its elements (Mechanism) nor the elements from the whole
(Hegelianism). Rather there exists a polarity: one has to see the whole
through its elements and the elements by way of the whole. One cannot travel
the route of grasping the whole synthetically out of the elements, nor the
route of grasping the elements by means of a derivation from the whole; there
remains only the circle. The infinite whole consists of the reciprocal determination of specific parts and wholes. We have to analyze *ad infinitum* and
relate all that is analyzed to its respective whole. For example, in biology all
particular-causal relations are held together by reciprocal action within a living whole. And in genetic *Verstehen* the "hermeneutic circle" is strength-

ened, where the whole is to be understood out of the particular facts, and, in turn, the whole is the precondition for understanding those particular facts.

This problem exists already in somatic medicine. . . . We find this opposition of the whole and its parts also in our grasp of the psychic life. Only here everything is scientifically less clear, more involved, more methodically multidimensional than in the somatic realm. . . .

If we call it "the whole of being human," then this whole is something infinite and unknowable as a whole. It is constructed out of a plethora of particular psychic functions. . . . Thus we can think of these particulars in isolation, e.g., as individual functions of the psyche, or as tools of the personality. In this way we can also contrast illness of such particulars, e.g., of memory, with fundamentally different deviations which from the start appear as located in the whole and do not seem to originate in individual parts of the psyche. . . .

This general contrasting of being-human as a whole with the individual parts of the psyche is not the only direction analysis can take; rather, there are many kinds of elements and wholenesses for psychological comprehension. Phenomenological elements are contrasted to the whole of the momentary state of consciousness, a specific performance to the over-all performance, the individual symptoms to typical syndromes. More comprehensive wholes are the constitution of man, the complex unity of his disease, his biographic totality. But even these empirical wholes are still relative; they are not the absolute whole of being human. This, the Encompassing of being-human, originates in a freedom which does not exist as object for the empirical study of man.

Our scientific endeavor progresses only when it analyzes, relates particulars to each other; but it withers and cannot differentiate between essential and non-essential if it goes no further, for then it slips into the comfortable state of merely enumerating scattered particulars. It must always be impelled by the idea of wholenesses, but we must not succumb to the temptation of wanting to grasp them directly in facile anticipation. In such anticipation one is intoxicated by phrases, but at the same time one's view is restricted through a presumed mastery of the whole, through a supposed vision of the all-embracing powers of the soul. Finally, our research must preserve, as a last horizon, the consciousness of the encompassing nature of being human, where all that can be empirically investigated in man is always merely a part, an aspect, relative even if it is the most empirically inclusive wholeness of all.

At the limits of all knowledge about man there remains the great question as to what man really is.

Inevitable Logical Deviations to be Overcome

For knowledge to result it is not enough that the determination of facts and the line of thought in an investigation be "correct." Even in correct research there are wrong paths on which we become stymied without really knowing why, on which even heroic efforts seem to come to nought. This is an experience common to all researchers. We must learn to recognize such dangers by understanding their nature. I shall attempt to point out some of them.

1. The Slide into Endlessness

The researcher is bound to have a certain recurrent experience: He must temporarily embark on and attempt an endless path in order to be brought up short, and—full of the material he has found along this path—gain the insight that orders, classifies, consolidates, epitomizes. Every step in the direction of genuine discovery is the overcoming of endlessness. It is a fundamental error in one's attitude as a researcher—an attitude which is basically one of laziness despite all seeming industriousness—not to be aware of this endlessness after a while and to remain sterile in mere repetition. One must stop short and be able to desist, must feel the prod of the task at hand and discover, in the endlessness experienced, the point of departure of new discoveries. True, one always needs to enter into the endlessness for a stretch. Each work of discovery is followed by merely analogical labors that do the same thing over again with different material, that confirm and broaden them until they disclose the endless in the repetition. But the steps that carry one forward, the pulse, as it were, in the rhythm of research, occur out of the consciousness of the research situation in awareness of its import. Then an inspiration comes to the rescue of the researcher with the solution of a mystery within the endless, of which, until now, he was vaguely conscious. At this point the clear question will emerge, together with its answer.

The principle underlying these remarks regarding the dangers of endlessness is the following insight: Reality in its concreteness, mental activity in its possibilities, are infinite. Cognition is the discovery of conceptions in which the *infinite* is mastered and overcome by *finite insights*, but in such a manner that each such productively grasped finitude is appropriate to the nature of the object, arises from it and is not forced on it. . . .

2. The Impasse of Absolutization

Almost each method and object of research tend to be absolutized and thereby to be taken as the only authentic, the essential, the central one. It is believed that thereby one has finally hit on the right path and wants to arrange all findings with this central point of view in mind which is now regarded no longer as methodical but ontological. It is believed that one is taking hold of reality itself, is no longer moving within a manifold of methods doing research from various perspectives. In actual fact, however, the result is always the absolutization of partial insights, for all knowledge is particular. In order to avoid this error it is important to master all the methods and points of view, not to play one off against the other, not biology against human studies [*Geisteswissenschaften*] or vice versa, nor psyche against brain, nor classification of disease against its phenomenology. For absolutization is the wellspring of prejudice.

The theories of psychopathology and psychology, too, have come into being out of the wrongly satisfied need to grasp the whole with one single way of explaining all, with only a limited number of elements. The results are construed "systems," rough classificatory concepts, a seemingly final description of the whole that can be further elaborated in its details only. The theories of the natural sciences always serve as their models. We demand instead an overview of the methods and viewpoints which are to be clearly distinguished and not confused, and are not to be absolutized beyond the limits proper to them; within their limits, however, they should be applied properly and according to plan.

From its very conception this book was meant to be an enemy of all fanaticisms which—because of people's desire to assert themselves—are so strongly inclined to absolutize one particular conception. While this is almost unavoidable and even meaningful when we are dealing with the enthusiasm of the researcher engaged in a specific task, who at the stage of discovery follows up all possible leads, we must reject it completely when the creation of the total picture is at stake. The struggle with one's own fanaticisms—and who does not himself tend in that direction!—is the precondition for creating a whole, insofar as the whole is to originate from the idea of the whole and not out of an absolutization. This whole can never be complete. In contrast with the closed and completed nature of a theoretical construct that is based on a supposedly known objective principle, our idea of the whole points, perspectivally, in many different directions, demands freedom of movement on different levels . . . , and yet keeps a firm grasp on the systematic knowledge gained up to now, and succeeds in being disciplined and not chaotic.

Nonetheless it is still a tricky business to attempt to build the manifold of research into a unified whole. . . . The structure of the whole would indeed turn out to be a forced one if it were ontological in nature; therefore it cannot be in the form of a total knowledge of Being but only of total consciousness of method within which all possible knowledge of Being must find room. Consciousness of method itself must be so constituted as to remain open and leave room to accommodate new methods.

It it therefore the fundamental position of this book to fight all absolutization, to point out endlessness in research, to throw light on obscurities—but to acknowledge all genuine experience, to comprehend it in its own way, to understand and incorporate all possible knowledge and to assign to it the place most natural to it within the framework of our methods.

3. Pseudo-insight through Terminology

Clear cognition is reflected in precise terms. Felicitous or infelicitous formulations of concept and expression are extremely important for effectiveness and dissemination, for comprehensibility or incomprehensibility of insights. But terminology can be appropriate and expressive of the essence of a
thing only where cognition itself is clear and precise. Time and again the
demand is voiced for a uniform terminology of psychological and psychopathological concepts; the difficulty here lies not in the choice of words but in the
concepts themselves. If the concepts were clear, finding a proper terminology
would be easy. . . . We still lack the generally recognized concepts that
would have to be given names. . . . Today it is still possible to take psychological terms in all the multiplicity of meaning they carry in general usage, and
to transplant them directly into the language of research and discussion. Yet
fruitless attempts are made time and time again to propose a multitude of new
terms instead of continuing with research. . . .

Methodology: Critical vs Aberrant

Methods should not enmesh us in empty thought possibilities that yield
neither perceptions nor experiences. The value of methods becomes evident
in what they help us see, judge, and accomplish in our dealing with people. It is
thus the purpose of the critique of methods to examine an item of knowledge
as to its origin and derivation, to understand the impossibility of gaining
knowledge through the wrong method, to make us aware of the order of
knowledge in the diversity of methods, to clear the roads of cognition, to make
them passable and easier to follow.

As every road to scientific knowledge, so also the methodological one harbors dangers peculiar to it. There is the possibility that the methodology will
deteriorate to the level of a vacuous formal calculus of concepts. No matter
how skillful, such reckoning which can never penetrate beyond the surface,
this mere pushing back and forth of concepts, is destructive in its effect. Actual
perception is and always remains the wellspring of our knowledge. Of course
it may happen that a certain author, though able to see something novel, is not
able to find the best conceptual formulations. Even though he may be right in
his insights, formal logic can be used to demonstrate—albeit only superficially—contradictions and inaccuracies in his formulations. In fruitful criticism, on the other hand, we grasp what is essential and to the point, and
restrict ourselves to improving the formulations and clarifying the method.
This necessary though formal correction presents a danger, however, if it
causes us to overlook the essential meaning of the new insight. . . .

Methodological discussions have meaning only if they are based on concrete material and their effects are demonstrated at the same time. Methodo-

logical abstractions, devoid of perceptions, are tedious. Only concrete logic has validity in empirical science. Mere argument without factual investigation or presentation of concrete material lack a solid foundation. Inventing methods that are not, at the same time, or perhaps cannot ever, be applied concretely only leads to empty methodological cant.

There exists a kind of methodological discussion which operates with mere categories and thereby negates, on purely rationalistic grounds, any positive attempt at cognition, and yet is sterile in spite of its seeming correctness. One example of this is the typical objection advanced against precise differentiation of concepts: It is claimed that one divides what is really "one" (such as body and soul, science and life, personality development and morbid process, or perception and conception, etc.). Or it is said what has been divided is connected by "transitions" which make the divisions actually illusory. No matter how true this thesis of oneness generally, its application to the cognitive process is usually untrue. Cognition proceeds through differentiation. True unity is the encompassing unknown that precedes knowledge; it is ever the idea that challenges us to join together, under clearly articulated points of view, what has been separated. However, cognition itself cannot anticipate this unity; it is achieved in practice, in the actuality of living human beings. Cognition differentiates, is particular and structured, fruitful through opposites, and through all this remains open for movement toward unity. The talk about transitions is usually the result of lazy thinking and observing. The consequence of this negative rationalistic pseudo-critique of methods is not at all the strengthening of genuine unity but rather confusion. This amorphous enthusiasm for unity leads to a muddle in which blindness rules instead of a breadth of cognition in full control of its tools. . . .

Dogmatics of Being vs. Methodological Consciousness

In 1913 [in the first edition of the *General Psychopathology*] I described the meaning and purpose of my methodological systematics as follows: "Instead of doing violence to the whole field of inquiry by employing a system based on a theory, the attempt will be made to separate clearly the individual ways of research, points of view, methods. In this way they will be clearly brought out and the many-sided nature of psychopathology will be exhibited. For this reason no theory nor any point of view at all will be excluded. Each view of the whole needs to be taken up, grasped in accordance with its importance, its limitations, its validity. That which encompasses them all, however, is and remains the inquiring mind, for which any picture of the whole is valid from a certain standpoint only, which would like to dominate these pictures of the whole in their totality, and yet, in the final analysis, is able to arrange them only according to the methods and categories in which they originated.

"We shall indicate the paths by means of which we arrive at the perception of different facets of the psyche. Each chapter of this book will exhibit such a facet. Instead of finding a system of elements and functions that guides the direction of analysis uniformly and everywhere in psychopathology, (as the theory of the structure and bonding of atoms in chemistry), we must be satisfied with merely carrying out different modes of viewing the subject matter. Instead of a theoretical order we can possess only a methodological one."

In this self-characterization there is expressed a scientific antithesis that must be seen in very radical terms. Either one believes that one already possesses, in what is known, *Being in itself* and in its entirety, or one realizes that cognition has a *perspective* character, that it is both methodically founded and limited. Either one seeks contentment in [firm] knowledge about *Being*, or one knows oneself to be within the *open horizon* of infinite movement [of cognition]. One either has one's center of gravity in a *theory of Being* that one believes one recognizes, or in the *systematics of deliberate methods* with which one throws light into the infinite darkness. Either one abandons all *methods as* nothing other than a *temporary* necessary *framework* in order, as is believed, to possess the object itself that one has conquered; or one dissolves again all *dogmatics of Being as a temporary unavoidable error*, in favor of the movement of cognition which is never straight-forward or finished but is open to limitless experience and exploration.

Methodological consciousness keeps us in readiness vis-à-vis the reality that must always be grasped anew. *Dogmatics of Being* closes us off in a knowing that drapes itself like a veil between us and all new experience. In this way the fundamental attitude of methodology finds itself over against the absolutizing attitude, the basic attitude of research over against the fixating stance. . . .

Methodological Order as Principle of Arrangement

Methodological ordering means bringing to consciousness all modes of perception, forms of observation, modes of thought, paths of research, fundamental attitudes of cognition, and to practice them on the experiential data proper to each in turn. In this way differentiations are made decisively, the organs of perception and research are developed in their purity, the limits that show themselves in each instance are discerned, the possible perceptions of the whole are attempted and at the same time relativized. Schooling in [the use of] methods leads to reliable critique in regard to the significance and limits of all knowledge and promotes openness in the appreciation of facts.

Actuality confronts us in the form of an individual whole, as a live human being. In cognizing, we take apart; and each actually determined fact has been arrived at by way of a certain method. From this follows first of all that all cognition affects only the particular; we have never even seen the whole prior to dismembering it. By the time we regard it, it is already taken apart. Secondly, fact and method are closely connected. . . . There is no radical division between fact and method, rather one is by way of the other.

Therefore a structuring according to method is at the same time the appropriate structuring of reality as it is for us. Such structuring is the motive function of cognition in which empirical being becomes evident for us. The basic kinds of facts are perceived through the arrangement of methods as well as the presentation of what can be seen through them. . . . Methodological arrangement introduces a structure to the factual material that accords with the material itself. . . .

An ordering of our knowledge seems much simpler where there exists a *theory of Being*. A few principles and elements put us in possession of the whole. I have actuality itself within my grasp. This is the reason for the fleeting success of suggestive systems in which the subject matter itself seems to have been basically comprehended, where anyone coming along is able to take hold of the whole, believes he has found a firm footing right in the center of actuality, seems to be doing cognitive work while being busy merely with thought that is repetitious, confirming, applying, and elaborating. *Methodological* structuring, on the other hand, is more difficult but it is truer. It is neither suggestive nor comfortable, cannot be achieved quickly, does not permit any grandiose mastery of the whole. But it practices true cognition, brings to life the motivations for inquiry, demands one's own competence. Such structuring demonstrates what has been gained, shows what appears when specific paths are pursued and remains open for the whole of being-human.

Methodological arrangement and ordering in a work dealing with psychopathology in its entirety is, therefore, an ongoing task. It does not imply the design of a finished model but the constant effort to lift the structural ideas out of the actual research, to make us aware of them and to interconnect them. . . .

Empiricism and Philosophy

In the first five parts it is my intention to be a radical empiricist, to wage a successful battle against the emptiness of speculative deliberation, against theoretical dogmatism, and against absolute knowledge of Being. In Part Six (and in this Introduction) on the other hand, I discuss philosophical questions which the psychopathologist cannot but clarify for himself. For not only does unprejudiced empiricism bring us to the genuine limits [of scientific knowledge] where philosophizing begins, but only philosophical consciousness in its turn makes possible a reliable empirical attitude toward research. The relationship of science and philosophy is not so constituted that philosophical studies could be directly applied in science—it is an always unproductive, albeit oft repeated, endeavor to give philosophical names to empirical facts—rather it is such that philosophizing brings about an inner attitude that is beneficial to science through the setting of boundaries, through providing inner guidance and the driving force of a limitless desire to know. . . . The psychopathologist must concern himself with philosophy not because it might teach him something positive as regards his field but because it clears the inner space for the possibilities of knowledge.

II.

Philosophical Foundations

EDITORS:
The three selections which follow are quite different from each other. They come from works distinct in kind and written at different times. They are also different in content. The first, "Kant: The Phenomenality of Being," is taken from the first of Jaspers's two main works of philosophy, his *Philosophy*. In it Jaspers develops his concept of 'transcending' thought in connection with an interpretation of Kant's distinction between 'thing-in-itself' and 'thing-in-its-appearance,' with special reference to the "Transcendental Deduction" of the *Critique of Pure Reason*. —The second is a selection from Jaspers's other main work of philosophy, *Von der Wahrheit* (Of Truth), published in 1946. In these few pages Jaspers states as explicitly as anywhere the nature and meaning of what he regards as the "basic philosophic operation" of thought. —Finally, the third selection is taken from Jaspers's interpretation of Plato's theory of Ideas in his *The Great Philosophers* (1957).

As different as these three passages are in content and respective contexts, they are nevertheless to be regarded as three versions of the same train of thought: Thought—in particular, concrete and positive thought—takes place within an infinite context, or, as Jaspers says, an "open horizon." When questions of the truth, or the significance, or the value, or the relation of concrete thoughts are raised, thought steps into, or "transcends" to, that infinite context which places concrete thought into perspective. This step is, to Jaspers, the distinctive philosophic step. Philosophical thought, to be clarifying and critical, is to be understood in its distinctiveness and is to be undertaken deliberately. It is to be recognized as a thinking about concrete thought, and not as another kind of concrete thinking. Philosophy proceeds at a different level. However, the philosophic operation and the content of philosophical thought are unavoidably expressed in the form of concrete thought; therefore philosophical thought is liable to be misunderstood.

All these features of the "basic philosophic operation" can be recognized in each of the following three selections. In Jaspers's philosophical development the identification of the 'basic philosophic operation' is tied to his interpretation of Kant's theory of the phenomenality of Being as expounded in the "Transcendental Deduction." Jaspers's presentation of the "basic philosophical operation" in the *Philosophy* in connection with an account of this interpretation of Kant, and our inclusion of this section in our Reader is no accident. Jaspers's preoccupation with Kant is in fact as much a foundation of Jaspers's philosophy as the related "basic philosophic operation." Jaspers's recognition of this basic step in all significant philosophizing is meant to be demonstrated representatively in the selection dealing with Plato.

Selection 3

KANT: THE PHENOMENALITY OF BEING

EDITORS:
This selection is from Jaspers's *Philosophie*, Vol. I, *Philosophische Weltorientierung*, pp. 40–44; translation in English by E. B. Ashton: *Philosophy*, Vol. I, *World Orientation*, pp. 79–82. Ashton's translation of the following has been emended by the editors.

TEXT:
It becomes a puzzle how we know an object that can never be identical with us and will always remain strange. We cannot step outside of the subject-object relation. Whatever we may be thinking about this relation, we can never help thinking of something objective again and thus presupposing and at the same time establishing the very relationship we want to comprehend. This is why we tend to move in the subject-object relationship as that which cannot be questioned, as though it were a matter of course. To grasp it directly, we must try to go beyond all objectivity.

Kant has given us a marvelously illuminating demonstration of such transcending to nonobjectiveness. Before him, what lies beyond the things of the world had been conceived as transcendence, and in metaphysics men had tried thinking about it. Substance, monad, God—all of these could be defined in principle. Kant changed the direction of transcending. His object was neither a thing-in-itself of the things in the world nor an immortal soul; he recognized the impossibility of their cognition as objects. His transcending had neither an objective nor a subjective goal; it had no goal at all. He carried out what he called the "transcendental method" and distinguished it from transcending to a being of things in the beyond, but in the method he held on to transcending as such, whereby all existence became appearance. Here we come upon the well-known Kantian concepts of the conditions of all objectiveness, which themselves are not objects, of the *a priori* of the categories derived from the unity of apperception—a unity which is not the category of unity, however, but its ground.

This is Kant's dilemma, this impossibility of discussing the premises of all objectiveness otherwise than in concepts that cannot but objectify. He always wants to transcend, but with the first words into which he puts his transcending he slides back into the immanence and particularity of something objective. This, then, makes for the infinite toil in the *Critique of Pure Reason*, notably in the chapter on the "transcendental deduction," which he himself declared to be the most profound. No definite insight resolves these difficulties. They are not objectively resolved at all; their only solution lies in the act of transcending itself—which act Kant, by his laborious, constantly renewed and rephrased disquisitions, stimulates without being able to perform for us.

For it is here, at a formal, seemingly still rather unsubstantial boundary, that we come—not to know, but most distinctly to be aware of the difference between true and false transcending. False transcending takes me to an object beyond the boundary, an object which I then "have got." Misunderstanding Kant, I "have got" the *a priori*, the transcendental unity of apperception, and so forth, as solid, definable concepts of something. But true transcending only occurs on the borderline of object and nonobject, in passing from one to the other. Those concepts are functions rather than insights, tokens rather than objects. I cannot possibly understand the Kantian thought if I *falsely try to bring it nearer by objectification*. This leads to the typical and necessarily recurring misconceptions whose inevitability Kant's own words portend, the best-known of which are the *psychological-anthropological* one and the *methodological-epistemological* one. Either will prevent me from transcending—the first by having the world spring from the cerebral and psychological development of man, and the second by turning methodological preconditions of cognition into preconditions of the existence of . . . objects of experience.

Yet both misconceptions, despite their vain attempt to make objectively conceivable what is true only as philosophizing, retain the circle which is the necessary expression of any communication of transcending . . . They do it in rather crude forms: the brain produces the world of which it is a part and a product; the methods produce the object whose cognition leads to the development of methods. Circles, in almost explicit formulations, occur in Kant's own words. Their only function is to serve as signs of his transcending.

The circles in that Kantian thought can make me aware of the limits of mundane existence. With its help I can ascertain that the world is not all, that it is not being-in-itself, that it is not the very ultimate. But since I can neither cross the limits to reach Being that is not world nor have in the world an adequate expression of transcending, that thought lies solely in transcending itself. Without that, it is nothing. Transcending gives me no insights which I then possess; instead, it shifts the posture of my consciousness. I get an inner jolt that will effect a change—a merely formal change, at first—in my attitude toward everything objective.

Reasons cannot compel true transcending. There is an essential difference between this and the finding of insights. If I experience the "*eureka*" in scientific research then it makes me want to tell about it, to communicate what I have found. But in transcending, when the origin of Kant's transcendental deduction becomes clear to me, I am taken aback and silent, I seem to be having and to be asking at the same time. A man to whom this has happened will no longer be satisfied with merely intellectual, philosophically unsubstantial interpretations aimed at results that he can know and that will have final validity. To enter into transcending means, instead, to climb the path to the freedom of philosophizing. . . .

It transforms itself into a consciousness of the *phenomenality* of all existence. This consciousness envisions neither two worlds nor the one world. To transcend from existence to Being is not a matter of being in the world, nor a matter of being beyond the world. Transcending, rather, has the result of the naive being in the world turning into a knowing one. And the knowing being in the world takes place only because a virtual—though never actual—being beyond the world has been experienced which brings our very being in the world primally to consciousness. No psychology can describe this unique sense of moving between being in and being beyond the world. It is an act of freedom out of one's absolute consciousness. . . .

If the transcending consciousness is expressed in the statement that the world is appearance, still nothing can be found that it might be the appearance of. It is not appearance in the sense of the category "appearance," not like a thing in the world of which I can say—as of color, for instance, as contrasted with the underlying process of physical motion—that this is how the object appears to me while at the same time I can get a clear conception of the object itself that appears in this way. If we call the world appearance, then that of what it would be appearance is, in principle, not an object and not a possible object; as such it is not even in the categorial sense of a definite being. World as appearance is merely the expression for the consciousness of limits or for that transcending that brings the world quasi into suspension for me, and me in it, without leading me out of it toward an other. Therefore, in the world the statement that the world is appearance has no meaning. Such meaning is derived solely from its limits.

The transcending thought can be expressed in the formula: *no object without a subject*. Yet this will promptly lead to misconceptions, as if the subject or . . . consciousness existed in themselves and were the preconditions of everything objective. Hence the reverse of the statement is equally correct: *no subject without an object*—for there is no consciousness without something to which it is directed. Anticipating the accusation that he does away with the actuality of the world and replaces it with the subjectivity of appearance, Kant had elaborated with unsurpassed clarity that the subject or the I—as I observe myself—is, exactly like the objective thing, merely an "I, as I appear to myself." Both subject and object are appearance (if I must express my mental transcending of the whole world in words such as these that are bound to be misunderstood). This consciousness-as-such is not an empirical subject, not consciousness in a psychological sense, but the name given to the existence of the world in that subject-object dichotomy which I must enter in order to partake of this world at all.

Selection 4

THE NATURE AND SIGNIFICANCE OF
THE BASIC PHILOSOPHIC OPERATION

EDITORS:
The following selection has been taken from *Von der Wahrheit*: p. 37–42. The translation is provided by the editors.

TEXT:

The Basic Philosophic Operation

The question is: what is Being? A question must be asked about this question, namely: how can I, how must I think about Being?
A. Everything that becomes an *object* for me emerges toward me from the obscurity of the world in which I live and which, by living, I clarify. An object is a *determinate* being. It is related to other objects from which it is distinguished; it is also related to me, whom it confronts as something which is being thought. An object is *not everything*; no matter how large, it is contained within a more comprehensive Being; it is *not the whole*. Being itself cannot become manifest as an object.

Whenever I attempt to think Being, e.g., as matter, or energy, or mind, or life—all imaginable categories have been tried—it turns out that I have absolutized into Being itself one mode of determinate Being occurring within the whole of Being.

Immediately experienced Being is appearance which points to something else; Being itself which is known mediately is not experienced as itself. Being, which is simply Being itself, cannot occur in the form of an object, immediately or mediately. It cannot be grasped as an object is grasped.

No matter what is grasped by means of knowledge, it turns out that the Being which I know is not Being in itself nor Being which I myself am. Our knowledge has no foothold in some determinate Being. Rather, it is as if Being retreated before the grasping will to know, always leaving us holding only remnants and traces of itself in the form of objects. No Being that is known is *the* Being.

B. Everything that becomes objective for me is comprised in a relative wholeness of our world, in which we live. We behold this wholeness and are sheltered within it. It encloses us as if in a *horizon* of our knowledge.

Every horizon encloses us, denying us the prospect beyond. Hence we press on beyond every horizon. But no matter where we go, the horizon, constantly encircling whatever has been attained, goes with us. It is always there anew and, because it is horizon and not completion, forces us to give up every resting place. We can never stand at a point where the limiting horizon would cease, and at which there would open to our view a whole which is horizonless, closed and thus not pointing beyond itself. Neither do we gain consecutive standpoints whose totality—achieved by moving through the various horizons like in the circumnavigation of the globe—would give us the one closed Being in a system of Being. For us Being remains *open*; it draws us on all sides into the unlimited. Ever so often it lets something new come our way in the form of specific determinate Being.

C. We have been proceeding, in our cognition, from the *indeterminate whole* of our world (in which we live immediately), to the *determinate object* (which occurs in the world and from which it emerges toward us), and thence to a *closedness of the world* as deliberately grasped (in different systems of Being) within its horizons. At each of these steps we confront Being, but at none of them do we possess Being itself, for each time we see the possibility of going further into Being, beyond the appearance of Being that we have gained. Determinate, known Being is always encompassed by something more comprehensive. Each time we grasp positively something particular—and every thought system of the whole of Being is also such a particular—we experience at the same time what Being is not.

As we become aware of this experience, we ask once more about Being which retreated from us even as the appearances which approached us become manifest. This Being, which is neither an—as such restrictive—object nor a whole that is formed within an—as such limiting—horizon, we call the *Encompassing*.

The Encompassing can be sensed because there is a horizon, i.e., something always shows itself beyond each horizon which encloses each attained horizon without itself being horizon. The Encompassing is then never the horizon within which our knowledge is located and in which we encounter any definite mode of Being, for the Encompassing is never visible as a horizon. What encompasses, then, is Being, from which—as that which encompasses absolutely—all new horizons emerge.

The Encompassing thus always only *gives notice* of itself—in what is objectively present and within the horizons—but itself never becomes object and horizon. We do not encounter it itself but we encounter everything else within it. The Encompassing becomes present for us, albeit indirectly, through our approaching and transcending every horizon from within the Encompassing. Within each horizon we grasp things as these and those definite objects, which yet are not only what they immediately appear, but which become transparent through and by way of the Encompassing.

We carry out the basic philosophical thought by means of thinking beyond every definite being, beyond every discernible, hence definite, horizon, toward the Encompassing in which we are and which we ourselves are.

The Encompassing is that in which all Being is for us. Said in another way, it is the very condition under which Being becomes Being for us. It is not everything in the sense of the sum total of Being, but rather the whole— which remains open for us—as the ground of Being.

D. It is the Encompassing that we search for when we engage in philosophical activity. Since it is encompassing we shall not grasp it in the manner of something in the world which we encounter—it is, after all, that in which we encounter everything else and which cannot adequately be cognized as an object. Rather, we become aware of it in thought only as a limit. We would like to go beyond all beings which occur within horizons, and beyond all horizons to behold Being itself; we would like to go beyond our own existence in order to learn what we really are.

We do not reach this goal if we leave our world behind and its mode of objective thought, and relinquish all horizons. As soon as we try such a path we tumble into the void of meaningless reverie. We must stay in the realm of knowledge which is distinct because it is directed toward objects; but in and with such knowledge we penetrate to its very ground. In thinking beyond knowledge we always remain within it, always remain bound to what we make transparent by going beyond it and which we yet wish to regard from a distance as if we were no longer merely in it, or else wish to regard from the depth by which all this knowledge is supported and penetrated.

The Meaning of the Basic Philosophic Operation

A. The thought of going beyond beings toward the Encompassing is a simple one but one that is infinitely rich in consequences. It serves to liberate us, in our consciousness of Being, from bondage to any specific knowledge; we wish to gain the *breadth* of Being without such constraint.

It is a thought which turns us around, releasing us from all specific beings, and forcing us to re-turn from every solidified position.

The thought itself does not show us a new object. Seen in the light of usual knowledge of the world, it is empty. However, by means of its form it opens up the simply universal possibility of Being.

The thought awakens us so that we learn to listen to that which authentically is. It enables us to perceive origins.

B. Since the thought—if it is really carried out and not merely thought externally—turns us around, it is highly *unnatural* in comparison with our customary lives. Our natural comportment in the world is devoted to the specific things and purposes that occupy us. We do not ask about the sense in which we have, mean, want, or maintain what there is. Occupied with the concrete questions of the world we do not inquire about us, the questioners, nor about the world as a whole. Or else, we ask about us but only as far as we are specific individual beings among other beings; and we ask about the world but only as far as it becomes, in its totality, an object of research. Ruled as we are by what concerns us in practical life and in research, we do not approach the limits at which our whole doing and knowing is subjected to questioning and at which our knowledge of Being is turned around and we become aware of the really encompassing.

C. This simple thought of the Encompassing is one that *somersaults over itself*. Even though we must think it in order to reach, beyond all horizons, Being itself and our own essence, it seems at the same time that such thought is impossible. Becoming aware, as we turn, of the Encompassing, we seem to lose everything in the process. We are to carry through a thought in which no object remains for us.

We are, after all, tied to the form of our thinking in such a manner that whatever we want to cognize we must turn into determinate objects. If we want to think the Encompassing, this also immediately becomes *object* for us, i.e., the Encompassing is the world, is the Being which we are, is consciousness-as-such. Thus by clearly thinking the Encompassing we are doing exactly that which should be overcome by our thinking it. When we seek in the Encompassing the ground of all, we can no longer have any object before us save this Encompassing. But as we think it we cannot help but think it with the aid of determinate being-contents.

This has consequences for the way in which the thought of the Encompassing makes its appearance.

In carrying out this thought all definite objectivity which is indispensable on the way toward it, must *disappear*. Only as it disappears do we become aware of Being itself, which is now no longer some definite being but the ground of Being. Every statement that refers to the Encompassing thus contains an absurdity within itself: it demands that something non-objective be thought in the form of the objective. Philosophizing is possible only because this is possible. But because it is difficult—not for the understanding (for which it is altogether impossible) but for our thinking nature itself which, as it were, is broken open by it in order for it to become wide and bright—philosophy is inaccessible in a manner which differentiates it from every object of knowledge that can be apprehended merely by way of the understanding.

If, further, the thinking of the non-objective is expressed in terms of objectivities, then every sentence expressive of such thinking is necessarily such that it can be *misunderstood*. It may appear as if another new kind of object had been added to all the others that are susceptible to research. We remain inclined to apply the modes of cognition that are usual in our world to everything and to expect them also in the objective statements of philosophizing; but then the thought of the Encompassing is understood erroneously as the thought of something which we actually encounter. A knowledge of the Encompassing is crystallized out in accordance with the objective mode of cognition, which we now supposedly know or are able to survey. Instead of becoming aware of the Encompassing in a thought that turns us around, we would be left, in the wording of isolated statements, with a sham knowledge of the whole of the Encompassing.

It is, however, the very task of the basic philosophic thought to lead us beyond every specialized knowledge that pretends to being knowledge of everything and the whole.

D. The operations that cannot be carried out in accordance with customary cognition because they would conflict with the laws of non-contradiction, can yet be carried out in the realm of philosophy as the *elucidation* of a *consciousness of Being* that cannot be compared with determinate knowledge. This consciousness of Being is the fundamental mood, or attitude, or frame of mind of the philosophizing person. For the thought of the Encompassing is a first clarification of this fundamental frame of mind. In philosophical logic it develops into thought processes to which it gives content. It is ground as well as consequence of this thinking.

E. The thought of the Encompassing itself shows us *no new object* and *no new method*. Impelled by the quest after Being, we have searched for but have found no special method by which we could now find an answer to this question. Rather, starting from that thought, we are to illuminate the methods—which seek their goal in definite forms and in various ways—to fulfill them according to their meaning and to lead them beyond themselves.

Instead of creating new methods and a new object, the fundamental thought has to penetrate all kinds of thinking, realize their significance and bring about awareness of their limits. Instead of proceeding by way of mysticism to the realm of the other-worldly, the fundamental thought must find its certainty in all modes of objectivity, in all methods, and all kinds of objects.

While the fundamental thought loosens the bonds to what is thing-like, such as objects and material realities, it changes them in accordance with their meanings. One must find out, in the process of philosophic logic, how all beings are, as it were, regained through thinking the Encompassing, and how the thought of the Encompassing is confirmed in the comprehension of beings.

While the thought of the Encompassing liberates us from absolute subjugation to a knowable order, it yet lets us grasp all meaningful order. However, such order is grasped as tool or path or schema, and not as ontology, theology, or system. It teaches us to grasp in play what has the seriousness of a language, teaches us to soar without sinking into the bottomless, to let ourselves be supported without taking root.

Through the transcending thought we enter the Encompassing, without however having attained anything in this way. But all that is for us as something that is known, gains depth by reference to the Encompassing out of which it approaches us; it heralds Being but is itself not Being.

The fundamental thought and its development create for us the free space in which philosophic logic can develop.

Selection 5

THE TURNING

EDITORS:
The following consists of selected passages from *Die grossen Philosophen, Erster Band*, pp. 273–77; in English translation by R. Manheim: *The Great Philosophers*, Vol. I, ed. by H. Arendt, pp. 141–45. Translation by the editors.

TEXT:

The Dogmatic Interpretation of the Theory of Ideas

In view of the manifold meanings embodied in the theory of Ideas, any attempt to reduce it to a principle and interpret it as a whole is futile.

It is futile to give a fixed meaning to the Ideas. They are not real figures, not objective constructs, not things to be apprehended intellectually analogously to things apprehended by sense perception; they are not representations, not ideals created by our phantasy, not concepts nor demands on us—rather they are all of these as well.

It is futile to attempt a systematization of the Platonic theory of Ideas. To make one direction of thought, one mode of its representation into a doctrine, does not make sense. Plato goes in many different directions.

Neither do we understand the theory of Ideas as embodying a development of Platonic thought in which it is brought from its beginnings, in several steps, to maturity and perfection. Of course Plato's thoughts about the Ideas unfold in the progression of dialogues during the course of forty years. But there is no unified theory of Ideas, only a complex of notions, some of which run through the whole work from the earliest dialogues, while others make their appearance later. The Ideas play an essential role in the ascent of thought toward true Being, but their expression changes according to the manner in which this ascent is communicated. When they become fixated in a doctrine and as such pose insoluble problems, they become an object of criticism for Plato. He calls them in question and asks: Are the Ideas only of the good, or also of the bad? How are all the many Ideas related to one another? How can they be and at the same time not be?

The Ideas are not only archetypes, patterns, species, unities. Ultimately, as forms of all existents they become numbers (not as quantities, but as individual primal forms). They are arranged in different ways. In later dialogues they are not even mentioned, and in a very late one (*Timaeus*) they reappear in their simplest form, namely as the models that the Demiurge contemplates while fashioning the world. A line seems to run from the perplexities (particularly in the early dialogues) to the theory of Ideas and thence to the ineffable. The frame seems to grow steadily wider, the space more open and at the same time more richly inhabited; as to the solution, it is never complete in the progression of our thinking. . . .

The Allegory of the Cave

The theory of Ideas is brought home to us most forcefully in the famous Allegory of the Cave (*Republic*, Book VII). It is the parable of our human situation and of the meaning of the knowledge and the action possible in it. . . .

The implications of this parable are astoundingly rich: the parable of the [two] worlds and the modes of knowledge proper to each; —the parable of the kinds of human existence and of the two kinds of blindness springing from opposite causes; —the parable of the modes of truth; —the parable of transcending as the essence of human being and knowing. . . . As a whole, the parable with its interpretation remains unforgettable. It is a masterpiece of philosophic invention and provides us with an approach to thoughts that cannot be expressed directly. . . .

Let us single out three moments of the parable that generally determine Platonic philosophizing: the turning, the levels of cognition, the twofold direction of human life.

The Turning

Man's insight is bound up with a turning (*metastrophe, periagogue*). It does not occur as a gift given from the outside, nor through the insertion of eyes (these are in place already), nor through the implantation of a seed. Rather, it occurs as it did in the cave, when the turning of the eyes could be accomplished only by turning the whole body; knowledge, together with the soul, must turn from the realm of becoming toward Being. Accordingly, education (*paideia*) is the art that brings about such turning. Because of its divine origin the faculty of rational insight is always present, its power hidden. But it becomes beneficial only through the turning; otherwise this same faculty is harmful.

The Doctrine of Levels

Knowledge advances by steps. From sense perception it proceeds to pure thought (in mathematics)—from pure thought to the Idea (from mathematical knowledge to dialectic science)—from the Idea to the realm beyond Being (from the Ideas to the Idea of the Good).

Or, phrased differently: From sensory experience it progresses to true opinion (*doxa alethes*). . . . From *doxa* it continues by way of the sciences to the next higher level where the Ideas shine in their pure light, and from there to contact with that through which the Ideas are able to shine and exist.

According to how they are seen, these levels are either levels of cognition, or levels of man's comportment in the whole of his condition, or levels of beings. This ascent is at the same time a deepening of cognition, of becoming oneself in the purity of soul, of attaining the vision of the highest. . . .

As we linger on the lower levels, we have the tendency to speak as if the higher ones did not exist. But our discourse on these levels can achieve truth only through guidance from above. If this guidance is lacking, then the sham of endlessly changing information gains the upper hand. We remain perplexed and obstinate because we lack the inner relationship to that which must guide everything if truth is to prevail.

We are directed toward the higher levels, to attain them by rising. By themselves, the lower levels remain in the incomprehension of ignorance. The consequence of this is, that whoever transcends the unavoidable lower levels in order to make the higher objects themselves speak to him, and therefore ventures onto the higher level of cognition proper to them, finds himself in a strange situation. For here the person attached to the lower level, the "one versed in confutation, has the advantage, if he wants it, and presents him who expresses his thoughts in the form of speech, writing or response, to the majority of his listeners as a bungler. . . ."

Two Necessary Directions in Human Life

Two directions open up for the comportment of the thinking soul: from the world of appearance out into the eternal world (*Phaedo*), and from the vantage point of the eternal world again to see, to comprehend, and to shape the world of appearance (*Republic, Laws, Timaeus*). Both motions take place in Platonic philosophizing: philosophizing in the direction of Being and with Being as the point of departure. Man is "here" in the world; he must look beyond the world "to there" in order, by touching the essential, to become essential himself. On this ascent of thought there follows man's reentry into this world: out of his turning away from the world comes his re-turn to the mathematical and mythical comprehension of the cosmos (*Republic, Timaeus*); his turning away from the life of the *polis* and toward the eternal regions obligates him to return again to the life of the state (*Republic, Laws*). Plato's ascent does not lead to an abandoning of the world, nor to ecstasy bereft of communication, nor to deification. If one compares Plato with Plotinus, one finds the common element to be the release from attachment to the world. But while, for Plotinus, this solution is sufficient in itself, Plato's philosophizing shoulders its task within the world. But he can fulfill this task only because he is at home in this place beyond the stars whence come norms and guidance.

Part Two

WHAT IS MAN?

EDITORS' INTRODUCTION TO PART TWO:

In the first quarter of the twentieth century some secular European thinkers, facing the apparent impasse which Western philosophy had reached and the malaise of the Western spirit associated with it, attempted a fresh start. Among those who achieved special prominence are Husserl, White-head, Moore, Wittgenstein, Heidegger, and Jaspers. The approach taken by each of these is distinct. Heidegger and Jaspers are often associated because they, together with certain others, chose a fundamental treatment of the question of man as their point of departure.

Before Jaspers can attempt to make any fresh start in philosophy he must first identify the new situation as it arises from the impasse reached by philosophy. In the main this diagnosis centers around two aspects of the modern situation as it pertains to philosophy. The first one makes manifest the prevalent loss of faith, the loss of grounding in truth by which man can live his life, can associate with others in trust, can accept obligations and defy or defer to authorities. Connected with this are certain discrepancies, for example those between professed beliefs people hold and their life practices as well as their conduct of affairs, which supposedly provide the testimony to their beliefs. It is the apparent failure of transmitted beliefs and the discord which their reception provokes—whether within public life, the life of the spirit, the life of the intellect, or their reflection in philosophy—that needs to be clarified. For Jaspers, this clarification, together with its implications for the possibility of philosophy, is associated with Kierkegaard and Nietzsche.

The other aspect concerns the relevance to philosophy of critical "reflection," especially in the mode of stringent scientific thought. Science and the critical intellect are treated in various ways in several parts of this Reader. In this part we present Jaspers's treatment of the question insofar as it serves to characterize the new situation and what this situation requires of philosophy. What it requires, in Jaspers's view, is a fundamental inquiry into what it means to be human, into those dimensions of being human where the concerns for truth and the impulses of critical reflection arise and whereby man is a participant in the realization of truth and is affected by actualities such as the malaise of the modern situation. The new situation raises the question of man in a distinct way, requiring a new perspective on man. By means of original explorations and conceptions Jaspers provides such a new perspective on man, which then serves him as a point of departure for what he regarded to be a possible fresh start for philosophy. As may be discerned in the different parts of this Reader, this fresh start entails a transformation of philosophy. The fundamental explorations that were commenced with *Psychologie der Weltanschauungen* (1919) were furthered by Jaspers's teaching and through conversations that took place in the 1920s, especially between him and Heidegger, and culminated in the publication of *Philosophie* (1931).

The following selections are presented in two sets. The first set, "The New Situation," presents Jaspers's juxtaposition of Kierkegaard and Nietzsche, as well as an excerpt from *Man in the Modern World* under the title "In Search of a New Perspective on Man." The second set of selections, "The New Perspective," presents some of these basic explorations to be found in Jaspers's new approach to the question of man; these selections are from *Philosophy*, Vol. II.

I.

The New Situation

Selection 6

KIERKEGAARD AND NIETZSCHE: THEIR HISTORIC SIGNIFICANCE

EDITORS:
The writings in Part Two, more than those in the other parts, represent Jaspers's contribution to Existential Philosophy. The following selection reflects this fact in a distinctive way. The special preoccupation with Kierkegaard in recent philosophy began when the development of Jaspers's philosophy was impelled by his study of Kierkegaard. It was his friend Erich Frank who told him about Kierkegaard close to the outbreak of the First World War, in July 1914. Frank reports that "Jaspers caught fire at once," and goes on to claim that "it was in this discussion that the movement of existentialism was started."[1] In Jaspers's own judgment it was the publication of his *Psychologie der Weltanschauungen* (1919) and, within this work, the juxtaposition of Kierkegaard and Nietzsche that decisively marked the inception of what Jaspers preferred to call "Philosophy of Existenz." "In *Psychologie der Weltanschauungen*" Jaspers writes, "I juxtaposed Kierkegaard and Nietzsche despite their apparent discord (the one a Christian, the other an atheist). Today they are connected as a matter of course, so that mention of the one serves as a reminder of the other."[2]

Jaspers worked out the juxtaposition of the two and of their significance as regards the modern state of mind and, relatedly, of philosophy, in several versions. The following version is considerably more mature and elaborate than the original one in *Psychologie der Weltanschauungen*. It is excerpted from the first and the last of a series of five lectures Jaspers held in Groningen in 1935 under the title "Reason and Existenz." In these lectures Jaspers presented a first outline of his later philosophy, whose main published work is the massive *Von der Wahrheit*. Thus the juxtaposition Kierkegaard-Nietzsche heralded both major waves of his philosophical exploration. At the time of those lectures Jaspers was also finishing a large book on Nietzsche

(1936), a work published in deliberate counteraction to the attempted misappropriation of Nietzsche by the ideologists of the National-Socialist regime. It was soon after (1937) that Jaspers was dismissed from his academic post by the regime for reason of "political unreliability." But even though Jaspers published much on Nietzsche and hardly anything on Kierkegaard, it is the latter whose influence on Jaspers was stronger, though more limited in scope.

The following selection consists of pp. 12–29, 35–40, and 127–130 of *Vernunft und Existenz*; in English translation by William Earle: *Reason and Existenz*, pp. 23–39, 45–49, and 127–130. The selection has been retranslated by the editors.

TEXT:

Derivation of the Present Philosophic Situation

The present philosophic situation is determined by the fact that two philosophers, Kierkegaard and Nietzsche, who did not count during their own lifetime and remained for a long time without influence in philosophy, are constantly growing in importance. Whereas all the philosophers after Hegel recede into the background next to Kierkegaard and Nietzsche, they stand before us today basically unquestioned as the really great thinkers of their time: Their influence as well as the opposition to them attest to this. Why are these two the philosophers of our age who can no longer be ignored?

Regarding the situation of philosophizing as well as of real life, Kierkegaard and Nietzsche articulate the impending calamity which at that time no one had become aware of (except as momentary, quickly forgotten presentiments) but which became clear to them.

The question as to what this calamity really is, is still open today. A *comparison* of the two thinkers does not answer this question, only makes it clearer and more urgent. This comparison is all the more telling because there could not have been any influence of one on the other, and because their differences make their common ground appear all the more impressive. This affinity between them (against which their differences assume secondary importance) in the whole course of their lives, down to the particulars of their thinking, is so compelling, that their essential character seems to have been born out of the needs arising from the spiritual situation of their century. Through them Western Philosophy received a jolt, the final importance of which cannot as yet be measured.

What is common to them both is their thinking and their humanity, both of which are indissolubly related to the present age and understood in this way by both. Let us, therefore, first present what they have in common in their *thinking* and in the *actuality of their thinking Existenz*.

The Common Features of Kierkegaard's and Nietzsche's Thought

Their thinking creates a new atmosphere. They cross all the limits that, before their time, were beyond question. It is as if they are no longer deterred in their thinking by anything. All that exists is as if sucked into a dizzying vortex. In Kierkegaard, it is an otherworldly Christianity which is like a nothingness, and which shows itself only in negation (the absurd, martyrdom) and in negative decision. In Nietzsche, it is a vacuum out of which a new being is to bring itself forth in desperate violence (eternal recurrence and Nietzsche's corresponding dogmatics).

Both of them question *reason* out of the depth of Existenz. Never before has a thoroughgoing resistance to mere reason, carried out on such a high level of actually accomplished thought possibilities, been so radical. This questioning, however, never implies a hostility toward reason—rather, both seek to appropriate, without limitation, all modes of rationality. It is not a philosophy of feeling—for both strive constantly to find the concept that will express it. Least of all is it dogmatic skepticism—rather, the whole of their thinking is directed toward authentic truth.

They do not bring forth a few doctrines, or a basic position, or a picture of the world. Instead, in a spiritually magnificent fashion, and carrying through a lifelong earnestness of philosphizing, they bring forth a new comprehensive thought-attitude for man within an endless reflection that is conscious of not being able—as reflection—to gain any ground. Their nature is not characterized by anything in particular; no definite doctrine or summons is to be drawn from them as something that can be isolated and fixed.

Out of the consciousness of their truth they both are suspicious of truth in its more naive form of *scientific* knowledge. Not that they doubt the methodical correctness of scientific insight. But Kierkegaard is astonished at the learned professors: for the most part they live their lives and die, imagining that things would continue this way; and that, if it were granted to them to go on living, they would comprehend more and more in a continued direct ascent. They do not experience the maturity by virtue of which there comes a critical turning point, where, from this point on, it is a matter of comprehending, increasingly, that there is something missing that cannot be comprehended. Kierkegaard believes this is the most terrible way to live: to enchant the whole world through one's discoveries and cleverness, to explain all of nature, yet not to understand oneself. Nietzsche is inexhaustible in his devastating analysis of the types of scholars who lack the real sense of what they do, who are not able to be themselves, and yet believe they can grasp, with their ultimately vain knowledge, Being itself.

Because they both question the ability of all self-enclosed rationalities to communicate truth as a whole, they become radical opponents of the "system," i.e., that form which philosophy had assumed through the millennia and which led to its last burst of glory in German idealism. For them, "system" implies distraction from actuality, and hence lie and deception. Kierkegaard understands that for God existence can be a system, but not for an existing spirit; system and closedness correspond to each other, but existence is exactly their opposite. The philosopher who builds a system is like a human being who builds a palace but lives in the adjoining shanty: this phantastical creature does not himself inhabit that which he has thought up. Yet a man's thoughts must be the edifice in which he lives; anything else would be perverse. The fundamental question of philosophy, i.e., what it is itself and what is science, is posed anew and relentlessly. Nietzsche wants to be better at doubting than Descartes; in Hegel's foundering attempt to fit reason into the developmental process, he sees a Gothic attempt at storming the heavens. For him the will to create a system shows a lack of integrity.

Both express in the same way what they understand knowledge really to be. For them it is nothing other than *interpretation*.

Interpretation, however, has no end. Existence, for Nietzsche, is capable of an infinity of interpretations. For Kierkegaard, whatever has happened or was done in the past is always open to fresh understanding: as it is interpreted, it becomes a new actuality that has been hidden until then. Therefore temporal life can never be quite comprehensible to man; no man can penetrate absolutely his own consciousness.

Both use the simile of interpretation for knowledge of Being, moreover in such a manner as if Being were deciphered in the interpretation of interpretation. Nietzsche wants to strip the original text, *homo natura*, of succeeding layers of writing and to read it in its actuality. Kierkegaard assigned no significance to his writings other than that they are to be rereadings of the original texts of individual human conditions of existence.

Connected with this fundamental thought is the fact that both Kierkegaard and Nietzsche—these most open and candid of thinkers—show a seductive penchant for *concealment* and the mask. For them, the mask is necessarily tied to being true. *Indirect communication* becomes the only way of communicating genuine truth; and indirect communication, as expression, belongs to the indecisive nature of truth in temporal existence, in which it must still be grasped in the process of becoming out of the wellsprings of each Existenz.

In their thinking, both encounter that ground which, in man, would be Being itself: Kierkegaard counters the philosophy that has asserted, from Parmenides through Descartes to Hegel, that "Thinking is Being," with the proposition: "As you believe, so you are," "Believing is Being." Nietzsche sees the Will to Power. But faith as well as Will to Power are mere *signa*, themselves not showing directly what is meant but themselves capable of limitless interpretation.

For both, *honesty* is the decisive motivating factor. For both of them it is the expression of the ultimate virtue to which they submit. It remains for them the minimum measure of the unconditional that is still possible within the confusion where all content becomes questionable. But it also becomes the vertiginous demand of a truthfulness that brings even itself into question, which is the opposite of that expedient brute power that believes it possesses the truth clearly in barbaric certitude.

It is a valid question whether anything at all is being said in thinking such as this. Indeed, both Kierkegaard and Nietzsche are conscious of the fact that the comprehension of their thinking is not open to man merely as thinker. Rather, it is a matter of *who it is that understands*.

They address the *individual* who must bring with him and must bring forth out of himself what they can say only indirectly. Kierkegaard believes in Lichtenberg's epigram which he cites: Such works are mirrors; if a monkey peeks in, no apostle can peek out.[3] Nietzsche considers understanding him a distinction that has to be earned. He states that it is impossible to teach the truth where the manner of thinking is base. Each seeks the readership appropriate to him.

Kierkegaard's and Nietzsche's Thinking Existenz

The mode of thinking thus characterized is founded on Kierkegaard's and Nietzsche's Existenz insofar as they belong to the present age in a manner peculiar to them. Neither one of them brings an era to its culmination; they do not construct a *world;* they do not create for one last time a *picture* of a world in passing. Thus no single thought, no system, no calling is in itself decisive for them. They do not feel themselves to be a positive expression of their time; rather, they express their time negatively through realizing in their very being what it is: an age each completely rejected but one both recongized for what it is, an age of decadence. It seems to be their task to carry out the *experience of this epoch to its very end* in their own persons, totally to be its very actuality in order to overcome it. At first they succeed in this endeavor involuntarily, then consciously by being representatives of their time but as the *exception* that causes scandal and offence. Let us look at this more closely.

Both of them become aware of their *task* early, at the end of their youth, but so far only vaguely. A *decision* on their part—one encompassing the whole person, quiet, often not even conscious, at other times a decision forced out of themselves—drives them into the most radical solitude. Without position, unmarried, without active participation in life, they yet seem, as the great *realists* which they are, to be in touch with the genuine actuality deeply below the surface.

They find this actuality in their basic experience of the age as the age of *ruin*: as they look back on the millenia to the beginnings of ancient Greece, they sense the end of this whole historical process; at the turning point they draw attention to this very moment but without pretending to comprehend the meaning and course of history in its entirety.

The attempt has been made to understand this age on an economical, technical, historico-political, and sociological level. Kierkegaard and Nietzsche, on the other hand, believe they can discern, as it were, a *substantial* modification in the very nature of *man*.

Kierkegaard regards all of the Christendom in its present actuality as a tremendous deception, in which God is made a fool of. This Christianity has nothing to do with the Christianity of the New Testament. There are only two paths open: either to keep up the deception through artifice and to cover up existing conditions—then all is lost; or to admit honestly to this wretched state of affairs, i.e., that at the present time there is in truth not a single individual born any more who is fit to be a Christian in the meaning of the New Testament, that none of us is fit for it but merely lives a pious, watered-down version of Christianity. When we admit this, it will become evident whether there is something true in this honesty, whether it has the approval of Providence; if not, everything must break down again so that in ensuing horror individuals may arise again who can be bearers of the Christianity of the New Testament.

Nietzsche summarizes the historical situation of the time in the one phrase: God is dead.

Thus in their basic substance both have in common a historical judgment about their time. They see the impending *nothingness*, but both still possess knowledge of the substance of what was lost. Neither one of them wants nothingness. Even though Kierkegaard presupposes the truth or the possibility of the truth of Christianity, and Nietzsche, in contrast, ascertains not merely that godlessness represents a loss, but seizes it as the greatest opportunity, they both still have in common the will to the substance of Being, to the nobility and value of man. They do not invent any programs for political reform, indeed make no programs at all, do not concentrate on particulars; yet through their thinking they want to make something happen, the nature of which they cannot foresee with any certainty. Nietzsche sees in this uncertainty his long-range "higher politics"; for Kierkegaard it means becoming a Christian in a new form which is indifferent to all worldly concerns. As both of them face their own epoch, they are gripped by the question: what will become of man?

They themselves personify *modernity* in a form that overturns itself; themselves foundering, they overcame themselves by having lived through it to its very end. However, they do not experience their epoch's plight passively but are themselves active, doing completely what most people halfway allow to be done to them. We see this in the first place in their *unlimited reflection*;

then, as a counter-thrust, in their drive toward the *wellsprings*; and finally, in the way in which, sinking into the bottomless, they grasp for support within transcendence.

Since Fichte the age of *Reflection* has been characterized as reasoning without commitment, as the dissolution of all authority, as the abandonment of all content that gives to thought measure, aim, and meaning; in this way, having become an indifferent game of the intellect and with nothing to restrain it, reason now fills the world with noise and dust.

Kierkegaard and Nietzsche however do not turn against reflection in order to destroy it; but, in order to overcome it, they engage in it to an unlimited extent and master it. Man cannot return to an immediacy without reflection, without losing himself; he can, however, follow this path to its end so that, rather than to succumb to reflection, he can reach his own foundation by means of it.

Thus their "infinite reflection" has a twofold character. It can lead to total ruin or it may become the condition of authentic Existenz. Both of them express this, Kierkegaard most clearly:

Reflection, as such inexhaustible, cannot be stopped through itself. It is faithless for it prevents all decision; it is never finished and can, in the end, become "dialectical prattle"; thus Kierkegaard calls it the poison of reflection. The fact, however, that it is possible, indeed necessary, is substantiated for us by the ambiguity inherent in all existence and action: for reflection, everything can always mean yet something else. This situation can be exploited on the one hand by the sophistry of existence as well as by the Existenz-less aesthete who only wants to savor everything in a novel and interesting way: no matter how decisive a step he takes, he reserves for himself the possibility of interpreting the matter in such a way that, at one blow, all is changed. On the other hand, however, we can seize this situation in a truthful manner, knowing that, insofar as we are honest, we live in the "sea of reflection where no one can simply call out to the other, and all sea-marks stand in dialectical relation to each other."[4]

Without infinite reflection we would slide into the tranquility of something fixed that, as the stable element in the world, would be absolute, i.e., we would become superstitious. An atmosphere of unfreedom comes into being together with such fixation. Therefore, infinite reflection, precisely through its limitlessly mobile dialectic, is the condition of *freedom*. It bursts open every prison of the finite. Only by means of it can infinite passion arise out of passion in its immediacy. Passion in its immediacy is unquestioning, and hence still unfree. But in infinite passion the immediacy is retained throughout the questioning, and the passion becomes genuinely faithful by being grasped in freedom.

However, in order that this freedom not come to nought in empty reflection but rather fulfill itself, infinite reflection must *run aground*. Only then can it start out from something or exhaust itself in the decision of resolve and faith. As untrue as is the arbitrary and forcible discontinuance of reflection, so true is the ground out of which it itself is mastered by something that comes to meet Existenz. In this encounter Existenz is given to itself as a gift so that by giving itself up to infinite reflection, it fully masters it.

Reflection, which can dissolve into nothingness as well as become the condition of Existenz, is designated as such in the same way by both Kierkegaard and Nietzsche. Out of it, they have carried out the thinking which they communicate in their works, in its immense richness. This thinking is, according to its meaning, possibility: "Running aground" can merely be indicated and made possible in it, but cannot be carried out by it.

In their thinking, both of them are also aware of their knowledge about the *possibilities* of man, aware of what they themselves are not yet when they think it. Consciously to know possibilities is not untrue—in analogy to fiction—but it is reflection that awakens and questions. Possibility is the form in which I am permitted to know what I am not yet, and the preparation for Being itself.

Kierkegaard frequently calls his method "experimenting psychology"; Nietzsche calls his thinking "(at)tempting."

Therefore they like to leave what *they themselves* are and what they are ultimately thinking *concealed* to the point of being unrecognizable, and let it appear sunk down into incomprehensibility. Kierkegaard's pseudonym writes: "The something. . . . , which I am, precisely that is a nothing"; it gives him great satisfaction "to hold his Existenz at the critical zero, . . . between something and nothing, as a mere *perhaps*".[5] And Nietzsche likes to call himself a "philosopher of the dangerous *Perhaps*."[6]

For both, reflection is primarily self-reflection. To understand oneself is for them the way to truth. But they both experience how, on this way, one's own substance can disappear, how the free, creative self-understanding can be replaced by an unfree preoccupation with one's own empirical existence. Kierkegaard knows the horrible state when everything "disappears before a morbid brooding over one's own miserable history."[7] He seeks the way "between this devouring of oneself in self-contemplation as if one were the only person who ever existed, and the scanty comfort to be found in the general human condition of *commune naufragium*" [general shipwreck].[8] He knows the "unfortunate relativity in everything, the endless questions as to what I am." Nietzsche expresses it in the following manner:

> Between a hundred mirrors
> before yourself false. . .
> strangled by your own rope
> Self-knower!

Self-hangman! . . .
Between two nothings
curved inwards,
A question mark . . .[9]

The epoch, no longer able to find its way in the multiplicity of its reflection and verbal rationalization, is eager to leave reflection behind and press on to the *origins*. Kierkegaard and Nietzsche seem to anticipate this move, too; only the later generations looked everywhere for primal sources in the *verbal*, in the aesthetic *attraction* of the immediately striking, in general *simplicity*, in unreflected *experience*, in the existence of the *things closest to us*. It would appear as if Kierkegaard and Nietzsche already served the same cause; they both lived with an awareness and passionate love that was at the source of possibilities for human communication. . . .

In fact, they travel the most radical road to the origin, but in such a manner that for them the dialectical movement never stops. Their seriousness is abrogated neither in an illusion of dogmatic rigidity of a supposed origin, nor by language, aesthetic attraction, or simplicity becoming an end in itself.

Both travel a road that would be unbearable for them without support in the transcendent; for they do not reflect, as do the average moderns, within the obvious parameter of vital needs and interests. Kierkegaard and Nietzsche, for whom it is an all-or-nothing matter, dare to be without limits. But they are able to do this only because they are, from the very beginning, rooted in that which is also hidden from them: both speak already in their youth about the *Unknown God*. Kierkegaard, as late as age twenty-five wrote: "Disregarding the fact that I am still far from understanding my inner self, I have . . . worshipped the unknown God."[10] And Nietzsche, at twenty, wrote his first unforgettable poem, "To the Unknown God," which ends as follows:

I want to know you, unknown one,
Who reaches deep into my soul,
Who sweeps through my life like a tempest,
Incomprehensible one, my kin!
I want to know you, even serve you.[11]

They can never confine themselves to the finite and the understood, hence trivial, because they reflect without limit; but they cannot bear to remain in reflection, either. Precisely because he is completely given over to reflection Kierkegaard says: "When I am bereft of the religious understanding of myself, then I feel like an insect must feel with which children are toying: just as cruelly does life seem to deal with me."[12] In terrible solitude, understood by just about no one, not geniunely attached to any human being, he calls out to

God: "God in heaven, if there were not after all a most inward center in man, where all this can be forgotten . . . who could endure it!"[13]

Nietzsche is aware at all times that he navigates on the seas of infinity, that he has abandoned solid ground forever. He is aware that something did not yet exist for Dante and Spinoza that he knows as his solitude; somehow they had a god for companionship. But Nietzsche, almost destroyed in his solitude, without people and without the ancient God, beholds Zarathustra and conceives eternal recurrence, this thought that makes him tremble with awe as it confers happiness upon him. He lives all the time like someone who is mortally wounded. His problems make him suffer. His thinking is his way of pulling himself together: "If only I had the courage to think all that I know."[14] But in his limitless reflection, there are revealed to him, after all, these contents that satisfy him so deeply and are indeed transcendent.

Thus both perform a leap toward transcendence but to a form of transcendence where, in truth, no one is likely to follow them: Kierkegaard toward Christianity, conceived as absurd paradox, as the negative decision to give up the world completely and as necessary martyrdom; Nietzsche toward eternal recurrence and the Superman.

Thus precisely those thoughts of Nietzsche's, which for him are his deepest, can cause us to be overcome by an emptiness, and Kierkegaard's faith can cause an uncanny feeling of strangeness to come over us. In the symbols of Nietzsche's religion, with his will toward immanence (in addition to the eternal circularity of things; the will to power; yea-saying to Being; the lust of deep, deep eternity) there is no longer a transcendent content if they are taken in their immediacy. Only in a roundabout manner and with difficulty can one derive interpretively an essential content from these symbols. For Kierkegaard, who breathed new life into the profound formulas of theology, it can appear to be a tremendous feat on the part of someone who might even be an unbeliever, to force himself to have faith.

Precisely because of the seemingly total essential difference between the Christian faith of the one and the emphasized godlessness of the other, the similarity of their thinking is more characteristic of them. In an age of reflection that exists in an actual state of unbelief but pretends that all the past still endures, the rejection of faith and forcing oneself to believe belong together. The godless can appear pious, the believer impious; both stand within the same dialectic.

What they create out of their existential thinking they would not have been able to achieve without being in full *possession of their heritage*. Both are imbued with an education based on antiquity. Both have been raised in Christian piety; their motivations are unthinkable without their Christian origins. Even if they passionately resist these currents of tradition in the form it has assumed over the course of millennia, they still find a historical, for them ineradicable, support in this origin. They commit themselves to an origin that fulfills their own faith: Kierkegaard to the Christianity of the New Testament as he understands it, Nietzsche to a preSocratic Hellenism.

But nowhere, neither in finitude nor in a consciously grasped origin, nor in a decisively seized transcendence, nor in a historical tradition, is there a final anchor point for them. It seems as if their existence—because both live through all the sense of loss inherent in their times to the very end—would therefore be a shattered existence in whose very *shattering* a truth would be revealed that could not be expressed otherwise.

Even though they gain tremendous sovereignty of character, there is at the same time inflicted on them a solitude that places them beyond the world; they are as though *banished*.

They are *exceptions* in every sense of the word. Physiologically they do not measure up to their nature: Their physiognomy is confusing because they look undistinguished in relation to who they are and does not leave the imprint of a prototype of human greatness. It is as though they lacked something in sheer vitality. They seem eternally young, as spirits who have strayed into the world, lacking reality because they lack a world.

In their presence, people around them feel attracted in a mysterious way, feel for a moment as if raised to a higher level of existence, but no one ever genuinely loved them. . . .

Both are irreplaceable for us as shipwrecks who have dared to be just that. We orient ourselves by them. They bring us tidings of something that we would not have become aware of without such sacrifice, of something that seems essential to us but which we cannot, to this very day, grasp adequately. It is as if truth itself were speaking, stirring up a disquietude that attacks the very depths of our consciousness of Being. . . .

The modern age, precisely in its deterioration out of negligence, has nurtured itself on them. Their reflection, instead of remaining in the seriousness of infinite reflection, has become a means of sophistry in careless talk. Their words as well as the whole phenomenon of their existence were relished as a grandiose aesthetic attraction. They caused the dissolution of all remaining ties on the part of those who are not guided to the wellspring of true seriousness but wanted to clear the path for capricious choice. Thus their influence, contrary to their very being and thinking, turned into an immeasurably destructive one.

The Significance of the Philosophic Situation Brought About by Kierkegaard and Nietzsche

The significance of Kierkegaard and Nietzsche becomes evident through what has become of them in the course of time. Their effect is immeasurably great—greater still in thought in general than in the field of philosophy,—but infinitely ambiguous.

What Kierkegaard really signifies is clear neither in theology nor in philosophy: Modern protestant theology in Germany, insofar as it is authentic, seems for the greater part to be under the direct or indirect influence of Kierkegaard. He, however, issued a pamphlet in May 1855 as the summation, on a practical-active level, of what he wanted to achieve with his thought. The motto was: "But at midnight there is a cry" (Matthew 25:6), and he wrote: "Because you no longer participate in public worship as it is practiced at this time . . . you have invariably . . . one great guilt less: you do not participate in making a fool of God by passing off as New Testament Christianity what is not that at all."[15]

In modern philosophy, some decisive impulses have been developed because of Kierkegaard. Some of the most essential basic concepts of present-day philosophizing, especially in Germany, have their source in Kierkegaard, this Kierkegaard whose very thinking seems to dissolve previous systematic philosophy, who repudiates all speculation and who, when he does give recognition to philosophy, says at best: "Philosophy can watch over us—but cannot nourish us."

It may well be that theology as well as philosophy, when they follow Kierkegaard, hide something essential from themselves so they can use his concepts and formulas for their own quite different purposes. Thus it may well be that within theology even a non-believing theology could—by using Kierkegaardian methods of thinking which have been refined for this purpose—set forth a way of expressing faith through dialectical paradoxes, which would make it rationally compatible for it to consider itself as adhering to the Christian faith.

Thus, also, it may well be that philosophizing based on Kierkegaard is secretly nourished by the Christian substance which it ignores when it speaks out.

Nietzsche's significance has remained just as unclear. The kind of effect he has in Germany has been achieved by no other philosopher. But it does seem that every position, every Weltanschauung, every conviction claims him as authority. It could be that all of us do not yet know what this thinking as a whole comprises and achieves. Therefore it is the task of everyone who lets Kierkegaard and Nietzsche be of importance to him, to be honest about the question: how does he really deal with them, what is his relationship to them, what are they to him, what does he make out of them?

The effect common to both of them, to enchant and then to disillusion, to seize and then abandon dissatisfied, as if heart and hands remained empty, is merely the clear expression of their own will: all depends on what the reader in his own inner action makes of what they communicate, in a situation where one does not find the sort of fulfillment one usually does through either some cognition, or a work of art, or a philosophical system, or a piously accepted prophecy. They suspend all satisfaction.

The two are indeed exceptions but they do not provide a model to follow. Whenever someone has imitated Kierkegaard or Nietzsche, even if only in style, he has made himself ridiculous. What they themselves did was to just miss, at certain moments, the fine borderline where the sublime turns into the ridiculous—what they did was possible only that one time. True, all greatness is unique and can never be repeated in identical form. But in our attitude toward their uniqueness, it is one thing to live in its presence, and, appropriating it, remake ourselves; and essentially another thing to regard it as a far reference point which changes us even as it increases our distance from it.

They dismiss us without giving us an aim and without assigning us definite tasks. Through them, each of us can only become what he is himself. But what that is, in those who follow them, has not been decided to this day. The question is how we who are not exceptions should live yet seek our inner path as we look at these exceptions.

We are in a spiritual situation where merely turning our glance away from them becomes the seed of dishonesty. It seems as if it is they who fully *force us out of a certain thoughtlessness* that, without them, seems to remain even in the study of the great philosophers. We cannot calmly proceed in the continuity of traditional conceptualization. For, through Kierkegaard and Nietzsche, a mode of the thought-experience of Existenz has become effective, the full consequences of which have in general not yet come to light. They have posed a question that is still impenetrable but which one can feel; this question is still open. They have made us aware and have indeed brought it about that there is no longer any self-evident ground under our feet. There is no longer any background to our thinking that remains untouched.

There are two equally great dangers in an individual's preoccupation with them: to become addicted to them, and; not to take them seriously. One's relationship to them is inescapably ambivalent. Neither of them constructed a world, but even though they appear to invalidate everything, they are positive spirits. If we really want to get close to them, we must realize a distinctive, novel relationship to them as creative thinkers, a relationship that is different from the one we maintain to all other great thinkers.

Supposing—in consideration of the times and the way of thinking created by Kierkegaard and Nietzsche—the question is asked: *what now?* In response, Kierkegaard refers us to an absurd Christianity in the face of which the world sinks out of sight. And Nietzsche points to the distant, whose indistinctness does not manifest itself as a substance out of which we could live. No one has accepted their answers; they are not ours. In the light of what they are for us, it is up to us to see what we become through ourselves. But this can in no way be planned or determined in advance.

Thus we would err if we were to believe that we could deduce, from a *world-historical* survey of the development of the human spirit, what should happen next. We do not stand outside like a god—who is thought to do just that—who, anticipating all, would perceive the whole. For us, rather, the present cannot be replaced by what is supposed to be a world history from which we derive our place in life and our task. . . . No one knows the aim and purpose of man and his thinking. Since existence, man, and his world have not come to an end, there can be neither a completed philosophy nor an anticipation of the whole. We humans make plans with finite purposes; the outcomes always include something quite different from what anyone had intended. In the same way, philosophizing is an activity that calls forth man's inwardness which is unaware of its ultimate meaning. Thus man is not able to derive the present task as something particular from the anticipated whole; rather, it is brought to consciousness out of the origin experienced in the here and now, and out of the content as yet indistinctly willed. Philosophy as thought always is, at the same time, the consciousness of Being that is integral for this moment, which knows that—in the form of expression—it would not endure as something ultimate.

Rejecting a supposed overview of the spiritual and actual total situation, we philosophize in the knowledge of a situation that leads us once more to the ultimate limits and origins of being human. Today, no one is able to develop completely and definitely the tasks for thought which arise therein. We live, so to say, in the breakers of possibility, constantly under threat of being tossed over but always ready to get up again in spite of it. We are ready, in philosophizing, to carry out, in the presence of that which puts everything into question, our most actual thoughts, i.e., those that elicit our humanity. These thoughts are possible for us when the horizon is limitless, the actualities clear, and the authentic questions are revealed.

The Task: To Philosophize in View of the Exception Without Being an Exception

We have taken a look at the situation created by Kierkegaard and Nietzsche for philosophizing within the actuality of this epoch. Because of them there has arisen a new situation of being able to think and having to think in a way that cannot be understood by drawing an analogy with any other historical set of facts. True, it appears that, from time to time, one would like to shake both of them off impatiently. But since they have not been truly penetrated or really caught sight of in their actuality and in their thinking, they come back to us, even greater and more impressive than before. The ambivalence of their effect—which is as grandiosely awakening as it is radically destructive—has existed now for half a century.

Philosophically we have had to guard ourselves against their being misunderstood in order to experience all the more decisively the inescapable challenge they left behind. We have had to guard against nihilistic, sophistically

twisting, ways of using their thoughts and words, ways that seduce us to endless reflection or overpower us by their suggestiveness.

Over the past decades one could observe the impotent and fruitless restriction of truth to the so-called but only seemingly rational, and the alternative,
equally fruitless, rejection of reason into which trust in an inadequately
grasped reason could easily be transformed. Hence, the philosophy which
now is called Philosophy of Existenz has no desire to be one of the chaotic
anti-rational movements. Rather, it wishes to be the counterblow against the
chaos and ruin that can appear both in the guise of intellectual reasonableness
and open anti-reason. In the Philosophy of Existenz the clarity of transcendentally oriented life shall again become communicable out of original decisiveness, in articulated expression, and as a philosophizing in which we actually live.

What is philosophy? What will become of philosophy? To ask these questions again, in the situation in which thought finds itself today, means that we
actually consider ourselves as standing at an end point. In the case of Hegel we
mark the end of Western philosophy regarded as objective, self-assured, absolute rationality; philosophizing according to him is, in the final analysis,
knowledge, in the present, about the whole of bygone substance. In the case of
Kierkegaard and Nietzsche we reach the end of the possibility of questioning,
by means of limitless reflection, on the part of exceptions which are devoid of
communication and either with God or with nothingness. To study thoroughly both modes of coming to an endpoint is the condition—not only for
acquiring the intellectual means for philosophizing but, essentially, in order
not to arrive superficially in easy affirmation of nothingness, but rather inwardly in one's own experience—at the point where one really knows: One
cannot go beyond this point. In fact, we are not facing nothingness but standing again, as at all times when human beings exist, before our primal source.
The new philosophizing grows out of this experience, and we will present a
picture of its possibilities.

Philosophy after Kierkegaard and Nietzsche cannot consist in characterizing what they had thought in the form of a coherent thought structure; this
would dislocate them from the ground on which they stood. Instead, one must
let this ground itself become effective. Our task is: to philosophize, *without
being an exception, in view of the exception.*

The truth of the exception for us consists in a permanent putting-
everything-to-the-question, without which we would sink back into more or
less crude, foregone conclusions of a complacent frame of mind that does not
think radically. By its knowledge about the exception our soul, instead of en-
capsulating itself in a new narrowness, can remain open for possible truth and
actuality that can still speak to us even in despair, in suicide, in the passion for
the night-side of life, in every form of negative resolve. Seeing the counter-

rational rationally not only shows us the possibility of the positive in the negative, but also the ground upon which we ourselves stand. Without the exceptions there would be lost to us an indispensable approach to truth. Their seriousness and unconditionality constrain us to use them as standards although we do not act in accordance with the contents they realized. The difficulty of our philosophical situation is created by the fact that we owe to Kierkegaard and Nietzsche something new that is possible through laying the deepest foundations, and yet we do not follow them in essential decisions.

The philosophizing which owes its impulse to them will, in contrast to their lack of communication, be a communicative philosophizing; otherwise it would be a vain effort since the exception cannot be repeated. In contrast to the negatively limitless radicalness of the exception, this philosophizing will be committed to the communicability in all modes of the Encompassing. Over against the risk of their worldlessness . . . it will issue forth out of the will to commitment in communication as actualization in time.

From this attitude there emerge some necessary, early, basic characteristics of contemporary philosophizing:

1. Since it does not mean to be the philosophizing of the exception but open to all, it considers itself true only if it can be translated into the actuality of many, that is, if the possibility of reason in its widest compass is brought methodically to self-consciousness.

2. Only in light of the exception, which accomplished the seemingly impossible, do we find our way back, without self-deception, to the being of a universality within the *history* of philosophy that has once more been transformed for us.

3. In face of the exception, whose thinking is indeed not solely philosophizing but changes abruptly into un-philosophy—whether of the faith of *revelation* or of *atheism*—philosophizing becomes aware of moving between these two possibilities that concern it essentially and constantly put it in question.

4. With this, philosophizing must reassure itself anew of the ground of its own fundamentally *philosophical faith*.

As we travel these paths of philosophizing we feel as if we were once more looking for the calm of Kant and Spinoza, of Nicolas of Cusa and Parmenides, and turn away from the irrevocable disquietude of Kierkegaard and Nietzsche. The latter, however, remain, like flickering beacons, the constant guides without which we would succumb once again to the deception of teachable philosophical knowledge, which as such lacks power.

NOTES

1. "Erich Frank's Work; an Appreciation by Ludwig Edelstein," in Erich Frank, *Wissen, Wollen, Glauben*, Artemis Verlag, Zurich Stuttgart 1955, p. 419.

2. Karl Jaspers, "Vorwort zur vierten Auflage," *Psychologie der Weltanschauungen*, Springer-Verlag, Berlin Heidelberg New York 1971, p. x.

3. Cf. Kierkegaard, *Gesammelte Werke*, vol. IV, Diedrichs, Jena, p. 8.

4. Emmanuel Hirsch, *Kierkegaardstudien*, Guetersloh 1933, vol. I, p. 298.

5. Kierkegaard, *Gesammelte Werke*, op. cit., vol. IV, p. 247.

6. *Friedrich Nietzsche's Werke*, Naumann Verlag, Leipzig, vol. 7, p. 11.

7. Kierkegaard, *Tagebuecher*, Innsbruck 1923, vol. I, p. 92.

8. Op. cit., p. 88.

9. *Friedrich Nietzsche's Werke*, op. cit., vol. 8, pp. 422, 424.

10. Kierkegaard, *Tagebuecher*, op. cit., p. 35.

11. Nietzsche, *Jugendschriften*, Munich 1923, p. 209.

12. Kierkegaard, *Gesammelte Werke*, op. cit., vol. IV, p. 332.

13. Kierkegaard, *Tagebuecher*, op. cit., p. 259.

14. Nietzsche's letter to Overbeck, dated February 12, 1887.

15. Kierkegaard, "This has to be said; so be it now said," *Attack Upon Christendom*, Princeton University Press, Princeton 1946, p. 59.

Selection 7

IN SEARCH OF A NEW PERSPECTIVE ON MAN

EDITORS:

In the following selection Jaspers develops the view that in the modern disarray of the truths one might believe in and the concomitant devaluation of man, the individual is left to his own devices. Philosophically this entails a fundamental re-view of the question: What is man? In our times, Jaspers maintains, such a re-view is the task of Existenz-philosophy. Before he directs our attention to this task he disposes of the prevalent claim that today empirical sciences are the provenance of a comprehensively fundamental answer to the question of man: "When, by means of absolutization, they are meant to cognize the being of man in its entirety, they must be rejected as utterly inadequate substitutes for philosophy." On the other hand, even as we are directed to the explorations of Existenz-philosophy, Jaspers cautions us that these explorations are not to be regarded as an absolutization of man: Existenz-philosophy is an "advance toward Being itself"; it "is the philosophy of man's being which leads beyond man."

The selection is taken from a little book that appeared concomitantly with the three volumes of *Philosophy* in 1931 under the title *The Spiritual Situation of our Time*. The book was meant for and was read by a much wider audience than the large volumes that it accompanied. For many Germans it was a *vademecum* on their dismal journey through the years of the Nazi regime. It was also the first book by Jaspers to have been translated into English.

In the original the following excerpt appears on pp. 158–64, 173, and

175–80 of *Die geistige Situation der Zeit*; in English translation by Eden and Cedar Paul: *Man in the Modern Age*, pp. 157–62, 172, and 174–78. This excerpt is an emended version of the English translation.

TEXT:

A. Current Conceptions of Man's Being

The unsheltered individual gives our epoch its physiognomy: in rebelliousness; in the despair of nihilism; in the perplexity of the multitude of persons who remain unfulfilled; in a search along false paths on the part of those who renounce finite goals and withstand harmonizing lures. "There is no God," cry the masses more and more vociferously; and with the loss of God the value of man is also lost. Any number of human beings are massacred because they are of no account.

The aspect of our world in the coerciveness of its life-order and in the instability of its mental activity renders it impossible for being to retain a satisfactory grip upon the extant. Our representation of the outer world tends to discourage us. We have a pessimistic outlook; we incline to renounce action. In other cases, however, despite our gloomy picture of the world in general, we preserve an indolently optimistic consciousness of our own personal joy in life and are satisfied with our contemplation of the substantial—for such an attitude is common enough today. But pessimism and optimism are both oversimplifications, and are the outcome of evasions.

In actual fact, however, the demands which the situation makes upon man seem to be so exacting that none but a being who is more than man is capable of complying with them. The impossibility of complying with these demands can tempt us to evade them, to accommodate ourselves to that which is merely present, and to set limits to our thoughts. One who believes that everything is in order and who trusts in the world as such, does not even need to be equipped with courage. He complies with the course of events which (so he believes) work for good even without his participation. His alleged courage is nothing more than a confidence that man is not slipping down into an abyss in which he would be lost. One who has genuine courage is one who, inspired by the anxiety of sensing the possible, takes hold in the knowledge that he alone who wills the impossible can attain the possible. Only through his experience of the impossibility of achieving fulfillment does man become enabled to perform his allotted task.

Contemporary man does not receive his imprint simply from the fact that he assimilates whatever, in the form of being, comes to him out of the tradition of his world. If he gives himself up to this tradition alone he dissipates himself. He is, in a new sense, dependent upon himself as an individual. He must help himself, seeing that he is no longer free by assimilation of the all-permeating substance, but is free in the void of Nothingness. When transcendence conceals itself, man can attain to it only through his own self.

If man is to help himself, his philosophy, today, must take the form of a study of what is our present conception of man's being. The old antitheses— the contrasted outlooks known respectively as individualism and socialism, liberal and conservative, revolutionary and reactionary, progressive and re-versionary, materialistic and idealistic—do not fit any more, although they are still universally flaunted as banners or used as invectives. An examination of various world views, as if there were several among which to choose, is no longer the way of attaining to truth. An expansion of vision and cognition to all that is possible has culminated today in the lack of commitment in which there is an untransferable choice left, between Nothingness, on the one hand, and, on the other, the absolute historicity of one's own foundation, which is at home in all possibility and conscious of binding limits.

But the question of man's being, which is to lead us out of the dogmatism of the objectivity of fixed alternative world views, is not, as such, by any means unambiguous.

Man is always something more than what he knows of himself. He is not what he is simply once and for all, but is a path; he is not merely a determin-able fixed existence, but is, within that existence, endowed with possibilities through freedom. Out of this freedom he decides, even as he acts, what he is.

Man is not a rounded-off existence which repeats itself from generation to generation, nor is he a luminous existence, transparent to itself. He "breaks through" the passivity of perpetually renewed identical circles, and is depen-dent upon his own activity, to continue this movement toward an unknown goal.

Consequently, there is a profound cleavage in man's innermost nature. No matter how he thinks himself, in thinking he sets himself against himself as well as against the other. He sees everything in opposites.

Every time the meaning is different according to how he sunders himself into spirit and flesh, into understanding and sensuality, into soul and body, into duty and inclination—also into his being and his phenomenal aspect, into his actions and his thoughts, into what he actually does and what he thinks he is doing. The decisive point is that he must always be setting himself in oppo-sition. There is no being human without cleavage. Yet he cannot rest content in this cleavage. The way in which he overcomes it, constitutes the way in which he comprehends himself.

In that respect we find that there are two alternative possibilities which must be adequately discussed.

Man may make himself the object of cognition. He then regards as his true being what, in daily experience, he recognizes as his existence and its underly-ing ground. What he phenomenally is, that is his consciousness; and his consciousness is what it is in virtue of something else, in virtue of the sociological circumstances, in virtue of the unconscious, in virtue of the vital nature. This other is, for him, Being, whose essence is reflected for him phenomenally as consciousness.

The purpose of this mode of cognition is to overcome this tension through being becoming identical with consciousness. The idea of mere existence as completed in a state wherein there are no tensions is, in this mode of cognition, involuntarily regarded as attainable. There is deemed possible a sociological order wherein all will enter into their rights; a mind wherein the unconscious and the conscious will be amicable companions as soon as the former has been purged of all its complexes; a racial vitality which, after an efficient process of artificial selection has done its work, may be considered noble and healthy and thus perfect itself as existence, satisfied in having turned out well. In these circumstances which, in an ambiguous sense, are called natural, i.e., both necessary and true, there will no longer be any unconditionality of temporal life, for unconditionality arises only out of the tension in which self-being forcibly takes hold of itself. Rather, knowledge about natural being-human turns against self-being as against something lost, extravagant, morbid, and self-exclusive.

This is the course taken by the second possibility. Here are found the tensions that are the limit situations which cannot be eliminated from existence once and for all, and become manifest with the decisiveness of self-being. If man be no longer recognized as Being (which he is), then he brings himself, in cognition, into the suspension of absolute possibility. Therein he experiences the appeal to his freedom, in virtue of which he becomes, through his own agency, what it is possible for him to become but what he is not as yet. As freedom he conjures up being as his hidden transcendence.

The meaning and aim of this path is transcendence. In the end, that which is authentically itself experiences shipwreck as mere existence. From here on, the absence of tension is considered as a path of where, believing to have overcome the limit situation, one merely conceals it from oneself and suspends one's temporality. All cognition in the world, human cognition included, is a particular perspective by means of which man is given the scope of his situation. Cognition is, therefore, in the hands of the man who can reach beyond it. But he sees himself as thoroughly incomplete and insusceptible of completion, at the mercy of some Other. By thought he can do nothing more than throw light upon his path.

Due to the fact that man, finding that, in all his cognizing, he is himself not yet cognized and then incorporates the cognition of objects into the process of his philosophizing, he once more experiences a breakthrough, this time through his own efforts. That which he had lost when he was wholly thrust back upon himself, may now become once more manifest to him in a new form. Only during a misguided moment of despair concerning bare existence did he consider himself identical, as knower, with the origin of all. When he treats himself seriously, he receives back in turn what is more than himself. In the world he grasps anew the objectivity which had threatened to petrify into indifference or to be lost in subjectivity; in transcendence he grasps being which in the freedom belonging to him as phenomenon of existence he had confused with himself as self-being. . . .

The cognitions of being human which could be grasped in particular trends have become, as sociology, psychology, and anthropology, the typical modern sciences. When, by means of absolutization, they are meant to cognize the being of man in its entirety, they must be rejected as utterly inadequate substitutes for philosophy. Only out of a radical reorientation does that philosophy arise which, at the present time, is known as Existenz-philosophy. It finds the material of its expression in those areas which, since they deal with the knowledge of man, are simultaneously bounded and safeguarded by it. But it goes beyond these in its advance toward Being itself. Existenz-philosophy is the philosophy of man's being which leads beyond man. . . .

Without sociology, no political program is possible. Without psychology, no one can ever succeed in mastering the confusion that prevails in his relationship to himself and others. Without anthropology, our awareness of the obscure foundations, where we are given to ourselves as a gift, would be obliterated. In each of these instances the range of cognition is restricted. No sociology can tell me what I will as destiny; no psychology can make it clear to me what I really am; the authentic being of man cannot be the result of racial breeding. In all directions we reach the limit of what can be planned and made.

Cognitions are indeed the impetus that makes us act in order to bring about the desired course of our existence. But man can only truly be when he distinguishes genuine cognitions from mere possibilities. . . .

B. Existenz-Philosophy

Sociology, psychology, and anthropology teach that man is to be treated as an object concerning which something can be learnt that will make it possible to contrive its modification. In this way one comes to know something about man, without coming to know man himself; yet man, as a possibility of a creature endowed with spontaneity, turns against being regarded as a mere result. The individual cannot accept as compellingly valid and exhaustive whatever construct he is transformed into on the basis of sociology, psychology, or anthropology. By taking hold of the actually cognizable as something merely particular and relative, he emancipates himself from that which the sciences apparently would like to agree upon about him once and for all. He perceives that the transgression of the limits of the cognizable by way of the dogmatic assertion of known being is a deceptive substitute for philosophiz-

ing, and that those who wish to escape from freedom seek justification for
their action in a spurious knowledge of Being.

For his actions in every situation and in all occupations, man needs a specific, expert knowledge concerning things and concerning himself as existence. But expert knowledge alone is never adequate for it only becomes significant in virtue of him who possesses it. The use I make of it is determined
only by my genuine volitions. The best laws, the most admirable institutions,
the most correct results of knowledge, the most effective technique, can be
used in a spirit opposed to them. They are destroyed unless human beings
fulfill them to contain a rich actuality. What actually happens, therefore, cannot be modified by an improvement in expert knowledge; only by man's being
can it be decisively altered. A man's inward attitude, the way in which he is
conscious of his world, the kind of things that satisfies him are the wellsprings
of his actions.

Existenz-philosophy is the way of thought by means of which man seeks to
become himself; it makes use of expert knowledge while at the same time
going beyond it. This way of thought does not cognize objects, but illuminates
and brings about the being of him who thinks in this way. Brought into a state
of suspense by going beyond all cognition of the world (in the form of a
philosophical world orientation) that fixates being, it appeals to his freedom
(as illumination of Existenz) and clears the space for his own unconditional
action through invoking transcendence (as metaphysics).

This Existenz-philosophy cannot achieve a finished form in a particular
work, nor can it acquire final perfection as the life of a particular thinker. Its
origin in modern times as well as its unparalleled elaboration are to be found
in Kierkegaard. During his lifetime he was a sensation in Copenhagen, but
soon passed into oblivion. Shortly before World War I, he became better
known but his period of decisive influence has only just begun. Schelling, in
the later development of his philosophical thought, entered paths on which,
existentially, he broke through German idealism. But whilst Kierkegaard
sought vainly for a method of communication, and made do for this purpose
with the technique of the pseudonym and his "psychological experimenta-
tion," Schelling, on the other hand, buried his genuine impulses and visions in
the idealistic systematics which, having developed it in his youth, he clung to
and could not overcome. Whereas Kierkegaard consciously meant to deal with
the most fundamental problem of philosophy, that of communication and, by
dint of his intention of actually wanting indirect communication, arrived at a
strangely misshapen result (which nonetheless cannot fail to arouse the
reader), Schelling remained, in a manner of speaking, unconscious, and his
meaning is only discoverable to those who approach him through prior
knowledge of Kierkegaard. Nietzsche travelled the road through other beginnings and without knowing the Existenz-philosophy of these two earlier

thinkers. Anglo-Saxon pragmatism was a sort of preliminary stage. In demolishing traditional idealism, pragmatism seemed to be laying new foundations; but what it built thereon was nothing more than an aggregate of insipid analyses of existence and cheap optimism of life, and was no more than the expression of a blind confidence in the contemporary confusion.

Existenz-philosophy cannot discover any solution, but can only become actual in the multiplicity of thought proceeding from each respective origin in the course of communication between two people. The time is ripe for it but it is today even more visible in its failures than in its successes, and has already succumbed to the tumult that transforms everything that enters our world into ill-tuned noise.

Existenz-philosophy would be instantly lost if it were to believe, on its part, that it knows what man is. It would then once more provide the basic outlines for the exploration of human and animal life as types and would thus again become anthropology, psychology, sociology. The only possibility for it to have meaning lies in remaining without a fixed foundation in its relation to objects. Its role is to awaken what it does not itself know; to illuminate and move but not to fixate. For the man on his journey through life it expresses that which enables him to maintain his direction; it is the means whereby he is able to preserve his sublime moments so that he can realize them throughout his life.

Existenz-philosophy may lapse into mere subjectivity. Then self-being is misinterpreted as being-I, which solipsistically closes itself off as an existence that wishes to be nothing more. But genuine Existenz-philosophy is that questioning which is also an appeal in which today man is again seeking to come to his true self. Obviously, therefore, it is found only where people still wrestle to attain it. Having been mixed together, in a most bewildering manner, with sociological, psychological and anthropological thinking, it is now plunged into a sophistical masquerade. Now censured as individualism, now used as a justification for personal shamelessness, it becomes the perilous foundation of a hysterical philosophizing. But where it remains genuine, it makes a person uniquely sensitive to the appearance of the authentic human being. Because it remains without an object, the illumination of Existenz leads to no result. The demand for it is contained in the clarity of consciousness but its fulfillment is not attained. As cognizing individuals we have to be content with this. For I am not what I cognize, nor do I cognize what I am. Instead of cognizing my Existenz, I can merely inaugurate the process leading to its clarity.

Knowledge of man reaches its end if its limit was conceived to lie at the boundary of Existenz. The illumination of Existenz, which goes beyond the bounds of man's knowledge, remains inadequate without the next step. On the basis of the illumination of Existenz we must move into a new dimension whenever we attempt a metaphysic. The creation of the metaphysical world of objects, or the manifestness of the origin of Being, are nothing when they are divorced from Existenz. Psychologically regarded, it is only a construct, consisting of shapes engendered by fantasy and strangely moving thoughts, of the contents of tales and inventions of Being, which vanish into thin air in the face of any knowledge that attempts to grasp them. In it man attains peace or at least the clarity inherent in his unrest and danger, when authentic actuality seems to reveal itself to him.

Today the attempts at metaphysics are, in their existential nature, as confused as is all philosophizing. But it has become possible to do metaphysics in a purer, even though more limited, manner. Because compelling empirical knowledge can no longer be confused with it, it is not possible any more to do metaphysics after the manner in which one arrives at scientific knowledge. Rather, it must be approached from an entirely different direction. Metaphysics is therefore more dangerous now than previously, for it readily leads either into superstition accompanied by the repudiation of science and truthfulness; or it leads us into a helplessness where we believe that nothing can be achieved any more since the aim of metaphysics is knowledge, but knowledge cannot be attained through it. Only when these perils have been recognized and surmounted on the basis of Existenz-philosophy, does the idea become possible of the grasping, in freedom, of metaphysical contents. What the millennia have disclosed to man of transcendence could once again become articulate after it is appropriated and transformed.

II.

The New Perspective

EDITORS:
The six selections of this sub-part are from *Philosophy* (1932), Vol. II, *Illumination of Existenz*. The topics of the selections are the distinction of existence (*Dasein*) from Existenz, communication, historicity, freedom, limit-situations, and absolute consciousness (including faith and love). These concepts have, in the meantime, come into common usage in philosophical and other literature, especially in "existential" thought. In fact the volume, together with certain works by other authors[1] of that time, is regarded as the foundation of the movement of "existential philosophy" which focuses primarily on man's existing in time. However, it would be a misunderstanding to take this fact as constituting the main significance of this volume. According to Jaspers's own conception it is the second of three volumes whose respective topics are not miscellaneously juxtaposed. The topics—world, man, God—are, rather, tied to each other by virtue of a unitary conception of philosophy that is their common leitmotif. The principle pervading all three volumes is that of "transcending." In transcending, freedom, articulated as thought, breaks through the confines of determination and keeps open the options for man's concrete enactment. The modes of transcending stressed in the respective three volumes of *Philosophy* are indispensable to each of the other, whether it be "world-orientation" (Vol. I) or "illumination of Existenz" (Vol. II) or the "metaphysics" of "transcendence" (Vol. III). Jaspers says, "Without Existenz, world orientation would be senseless, and transcendence would turn into superstition. Without world orientation Existenz would be vacuous, and transcendence would remain without a voice. Without transcendence Existenz would lose its genuine self-being and world orientation, its potential profundity."[2]

It is the function of the second volume, from which the following selections are taken, to develop the philosophy of man in a way that accounts for man being "more than he knows, and can know, about himself," for man being a career of freedom, action, and enactment, for man becoming within time, for man being with others and in confrontation with situations. The philosophy of man is here conceived in a way that does not confuse philosophy of man with the actuality of man. Philosophically we can speak of man only as a possibility. Philosophy can aid in evoking, in fostering, and in clarifying self-hood, but it cannot determine its actuality either cognitively or concretely. Hence—in distinction to the scientific approach to aspects of "human nature"—this philosophy of man speaks of man only as "possible" Existenz; and it is published under the title of mere "Illumination of Existenz."

NOTES

1. Franz Rosenzweig, *The Star of Redemption* (1921); Martin Buber, *I and Thou* (1923); Gabriel Marcel, *Metaphysical Journal* (1927); Martin Heidegger, *Being and Time* (1927).
2. *Philosophy*, vol. I, in German: p. 52; in English: p. 89.

Selection 8

EXISTENCE—EXISTENZ

EDITORS:

In the following selection Jaspers presents the distinction between existence and Existenz. Existence is man as object, man regarded as a being among other beings in the world. Existenz is man as non-objectifiable self. In connection with this distinction Jaspers discusses the methodological problem of thinking and speaking of Existenz, which cannot be objectified and which, insofar as it is thought, is merely "possible" Existenz and never its actuality.

A note on terminology: In this book we retain the usage—found in past English translations—of Jaspers's word "Existenz." We use "existence" to translate Jaspers's "Dasein." In our translation the adverb "existential" is correlative with "Existenz," and not usually with "existence" (*Dasein*).

The passages of the selection are from *Philosophie*, Vol. II, pp. 1–11 and 13–21; in English translation: *Philosophy*, Vol. II, pp. 1–20. What follows is a translation by the editors.

TEXTS:

A. Existence in the World and Existenz.

If by "world" is meant the sum and substance of all that can become accessible to me through my cognitive orientation and which has a content that is cogently knowable by anyone, then the question arises whether world-being exhaustively covers all Being and cognitive thinking ends with world-orientation. That which, in the language of myth, is called soul and God and in philosophic terms Existenz and transcendence, that is not world. These do not exist as knowables in the same sense as things in the world, but they could exist in a different way. Even though they would not be known, they would not be nothing, and even though not recognized, they would be thought.

A fundamental philosophic question is entailed by the question: What is there vis-à-vis the entire world-being?

It is the Being which is not within the appearance of existence, but which can be and ought to be, and hence decides in time whether it is eternally.

This Being is myself as Existenz. I am this Existenz insofar as I do not become an object for myself. In Existenz I know myself to be independent even though I am unable to perceive that which I call my self. I live my life based on the possibility of my Existenz, and I am myself only in its actualization. It eludes me whenever I want to grasp it for it is not a psychological subject. I feel much more rooted in the possibility of my Existenz than where, regarding myself objectively, I comprehend myself as to my disposition and my constitution. In the polarity of subjectivity and objectivity Existenz appears to itself as existence yet it is not the appearance of something that might at some point be an objective given or upon reflection be disclosed as a substratum.

Thus it is not my existence that is Existenz but man in existence is possible Existenz. Existence is present or absent, but Existenz—since it is possible—by its choices and decisions takes steps toward its being or away from it into nothingness. Between my existence and other existences there is a difference of scope, ranging between narrow and broad world-being; but Existenz is essentially different from other Existenzen because the ground of freedom is different. As Being, existence lives and dies; Existenz knows no death but relates to its Being by soaring upward or plunging down. Existence exists empirically, Existenz solely as freedom. Existence is wholly temporal, Existenz is in time, yet more than time. My existence—inasmuch as it is not all existence—is finite and yet enclosed within and for itself. Existenz, too, does not exist for itself alone and is not everything; for it can only be as it relates to other Existenzen and to transcendence; in facing the latter as the totally other, Existenz realizes that it exists not merely by virtue of itself. However, whereas one can call existence infinite since it is the relative roundedness of something endless, the infinity of Existenz, not being rounded, exists as open possibility. For existence, action based on possible Existenz is problematical because existence, concerned with enduring in time, must turn against the unconditional whose path it sees as doubtful since it may be detrimental to existence and lead to its destruction. In my concern over my existence I would like to make my existential acts conditional on the continuation of this existence. For possible Existenz, however, the unconditional grasping and enjoyment of existence already constitutes defection because possible Existenz, for its part, subjects the actuality of its existence to conditions where it understands itself as unconditional. But in my unconditional sheer will to exist I must despair when my existence is revealed to me as being the actuality of complete shipwreck.

The fulfillment of existence is world-being. For possible Existenz the world is the arena in which it appears to itself.

The world as known is alien. I remain at a distance from it; that which understanding can know and that which can be experienced empirically repel me because they are merely that and nothing else; to me they are the Other. I, for my part, am a matter of indifference to them and subject to all-powerful causality in the realm of actuality and to the constraints of logic in the realm of validity. I am not at home in it; I do not hear the speech of my kin. The more decisively I comprehend the world the more outcast I feel in it; for the world, as the Other, as nothing but world, is bleak. Unfeeling, neither compassionate nor pitiless, subject to laws or floundering in coincidence, it is unaware of itself. It cannot be comprehended for it confronts me impersonally; it can be explained in its particulars but can never be understood in its totality.

However, I know the world in yet another way. Here it is akin to me, I am at home, indeed secure in it. Its laws are the laws of my reason. I find tranquility as I adapt myself to it, fashion my tools and proceed to cognize this world. It speaks to me in my idiom; there is a life in it in which I participate. I surrender to it and yet am wholly with myself even as I am in it. It is familiar to me in small and present things, and I am transported by its grandeur. It makes me content in my surroundings or wants to tempt me into its far reaches. It does not travel along expected paths but when it surprises me by unexpected fullfilments and incomprehensible denials I keep trusting it even in my downfall. . . .

Thus possible Existenz differentiates itself from the world so that it may then genuinely enter into it. It detaches itself from the world so that, in grasping it, it may gain more than the world can be. Existenz is attracted by the world as the possibility of its defection into mere existence. World and Existenz stand in tension with each other. They can neither become one nor can they be separated one from the other.

This tension is presupposed in philosophizing out of possible Existenz. World as that which can be known and Existenz as that which is to be illuminated are differentiated dialectically and again taken as one. . . .

B. *The Dissatisfaction of Possible Existenz in Worldly Existence.*

1. The Doubt in the Being of Existenz.—If Existenz is set off over against existence, world, and the universal, then nothing seems to be left over. If it does not become an object, the attempt to grasp it in thought seems doomed to fail. Since such thinking can never achieve a result or gain permanence, the attempt at thinking Existenz seems perforce to destroy itself. We can doubt the being of Existenz in every respect, and our healthy common sense makes us demand that we stick with the objective as being the true and actual. Is our attempt therefore due to a figment of our imagination?. . . .

Since Existenz is inaccessible to the person who searches for it by means of the objectivizing understanding, it remains subject to permanent doubt; but even if no proof can force me to acknowledge the being of Existenz, I still have not come to the end of my rope in my thinking; for I can surpass the limits of what can be objectively known by a leap that goes beyond the rationally explicable. Philosophizing begins and ends at a point that is gained by this leap. Existenz is not the goal but the origin of the philosophizing which takes root in Existenz. An origin is not the same as a beginning beyond which I would always have to ask for a still earlier beginning; it is not an arbitrariness on my part in which I would have to despair; it is not a will that results from the endlessness of questionable motives. It is Being as freedom to which I transcend when, in ignorance, I come to myself in my philosophizing. The helplessness of philosophizing in a state of doubt about the origin is the expression of the helplessness of my self-being; the actuality of my philosophizing is the incipient soaring upward of this self-being. Therefore, the precondition of philosophizing is the grasping of Existenz, which, at first, is merely the striving, in darkness, for meaning and support, which—as I experience it in the form of doubt and despair—directs me back to its possibility and then comes forward as the incomprehensible certainty that is illuminated in my philosophizing.

2. Dissatisfaction with Existence as the Expression of Possible Existenz.
—If I permit, either in theory or practice, existence in the world to be everything for me, I am overcome by dissatisfaction. This is a negative origin; as I set off Existenz against existence in the world, this origin makes me aware of the truth of this differentiation. Since the world cannot be known completely, since no possible correct ordering of existence is final, and since no final goal in the world is discernible as the one goal for all, my dissatisfaction is bound to become all the more decisive the clearer my knowledge and the more honest the sense of my actions.

This dissatisfaction cannot be sufficiently explained. It is the expression of the being of possible Existenz which—when it expresses its dissatisfaction—understands itself and not something other. Thus, dissatisfaction is not the impotence of knowledge, nor the void I encounter where I stand before the abyss of nothingness. Instead, as this dissatisfaction, it becomes the spur propelling me forward in the process of becoming.

Such unexplainable dissatisfaction reaches beyond mere existence. It accompanies me into the solitude of the possible before which all existence in the world disappears. This solitude is neither the resignation of the scholar who despairs of achieving genuine cognition of Being, nor is it the joylessness of the man of action who has come to doubt the meaning of all action, nor is it the suffering of the man in flight from himself who cannot bear to be alone. Rather, having endured all these disillusionments, it is my dissatisfaction with existents altogether and thus the call to me to exist out of my own origin. With the realization that dissatisfaction is a condition inadequate to existence, I have placed myself in opposition to the world; and now, in the overcoming of all disappointment by my own freedom, I return to the world and thus to other human beings together with whom I become certain of my origin. However, I cannot comprehend all this in reflective cogitation; rather, having been left in the lurch precisely by thought, I comprehend it in the actuality of my action and shipwreck. . . .

This dissatisfaction can be expressed and understood only out of the dissatisfaction of possible Existenz—whether it be theoretical dissatisfaction in mere knowledge and observation of all things in the world, or practical dissatisfaction in the mere execution of one task within an ideal whole. It is never motivated by generally valid reasons; these have, instead, the tendency to seduce us into a state of satisfaction and tranquility within the totality of an existence in the world permeated by the Idea and transformed into Spirit. The dissatisfaction of possible self-being has broken through existence in the world and has thrown the individual back upon himself and into the origin from which he can take hold of his world and can become actual as Existenz in togetherness with the other human being. . . .

C. *Methods of Illumination of Existenz.*

Thinking which illuminates Existenz directs itself to the actuality of such existing. In its historic situation, such actuality is a transcending to oneself. The illuminating thought, however, needs as its vehicle an objective thinking by means of which it transcends to that original transcending of Existenz itself. In the illumination of Existenz philosophic thought as such—if it is merely thought in pure objectivities—is bereft of its transcending and thus misunderstood. If, however, it is thought by transcending, then it is an act not, to be sure, of the actuality of Existenz but of its possibility. Once illumination of Existenz has become such a possibility it has been appropriated in a first transmutation. Existenz itself, however, exists only as the actuality of real action. To be sure, the appropriation of such possibility can initiate, in inner action, the second transmutation of thought illuminating Existenz; but one has to differentiate between what merely inspires me from what I actually become. As we philosophize we merely turn toward Existenz; we are not yet our being, we only think it. Therefore, if I understand myself in these thoughts as someone who thinks his possibility, I do indeed appropriate these thoughts in a manner exclusively my own; and without such appropriation, thoughts illuminative of Existenz would be thought in general terms only and would thus have no meaning, indeed would remain incomprehensible. But the first appropriation still requires that which is authentic, of which one can have just an inkling since it has not yet become actualized.

Statements about Being within the framework of philosophizing that illuminates Existenz concern freedom. As expressions of transcending thought they state what can come to be out of freedom. Their criterion of truth is— rather than an objective standard according to which a statement is either correct or false, or instead of a given phenomenon whose characterization in the statement is to the point or unsuitable—the will itself which affirms or rejects. In freedom I examine, through my own agency, what I not only am but am capable of being, and what I want to be but can only want in the luminousness of consciousness. At its decisive points, philosophizing as illumination is itself already an expression of the will on the part of freedom.

The form of every statement is tied to objective contents and, as such, to a universal meaning. If, however, we search for illumination of Existenz in this statement, then its meaning, which goes beyond the universal nature of such meaning, is no longer generally comprehensible. Thus the thinking and speaking that illuminate Existenz are universally valid and yet at the same time replete with a content that is totally personal and unique for each individual. The universal as merely universal here remains hollow, as it were, and its sense is misleading. On the other hand, Existenz would remain unreal without language, i.e., without some universal expression, because it would lack certainty of itself. . . .

Possible Existenz, comprehending itself thus in thinking, considers the universality of its thought as valid because it has already given content to this universal; yet at the same time possible Existenz knows that the merely universal, knowable by all in an identical way, provides us with insight that is different in character. In uttering the universal as the form of Existenz-illuminating thinking, possible Existenz turns toward itself as well as to others in order that it may come to itself in both. Such utterance directs itself toward others and not—as does scientific cognition—toward any and all. Not every person, insofar as he represents just anyone at all, can be in agreement with it; solely that single one can agree with it who sees as possibility what is not directly expressible in universals but is, properly, within himself the complement to such a universal. For the thinking that illuminates Existenz has two sides, one of which, by itself, is untrue (the solely universal), and the other, by itself, is impossible (mute Existenz). As a whole they come together fortuitously in an expression that goes beyond what can be attained by method. To be sure, such thinking is methodical inasmuch as it can be tested as to its truth and presented in its relationships; but the formulations that carry it are the interlocking handholds of possible Existenz urging on toward communication. It is a thinking in which, as it were, two wings are beating; and this thinking can be successful only when both of these wings—namely possible Existenz and the thinking of the universal—are really beating. If one of them fails, illumination, attempting to soar upward, plummets to earth. This illumination constitutes philosophizing; in it, the two wings of philosophizing meet, i.e., the universal and I myself. . . .

1. *Leading up to the Limit.* Man uses negative methods in dealing with objects in order to distinguish himself from them as that which is not Existenz. We traverse a region of objects, progress step by step as far as the boundary where no more objects appear and only a void remains unless this void is given content out of a different origin. At this point the call is sounded to transcend. If such transcending takes place in a leap out of the universal, then this is the second wingbeat accompanying the first; in the first wingbeat the object was thought merely for the purpose of excluding it because it was not what we meant when we grasped Existenz. Such argumentation cannot coerce truth; rather, in breaking through existence in the world, it means indeterminately to hit upon possible Existenz.

2. *Objectification in Psychological, Logical and Metaphysical Speech.* . . . In logical determination one speaks of possible Existenz by means of abstractions which, however, instead of grasping an object, are cancelled out in use and in this way acquire an illuminating function. A knowledge seems to coalesce, though precisely in the light of not-knowing something that yet is present. The logical determinations are the universal; not-knowing lies in the movements of possible Existenz that still must give content to this determination. The argumentations do not proceed in linear combinations whose end result is truth. Thinking would needs get bogged down in empty argumentation; but as argumentation that is filled with existential meaning it can, through the manner in which it founders, be the expression of the self-illumination of possible Existenz. Such argumentation cannot produce evidential proofs; it can only aim at convincing by means of an appeal.

What is objectively a logical circle is a means of reversal that, at the same time, effects a representation. In this circle what is expressed objectively loses its ground and disappears while what remains is precisely the point in question. I can say, for example, that I am as Existenz only through an other Existenz, just as this other Existenz is solely through me, that there is thus no Existenz as such but only through and in communication. In this case the meaning of what I have said cannot be considered to be objectively valid truth. Rather, the being-through-each-other of the I and the other in communication can—if thought in objective terms—be only considered as a circle. If, however, we think of these terms in polar relationship erroneously as existents that are solid in themselves and reciprocally effective, then, to be sure, it is possible to make assertions about objectively observable processes of exchange between them and about the influence of one upon the other. This objectively comprehensible mode of being-through-each-other would apply only to psychological—and as such investigable—existence; in it, the I and the other are two things, both of which change as they interact. However, the existential being of the I is itself only when it is with the other and never in its prior isolation. Communication, or the readiness to communicate, becomes the instance of the birth of the "I myself" in the phenomenal realm. Hence, if the supposition of the two entities as Existenzen (rather than mere existences) were to fall away, then the notion of their being-through-each-other, being only an objective notion, would be meaningless. The construction of such circles is, however, an attempt at explication of the being of Existenz in communication, as over against the cognoscibility of vital existence in its interaction. From the standpoint of objective knowledge the being that arises out of communication is nothing; yet it is to become indirectly expressible in the determinations of the being-through-each-other in which we transcend to it. This attempt, though, objectively, it collapses, demonstrates the illumination of the certainty of self-being effected in communication.

Another way of expressing Existenz through universal categories is by means of the logical contradiction of statements in which, however, an actuality is present. There is tension between the two pairs of contradictory concepts; yet it is precisely this concept-pair in its wholeness that furnishes us with a possible expression of Existenz. This tension fulfills its expressive function adequately at this point by making it impossible for the understanding objectively to fixate and define Existenz.

An example of such a concept-pair of contradictories which are always existentially related would be temporality and eternity in historic consciousness; however, only temporality is objective actuality. The temporally objective side taken by itself is, as it were, stripped of its soul; and eternity as such is nothing. . . .

3. *Conceiving of a Universal Specific for the Illumination of Existenz.* Speaking in psychological, logical, or metaphysical terms always presents the possibility of sliding back, in the following manner: the universality used in this speaking may remain detached as such; if this is so then illumination of Existenz did not succeed. Or Existenz may resonate in the universal as an other in which it appears to itself, but it may exhaust itself. In the latter case the universal continues to exist alongside the philosophic thought, though as this universal.

A last and authentic way of Existenz-illuminating speech is different because of a universal that cannot even occur in the kind of knowledge that orients us in the world. Its categories lack the power to determine new objects and are therefore mere signs. This universality does not at all exist in a detached state. For example, there "is" no Existenz, no self-being, no freedom, no existential communication, no historicity, no unconditional acts, no absolute consciousness. Debased into an object of knowledge about human existence, these words mean something utterly different which, if designated by existential signa, merely lead to confusion. For illumination of Existenz expresses by means of signa what is true being for possible Existenz. It does not do so as an indication of what objectively is. Rather, it does so as what I cannot grasp without genuinely willing it since I am it already according to my possibility. Hence, the signa as universal designate freedom as the activity of that being whose being depends on itself.

The signa that are specific for the illumination of Existenz derive their words—at least on the surface—from the objects of world-orientation, this derivation being often characterized specifically by the adjective "existential." But their purpose is not to become, finally, object-forming categories but signs for the thoughts that call forth existential possibilities. As signa that have a universal side that, as such, is no longer wordly being but is already existential. In order truly to think them, there must needs be an echo of the universal statement in Existenz, for without Existenz the signs are not only empty but are indeed nothing.

Thus, in the illumination of Existenz I speak about the Self as if it were a universal whose structures it exhibits; but I can only mean my own self for which there is no substitute. For I am not the "I," but I myself. To be sure, I search for *the* Self, but in order to find *my* self; and I search for *my* self for the sake of *the* Self. If I ask about myself then I learn through my own inner source that I cannot at all *speak* of myself as that which is incomparable. *Self* becomes the signum through which I reach that which I can think as combining my self and the Self into one. In illumination of Existenz I speak further about the many Selves as Existenzen; but I cannot mean it in just this way for the many Selves do not exist as instances of a universal. In illumination of Existenz I also speak about communication and mean my communication; in the same way I mean my freedom, my historic consciousness, my limit situations—and yet can speak of them only in universals. . . .

In order to make clear the universal nature of Existenz-illuminating signa, let us contrast the temporal appearance of possible Existenz with temporal existence as universally valid objectivity, i.e., concepts of Existenz with the Kantian categories.

Both, the objective actuality of the world and existential actuality, are phenomena in time. Kant conferred on his categories, which are determinative of objective actuality, their applicability to the material of sensuous perception by linking them through the mediation of time in the Schemata, as he referred to them. It is possible to contrapose these Kantian Schemata of objective actuality with completely heterogeneous Schemata of existential actuality because both require time as their medium. This parallel, whose principle is contrast, may be strange but is significant; it can be expressed in brief formulas (see Kant, *Critique of Pure Reason*, B, pp. 176 ff.):

Objective actuality is subject to rules and can be cognized under those rules; existential actuality is without rule and absolutely historic.—The rules of actuality are causal laws; whatever happens has its cause and effect in time sequences; existential actuality, however, appears for itself in time out of its own origin, i.e., it is free.—Substance is that which endures in time; it persists, is neither increased nor diminished; in time as appearance, Existenz disappears and commences. Objective duration, however, has a contrasting parallel corresponding to it, namely authentication in time.—The reciprocal causality of substances (mutual effect or community) is counterposed by the communication of Existenzen.—Objective reality is that which corresponds to any sense perception at all; existential actuality is the unconditionality at the decisive moment; empirical actuality is counterposed by the content of the decision.—The objectively determined magnitude in quantitative relation is counterposed by something that is called niveau or rank of Existenz that cannot be determined objectively.—Objective possibility as the correspondence of representation with the conditions of the time is contrasted with the possibility of choice as the undecided nature of the future which is my Existenz itself.—Necessity (existence of an object at all time) is counterposed by the fulfilled time of the moment (instead of endless time).—Time as such (in Kant as the form of duration whose correlate is substance) is counterposed by this fulfilled time in the form of the eternal present. The former is something objective, measurable, is an experienceable actuality; the latter is the depth of Existenz out of original freedom. Time-as-such is validly present for everyone; together with choice and decision, which are the appearance of Existenz, fulfilled time becomes a here-and-now. Existenz has *its* time and not time-as-such. The latter is valid for consciousness-as-such, the former solely for Existenz in its historic consciousness.—In the realm of objective substances, nothing new can come into being. . . . In the existential realm, on the other hand, there is no objectivity that has final duration; there are, however, leaps and new beginnings of Existenz within its appearance.

Kant himself explicitly rejects several of the existential signa upon testing them against his objective categories. For example, he gives the reasons why there are no leaps (in time) in the world and no gaps (in space); why there are no coincidences, i.e., no blind chance operative in events; why there is no fate, i.e., no necessity that would not be necessarily comprehensible in accordance with rules. Indeed, none of that exists in a world taken as objective or as the object of cognition. But whenever an explication of Existenz is attempted, all these words return. There are not two worlds in juxtaposition; there is only one world. In a completely different dimension, explicable only in seeming parallel (parallel only because objective concepts and categories are unavoidable as vehicles of expression) and in a different sense and in different forms, depending on the demands of the cognition of objects, Existenz is illuminated for us without being cognized.

D. *Ambiguousness and Misunderstanding of Existenz-Illumination*

. . . . As I attempt illumination of Existenz I must speak in objectivities. For this reason everything that is meant to be existential-philosophic must needs be misunderstood if taken as psychology, logic, or objective metaphysics.

The consequence of this is that the most extreme opposites are confused with each other:

1. The blind impulsiveness of the moment that is given expression in the emotionality and arbitrariness of wanting something for the mere sake of wanting it, the impenetrable vital strength of naked life and one's intoxication with this life (without faithfulness and form and without their formative effect on the course of existence) stand over against something that objectively is just as irrational, that constructs its actuality out of the origin of freedom, is tied to itself and forgets nothing; what, objectively can be taken for arbitrariness is then embedded in the—not logical but existential—consistency of a life. This life knows the consciousness of eternal certainty that stands in contrast to the fleeting intoxication found in the pseudo-certainty of immediate satisfaction.

2. If I say about someone that he always speaks about himself even when he discusses the most factual problems, then this may mean either of two things: it may imply the reproach that he remains within the realm of egocentric selfishness of empirical individuality; or it may mean my deepest agreement that he speaks in a manner that is truthful and committed, i.e., out of his Existenz. The fact that someone takes himself infinitely seriously may mean either the vain narrowness of empirical individuality, or it may mean that which is decisively at stake, namely his concern about his authentic self.

3. In the life of science the following look so much alike objectively that they are easily confused: one is the personal interest, on the part of a scientist, in achieving a certain result, an interest which is not objective and whose motives have a source outside of science; the other is the enthusiastic love that forms the basis of research. Both of these stand in contrast to impersonal achievement which, lacking content, is only incidentally useful for something else. The objectivity of the idea which, in the service of an Existenz, dominates a piece of research, can be confused with the pseudo-objectivity that serves as a false front for endless argumentation, justification, and permanently valid results.

4. There is an absolutely independent point in Existenz where it is at rest

itself. (This is the point from which it enters necessarily into communication.) Objectively similar and thus deceptive and easily confused with this is the self-encapsulation practiced before others for the purpose of safeguarding merely empirical individuality and sensitivity (out of which communication is no longer possible).

5. The historicity of individual Existenz in its objective distinctiveness is the appearance of its being. It is a distinctiveness which is objectively the same but possessed of beautiful though endless diversity and becomes the object of attraction, curiosity, and gratification. Absolutely historic Existenz, however, as the appearance of something distinct, concentrates itself in this appearance while the endlessly distinctive remains chaotically ephemeral.

These confusions are examples of the thoroughgoing ambiguity of Existenz in this appearance and of the statements about it. This ambiguity cannot be removed by knowledge but only by possible Existenz responsible for itself. Therefore, in mistaking one for the other—even though this cannot be understood by the mere understanding or prevented by it—we become guilty and are held accountable. The critical consciousness of possible Existenz stands, as it were, between two worlds which, for the mere understanding, seems to be one: the world of the appearance of vanity and that of the appearance of Existenz.

Selection 9

COMMUNICATION: THE LOVING STRUGGLE

EDITORS:

In the following selection Jaspers develops the existential phenomenon of communication, according to which the human being, what he actualizes and what is actualized through him, is primally a matter of being with others, and being so communicatively. Communication that is existential is loving, but not "blindly" so; rather it is a matter of presenting the other with challenges, and being challenged oneself, of vying with each other in the actualization of truth. Communication is a struggle, a loving struggle. The importance Jaspers attaches to the conception of Existenz as communicative can be seen in the recurrence of the theme of "communication" in a variety of contexts in this Reader. In particular, "communication" plays a major role in Jaspers's theory of truth for man in time (see Part IV).

The following excerpt is from *Philosophie,* Vol. II, pp. 61–67; it has been translated by the editors. In the English edition of *Philosophy,* Vol. II, it can be found on pp. 56–61.

TEXT:

A. Solitude—Union

With respect to myself, communication involves both being-oneself and being-with-the-other. If—as someone who stands on his own—I am not also independently myself, then I lose myself completely in the other; communication would then cancel itself at the same time that it cancels me. Conversely, if I begin to isolate myself, communication becomes more impoverished and empty. In the extreme case where it is broken off absolutely, I cease being myself because I will have vanished into the emptiness of a geometrical point.

Solitude is not identical with being isolated in a sociological sense. If, for example, a member of a primitive society, who does not have the self-awareness of standing on his own, is expelled from this society, he either continues to live inwardly within this society or he has an unclear awareness of the desperation of not-being. He is not solitary, neither within the sheltering society nor in his state of being excluded, because he is not an I for himself.

It is only in the clear awareness of more highly developed conditions that one can say: Being I myself means being solitary, but in such a manner that in solitude I am not yet myself; for solitude is the consciousness of being ready for possible Existenz, which can be realized only in communication.

Communication always takes place between two who enter into a bond with each other but have to remain two—who come to each other out of solitude and yet know solitude only *because* they stand in communication with each other. I cannot become a self without entering into communication, and I cannot enter into communication without being solitary. In any suspension of solitude by communication there grows a new solitude which cannot disappear without myself ceasing to be the condition of communication. I must desire solitude if I dare to exist out of my own primal sources and thus to enter into the deepest communication. True, I can give myself up and, abandoning distance, dissolve in the other; but, as water that is not dammed flows along weakly in a thin rivulet, so does the I weaken which does not desire any longer the rigor of being itself and of keeping at a distance.

In existence, the polarity of enthusiastic yielding up of one's self and the strict keeping to oneself in solitude cannot be suspended existentially. Possible Existenz can be found in existence only as the movement between these two poles in a course whose origin and goal remain obscure. If I do not want to put up with a solitude that I have to keep overcoming anew, then I choose either chaotic dissolution or fixation in self-less forms and tracks; if I do not want to risk surrendering myself, then I become nothing, a petrified, empty I.

In the existence of the self, therefore, a restlessness prevails that is relaxed only momentarily to arise soon again in a new form. Yet this movement does not constitute the endless repetitiveness of being hopelessly driven. Rather, in this movement possible Existenz embarks on a direction and on an ascent whose goal and ground are not palpable to any insight but, in transcending, illuminable to Existenz.

This communication of solitude is opposed by a fundamental attitude, alien in its very origin. This attitude argues: that such communication is only the hopeless attempt at a community of the solitary; that it consists merely of a willful self-being whose eyes are shut to the truth which lies in genuine community; that this culpably solitary individual creates a philosophy for himself to feed his delusion that he has companions in his solitude. But to the question, what, then, is genuine community? this attitude replies: whatever is capable of uniting all men. This is then held to be either the truth of revelation, which is to be followed obediently in the community of believers; or it is an idea of a right world order, or of a nation-state taken as all the forces of nation concentrated into the power of a single will; or of a movement of world-conquest as the key to mankind's happiness. Man must renounce himself, so claims this attitude: when I serve the whole, then I stand within true community; to be oneself means to be self-less.

Both philosophy's attitude toward communication and its opponent's agree on the same thesis: Truth is that which brings about community. Furthermore, religion and philosophy agree that the merely intelligible creates only pseudo-communities based on what is known objectively. The intelligible, it is true, is the vehicle of community within the realm of the incomprehensible which the intelligible brings into a unending process of clarification. The merely intelligible however becomes, as a known, noncommittal because it creates a distance from self-being: when it becomes the most important thing it weakens community. If everything were to be rationalized until it is as clear as pure water, communication as community would vanish.

A parting of ways occurs with respect to the location and origin of the incomprehensible that founds community. For a philosophizing existence it lies in the actuality of the self-being of persons who actually encounter each other; for an obedient existence it lies in an objectively fixed divine revelation or in an authoritatively established right view of the world, such as Marxism. Either the historic actuality of my communication with actual people, to whose self-being I am indebted for my own self-being, means more to me than what I can learn as objective truth; or I let my possible communication with men be submerged in a generalized love of my neighbor extended to all, which has its anchor point either in a worldless love toward the deity or in a reasoned but nonetheless incomprehensibly mysterious awareness of the destiny of mankind. Either I continuously risk solitude anew in order to achieve self-being in communication, or I have suspended myself with finality in another being.

This division is deepened in that attitude which holds that a community of all mankind is possible. To be sure, empirical observation supports the truth of the proposition which obtrudes itself on us time and again, that the greater the number of people who understand something, the less substance it has. However, since philosophic truth sees all human beings as possible others with whom it remains our task to communicate, it cannot set aside the challenge that the most profound truth is the truth which all people could understand and thereby become a single community. In this dilemma the fundamental convictions part company; one wants to compel unity by force and contents itself with the most superficial comprehension, indeed with uncomprehending obedience; the other conviction refuses, for the sake of truth, to engage in illusory anticipation and therefore accepts what exists in fact and is mastered only in an uncharted process of true communication. To be sure, the community, which makes existence possible through the order it imposes, must have aims and purposes understandable to all. But it is precisely not this community in which I achieve awareness of authentic Being; I achieve it rather in the order of a world of men in which even those who cannot understand each other yet respect each other. In this world the task remains: to come closer and closer to each other in an ever-widening perimeter of communication.

The choice, which is the possibility of Existenz in the tension between solitude and communication, is not meant to be universally valid for everyone. It is, however, meant unconditionally for self-being regarded as taking hold of that Being which is accessible to it, the Being within man.

B. *Manifestation—Actualization*

In communication I become manifest to myself together with the other. At the same time, however, this manifestation is the actualization of the I as a Self. If I believe, for example, that manifestation represents an elucidation of my innate character, then I abandon the possibility of Existenz which, to the contrary, creates itself in the very process of manifestation through self-elucidation. For objective thought, to be sure, only that which is prior can become manifest. A manifestation, however, which brings about Being together with this becoming, is like an emergence out of nothingness and thus not like what we mean by mere existence. Suppose I assume the standpoint that I am the way I was born; that I can get to know my endowments in the course of my life, but I remain what I am. In this case I observe myself from a psychological standpoint and presuppose that complete empirical knowledge could tell me early on in life what I am. This is correct as far as faculties and traits are concerned; to know these belongs to orienting myself in my situation. But consciousness that is decisive of possible Existenz takes hold of these givens; to seek clarity about them is merely the presupposition of existential manifestation through which it becomes clear in the world not only what I am as empirical existence but what I am myself. For this manifestation, the acknowledgment of real limits in the situation of the given means that I derive from the given merely the material of another kind of actualization after all. Therefore, since no knowledge is final, such an acknowledgment of the given includes the possibility of transcending these limits, a possibility improbable for him who sees things only empirically.—The existential will to manifestness comprises apparent opposites: an inexorable clarity about the empirical and yet the possibility of becoming, in this way, what I am for eternity; being shackled by the inescapable nature of the empirically actual and yet the freedom to transform it by taking hold of it; and an acknowledgment of being-thus yet denying all fixity of being-thus.

This will to manifestness risks itself totally in communication in which alone it can realize itself: It dares to risk any being-thus, knowing that precisely thereby Existenz finally comes into its own. On the other hand, the will to concealment (to mask, to the throwing up of defensive walls) only seems to enter into communication and does not risk itself because it confuses its being-thus with its eternal being and wants to save its being-thus. For it, manifestation would equal destruction, while for self-being manifestation means grasping and overcoming the merely empirically actual in favor of possible Existenz. For in manifestation I lose myself (as established empirical existence) in order to gain myself (as possible Existenz). In concealment I preserve myself (as something existing empirically) but must lose myself (as possible Existenz). Manifestness and existential actuality are related in that they seem to emerge jointly out of the void and are self-sustaining.

This process of actualization as manifestation takes place not in isolated Existenz but only together with the other. As an individual I am for myself neither manifest nor actual. The process of manifestation in communication is that unique struggle which, as struggle, is also love.

C. Loving Struggle

No matter what its object, communication regarded as love is not blind love but a combative love that is clear-sighted. It calls in question, makes things hard, challenges, and tackles out of its possible Existenz the possible Existenz of the other.

The struggle in this communication is the struggle of the individual for Existenz, which is at once the struggle for one's own and the other's Existenz. By contrast, in the struggle for existence any weapons may be used, cunning and deception become unavoidable; one treats the other as the enemy, as wholly other, the way one treats recalcitrant nature. The struggle for Existenz is infinitely different: Here we are dealing with utter openness, with exclusion of all force and superiority, with the self-being of the other as well as my own. It is a struggle in which both sides dare, without reserve, to lay themselves open and to let themselves be called into question. If Existenz is possible then it will appear as an attaining of oneself (which never becomes objective) through struggling surrender (which though it becomes objective in part, remains incomprehensible if its motives are sought in existence).

There exists an incomparable solidarity in the struggle of communication. It is this solidarity that makes possible the most extreme questioning because it sustains the venture, turns it into a joint one and is coresponsible for the result. It limits the struggle to existential communication, which always is the secret of two; thus, those who are the closest of friends, as far as the public is concerned, are the ones who wrestle with each other with the utmost decisiveness in a struggle in which both share gain and loss.

One could draw up rules for such a struggle for manifestness. Superiority and victory are never desired; where these occur, they are perceived as disturbance and guilt and are themselves fought against. All cards are laid on the table and no calculating reserve is practiced. Mutual transparency is sought not only in the respective objective contents but even in the means employed in asking and in struggling. Each penetrates into himself together with the other. It is not the struggle of two Existenzen against each other but a joint struggle against oneself and the other; but the struggle is waged solely for the sake of truth. This struggle can take place only on a level of complete equality. If there is a difference in the technical means of battle (in knowledge, intelligence, memory, proneness to fatigue), both will equalize the level by handicapping their powers. But equalization demands that each of them make it existentially as difficult as possible both for himself and for the other. Here chivalry and all forms of relief are valid only as a temporary safety measure— with the approval of both—in times of trouble which occur in the phenomenon of our existence. If it becomes permanent, communication is cancelled. Making things difficult, however, applies only to the innermost grounds for deciding within the substance of decision. Where greater strength of psychological equipment carries the day, where even sophistry is possible, there communication ceases. In existentially struggling communication each puts everything at the disposal of the other.

Nothing that is felt to be relevant may remain unanswered in communication. Existing, I take seriously the phrase I have heard, in its nuances, and react to it; perhaps the other is posing a question, consciously albeit indirectly, and wants an answer; perhaps instinctively he wanted to keep silent and did not seek an answer but now must listen to it. What I myself say is intended as a question; I want to hear an answer, not merely talk the other into something or force something on him. It is an essential part of true communication to pose questions and give answers without limit. If answering is not carried out at that very moment, it remains a task that will not be forgotten.

Since the struggle takes place on an equal level, recognition is inherent in this very struggle, and calling the other in question comprises affirmation. Therefore, in existential communication solidarity is manifested precisely in the most heated battle. Such struggle, instead of causing separation, turns out to be the way of binding Existenzen together in truth. Thus it is a rule of such solidarity that these persons trust each other absolutely and that their struggle is not an objective one visible to others; such visibility could lead to the formation of parties. It is a struggle for the truth of Existenz and not about what is universally valid.

Finally, truthfulness in struggling communication cannot be achieved nor the freedom of Existenz to Existenz be assured without the recognition of certain actualities, namely mental ones that are laws unto themselves, and psychological drives, both of which center the self onto itself and isolate it. These forces disturb and hobble and hinder the free activity of communication to which they set limits or to which they tend to attach conditions. Man cannot control such powers without recognizing and exposing them; though he may be free of them at high points of his Existenz, he will sink back again not knowing what is happening to him.

Selection 10

HISTORICITY

EDITORS:

Jaspers's conception of historicity is as decisive for the "illumination of Existenz" as it is difficult to formulate and to grasp. Basically it is meant to suggest how Existenz, in its radical distinction from existence (see Selection no. 8), can be regarded as requiring existence as the vehicle of its actualization. By virtue of his decisions and actions man participates in the determination of his essential being, or, in Jaspers's idiom, man decides in time his eternal validity. In this sense the exploration of the phenomenon of historicity involves the imagery of the "unity" of opposites like "time and eternity," "necessity and freedom," "existence and Existenz." In this sense also, as some readers will discern, the influence on Jaspers of Kierkegaard's *Sickness Unto Death* is particularly pronounced here.—According to Jaspers the historicity of Existenz cannot be adequately conceived through categories such as individuality (vs. universality), or membership within a whole. Historicity is conceived by Jaspers in distinction to the idealistically conceived universal, whose concretion is the historic individual. It is not without significance that during the semesters when Jaspers worked out his "illumination of Existenz" he conducted a series of seminars on Hegel.—By effecting a dissociation of "historicity" from the categories of quantity, Jaspers has also distanced himself from

the frequently encountered association of the existential self with individualism. This is stressed by the following consideration: In the structural sequence
of Jaspers's "Illumination of Existenz" the phenomenon of historicity (of the
ineluctable and irreducible moment of one's choice) is juxtaposed to and follows the phenomenon of communication (one's being with and with respect
to others).

A note on terminology: In this book, "history" is the translation of
Geschichte and *Historie*. "Historicity" stands for *Geschichtlichkeit*. "Historical" is the adjective that correlates with "history," "historic" with "historicity." The only available adverb, "historically," is correlative with either of the
two nouns; wherever its reference to "historicity" is important, we avoid the
use of "historically."

The following passages, which have been translated by the editors, are
selected from *Philosophie*, Vol. II, pp. 118–19, 122–24, 126–27, 130–34. In the
English edition these passages appear in *Philosophy*, Vol. II, pp. 104–05,
107–09, 110–11, 114–17.

TEXT:

A. Historical Consciousness and Historic Consciousness
(History and Historicity)

Knowledge about history we call historical consciousness. But such knowledge is not knowledge about something that happened the way something is
happening all the time and everywhere; rather, it becomes such knowledge to
the extent to which it grasps what has happened in the past as the objective
preconditions of our present existence, and at the same time understands it as
an other which, having existed, was by itself a unique event and the only
one of its kind. This historical consciousness finds fulfillment in the historical sciences. It proves itself in the all-embracing panoramic view of
world-history and in the—always merely limited—ability to interpret out of
its past what exists today. Yet with historical consciousness we merely stand,
knowing and searching, facing a past event, regarding it and questioning it as
to its causes. Even the contemporary event, when it is objectified in this
manner, is regarded as if it had occurred in the past. Furthermore, historical
knowledge is directed toward the public realm, to the sociological, the political, to institutions and customs, to efforts and effects. It does not exist for me
as this particular person but as the individual instance of a contemporary
human being or even as the instance of man generally who just happens to be
alive today and who, therefore, while limited in knowing the *contents* of what
has occurred up to now, is not limited as to the mode of knowing. In such
knowledge, I as an individual am not myself but consciousness-as-such, as the
one who knows I am separate from the object that I know.

Historic Consciousness proper is different; with it, the self becomes aware of its historicity which alone is actual. Historic consciousness of Existenz must be personal in its origin. With it, I am conscious of myself in communication with other historic self-beings. Within the realm of appearance as I-myself, I am bound in time to a succession of unique instances of the situations and givens in my life. Even though the historicality of objects, as I know and mean it, is historical for me and not for itself, I know myself in my historic being as historicity for myself. Here, being and knowing are inextricably bound to each other at their origin. That which we then differentiate in thought, i.e., historic being and our knowledge about it, are existentially so much alike that the one cannot be without the other: there is no historic being without knowing, that is, without clear comprehension and involvement; and without historic actuality there is no knowledge. To divide the two would turn me into an object that is known. What I know about myself theoretically has become something particular and an object, something no longer I-myself. As I grasp and accept it, it becomes myself again, fused into the active historic process of my possible existing. This identity of the self regarded as knowledge in historic consciousness and as historicity in becoming actual, cannot be presented in a way where it can be thought without contradiction. In Existenz, it is that which is most certain, most lucid; in theory, it is most incomprehensible. . . .

B. *Historicity as Unity of Existence and Existenz*

The unity of historic consciousness can lend absolute weight to existence as it is grasped by self-being, yet at the same time it can keep it as a suspended relativization of mere existence. Existentially grasped existence is recognized by the individual as infinitely important and as taking place, in true communication, between two partners; yet at the same time, to the individual facing transcendence, existence is vacuous. To stand in this tension is historicity: in the uniqueness of temporal actuality the depth of authentic Being becomes irreplaceably present as if arising from its very ground.

Thus, in historic consciousness I know myself to be primally tied to existence, yet in existence I also know myself as an appearance of possible Existenz.

Chained to existence I am devoid of Existenz as long as existence as such becomes absolute for me, in the sense that I am not aware of it any longer as appearance. This is the way it is in circumstances lacking clear historic consciousness, in which man already loses himself when he is brought out of his own particular world in which he has been existing, into another one; or, when he cannot confront an environment in which he has experienced something crucial because, chaining himself to matters of the senses, he becomes addicted to them as if they were his whole life plain and simple. But even such ties are existential if I admit them and hold on to them, as long as I also confront them as an existence through which I am not simply compelled; these ties are no longer chains for me if I knowingly reach beyond them; for they are loosened by my free appropriation of existence, which is the historic determination of myself.

A process is set in motion which brings about a hierarchy both of the determinations of my situation and of my chances in the objective conditions of the givens which consist of my traits and the people I encounter. For in the world in which I live I am not present everywhere as I myself with the same degree of unconditionality. The only thing essential for me is that, as appearance of myself, I am—at some point, without being objectifiable—at once both existence and historic determination. There is no criterion for deciding where the unconditional point of the identity is grasped; rather, in this grasping Existenz realizes its essence by virtue of its destiny.

If Existenz wanted to keep itself free in an absolute sense, if it did not want to grasp any existence as its appearance, it would step beyond the world and tumble into a bottomless void. But only by being and doing something unconditionally in existence can transcendence manifest itself to me also as the non-being of the world; it does so only if I also know existence to be appearance. Each betrayal of transcendence becomes present to me in the form of the betrayal of an appearance within existence, and I pay for it with a loss of Existenz. Existenz would be annihilated if nothing remained but existence, where everything has the same level of triviality and when I am no longer certain of any transcendence because nothing remains unconditionally valid for me.

Thus in historic consciousness the unification of existence and Existenz is primally carried out in such a manner that the actual condition of being bound is accepted as one's own. Out of my freedom I am identical with the historic particular while at the same time the possibility is open to me of not identifying with it.

We do not exist without phenomenal objectivity. If, however, we posit it absolutely, as distinct from the historic moment and the definite situation, then we attach our Existenz to something that is generally true, something that exists outside of time and actuality, and in the face of which we ourselves have become indifferent not only as existence but as Existenzen. But should we once more reduce all objectivity in the phenomenal realm to mere existence in its conditionality, then we *lose* Existenz because we lose unconditionality and with it every primal source. It is the concentration of unconditionality on the historic concrete present that allows unconditionality to remain as the sole truth. The truth which Existenz, in coming to itself, attains here lies only in the phenomenon; but this phenomenon as such, objectively thought and held fast, is not this truth. It was this truth only because it contained transcendence at the same time. That, however, was historic; it was not general as this objective phenomenon regardless of how and where it may occur again.

Historic self-becoming is, then, not a matter of attaining to something enduring which can be possessed and expressed. Rather, it is a matter of actualizing an Existenz which, as (phenomenal) existence, is open to question and exposed to temptation, and which in the state of phenomenality is in jeopardy of dissolution into nothingness. The greatest illusion arises precisely at that point of unconditionality where in historic situations appearances are taken as absolute and where they then can be fixed as mere appearances, as empty shells in the flow of time. It is important to *relativize* once more all that appears out of the absolute origins of historic self-becoming. One must not be content with any appearance as something enduring, something that becomes universally valid; and yet, insofar as one exists, one cannot but be always absolutely identical with an appearance. . . .

C. *Historicity as the Unity of Time and Eternity*

Existenz is neither timelessness nor temporality as such, but the one in the other, not the one without the other.

Existing is the deepening of the moment, such that the temporal present is the fulfillment which, containing both the past and the future, is diverted neither to the future nor to the past. Not to the future—as if the present were merely the passage and stepping-stone in the service of something still to come; such a relationship would have meaning only in regard to certain achievements and particular goals when path and goal are embedded as a whole within the compass of existing. Not to the past—as if the purpose of my life were merely the preservation and repetition of a past completion; such a relationship is truly meaningful when it serves to awaken and to facilitate assimilation, but not in such a manner that the whole life of self-being— which exists out of its own origin—could be exhausted therein.

That moment, as the identity of temporality and timelessness, is the deepening of the actual moment toward the eternal present. In historic consciousness I am aware of both *in one*, the transitoriness as appearance as well as the eternal being which is present through this appearance: not in the sense of a timeless validity that could by chance be grasped now, and later possibly grasped in the same way; also not in the sense where temporality and timelessness would be juxtaposed in their disparateness; but in such a manner that the uniquely fulfilled temporal particular is grasped as the appearance of eternal Being. This eternity is bound absolutely to *this* moment.

The moment as mere instance of the temporal is fluid: conceived objectively it is merely transient, it is nothing; it may be desired as an isolated experience, yet as mere experience it must become worthless through lack of commitment and by virtue of self-sufficiency. Rather, what matters is that the moment proves itself as a historic phenomenon of Existenz through belonging to a phenomenal continuity. The moment proper, as the sublime moment, is the pinnacle and articulation in this existential process. It is not a means nor does it have significance in its own right; i.e., it cannot be separated from being substantially bound to sequentially appearing Existenz in time. Over against the mere moment and the delights of time stands Existenz. Existenz, to be sure, is present in the moment but not perfected in it. It brings forth the moment and makes it its own. And Existenz knows itself as quietly inexorable and silently reliable by virtue of the continuity that illuminates the moment. Only here does the historic character of the appearance of Existenz become clear: Existenz does not arrive at appearance in an immediately finished form but achieves appearance through the steps of its decisions taken in the span of time. Its appearance does not consist of the individual moment but of the historic sequence of moments, one with the other. This one-with-the-other is present to each moment—in the wait for the great moment by virtue of a stance that does not squander itself;—in relating the present high point to its presuppositions which are guarded and not given away;—in a life that goes on, which is lived out of a sublime moment, which, though passed, perdures as the standard for the present. . . .

D. *The Historic as Distinct From the Irrational and the Individual*

Being as thought Being is either a universal or a whole. Being as grasped in historic consciousness, however, is never the universal, but neither is it its opposite; the universal constitutes its content, but in its intrinsic nature historic consciousness knows itself as reaching beyond content. Being in historic consciousness, furthermore, is never the whole nor its opposite, but is a becoming aiming toward wholeness, yet one that also refers to other wholes and non-wholes. No historicity is all-encompassing, neither as the universal nor as the one wholeness, yet it cannot be expressed by negating either the universal or the whole.

For historic consciousness the surrender to the universal represents a transition. If the universal were simply the true, assuming the true can be known, then the individual, as the self, would only be something added, incidental and interchangeable; for it would itself be the universal and thus everywhere. In becoming, the self must be the true without being able to *know* it. Out of this self I take hold of my situation, which I do not know beforehand but get to know only in the very act of taking hold of it. All knowledge of the universal is merely a presupposition that shows us possibilities and is our touchstone for the particular. It is impossible to live within the universal as the *absolute* without the self disappearing into thin air as a self.

If the historic component of Existenz is not a universal, then it is said to be irrational. This designation is not false but misleading. The irrational is something that is only negative, e.g., matter in relation to universal form, the arbitrary in relation to lawful acts, the accidental in relation to necessity. As the negative, the irrational is always the remainder, that which could not be penetrated or has to be repudiated. Thought strives toward limiting this remainder to a minimum, and rightly so. For thought, irrationalities are not something in their own right but, as mere negatives, the limit or the indifferent raw material of the universal. The absolute historic, however, being positive, is itself bearer of the consciousness of Existenz; it is source and not limit, origin and not remainder. Non-transferable, it becomes a singular standard. It is that which is authentically true through which every mere universal is degraded to the level of correctness, and all ideality is reduced to being penultimate. Not recognizing the absolutely historic merely means not being able to translate it either into the universal or its negation. Recognizing it means partaking in the process of self-illumination on the part of possible Existenz through its own actualization, a process in which it is responsible for itself. Existentially, the universal and the non-universal sink to the level of a means of expression and appearance.

Not only are the limits of the universal irrational, but also such non-rational universalities as validities in the form of poetry and art. Historicity, however, not possessing a universally valid form, has a ground that is always becoming clearer but is never fully clear. Its medium is the rational as well as the irrational that has assumed form. It is supra-rational and not irrational.

Knowledge about the irrational as the negative of the universal or as a universality that is not rationally valid can lead to a kind of thinking that seeks to incorporate the irrational in the Concept. Such thinking, developed with virtuosity by Hegel, is able to express in a unique manner philosophically relevant matters. However, it skirts the originally historic consciousness which, in thinking, expresses itself not through objectifying a subject matter but in its appeal to possibility. Existential historicity, though seemingly extremely close to the historic, may quickly find itself far removed from it by virtue of the illusion of knowledge.

The individual, too, is irrational. True, a single Existenz in its existence is an individual, yet to be an individual does not mean being Existenz. Individuality is an objective category. It is the one thing at a given time insofar as this thing—because of the endless nature of actuality—cannot be reduced to general laws. Because it is endless it is also unrepeatable and unique. Furthermore, a living individual is, in its indivisible unity, a whole yet cannot be generally grasped because its endlessness turns into infinity. Such concepts of the individual are again expressions of the residue that remains when actuality is to be understood as general.

The idea that the historic individual is constituted by reference to a specific meaning pertains only to the logical structure of objectifying historical representations (e.g., in accordance with the choice of subject, the structure of coherences, the distinction between important and unimportant facts). However, this idea does not at all touch upon the uniqueness in historic consciousness; rather, it dissolves historic consciousness into a new generality that was realized only once, while it obscures the consciousness of Existenz.

Thus the historicity of Existenz is not yet the non-universal, neither as the irrational nor as the individual. In both instances it would be either mere limit and remainder or a new mode of the universal. In either case the historicity of Existenz would be transformed into an objectivity that would have to be expressed in negating formulas or in general references. Its own positive nature serves to shut it off from objectivizing cognition. Thus all statements about historicity, taken literally and logically, must turn out to be untrue, for they always assume the form of universality (one can think and speak only in this form); historic consciousness itself is primal only in its uniqueness. If it were an instance of a general sort, or the actualization of an atemporally valid determination, or the approximation of a type, then in each case it would not exist out of its own origins but would be subsumable under a higher order. Historic consciousness would be an object rather than that which penetrates objectivities as its appearance. Therefore, the method of explication could only be the following: To lead us to the limits by means of the universal. Historic consciousness can shine forth only by way of a leap—not of thought but of consciousness itself, only through the translation of thought into the actuality of consciousness. In each case this leap must succeed in a manner incomparably its own, for I can comprehend only myself in my historic consciousness and in this manner become open to the other in his historicity. The universal—in negation, circular relationships, images, and inadequate application of categories—remains the way, as the form of imparting information, and the means of awakening.

E. The Historic as Distinct From Being a Member Within a Whole

As historic I exist in specific situations facing specific tasks. Historicity is my rootedness in the unique situation of my existence and the singularity of the task that lies before me, even if it appears to my consciousness in the form of a general task. Such fulfillment of my existence seems tied to the wholeness in which I, as its member, have my appointed place, and out of which grows the peculiar nature of my task. But my place is not ascertainable as a location within a closed world. If I were to understand my rootedness in this manner, I would dissolve into a new universality as into an absolute whole. However, it is the absolute historicity of my rootedness that simply cannot be subsumed under a universal nor integrated into a whole. Subsumption and integration exist only in a relative sense for the aspects of existence. Only in our imagination could we develop an order of the whole and of all existences, seeing existences as arranged in accordance with the distribution of assigned places within a whole. In this unreal phantasy, actual Existenzen with whom I am in communication, and thus also I myself, would be excluded. However, blind faith in such a whole, even unawares, does away with historicity in its profundity, for this exists in the togetherness of Existenzen in individual wholenesses achieving objectivity; it does not involve any wholeness of the world or that of a realm of the spirit closing in upon itself. Instead of the totality of a possible world existence in which all individuals are done away with by turning them into mere members, there exists for Existenz only the transcendence of the One, the appearance of which is itself historic. All that is universal and whole remains subordinate and is not to be mistaken for transcendence. Only as possible Existenz do I grasp the universal and the wholenesses accessible to me. Passing through them I take upon myself my existence, which then becomes the historicity of my Existenz. It can be expressed in phenomenal form but cannot be objectified in its Being.

A wholeness that is one unconditional wholeness for all would signify the possibility of an ultimate goal that would function as the purpose of temporal existence. If one believed in a double world in the sense of a world beyond this one, then that would be either the proper ordering of this world or a world of eternity existing beyond. However, given the primacy of historicity, the possibility of a proper ordering of the world collapses and the idea of eternity becomes a cipher. There is no one ultimate goal for all. This does not imply a denial of all that is universal and whole; its import is retained in its particularity. Indeed, an ultimate goal is even historic if I take it upon me and will it as something given and necessary. However, it cannot be derived from the historicity of Existenz because within Existenz no whole encompasses everything. Not only do I partake in communication with strangers but they and I are together in some Other that at first is Existenz-less for us, in the form of empirical actuality, of universal validity, of particular wholenesses as we find them or bring them forth.

Historic consciousness as a being realizing itself is not a possible standpoint that one could classify in juxtaposition to other standpoints. Historicity, as the consciousness of an origin that cannot be fathomed in itself, cannot be expressed adequately as an origin that is known phenomenally. Historicity comes to itself only in its actualization. If it were not to revolve within the circle of self-elucidation through communication but to expand the circle indefinitely in the form of phenomenal existence in the world, historicity would become an objective solid structure in which it would become lost. It is impossible to discover what lies beyond the origin; for, existing, I cannot step behind myself, which is something I can do as consciousness-as-such. Then I would lose the origin and become a geometrical point I-as-such; I would no longer be myself.

Selection 11

FREEDOM

EDITORS:

Awareness of freedom pervades Jaspers's thinking. The following passages are taken from one of his explicit treatments of "freedom." In our selection two aspects of Jaspers's conception of existential freedom are stressed: First, the historicity of freedom, i.e., its actuality in dialectical tension with the situational constraints of "necessity." Second, the relation of awareness of freedom to the awareness of transcendence, i.e., the dialectic of groundedness and independence.

The selection is from *Philosophie*, Vol. II, pp. 190–200. The version in *Philosophy*, Vol. II, is on pp. 166–74. Translation by the editors.

TEXT:

Recent physics is useful for philosophizing about freedom in that it prevents, on its own terms, the absolutization of its world into a being-in-itself in which we are entirely enclosed. It presents palpably and hence effectively what Kant had presented philosophically and hence cogently, namely the insight that Being is not exhausted by Being regarded as the lawful state of things.

Kant's specific solution for the question of the relationship between freedom and existence in the world is to differentiate kinds of being: phenomenon and thing-in-itself. He said: the same thing that, to me, is as phenomenal object completely subject to causal laws (the psychological individual and his empirical character), is in itself free (intelligible character). We can revoke this solution insofar as there is contained, in this formulation, an objectification into two worlds, for there is only one world of objects. But insofar as it is merely an unavoidable objectivizing formulation for the Being of freedom, it remains true for us. Freedom is not allowed to enter, as it were, through a gap in a world otherwise ordered by law. Its objective rescue always turns out to be so pitiful that it is served just as well if it is not rescued at all. But even worse: its objective rescue makes freedom itself into something seemingly objective and thus heterogeneous to itself.

Origin of the Consciousness of Freedom

Freedom is not external to self-being. There is neither space nor opening for it in the world of objects.

But if I were to know the Being of transcendence and of all things in their eternity, then freedom would become unnecessary and time would be fulfilled: I would stand, in eternal clarity, where nothing needs to be decided any more.

But as I am in temporal existence, I only know existence as it manifests itself to me in world-orientation, and not as Being in its eternity.

I, however, must will because I do *not* know. The Being that is inaccessible to knowledge can reveal itself only to my volition. Ignorance is the origin of having to will.

This is the passion of Existenz, that it does not suffer absolutely under ignorance because it wills in freedom. The thought of an inescapable unfreedom would make me despair over my ignorance.

The origin of freedom excludes it from the existence which I can investigate. The being within existence that I myself can be has its foundation in this freedom.

Freedom and Necessity

Every mode of freedom has meaning with respect to some constraint which, as necessity, constitutes resistance to it, or functions for it as law, or gives it impetus; consciousness of freedom unfolds in opposition to necessity, or in union with it. A freedom that has overcome all opposition is a phantom.

The Resistance of Necessity

What merely happens is not free. What I comprehend as nature is determined in its happening by necessity. As caused it is exempt from arbitrariness. Its existence is determined, in the way it is, through an other.

If I call everything actual "nature," hence identify all Being with this mode of necessary existence, then I am myself nature. If I affirm Being as nature because of the exclusiveness and uniqueness of this necessity, then nature as such is good and I am good the way I am. Surrendering, I abandon myself to my instincts, urges, inclinations, moods, and place my trust in the ever recurring beautiful moment. But once I argue, I justify. Instead of justifying myself as freedom out of myself, I—who am removed from all natural context—justify out of something other than the given, in which I myself am given. Because something is actual it is good (naturalistic ethics).

However I cannot stay with this view. I maintain the autonomy of judging and willing over against natural actuality. Actuality as such is questionable; I see it either as indifferent, as neither good nor evil, or as essential and radically corrupt. What matters to me is not to go along with it but to actualize something that exists not only because it issues from actuality as such. What is good cannot be proven or justified out of an actuality but shows itself to be so in its actualization. The judging will rests on a foundation counter to actuality even if it founders in this actuality. That something is natural is no criterion for this will; that something is unnatural or not actual or impossible is no reason against it. It is in spite of everything. It takes hold of what is unnatural if it can be posited as true on the basis of an original Existenz. Such an ethos often merely negates; its substance, even if actualized objectively, is simply transcendent. The harshness and violence that alienate us from the world and from an existence that can come to itself only in the world, are the conditions of the consciousness of total independence (heroic ethics).

The differentiation of "natural" from "unnatural" is made possible by a double meaning: the natural is, first, what is merely actual, and second, what is normative. One cannot separate decisively in concrete situations the naturally actual from the naturally normative. In each instance the natural is also an actual that, as such, binds me (whether I affirm or deny it), and in each instance the actual as such has some kind of quality of demanding. I am neither a mere link in the process of nature nor am I in opposition to nature as something totally independent. The above differentiation into naturalistic and heroic attitudes refers only to conceptual extremes: in the one instance, the boundary at which the given of nature has not yet come into serious conflict with the consciousness of freedom; in the other, the boundary where a self-isolating consciousness of freedom has progressed to scorning every thing that exists as a natural given (both within me and external to me). These extremes illuminate the situation which I always experience *between* them. Being grounded in an absolute, freedom is relative in the world. It is always confronted by a natural given which signifies for it dependence, resistance, impetus, material. But freedom is also not nothing; rather it consists in its setting itself over against mere nature, even if only in differentiating oneself through knowledge.

Vis-à-vis the givenness of nature the will acts out of transcendental freedom in its knowledge of another necessity that is not subject to the laws of nature but to those of the "ought." This necessity is formulated in propositions as commandments or prohibitions. Consequently these validities, which originated in freedom through the acknowledgment of their evidence, become a confining burden of legality. Conflicts arise to counter them, out of original existential freedom. A newly emerging freedom finds itself faced with a necessity which earlier had itself sprung from freedom. It must prevail against rigidified demands in order to create new forms of validity.

Thus existential freedom sees itself between two necessities, the lawfulness of nature as the irremovable resistance of actuality and the lawfulness of the "ought" as the rigid form of rule, and is in danger of being quashed between the two. But if it were to remove itself totally from them instead of moving in closest proximity to both, it would be bound to lose itself in fantasy.

The consciousness of freedom that would seek to found itself completely on itself would not be able to sustain itself in such radical autonomy. It could endure only if an absolute freedom were to prove itself in it which would absorb all Being.

The Phantom of Absolute Freedom

The idea of an absolute freedom is directed toward a Being which suspends the limitations of all freedom without suspending freedom itself. Every freedom that is the freedom of an individual, must take its stand within an opposition, must unfold itself in process and struggle and, hence, must always be limited. Absolute freedom would be the freedom of a totality that would have nothing external to it and all oppositions within itself. If there is absolute freedom, then what-is-in-itself is this freedom. This notion of absolute freedom has been developed most completely by Hegel:

What confronts the subject no longer contains anything alien, hence it has neither boundary nor barrier; rather it finds itself there in the object. If this succeeds the subject is satisfied in the world and every opposition and contradiction is solved. To be in the totally other and yet in oneself, that is freedom. A freedom that is only subjective would be unfreedom because it would be confronted by what is merely objective functioning as necessity. Freedom is reconciliation; it is completed in man's pure thinking in which spirit thinks itself. This pure thinking as absolute freedom is philosophy, which has no object other than spirit or God and hence is divine service. But man cannot endure in pure thought but needs sensuous existence. Therefore there unfolds, in sensuous existence, a hierarchy of relative freedoms and satisfactions which achieve true reconciliation only in the pure thinking of the philosopher or in its precursor, religion. Thus there is the immediate gratification through the resolution of the antithesis in the systems of sensual needs (but these are gratifications of a finite and limited sort; because the gratification is not absolute, it proceeds, without respite, to a new state of need). Then there is the spiritual gratification and freedom in knowing and willing, in information and action. The ignorant person is not free for it is an alien world that confronts him; the desire to know is the striving to do away with this unfreedom. The aim of the person who acts is to achieve actuality for the will's reason. This actualization of freedom takes place in the life of the state. But even here there is everywhere opposition and contradiction because action stays in the area of finitude. The gratification remains relative. Only in the region of truth is absolute freedom in itself, a freedom that is actualized in religion and philosophy.

Thus Hegel. Obviously this absolute freedom is either a myth about the Being of the divinity thinking itself (and has meaning here as a cipher), or it is the illumination of a form of absolute consciousness which is actualized in cognition (and here hits upon a truth); in both instances it is meant to be actual freedom. But it is not what it pretends to be; for neither in myth nor in contemplative experience of absolute consciousness can man grasp the Being of freedom in such a manner that—as this content would demand according to its meaning—he could remain with it. In thinking absolute freedom he enters a realm that, in fact, is not absolute but has something beyond it into which the thinking person promptly relapses.

Furthermore absolute freedom is not given in freedom insofar as in it Existenz is suspended in favor of something universal and total; not only subject and object disappear but, together with all opposites, Existenz itself goes up in smoke.

Finally, absolute freedom does not make sense: for freedom becomes empty when it has no opposition; it is within opposition as process. It cannot remain in what has been achieved; its own substance is present in its disappearance; its place is in the appearance of Existenz within existence, and neither in transcendence nor in nature. Its ultimate purpose may be to want to sublate itself; but the goal for which it sublates itself is no longer freedom but transcendence.

The Unity of Freedom and Necessity (Freedom and Constraint)

Whereas freedom in its objective existence might appear to be arbitrariness, it knows itself in its existential origin precisely as necessary. But if the identity of freedom and necessity is effected only in the origin of the individual, then it, too, is not absolute freedom.

The necessity which was injected into my future actions by what I had done up to now is my own necessity that at the same time determines me through myself as if it were not my own. Each existential choice illuminates itself as something final which, once carried out, cannot be unmade. Though free in my choice I bind myself through it, carry out and bear the consequences. Only the clear consciousness of this choice makes it an existential one. In this way every one of my decisions becomes a new ground in the shaping of my historic actuality. Henceforth I am not bound by the empiric actuality that came to be thus by virtue of my actions but by the step that I as my self-creation took within myself at the moment of choice. I became the way I had willed myself to be. Even though, in time, there always remains possibility, my being is now bound through itself and yet free at the same time.

This necessity, which is present in each new choice as a constraint by means of my own historic ground, brings into the open the deeper necessity that is present in the consciousness of "here I stand, I cannot do otherwise," i.e., in the consciousness of "having to"; and this is bound up with the most primal decision of freedom on the part of Existenz. This is the point where these strange expressions make full sense: man chooses to do what is necessary but there is no question of "free" choice; absolute freedom is absolute necessity;

there is no choice in the greatest decisiveness to do the right thing. Such necessity is never comprehended or deduced; necessity of nature and of the law of the "ought" can be grasped objectively and validly, but existential necessity cannot: hence the risk of total commitment as the high points of decision; hence the impossibility of bringing about the decision from the outside and by way of reasons; but hence also the depth and certainty of the original consciousness of Existenz in making this decision.

Freedom and Transcendence

Freedom and Guilt

Because I know myself to be free I acknowledge myself to be guilty. I am responsible for what I did. Since I know what I did I take it upon myself.

Nowhere can I find the source where my responsibility first began. I cannot limit my guilt in such a manner that I know a beginning from which point on I first became guilty.

In the guilt that I already bear when I become aware of it, I do not want to become guiltier if I can avoid it; yet I am ready once again to take upon myself any unavoidable guilt.

In it I experience, in spite of the clarity of my free decision and through this decision, the limitation of my freedom; and nonetheless I acknowledge it as my own doing, and together with this limitation, as my guilt. I take upon myself what, according to all my knowledge, I could not have avoided. Thus I take upon myself the primal source of my nature which is prior to every one of my actions as the ground out of which I willed and had to will; thus I furthermore take upon myself within actuality what I must do without being able to do otherwise in any one situation. It is as if I had chosen myself the way I am prior to time, and as if I acknowledge this choice—which in fact never took place—by my act of taking it upon myself, to be mine; and it is as if I felt in my consciousness of guilt the actualities in which I find myself to be, nonetheless, my own doing.

If I knew the beginning of my guilt it would be limited and avoidable; and my freedom would be the possibility of avoiding it. I would not need to take anything upon myself, neither myself, in the sense of choosing myself in what I am not conscious of having done; nor would I need to take this existence upon myself, which I enter and for which I become responsible as I act.

In my freedom I come up against an other—the necessity for guilt—which seems to suspend this freedom. Yet this other exists for me only by my taking it upon myself and thereby, through the acknowledgment of guilt, preserving my freedom.

Within my freedom my guilt is always a specific one and is thus something that I attempt not to bring upon myself. *Through* my being free my guilt is the undeterminable and hence immeasurable one which becomes the ground of all particular guilt insofar as it is unavoidable. Whereas, being free, I struggle against becoming guilty, I am guilty through my very freedom. But this guilt I cannot escape without incurring the guilt of denying my freedom itself.

For we exist in a state of activity which is its own ground; otherwise we are not, because passivity is vacuous. I *must* will; because willing must be my ultimate if, in the end, I will *to be*. In the way in which I freely *will*, however, transcendence can manifest itself to me.

Dependence and Independence

I am responsible for myself as I am and yet discover only in being free who I am. Heretofore I seemed to be standing wholly on my own feet; but now I ask about my ultimate dependence and independence.

Either I am totally dependent: A God has cast me into existence. I myself am not at all my will. My will would not be of any help to me if the divinity would not move it. Whoever is not granted this undeserved grace is lost.

Or, my consciousness of being a self silently argues against such dependency. In my will I create myself, to be sure, not all at once but in the continuity of a lifetime; to be sure, not arbitrarily out of a void but with the historic ground of my being-thus which offers me indefinite possibilities for free transformation. I know I have a core that is independent. Only from this core am I related to transcendence which has wanted me to confront it freely because I cannot be myself in any other way. I am myself responsible for what I want and do and what I am out of my source. I also have to be responsible for my empirical existence as if I had chosen my nature, and bear the guilt for this choice. For there is in me a primal source that is wholly myself, from whose perspective I see my appearance—though in a condition of guilt as an existence that I have to mold. Freedom demands that I transform all that I am into *my* freedom and guilt.

We recognize both of these metaphysical positions, absolutized respectively into grace and autonomous freedom, in their rational definiteness and unequivocal straightforwardness as necessarily inadequate ways of expressing the mystery of the transcendent ground. In consciousness of grace we deny freedom in favor of the solely acting divine will, as if in this form *without* freedom there could still be guilt; in autonomous consciousness of guilt we affirm freedom in favor of our own responsibility, as if, without transcendence, there could still be guilt *in* freedom. It is only the tension between these two ideas that expresses the conscious experience of the will's impotence in the transcendent relatedness of Existenz, together with experiencing the will's freedom in the unlimited responsibility of my actions and my being.

Transcendence in Freedom

If there were no transcendence then the question would be why should I will; for it would be merely arbitrariness without guilt. Indeed I can will only when there is transcendence.

But if there were simply transcendence then my will would disappear in automatic obedience. If, on the other hand, there would simply be no transcendence then my mere will could not call it forth.

Just as freedom is already present in my question about it, the possibility of transcendence can be only in freedom itself. By being free I experience in freedom—but only *through* it—transcendence.

In its actualization freedom is never complete; rather, in its most decisive actualization it is, as regards itself, faced with the most profound lack: I am actual but never complete, nor do I approach possible completeness. In my actualization I am related to my transcendence out of my failure which, being freedom, is guilt.

As free I confront transcendence but am not detached from it. For since, in facing it, I cannot point to myself as a perfection, no matter how transitory in nature, I am actual for myself in my freedom as uncompletable, I am free in my "having to," of which I become conscious as my guilt; but this being-actual is itself already within its transcendence. Transcendence is not my freedom but yet is present in it.

This freedom, reaching forth, conscious of the necessity which I am myself by creating it, this remains for me the existential primal source beyond which there is no freedom.

It is precisely in the source of my self-being, in which I mean to reach forth beyond the necessities of the laws of nature and of the "ought," that I am conscious of *not* having created myself. When I return to myself as the authentic self, into the darkness of my original volition, a darkness that can only— and then never completely—be illuminated, then it may be revealed to me that: *where I am wholly myself I am no longer only myself*. For this authentic "I myself" in which, in fulfilled historic present, I say "I," I seem to be through myself; and yet I surprise myself with it. Following an action, I might know: I was not able to do this alone; I could not do it once more in this way. Wherever I was authentically myself in my volition, there I was given to me in my freedom at the same time.

What I become I am through an other, but it does so in the form of my being-free. The antinomy: what I am *out of* myself I cannot be *solely* through myself; since I am out of myself I am guilty; since I am it not only through myself, I am what I wanted to be through being bestowed upon me. This antinomy is the expression for the union of consciousness of freedom and of necessity in transcendence. By taking hold of myself out of freedom I took hold thus of my transcendence whose evanescent appearance I am myself in my freedom.

In existence I can lose freedom by losing myself. But only in transcendence can freedom be sublimated. Through transcendence I am as possible Existenz, i.e., as freedom in temporal existence. My decision in favor of freedom and independence over against all structures in this world, against all authority, does not mean that I decide against transcendence. The person who stands completely on his own feet experiences, in the face of transcendence, most decisively that necessity which places him wholly into the hands of his God. For only now does he become conscious of his freedom as the temporal phenomenon that has the urge to sublimate itself. Freedom has its own time. It is still something on a lower level that seeks to destroy itself. However, this thought has meaning only for the transcendent conception of an end of days; it has no meaning in the world.

Selection 12

LIMIT SITUATIONS

EDITORS:

The conception of "limit situations" is, next to the juxtaposition of Kierke-gaard and Nietzsche, the main contribution of Jaspers's *Psychologie der Weltanschauungen* to the inception of Existential Philosophy. In *Philosophie*, Vol. II, Jaspers presents a better defined, less diffuse, treatment of "limit situations"; the two excerpts which follow are from this version. The first excerpt deals with the general conception of man's situationality and the limit situations which are the confines of his being as Existenz. The second excerpt presents one of the four limit situations that Jaspers discusses in *Philosophie*, Vol. II, *viz.*, guilt.

The excerpts are, respectively, from pp. 203–09 and 246–49. In *Philosophy*, Vol. II, they appear on pp. 178–83 and 215–18. The translation of what follows is provided by the editors.

TEXT:

A. Situation and Limit Situation

Situations such as: that I am always in situations, that I cannot live either without struggle and without suffering, that I ineluctably take guilt upon myself, that I must die—these I call limit situations. They do not change except in their appearance; as applied to our existence they possess finality. We cannot gain an overview of them; confined within our existence we see nothing else behind them. They are like a wall against which we butt, against which we founder. They cannot be changed by us but merely clarified, yet they cannot be explained or derived from an Other. They go together with existence itself.

The word *limit* expresses that there is an Other, but tells us at the same time that this Other is not for consciousness within existence. Limit situations are not situations for consciousness-as-such because consciousness—knowing and acting purposefully—can take them only to be objective, or merely avoids, ignores, or forgets them. Consciousness remains within the limits and is incapable of even approaching questioningly the origin of these limits. This is so because existence as consciousness does not grasp the difference; it either is not touched by them or—as existence without elucidation—it is reduced to helplessness and dull brooding. Limit situation belongs to existence as the situations belong to the consciousness that remains immanent.

B. Limit Situation and Existenz

As existences we can evade limit situations only by closing our eyes to them. In the world, we want to preserve our existence by expanding it; we relate to it unquestioningly, either mastering or enjoying it or suffering under it and succumbing to it; but in the end there remains nothing for us but to surrender to it. Thus we react meaningfully to limit situations not by planning and calculation in order to overcome them, but by an entirely different sort of activity: namely, by *becoming the Existenz possible within us.* We become we ourselves by entering into the limit situations with open eyes. Only superficially discernible by knowledge, they can be sensed as reality solely by Existenz. To experience limit situations and to be Existenz are one and the same. Out of the helplessness of existence, Being soars upward within me; this is Existenz. While questioning about Being in limit situations is alien to existence, within such situations self-being can become aware of Being by means of a *leap*: the consciousness that usually merely knows about limit situations is all at once fulfilled in a unique, historic, and irreplaceable manner. The limit then enters upon its real function: to remain immanent and yet to point toward transcendence.

C. The Threefold Leap of Existenz Evolving in Limit Situations

Although I am in and of the world, I am able to take my position over against everything. Not wanting to participate in the hustle and bustle, it is possible for me to be in the world and at the same time stand outside of it if—not as existence but in contemplation—I push on toward an Archimedean point, the vantage point from which I see and know what is taking place. With startling though empty independence I confront my own existence as if it were someone else's. I am as if I were outside my existing life, and step from here into the world in order to orient myself in it; I no longer do this as someone living for his own particular purposes in his situations but as myself for the sake of knowing all and the whole which, as knowledge, is sufficient unto itself.

Thus I conquer my own being in absolute *solitude*, in which—in view of the questionable nature of worldly events, of the passing away of everything and thus also of my own existence—I stand beyond the world and yet stand before myself as if I were a safe island in the midst of the ocean; from here I cast my gaze aimlessly around the world like a billowing mist that fades into the boundless watery wastes. Nothing really concerns me but I look at everything, conscious of my knowledge that is my secure anchor. Yet behind this enclosure of my self-being I embody the universal desire to know. Unmoved I gaze at the positive that I recognize as valid, certain in this knowledge that constitutes my being. The substantial solitude of him who knows universally, apart from any situation, is like the naked eye that looks at everything but not into itself and that encounters no other eye. At home in the solitude of its self-being, it is like a being dwindling to a pin-point, without content other than the quietude of its gaze. *Sic fractus illabatur orbis, impavidum ferient ruinae.*[1]

There is no finality in this solitude, for it harbors other possibilities. It is, after all, the eye of an existence that breaks forth, in this solitude, beyond itself in a first leap. It does not really stand at that outer point, but merely seeks the path thereto; and while it thinks the completion of this path it makes itself ready to enter the world anew. For after this first leap out of the world I yet remain existence, involved in situations as possible Existenz concerned with what actually is. Solitary self-being becomes knowledge that makes me authentically open, in existence, to limit situations; it can be the naked eye only in transient moments. As possible Existenz, sheltered as within a seed in the solitary punctuality of having stepped outside, I make a second leap, the leap toward elucidation. Philosophizing self-being makes the limit situations intelligible to itself as possibilities that strike the very essence of its being, the same limit situations which in its unperturbed cognition it had dismissed as alien to it. No longer is the world merely an object of knowledge for me to which I may permit myself to remain indifferent; rather, in it I find my very own being in which I am deeply stirred. The fearless overcoming of the blind helplessness of existence becomes the source of fear for that which is truly important in existence and which is called in question in limit situations.

After having attempted to attain knowledge divorced from situations, I once more make my situation my object only to learn that there are indeed situations from which I cannot escape nor can they become transparent to me

1. "If the round sky should crack and fall upon him, the wreck will strike him fearless still." Horace, *Odes*, III.iii.7.

in their totality. Only where situations are completely transparent to me do I knowingly escape them. Wherever I do not master them through knowledge I can only grasp them existentially. At this point there occurs a separation between my worldly being—which I can abandon knowingly since it is one merely specific dimension of being—and Existenz—which I cannot, through contemplation, get out of but which I can only be or not be. One cannot gain an overview of one's being-in-situations, since: the world of my world-orientation is not a closed one; the historic actuality from which I come does not become whole; it is not possible to think a realm of Existenzen pictorially and constructively; and the multiplicity of truths cannot be known as multiplicity but can only be sensed within the self-being of one truth. The leap out of the solitude of knowing self-being into the consciousness of its possible Existenz leads us, instead of into valid knowledge, into the elucidation of non-transparent limit situations.

However, as elucidating contemplation, the elucidation in thought of limit situations is not as yet existential actualization. When we consider limit situations we do this not as Existenz—which comes to itself only in its historic actuality and no longer meditates in detached calm—but as possible Existenz, merely in readiness to leap, not in the leap itself. Contemplation lacks the finite as well as the actual situation that constitutes the embodied appearance of Existenz. Contemplation suspends the actuality of the one who contemplates and is mere possibility. Although not yet Existenz, it has the character of relevance for Existenz because it is more than mere objective representation of situations. What I know prepares me for what I can be; and I know only by achieving dot-like Existenz but I am not yet what I—philosophizing—know.

Even though limit situations can be grasped objectively in the manner of general human situations, they truly become limit situations by virtue of one unique transforming act in one's own existence through which Existenz becomes certain of itself and distinctive in its appearance. In contrast to the actualization in a finite situation that is particular, transparent, and merely one instance of a universal, actualization within the limit situation is directed toward the whole of Existenz, incomprehensibly and irreplaceably. No longer do I find myself as an individual living thing in special situations that interest me only in a finite way; instead, I grasp the limit situations of existence as an infinitely concerned Existenz. This is the third, and essential, leap in which possible Existenz is transformed into actual Existenz.

In limit situations, each form of the leap leads me out of existence to Existenz—to Existenz as a germ enclosed in the seed, to Existenz as elucidating itself as possibility, to Existenz as actual. After the leap, my life is something other to me than my being in the sense of merely existing. When I now say "I am," this statement has a new meaning. The leap to Existenz is not like the growth of a living being, which proceeds step by proper step, each in its time, by reflex action that follows discoverable laws. Rather, it is the conscious inner act through which I step out of a Heretofore into an Afterward, so that its origin is indeed I myself as my beginning, but in such a manner that even in this beginning I know myself as having been before. Emerging from the possibility of self-being which I did not create, I attain, by the leap, my actuality in which I become aware of myself as having given birth to myself by my own act.

These three leaps take me from my existence in the world in the face of the questionable nature of everything to the substantial solitariness of one engaged in universal cognition; from the contemplation of things in the face of my necessary participation in the world of shipwreck to the elucidation of possible Existenz; from existence as possible Existenz to actual Existenz in limit situations. The first leads to philosophizing in images reflecting the scheme of things, the second to philosophizing that is elucidation of Existenz, the third leap takes us to the philosophic life of Existenz.

Although they are tied to each other, they do not represent an ascending sequence which proceeds in only one direction; rather, each leap is alternately an impulse for any other. The *solitariness of a point-like self-being in knowledge* is not only a refuge serving to preserve myself as possibility in situations of failure, but has positive import. Even when self-being, seeing before itself the actuality of Existenz, yearns to quit this solitude, it yet has self-value; otherwise it could not maintain itself as a state of readiness for the leap. Even though solitude vanishes before Existenz, it is yet the condition for it. Only he who has been absolutely alone can become Existenz. The disappearance of solitude, however, is like an offering-up of independent non-involvement in the world, a world that remains as possibility even when it is given up as Being.

Elucidation of Existenz as philosophizing thought creates the space in which Existenz is able to articulate its own decisiveness. Without it, Existenz remains dark and uncertain. Out of this elucidation it draws the awareness of self-certainty. In it there is contained a life of possibility that makes me sensitive, a life of preparation even for that which may never become actual; the breadth of humanity is in it as the breadth of knowledge is in the dot-like solitude.

Actual Existenz is historic actuality that ceases to speak. Its silence goes beyond knowledge of the world and philosophizing about possibility. Containing both and leaving both behind, it stands at the point where all thought is most open. If this actuality of Existenz is lacking, then its possibility is also absent. It is this possibility, however, that is the minimum of its actuality within those who know and philosophize.

Each form of the leap turns into a skid whenever these forms lose their relationship to each other. Knowing self-being can turn into the hardened egocentricity of the non-involved, into the indifference of the "that's the way it is," which, heartless, has become merely knowledge without Being. The philosophizing that illuminates limit situations can luxuriate in possibility and thus close itself off from all actuality; it can become shameless by merely thinking the existential without being ready and available for Existenz. And an immediate actuality of Existenz can become submerged in the bewilderment of passion, in a state of radical agitation without the clarity of transcendence.

D. The Duality of Mundane Being

As existence, I find myself in situations; as possible Existenz within existence, in limit situations. The leap is followed by an insoluble duality: to be no longer merely in the world and yet to exist only in it insofar as I appear to myself. To all appearances this duality can be relinquished in favor of one side, but with the consequence of losing the limit situation: either I step completely out of this world in uncommunicative and worldless mysticism, or I immerse myself completely in the world and arrive at what is, in effect, positivism.

The *mystic*, however, actually continues to live in this world. Either his mystical state of being beyond the world and his daily life coexist unrelatedly. In this case, the mystical becomes for him an experience of intoxication or ecstasy, while in his daily life he descends to the level of merely-being-in-the-world; here, the covering up of the limit situation lies at the bottom of this unconscious contradiction. Or, his daily life and mystical experience are intimately related as the phenomenon of this being-beyond-the-world; in this case it enters the duality which, within the limit situation, constitutes the essence of mundane existence for Existenz.

Conversely, the *positivist* cannot find rest in a world that is mere world. Constantly fleeing before the threatening limit situation, he chases after novelty until he stops in his tracks and finds himself in the crisis out of which he emerges as possible Existenz and now sees the world as his limit.

Existence regarded as possible Existenz passes through moments of mysticism and of positivism; using them as springboards, it returns to the duality. This duality can be expressed only indirectly in the phenomena that have an immanent incomprehensibility. Through it, seeming contradictories can coexist. The strength of this contradiction, insofar as neither side is weakened, is the truth of Existenz: Everything in the world is completely indifferent and everything in the world can assume decisive importance. Existentially, I am supra-temporal as phenomenon by remaining altogether within temporality. The fact that time has no essence constitutes, within the phenomenality of

Existenz, its absolute importance which it gains through existential decisions. The passion of my acts combines with my awareness that all is vanity, but in such a manner that the seriousness of the act is deepened and the act itself is not impeded. . . .

E. Guilt

Every act has consequences in the world that the agent did not know about. He is frightened by the consequences of his deed because, even though he never thought of them, he knows himself to be their originator.

Through my very existence, the conditions of my life involve the struggle and suffering of others; in this way I am guilty of living through exploitation. Yet I, too, pay the price through my own suffering, through arduously laboring for the essentials of life, and finally through my perishing.

The motives of my actions and feelings—arising as they do in the original impulses of situations—are so ambiguous, due to the manifold possibilities of what is desirable as well as the expectations fed back to me by my environment, that clarity of decision is possible only in rare moments, or only seems to be possible through blind rational abstraction. In a way, I live within the fabric of an existence that always becomes entangled even when there is a minimum of active life, in which Existenz strives to achieve that purity of soul that is the innocence of simple non-ambiguity. However, the impurity of the Being submerged in existence arises again within existence as soon as it is overcome. Not only do I have to cast off the dross but, for the duration of my life, shall always see new dross forming. I don't even know what that pure soul is, about which I, as possible Existenz, am concerned. Rather, I am thrown back on my concrete conscience, which leads me and which, in the deepest recesses of my feelings, finds me guilty in some sense. Purity of the soul is the truth of Existenz, which must risk and realize impurity in existence in order that—always guiltily—I may take hold of the actualization of purity as my unending task within the tension of my temporal existence.

If in existence I am possible Existenz, I become actual through the One. To take hold of the One means to reject other possibilities, even though done tacitly and, in the sense of rational morality, guiltlessly. This Other, however, are human beings, Existenzen that are compossible with me. Reason believes that the simple solution lies in giving each his due; but finding Being in this meting out of abstract rights is tantamount to doing away with all existential actuality. I must choose either the multiplicity and interchangeability of the many—but with the consequence that everything is as nothing—or the One. If the latter, it follows that I betray the Other which has come, as possibility, to challenge me, and thus I betray what could have become actualized if only in a momentary, fleeting beginning. Through exercising the most profound decisiveness in the actuality of existing, I take upon myself an objectively incomprensible guilt; this guilt, unintelligible to me, threatens in the silent recesses of my soul and smashes most radically any self-righteousness my actualizing Existenz may have.

By actively taking hold of life myself, I take away from others; I allow, through my entanglements, the impurity of the soul; I wound the Other by my exclusive actualization and consequent rejection of another's possible Existenz. If I am shocked by these consequences of my actions, then I might well think to avoid this guilt by not entering the world and thus not doing anything. In that case I would deprive no one, would remain pure, and would, by remaining within the universal possibility, reject no one. But not acting is itself an action, namely an omission, which itself has consequences, to wit: Consistent non-action absolutely adhered to would necessarily lead to rapid destruction; it would be a form of suicide. Not to enter the world is to withhold oneself from the demands of an actuality that approaches me as an obscure challenge to risk and to find out what is to come next.

In my situation I bear responsibility for what happens because I do not intervene; if I could do something and don't do it, then I am responsible for the consequences of my inaction. Thus, acting and not acting both have consequences; in each instance I am unavoidably guilty.

In this limit situation it remains for me knowingly to allow for whatever happens through my agency, even though I do not positively intend it. Insofar as the agent consciously permits these consequences because he desires the act for the sake of other consequences, he is regarded as lacking conscience. In the limit situation, however, he regards himself as responsible for his act. Responsibility is the readiness to shoulder one's guilt. Through responsibility, phenomenal Existenz stands under unrelieved pressure.

I can remove myself from such pressure by living without this limit situation. Thus I can say, albeit, untruthfully: that's the way it is; one can't change things after all; I am not responsible for existence the way it is; if this makes guilt unavoidable, then it is not my guilt; then it is a matter of indifference if the guilt devolves on me since, in principle, I am guilty through no fault of my own. Therefore I do not let the consequences of my actions weigh me down, consider it all right to live by exploitation, am not concerned about the impurity of the soul—which I observe and establish with calm detachment—and am no longer able to understand at all how that obscure rejection of existential possibility can be guilt.

I manage to hide the limit situation from myself in a still more radical manner by not even seeing this course of the world. I may hold that we produce for, are of service to and take advantage of, one another in mutuality, and that the inherent exploitation is cancelled out by an order based on law. Or I attempt to escape by assuming that to be my Being which—in an abstract, moral, non-deviating way—I declare to be my motive. This Being I confuse with my phenomenal Existenz fighting for its purity. I deny the obscure claim that actuality has on me as possible Existenz and do not even become aware of the fact that I have failed myself in respect to it.

Finally, I do away with the limit situation by interpreting each instance of guilt as merely a specific and thus unavoidable one. I have incurred either a single specific guilt that I could have also avoided, or I am conscious of no guilt at all and my conscience is clear. Optimistic, I envisage a possible life without guilt and all guilt as unique, something I can atone for in order to cleanse myself of it.

When such veiling of untruth becomes impossible for Existenz in the limit situation, then I lose a support in my innermost depths; I am I myself, but I am guilty. From now on I can live only in the tension in which I seek to raise myself up. It is no longer a matter of becoming free of guilt, but of actually avoiding avoidable guilt in order to reach genuine, deep, unavoidable guilt. But even here I cannot find rest. Responsibility is intensified to its existential pathos of shouldering the inescapable guilt that we would ordinarily shun only to become, thoughtlessly, passively, entangled in some paltry guilt. Exploitative utilization obliges me to do something in turn. Impurity leads to the demand to will only in the most lucid actuality so that the original volition attains clear expression. In the actualization of Existenz in the One we find the true ineluctable guilt, namely that we have rejected other possibilities of Existenz.

Selection 13

ABSOLUTE CONSCIOUSNESS (LOVE, FAITH)

EDITORS:
"Absolute consciousness" refers to consciousness of Existenz with respect to the source of its being. This consciousness is "absolute" because it is not consciousness of something to which one is related intentionally, cognitively, or experientially; Existenz is not an object and is not its own object. And Existenz is historic: In idealism the person can know itself as the concretion of an absolute universal consciousness. However, such knowledge, even if it were to affect the substance of one's choice, does not mitigate the responsibility for one's choice. Hence to Jaspers the person, seen as Existenz, is—as historic—himself an absolute consciousness in that he taps the sources of his being originally, without recourse to mediation, ultimately in ignorance, at his own risk, and essentially involving free choice. In discussing absolute consciousness, therefore, Jaspers continues the distinction between the existential and

the idealistic conception of the person which was begun in Selection 10. Though absolute in its objectlessness, the absolute consciousness of Existenz—which gains its being in a temporal career of actualization—requires the concreteness of objects for its verification, and it requires the idiom of objectivity as a vehicle of its articulation. Hence the importance of love and faith as forms of the fulfillment of absolute consciousness, and of action for the testimony of love and faith.

The following excerpts are taken from *Philosophie*, Vol. II, pp. 255–68 and 276–82. In *Philosophy*, Vol. II, they can be found on pp. 223–34 and 240–46. The following translation was prepared by the editors.

TEXT

INTRODUCTION

A. Consciousness as Living Experience; Consciousness-as-Such; Absolute Consciousness

As *living experience*, consciousness is the actuality of individual existence. As *consciousness-as-such* it is the one universal condition of there being objects for knowing subjects. As *absolute consciousness*, it is the certitude of being on the part of Existenz.

Absolute consciousness, first of all, is not experience and thus not an object of psychology. It stands at the limit of what can become experienceable actuality for psychology, since it is not for an observer but within the observer as that which gives direction. It cannot be understood out of some Other because its source is within itself. However, it is not the limit of the understandable, e.g., the givens of drives and experiences that can be described and which are then the starting point of understanding; rather, it functions as the limit that reaches beyond experiencing existence, penetrating and transforming it. Invisible to the psychologically objectivizing eye, it changes all psychological cognizability into something peculiarly incalculable. It is the incomprehensible that brings forth the mode of the certainty of Being in consciousness; as such, it is comparable to the totally heterogeneous and incomprehensible—yet investigatable—causal connection of things on which all psychological comprehensibilities completely depend in their being. Even though it does not become the object of psychological knowledge, absolute consciousness either stamps psychic existence as the appearance of authentic being or relinquishes it to the indifference of endlessness. Absolute consciousness is never over and finished, as is a living experience even if it persists as a cause; rather, as the appearance of existential being absolute consciousness is more than living experience. Therefore, it is not bound to living experiences in the manner of motivating affects; it is, rather, the steady substantial ground that resonates softly, but always decisively, in our feelings. Absolute consciousness forms the background to silent and reliable commitments.

The phenomena which are the objects of psychology (living experience, consciousness, sensation, perception, impulse, volition) are, as the appearance of Existenz, the presence of the unconditional which I myself am. It is the being for which I am responsible and in which I encounter my self as my own being. It is positive fulfillment through the experience of inner action. Therefore, it is not merely living experience but freedom.

Secondly, absolute consciousness is *not consciousness-as-such* and thus the object of the analytic of *Dasein* and of logic. When one thinks of consciousness-as-such as the condition of all objectivity, and of its forms and rules, one already transcends all objectivities; yet the thinking of absolute consciousness transcends once more this consciousness of the general and timeless as being general and timeless, and for which the individual consciousness is merely one incidental place for its appearance. One transcends it to the individual, historic in his appearance in time, insofar as he is unconditionally out of himself yet not general, irreplaceable yet, as mere empirical existence, irrelevant. As I attain consciousness-as-such by transcending all objectivity, so do I reach absolute consciousness by *transcending* this universality *back into temporality*. In this way, temporality, without ceasing to be empirical, has also, through being unconditional, gained a new character that belongs to it not immediately but only by virtue of this twofold transcending. Brought about by that transcending that reveals me to myself, it is separate from all the immediacy of my existence. When I become certain of myself as fulfilled freedom, then I experience actively what absolute consciousness is; yet I never have before me my absolute consciousness in itself. . . .

The word *consciousness* contains an ambiguity: it seems that absolute consciousness could be brought about like a psychological condition, yet absolute consciousness knows itself precisely as not being the condition of a living experience. There is yet another ambiguity: it seems as if absolute consciousness could be a *knowledge of something* that is an absolute being; but all knowledge of an object is to it merely the way to self-illumination and communication. As an observer doing empirical research, for example, I can probe religions and philosophies (in which the clearest certainty of absolute consciousness is manifested) as to what psychological *conditionality*, hidden beneath explications of meaning and dogmatic symbolism, they in fact strive for as absolute consciousness. And I can equally ask about the objects in which both know their truth to be absolute. But in the state of consciousness (such as in the certainty of salvation, in the dissolving acosmic feeling of love, in ecstasy) and in the object (such as the gods, the absolute spirit, the trinity, the legalism of cultic acts and rites) I merely grasp externals. The sense of knowing these externals may be that of finding the authentic point of contact, the point at which, based on my possible absolute consciousness, I enter into communication with the other, which is not a matter of understanding or of comprehending, but of experiencing my origin in becoming myself.

B. *Absolute Consciousness and Existenz*

Absolute consciousness does not exist as universal form; form and content are not separable in it. The content itself at its original appearance is absolute consciousness as certainty of Existenz; it is not the knowledge Existenz has about itself. Just as consciousness is not an object but knowledge about an object, absolute consciousness is not the being of Existenz but its certainty, not authentic actuality but its reflection. Existenz gains certainty of itself by ful-filling the consciousness that awaits it, so to speak, and which is the possibility of becoming aware of Being within existence.

Absolute consciousness is not a "life style," not an "attitude," nor a "spiri-tual posture." Life style is the objective rule governing one's behavior in the form of custom, of conscious discipline, of a meaning that can be expressed. Attitude concerns the possible stance—determinable in objective analysis—assumed by a subject in relation to objects and to himself on the basis of standpoints expressed by him. Spiritual posture means being jolted by ideas into activity, a jolting that can be realized as typical even though it cannot be defined. Existential stance or absolute consciousness, in contrast, is the effec-tive basis of these objectifiable attitudes regarded as the reflection of Existenz in its unconditionality. It is the boundary into which issue life style, attitude, and spiritual posture. To these, as its derivations, absolute consciousness supplies the content.

"Absolute consciousness" is meant to be the all-inclusive signum for the consciousness of Existenz, the consciousness of authentic Being out of its un-conditional origin. Insofar as I, as empiric existence, have nothing to hold onto and am searching, I find in it my support and my contentment; insofar as I am restless, I find peace; insofar as I am enmeshed in strife and tension, I find conciliation; and insofar as my questioning is genuine, I find decision.

The illumination of absolute consciousness leads us to the unavoidable illu-sion that we can yet again comprehend it in general and hence in knowable forms and to differentiate in it conscience, love, faith, etc. These, as forms, however, are not what is intended with them in illumination. They are not adequate to their object as are categories; they merely point to something immaterial, completely of the present, existing as freedom, which achieves no being other than that present in its own acts.

The fact that I cannot know the motivating origins in absolute conscious-ness signifies the following: I come forth but cannot turn around; I come hither but cannot step upon the ground. Although I cannot know either its being or its non-being, I can yet sense it as possible Existenz that stands in relation to itself and to the other Existenz. I am aware of its non-being by the void in me in which I want to flee from freedom and cling to objectivities; I feel it in the other when he cannot be addressed by me, when he escapes me, so to speak, as if he himself were not here at all; when I, as myself, try to find a relationship to him as self and am forced over and over again to turn him into an object. When communication is successful, whatever is present in the other as absolute consciousness but never grasped as one's vis-à-vis, is, at the same time, also covered up in the illuminating discourse about it.

Nonetheless I do not content myself, in my philosophizing, with silence.

C. Certainty of Being in Absolute Consciousness and in Philosophizing

Wherever and whenever people philosophize they search for the certainty of Being; they do this in spite of the impossibility of such knowledge and the resultant obliqueness in the form of expression, their ground and reason being the incompleteness of each Existenz. Existenz that is fulfilled to the point of clear actualization would not philosophize; the impetus comes from the tension between absolute consciousness and consciousness as mere existence, between the truth that is in the process of becoming but not in the state of being, and the established truth of cognitive cogency.

Existenz's original certainty of being wants assurance; for since it both grasps existence and detaches itself from it, it remains uncertain and ambiguous. Without thinking itself it lacks security in itself. Certainty seems to slip through its fingers.

In philosophizing, consciousness of being becomes a clear thought construct. Either Being is thought as the absolute Being of transcendence, and everything that exists is developed out of that in which it is sublimated at the same time. Being itself seems to be the object of thought. Or, on the other hand, Being as existence is construed on the basis of consciousness-as-such in which everything that is to have being for us must come before us as object. As Being assumes the shapes of empirical phenomena it becomes accessible to our orientation in the world through penetrating research. These two directions of philosophical thought impel each other, and purportedly produce knowledge about the being of which I am the observer. To be sure, I am included in this knowledge in accordance with the form of my being subject, but not as this particular historical actuality which I myself am. With such knowledge ontological consciousness does not constitute the end of philosophy but the articulated consolidation of its beginning, at which it stops.

Philosophizing returns from ontological consciousness to the assurance of Being which is verified as the actuality of the self-illuminating presence of this historic self-being. Ontological consciousness is preserved as a possibility of reading the cipher-script wherever it means to aim at absolute Being. It is also preserved as the unlimited will to know all the being of the world in its respective determinacy wherever it directs itself to existence. But the truly philosophical consciousness turns both into its medium. As such they lose the solidity that comes with a conclusive knowledge of Being. For the assurance given by Existenz's original certainty of Being cannot rest content in the objectivities of the absolute certainty of transcendence and of being-world. This certainty of Being cannot be true as mere knowledge of Being but only in unity with the concrete historic present of self-being; not as mere knowledge but as a knowledge that is also action. Therefore, philosophy as it is expressed must have a form capable of sublimating what is fixed, of merely addressing possible Existenz, of merely invoking the Being of transcendence. It must preserve the form of potentiality in which all actualized knowledge is enclosed as step or as an articulation. Existential certainty of being which aims at assurance through thought is, from its very origin, a philosophic act; it is a thinking that, in philosophizing, projects its thought ahead and behind itself in order to exist more decisively in its actuality.

To make absolute consciousness—this certainty of Being which, through the tension between it and uncertainty, is the source of all philosophizing— the central theme of philosophizing rather than merely to do philosophy based in it, seems like a *salto mortale* in empty space. It is as if I were to turn around after all to look at what no eye can penetrate, as if I were to set foot upon that ground whence I finally come when I am truly myself. Absolute consciousness—inconceivable as object, unfathomable as existence, unimaginable as experience—seems like nothing.

But just as consciousness-as-such is the condition of all objectiveness in the world, absolute consciousness is the reflection of the source of the comprehension of each wordly existence in its non-objective historic depth, the source of the unconditional acts of Existenz as well as of the manifestation of transcendence. It is the consciousness of my essence. As the illumination of Existenz is the axis of our philosophizing, so absolute consciousness penetrates to the innermost recesses of Existenz itself.

We must attempt to find signposts that point toward this source. The paradoxical nature of philosophizing as evident in saying and not-saying, in the circle and disappearance of what is meant, tells us that this task can never be completed.

We bring to mind absolute consciousness in its three aspects: in its movement out of a primal source regarded as ignorance, vertigo, anxiety, conscience; in its fulfillment as love, faith, fantasy; in safeguarding it in existence as irony, play, sense of modesty, self-possession.

THE MOVEMENT WITHIN THE PRIMAL SOURCE

Since I cannot know absolute consciousness as empirical existence and indeed it cannot become my possession by way of knowledge, it can have being for me only as I struggle to attain it. Thus absolute consciousness, which I can take hold of only in this movement, occurs together with my awareness of the inherent dangers: I can gain myself but also lose myself; I can either become myself but also dissipate myself.

One can discuss these movements but not as if they were rules in accordance with which they could be effectuated. Since their true content is in each instance historic, they are not transferable nor can they be steered by technical means, nor repeated in identical form. But as the individual thinks them he can, by transforming what he thinks, affirms his own primal source.

Out of the negative and by means of it, the movement brings about the positive as possibility, i.e., in (a) ignorance, . . . in (b) anxiety. It is precisely through the experience of these that the movement impels us to abandon the depths and to soar upward. In the face of what emerges here, the movement calls forth, in our conscience, the criteria for differentiating and the demand for action.

A. Ignorance

1. Ignorance as the Turning Point within the Primal Source. Ignorance as a merely negative statement would, taken by itself, be nothing. As the movement of absolute consciousness, it is not the general knowledge about ignorance that precedes my knowing, but the acquired ignorance that comes to itself in each instance of sublimating objective knowledge. It is not the empty negation of knowledge that precedes the attempt to gain knowledge, nor a self-denial for the purpose of avoiding all specific actuality; rather, its content is determined in each instance through the criterion of knowledge in which it finds itself as ignorance. In simple terms: since ignorance is nothing, such frequently occurring phrases as "this cannot be cognized, cannot be grasped conceptually, cannot be expressed" are empty words if one lets the matter rest right there. Since these expressions have import only in connection with the knowledge which they were instrumental in surmounting in the direction of ignorance, such ignorance is substantive only insofar as it is specifically produced by way of that cognitive content. Only that ignorance which is achieved on the basis of the most all-embracing knowledge is authentic ignorance.

Acquired ignorance, however, is not a resting place but is the turning point in the movement; as this turning point is reached, the return out of it is also initiated. One cannot remain at this point but is driven to knowledge and certainty which carry within them the origin of the movement that is derived from it.

For this reason it is not enough to give up trying after many unsuccessful attempts at achieving knowledge and to be reduced to knowing that I do not know. This kind of ignorance would remain without connection to knowledge; it would be unmoved and unmoving. Nothing can be undertaken with it because it is merely a stopping point. What is important is really to know what one is capable of knowing in order to arrive at genuine ignorance. This does not destroy specific knowledge but, because it is insufficient, one overcomes it by transcending its boundaries. In this case ignorance is not indifferent ignorance, left behind at the boundary by the cognizing individual; neither is it the empty ignorance grasped as the last remains of his being by the person who has given up; instead, it is the ignorance in motion that drives us back again.

It is also not the ignorance of uncertainty in regard to finite things, an uncertainty that can be surmounted by specific knowledge; rather, it is insurmountable ignorance which is experienced all the more decisively the clearer authentic knowledge becomes. It is the depth that is not entered except at the turning point of movement, one that never finds its fulfillment there but in that to which it returns.

2. Wanting to Know in Not-Knowing. This takes place if I reach the depth of absolute consciousness as ignorance not by way of resignation, arguing that after all I cannot know, but when I reach it precisely through my desire to know which propels me onward with ever greater force as I attain the turning point. Even where I cannot know anymore I cannot give up wanting to know; even in my ignorance I still want to know. I cannot bear not knowing as long as I go forward goaded on by my original desire to know.

The pathos of wanting to know in the area of world orientation lies in the critical limitation of its meaning and its possibilities. But wanting to know as such has no limit; it transcends all boundaries; it does not want to founder, yet founder it must.

Thus the courage to truth does not lie in the blindness of laying claim to a knowledge about being in itself. It is to be found instead in the openness of an unbounded will to know that sees itself as foundering out of necessity. This will to know cannot become attenuated in ignorance. It would weary to the point of no longer wanting to know only if my Existenz itself were to weary also. Thus ignorance, as the movement of Existenz, does not bring certainty into my exploration of what knowledge is possible for me but brings into sharp focus in me each decisive mode of knowledge.

3. Certainty in Ignorance. Absolute consciousness turns into certainty in ignorance not as the knowledge of something but as the decisiveness of my own inner acts and my exterior conduct.

This certainty is kindled by the ignorance of the will to know. Out of this certainty a new passion is introduced into the sovereign will to know, a passion to arrive at that ignorance in which there is operative, instead of the possibility of a return to knowledge, the primal source of existential certainty. It is a passion in which the fact that Being cannot be known is not only tolerated but is grasped as the price to be paid for the certainty of authentic self-being in regard to its transcendence. Again I do not take hold here of ignorance for its own sake since, it being emptiness, I could only drown in it. Rather, I grasp it because it is the situation of the turning allotted to me, in which I must find myself in spite of, as well as over against, ignorance.

In this ignorance I become certain of myself even though the facts—that I love and have faith, that I can live in limit situations after all, that the Being of transcendence becomes palpable in my inability to think farther—remain inexplicable. Knowledge in the world founders on the impenetrable recalcitrance of the Other which I think of as beyond my thought, as matter which I think of as if through non-thinking. In like vein, as long as I do think, I silently think the unthinkable, the deity, as the incomprehensible that conceals itself from me in the brightest light as well as in the blackest depth.

In ignorance, Existenz as freedom is referred back to itself. If absolute knowledge existed in an objectively fixed form either as a proposition for cognition or as a purpose for action, then the absolute consciousness of Existenz would be abolished. All that would remain would be a consciousness as such into which would enter an absolute that had now become objective. Existence would turn into a marionette theatre whose puppets would be controlled by these objectivities.

Because Existenz, through its certainty, must first fulfill the ignorance in which it experiences itself, knowing that I do not know is a general formula for the absolute consciousness which—as the actual certainty of ignorance—is historic and not interchangeable. Actuality as certainty and the ignorance of consciousness bring each other about, each affecting the other, in concrete uniqueness. This is the point of origin without which the philosophic thought directed toward it would remain an empty game.

B. Anxiety

The movement of fright, expressed as vertigo and shuddering, become, in anxiety, the turning point where I become conscious that I can be annihilated. Anxiety is the bewilderment and dread of freedom in which I am faced with making a choice. I can attain the decisiveness of absolute consciousness only by way of overcoming this anxiety.

Seen from the vantage point of existence, all anxiety originates in the underlying fear of death. Detaching oneself from the fear of death would dissolve all other anxieties as well. But the blind fear of the animal and the open-eyed anxiety of man both belong to existence since they are necessary for its preservation. By instinct or foresight existence counters any threat and

calculates how it can be diminished. Even small things are the objects of anxiety if they indicate the possible approach of a threatening actuality or merely
remind us of it. The anxiety that is the all-pervasive consciousness that everything finite is ephemeral has no object. . . .

The fears of mundane existence are essentially different from the existential anxiety caused by the possibility of nothingness. I stand at the edge of the
abyss: not only will it come to pass that I soon will no longer be here but I will
literally not be at all. I am no longer concerned about my existence, am no
longer afraid of physical death, but experience the devastating anxiety of losing myself and bearing the guilt for it. I become aware of the emptiness of
Being and of my being. The vital despair associated with the situation of
having to die is no more than an analogy of the existential despair I experience
since I lack the certainty of self-being. I do not know what I ought to want
because I would like to grasp all possibilities and not forgo any; and yet I do not
know of any one of them as one that really matters. I can no longer
make a choice; instead, I submit myself passively to events as they come about.
Aware of my existential non-being I take flight before this awareness and
throw myself blindly into random activity.

Anxiety about genuine Being is not concerned with planning ahead or calculation, nor with external threats. Here one must face up to the possibility of
non-being and realize that there exists no caring agency which could lessen
this possibility. Absolute consciousness is illuminated solely in self-becoming
through historic communication of Existenz with Existenz. And it is absolute
consciousness that also makes for a sort of suspendedness in finite existence
that constitutes the attitude of tranquility.

No automatic procedure will ever bring us back out of the state of anxiety.

We saw that the fears of mundane existence cannot be overcome by objective certainty; we can never disprove our cares and concerns with rationally
cogent arguments; all misfortune lies within the realm of possibility, and in
the final analysis we can be certain that what is most terrible for existence will
come to pass. Seen rationally, despairing melancholy that faces the possibility
for these fears is always justified. The only way to surmount such fear is to
relativize it in the process of mastering the ways of knowing, a mastery based
on the certainty of Being that can grow out of existential anxiety. Then self-
possession can be attained which, though it does not eliminate fear, contains
it.

There is even less likelihood that existential anxiety can be overcome by
objective certainty even though, in our bewilderment, we may seek it in the
objective guarantees of earthly authorities. But all they are able to offer the
individual who has once lived in freedom with himself is a desperate kind of
certainty. Rather, absolute consciousness must ever renew itself primally; in
its assurance, it remains bound to actual fear. For this reason surmounting

such fear does not mean abolishing it. It is possible out of empty indifference positively to want this fear in order to come to oneself again. The courage to fear and to surmount this fear is the condition for the authentic question about true Being and the incentive to move toward the unconditional. That which may destroy the individual is also his path toward Existenz. There is no freedom without the threat of possible despair.

Within the limit situation anxiety may remain as a destructive vertigo. If the individual persists in despair without faith, no rational reason can move him. Even his negative faith, in which he feels himself guilty for his lack of faith, fails to force him into faith. The person isolating himself from his origin fails to find fulfillment. His good will seems to accomplish nothing. Instead of completing the movement through the turning point, man has been given the task of bearing the dreadful emptiness whose resolution seems impossible to him until it is conferred on him as if it were a gift.

The surmounting of anxiety in absolute consciousness is the criterion of philosophic life, a criterion that, though not objective, is experienced in one's innermost being. He who seeks the way to absolute consciousness out of his own primal source, without objective guarantees against anxiety, lives a philosophic life. For him, philosophy is that which is communicated to him in rational illumination along this way. He to whom objective guarantees give certainty lives religiously; the rational illuminations found along this way are theology. In both ways, each individual, as soul, struggles to attain Being as it is reflected in his absolute consciousness, a consciousness to be attained by him in his movements out of the turning point.

FULFILLED ABSOLUTE CONSCIOUSNESS

Our thinking is natural and is itself whenever it directs itself toward definite individual objects and articulates its forms of thought. But when it turns back from all objectivity and presses on toward origins, when, in other words, it becomes philosophic, there thinking either becomes dogmatic and untrue through mistaken objectivity, or it becomes all the more strained, more indirect; the closer this thinking approaches the origin out of which I can be but which I cannot know, the more impossible it becomes to carry this thinking out. Here simply anything can be misconstrued; to the understanding, all that remains are empty names designating that which does not exist for it. Carrying out in thought the fulfillment of absolute consciousness would bring us closest to the origin; thus it is precisely here that the difficulty will become greatest. This will manifest itself in an aggregation of utterings that will occur rather than in a movement that can also reverberate in the thinking of an Other.

This original source, awakened by the movement . . . , is, in its reflection, the fulfilled absolute consciousness.

Beyond the world, fulfilled absolute consciousness would be a matter of incommunicable mystical union with transcendence in which the I, giving up itself and all objectivity, is engulfed. For Existenz, however, it is a phenomenon in the world in which it becomes objective for itself through acting and objective thinking.

Absolute consciousness can be illuminated as the love which, when active, is faith and leads to unconditional action and which, in contemplation, becomes metaphysical incantation. What grows out of love will stand in indissoluble correlation to it.

To distinguish absolute consciousness in itself means letting it somersault twice: first into an objectlessness of movement and then into an inadequate objectivity. Thus, one can speak of absolute consciousness as if it concerned psychological phenomena. The desire to speak, therefore, is curbed most strongly when it comes to the fulfillment of absolute consciousness. The gap between actuality and language, unbridgeably wide in all illumination of Existenz, is like a wound. Philosophy, as the will to the greatest degree of directness, yet with the knowledge of its impossibility, defies—in its articulation by means of some sort of universal—the restraint of the act of silence demanded within concrete actuality.

Love

Love is the wholly underivable, yet most palpable and hence entirely incomprehensible, actuality of absolute consciousness. Here we find the source for all content, here alone the fulfillment of all searching.

Without love, conscience remains at a loss. Without it, conscience is reduced to the confines of emptiness and formality. Through love, the despair of limit situations is overcome. Inspired by love, ignorance turns into fulfilled reality; love is the bearer of ignorance while ignorance, in being borne by love, is the expression of this love. Love is the return, out of vertiginousness and dread, into the certainty of Being.

Deep contentment of being is encountered in existence only when love is present; the pain of existence lies in my having to hate; the emptiness of non-being is contained in the stale indifference in which I neither love nor hate. In love I attain the heights, in hatred and lovelessness I plunge downward.

The lover does not exist in a realm beyond sensuality, in a world beyond this one; rather, his love is the unquestioned presence of transcendence in immanence, the miraculous here and now; he believes that he beholds the suprasensual. Only in love and nowhere else is Existenz certain of its Being as founded in transcendence, and no act of true love can ever be lost.

Love is infinite; the lover does not know, in concrete objectivity, what and why he loves, nor can he find, in his love, the foundation on which it rests. Yet even though love fails to be its own foundation, that which is essential is founded in it.

Love is clairvoyant. It is open to all that is. It does not shut out, but is capable of relentlessly wanting to know; for it can bear the pain of negativity since this is an aspect of its being. It does not blindly accumulate all that is good, neither does it create for itself an enfeebled perfection for its own edification. But he who loves sees the being of the other, a being which he affirms, without firm foundation and unconditionally, as original: he wills it to be.

In love there lies a soaring upward as well as a gratification in the present: movement as well as rest, improvement as well as goodness. The enthusiastic striving that never seems to reach its goal is itself the present which in this form—as temporal phenomenon—is always at the goal.

Love that finds fulfillment in the present is merely a peak and a moment; it is as if surrounded by a homesickness. Only the love that is utterly of the present can rid itself of this feeling.

Love is repetition in the form of faithfulness. However, in each instance, the objective sensuous present and I myself, as I used to be, are irretrievably past. Repetition is the eternal single source of love cast into a shape which is of a particular time.

Love is becoming and offering-up of the self. Where I give myself truly, totally, and without holding anything back, there I find myself. Where I turn back to myself and hold on to my reserves, there I become loveless and lose myself.

Love finds its depth in the relationship of Existenz to Existenz. In this loving relationship, all existence becomes as if personified. To him who looks at nature through the eyes of the lover are revealed the soul of the landscape, the spirits of the elements, the genius of each place.

In love there is uniqueness. What I love is not something general but something that has become irreplaceably present. Lover and beloved are bound together, each to the other; their relationship can be preserved only on the basis of this uniqueness.

In love there is absolute trust. The fulfilled present cannot be deceptive. Loving trust is not based on calculation and securities. My loving is like a gift bestowed upon me and yet it is my being. In love I possess a certainty that cannot be deceived, and I become guilty in the very roots of my being if I mistake this love for something else. True love, in its clairvoyance, cannot be mistaken. Nonetheless, not being deceived is like a miracle for me for which I can take no credit. Only by being truthful and by acting honestly in my day-to-day affairs can I prepare the ground for the possibility that love will seize me at the right moment, a love before which these preconditions recede into nothingness.

Love is found in struggling communication but may deteriorate into a communality of possession without struggle or into loveless quarreling. Love is found in reverent admiration but may deteriorate into dependence in the cult of authority. There is love in compassionate helping but it may deteriorate into the self-indulgence of indiscriminate pity. Love is found in beholding the beautiful but may degenerate into an aesthetic and noncommittal attitude. In the limitless possibility of its readiness it is still without an object but may deteriorate into intoxication. Love is sensual desire but may degenerate into hedonistic eroticism. It is found in the original desire to know, a desire that seeks openness, but may deteriorate into empty thought or curiosity. That which one could call the body of love assumes innumerable shapes. If this body becomes independent, then love is dead. Love can be present anywhere; without it, all is vanity. Love has overwhelming power and can still be authentic even where it is attenuated into humaneness and love of nature; on the basis of these the flame of love will once more be kindled.

Faith

Faith is love's explicitly conscious certainty of Being. Faith, having attained independence, animates out of its certainty the love that originally gave rise to it.

Further, love is the certainty of Being that becomes active in unconditional action. By rights, knowledge and its consequences should make it impossible to go on living; but faith means knowing and yet being able to live.

As a source, faith is also underivable. I do not will it but it is the source of my willing. There is no proof for it but it is understood in each instance in its objectification as a specific thought or image. As it illuminates itself, it proceeds toward generality.

Faith must be questioned in two respects: what is man insofar as he has faith, and what is it that one has faith in? Seen subjectively, faith is the way in which the soul is certain of its being, its source, and its destination without having concepts adequate to this. Objectively, faith is expressed as content which, as such, remains incomprehensible by itself and indeed disappears again since it is merely objective.

(i) *Faith in Something*. Faith in its appearance is not a matter of believing something but believing in something. In faith one does not possess an uncertain knowledge of an object, such as believing that something exists that is not visible; faith is, rather, the certainty of Being within present existence, where one believes in that existence as the appearance of an Existenz or an idea. Instead of leaving, in uncertain knowledge, this world in favor of a world beyond this one, the man of faith remains in this world; in it he perceives what he can believe in its relationship to transcendence. In this way he believes in a person and believes in objectivities which for him are the appearance of an idea in which he participates, such as fatherland, marriage, science, vocation.

Faith within the parameter of a fulfilling idea can unite me in an objectified cause shared with others. However, the faith in another human being as Existenz is the precondition without which the faith in ideas loses its foundation. In this case faith rapidly lapses into the activity of an existence that is now merely objective, subject to an enforced order, and under rules that are tolerated and obeyed out of sheer habit. An idea is true and effective only when it is actualized in human beings as Existenzen, where it is believed within the actuality of a single individual. Where Existenzen are destroyed and mere individuals remain, the ideas cease to be. But even where the ideas collapse, the faith in Existenz on the part of each man still remains as a possibility. In a world that is going under there still remains the love from one Existenz to another; poor, because it lacks the space of objective existence; mighty, because it is still the source of certainty of Being. Out of this Existenz new ideas can be born in this world that is handed to us, is penetrated by us in action and knowledge and is then again transformed by means of these ideas.

On the foundation of our faith in ideas and in Existenz there arises our faith in transcendence. Possible Existenz has a consciousness of transcendence that is prior to all objectification. Even before any definite transcendence is conceived of, Existenz is sheltered in it or stands in tension to it. This shelteredness or its endangerment assumes the particular historic form of objective self-illumination which, when structured and systematized, becomes metaphysics and theology.

If one concentrates on the objective content as such, there ensues an adulteration such that the illumination of faith is turned into a subsisting object. Faith is then supplanted by a superstitious knowing. It becomes rigid, nourished out of something known rather than out of the certainty of Being, out of a constricting fanaticism rather than out of love; together with its origin in love, faith would have lost its content.

Faith ceases to be when it leaves this world, for it loses itself in mystical union with Being. When I give up myself and the world, when I become one with the deity and myself become God, then I no longer believe. Faith is alien to mystical union, which does not believe but instead possesses. Faith, however, is the certainty of Being in its appearance; it is faith in a divinity that conceals itself so completely that, the further our knowledge progresses, the more improbable this divinity becomes. Faith is certainty coupled with distance.

(ii) *Faith as Something.* Faith slips through my fingers when it attains the certainty of rational cogency. Where I know and have a reason for knowing, there I do not believe. The acknowledgement of what is objectively valid does not involve the Being of Existenz. Thus, whenever faith pretends to objective certainty, it is untrue. Faith is a risky undertaking. The substratum of authentic faith is a total objective uncertainty. If the divinity were visible or provable,

I would not need to have faith. Rather, seeing all objective wellsprings of faith dry up is the experience in which the freedom of Existenz becomes aware of its origin as it relates to transcendence.

Knowledge is directed toward finite things in the world, faith toward authentic Being. Knowledge, for all its certainty, is subject, in its infinite progression, to critical doubt. An act of faith takes place when this faith proves itself as the power of Existenz.

What I believe—as it addresses me in the form of objectivities—I am through my self-being; not passively, not objectively, not as someone who merely receives. Rather, I am this faith in my essence for which I know myself to be responsible even though I cannot force this faith out of myself by means of willing or understanding.

My conscience tests the truth of my faith in its objectification, in view of the historic situation. All rational testing, on the other hand, merely exposes faith to be the underivable primal source.

Faith is trust in the form of indestructible hope. In it, my consciousness that all appearance is uncertain, is resolved into my trust in the ground of Being. The certainty of Being achieved within it knows itself to be face to face with transcendence, without any sensuously real relationship to it resulting in a deceptive truth.

(iii) *Active Faith.* As the certainty of Being, faith is found in the origin of unconditional action; it exists as historicity.

In action—provided it does not take place accidentally and for immediate purposes but rests on a deep fundament that binds and leads me without having such a purpose—faith constitutes my readiness to bear all. In faith, I am able to unite purposeful activity with the certainty that I act in truth even when everything fails. The unfathomable nature of the deity gives me tranquility and the motivation to do what I can for as long as it is possible.

In existence there is no certain prognosis; everything lies between the boundaries of very great probability and improbability. As existing life we seek certainty but we despair because of its impossibility. Faith, however, enables us to renounce certainty within the phenomenal realm. In all peril it holds fast to possibility; within the world it knows neither certainty nor impossibility.

Such active faith proves itself most decisively when the active realization of its historic uniqueness joins together with my—apparently contradictory—consciousness of the eventual annihilation of everything, of those closest to me, of myself, of my people, of every objectivization and realization. When this consciousness is preserved in its purity by not allowing any fixation in a world beyond (in the form of an enduring realm) or in this world (in the form of the continued existence of one's people, or of the endless progress in the realization of ideas), then faith in a transcendent certainty of Being becomes possible, a faith where I am bound together with the deity in a relationship no longer tarnished by other interests.

What I believe—as it addresses me in the form of objectivities—I am through my self-being; not passively, not objectively, not as someone who merely receives. Rather, I am this faith in my essence for which I know myself to be responsible even though I cannot force this faith out of myself of willing or understanding.

My conscience tests the truth of my faith in its objectification, in view of the historic situation. All rational testing, on the other hand, merely exposes faith to be the underivable primal source.

Faith is trust in the form of indestructible hope. In it, my consciousness that all appearance is uncertain, is resolved into my trust in the ground of Being. The certainty of Being achieved within it knows itself to be face to face with transcendence, without any sensuously real relationship to it resulting in a deceptive truth.

(iii) Active Faith. As the certainty of Being, faith is found in the origin of unconditional action; it exists as historicity.

In action—provided it does not take place accidentally and for immediate purposes but rests on a deep fundament that binds and leads me without having such a purpose—faith constitutes my readiness to bear all. In faith, I am able to unite purposeful activity with the certainty that I act in truth even when everything fails. The unfathomable nature of the deity gives me tranquility and the motivation to do what I can for as long as it is possible.

In existence there is no certain prognosis; everything lies between the boundaries of very great probability and improbability. As existing life we seek certainty but we despair because of its impossibility. Faith, however, enables us to renounce certainty within the phenomenal realm. In all peril it holds fast to possibility; within the world it knows neither certainty nor impossibility.

Such active faith proves itself most decisively when the active realization of its historic uniqueness joins together with my—apparently contradictory— consciousness of the eventual annihilation of everything, of those closest to me, of myself, of my people, of every objectivization and realization. When this consciousness is preserved in its purity by not allowing any fixation in a world beyond (in the form of an enduring realm) or in this world (in the form of the continued existence of one's people, or of the endless progress in the realization of ideas), then faith in a transcendent certainty of Being becomes possible, a faith where I am bound together with the deity in a relationship no longer tarnished by other interests.

Part Three

WHAT IS PHILOSOPHY?

EDITORS' INTRODUCTION TO PART THREE:
The selections of Part Three present Jaspers's basic conception of the nature,
the import, and the very possibility of philosophy. Jaspers's work on this
conception (like the "illumination of Existenz" in Part Two) is keyed to the
requirements of man's temporality, i.e., the circumstance that man lives in the
present, on the foundation of the past, and with respect to the future. It is the
actualities of the present situation with its dangers and chances that one addresses in one's philosophizing. Hence Jaspers's conception of philosophy
deliberately proceeds from his ascertainment of decisive aspects of these features of the situation. Here is one example: The truths human beings live by
(whether realized merely by life-style, or articulated in myths, symbols, a tradition of belief, an institution, spiritual heritage, or a finely worked system)
are multiple and various. No adherents of differing truths are, in today's
world, so distant from each other that they cannot affect each other,
particularly if truths exist in league with the exercise of political power. Yet it
must be possible to devise the means of living with one another without
gainsaying the truth of the other or denying him his right to live by it. How
can this possibility be realized? To indicate and to articulate it defines, in
essence, what Jaspers regards as the present task of philosophy.

Jaspers's elaborate conception of philosophy in light of its present task is
presented here in four subparts:

The first, "Introduction," consists of two selections, one dealing with the
challenge which the present situation presents to philosophy, the other with
the distinctness of philosophy vis-à-vis modern science and religion.

The second subpart ("Periechonotology: The Systematic Task of Philosophy") presents excerpts of Jaspers's theory of Being, both its substantive
elaboration and its significance. Jaspers regarded his approach to Being as
"encompassing" (periechontology means the doctrine of the Encompassing)
to be foundational for all aspects of his philosophy; this can be seen from the
fact that little essays on periechontology appear in many of his later books.
The English reader knows this theory only from these minor publications.
The main statement of periechontology is contained in *Von der Wahrheit*,
from which excerpts appear in this subpart for the first time in English translation. A more elaborate comment by the editors will be found at the beginning of this subpart.

"Philosophy and Its History," the third subpart, affords some glimpses
into how Jaspers sees philosophy (whose tradition has become problematic,
which, in turn, has occasioned Jaspers's radical redirection) come to terms
with the heritage of its past. The essay on the meaning of greatness in philosophy is to be understood as integral to Jaspers's conception of philosophy; it
appears here in English translation for the first time.

Finally, in the fourth subpart, entitled "Philosophy in its Everyday Mode," the reader may see how Jaspers regards philosophy as grounded in and as issuing into the concreteness of life.

I.

Introduction

EDITORS:

The two selections of this subpart differ in form from each other. The first is a lecture delivered in 1954 to a general radio audience; the second is an excerpt from Jaspers's last large book, published in 1962. Yet the two form a coherent background to what Jaspers regards as the task of philosophy in the present age; thus they form a statement of what animated his own philosophical endeavor, especially in its later phase.

The first selection, "The Present Task of Philosophy," reflects Jaspers's view of the political import of philosophy. Intended or not, a philosophy contains the seeds for potential political effectiveness. It also means that precisely for this reason philosophy must engage in its critical enterprise with respect to the challenges of political realities. For Jaspers the main political challenges presented to philosophy by modern realities are the tenuous chances of freedom and the dangers of totalitarianism. Freedom, to Jaspers, is essentially tied to a vigorous assertion of philosophical thought in its distinctness from intellectual thought (consciousness-as-such, science) on the one hand, and doctrinal faith on the other. In his analysis, detractors of the distinctness and significance of independent philosophy, whether on the basis of an absolutization of science or of a religious doctrine, in effect foster totalitarianism at the cost of freedom. Against such danger, Jaspers holds, in an oft-quoted passage, "philosophy must not abdicate, least of all today."

It is a basic task of philosophy, therefore, to clarify its distinctness vis-à-vis the development of modern science and the theology of revealed religion, regarded as source of truth in turn distinct from philosophy. This is the topic of the second of the following selections.

Selection 14

THE PRESENT TASK OF PHILOSOPHY

EDITORS:

This selection appeared in *Philosophie und Welt*, pp. 9–20; in English translation by E. B. Ashton, *Philosophy and the World: Selected Essays*, pp. 3–14. Except for a few emendations, Ashton's translation has been retained.

TEXT:
What is the task of philosophy today? We know the familiar answer: None—
for it is not actual, the private business of a guild of specialists. These philosophers, we are told, occupy university chairs dating from the Middle Ages and
meet in futility, at conventions which are the modern occasions for showing
off. Their monologues are attested to by a voluminous literature, scarcely read
and rarely bought, except for a few fashionable publications with snob appeal.
If the press, as the organ of public opinion, takes note of these books and
periodicals which gather dust in libraries, it does so without real interest. All
in all, we hear, philosophy is superfluous, ossified, behind the times, waiting
only for its disappearance. It no longer has a task.

Against such strictures we may point out, first of all, that not everything
which goes by the name of philosophy should be confused with philosophy
itself. Philosophy exists wherever thought brings men to an awareness of
their existence. It is omni-present without being specifically identified. For no
man thinks without philosophizing—truly or falsely, superficially or profoundly, hastily or slowly and thoroughly. In a world where standards prevail,
where judgments are made, there is philosophy. There is as much of it in the
cohesive faith of the Church as in a conscious, self-contained philosophical
faith; there is philosophy even in the belief of the unbeliever, in nihilistic
disintegration, in Marxism, in psychoanalysis, in the many precepts for living
that are now popular, such as anthroposophy and others. The very rejection of
philosophy goes back to a philosophy that is not aware of itself. The task of
the professional philosophers on their lecture platforms is to illuminate this
omnipresent, inescapable philosophy, especially through the tradition of the
great, historic philosophical figures. This is subservient but respectable work.

The two huge powers now ruling the globe are the worlds of freedom and
of totalitarianism. To keep them both in view is essential for our philosophical consciousness, for today they govern even the reality of philosophy. Philosophical thinking has contributed to the course of these realities, and its
strength or weakness will help to decide the way of our future.

On one side lies the freedom of possibilities; on the other, the absolute
power of a single spirit. On the one hand lie inquiry and discussion and a
constant battle of minds and things; on the other, a total knowledge and a
battle of intrigues. With the one lies planning in particular areas, aware of
limits beyond which we cannot plan; with the other lies total planning, unaware of limits. With the one lies variety to the point of anarchy; with the
other, uniformity to the point of creating an ant society of men who are no
longer human, who have become materiel, intrinsically irrelevant, fodder for
the machinery of a party, a bureaucracy, an army or a police.

Totalitarian regimes proceed on the premise that they know the course of
history and of nature. On the basis of this total knowledge they engage in total
planning. Yet no man can actually grasp the whole, either in thought or in

action. If one means to do so anyway, he may be capable of conquering the world by force—but his hold on it will be like the murderer's hold on the corpse, not like that of a man who joins with others in a bond of destiny to shape their common world.

Whoever means to grasp the whole with his supposedly total knowledge is philosophizing in reverse, so to speak. For all its logical and dialectical intensity, his formally consistent thinking is uncritical. For he is untouched, and thus not refutable by actuality, and he fails to clarify the premises of his own faith—for instance, of his faith in a coming salvation—this utterly vague concept for whose actualization he considers it necessary to lie, even though claiming that it will be automatically brought about by the magic process of dialectical history.

In the realm of totalitarianism, philosophy is publicly at an end. National Socialism declared it a thing of the past, replaced by a race-oriented anthropology and a politically guided science. In Bolshevism its place has been taken by Marxist doctrine; at East German universities, therefore, the basic course of studies for everyone is not philosophy but Marxist sociology. National Socialism and Bolshevism claim absolute truth for their doctrines. Any resistance to this truth must be liquidated. Unbelief can only be due to ill will, to congenital inferiority, to a false class or general consciousness.

What task can a philosophizing human being set himself under this violent terrorism? History tells of martyrs; it tells of lonely men going into the desert, or into the forest. But these, till now, were acting visibly, borne by a world that knew them. The fundamentally new fact is that today large numbers of men simply vanish and are never heard of again. The individual's impotence is complete. While he exists, he can withdraw to the absolute seclusion of the most private sphere—if he is granted a trustworthy friend or wife or husband, in the sense of Nietzsche's word, "Truth begins with two." For the wholly forsaken individual may cease to trust himself, may begin to doubt evident truth if he alone sees it and can no longer discuss it. The individual seems to be capable of taking utter absurdity for truth if an overpowering environment forces it upon him by its lasting influence. Under this suggestive compulsion, and under the threat of soundless destruction, there remains but one actuality to his philosophizing: the essentially invisible, that which to the so-called realists is an illusion, a mirage, a dream—divine Transcendence. And there may remain a sense of self-conservation, of being ready for the moment of a deliverance which is still possible, however unlikely. Philosophy, by its way of thinking, should strengthen the powers of resistance to the cynical propaganda of a public life that has become monotonous, to the lure of yielding to the faith in absurdity which reaches so dreadful a climax in the confessions at show trials.

In the realm of freedom everything is different. No one here has the human world in his hand, as though standing outside it. Here man seeks to join others in taking hold of his world; here he struggles for existence and competes for influence in a framework of legal rules. Uniting with the creating strength of all, he makes his way through time without a man-made, self-arrogated, totally knowing and planning supreme authority. Injustices remain; by better laws, man seeks to reform them into better opportunities for all. He remains en route, advancing in reverent dissatisfaction. The specter of an ultimate totalitarianism may loom even in this world of freedom, but here is seems inconceivable that it will last; it would have to explode, to leave a desert behind—from which the past would not be restored, however, but something new, incalculably different, would emerge.

Here in the realm of freedom, philosophizing occurs under very different conditions, in a wealth of possible ways. Here, too, the individual of today knows the impotent feeling of being one among billions, reduced to the vanishing point in the effect of his actions. Yet this feeling of impotence differs essentially from a subjection to totalitarian power. If individual action in the realm of freedom seems so trivial as to be meaningless for the course of events, this is exactly why one vote in a free ballot may seem too infinitesimal to count—and yet, all these single votes decide the outcome. The will to power gruffly spurns this fact. But the will to humanity, the consciousness of our link with all others, makes us solemnly and responsibly cast our vote as a joint decision, vital in its very infinitesimality; it makes us live throughout our existence as the trifle that helps bear the whole. It is in such impotence that freedom lives.

Yet the free world also contains all the forces which purposely or unwittingly seek to kill freedom. Many a man who inveighs against totalitarianism will in fact promote it by his way of thinking, because his own attitude is not grounded in true, trustworthy Existenz but edges surreptitiously toward obedience and force. He would take their side in a crisis, as a matter of course. It is in moments of crisis that the veils suddenly fall, and man reveals his true nature.

Many a professor of philosophy has expressed the view that philosophy should have but one representative at the university, that several would sow confusion in the student body. Some even wanted entire countries limited each to one philosopher—meaning themselves, of course—on the ground that only one philosophy was true. However heterogeneous the doctrines of the philosophers making such claims, their way of thinking is identical. They blaze a trail for totalitarianism.

One great task of philosophizing today is to discern these forces lying in wait to destroy it—forces so seductive in appearance and so roundabout in their effects, forces which contain truth but keep twisting it, forces which capture great talents. They may be called Luciferian; for in their consummate faithlessness, which stops at nothing, they can be most brilliant, notably in the arts and letters. Their wit and vigor of expression can be striking and befogging at the same time. They can be compelling in their extreme cynicism, whether garbed in the uninhibited *élan* of a mythology of nature or in the fierce language of terror or in the peculiar truthfulness of radicalism. At the root of all this lies a mendacity that will employ truth itself for lying ends. These forces use the intellect to destroy reason. They call for freedom so as to abolish freedom. Their insincerity twists the meaning of words and makes language itself untrue—a tool of deception rather than of communication. They are exciting, but their disciplined techniques lead into a void where thoughtlessness, along with the horror of enormity, will make men ready to submit. All these phenomena are like exercises for the surrender to totalitarianism.

The task of philosophy is the intellectual struggle against these forces. Each of us can gain freedom of thought only in a constant conquest of these enemies, within ourselves and in any public encounter. Hence any intellectual act today is bound up with the responsibility for the freedom of man—a responsibility which can materialize only with every man's free judgment in public debate, and without any censorship presuming to act as a selecting and prohibiting authority. Yet the fight that is being waged against totalitarian un-philosophy carries within itself the seeds of a great danger: the foe I am fighting compels me to take up weapons which do not suit my own mentality. In combat against the violent, declaratory spirit, a fundamentally liberal, communicative mind may well forget to be tolerant of total intolerance. It wants to communicate, but finds itself facing an actual rupture of communication as the other constantly dodges, stops talking, digresses, distracts, and deceives. The enemy dictates the mode of combat, and this in turn affects the combatant's nature. Even in victory, freedom would lose the battle if it permitted itself to undergo such a change.

The idea of chivalrous combat was to keep even the combatants linked by common standards. But total combat regards opponents as nothing but fools, frauds, or criminals, compelling them in turn to apply such categories to the functionaries of totalitarianism. Total combat knows no obligations imposed by a common superior authority. Such ruptures among men have dreadful consequences; they bring back the condition of beasts engaged in an out and out fight for existence. The mode of intellectual combat prepares for this condition and anticipates it. Experiences of this sort may well fill us with horror. In harmless discussion, the kind of polemics to which our partners resort may give us the feeling of an encounter with potential totalitarian propagandists and killers—without letting us know whether we should expect this of the individuals themselves.

An important factor in the present intellectual calamity is the reign of a nebulously scientific thinking. We believe in science. It is the authority on which we stand.

Let me cite some examples. Bertrand Russell, the eminent British philosopher and logician, looks at the end of his survey of Western philosophy for a unification of mankind by science. Oddly, though, science has always united only the intellect of men, not the living, historically rooted, entire human beings. If we take the effects of physical knowledge, for instance, we find that as a result of the accord among scientists, scientific discoveries from the stone axe to the atom bomb have been employed as weapons against each other. Agreement on scientific knowledge unifies views; it does not harmonize minds. We abuse science if we want it to do more.

The Modernist Creed of 1910 contains this sentence: "I believe that, as the cause can be known by its effect, God can surely be known, and proved as well, by the visible works of Creation." Is it not curious to be asked to believe that God's existence can be proved? What can be proved should not require belief. We need no creed where the intellect cogently affirms its content.

A third example is the thinking of the totalitarian regimes. They claim to be based on science, but demand faith in that science. They maintain, for instance, that nothing exists but this world and what man can do. Science, not revelation, is to be his ground. Oddly, however, this science is definitive in its basic perceptions. It already knows everything. This I am supposed to believe; I must not raise further questions, must not doubt or test any more—in other words, I must refrain from further scientific inquiry, except about technological inventions of instant material utility.

Yet what Bertrand Russell and the authors of the Modernist Creed and the epistemologists of totalitarian science have in mind is something other than science. The thinking they mean is tantamount to believing. Lord Russell has faith in the power of scientific integrity as the one, all-unifying human reason. The authors of the Modernist Creed have a philosophical faith, ascertained in forms of thought which do not know a thing but do illuminate the consciousness of the believer. The dogmatic Marxist believes in his knowledge of the necessary course of history, the dogmatic National Socialist in his knowledge of the natural laws prescribing the survival of the fittest. Both merely want to speed up what will happen in any case, and to do so by exterminating the inferior beings, classes, and races whose resistance to the course of events marks them for destruction. Both submit faithfully and obediently to premises which they regard as knowledge.

However disparate, these examples indicate one point which throws our modern consciousness into confusion. Instinctively we want to know, to have as knowledge, what is actually pure faith. But faith is man's inescapable, basic essence. Knowledge can never replace it—though in this case it falsely poses as knowledge. I am asked to expect of science what it can never do. I am supposed to believe even what I can allegedly know. Absurd beliefs are said to be findings of science. Expressions of something that is beyond scientific knowledge are pronounced as if it were scientific knowledge. All this happens under the pressure of scientific superstition, our modern overestimation of the capabilities of science.

Philosophy's present, great, by no means accomplished, mission is the clarification of its own relationship with science—that is to say, of the ways of thinking and cognition as such. While the thorough, perceptive performance of this task may be a matter for experts, the concept of its simple solution is a matter for us all. This solution would deliver us from scientific superstition and thus allow us to establish the meaning and the limitations of the magnificent and vital modern sciences, as well as to find, in the possibilities of real philosophizing, the way to our self-assurance.

The question of science is one of the great tasks of sober philosophical investigation. There is another task, with which philosophy is charged by the new state of society in the free world—by the fact that the masses today play a part, and in elections a decisive part, by their own knowledge and will, not merely by having their forces committed by a will not their own. Today philosophical ideas can only take effect in the world if they reach a majority of individuals. For the present situation is this: the masses of the population, though they can read and write, remain far from the full scope of Western education, and yet they share in information, participate in judgment, have a hand in action. Their ability to live up to these new opportunities will grow as fast as they attain to the full measure of sublime views and critical distinctions. For the contemplative hours of all men, therefore, the essentials must be made communicable—as simply and clearly communicable as can be done without sacrificing depth. Today many people do not yet really know what they want. Propaganda playing on their interests, exploiting forces, disregarding truth or falsehood, can take hold of their unthinking, unresisting souls. Truth itself, if it wants to be heard today, cannot help taking the form of propaganda. The great task of creative thinking, therefore, is the reduction of truth to forms simple enough to find an echo in each individual's inborn reason. Simple thoughts are of the essence, thoughts that strike the emulator with the clarity of the operation, at the point of inner action rather than mere knowledge—at the point, that is, where reason comes fully awake.

Against the view quoted earlier—that philosophy is at an end—I trust I have pointed out a few challenges which make philosophy today a matter of true humanity. It has the task of keeping individual thought—and thus individual being, which totalitarianism would extinguish—alive against an allegedly total knowledge. It is to remind every individual that he can be himself, and that to give up this chance means to cease being human. Our common future depends upon the actualization of rational thinking, in the clarity of will and from the depths of responsibility.

We who are professionally charged with the cultivation of philosophy as a subject to be taught are far from doing what the situation demands. Yet the little which many attempt, with the best of intentions, should not be held for naught.

Selection 15

THE MODERN TRIPARTITION: SCIENCE, PHILOSOPHY, THEOLOGY

EDITORS:

The following selection is a summary of Jaspers's thinking about the development of modern science as a distinct mode of thought and about the consequent re-definition of the nature and scope of philosophic thought. It is also a culmination of Jaspers's conception of philosophy as distinct from and with respect to the revealed faith of doctrinal religion. The selection, translated by the editors, is an excerpt from *Der philosophische Glaube angesichts der Offenbarung*, pp. 95–103. This was Jaspers's last large published book of philosophy and his major effort to confront revealed faith with philosophic faith. The work was translated by E.B. Ashton and appeared as Volume 18 of *Religious Perspectives*, ed. Ruth Nanda Anshen. In Ashton's translation the selection appears on pp. 50–55.

TEXT:

A vast spiritual corpus of philosophical and theological thought, created over a period of three millennia, addresses itself to us. It is not merely an object of our admiration for it contains the truth which we must, time and again, save from oblivion and make our own.

However, a change has taken place in the way we think, in the order and structure of our thought and cognition, which throws a new light on everything. This change was brought about by an event whose development over the last few centuries existed previously, also among the Greeks, merely as crude preparatory beginnings. This event is modern science.

Modern science is, first of all, methodical cognition combined with knowledge of the method which is used. Secondly, it gives compelling certainty: no one who understands it can avoid this cognition save by doing violence to it by his untruthfulness. In the third place, it possesses universal validity, not only —as did all previous cognition—in its claims, but in actuality: scientific knowledge alone is accepted far and wide as comprehensible to everyone. Fourthly, it is universal: it encompasses everything that is real and thinkable.

The experience of modern science brings about a state of mind which we call the "scientific attitude." For this scientific attitude knowledge also means knowledge of its own limits: it knows with certainty even its uncertainty, it sees the scope and the presuppositions of every method. It recognizes that its kind of cognition can succeed in every instance only through limitation and renunciation and can never reach the totality of Being.

Within its limits, science possesses compelling validity and is thus unavoidable. If we attempt to avoid it we become untruthful. The truth which is accessible to us, however, embraces a wide area outside the sciences, in philosophy and theology. Yet if this truth, in its statements, violates scientific cognition, it ceases to be truth.

The universal scientific attitude has become possible in our age and has been realized here and there as a state of mind. To be sure, all the sciences are paths toward it but even today this attitude has not been generally and reliably adopted. Scholars and scientists sometimes actualize it only in their own field of study. Ordinary and public thought partakes more of uncritical enlightenment than of this scientific attitude.

The universal scientific attitude is not the same as universal science. For a long time philosophy considered itself to be the universal science and had its own world view accordingly. Both have been destroyed by the modern scientific attitude. Through it, all traditional truth has been transposed, as it were, into a different condition. Just as a single hormone is able to transform a whole organism without destroying it, the modern scientific attitude has transformed all traditional thought. But the latter, with its imposing truth, need not be given up for it is the bearer of our humanity without which we would lose ourselves. But the day of the modern scientific attitude has come. It is by no means deadly where it is actual in its purity. It becomes deadly, however, when it is denied. For in such a case, i.e., in an atmosphere of dishonesty or in a state of confusion engendered by false enlightenment, the wellsprings of faith of philosophy and theology cannot long exist in a form inimical to science.

Both philosophy and theology must change their form, their awareness of themselves, and the clarity of their methods in the light of the new situation created by the universal scientific attitude. Philosophy itself can no longer be equated with science for it is an independent source standing between science and revealed faith. The truth of this is decisive for the treatment of all of our questions.

1. *The Modern Development of Science*

This is the result of the last few centuries: Great scientists have striven for autonomy, independence, the accuracy of scientific cognition in all areas, i.e., universally. They have achieved their aim in many of these areas even though they have not, as yet, realized it generally.

Together with this realization it became obvious, however, that the question as to the meaning of the sciences (why they should be at all, what impels men to serve them) could not be answered by recourse to science itself. The answer that science exists for its own sake did not avail against the attacks on it, to wit: that it indulges in superfluous labors, is a knowledge of things not worth knowing, produces ways of thinking detrimental to life, turns human substance into an empty shell, and finally, that it leads to the destruction of human existence altogether. The argument regarding science for its own sake indeed pointed to a basis in faith which is to be found in philosophy.

2. The New Experience of the Independent Stance of Philosophy

The sciences became aware of their limits through self-criticism; but through such self-criticism there also became apparent, in a new way, the independent stance of philosophy. The latter cannot be called a science in the same sense as the word is applied to the modern sciences. Rather, those which belong to them no longer belong to philosophy. What does remain within philosophy—and has always been its substance—is a cognition which is not universally valid for every intellect, but is a movement of thought illuminating philosophical faith.

Historically, philosophy has carried along the sciences within itself up until the more recent centuries as if philosophy and science were one. As long as they were considered a unity because both employed "natural reason," the problem of the independent stance of philosophy and the differentiation of philosophy and science did not exist.

Yet despite their subsequent separation, based upon the realization that their truths have totally different origins and their methods of cognition must therefore be separate, there is in fact an indissoluble bond between them. The notion that there ought to be science at all, the seriousness and the danger inherent in the desire to know (the *sapere aude*), and the absolute commitment: all these originate in faith and can be illumined solely by philosophy.

The origin of philosophy has been separate and independent throughout the centuries, indeed has been thus since the beginnings of Greek philosophy. It was incorporated into the thinking that is based on faith in revelation but then its independent origin in faith was disavowed. Philosophy has its own imposing tradition based on its writings which are an analogue of the Holy Scriptures; it continues to flow, as a stream fed by its own source, within revelational thinking in spite of the idea of revelation.

By virtue of their own insights philosophizing men base themselves on this great and unique tradition which is theirs and out of which almost all theological thought exists *qua* thought. In this way they are able to counter the tendencies to let philosophy disappear in favor of the exact and cogent authentic sciences on the one hand, or in favor of obedience in faith and cognition through faith on the other.

What is decisive for the truth of their thought is different for the sciences from what it is for philosophy. In the sciences the decisive point rests completely in the objective area, in thought, in judgment. In philosophy it rests in the actuality of inner and overt action, in the condition of the soul, in decision.

In the sciences, verification is dependent on objective research, on investigation, experiment; in philosophy, on the actuality of Existenz.

In order to attain the actuality relevant to philosophy one must prepare for it by doing preliminary work in philosophy: in philosophical logic, in discourse with the great philosophers, in the philosophic thought structures as a language which—if attended to properly—enables man to ascend to the heights of philosophy.

3. Under What Circumstances the Sciences and Philosophy Turn against the Revelational Knowledge of Theology

When philosophy began to reassert itself, the opposition to faith in revelation became articulated.

Whenever statements are made in theology in the name of faith in revelation about empirically determinable, universally valid facts, there theology is in the wrong vis-à-vis methodically cogent science. Whenever such science contradicts theology, the person who thinks in scientific terms and adopts the scientific method is forced to realize that science is in the right: he has the choice only of following science or of committing the *sacrificium intellectus*. Such a sacrifice is intolerable for a rational Existenz; but acknowledging scientific cognition as correct by no means spells the end of revelatory faith. For the latter cannot be attained by scientific cognition and remains untouched by it. Whenever revelatory faith gives up the aberrations that have constantly crept in due to the mistaken notions it has of itself, science can neither cognize it nor fight against it. Whenever the knowledge of science comes up against statements of faith, then faith is the loser. But this is the case only when faith has let itself become involved in an appearance of thinking which is no longer faith.

Things are different, however, when philosophy tries to defend itself against revelatory faith that denies it. Here knowledge does not confront faith but faith confronts faith. However, the adversary stance of philosophy does not imply the negation of revelatory faith but the refusal to adopt and follow it. Only a dogmatic theology and a dogmatic philosophy, both of them disastrously insistent on the untrue absoluteness of their allegedly known ground, exclude each other. Revelatory faith and rational faith as such stand in a polar relationship toward each other, are affected one by the other, understand each other—not completely, to be sure, but they never give up trying to understand one another. What an individual rejects for himself he can yet acknowledge in the other person as that person's faith.

4. *Current Misconceptions about Contemporary Philosophy*

The purification of cognizing consciousness has been accomplished in principle under conditions set by science and with respect to the primal sources of philosophy. But so far it has become widespread neither in contemporary education, nor among scientists, nor among all philosophy instructors, nor in the thought of all nations. Thus, what has been overcome in principle is in fact still held valid as the opinion of many people.

In this way philosophy today is forced into a wrong position by theology and academic philosophy as well as by conventional public opinion, dealt with as if it were a science and classified as one department within a faculty. Philosophy is treated as an objective science that cognizes its objects by way of reason in a universally valid manner. Thus, it is expected of philosophy that it register progress like any other science and therefore always represent its most recent and—up to now—highest standpoint. Philosophy is then questioned about its latest results since one would like to make use of them. Or philosophy is despised since the expected progress does not occur and it does not "know" anything after all. However, for reasons of traditional respect, this latter attitude is not expressed; instead, people no longer pay any attention to this obsolete business.

Philosophy itself has acquiesced in this kind of image that is presented by many of its own representatives. It has gotten itself into this position by forgetting what it stands for. This image became possible because of the belief that man bases himself and all his thoughts and actions on the pure understanding. This basis as a whole was supposed to be philosophy. Over against this philosophy, beyond the understanding, one sees the "emotive" which does not concern scientific philosophy. Or there is talk about a "private metaphysics" about which one should not speak. Or the mystery of faith is considered to be something incomprehensible which, as Hobbes phrased it, had to be swallowed like pills which are good for one but which must not be chewed because their vile taste makes one spit them out.

The truth is that philosophy is founded on assurance through thinking, on something which becomes understandable to man through reason making use of the intellect, and that this does not come into being out of a void.

Philosophy has been lost sight of. Why? Because in our time philosophy, forgetting itself, no longer does justice to its task. It no longer illuminates that out of which man lives; it fails to engage in the thinking that sustains man's life by virtue of this illumination. It fails to take hold, in thinking, of its own source. This is what occurs when it is reduced to mere specifics that are the objectivity of putative knowledge, into endless deliberation without fulfilling substance. Its thinking loses the strength for the accompanying inner action. The thinking of philosophizing man no longer originates in his total involvement. His thinking becomes noncommittal and existentially feeble even if it is logically acute and literarily accomplished. It is philosophy no longer.

Once before, in late antiquity, in the time of St. Augustine, a similar situation existed. The philosophy of his day had fallen into comfortable, rational conventions, had become repetitive in the endlessness of thoughts, in dogmatism and skepticism, addicted to the mere formulation of academic doctrines and didactics. Such philosophy could no longer satisfy the seriousness of Augustine no matter how highly he regarded the philosophical seriousness of neoplatonic speculation. In Augustine philosophical thought regained its full earnestness. Augustine's new, original philosophy absorbed the contents of biblical thought and revelation, drawing on the entire spectrum of biblical texts. It was as if Christian faith—at that time still in the process of becoming and thus still full of vitality—had transfused its blood into philosophy.

A thinker such as Augustine did not—as happened later on—separate philosophy from theology, indeed not even the natural from the supernatural. For him, philosophy and theology were one, as later, in a different way, they were for Scotus Erigena, Anselm, Nicholas of Cusa. In the light of their philosophies, the following may be asked: Is not revelation itself a natural event? Is the natural itself not supernatural? Natural reason (the *lumen naturale*) is, after all, itself founded in the supernatural.

When the differentiation of natural cognition and revelational cognition had at last been carried out with finality, philosophy at first seemed to have gotten lost in the process and abandoned in favor of mere intellectual cognition on the one hand and the mystery of revelation on the other.

Philosophy had to remember and reflect anew upon itself and upon its origin. Intellectual cognition, i.e., science, is valid in the same way for all men, hence also for theology and philosophy. But when philosophy is divorced from both revelation and theology as well as their ground in the Holy Spirit, it comes to know the testimony of its own spirit, of reason, of Existenz. For individuals this testimony may be the source as well as the last resort of insight and decision. Philosophy had to realize, in the light of revelatory faith set down for all time, that it can no longer become one with it in the way it could do so once upon a time when this faith was still in its infancy.

II.

The Systematic
Task of Philosophy
Periechontology:

EDITORS:
Except for 29, all the selections of this subpart are taken from Part One of *Von Der Wahrheit* (*On Truth*), entitled "The Being of the Encompassing," Jaspers's main statement of his periechontology. It is, in his words, an essay at a radical theory of Being. We ought to understand it as an elaborated consolidation of his treatment of Being as it developed from achievements of his earlier philosophy. Let us explain:

Jaspers's earlier main work, the three volume *Philosophy*, may be regarded as a reorientation of the philosophical question of Being and truth. This question may now be formulated thusly: how can we, as Existenzen, direct ourselves toward what is and toward what is true? The features of being as Existenz is the distinct achievement of the second volume of *Philosophy* (*see* selections 8 to 13). In a radicalization of Kant's Copernican Revolution, the question of Being is now found to be located within the perspective of the one who, in one form or another, is concerned over the question, i.e., within the perspective of the challenges of our respective situations, especially limit situations, within which we unfold our careers as human beings, of our growth and failures with respect to the chances of communication with others, etc. Yet such a redirection of the question of Being can lead to its dissolution. The question of Being retains its validity when it is pursued with respect to the unity of Being. Hence something else had to be worked out by Jaspers in order for the redirection to lead to a radical reopening of the question of Being with respect to its unity. For Jaspers this occurred in the year following the completion of *Philosophy*, 1931–1932. In that year he worked out a conception of Being for man in time, according to which Being in its unity is absolutely transcendent, thus "encompassing" its being for man, and is for man primordially divided into modes of Being which in turn are "encompassing." In Jaspers's conception, a radical theory of Being consequent upon the reorientation of the question of Being achieved in *Philosophy* will try to identify the spaces in which Being and its truth become manifest. It will attempt this identification by means of communicative reference to the testimony of mankind's hitherto achieved realization of truth and Being. What, in his study of this testimony, Jaspers discerns as the various modes of the Encompassing, is— explicitly or implicitly, as the case may be—recognized in his *Philosophy*. Readers of excerpts from *Philosophy*, such as Selections 8 to 13, will notice that Jaspers operates in his earlier work with concepts pertaining to the modes of the Encompassing, such as existence, Existenz, world, etc. However, in his periechontology these concepts are subjected to a fundamental analysis as modes of Being regarded as encompassing. It is in light of this that Part One of *Von der Wahrheit* is an elaborated consolidation of his earlier thinking about the redirected question of Being, a consolidation made possible by the conception of the Encompassing. In this sense it is foundational for all aspects of his philosophy.

In English translation there have so far been available only some summary versions of periechontology which Jaspers had included in various smaller publications. Selections 16 to 28 are excerpted from *Von der Wahrheit* and have been translated by the editors for this Reader for the first time.

A note on terminology: "*das Umgreifende*" is here translated by "the Encompassing." In this we follow most translators. One exception is Ralph Manheim, one of the earliest translators, who uses "the comprehensive" (*The Perennial Scope of Philosophy* and *Way to Wisdom*). We prefer "Encompassing" because it evokes more readily than "comprehensive" the imagery of the open horizon intended by Jaspers (*see* Selection 4).

Selection 16

PERIECHONTOLOGY (1): PRELIMINARY DISTINCTIONS

EDITORS:
Jaspers's operation with the term "encompassing" is introduced in Selection 4. In the following selection Jaspers shows how Being, regarded as encompassing, shows itself to our human subject-object dichotomy as primordially divided into modes, which in turn are encompassing. The selection is excerpted from *Von der Wahrheit*, pp. 47–50, translated by the editors.

TEXT:
As soon as I attempt to illuminate the one Encompassing according to its content, it splits into the modes of the Encompassing. We are left not with a single ineffable constituting an indeterminate and unfilled dimension but rather with an Encompassing divided, as it were, into distinct spaces. . . .

We arrive at the modes of the Encompassing by taking the following steps in our thinking:

The First Step

We live in the world but do not have the world before us as if we stood outside of it. Everything we can cognize is in the world but never is the world. The world as a whole cannot be an object for us. Kant understood this when he stated: the world is merely an idea. If we attempt to understand the world as a whole, it defies this attempt at knowledge and our thinking becomes entangled in insoluble contradictions (the Kantian antinomies). The world is the Encompassing in which and out of which all being-world presents itself to us in the form of particular objectivities. Designating the world as idea expresses its character as being encompassing.

All cognition of the world (i.e., all being-object) is, for us, conditional upon our cogitative consciousness. For example, the unity of any object at all is, in its apperception, conditional upon the respective unity established by the unity of consciousness-as-such. Expressed differently: all "being-for-us" is an appearance of "being-in-itself" in the form in which it presents itself to our consciousness-as-such. The development of these notions in Kantian philosophy brings about this jolting of our consciousness of Being: it produces and illuminates our knowledge of the phenomenal nature of being-world by our becoming aware of the Encompassing of consciousness-as-such.

Thus we have seen the Encompassing appear in two modes: The Encompassing in which Being itself appears is *world*; the Encompassing which I am and which we are is *consciousness-as-such*.

The Second Step

The Encompassing which I am is more than consciousness-as-such.

I am also *existence* which suppports my consciousness. We can regard ourselves as actuality only by taking the step from mere consciousness to actual existence. This is the existence that has a beginning and an end, labors and struggles in the world surrounding it, or tires and gives in, enjoys and suffers, experiences fear and hope.

As actuality, however, I am not only existence but am actual as *spirit*; all that is thought by consciousness and all that is actual as existence can be taken up into the spirit's ideal totalities and become the movement—revolving in itself and penetrating itself—out of which grows the construction of worlds such as those of communities, of works, of the professions.

The Third Step

Altogether, these modes of the Encompassing constitute what is undoubtedly present. They comprise the *immanence* of what I am, namely existence, consciousness-as-such, spirit, and of what becomes object for me, namely being-world. One can ask further if such immanence is sufficient unto itself or whether it points to something else. Indeed, men have maintained that there is only immanence, and they believed that they were living lives based on this knowledge. For such an attitude immanence would suffice and beyond it one would see nothingness. But throughout all periods of history there have been men who have taken the leap out of immanence and beyond it. Immanence was not enough for them. They became aware of being lost in it and they came to understand that immanence does not exist out of itself and cannot be comprehended out of itself. Hence, they took the *transcending* leap, all in one: the leap from the world to the *deity* and from the existence of the conscious spirit to *Existenz*. Existenz is the self-being that stands in relation to itself and thereby to transcendence; it knows itself as given to itself through, and bases itself on, transcendence.

The Fourth Step

Not only are there several Encompassings but in all the modes of the Encompassing we encounter a multiplicity. A manifold may come apart, contraries seem to destroy or exclude each other.

It is possible to move within a multiplicity, to let its components exist side by side, not to be affected by anything alien, to live unquestioningly within mere aggregation. But when I experience aggregation as insufficient, a decisive leap becomes possible for me, and when I have become fully aware of that insufficiency, the leap becomes a necessity: this is the case when I can no longer rest content in the side-by-side, when I can no longer contain my urge to experience everything in relation to everything else, to grasp for unity and to bring it about.

This leap leads me into *reason*. Reason wills—and is—the bond between all the modes of the Encompassing and all phenomena within them. Here a silent restlessness, springing from its own origin, lies in readiness. But it is only through living Existenz that this reason in me is set in motion as the Encompassing which, open in all directions, wants to join together everything there is.

PERIECHONTOLOGY (2): THE ENCOMPASSING WHICH WE ARE OR CAN BE

EDITORS:
Existence (*Dasein*), consciousness-as-such, spirit (*Geist*), and Existenz, which are familiar modes of Being, are here presented as the subject-modes of the Encompassing, as encompassing modes of being human. The first three are

characterized as immanent modes, i.e., as modes to which some form of objectivity is proper. Existenz is the transcendent mode of being-human, in that no norm of objectivity is proper to it save its appearance within the other modes, in particular existence, which Jaspers has already touched upon is Selection 8.

Selection 17

EXISTENCE (*DASEIN*)

EDITORS:

The following excerpts of Jaspers's treatment of existence in *Von der Wahrheit* is continuous with that of Selection 8. Like the latter it stresses that existence is insufficient as a mode of being-human, and urges beyond itself. Unlike in the earlier treatment Jaspers here inquires into the mode of objectivity proper to existence and, relatedly, into the scope of knowledge that is possible with respect to this objectivity. The excerpts are from *Von der Wahrheit*, pp. 53, 55–59, 62–64. The translation is provided by the editors.

TEXT:

Existence is the Encompassing which I am as a living human being, having a beginning and an end; as such it is the space of my actuality in which there is everything that I am and that is for me. . . .

Existence as Encompassing Origin, and Life as Object of Research

Only in ourselves can we be certain of what existence is. Encompassing existence can fundamentally and comprehensively be aware only of itself. However, within the space of the encompassing existence which we are we encounter something other that, encompassing itself, is also existence; and within this space we also become our own object as this existence which we are. Conscious of this, we see encompassing existence as a particular actuality occurring in the world. We call it "life," the life of man, of animals, of plants. But whatever becomes object for us as life is, as object, no longer the Encompassing. . . .

Life has become the subject of research through the objectification of something which as a whole is non-objectifiable. To be sure, through isolating and separating we achieve clarity about the living thing in its particular objectivity. What we grasp objectively as life is that part which is specific and tangible and grows out of our vague awareness of our encompassing existence; yet by doing so, we must needs abstract from this life. . . .

Does the Encompassing slip through our hands when life has become the subject of our research? Do we surrender the Encompassing when we achieve determination in the form of the object of research? This will occur only when this object of research is taken absolutely as Being; in this case its ground in the Encompassing is not thought of as a boundary, is not experienced as motivating actuality, indeed is no longer present in any manner whatsoever.

When we cognize objectively the Encompassing that we are as human beings, it, too, becomes something different for us from the things in the world. Insofar as we are capable of investigating ourselves, we are ourselves taken up into this being-world which for us is the incomprehensible Other, i.e., nature. In a turnabout of cognition which has been displaced from the Encompassing and included in objectivity, we now comprehend being-human merely as one manner of Being among others, namely, as human nature within nature in general. At this point we are no longer aware of ourselves as authentically human existence.

However, this turnabout is not necessary. Through research we penetrate into the Encompassing by gaining, through our awareness of the Encompassing, the motivation to continue research and discovery. Since the researcher stands within the Encompassing together with the subject of his research, awareness of the Encompassing is a guide for research. In objective cognition the limits are then recognized. Such a researched object can speak to us with a meaning which is not present in one that is taken as isolatedly knowable.

Hence there ensue both the depth and the shallowness of research: the depth of research which, taking place within the realm of this Encompassing, expresses it even though the Encompassing is not mentioned; the shallowness of research which moves endlessly in the immediate, the interest in which is bound to fade soon since the researcher himself is not moved.

Cognition brings about separation and cannot reclaim the one whole once it has been lost to cognition. *Illumination* remains within the whole, revolves internally, and does not arrive at any specialized cognition.

Cognition of life is concerned with specific, individual forms of reality. In taking hold of the object of research which is always determinate, I do not at the same time take hold of the Encompassing as an object of cognition; rather, it is abandoned unless it remains the space encompassing the researcher's knowledge. After I have carried out a separation in order to take hold of an object of research, I am no longer able cognitively to reduce what I have differentiated to a single ground. When with increasing cognitive clarity living existence has been split into distinct objects, I cannot regain the Encompassing, on the path of this cognition, through this cognition itself. The Encompassing itself is supplanted by the infinity of mutual relationships among the objects cognized in the separation.

The *illumination* of encompassing existence, on the other hand, does not take place by my regarding something else, alien or objective, but, by my becoming aware of what I am. . . . I live my life. If, merely looking at life, I become an observer, I become estranged from it and no longer find myself within the momentum of its actuality. If I throw myself into bodily passion, into thoughtless experiencing; if I entrust myself, without reflection, to the silent, unceasing happening within my life, then I remain in the darkness whose compelling presence excludes all cognition and all clarity. Or, if this immediacy is intended and is the result of my desire for experience, I end up in a state of confusion. After unsuccessfully taking hold of my life in its immediacy, the illumination of encompassing existence can take place only if I call to mind again my former awareness and remove again from definite, objectified knowledge of my life and life in general what had gotten lost in the determinacy of such knowledge. . . . Judging by scientific standards, I blur the boundaries of objects when I state propositions that illuminate existence; I transcend these boundaries and seem to confound their meaning. Hence, the propositions dealing with the illumination of existence have to be ambiguous and vague. . . .

Bearing in mind the relationship of existence to cognition and illumination makes it possible for us to fend off the false claims of research. We become sensitive to the inadequacy of objectifying existence and turn it into an object of cognition through the actual presence of our own existence. My existence as well as my awareness of the other's existence are conscious, as it were, that their salvation lies in fending off all absolutization of knowables. These always refer solely to the objective modes of appearance that stand forth from the Encompassing. Counter to all fixations of knowledge about the Encompassing and breaking through these fixations, the presentiality of existence shows itself as an urge toward actuality on the part of a possibility that is vague yet inexhaustible and that again encompasses that which has already been actualized. The "I am here" encompasses more than is manifested by anything known objectively. As actual existence I am always more than I know and can know about it. . . .

[For example:] My life is based on physical and chemical processes. Without them, it is not a real life. In these processes I recognize something by means of which life as Encompassing is made possible and through which it is conditioned. But this encompassing life is neither comprehended nor exhausted by these conditions. . . .

One must hold on to the character of the Encompassing in order to guard against the constant threat of sliding back into identifying it with a cognized object.

Even though I can never cognize my existence as the Encompassing, I am, in my constant present, this encompassing existence. Although we know about body and soul, life and consciousness, only in the way in which it is accessible to our consciousness, we look through all these knowables, as it were, at the encompassing existence which we are as a whole, undivided. In it, we are able to find ourselves through illumination even though we do not cognize it by surveying it as a whole.

Experience Bears Within Itself the Urge to go Beyond Itself

As existence I am conscious of myself. Human existence—and only human existence—knows death. As existence, man does not merely let things happen to him; he makes plans and takes concrete steps endlessly to broaden and transform himself.

And once again man is aware of himself as this particular knowing existence; he can know his knowing. There is something in him that can take him beyond existence. This new fundamental character of aware existence means that from its very origin it has a double nature.

As positivity of existence it can be as unfragmented as nature, can live out of the plenitude of being unquestioned matter of course. It is an ungrounded celebration of being a living existence. Happiness consists in simply existing. "We exist, after all!" is sufficient comfort even in the face of all that is menacing and destructive, indeed in the face of death.—As existence man knows himself as that which does not ultimately decide about himself; existence, at its very basis, is the event for which all plans and steps merely supply the space. No matter whether it has turned out well or badly, in each individual case it is, as existence, that which is gcod, that which wills itself. Whether healthy or ill, of this kind or that: as this particular existence it is always new, unique, original. In every case, because it is itself, it needs no other reason for its value; it is the irreplaceable, the affirmation, merely because it is.

Over against this we find the other fundamental characteristic of existence aware of itself, expressed as: Existence is fleeting temporal existence. In time it has no final goal, no end but its own perfection. Its success carries within it the germ of its destruction. As existence, existence is unable to fulfill its purpose. Specifically this means:

No satisfaction in life—be it ever so overwhelming and complete for an instant in time—is without illusion or without forgetting. In truth, it is impossible to represent graphically what happiness is; and under no circumstances can it be realized. For whatever it is that we consider to be happiness, it reveals itself as untenable because it is internally contradictory. It is the origin of its own destruction, is itself the source of new misfortunes.

Existence has no permanent state. Hence it is irresistibly impelled onward by changes which overwhelm it or which it helps to bring about. This unceasing forward movement remains confined to the particular in spite of all the energy expended; and in spite of the clearness of its individual aims, it moves, as a whole, with a staggering motion.

This twofold nature of existence—ungrounded, jubilant presentiality and unhappy transience—is possible only because existence can go beyond itself and thus points to an origin which makes its appearance in existence by way of another Encompassing. This origin reveals its presence in existence by the unbounded dissatisfaction experienced by man with himself as existence.

It appears that the fact of existence going beyond itself can remain hidden and unnoticed. Existence seems to contain the possibility to remain—or become—"mere existence." However, if I remain an existence without illuminating it in its totality, then I see the things in the world as an ongoing, opaque, and unquestioned reality; then what, unknown by me, has been passed on to me, possesses absolute validity; then I am claimed by objects, dominated by elemental drives and schemata of understanding—I am like the animals on which zoologists demonstrated this concretely; I am suffused by fear and thoughtless ephemeral happiness, in thrall to necessities that are unquestioned and therefore misunderstood; and all this occurs without my knowledge.

But my capacity never ceases completely to go, as existence, beyond this existence and thus sense it in its totality. If I am able, as existence, to experience it in this manner, then I am, at the same time, no longer just this existence. I can now illuminate it as the Encompassing which I am and into which I cannot lose myself totally because of my knowledge.

Steps Toward Finding Oneself as Existence

The self-discovery of existence is a deep mystery; for this existence is that pinpoint of light which, in existence, brings about—in the darkness of the unfathomable universe—its own appearance and that of the world. Only in the glow of this pinpoint of light which we are does the nature of Being become accessible to us. As we become aware of the accidental character of our own existence, it is brought home to us to an increasing degree that there is Being: it would be possible for me not to be; existence as such also might not be—but I am actual. This limit-thought which makes us sense existence in the mystery of its "that it is," also reveals to us that existence is not through itself.

The self-discovery of existence occurs in steps. Existence itself is life that has not been reflected upon; it means being driven by fear and jubilation; it is consciousness unaware of itself. Each further step derives its essence from another Encompassing that I am but retains that facet of existence which is proper to it. The thinking of consciousness-as-such is certain of itself as it thinks of an existence (*cogito ergo sum*). The notion that spirit is idea presents me with yet a new experience of existence: I am actual to the extent to which I am borne up and overpowered by ideas. I experience actuality as a tool in the service of ideas. Existenz comes into its own in the decisive resolve; it ties my existence to it, consuming existence in historic fidelity: I become aware of the possibility of losing myself into the void, of passing by my genuine actuality;

and yet I gain certainty of myself only in the real appearance of existence, which is the appearance of my Existenz.

Self-discovery is bound, in each instance, to sensing the other through which I am. In the drivenness of unreflected life I feel the ground of all life out of which I am; in thinking I am aware of the validities that emerge; in the spirit I sense the ideas that demand that I serve them; and in Existenz I experience the freedom in which I am given to myself as a gift.

Selection 18

CONSCIOUSNESS-AS-SUCH

EDITORS:
Consciousness-as-such is thought which receives its formal articulation in logic and finds its cognitive fulfillment in scientific knowledge. The nature of thought is a recurring topic in Jaspers's writing, and within the framework of his "philosophic logic" he devotes one of the three parts of *Von der Wahrheit* (pp. 225–449) to it. His treatment of consciousness-as-such as a mode of the Encompassing is very brief. In the following excerpts the stress is on the distinction of consciousness-as-such from the other modes of being-human, and their relation. They are from *Von der Wahrheit*, pp. 64–70. The selection is translated by the editors.

TEXT:
Consciousness means, first, the act of living experience, i.e., inwardness; second, the objective meaning of something, i.e., knowledge; and third, the becoming self-reflectively aware on the part of consciousness, i.e., self-consciousness.

Being for us is only what enters our consciousness, what becomes a living experience and an object. Whatever does not enter consciousness, whatever cannot be reached by knowing consciousness, is for us as if it were not at all. All that is to be for us must take on a form whereby it can be experienced or meant by consciousness: i.e., it has to be present within a temporal act of consciousness or be manifest through some mode of objectivity. It has to become language in some form of cogitability and thus gain a mode of being conveyed. The circumstance that all Being for us falls under the conditions which enable it to appear in consciousness keeps us in thralldom within the Encompassing of consciousness. Yet we are capable of clarifying these limits, and, aware of them, to become open for the possibility of the other which we do not know.

Consciousness of Existence and Consciousness-as-such.

. . . . Consciousness-as-such is the Encompassing which we are, not as the multiplicity of the living consciousness of countless individuals more or less similar yet different in kind, but which we are by virtue of participation in the one consciousness-as-such. Being self-identical, it is capable of meaning what is identical and to grasp it correctly. We find ourselves in this consciousness-as-such without any transition from existence; it takes us from the narrowness of individuation into the Encompassing of common knowledge of all Being in the world. Consciousness-as-such is the locality of valid thought.

Basic Characteristics of Consciousness-as-such

Consciousness-as-such, or thought, is the Encompassing in which Being as objectivity is manifest together with knowledge that is directed toward objectivity. The unfolding of consciousness-as-such takes place in the actualization of the forms of objectivity or categories. Hence, the history of thought is the history of consciousness-as-such in its manifestation.

In consciousness-as-such Being is, as it were, crystallized into certain forms, becomes necessary in certain coherences and movements, and is ordered in modes which are methodically accessible to consciousness.

Consciousness-as-such judges. Its judgment constitutes the recognition of a universal validity. A valid claim, which has no existence as timeless validity, attains the presence of existence in the actuality of judgment.

Knowledge, constituted by the meaning-directedness of thought to its content, is at the same time a knowing of knowing. The discovery of categories and methods in their actual use is followed by a deliberate knowledge of them. Consciousness-as-such is the clear-sightedness for everything and is at the same time clear to itself. It is the self-consciousness in one's knowledge of oneself.

The Scope of Consciousness-as-such

Consciousness-as-such is limitless. It comprises everything that, for us, can be meant objectively and can become present through objective meaning-reference, yet such that, in the act of meaning, a validity becomes present; namely the truth which is cogent insofar as we understand it. By virtue of consciousness-as-such we partake in a realm of fixed, valid meaning, and with it we reach as far as it is possible for any mode of universal validity.

We partake not only in correct cognizables, but also in a mode of law governing the forms of willing and feeling which are necessary and to be acknowledged as universally valid. Regarded in this way, truth, as formal correctness, is timeless, and our temporal existence is a more or less extensive actualization of this one timeless substance.

The limit of consciousness-as-such is Being, which as such is unthinkable for us, and which gives notice of itself solely where the meaning of truth proper to consciousness-as-such founders. . . .

Consciousness-as-such in the Service of and as Disturber of Existence

By no means is there an original accord of existence and thought. To be sure, one can show how thought leads to results which are useful to existence, and how the invention of tools has enabled man, as thinking existence, to become the master of nature; in this way cognition, which as such is independent of existence, can be of service to existence. However, it can just as well be shown how thought can disturb existence, can confuse the instincts of existence, deliver existence to illusion, cause counterpurposive destruction through false thinking, and how, through true insight, thought can not only fail to support existence but cause insecurity and wretchedness. The truth of cognition is by no means unambiguously good for *existence*. The relation of knowledge and existence is problematic.

This discrepancy is an additional indication of the distinctness of the sources of existence and consciousness-as-such. The duality of beneficence and disturbance by consciousness-as-such is a universal problem for all modes of the Encompassing.

Consciousness-as-such and the Other Modes of the Encompassing

In its relationship to all other modes of the Encompassing, consciousness-as-such is something adventitious. One might think that, as such, it would not modify what already is without it. It would then be nothing other than a noticing, observing, a cognitive registering of what is and what happens in any case. But this is not the way it is. Consciousness-as-such is nourished from all other modes of the Encompassing, yet it brings all of them to their full unfolding. It is not a mere spectator; its observation everywhere transforms what it observes. However, this modification can spell disturbance and ruin as well as a bringing forth and heightening.

The disturbance brought about by thinking consciousness is manifold. The originally secure, rich, and well-formed flow of lived experience is interrupted, overwhelmed, impoverished, and destroyed. Just as sudden attention to what I am saying or doing can be confusing, so it is everywhere in the Encompassing. Knowledge about things increases my care, anxiety, and suffering; it paralyses and shows the senselessness and hopelessness of everything. Missed possibilities of lived experience are replaced by mere knowledge and intention in order to feign to oneself and to others the appearance of what is not really happening but is merely wished; thus consciousness creates illusory substitutes for the actualities of life. When one investigates such representations, consciousness must seem like a disaster. Over against this, essential phenomena must be distinguished from subsidiary phenomena. Consciousness can fault, and can be used in faulty forms; it then becomes the source of particular untruth. However, this is possible only because it is the source of particular truth.

For consciousness is not only something adventitious but also something that awakens, impels upward, makes for development, and becomes the condition of new experience derived from all modes of the Encompassing.

What is raised to consciousness is no longer what it is or was without consciousness. In an authentic instance of being raised to consciousness there arises a new originality which can now become the ground for a new potential consciousness without limit.

Becoming conscious is the process through which man gains clarity about himself in his objective creativity. In creating tools, works, thought images, in all he produces, man works out and brings to clear consciousness what in this very process becomes actual out of all the Encompassing and did not exist before. But for itself alone consciousness-as-such cannot be the origin of contents. Clarity as such would be empty light, and that is no source of Being.

Selection 19

SPIRIT

EDITORS:
Even though Jaspers follows Hegel in his general characterization of spirit, spirit is for him not the absoluteness of Being but a subject-mode of the Encompassing. Hence the stress in the following selection lies not only in the basic characteristics of spirit, but in its distinction to other modes of the Encompassing. Such distinctions have been thematic in selections 10, 11, and 13, and other aspects will be found in subsequent selections, especially 19.

A note on terminology: "*Geist*" is here translated as spirit. At other places *Geist* is used in a sense which is more vague than here, especially in connection with *Geisteswissenschaft*; such less defined use *Geist* can be rendered by "mind."

The selection, translated by the editors, is excerpted from *Von der Wahrheit*, pp. 71–74.

TEXT:
Spirit is the Encompassing which we are as beings which actualize wholeness in a movement of understanding and being understood. This actualization occurs in one's inwardness as well as in the form of a world penetrated by spirit. Spirit is as actual as existence and as inward as thought (consciousness-

as-such) but, springing from another source, it is more than existence and thought.

Basic Characteristics of Spirit

Spirit is active, present, effective wholeness; it is active—in thought, feeling and deed—by holding together; it is present as guidance; it is effective through structure, measure, and the setting of limits.

This whole—itself not an object but a force that penetrates everything, attracts as goal, acts as a driving impulse within me, crystallizes into the objective forms of configurations and patterns—is called *idea*.

The idea exists only through the *movement* of its actualization; it must constantly recreate and reconstitute itself. This movement contains both a forward progression and a circular motion; in the mutual relationship of its members it is the unceasing expansion of what is enclosed.

Spirit is the *encompassing actuality* in which every Being essential for it was appropriated with understanding and all that is alien was excluded.

In its idea, spirit always has a specific content, is never mere form. These contents arise—infinite and not to be comprehended by any principle—from the depth of its encompassing essence, are actual in the obscurity of existence, are awakened by Existenz, and find their illumination in consciousness-as-such.

I am fulfilled by these contents, and I become intuitively aware of them in what is sensibly perceivable and objectively knowable. The contents are not knowledge of something but a present encompassing actuality which understands itself as it understands the other and, in this understanding, transforms itself.

The constant movement of the spirit arises from its contents by virtue of ideas and within specific encompassing actualities; but it takes place in a real world which is never solely spirit. Let us characterize this movement in greater detail:

Spirit informs a material. It orients itself by the evidence of the correct information produced by consciousness-as-such and by the reality of what is the other to it, namely, cognized and utilized nature. But from its own primal source it brings structure to this unlimited material. Its ideas create the connections among the multiple finite ends of my acts; they bring limiting form to the endlessness of consciousness-as-such, unity to the diffuseness of the knowable and experienceable. They overcome isolating tendencies through tendencies that bring together. Wherever idea is actualized, a hierarchy develops which assigns meaning that arises from the whole to individual acts and thoughts. The effective idea superimposes an invisible order on all wholeness which is merely thought; this order penetrates all order which is merely thinkable, mechanical, or technical; it creates an atmosphere, as it were, in which something happens that cannot be sufficiently explained by the understanding: it is that which builds up, determines criteria and aims, brings forth cohesive continuity, provides an interior bond.

Spirit does not find rest, neither as temporal duration through something firmly established nor in the form of transtemporal validity. However, its constant movement is not a matter of a happening but an impulse of reflected knowledge, i.e., spirit effects what is novel from an understanding of its realized knowledge and deeds, and such novelty becomes possible through the understanding of the spirit's past actualizations. In movement, spirit labors at itself by affirming and denying and bringing together of opposites; and it labors and struggles to bring itself forth.

Thus spirit is the activity through which it actualizes itself out of itself together with that which comes toward it; this takes place in a world which, although always already given to it, yet has to be transformed by spirit. It is the process of melting down and casting anew of a whole, never entirely completed, and yet always the specific completion of, an illuminated existence in a world. From a wholeness which is always actual as well as always shattering it urges onward to create itself over and over again out of the source of its actuality; because it urges toward wholeness it wants to preserve, heighten, give to each its place and its limit, wants to take on what belongs to its wholeness, and exclude what it cannot appropriate.

The above indications fulfill the task of intimating the dimension of spirit as an Encompassing in its own right. Knowledge about the spirit attained by means of what is objectively intuitable is indefinite, yet it grants us insight into what is peculiar to this primal source. However, this originality becomes clearer in explicit distinction to the Encompassing of existence and of consciousness-as-such.

Spirit and Existence

We are an encompassing actuality as existence as well as spirit. In contrast, consciousness-as-such—the encompassing possibility of knowledge—exists in each case merely as a focal point. Existence and spirit, on the other hand, are related in their actuality, for in existence spirit finds its vehicle and its vital power. Yet in each area of their relationship they also display the difference in their origin.

The wholeness of living existence is unconsciously impelled from the depth of an Encompassing, without understanding. The wholeness of spirit perfects itself in the light of the pervasive inwardness of motivating self-understanding.

Existence, in its individuality, is an enclosed configuration. The wholeness of the spirit remains unclosed within any confines, so also in the case of the individually existing spirit, and is the potentiality of development that is capable of breaking through them. . . .

Existence and spirit are bound to their ground. But as existence we are rooted in impenetrable darkness, as spirit in a primal source that becomes endlessly clearer, whose clarity increases endlessly and can in principle be complete. As existence we are, unknowing, tied to the ultimate grounds of matter, of life, and of the psyche; when we regard this Encompassing as an object, then we endlessly cognize ourselves only from the outside and only such that we split ourselves into segregated realities which can be studied only in their segregation. As spirit, on the other hand, we are, in full awareness, related to everything that is understandable; hence spirit transforms everything, the world as well as itself, into something that is understandable and does so by means of consciousness-as-such. When we, as this Encompassing, become an object, then we cognize ourselves from within as the one sole actuality for which all is spirit and which is spirit only.

Spirit and Consciousness-as-such

Spirit and thought are usually taken as being one and the same. While there is often thought without spirit, spirit is in fact never without thought; yet their primal sources are essentially different. Both are to be illuminated as Encompassings, but not to be reduced to each other. For both, the same expressions are to be used, but in a radically different sense:

"Being with oneself in the other." In thought, hence, in spirit, we are directed toward objects. There is a pervasive split between the thinking I and the thought object; and conversely, wherever there is this split, there thought (i.e., consciousness-as-such) is present.

But in consciousness-as-such the split is absolute. Its thinking is directed toward the object as toward an absolutely other. Spirit, however, though directed toward objects by way of consciousness-as-such, is in the objects with itself. For spirit the split is a bridge to its awareness of itself in the other.

Spirit assures itself within the Encompassing of its substance. Consciousness-as-such assures itself, in the forms peculiar to its encompassing being, of objective contents as something that, as such, is foreign to it. In brief: Spirit always deals with itself, consciousness-as-such with an other. . . .

"Actuality." Spirit is carried by the broad, structured reality of existence and is awakened through Existenz, which is effective in it. Consciousness-as-such, as existence, is like a focal point, not devoid of, but indifferent to, existence; it functions as a medium for spirit and is in the service of existence, but is itself not an authentic existent, though it is of immeasurable consequence to any sort of actuality.

Spirit is temporal movement, one that becomes actual precisely in full temporality. Consciousness-as-such takes place as thinking in time, yet with a sense of strangeness with respect to time in that it would bring its significance to completion as the atemporal presence of the correctness of thought. . . .

Objectification of Spirit

Existence, consciousness-as-such, and spirit become objects of research but each in its own way.

Consciousness-as-such becomes the object of its own exploration, yet such that it does not grasp itself but merely clarifies itself in what it cogitatively produces. The exploration of consciousness-as-such consists of the logic of objectivity, the forms of the categories and methods.

When objectified in research, existence becomes the subject matter of biology, psychology, and sociology. The spirit in its objectification also becomes an object for consciousness-as-such in some sciences. Thereby spirit loses the character of Encompassing and displays itself to research in its objectifications, i.e., in the finite appearances of its thoughts, works, deeds. As long as such research consists only of the cognitive work of consciousness-as-such, spirit is not discernible as such; instead, what is cognized is merely its objective product. . . .

Spirit understands both itself and the world in works that have become objective: in works of thought, of art, and of literature; in institutions, laws and constitutions; in professions; in customs and patterns of life. Its understandable movements take place only in its reaching for objectification and in the creation of new objectification.

Yet the objectification is not the spirit. A purely objective, rational, purposive, technical understanding of a work does not as yet constitute a partaking and a reverberation of spirit. Spiritual understanding, which also means partaking of its substance, passes through what can be grasped objectively and aims at the whole and the ground, at the substance of ideas.

The creations of the spirit are not another closed object for my knowing; they are, rather, a means and a guidepost for the spiritually live movement only in which spiritual creations can themselves become manifest again in their essence.

Selection 20

EXISTENZ

EDITORS:
Existenz is the topic of selections 8 to 13. The following selection deals with Existenz as distinct from the three immanent modes of the Encompassing

which we are or can be. It is excerpted from *Von der Wahrheit*, pp. 76–82, in a translation provided by the editors.

TEXT:

What I truly am, that is the Encompassing of self-being. Existenz is the source of true actuality without which that scope and actuality of existence would evaporate. As Existenz I can in no way become my own object of research, cannot know myself; I can only become actual or I can lose myself. I can never possess Existenz through my knowledge of it, yet it conveys the content of every mode of the Encompassing which I am. Where everything for which I reach in my desire to know vanishes, here is the axis, so to speak, around which everything turns, both what I am and what yields to me the authentic meaning of Being in the world.

The Gap Between the Immanent Modes and Existenz

. . . . Between the three modes of the Encompassing which I am as immanent being and the Existenz which transcends them all, there is a gap which is quite different from the gaps between the modes of the Encompassing discussed so far. When I become aware of the Encompassing which I myself am as Existenz, then I do not experience a new space filled with its own specific content and objectivity but a transcendent actuality which, although itself intangible, is to sustain everything:

1. The three immanent modes of the Encompassing bring me the actuality of the world as well as its scope. Existenz is the origin of authentic actuality without which all this breadth and actuality of existence would evaporate. It is only Existenz which truly gives voice to the contents and substance of the immanently transcendent. It is Existenz which animates immanence.

2. Existenz which actualizes the Encompassing which I myself am is really the capacity to be. It is always in the process of choosing whether to be or not to be and must decide about itself. I am not only here, am not merely the focal point of a consciousness-as-such, am not only the locus of intellectual movement and production but can, in all of these, be myself or be lost in them. . . .

Existenz and Existence

[Editor's note: the distinction between "existence" and "Existenz" as presented by Jaspers in *Philosophy* may be found in Part Two, selection (8) "Existence-Existenz."]

Existenz and Consciousness-as-such

As individual, consciousness-as-such is the shiftable focal point of a universal; Existenz is the irreplaceable historicity of a unique origin.

The Encompassing which we are is clear by reference to an other. However, this other, which is Being itself, is essentially different for consciousness-as-such than for Existenz. Just as I am consciousness only by casting my glance at objective being in its otherness and by dealing with it, I am Existenz only when I am at one with the knowledge about transcendence as the power through which I am authentically myself. The other is either Being in the world which manifests itself to consciousness-as-such, or it is transcendence which manifests itself to Existenz. This twofold other becomes distinct only through Existenz. Without Existenz, the meaning of transcendence would be lost.

For consciousness lacking Existenz at the limits of what is objective for it, there would be left only that which cannot be cognized, something thought to be fundamental, something yet to be conceived. But this non-cognizable could be a matter of indifference, at bottom may not concern me. It can be put aside.

Or, at the limit, conscious existence may encounter something uncanny and frightening. There are kinds of superstition and fear which can be investigated psychologically; these can be overcome through insight into the factual by means of consciousness-as-such and their illusory contents be made to disappear in the indifference of the non-cognizable. Solely through Existenz does transcendence become present, without this illusory superstition, as the authentic actuality.

Existenz needs consciousness-as-such in order to enter into the space of clarity which is its medium. Whenever Existenz cannot clarify, in this space, everything knowable and thinkable, it remains closed to itself.

Existenz and Spirit

Spirit already seems to bring with it the perfection of being-human. The magic of the spirit tends to be sufficient unto itself—whether in the richness of its content, the plenitude of its configurations, the level of its power of vision and performance, or in the actualization of its mental vitality in unity with existence. Whenever this is the case, then Existenz is like a counterweight to spirit. At the same time, however, Existenz is completely dependent on the spirit which, in its creativeness, brings to Existenz the configurations in which it can understand and actualize itself. Let us contrast the characteristics of the spirit with those of Existenz:

1. Becoming whole and being authentic. Spirit is the desire to become whole (but man cannot become a completed whole in time); Existenz is the desire to be authentic (but man cannot come into secure possession of his self in time).

Spirit is on the way toward becoming whole by means of talent and ability; as the medium of ideas it is creative genius. Existenz is on the way toward Being through the decision based on its resolve and is thus authentic self-being.

Spirit fulfills itself in constant motion, completes itself in ever new realities, moves forward yet is enclosed in a constantly revolving circularity. It makes no decisions but excels just as much in the service of the devil as of God. Existenz penetrates to its ground by decision coupled with exclusion, breaks through everything closed, desires nothing but the certainty of transcendence.

2. Certainty of Being.   Spirit is certain of its being in the richness of its essence and the unceasingly extended appropriation of its plenitude. But spirit is seduced into finding in this the tranquility of the certainty of Being, while at the same time wasting its substance in the unceasing novelty of its motion and in reality remains opaque to itself as regards the motives that set it in motion, motives which do not reside in spirit itself. This seduction of the spirit is all the more deceptive the more certain it is of its enjoyment of this plenitude.

Existenz achieves a certainty before transcendence which is never objective and therefore always remains in doubt, and assumes a life of risk on the strength of there being such transcendence. It is the seduction of Existenz to believe itself to be in possession of its being merely on the basis of its reflection on the certainty of Being. Whereas spirit can still be charming even in the exuberance of deceptive certainty, Existenz, deceived into self-certainty, loses itself in arrogance. It has surrendered its meaning and its actuality. It is a caricature of being-human, come about through the perversion of its highest possibility.

3. Understanding Spirit and Existenz.   Spirit is that which is understandable all the way through, is self-realizing in its wholeness, and can be illuminated in its ground, insofar as it contains it. Existenz, however, conceals in its ground something incomprehensible which, even though infinitely clarifiable, never possesses final clarity. It is that which breaks through every whole without ever reaching an absolute whole. If Existenz understands itself, then this is not an understanding that can be detached from that which understands, it is not an observing; rather, it is the primal source which comes itself first into being in understanding clarification. It is not like the participation in an other but is at once the understanding as well as the being of what is understood. It is not an understanding-in-general but is, by means of understanding-in-general, an understanding in the unique, absolutely present, in action, in love, in every configuration of absolute consciousness. It is the difference between the way in which I understand the love of the other and yet can never really understand it, and the way in which I understand my own love because I am actually it; or it is the difference between the way I understand an event or an experience by empathizing with anything at all, and the way in which I understand as only I can because even in my misunderstanding I know myself before transcendence.

For spirit, the perfect transparency of contents would itself become the primal source of Being. Existenz, on the other hand, remains, in spite of all intellectual clarification, the ever dark origin that cannot be sublimated.

4. The Universal of the Spirit and Singular Existenz. Spirit sublimates everything individual into the universal which it exemplifies, and at the same time into the whole of which it is a member. Existenz, however, cannot be sublimated into an other; it is responsible for itself, is not derived, is singular.

As spirit, the individual is not yet he himself but the unity of the randomly individual with the necessarily universal. As Existenz, the individual is the primal source which, being prior to the merely individual and the merely universal, animates both.

As spirit, the individual wants to derive completely his decision from the whole of which he is a member, or, with the aid of consciousness-as-such, from that universal based on which his decision turns out to be objectively correct. As Existenz, the individual takes hold of eternity by way of temporality; he does so through his underivably original decision, with which he is at one, so that he knows himself bound to it with his whole existence. He who himself actualizes himself beyond all time in time, becomes, as historicity, an origin in time.

5. Spiritual and Existential Historicity. Existential historicity is essentially different from the historic consciousness of the spirit. Spirit, looking back on its past, sees itself in its historicity as the transparent totality of what it has become. Existenz, on the other hand, is historical as eternity in time. It is the absolute historicity of its concrete existence in its spiritual opaqueness. Existenz is not merely the incompleteness of all temporal existence which, being incomplete, always wants to extend and transform itself into becoming spiritually complete; rather, in its incompletion, Existenz is truly penetrated temporal existence: it is the paradox of the unity of temporality and eternity.

6. Immediacy of the Idea and of Faith. The immediacy of the spirit is the burgeoning idea; the idea unfolds in the clarity of its universality. The immediacy of Existenz is faith; faith is chosen upon reflecting on its radically questionable nature. An idea is the plenitude of an internally articulated wholeness of immanent Being. Faith is the historicity of Existenz in the face of transcendence.

Through their respective movements, idea and faith arrive at their mediated new immediacy: the idea in the form of present fulfilling consciousness; faith in the form of a certainty which cannot be confirmed because it is void of criteria, yet existentially sustaining.

7. Spirit and Existenz as Indivisible. As we contrast spirit and Existenz we must not conceal in what way the two are dependent on each other.

Spirit is immanent, seems to be sufficient unto itself, but in the last analysis its substance and ground lie solely in the Existenz which sustains it. In the face of transcendence Existenz remains empty or perplexed unless spirit creates for it the configurations in which it assures itself of its transcendence. Existenz can only remain free and undeceived, can only then become lucid in its world and clearly decisive when it takes hold of the movements of the spirit and uses them as its material. Traversing spirit, going beyond it, and not caught in it, Existenz finds its way.

Selection 21

PERIECHONTOLOGY (3):
THE ENCOMPASSING THAT IS BEING ITSELF

EDITORS:
The following selection is brief but decisive for Jaspers's conception of Being and truth. The human being, whether regarded in one or in all of the modes of being-human, is not Being itself. This view is here presented in opposition to two thinkers for whom Jaspers has the highest regard: Nietzsche with his view that the truth of Being is interpretation; and Hegel, for whom the primacy of consciousness implies an idealistic conception of Being.

The passage to follow has been translated by the editors; the original appears in *Von der Wahrheit*, pp. 83–85.

TEXT:
We go beyond the Encompassing which we are when we ask whether this whole, consisting of existence, consciousness-as-such, spirit and Existenz, is Being itself, and whether Being is exhausted by this whole.

The following train of thought seems possible: Whatever is for us must enter our existence as actuality, our consciousness-as-such as the known, our spirit as a whole moved by understanding; whatever does not enter here is for us as if it were nothing, and what cannot enter here is nothing at all. If that is so then the next obvious step is to think that the entirety of the abode of the Encompassing which we are is at bottom itself all of Being. The thought of the Being of the other would then be merely a form of the self-presence of Being within this Encompassing, and would not represent a reference to a radically different actuality. Thus appearing in the Encompassing which we are would be all of Being. This was the intent of Nietzsche, who comprehended Being as interpretation and our being as interpreting; he regarded interpreting as the creative origin from which what is interpreted emerges as an illusory world. For him, interpreting is no longer the interpreting of something other; rather, he would reject another Being as an illusory world behind this world.

On the other hand, our cogent experience reminds us: Our interpretation does not bring forth the world and transcendence, but makes it accessible to us in a mode of its appearance which is for us and not in itself, and is always inadequate. In this appearance Being itself makes itself felt as that which is totally independent of us. Hegel's statement surely holds true, according to which "what consciousness does not know has no meaning and has no validity for it." But what does not enter our consciousness is an effective force, even if unknown. While we may one day become conscious of it, such a force, extending beyond our consciousness, remains something still unfamiliar to us. The unknown is operative at the limits of the most extended consciousness. It affects us, determines us, overpowers us without our knowledge but we can perceive it principally as two boundaries: each fact confronting us points toward the Being which we are not and which, in its totality, we call the world; and the Encompassing which we are cannot be comprehended out of itself but points toward an other through which it is. For Existenz, it is most clearly comprehensible that: it knows itself as given to itself; and the clearer it becomes to itself, the more decisively it stands vis-à-vis transcendence through which it is.

Being itself, in both of its configurations—world and transcendence—is palpable at the boundary because of the indicator pointing to it. In our thinking which illuminated us as the Encompassing which we are, it manifested itself at the ultimate, which now has to be discussed. In our natural attitude it has priority, for Being is not brought about by us and is not mere interpretation and being interpreted. Instead, it gives us the impetus to interpret and does not let us rest content with our interpretations.

Up to now, in our illumination of the Encompassing, the Encompassing which we are was considered the essential Being. Now, however, the Encompassing which is Being itself becomes that which truly is. On our road up to this point we took hold in ourselves of the conditions of all Being for us; on our present path, which is the polar opposite of the previous one, we stand before Being itself which, however, we do not grasp outright as such. Up to now the Being which we are became the all-embracing within which everything that is has its place. Now, however, the Encompassing which is Being itself towers before us overwhelmingly: before the Encompassing in which we are (world and transcendence) the tiny Encompassing which we are (existence, consciousness-as-such, spirit, Existenz) disappears. Each of the paths has its own truth. As we change paths, one of these Encompassings becomes all the Encompassing there is, to the detriment of the other.

Selection 22

WORLD

EDITORS:
The world is where the possibilities of being-human become concrete, and the world's objectivity is the content that fulfills man's cognitive capacity. The being of the world, particularly as related to the being of man, is a major topic of Jaspers's philosophy. Under the title of "World-Orientation" Jaspers devotes the first volume of *Philosophy* to this topic. In the following selection from *Von der Wahrheit* the emphasis is on being-world as encompassing; on the distinction of being-world from the being of man; and from the basis of these considerations, on three problems: the scope of our knowledge of the world, man's freedom, and the transformation of our consciousness effected by regarding the world as encompassing.

The passages to follow have been translated by the editors from *Von der Wahrheit*, pp. 87–94; 96–99; 103–07.

TEXT:
The world is, within itself, a being that encompasses. The illumination of this Encompassing presents us with new difficulties. We cannot irradiate it from the inside as we can the Encompassing which we are, completely present to us as it is. Rather, it has to be reached from the outside as that which is simply other, in the way in which we are reached by it or we collide with it. It is, in short, that out of which the phenomena in which world-being is accessible to us encounter us. We cognize a specific world-being within the space of the encompassing world which we penetrate without cognizing the world itself.

*The Encompassing World in Distinction to the Closed Universe
and to the Illusion of Mere Interpretation*

There are two divergent positions vis-à-vis the world:
The natural attitude of our thinking is as follows: The world is Being itself. The universe is a whole even without man. It would not change if man were to disappear. It is sufficient unto itself. Even the most insignificant things are what they are without man. The butterfly in the Brazilian jungle as well as solar systems and nebulae remain what they are even if never beheld by man's eye. And all this existing in itself, the universe, can appropriately be grasped in the one true concept of the world.

This is opposed by the following view: All world-being of which we know is man's interpretation. However, no underlying text, as it were, can be found.

There is only interpretation and no thing that is being interpreted. That which is underlying is itself, in the way it is thought by us, thought through an interpretation. There is no firm core of being-world, there is only the never-ending movement of ever different, ever new interpretation. In itself the world is nothing.

The response to this dissolution into illusion is as follows: All being-world of which we know is indeed being as it appears to man, or—if as yet unknown—can appear to man. Thinking man is the center to which every-thing is related. In considering the Brazilian butterfly, we have already con-joined it with the man who will one day enter that jungle, and the farthest nebula with the astronomer who will one day discover and study it. All that is enters as a reality in the realm of man's existence, becomes an object of his knowledge within the forms of his consciousness-as-such, becomes a medium of the spirit and the arena of his existential actualization. However, appear-ance is not illusion; rather, Being is disclosed within it. As regards cognition it must be said that, while as consciousness-as-such we produce everything we cognize according to its form—simply because it has to conform to the mode in which it can become an object for us—we produce, in its being, not even a speck of dust. Being itself, the world, is that which upon inquiry becomes manifest in the endlessness of its appearance while receding as it is in itself. It shows itself only indirectly in the form of what, in the progress of our experience, we encounter as determinate reality and of what we cognize as the specific law-like regularity of occurrences. The world reveals itself to us as the awesome other, which is without us but which, as it appears to our consciousness-as-such, can be investigated through the facts which approach us out of the darkness of otherness.

This encompassing world is neither a universe that can be known in a concept of the world, nor is it an illusion moving in endlessly varied interpre-tation. Every concept of the world is, rather, only a perspective on determi-nate objects, gained from specific standpoints and by means of specific meth-ods, though as perspective it is a real appearance.

Both of these one-sided views of the world either reduce the world to abso-lute Being in a concept of the world regarded as universe, or annihilate the world; the former is the absolutization of the world, the latter acosmism.

The world is encompassing, though it is a mode of the Encompassing all its own. We are ourselves encompassing. Both Encompassings are within each other (we ourselves are world-being); they are toward each other (world-being becomes an object for us); and they are over and against each other (we assert ourselves against the world in the manner of forming, or warding off, or incorporating; within the world we become restricted, overwhelmed, annihilated).

The Encompassing which We are, and the Encompassing of the World

The Encompassing which we are also becomes objective and, thus, cognizable to us in the form of being-world. As something that occurs in the world it
is an appearance to others and to ourselves. As such an occurrence within the
world we become something that is to us an other and strange, for as something thusly cognized we are not any more the Encompassing which we are.
Yet we are able to supplement it from within through the presentiality that is
proper to our being encompassing.

The authentic being-world is otherwise. It is the Encompassing which is
not us; it is the Being within the objectively knowable which appears within
this objectively knowable, yet without itself being in any way immediately
present or directly accessible to us. It is the other, not one's own,
Encompassing.

Through the circumstances that we appear to ourselves within the world,
the Encompassing which we are in no way becomes a mode of such being-
world. The Encompassing which we are and the Encompassing of the world
are there at the same time, together, but at their origins they are independent
of each other and, as it were, counterpoised. There is, in our encompassing
existence, an origin which finds itself in the world as if it had stepped into the
world. Consciousness-as-such is the condition for the world's appearing to me
and, as such, encompasses the entire world in its appearance. Spirit is being-
in-the-world through ideas, formed into and interpenetrated by wholeness,
where the ideas form the world and are not derived from it. All of this is
interwoven in the appearing objectivity of the world-being which can be investigated. Yet within it appears and remains the radical disparateness of the
origins of the Encompassing.

Two distinctions meet in such characterizations: first, the distinction between the Encompassing and its objective appearance; second, that between
the Encompassing of the world and the Encompassing which we are. Accordingly, there are two senses of "world," broad and narrow: in the broad sense it
means the mass of what is objectively knowable, wherein all modes of the
Encompassing appear; in the narrow sense it means the Encompassing which
is not us, the absolutely other, what is not present from within in the manner
of our own nature, what appears to us as that which is lifeless. If we call
being-world everything immanent which appears as object, then both the
Encompassing which we are and the Encompassing which is the world are
being-world. Both become appearance for consciousness-as-such as being-
world in the investigable realm of objectivity. In this sense "world" means to
us that possibility of experiencing reality in space and time which challenges
us to progress in our cognition beyond all limits. It is that which comes to meet
us from all modes of the Encompassing and becomes existence. It is that
which can be universally experienced by consciousness-as-such. . . .

What appears to me as object and thus as object of investigation in the world is therefore either a being that, in itself, is alien to me and accessible only as this appearance, or it is what I myself am and can be as the Encompassing which I am. And then, by way of the radically different approach of becoming aware, of doing, and of innner action, I know about this Being which, estranged from me, yet appears at the same time as an object in the world.

Throughout the course of the history of thought we encounter the big alternative: Whatever is—be it life, soul, God—must either have developed out of the world (out of that which precedes it in the world), or it enters the world from the outside as something other, something created. Aristotle already has the nous enter man from the outside ($\delta\upsilon\rho\alpha\tau\eta\nu$), but who for the rest, stands within the community of life.

The distinction of these alternatives does not apply in this form when we have assured ourselves of the modes of the Encompassing. The following principles take its place:

1. Whatever develops in the world out of something else is a specific event which I study as something that has become objectified and can never be the entire occurrence of an actuality.

2. Whatever grows out of a mode of the Encompassing is not yet the whole actuality, which is present only when all the modes of the Encompassing come together.

3. What is cannot altogether be comprehended in the world as a development of world-being—for example, there is no recognizable developmental sequence from the atom to the mind—but must, in the final analysis, be rooted in the origin of Being whose source is the Encompassing of all Encompassing. The manifestation of world-being is not a matter of what came first in the world and the development of everything from it; rather, it implies the becoming manifest of the Being which I myself am and to which I am bound and which I encounter in the world as world-being.

The presence of all the modes of the Encompassing prevents, in the first place, the isolation of the encompassing world-being; secondly the absolutization of the objectified world-being; and both together prevent my being chained to the world.

The Characteristics of the Encompassing of the World

World-being is the incomprehensible other, is itself neither a thing nor being-I. What the world itself is as being-encompassing-in-itself, that is the inaccessible mystery of being-other vis-à-vis the Encompassing which we are as well as vis-à-vis transcendence.

The Encompassing of the world is that which, in its obscure Being, cannot be made clearer by any means. It is the origin of all reality, of what we call matter. But whatever we may call it—reality, matter, substance, or what have you—it always means that our thinking collides with this impenetrable which embraces and pervades us. As soon as we cognize it we contain it, as object, within its proper categories, within space and time, causality and thingness, etc. Therefore, the encompassing world-being itself is more than reality, matter, etc., insofar as these are merely categories. It is the ground and origin of reality. This reality tames us, bodily carries us, simultaneously overwhelms us, or again sets us free. Encompassing world-being is ineluctable for one who is bodily present; and yet, in whatever mode it appears, it does so only for the present moment, for it is characteristic of appearance that it can constantly change as well as disappear. What was a matter of life and death just a short while ago can later lose its importance; but in another form this unassailable reality remains constantly present.

Even though the encompassing world-being may be referred to as the ground and origin, it is the radically other, even vis-à-vis transcendence. The world does not exist out of itself, is not *causa sui*. To be sure, it is precisely when we think the encompassing world-being that the world seduces us to think of it as the absolute (*natura sive deus*). But just as all appearances prove to lack a ground in themselves and point to their ground in the Encompassing, this Encompassing of world-being, in turn, is—though an origin—not an origin that brings itself forth and is complete in itself. Expressing this idea in mythical terms, we say: The world is created Being.

The Encompassing of the world-being is the abyss of plenitude out of which comes forth the infinitely abundant appearance of the world. But Being collapses, as it were, if this ground is considered to be identical with transcendence. Encompassing world-being addresses us in the language of the cognizability of appearances, transcendence in the language of ciphers. In world-being we find the ground of reality which we do not doubt for a moment; in transcendence we find the ground of actuality which we sense and out of which we are certain only at specific high points of our lives. The encompassing ground of world-being is so very powerful, so all-embracing as the creation of reality as such by transcendence; but it is so very dark, so impenetrable, so bottomless as the other of transcendence. God is more luminous than the world for the world deceives us through its cognizability in which it is not at all the world but an appearance, a façade which it presents to us, as it were, in order to conceal itself behind it. God does not deceive us by his cognizability; he conceals himself openly, lets us be certain of him without knowing him in some way or cognizing him. It is only when we consider cognizabilities to be the being of the Absolute that there is no God for us.

Encompassing world-being exists for us only in its appearances, and these can be clearly grasped only by way of the sciences. The Encompassing of the world itself cannot be characterized as can be the Encompassing that we are— by the presence of inner experience. It is that which is without our being it and which remains in its ground when we comprehend its appearance that emerges from it. Hence, its characterization will be a negative one and will stick to the appearances of world-being in the sciences. The intent of such characterization is to prevent the disappearance of the Encompassing of the world through the absolutization of appearance.

1. The Encompassing of the world is not an object of cognition. What does become the objects of cognition are the appearances encompassed by world-being and from which they emerge. . . .

2. We ourselves are, in the world, a part of the world. The Encompassing of world-being must contain, in any case, that which is the condition of what we are as existence, spirit, Existenz. The world makes possible that we are and what we are and can be. However, we must ask ourselves what this conditional relationship signifies. Did we, being world ourselves, originate in the world or are we, together with the world, rooted in a ground which sustains both, the world and ourselves? . . . .

But under what conditions in the encompassing world-being can there be that which we are even if it did not grow solely out of the world? This question allows us to sense the depth of the being-encompassing of the world yet without being able to grasp it thereby.

3. The Encompassing of the world can be touched only by transcending; it cannot be grasped through knowing. It is impossible therefore to transform the positive notions about the Encompassing of the world (which can be allegories and ways of illumination) into objects for the formation of hypotheses whose purpose is understanding the world. . . .

4. What is touched by transcending cannot be determined as an object or derived from an other. This is the place for symbols and myths. Thus we can speak about the creation of the world by means of transcendence, of the creation of worlds within the world, of the creation of existence and of the spirit. But these are images which express the enigma and augment it but do not solve it.

I do not cognize the Encompassing of the world through these images; however, they do furnish the substantial background of all cognition. My consciousness of the Encompassing of the world and in the world causes the unrest which keeps me from getting bogged down in a known but also the calm of belonging to a ground which is never exhausted by what I cognize as appearance. . . .

The Limits of Cognition of the World

Our awareness of the Encompassing world-being is called forth when we realize the limits of our cognition of the world. What we realized in its immediacy becomes indirectly tangible when, in actual cognition, we experience these boundaries as we collide with them. It is the task of philosophizing within the sciences to expose these limits. The following brief examples bear this out:

In research we presuppose that *the world is cognizable*. Without this presupposition all research would be meaningless. However, if we draw the consequences of this presupposition, we are bound to founder.

But this presupposition may mean two different things. First, it may mean the cognizability of objects in the world, and second the cognizability of the world as a whole. Only the first presupposition is applicable; for we can progress further and further in the world, cognize specific objects and even universal interconnections—which are always something specific in the world and not the world—without ever knowing how far this cognition in the world will take us. The second presupposition, however, is not applicable. That it is false is made evident by the radical insolubilities which, to be sure, set no limits to substantive research but demonstrate the limits of knowledge: no matter how great the progress of cognition it will never know the world in its totality. The world as the only one and as a closed whole evades cognition; indeed, it does not exist for us as something that can be thought and experienced without contradiction.

This limit becomes evident when one sees the false presuppositions about the cognizability of the world as a whole run aground on the facts of research. Let us look at this briefly. The false presupposition may, for example, assume the following forms:

1. "The world, as completed whole, becomes an object for us." This presupposition considers it to be a meaningful task to capture the world in an image of the world and believes that a single, true, comprehensive picture of the world can be achieved. It fails, however, because every totality of the world that has become our object must shatter, for:

(a) Statements about the world become entangled in *antinomies*, i.e., in antitheses both of which seem equally provable. Kant showed, for example, that the world is infinite or finite in space, can be thought—and is simultaneously unthinkable—with or without a beginning in time. However, if an object is constituted such that it causes, in statements about it, contradictory propositions, then it has ceased to be an object. In contradicting itself, it has disappeared as an object.

(b) The world is not an object but an *idea* in the Kantian sense. The significance of this statement emerges from the meaning of research.

Research is directed toward the things in the world. It remains *within* the world which encloses each of its objects as a still more extensive Being. It does not reach *the* world. As the exploration of things in the world it retains its meaning only if it is guided in each instance by an idea which gives it coherence and aim. For out of the world there comes toward it, as it were, what corresponds to its search for the systematic unity of the objects investigated, for example, the systematic order of all forms of living things, or the interrelation of all characteristics of the material world. If the idea disappears from scientific consciousness, then everything that is cognized shatters into pieces *ad infinitum* and is dissipated into instances of correct information lacking the meaning supplied by coherence. But even such ideas of research are still ideas in the world. It is always only the experiment and the experience of factual coherence that can teach us to what extent they are actual. The idea of the world, i.e., of the one world as a coherent, ordered whole, this idea of ideas, is limited to the task of seeking, with respect to everything in the world, relationships in all directions in order to counteract the constant falling apart of the world that occurs when the world becomes the object of research. In fact, relationships between objects in the world do become evident. But it remains the task of investigation to determine the kind and meaning of these relationships. The unity of the world remains a question always answered in the progress of research by the ideas guiding it and for which it has found systematic coherences of its results in the objectivities gleaned from the world.

Thus the world is called "idea" because it represents the task of progressing steadily in it rather than because it is a closed whole. Only *in* the world do we encounter all investigable Being. The whole world is never here for us as object. Objects are world-being, cognizable within the world. . . .

2. "The world is a series of events, continuous and complete in itself." This presupposition fails because world-being is as decidedly fragmented as it is continuous.

(a) The Fragmentation of Reality.—Physical abiological events, biological events, consciousness, and spirit are four realities of which each latter one is tied to the reality prior to it but not vice versa. They stand next to each other, each separated from the other by a gap; there is no continuity between them. They cannot be derived from each other, nor can they be understood as developing out of the prior reality. In the past, when little was known and scientific discussion was merely approximation, the separation between them was veiled by what was presumed to be transitions. Today the increasing clarity of empirical knowledge has made the gaps all the more decisively important and has taught us to see them in a more radical light. Based on our cognition, that is, in the foreground of what has become an object for us, continuity is not at all the pervasive characteristic of the world; instead, it is the gap which remains the basic feature of reality. As we come to know the world the principle of continuity fails because of these gaps.

(b) The Fragmentation of Methods.—Each method leads us to observe one world-being, not the world; a particular, not a totality; a perspective on the world, not the world itself.

For example, the method of investigating nature may be directed either toward the always uniform laws governing natural events, toward the natural forces that always remain the same, toward what is universal in their being: or it can use its method to focus on the uniquely occurring reality, perhaps on why the earth's astronomic cosmos has developed in just this way, or on the sequence of the different periods in the natural history of life. It is something radically different whether I investigate the chemical properties of sulfur, its place in the periodic table of elements, its compounds, or whether I direct my attention to the places in the world where sulfur occurs such as the masses of sulfur found in Sicily. The latter fact cannot be grasped by the cognitive means of the former. Thus there ensue two basic aspects. In geography, for example, there is research which presupposes that the same conditions prevailed at all times, that all that happened is to be grasped through the forces and laws operative also today; and then there is the research which does not consider this presupposition to be absolutely valid and searches instead for what is unique in the sequence of time and envisions an actual history of nature, of the earth, of life. These two directions of research cannot be conflated into a single whole. The natural scientist who works with general laws will consider the historical observation—insofar as it means to be something other than the mere application of general insights—to be poetry or a toying with the inconsequential. The scientist investigating the history of natural phenomena, in contrast, will see in generalizing cognition something one-sided, superficial, preliminary. To both, different aspects are revealed as the Encompassing of world-being becomes object for each, to neither does the world as a whole reveal itself.

This is the way it is everywhere. There is a split between the methods which cannot combine into a universal method of cognition.

To be sure, each of the two opposing ways of cognition is equally justified either in differentiating and finding splits everywhere or in building bridges everywhere and seeking unity. Only if one of the two ways is considered to be the only one leading to the true cognition of the world will either of the two sides do battle against the other one because it is false. But there is no procedure for making the two of them into a harmonious and non-contradictory whole. They are contraposed, then reverse to intertwine, and remain split in this split world in which even unity is manifest only together with separateness.

(c) Hence, no world-being as object of cognition is world-being as a whole. No being that can be investigated is the world itself. By investigating it I allow the world to *break apart* into modes of reality separated by leaps. As subject of research, I experience this breakup of the world as the fundamental trait of its appearance; and even though I hold on to the idea of the one world in its interrelationships and thus remain on the way to understanding what has come apart, I am never again able to reach the world in its oneness. . . .

4. "Our cognition coincides with the cognized object." This presupposition fails because all that is cognized is for us only one way of knowing the

object in its appearance. It is not the Encompassing of Being itself and does not bring us face to face with the whole. It is as if everything that we cognize were to become, through this cognition, the lifeless hull of the Encompassing. Solely in the movement of cognition and in proceeding beyond all definite and, as such, rigidifying cognition do we approach the Encompassing by way of cognizing without grasping it directly.

The limits of cognition of the world demonstrate the same thing no matter what form they assume: The Encompassing of the world is not exhausted by the totality of what is objectively investigable.

Phenomenal World-being as Bottomless, and Man's Freedom.

If the world, insofar as it is comprehensible to us, were a whole complete in itself, comprehensible out of itself, without internal contradiction, a harmonious total event, a thoroughgoing purposefulness in a fabric of causalities and having but one meaning, then this world would be Being itself besides which there would be no other. The world and God would be one, God would be nothing other than the world as a whole.

There is a stubborn tendency in our thinking to think the world as a whole at every level of our conception of the world as if it were Being itself. The principle of world-being is presented to us objectively as atom, matter, energy, as life, as process, so that everything which exists, including ourselves, is derived from known world-being as a whole.

But with the growth of clarity in critical cognition it becomes inescapably obvious that such cognized world-being does not become a ground on which one may step, conscious of now possessing Being itself. No matter how we attempt to do this, we always end up in the rigidity of a deception which wants to derive all Being from a being that has become objectivized and is categorically particular. We lose ourselves in such absolutizations which are mere figments of the imagination without gaining knowledge.

Therefore, we must take the philosophic step of completely removing the firm ground from under all objective, i.e., cognizable, Being. The bottomlessness of world-being must become manifest to us so that we may gain the truth of the cognition of the world. But together with the clarity of individual cognition the bottomlessness of the whole points to the Encompassing which sustains all appearance. The Encompassing of the world-being extends beyond cognizability even though it is endlessly manifest to cognition in appearances. When the false absolutization of the world is suspended and the Encompassing of world-being is made manifest, this does not imply skepticism as regards the reality of things; rather, it implies clarity about the nature of this reality and about the meaning of its being cognized.

This insight results in an awareness of Being which at the same time makes our freedom palpable. Through this freedom we become receptive to genuine

Being within the space of all cognizabilities. We are liberated for the world, for ourselves in the world, for ourselves in relationship to transcendence:

1. "We are liberated for the world." World-being without ground in the Encompassing is bottomless. By breaking through all firm ground we attain the realm of freedom. Through freedom we begin to understand the Encompassing of world-being because we advance, by way of all definite appearance and the ideas of world-being, into the ever-expanding space of this Encompassing. We then experience the Encompassing as promoting disquiet as well as supplying content. It is the ground of our unceasing movement in the world and causes us to experience, through each cognized world-being, the Encompassing of the world not only as palpable but also brighter than before; yet we cannot cognize the Encompassing itself.

2. "We are liberated for ourselves in the world." Through our world-being we penetrated to the ground present in ourselves as the Encompassing which we are. It is the origin of our becoming, as a sprout before it makes its appearance. There is something in us akin to a dark complicity in the creation of the world. This Encompassing which we are comes alive in the Encompassing of the world and manifests itself as our state of mind. It attracts us and fulfills us and does not allow us to become immersed any longer in the objectivities which are always finite and directed toward a purpose.

3. "We are liberated for ourselves in relation to transcendence." The suspendedness of world-being can make us become aware of the ground in us which still knows itself in Existenz even if it leaves the world. We are liberated for transcendence either on our way through the world or in direct relation to transcendence. To be sure, there is no unfolding for us if there is no embodiment in appearance in the world; for if the object and the appearance of I-being are lost, I can feel only in this disappearance what—unperturbed— is self-being before transcendence. But here, in the being of transcendence, man may find refuge. Then, when he again finds himself in mundane existence, he is once more faced with the ineluctable task of seeing what—out of the ever ambiguous certainty of the being of transcendence which he has experienced—arises for him on his way through the world; that is, how the Encompassing becomes manifest to him in finite cognition, actions, configurations.

The Modes of Knowing the World in the non-Presence and Presence of the Encompassing

When I have become aware of the Encompassing, the way in which I know world-being has been altered. To be sure, knowledge of the world is always the same as to content, i.e., that which is known definitely. But there is connected with all knowledge an experience of significance that usually remains unclear. What I know objectively and definitely is sustained in my experience of this knowledge by something of which I become aware only through this knowledge. This motivates me to gain such knowledge but does not itself become knowable. This experience of significance is decisive for the way in which I deal with knowledge, what my expectations are of this knowledge, what consequences I draw from it, and in which direction I attempt to broaden it. In what way this penetrating and motivating meaning sustains my knowledge is determined by whether the Encompassing is present or absent.

1. The non-presence of the Encompassing permits the absolutization of what is known. Then the following destructive effects of the rational take place. . . .

I cause confusion in the world, let everything become murky when, based on my supposed knowledge of the whole, I want to arrange everything properly and bring order into the world. This is the perversion of turning particular into absolute knowledge, of illumination into knowledge of the Encompassing as an object at my disposal, which will lead me into the wasteland where I want to do everything.

I destroy myself when, instead of being the Encompassing, being active as this Encompassing and opening myself up, I instead do violence to myself with finite purposes. In vain do I attempt to achieve intentionally, without paying heed to the ground, what can be given to me as a gift in the struggle of my innermost impulses.

I destroy the others when I, determining all purposes, make everything which ought to occur and ought to be done the object of my planning. Whatever bursts forth in creative impulses, unfathomable, out of the ground of the Encompassing, I can only ruin when I force it to become organized. Organization can supply merely the conditions of life; it cannot state purposes and enforce them by command. . . .

I lose the transparent ground in the Being of transcendence when I consider the contents of knowledge to be final and complete, for what is known then loses its transparency. I lose my sensitivity for that which addresses me in all world-being, for that out of which I myself live, that wherein my fidelity and truthfulness are founded, that in which my being human has its roots.

2. The presence of the Encompassing, on the other hand, has the following consequences for the way in which I know:

The world is no longer weighted toward that which is as such. It is, as it were, brought into suspension. Every controlling, constricting, total conception (whether mechanism or biologism or world process, etc.) is eliminated as is all rational, supposedly scientific metaphysics with its method of drawing probable conclusions about being as such. Every conception of the world is turned upside down, the falsity of all conceptions of the world is exposed.

Instead of a controlling total theory many theories are valid in accordance with the degree of their empirical fruitfulness. I limit myself to the mutual effect of theory and experience within the realm of progressive discovery; however, I reject all closed total knowledge.

Instead of a universal method of cognition there exists a multiplicity of methods.

Instead of Being itself there are levels and modes of Being.

Instead of an ultimate framework of knowledge there remains a radical openness, a readiness for new experiences in all modes of the Encompassing.

All meaningless strife is eliminated, that is, everything intended to make statements about the whole and the ultimate. What matters at the limits of knowledge (as opposed to the limits of action) is the understanding of the antinomies rather than the either/or.

Selection 23

TRANSCENDENCE

EDITORS:

Transcendence is the source of our freedom and, hence, the ground of human selfhood, of Existenz. This is the key to Jaspers's finely elaborated philosophy of transcendence. Volume III of *Philosophy*, entitled, *Metaphysics*, is devoted to this topic, and it determines much of Jaspers's later work, especially his controversy with revealed religion. In the following brief treatment of transcendence Jaspers distinguishes the two modes of the Encompassing that are Being itself, i.e., world and transcendence; discusses the relations of the thought-operation of transcending and transcendence and of Existenz and transcendence; and he summarizes the significance of the thought of transcendence. A number of subsequent selections function as elaborations on what is here summarized, especially Part IV, Subpart ii ("Metaphysical Truth: the Reading of Ciphers") and Part V, Subpart iv ("Philosophy and Religion").

The original of the following selection appears in *Von der Wahrheit*, pp. 107–13; the translation has been provided by the editors.

TEXT:

The Encompassing which we are has its limits at the being of the world and at transcendence. Here we do not encompass but are encompassed. The other which is not us is for us—insofar as we are existence, consciousness-as-such, and spirit—the perceivable, empirically experienceable other, which is called the world. It is for us—insofar as we are Existenz—the non-perceivable, empirically non-demonstrable other, which is called transcendence. That wherein and whereby we are *ourselves* and *free* is transcendence.

World and Transcendence

Throughout history there has been a fundamental position according to which only the world and not transcendence is valid: All that is, is world; transcendence is nothingness. However, since transcendence is accessible only through the world, it is—whether regarded as Being or as Nothing—to be clarified only in its relation to the world. Here three positions are possible:

1. What is, is pure immanence, is world-being.—Unreflected, this is historically the most pristine position. Later, after consciousness of transcendence has arisen, it is maintained against transcendence. The gods are beings in the world and belong to it. Cosmogony coincides with theogony. Man has arisen within the world and together with it. Man is a microcosm, i.e., the mirror image and representative of the macrocosm, comprising nothing, that is not also in the latter. Man, as it were, is everything. In this fundamental position it is left open how Being within world-being is conceived, whether as the sport of demons, or as life, or as mechanism of forces and elements. But always there is the absoluteness, the self-position, the exclusiveness of world-being, in the end regarded as the eternity of matter and as the recurrent cycles of aeons.

2. There is transcendence.—This position takes a new perspective on all that is world. Transcendence is the absolute other. Measured against the mode of world-being it is nothing, but this nothingness is the authentic Being measured against which all world-being is merely a secondary Being, a Being that is not founded upon itself. The world is created, is—as Being—the Being of transience, is unclosed and not comprehensible from itself, is for man the place of the language of transcendence. Man is created according to the image of transcendence, is his own origin within the world, while the world is the space where his freedom is actualized.

3. The objects of world-being are transparent.—The objects come into our presence from the dark of the Encompassing as aspects of what there is, or as language of a ground. Far from being closed within themselves, their isolation would render them groundless; if their transparency were to vanish, they would be endless, vacuous, untrue.

Yet we are constantly fettered to the objective, so that we may confuse it with Being itself. We are dispirited in such separation from the Encompassing, in such immersion in the foreground of Being. We come to ourselves through participation in the Encompassing, i.e., through life out of the primal source.

Hence, there is in us the unappeasable drive to Being. In one way it leads to mystical union with transcendence, which leads past and relinquishes all objects, and aims directly at the ground, the union with which takes place with the vanishing of the I and the world, devoid of object, speech, and image.

In the other way the manifestation of Being occurs through all modes of objectivity: objects become language in such a way that they aim at me out of the Encompassing and—constituted by me—cast beams of light into the Encompassing.

The way through the realm of objects makes both of these possible: on the one hand, the dispiritedness by which we regard ourselves as lost when objects are falsely turned into Being itself; and on the other, the fulfillment of life out of the Encompassing gained by entering such life in order to find tranquility in the One.

Transcending and Transcendence

A distinction must be drawn between transcendence of all modes of the Encompassing and authentic transcendence. We transcend to each Encompassing, i.e., we step beyond the specific objectivity in order to perceive what encompasses it; hence it is possible to refer to each mode of the Encompassing as a transcendence, namely in distinction to the objectivity which is tangible within that Encompassing. However, we call transcendence in the authentic sense only the absolutely Encompassing, the Encompassing of all that encompasses. Its substance is primally unique. In distinction to the universal transcendence which is proper to each mode of the Encompassing, it is the transcendence of all transcendences.

Correspondingly, the objects of world-being possess a twofold transparency. They are appearances out of the encompassing world-being and are in relation to transcendence. As appearances they let the encompassing world-being become manifest by way of their cognizability. As ciphers they speak the language of transcendence, a language of many meanings, as penetrating as it is non-cognizable. Through their cognizability shines the Encompassing of world-being. Through their being-ciphers the Encompassing of transcendence becomes perceivable, signifying to all modes of the Encompassing their grounding and their soul.

Let us compare the universal, inauthentic transcendence of each Encompassing with the authentic transcendence of the Encompassing of all Encompassings:

The universal transcendence can be brought to mind by penetrating it through cognition of the objects that issue from it. Authentic transcendence is not to be reached cognitively; it is only to be experienced existentially as something that offers itself gratuitously.

The universal transcendence of the Encompassing is an indubitable, yet an insufficient, never satisfactory actuality. The other, the one and sole transcendence, is the authentic actuality in which tranquility and grounding are to be found.

The modes of the Encompassing of existence, consciousness-as-such, spirit, and the world are in need of animation through Existenz which thereby pays regard to transcendence. The one transcendence is not in need, yet fulfills all need. All the Being of existence, of consciousness-as-such, of spirit, and of the world merely present forms of surrogation of transcendence or the material of its language.

The universal transcendence of all modes of the Encompassing is palpably present as the unobjective limit. Authentic transcendence is impalpably present when hearkened to by Existenz. It is nothingness as well as Being. It is, simply, to be doubted, and then it is as if vanished. For transcendence, unlike other modes of the Encompassing, has no body signifying its presence and solely proper to it, but speaks only through those other modes, enclosing and penetrating them.

Existenz and Transcendence

From the foregoing it can be seen that the world is Being for us as existence, consciousness-as-such, and spirit; and transcendence is Being for us as Existenz. For the former, transcendence is merely empty possibility, the unknown. Transcendence shows itself only to Existenz.

For Existenz transcendence is the other in which it is anchored. Where I am authentically myself, I am that not through myself. I have not created myself. Where I am authentically myself, I know that I have been given to myself. The more decisively I am aware of my freedom, the more decisively I am also aware of the transcendence through which I am. I am Existenz only together with the knowledge concerning transcendence as the power through which I am myself. Stepping beyond any specific world-being transcendence may—in distinction to the world—be either merely the—as such—indifferent unknowable, that which is thought as substratum, or awesome, inspiring fear and dread. Although transcendence vanishes in all appearances though never for itself, it is only to Existenz that transcendence authentically becomes that through which I am free.

For I am free only when I attain with myself independence from all world-being and from my own existence, i.e., when—in distinction to all existence, consciousness-as-such, and spirit—I stand before transcendence as that which authentically is. I can surrender completely only to transcendence, while any surrender to a world-being, regardless of the unconditionality of the commitment to it, remains under the conditions which issue from transcendence through the absolute consciousness of Existenz.

Basic Characteristics of Transcendence

Transcendence, the Encompassing of all Encompassing, is that which, as the absolutely Encompassing, implacably "is," even as it is not seen, vanishes as it is thought, and hides behind any image or configuration.

Unlike world-being, transcendence is not manifest in any adequate appearance. It eludes being thought, if thought means to grasp it without contradiction in the manner of a determinate object. In its appearance in the form of an image it is no longer present as itself, but merely in the form of a historic language that is at the same time man-made.

When it has become clear that any configuration of transcendence, any determinate thought about it, any image of it is also a matter of missing it, one speaks of it necessarily in negative formulations. It seems easier to say what it is not than what it is. However, even negative formulations become questionable if they are not only meant as general expressions of what is unutterable, but as defined by content: for, after all, what is there that transcendence could not only not be, but could not also be! The unending movement of thought, in saying and not saying, in expressing and revoking: that is the form which speaking of transcendence can take. In speaking of it we can find no firm place.

Even though transcendence cannot be reached in any thought, in any configuration, in any image, in any empirical reality, it is nonethless present as the authentic Being for which all those thoughts, configurations, images, and realities can be allegories.

The names for transcendence can endlessly be accumulated. The names normative in the West (Being, Actuality, Divinity, God) are indeterminate, yet by virtue of historical tradition they are solemn and infinitely full of content:

Insofar as transcendence is *thought* as the Encompassing, we call it *Being*. It is the Being that is subsisting, unchangeable, undeceiving. However, it is this tranquil Being, this liberating Being, only for abstract transcending thought.

Insofar as we *live* with transcendence, it is the *authentic Actuality*. It is perceivable to us as that which essentially concerns us, that which draws us to it, gives us firm ground.

Insofar as something demanding, something governing, something that surrounds us speaks to us in this actuality, we call transcendence the *Divinity*.

Insofar as we, in our singularity, know ourselves as *personally encountered*, attain a relationship to transcendence, we call it *God*.

Transcendence does not become an object as Being, Actuality, Divinity, or God, but these names indicate the experience in which it is touched upon. This experience is most decisive where transcendence no longer vanishes or hides, but where each mode of our being-encompassing vanishes before it.

The distinguishable experiences which touch upon authentic transcendence, such that in all clarification it yet remains hidden, and such that in all our experiencing we yet remain sustained, are as follows:

In formal transcending the Being of transcendence is ascertained by means of conceptually and methodically particular foundering movements of thought.

In existential relations—in defiance and surrender, in falling away and rising toward our essence, in obedience to the law of day and passion toward night—the actuality of transcendence is brought to actual presence for Existenz in its self-transformation.

We also touch upon transcendence by reading the cipher-script in everything that becomes objective and a living experience to us; such reading is the experience of the transparency of things so that they become comprehensible to us as a language of transcendence, to the extent that we become existential and by virtue of our becoming existential.

Transformation of Self-consciousness through Transcendence

If the aim of our life is to become open for the range of the Encompassing and, within it, for the primal sources, so that within the depth the grounding itself become effective for us, then this aim is attainable to the extent that we find ourselves within transcendence.

Once transcendence has become perceivable, it can become that out of which I live and toward which I die. Only it can effect the most profound agitation, only it can grant tranquility. I am with it when the *amor dei* takes hold of me, and my thinking proceeds from it when it is guided by my knowledge that is privy to creation.

Thus, everything in us is transformed when we address the Encompassing which is Being itself not only as the world but as transcendence. This is manifest in the manner in which we love or hate the world:

Once man has become conscious of the existence of the world as a whole, it is possible for him to face the world with love or hatred. Love of the world runs through millennia of Chinese life with magnificent continuity; hatred of the world became actual with magnificent radicality in gnosticism. The sense of desolation, which is always at the ready in man, and his fundamental sense of indignation bring about the rejection of the world.

The meanings of love of the world and hatred of the world differ according to whether the world is regarded as self-enclosed immanence or whether transcendence is regarded as well.

When the world is all of Being and this world is hated, such hatred of Being is despair and radical nihilism. When this world is loved then such love of the world resembles the love of God, but it is a love without God.

Where one is aware of the actuality of transcendence, hatred of the world is possible if one believes the gnostic notion according to which the world is a godless creation, brought forth by a fallen angel, a Luciferian, seductive formation of Being which is in fact thoroughly diabolical, not godly but counter to God.

Where the world is God's creation, then, if the world is loved, God is loved in it, and God is loved in his creation. The Divinity speaks in the splendor of nature and in the greatness and the possibilities of man. Here the world is rejected only when God and world are confused with each other or when world-being is falsely turned from secondary into primary Being; it is rejected in order to restore for consciousness what is authentic.

The world ceases to be only the world when it becomes the language of transcendence. But transcendence is perceivable to us only when it also speaks to us through the world. Hence, the possibility of the experience of divinity arises from a duality: there must always be a finitude, a presence, a knowable, a perceptible that addresses us as the vessel of transcendence, yet at the same time such that it is in truth a vessel in which an other is effective. We may not remain attached to some sensible finitude, and yet we must take it absolutely seriously and indulge it with the sort of unconditionality without which it could never be a vessel to us. There is no transcendence for us without it becoming palpable in the finite realm. By way of such finitude we are bound up with that through whose actuality all else is symbol.

The transformation of my consciousness of Being through transcendence loosens the adherence to embodiment without causing any weakening of actuality when embodiment assumes the function of symbol. Whatever authentic actuality takes hold of me and carries me away is present solely in the symbol.

Selection 24

PERIECHONTOLOGY (4): REASON— THE BOND WITHIN US

EDITORS:
Encompassing of Being presents itself to us primordially divided into different modes. Unity and openness are, for Jaspers, a motive rather than an actualization, and it is the motive of reason. Jaspers characterizes reason not only as "the bond of all modes of the Encompassing," but as this bond "within us." In this sense reason, as the motive of unity, becomes the task for man to effect unity. The task is informed by man's awareness of the multiplicity and disunity, defined by the challenges of one's historic situation and animated by the freedom of Existenz engaged in its actualization. This juxtaposition of "Reason and Existenz" not only is the title of a small work of Jaspers, but has gained currency as the main theme of his philosophy. It has certainly informed Jaspers's thinking about the meaning of truth (see selections 41, 43, 52) and its application to some realms of concrete concern, i.e., politics (see Selection 62), history, (see Selection 57) and religion (see Selection 66).

A note on terminology: The following selection concludes with a distinction between "reason" (*Vernunft*), "spirit" (*Geist*), and the "understanding" or "intellect" (*Verstand*).

The selection has been translated by the editors; the original is found in *Von der Wahrheit*, pp. 113–21.

TEXT:

Manifold are the modes of the Encompassing, and the appearance of each mode of the Encompassing is divided in its turn: Existence and spirit are dispersed into its [the Encompassing's] illimitable individualizations. Consciousness-as-such emerges as an infinite number of points that partake in it and are bound to existence. World-being is split into the multiplicity of its aspects transcendence into the variety of its historic appearances for the Existenz attuned to it.

We ask ourselves how all this comes together, joins, and finally attains unity. The ways in which the Encompassings and their unity are related will be our topic later on. At this point we are still discussing the Encompassing as such. To be sure, each Encompassing already brings about unity in its own peculiar manner but one that is limited to its own space. However, in the Encompassing which we are lies also the primal source of the unceasing drive toward unity, not only on the part of each Encompassing as such but of all the modes of the Encompassing which we are and which approaches us; for unity comes into being through Existenz and reason.

As Existenz I gain my ground by becoming I myself as I move through all the modes of the Encompassing without falling prey to the diffuseness that tempts me in all directions toward infinity.

Yet where I am truly I myself, there I am never merely I myself. I am myself only together with another self, am myself only in the actuality of the world for which I remain open without qualification, am myself only in my search for communicative association. It is not the tender mood of a universal bonding which brings me to myself; rather, it is the fertility of my ties with each and every mode of actuality as well as my following through on all the possibilities of bonding inherent in its movement and its structure. To the decisiveness of Existenz belongs also the wide range of its bonds. This is made possible by reason. Reason is the bond of all modes of the Encompassing and of all their configurations.

It is the distinguishing characteristic of our philosophic nature that we move within reason, that we allow the Encompassing of reason to become effective without limit. To illuminate the Encompassing of reason is the most essential feature of philosophic reflection.

a. Reason is the Bond. In every situation reason seeks to reclaim whatever there is from the diffuseness of mutual indifference and to bring it back into the movement of belonging to each other. From the absence of relation-ship, from the disintegration into mutual estrangement reason wants every-thing again to be of concern to everything else. Nothing ought to get lost.

In observing the sciences we find reason to be the bonding power vis-à-vis the endless accumulation of what can be known correctly. It is the incentive to go beyond every limit of a particular science, to search out the contradictions, to find relationships and complements. It functions as the idea of unity of all the sciences.

But reason pushes beyond the unity of scientific knowledge to the all-embracing union. In the illumination of the Encompassing it is reason which forces the progress from one mode to another, does not let any mode remain in its isolation, and urges the unification of all Encompassing.

Therefore, reason applies itself also to that which, according to the crite-rion of universal validity, is unfounded. It turns toward the *exception* which breaches the universal, and toward the *authority* which demands without be-ing understood. But it does not remain at rest with them as if it had reached its goal. They, too, measured against the demanding One, are still something provisional, belonging to temporal existence. But reason cannot find rest in something provisional, no matter how imposing its aspect.

Reason is attracted even by the most alien. It concerns itself even with that which actualizes itself by breaching the law of day, destroying the passionate attachment to night, and annihilating itself. This, too, reason wants to bring to being, wants to give it tongue, and wants to prevent its disappearance as if it were nothing. Reason pushes on to wherever unity is breached in order to grasp in this breach yet one truth of this breach. In the shattering of every unity which shows itself in this shattering to be preliminary and inadequate, reason wants to prevent the metaphysical breach, the tearing apart of Being itself and of the true unity. Thus reason, the primal source of order, accompa-nies even that which breaches order; it remains patient, constant, and infinite before all that is alien, before the invader, before the failure.

b. The Fundamental Attitude of Reason is Universal Living-with. Rea-son, as the constant forging ahead toward the other, is the possibility of uni-versal living-with, being there, of the ever-present attentiveness to whatever speaks and what reason itself gives voice to. Reason is hearing, but it is the unlimited hearing of all that is and can be. It hears what is a specific hearing; and it also especially hears that which is inaudible, what seemingly refuses to communicate but becomes audible through reason.

But reason is not an indifferent laissez faire in regard to everything which occurs; it is, instead, the openness of letting things matter. It illuminates not merely in order to know but is a probing that is like courting. Reason never turns into a possessive knowledge, which limits and fixates itself, but remains open without limits.

Hence, reason is the *total will to communication*. It wants to turn toward everything that is capable of expression, toward everything that is, in order to preserve it.

It wants to make authentic communication possible and, hence, seeks to realize the *honesty* whose attributes are unlimited openness and probing, as well as a sense of *justice* that wants all that arises from primal sources to attain its own validity, though also to let it founder against its limits.

There are moments when free reason reaches its highpoints in the mutuality of people who are, at the same time, strangers to each other—an encounter in the realm of absolute possibility. Reason is not yet love but it is the condition for the freedom, truth, and purity of love.

c. Reason Awakens the Primal Sources.   In its drive toward the One, reason is capable not only of hearing what there is, not only of being affected, but it sets *in motion* everything it encounters. Because it questions and gives tongue, it produces unrest which makes it impossible to rest satisfied with a knowledge, a fact, a being-such, a being which is not all Being. Hence, reason enables all primal sources to unfold, to open up, to give tongue, to stand in relation, to become pure. It makes possible the genuineness of the struggles that take place within and between the modes of the Encompassing and which for their part become the source of new experiences, of the One.

Reason, tied to Existenz, by which it is sustained and without which it would founder, makes possible for its part the truth of Existenz so that it may be actualized and become manifest to itself.

Even though reason does not bring forth anything through its own agency, it is precisely reason, present in the innermost heart of all Encompassing, that is able to awaken fully each mode of the Encompassing, to bring about its becoming actual and true.

d. In What Respect Reason is not Itself a Primal Source.   Reason is not itself a primal source as regards content. Rather, it is like a source that seems to issue from the one Encompassing such that all the sources from all modes of the Encompassing converge toward its openness in order that they be referred to the One, and thus be brought into relationship.

In this way reason points toward its source: toward that inaccessible One which operates by means of it as well as the otherness of the sources which become perceptible through it.

Reason is always too little when it is locked with finality into definite configurations, and it is always too much when it appears as substance in its own right.

Reason is the force which gathers, reminds, impels; it is limited by all that from which it derives its content; it teaches to go beyond each of these limits, for, attracted by the One for which it aims, it is expressive of a constant dissatisfaction.

e. Radical Detachment as the Way of Approaching the One. Reason wants to be able to follow, without restraint, the will to unity which does not forget anything and is open in all directions; it therefore demands and risks its detachment from everything finite and definite which tempts us to put it in place of the One and would thereby deceive us even it were the whole of the world.

Hence, reason animates the negative power of the intellect by which it is capable of disregarding everything. For the questioning intellect there is nothing that does not have some fault, nothing true that does not contain something false, no existence that is not ephemeral; everything that enters the world must perish. Reason takes hold of this negative not in order to give free rein to its destructive power but to find the positive in the negative. Reason may try to think the following: it would have been possible that there is nothing at all.—It does not think this thought as if it were an empty intellectual game but in order to experience groundlessness which only philosophic thought can bring to our consciousness, and to let us regain this ground through a new knowledge of Being. Leibniz, Kant and especially Schelling could ask the following question in this sense and let themselves be inspired by it: Why is there anything at all and not nothing? This question, in spite of its rational colorlessness, brings the situation home to us in which, for the first time, we really experience the being of Being as that which for us is incomprehensible and impenetrable, that which, prior to all thought, already is and comes toward us.

Further, the thinking of reason lies only in the movement which knows no stopping and no ceasing. The intellect, however, wants to preserve, either in positive or negative fixity; it wants to know the One or Nothingness and to possess the whole in the form of a doctrine. Reason, on the other hand, is constantly at work to overthrow the attainments of the intellect. It aspires to a unity that is not an overview of the whole which shows itself deceptively to the intellectual will to power by means of the mere intellect. Reason is nothing other than the impulse toward overcoming and connecting. There exists an intellectual pride of possession, but reason has no pride; there are only the movement which unlocks and the final tranquility of reason: This is not the tranquility of reason which supposedly relies on itself alone but the tranquility of Being itself becoming manifest to reason. . . .

Reason shatters restriction, dissolves fanaticism, does not permit being lulled by feeling or by the intellect.

Reason prevents us from suffocating in a mode of the Encompassing to which we surrender ourselves completely. We must not be strangled, not by existence in favor of the will to existence that, in its restrictiveness, asserts itself purposefully yet blindly; not by consciousness-as-such in favor of endless correctness; not by spirit in favor of a closed harmonious totality which it is

possible to contemplate but not to live. Everywhere, detachment does not lead
to nothingness but to authentic Being.

Behind each configuration of our finiteness, each of our acts and ways of
behaving, each historic unconditionality in its appearance, there is in us also
our knowledge about it which detaches and opens the door to the other. The
degree of decisiveness of this knowledge is the condition for our doing away
with the absolute impenetrability in us as well as with the rigidifying fixity of
not-being-able-to-hear-any-longer; it is also the measure of the extent to
which we become authentic human beings.

f. The Will to Unity. The will to unity emerges as the fundamental trait
of reason. But the vitality of reason lies in the fact that it cannot be satisfied in
a unity of intellect, not in a spiritual unity as such but only in the unity which,
beyond all premature and partial unity, is that unity in which nothing is lost
but all is preserved. Leaving behind all comprehensible intellectual unity and
unity of spirit in its completeness, the driving force of reason aims toward the
more profound unity for which all unities of intellect and spirit are merely
media and allegories.

Expressed more briefly: Reason seeks unity, not any unity at all simply for
the sake of unity, but the One which comprehends all. This One, though at an
unattainable distance, is present to us through reason as the propelling force
which overcomes all schism.

g. The Leap of Reason vis-à-vis All Immanence. We mentioned the fundamental traits of reason, namely the all-embracing will to unity and the negativity that overcomes and unlocks possibilities. But this characterization still
does not clarify the nature of reason in the way in which something can become clear to me.

Reason wants what seems impossible in consideration of dismembered
temporal existence. Whatever is its goal in the One cannot be represented
such that one could follow it as one follows a visible model. Rather, drawn
along by the One, reason enters into the free space of possibility in order, as it
seems, to find its way in groundlessness.

Like Existenz, reason is actualized by a *leap* from the closed immanence of
what is. In comparison with immanent phenomena such as the intellect, reason seems like nothing. If it is regarded as the Encompassing which we are, in
its character as incentive to search for and to actualize the One, then this
Encompassing has a transcendent primal source and yet manifests itself only
in the impulses, claims, and effects which we experience immanently.

h. The Atmosphere of Reason. There is, so to say, an atmosphere of
reason. It is disseminated where an eye, open to everything, beholds actuality,
its possibilities, and its unlimited interpretability. Here this eye does not become the judge and does not express an absolute doctrine but penetrates, with
honesty and justice, into everything that is, lets it come into its own, does not

gloss over nor veil, and does not make things easy by assigning merely one meaning to it.

The atmosphere of reason is present in great literature, especially in trage-dies, and belongs to all authentic philosophers. It is luminous in unique hu-man beings, such as Lessing, who affect us in the same way as reason itself and whose words we read just to breathe this atmosphere.

In my attitude of reason I want unbounded clarity, I want to grasp empirical actuality and the cogent validity of what can be thought, and to live in the consciousness of the limits; yet from all the sources, out of all the modes of the Encompassing, I press for their unfolding, and thus for their clarification in thought, and disavow thoughtlessness everywhere.

   i. Reason as the Source of Philosophic Logic. . . . . There is nothing human without thought, and thought is an unbounded space. Philosophic logic serves reason by searching out each mode of thought. Countering the inclination to consider one form of thought to be the absolute one, to be thought itself, it follows the impulse of taking hold of each possible form of thought and to reach the limits of each. Countering the inclination to design a system of all possible forms of thought, it follows the impulse to keep open, through knowledge and the penetration of the forms of thought already won, the consciousness that new ones are possible, i.e., to be open for the real discoverers who are the conquerors of new forms of thought. Thinking as such has no limits, but each form of thought has its own limits. Philosophical logic is in step with reason which resists being constricted into one form of thought.

   In philosophic logic the movement of reason enters all modes of the En-compassing, illuminates the thinking in them but does not carry out this thinking itself; rather, it presupposes it. Through logic reason is motivated toward unbounded liberating, toward breadth and unity. But it can merely illuminate and show the conditions; actualization within logic is not possible for it.

   Actuality occurs only in the concreteness of all modes of the Encompassing, out of the historic ground of Existenz which constructs and utilizes as its tool the philosophizing manifested in configurations of thought and in writings.

Historico-terminological Note

   1. "Understanding," "spirit," and "reason" have long been distinguished in German philosophy. However, common speech has not kept these words separated according to their deeper meaning. Hence, we must ever anew face the task of making them distinct. Understanding (or "intellect") means *objective understanding* by means of a comprehension which isolates. Spirit is thinking which unifies into wholes and lives out of complementing ideas. Reason is the perception which occurs when we are affected—in a way that unites everything—by each being and each possibility, by Being and by Noth-

ingness. The realm of understanding is the Encompassing of consciousness-as-such; that of spirit the wholenesses, rounded in themselves and excluding the other. Reason is the Encompassing which is adventitious to all the Encompassings and unites them.

2. Reason cannot be separated from the thinking of understanding. It is bound to it at all times.

Existenz can speak to us out of the depth of existence and spirit as an overcoming, shaping, sustaining; even so can reason speak to us out of the depth of common consciousness as an all-moving, a going-beyond, a uniting.

Within the medium of understanding, reason is more than understanding. It is "mysticism for the understanding" (Hegel), and yet it develops this understanding in all its possibilities in order to create its own communicability.

3. If we call the primacy of thinking in all modes of the Encompassing "reason," then more is meant by this than merely thinking. Reason is the thinking which goes beyond all boundaries, is ever-present and demanding; it not only grasps what is knowable in a universally valid manner or what is itself a being of reason in the sense of lawfulness and order of events, but it also brings the other to light. Reason confronts that which is utterly counter to it, touches it, and thereby brings it into being for the first time. Reason is capable of breaking through every mere "correctness" and every conciliatory, leveling totality. Where everything disintegrates, reason is the driving force. This force, however—analogous to the will-to-become-whole of the spirit, yet more than it, since it, too, is to be overcome—finds tranquility only in the absolutely One of transcendence. Hence, reason is no longer, as are consciousness-as-such and spirit, partially blind.

Through the primacy of thought and in constantly going beyond the limits, reason is able to clarify all modes of the Encompassing, without itself being an Encompassing like them. It cannot be grasped in the form of the modes of the Encompassing in which it moves.

4. In Kant and Hegel, "idea" has a heterogeneous meaning. In Hegel "idea" is the *idea of the spirit* which is closed off in itself and perfected; in Kant it is the *idea of reason* which, infinite and unlimited in its openness, ever remains a task for man.

Selection 25

PERIECHONTOLOGY (5):
DISTINCTIONS AND RELATIONS

EDITORS:
Since reason is the "urge toward unity" and as such the "bond of all modes of the Encompassing," the following question arises: Why distinguish among

the modes of the Encompassing and what is the relation between them? This is the topic of the chapter from which the following excerpts are taken. Included here is Jaspers's special interpretation of appearance, seen by him as a fundamental characterization of the relationship among modes of encompassing Being. This conception of appearance is continuous with Jaspers's interpretation of Kant's distinction between appearance and the thing-in-itself (*see* Selection 4).

The excerpts are from *Von der Wahrheit*, pp. 121–25, 127–29, 133–37. The translation is provided by the editors.

TEXT:

Remarks

We have attempted to look at the modes of the Encompassing in sequence. The separations between the modes of the Encompassing were absolute insofar as there were no transitions between them and they were separated by a gap. Yet they were not absolute since one mode constantly repulsed the other as being substantially different but also claimed it as its complement; for one mode points to the other. So far, however, the modes of the Encompassing stand next to each other like a mere multiplicity, like an aggregate.

The modes of the Encompassing could not be conceptually determined like elements of a thought construct with which, as fixed points, one could then continue to operate and, in constructing, to take in at a glance the whole of Being. Rather, the illuminating thought of the Encompassing was a circling within one Encompassing at a time; and here greater clarity can be achieved only if the circles become more comprehensive and richer.

The road of philosophizing on the basis of the Encompassing does not proceed from the fixation of elements to the construction of combinations; it does not deduce the whole from a few principles; rather, it takes the road which leads from the illumination of the spaces of the Encompassing, in which is contained everything which we are and which is for us, to the limits where the ultimate disunion becomes manifest and yet the unity of Being can become present to us. For this, philosophizing searches for the depth of the ground from which we come and to which we return. Its goal is a thinking which is possible for man and which unceasingly penetrates deeper and deeper, and not an impossible, commanding knowledge of Being.

In our presentation of the modes of the Encompassing we have up to now proceeded in a piecemeal fashion and have focused on each particular mode in turn. Such a presentation leaves us dissatisfied, because:

The separation of the modes seems questionable since what has been separated can also be conceived as coinciding. It could perhaps be said that existence cannot be separated from Existenz (for Existenz is nothing other than authentic existence); that world cannot be separated from transcendence (for transcendence is nothing other than the total manifestation of the world in its ground); that consciousness-as-such and spirit cannot be separated from each other (for they are the same thing seen from two sides, as are consciousness and the unconscious); that consciousness-as-such and spirit cannot be separated from reason (for reason is the actualization of consciousness and spirit).

Such identifications are in error because they do not go far enough. But hidden in their formulations lies the true impulse to search for that which comes through in these differentiations. The differentiations cannot be the ultimate step. Their apposition seems arbitrary as long as it does not become clear how these positions belong together.

Hence, it is necessary that we go more deeply into the differences as well as the relations between the modes of the Encompassing. Now that we have discussed the spaces of the Encompassing, we must attempt to illuminate the meaning and origin of the differentiations as well as the meaning and the modes of their relationship. . . .

Reasons for the Differentiation of the Encompassing

We may find the differentiation of the modes of the Encompassing to be questionable because we are not dealing with definable objects. Why is there for us not the one Encompassing but many modes of the Encompassing?. . . .

1. In transcending to the one Encompassing we always immediately encounter a particular Encompassing. Whatever remains over at the end, as we cross over, we consider encompassing, even if it proves to be a particular. In philosophizing, the modes of the Encompassing manifest themselves as a multiplicity. It is one of the fundamental experiences of philosophizing that, as we become aware of the modes of the Encompassing until we can go no further, each space of the Encompassing reveals, as it were, its peculiar light, its color, its basic character trait. To be sure, each Encompassing can be filled with a vast amount of content specific to it, a constant increment for us. However, everything which is for us and which we are can become appearance for us solely in these modes of the Encompassing or through them. No other modes became manifest to our observing awareness besides the seven modes of encompassing Being that we tried to illuminate.

2. No matter in what way we illuminate the Encompassing for us, it is, each time, in one sense everything. Everything else is in it and cannot be separated from it. But it is precisely because this quality of being everything manifests itself severally and each time with a power of persuasion belonging to this Encompassing, we are forced to acknowledge this multiplicity. Everything is existence or is in existence. Everything is for consciousness-as-such. Everything is spirit; only what belongs to spirit has substance, whatever lies beyond it remains inconsequential or is nothing. Everything is world. Every-

thing is transcendence. One can start out from each Encompassing as the first, and in it one can encounter all the other Encompassings. Accordingly, many sequences of representation can be carried through.

For example: We look around in order to see what other Encompassing is present in existence besides existence. To existence as such belong life, soul, consciousness. Other Encompassings appear in existence, namely, consciousness-as-such and spirit. Existenz manifests itself through all of these out of its ground and sets reason into motion. Being becomes evident in existence, and through the other modes of the Encompassing to be encountered in existence, as world and as transcendence.

I may also take as my point of departure consciousness-as-such or Existenz or any of the other modes. There is no point in playing them off against each other for they are ramifications of our representation, the reiteration of which makes the multiplicity all the clearer.

3. The different modes of the Encompassing do not allow their derivation from each other, neither the one from the other nor of all of them from a superordinate mode. They are non-objective signa of the furthermost and particular spaces in which we find Being and ourselves.

4. Since, in concrete illumination, the one Encompassing is always only one mode of the Encompassing, and next to which other modes immediately become evident, the One can be experienced only through moving from one Encompassing to the other. We cannot think or intuit anywhere in the world a One without taking the roundabout way over what is split apart, which then becomes a unity. In the illumination of the Encompassing this primal phenomenon is repeated: even in transcending thought no one is illuminated save by way of what is differentiated.

5. The modes of the Encompassing differentiated by us are historic in their being thought; they are the result of our Western educational process. Our ancestors lived and thought within their spaces. These modes were consciously adopted by their thinking. We woke up in these spaces. Through them we have experienced the primal sources accessible to us. The purpose of our thinking of the modes of the transcendence is to preserve what has already been thought and to comprehend it into a unity.

6. The truth of the differentiation of the Encompassings becomes evident only in the course of carrying it out. In the last analysis, the basis of our right to make this differentiation lies, for the whole of the philosophic enterprise, in what is illuminated by the differentiation, what it is possible to ask and to answer by means of it, what scope of Being is made manifest by it to our consciousness. But it is the nature of our philosophic situation that it will not be possible for this justification to be absolute or the doctrine of the modes of the Encompassing and their differentiations to be final. . . .

The Mutual Relationships of the Modes of the Encompassing

The relationship of the Encompassings to each other cannot be conceived as the relation of species to genera. The common denominator of the "encompassing"—an unavoidable way of speaking—must not seduce us into seeing in the modes of the Encompassing variations of something common to all. To be sure, the "Encompassing" is the expression of something in common, namely, that which is to be found at the limits, something non-objective; but the Encompassings encountered at the limits are essentially different. Even though growing out of a single primal source, they are not derivable from this one source and cannot be conceived as a series of variations of something basically the same. The One shatters in our hand if it is to be understood as the relationship of species to genera. Each Encompassing and the relations between them can be illuminated only by a thought process specific to it. What these relations are can only be clarified through reflection in the way in which we become conscious of them:

1. The relations are present through our effecting them. We are going to attempt to illuminate the mutual relationships of the Encompassings as "objectifying," "meshing," "appearing." It is unavoidable to speak of these relationships in terms taken from world-being; yet they are different in essence from all relationships that we know in the world. None of the relations can be observed adequately as an object, none can be investigated like an object as to its performance, none can be cognized as a necessary event determined by laws.

But all of these relationships are very close to us, indeed are immediately present. For we are they. They have either been effected by us or have been grasped by us in our action as an other, or we have experienced them as a gift in our freedom. None of these relationships is passive like a natural event, each is actual only through an activity on our part. We are the midwives, as it were, of each relationship. . . .

The relationships in the Encompassing are themselves encompassing. They are original, thus cannot be objectified nor derived; they are, however, to be illuminated in their presentiality.

2. The illumination of the relationships takes place through a transcending as the modes of relatedness are differentiated.

The relations of the Encompassing cannot be comprehended in the categories through which we think relationships in the world, such as causality, part and whole, etc. But since we must think everything that we think in such categories, the relationships of the Encompassing are also thought in categories that are in themselves immanent, particular, intelligible (such as meshing, appearing). However, as we make use of them when we want to aim for the Encompassing in transcending, we do not really mean to refer to them as they are but to something in them which can only be expressed by them and which, in being expressed, is immediately misunderstood if the statement is no longer understood as transcending. . . .

Only through the differentiation of the modes of the fundamental relationships does this relatedness itself become clear. This is neither an indefinite, general, mere relatedness nor a series of definite, definable relationships. Rather, it lies in the modes through which, in prelogical Being, the spaces of the Encompassing are each gripped by the other. We are aware of this gripping without seeing it before us. It is neither phenomenologically intuitable nor can it be disclosed through constructive procedures; rather, we are sure of it out of the very grounding of our consciousness of Being as we express this analogically by means of categories that are valid for objects in the world. . . .

Appearance: The Relationship Among the Modes of the Encompassing

Appearance must not be simply understood in the way in which something underlying in the world (such as physical waves) appears to us (such as sound or light). Rather, we transcend from this "appearance," which is a relationship within the world, to a relationship of Being to world-being. The latter relationship is itself inaccessible, and only in analogy to the former relationship is it an "appearance." Becoming-appearance is a relationship in the Encompassing reached through transcending and expressed by the category "appearance."

However, we speak of "appearance" as a fundamental relationship in the Encompassing in a multiple sense:

First: The becoming-appearance, for us, of world-being, i.e., (a) of encompassing world-being, (b) of the Encompassing of the Being which we are as existence, consciousness, spirit.

Second: Self-being (Existenz and reason) bringing about its appearance.

Third: The appearance of transcendence in immanence by way of a language which we—as possible Existenz—can understand.

1. *Becoming Appearance.*

(a) The Encompassing of the world itself appears to us as objectification: nature, inaccessible as it is in itself, appears in the investigable actuality of nature.

(b) The Encompassing which we are appears to us as world-being and is objectified as an investigable objectivity in the world: The three modes of the Encompassing which we are, namely, existence, consciousness-as-such and spirit, become the object of our orientation in the world. In this objectification, where they become the objects of research, these modes no longer are the Encompassing itself but have become appearances.

As objects of research they have become a single world-being amongst others. They are then encompassed by the world; this world, together with them and with its own objective appearance, is itself contained within the Encompassing of consciousness-as-such and constitutes the totality of objects. . . .

2. *Bringing about One's Appearance.* We appear to ourselves in the world by bringing about our appearance. This appearing-to-oneself is a relation consisting of our enactment through ourselves and not of a passive happening of becoming-appearance. Being manifests itself to us in that we do something with ourselves . . . We take possession of the existence in which we come to ourselves; we choose it and thereby transform it; we subject it to conditions. We obey the impulse of reason to let ourselves be infinitely concerned. We experience limit situations and attain our heights out of the primal source which lies neither in existence nor in knowledge nor in spirit.

Existenz enters the world through the three modes of the mpassing which Encowe are. It actualizes itself in existence, illuminates itself in consciousness-as-such, and manifests its substance in spirit.

Existenz and reason never become directly the object of our orientation in the world but only to the extent to which they have brought about their appearance in existence, consciousness-as-such, and spirit; they then become appearance for knowledge not as themselves but as these three modes. . . .

3. *The Appearance of Transcendence in Immanence.* If we consider the existence of a thing as object for us to be its direct appearance, then all appearance of transcendence in the immanence of existence must be indirect. Either all objectivity disappears, and transcendence is present in mystic union, or the objects in the world become, as it were, a language of transcendence. Only Existenz is capable of hearing this language and to understand it in that particular way where its substance always remains equivocal, while actuality possesses the greatest certainty. If we characterize the appearance of transcendence by the manner in which we relate to transcendence, then three modes emerge:

(a) Transcendence appears through the Encompassing of world-being and through the Encompassing which we are. In order to experience transcendence in its purity, the following differentiation is needed: with respect to the finite objectivity we are assured of the corresponding Encompassing; or, conversely, the modes of the Encompassing are present to us through particular objectivity. However, transcendence does not speak directly through individual objects but indirectly through the Encompassing. Hence, it is the very first precondition for my authentic hearing of transcendence that I experience the Encompassing in the object in order to perceive transcendence in all Encompassing.

If I want to possess transcendence directly in the particular object instead of listening, through the Encompassing, to the Encompassing of all

Encompassing, then I fall prey to superstition. If in the world, however, I turn with faith toward transcendence, then I touch it in a twofold way, i.e., contemplatively in the reading of the cipher-script, actively in existential acts related to transcendence.

Transcendence appears first of all as the cipher-script of all world-being. In it can be felt, as it were, the soul of things; and transcendence speaks in these souls. These souls are tangible to us, who are life and spirit, in an immediacy which is akin to perception. But we are seduced by ecstatic, aimlessly changing, extravagant feelings if we do not hear transcendence in these souls and do not read the cipher-script which is the language of transcendence. Only if we do, do we become ourselves and achieve structure within the fluidity of a world replete with souls.

Secondly, transcendence appears through the actuality of the Encompassing which we are as existence, consciousness-as-such, and spirit insofar as Existenz achieves in them its enactments in regard to transcendence. In falling away and rising, in defiance and surrender, in obedience to the law of day and abandonment to the passion of night, in dissipation and carried away by the One—Existenz transforms into historic experience whatever it has the capacity to hear of transcendence despite the lasting ambivalence in which transcendence stays hidden from temporal being. The appearance of transcendence, which gives a fundament to everything, takes place within the freedom in which I am given to myself as a gift; and together with the substantial grounding in me I experience the transcendence through which this freedom has come into being.

In both cases—in the reading of the cipher-script as well as in existential relation to transcendence—Existenz takes hold of transcendence, proceeding by way of the totality of appearances, the appearance of world-being, and the appearance of the Encompassing which we are.

(b) Transcendence appears in the Encompassing of consciousness-as-such through foundering movements of thought. Instead of relating only by way of the world, relating to transcendence can also happen, as it were, before, outside of, or without the world. A consciousness-as-such devoid of reference to the world assures itself through abstract movements of thought; it does this, however, in such a manner that it knows about transcendence not as the result of thought—which would founder against contradictions and tautologies—but such that it gains its certainty in the very enactment of transcendent Being. That one can, and indeed must, think in this manner, is an indicator pointing to transcendence.

Such speculative thinking opens up the space in which Existenz is related to transcendence through thought and is close to it in the primal bond of its capacity to think. To objective thought such thinking can appear to be vacuous since in it no reality is cognized and one is left with no organized object. The capacity to think in this way is an invaluable path on which transcendence appears to man.

(c) Transcendence is present in mystic union accompanied by the disappearance of all appearance. The presentiality of transcendence occurs in retreating from all Encompassing, that which is world and that as which we are in the world, through the unification of ourselves with transcendence yet without time, in the disappearance of every mode of being-I and of all objectivity.

It is impossible to doubt that mystics have experienced what they have expressed without being able to describe it. What that is remains inaccessible to the human being who lives in the world. The mystic, too, having once more awakened to the world, can merely report what he really no longer understands; however, in his memory he carries with him an experience which from this point on dictates the importance of everything else. Guided by it, he now allows his life to take place as a new life within the world.

Selection 26

PERIECHONTOLOGY (6): TRANSCENDING AND OBJECTIFICATION

EDITORS:
In the following selection Jaspers addresses the paradox of the kind of thinking which makes the philosophy of the Encompassing possible. By virtue of such thinking we transcend determinate objectivity, yet as thinking it is bound to the idiom of determinate objectivity. The thought of the Encompassing would miss its mark if it were to be objectified, yet such objectification seems unavoidable. Since Jaspers identifies the erroneous objectification of thought about Being with ontology, the present selection affords him the opportunity to define the distinction between ontology and periechontology.

The selection appears in *Von der Wahrheit* on pp. 152–61; the translation has been prepared by the editors.

TEXT:
Our thinking is object-directed and requires sensible intuition even as it thinks the Encompassing. Thus when we search for the encompassing Being we must transcend the indispensable realm of objectivity. In this process two things occur together: the realm of objectivity in its finitude comes forth out of the Encompassing, and, in taking hold of this realm, we transcend it and grasp Being.

Man assures himself of the Encompassing within the realm of objectivity in three ways . . . :

1. By means of consciousness-as-such and spirit, man—as Existenz—grasps out of the sources of the Encompassing in finite configurations within the world what, for him, is not this finitude as such, but the presence of Being itself as tied to historicity.

2. For research, the Encompassing itself becomes the object insofar as it becomes appearance in the world. It is comprehensible in its having become objective. Appearance is empirically cognizable ad infinitum.

3. In philosophizing we become aware of the Encompassing through transcending trains of thought. These take place in the medium of objectifications that have come about through the first two ways and with the kind of clarity that must lead from the thinker's awareness of Being to the fulfillment of thought. In this transcending reflection there arises a doctrine of the Encompassing which will now be discussed in greater detail.

1. The first way concerns the circumstance that the consciousness of Being is tied to the historic objectification arising from the origins of the Encompassing. It is a fundamental necessity of our being-human that everything that is for us must tie itself as well as us to finitude, to time, to intuitability, to being thinkable, in order to enter our world and our nature. Whatever does not enter such a bond with finitude remains vacuous or its bond is inadequate (without any bond it would not exist at all for us), and thus it remains abstract, lacks credibility because it is not immanent, and is therefore mere possibility, empty and without a foundation. We become our actual selves only through tying ourselves to finitude.

However, if finitude as such is taken as absolute, we lose that which we express through it. We experience our dissipation by becoming immersed in the merely finite. In this way, truth frozen within indispensable finitude can also be lost. This is shown by the development of forms that have become objective such as authorities, concrete deities, cults and rites, creeds, laws and doctrines.

The primal source of the Encompassing is active in us in its pure form only when our ascent out of finitude occurs within our attachment to finitude, i.e., when we achieve historicity.

Faced with the danger of becoming lost in frozen finitude, we proceed to reject all finitude. For an instant we desire a religion without images, an ethic without laws, a mysticism free of the world, deeply motivated toward them as the purest truth. But we come to realize that here, too, the finite bond—against our will and counter to our first motivation—has led right away to a narrowness, indeed to a radically destructive narrowness: in using words and laws against images, in laws hostile to law, in forced mystical experience. . . .

We are inclined to want to have the essential sensibly, indeed palpably, present to us. To be sure, this inclination becomes an elemental desire for something like a sign that I hold on to in my distress. I am impelled toward the beloved tomb which I approach in order to experience peace; toward a document, to something I can carry with me. But I take the great step toward freedom if I am able to bear up without such localization and absolutization (but also capable of carrying out ingenuously the transformation into the sensible without being constrained by it), if I am able truly to expose myself to the world as being-world. This freedom, too, cannot be dissociated from finitude. It can merely loosen the absolute fixation in order that I experience the truth of the Encompassing in all its modes and thus also in its sensible form. Then and only then will it not arrive at the illusory neglect of any form of actuality at all and yet will not become engulfed in any form of finite reality. . . .

2. The second way concerns the objectification of the Encompassing into an object of research. The Encompassing seems to become an object of investigation. The world is strange to us and becomes objectively investigable in the form of nature. The Encompassing that we ourselves are, i.e., existence, consciousness, spirit, are considered empirical objects and as such become the subject matter of biology, anthropology, psychology, sociology, *Geisteswissenschaften*. But whenever we have before us something as the subject of our research, it is no longer the Encompassing but an appearance of the Encompassing, a Something in the world, a mode of Being in its intuitability, in its being thought and cognized; it has become, as it were, something rigidified. . . .

Because all known Being is appearance, known Being cannot be Being itself. Being in itself never is in the form in which I can know Being; and in the form in which I know myself (i.e., as I appear to myself), I am never authentically I myself. Knowledge is never a knowledge of the Encompassing; rather, all known Being is what it has turned into in the process of becoming appearance. However, what this appearing is, remains—itself an encompassing—an impenetrable mystery.

The question arises as to how *Being* and its *appearance* relate to each other in the research object.

Cognition of appearance does not include the appearing Encompassing as, let us say, the foundation that has now been disclosed. Rather, all that is thought of as being fundamental is an auxiliary construct which still belongs logically to this appearance.

Nonetheless we are aware of sensing Being in the abundance of appearances. But there remains an absolute leap between Being and appearance. For all our sensing of Being, the experience of its presence is as such not cognition; rather, cognition becomes a means—in an awareness that is not cognition— of making this experience broader, richer, and fuller. . . .

If the subject matter of research is to remain imbued with content and the Encompassing is to become clear, then they must be indissolubly related.

Knowledge about appearance, gained in research, is essential for awareness of the Encompassing. The boundless movement of research is taken up into the space which is nowhere known but becomes present to us as that which illuminates further all that is known and which itself becomes clearer and clearer through this knowledge.

Awareness of the Encompassing influences decisively the way research is conducted with respect to the phenomenal realm. Out of this awareness the pertinent questions arise, I am led to choose what is essential, I am given the incentive to move toward what concerns me and to penetrate in depth the subject in question.

The clarity of my consciousness of Being calls for the distinction in thought between the Encompassing and cognizable appearance and forbids me to confuse their significance; such confusion would prevent the purity of my cognition as well as the depth of my awareness. However, their relation within the Encompassing, brought about through the appearance of Being and through objectification for consciousness, becomes all the more powerful as the Encompassing and the objectification of research are intertwined and thus realized.

For us, Being resides in this intertwining of the Encompassing and objectification, of the process of appearing and knowing directedness toward appearance. This interweaving on the one hand allows cognition unlimited progress, free in everything that becomes an object, but on the other hand sets it an insurpassable limit in the Encompassing, a limit which gives wings to the meaning of cognition.

To be sure, if I consider the content of knowledge to be actuality as such, I pass by genuine actuality. But over against what is specifically known, the Encompassing leaves me open to this actuality through the knowability of phenomena. . . .

However, the separation of a cognition that has before it only objects of research lacking transparency, from an awareness of the Encompassing that is meant to be sufficient unto itself, causes both to founder:

For the objects of the sciences in their endlessness become indifferent if their being cognized does not serve to enhance the breadth and fullness of the Encompassing in its presentiality. All modes of the Encompassing collapse, as it were, if they—having become the objects of research—are to be no more than that.

3. The third way concerns the objectification of the Encompassing in philosophic doctrine (Ontology and Periechontology). In deliberate philosophizing we think the Encompassing. The Encompassing cannot be grasped as a known like an object of research; rather, it is illuminated in philosophizing. However, by thinking the Encompassing it becomes objectified in some manner as we philosophize. To be sure, objectification is an indispensable tool of transcending thought. But the danger is always present that such objectifi-

cation of the Encompassing, instead of being a passing means of thought, becomes that which is thought. In this reversal, thought then becomes a doctrine in the world.

We cognize objects in the world by deriving them from each other. Whatever comes before us is comprehended in such a manner that it is comprehended out of an other. Our objective cognition compels us everywhere toward derivative connections, in the area of reality toward causal connection.

The philosophic connection of the Encompassing, on the other hand, implies an illumination of the spaces out of which the primal source emerges to confront us. These are spaces in which knowledge becomes possible but which themselves cannot be known. Hence the Encompassing—contrary to all knowability—has as its fundamental characteristic that (a) it can itself not be derived, and (b) nothing else can be derived from it.

(a) Since the Encompassing is not comprehended like an object in the world, it cannot be derived. It does not originate in something more primal; one cannot go beyond it but it is illuminated as we go beyond objectivity. Thus, it is that beyond which there is nothing. Neither could it possibly be derived from something specific that occurs within it. This impossibility always remains the same but can be expressed in its various modifications:

If we call the Encompassing "thinking," then we must say: thinking cannot be derived from something that is thought. If we call it our consciousness, then we must say: this, our consciousness, cannot be derived from a being that is an object for consciousness. If we call it the whole, then we say: this whole cannot be derived from a singular, no matter how comprehensive. In short, our being cannot be derived from beings that are for us; I myself cannot be derived from that which comes before me.

It is just as impossible to derive Being itself from beings that we cognize. If we call the Encompassing Being, then we must say: Being cannot be derived from the many beings. If we call it being-in-itself, then we must say: Being-in-itself cannot be derived from objective phenomena. If we call it transcendence, then we must say: the unconditional, which rests solely within transcendence, cannot be derived from the objective nature of the world, existence, spirit.

Again and again something surfaces in thinking man that reaches beyond all that can be thought either as he himself, or as Being that is not he at all, or as the unconditional that takes hold of him.

(b) Since the Encompassing does not become an object in the world, nothing can be derived from the Encompassing. It is not an object from which other objects originate, nor can it give rise to a proposition from which follows a set of other propositions.

There was the tendency in philosophy to derive from simple Being (which was how the Encompassing was conceived) the particular being as we cognize it in the form of an object. The world, ourselves included, was thought as originating from sources that were presumed to have been cognized in just the same way in which we comprehend things in the world out of their causes. But every object that is thought, no matter how comprehensive, every conceptual whole, indeed every Encompassing that is thought of as an object, remains, as such, an object, an individual, since it exists vis-à-vis other objects beyond itself and us. The Encompassing can never be cognized as a Something from which an Other can be derived.

Accordingly, these are the two fundamental characteristics of the Encompassing: *The* Encompassing cannot be derived, neither can anything be derived *from*, the Encompassing. No matter whether the Encompassing is derived from something else or whether a particular is derived from the Encompassing, in each instance one errs by turning things around: Derivations are put in place of fundamental connections, knowledge of coherences which occur is put in place of what is to be enacted. In each case, the basic error consists in making a science out of the illumination of the Encompassing by means of a supposed cognitive objectification. However, Being can indeed be illuminated but it cannot be cognized. It is cognized solely in its appearance insofar as we grasp the latter by extending our research into the limitless.

The scientific cognition of the one Being and of its structure by derivative means (i.e., deduction or construction) of all that is, from principles which are thought to be objectively adequate, is called *Ontology*. While the name originated in the sixteenth century, the subject in its main features has dominated almost all of philosophy since the time of Aristotle.

The road we take is the one of illuminating the Encompassing for which we search as that which shelters all origin within it and yet can never adequately become our object. If we call the doctrine which comes into being on this road *Periechontology*, in contrast to Ontology, we arrive at the following summary juxtaposition:

Ontology	*Periechontology*
1. Ontology displays Being as ordered with reference to diverse *objects* or meaning-units.	1. It illuminates a *space* in which we then find that all Being approaches us in it.
2. Everything is what it *is*.	2. Everything that is is *permeated* by the Encompassing; if it were not, it would be abandoned by it and as if lost.
3. There occurs a clarification of what is meant by *statements* or can possibly be meant by them.	3. There occurs a clarification of the *whole* in which we find ourselves as well as everything else.
4. It provides *objective* clarification.	4. The clarification it provides is *non-objective*.

5. Its symbol: an *organized chart* (analogous to Greek meandering ornamentation).

6. It demonstrates what, in immanent thought, is *virtually* visible.

7. Being is thought of as *genera* which, together, *do not constitute a genus* but their relationship is that of the *analogy* of Being.

8. The inability of defining the "first" is overcome by analysis of the *different meanings of what there is* and by the weeding out of the non-authentic meanings.

9. Ontology tells us what is; it provides a determinate framework and an edifice for what is. It aims toward a *system of Being*.

10. That which comes first in accordance with its subject matter, i.e., the *principle of all Being*, becomes its object and topic.

11. All that is is *derived* from this principle.

5. Its symbol: a dynamic *interweaving of relations* (analogous to Nordic ribbon ornamentation).

6. It makes palpable what, in transcending thought, is hit upon *indirectly*.

7. Being is thought of as that which is *prior* to all particular beings or as a receptacle and as *conferring* meaning, which in turn cannot adequately become an object.

8. The inability of defining the "first" is overcome through the *unitary thought of the Encompassing in all its modes* (by transcending, within every presentness, to beyond all objectivity).

9. Periechontology tells us what Being consists of, provides us with no determinacy of Being, constructs no edifice. It aims at a *systematics of what is*.

10. That which is first for us, i.e., *how we encounter ourselves in the Encompassing*, remains the boundary for us which we cannot cross philosophically.

11. We are never able to take hold of the Encompassing in such a manner that we can derive anything from it. The First remains for us the historic presentiality of our experience of existing, of idea, of love: in it, we come to ourselves. Our philosophic consciousness illuminates and makes these possible. What is, is for us not as the Encompassing that we know but as the presence of the Here and Now in its depth down to its origin.

The caesura in our thinking that takes place as we turn from ontological to periechontological philosophizing can hardly be overestimated. When constructs of the whole are no longer valid, when no picture of the world is absolute, when a closed doctrine of categories is no longer possible, then we are thrown back on what is totally in the present. In this presentiality there takes place—in an atmosphere of openness to everything where reason serves as the universal bond—the trenchant decision of Existenz by way of its historic irreplaceable act.

However, where we touch upon the deepest truths, the most serious misunderstandings are possible. That which is present is turned back from the depth of openness into the insignificance of the momentary, from existential fulfillment into the mere vitality of existing. Choices made in the historic present are turned into objective, commensurable decisions proper to the weighing of alternatives on the part of the interfering and calculating intellect. The openness to everything, originally a state where we let everything affect us, turns into a neutral—albeit always merely apparent—understanding of everything. In philosophy, illumination turns into doctrines of derivative constructions, systematics becomes system, and the illumination of the modes of the Encompassing is transformed into a series of pseudo-ontologies.

PERIECHONTOLOGY (7): THE USES OF PERIECHONTOLOGY

EDITORS:
To view Being as encompassing one's realization is regarded by Jaspers as being primal. Periechontology clarifies such a view with respect to mankind's vast and varied experience. Periechontology would not be successful if it were to present a finished theory of Being—as if it were possible for a human being to have an overview of human realizations of Being. Periechontology is, like all human realizations, historic, and its formulation an ongoing task. Its aim is to open the dimensions of Being in which human realizations of truth take place and encounter each other. Periechontology can thus provide a basis for human beings of fundamentally different perceptions of Being to meet, if not in like-minded communion, at least in communicative solidarity, each vying with the other for the clarity of his truth in a space encompassing both.

The following two selections spell out two aspects of Jaspers's thoughts on the significance and uses of periechontology. In the first, "The Relation of one's own Philosophy to the Tradition," Jaspers speaks of periechontology as functioning as an "ingenuous" synthesis open to any truth whatever, past or future. The second selection is entitled "The Idea of a Common Fundamental Knowledge." In it Jaspers examines the possibility of periechontology to function as a common fundamental knowledge "in which we meet," yet in such a way that "we let each other be free as to the incommensurably many and separate sources out of which we live." This idea seems to be inevitable. Yet it is problematic, hence Jaspers subjects it to scrutiny and in the end proposes the project of a periechontological, general, fundamental knowledge as a "means of Communication."

Selection 27

THE RELATION OF ONE'S OWN PHILOSOPHY TO TRADITION

EDITORS:
The following selection has been translated by the editors from *Von der Wahrheit*, pp. 190–93.

TEXT:
The doctrine of the Encompassing presents, as it were, an outline of Being. From its beginning philosophy has been thinking in configurations of such outlines, which are expressions of fundamental knowledge. Let us inquire into how one's own outline is related to those which have been handed down.

A. The Outline of Being in Actual Philosophizing and in Knowledge of Philosophy

Man always lives with some outline of Being. Within its framework he becomes aware of Being as he thinks and expresses it. The actuality of such an outline within one who knows it has a wider significance than specific items of knowledge. It is the pervasive form and the condition of his knowledge, the mode of his relation to the divinity or to nothingness.

In philosophical reflection, the fundamental knowledge that is effective in thought turns into a *known* outline. A known outline is the guideline which one's movement of thought will follow as he seeks for himself an explicit articulation of Being. However, there is originally more in the outline than what is left of it in the purely objective meaning of what it expresses. Hence, once it becomes separate in the form of a cogitatively objective opinion of what Being is, the outline loses its authentic significance; it can be understood only together with the actuality of the being-human which assured itself of its

fundamental knowledge by means of it. Such tension between interchangeable cogitative objectivity and actual knowledge of Being is peculiar to all
philosophizing. At all times philosophy is whole in what is thought only
through its fulfillment by a human actuality that thinks it. Hence we seek to
penetrate through the expressed concepts to the origin, whenever, understanding, we grasp within the Being of the thinker what has been philosophically transmitted. When we succeed in touching this origin, we hear out
of our own origin the foreign one that is related to us. Only then do we arrive,
on the basis of the conceptual outlines, at communication which alone hits on
what matters. No authentic philosophic thought can be mastered; we can
penetrate it, but we cannot adequately subsume it under an already formulated
type. The surface of what had been thought is the historical textual material
which we can examine, order, and survey according to its rational objectivity.
In this way, what in itself had been historic becomes for us historical. Thus,
what in itself had been immediate relation to God and thereby the living
completion of the whole truth turns for us into a mere mode of knowledge of
Being as it relates to the divinity.

This is the basis of the injustice and inadequacy inherent in the assimilation
of the past. For the one who philosophizes and who lives with his own fundamental knowledge of Being, the question of how his own outline relates to
those which have been handed down to him is an indispensable one. By regarding the others, he gains clarity about himself. He brings the others into
his perspective, assimilates them, and either recognizes them as to their sense
and truth or rejects them at their source. He is bound thereby to rob them of
some essential meaning which accrues to his own outline. Only one's own,
actually lived, fundamental knowledge can be adequately effective in the articulation of the outline. This injustice is all the more palpable since the one who
assimilates the outlines of others owes his own philosophic insights to those
from whom he seems to depart. He will strive for the highest measure of truth
by looking for forms through which his own outline retains the sort of flexi-
bility which makes it possible for the truth of the other's outline to become his
own truth.

B. The Image of the History of the Philosophy of the Encompassing

Every philosophy has been, in fact, a philosophy of the Encompassing. The
Encompassing itself appears in the actuality of becoming human. Awareness
of the Encompassing arises from such experience when we are grasped by its
actuality by virtue of reflection which in turn deepens the experience and
drives it forward.

The truth of such philosophizing is perhaps most comprehensive at the
beginning, when thought seeks nothing but Being itself and avoids as yet all
distinctions, in order to find itself bodily wholly in transcendence by virtue of

the cipher which it produces. The flaw in this comprehensive beginning is its lack of distinctions and, hence, its lack of definition.

Thence ensues the movement of the history of philosophy:

The movement is one of creative clarification and, soon thereafter, one of falling away. What has been grasped philosophically loses its substance in the transformation of language into an objective content of knowledge. But there follows a rallying of the creativities of thought, of philosophic truths and original primacies from this evermore extensive falling-away, a rallying to new knowledge about the Encompassing. The language of this knowledge reaches us, since the beginning, from all authentic philosophic points of departure and fades away in the conceptions of the common heritage and mode of speaking.

One way of falling away consists in becoming ensnared in the absolutization of an Encompassing in the form of knowledge about it. Restoration takes place by stressing the other, neglected Encompassings, e.g., by stressing thought over against mere nature, vital life over against mere thought, spirit over against merely known objectivity, Existenz over against mere contemplation.

The truth of any contemporary philosophy can unfold only in continuity with the entire tradition, through the clearest knowledge about the Encompassing and its modes. Whatever existed originally must be included. What is true can reach the light of day only as the sum-total of the entirety of Western thought, indeed of the thought of mankind. However, this truth cannot be attained by throwing together or by grouping results but must be restored from the sources of such thought. From these sources philosophizing must always come to life anew; it must not rigidify in these results, must not lose its substance through conceptualization and thereby become, though ostensibly comprehensible, in fact incomprehensible. In this way we can distinguish between what is gathered together from the depths and what is the mere assemblage of superficial manifestations, and thus between originality and eclecticism.

In its ramifications, my basic thought is only seemingly new. It cannot be authentically new, for I have spent my life conscious of finding age-old truth. In philosophy, being new speaks against being true. True novelty may appear once in millennia. The novelty of my philosophizing has not even a trace of an absolutely new creation, as was the case in the history of philosophy with the pre-Socratics, with Kant. My philosophizing, rather, is nourished at every step by the heritage. I regard my thinking as the natural outcome of Western thought until now, the ingenuous synthesis by virtue of a principle that enables us to admit all that is true in any sense whatever.

I see in this mode of philosophizing the point of departure for future thinking, making possible that which is yet to be envisaged. For it does not bring to a conclusion, but outlines spaces into which research and life, Existenz and history can step forth unhindered, yet under the guidance of the high expectations that have become articulated in history.

Such philosophizing can be the key to an authentic understanding of past philosophy and can provide the possibility of assimilating the best tradition.

A world history of philosophy, planned out in this sense, is reserved for another work.

Selection 28

THE IDEA OF A COMMON FUNDAMENTAL KNOWLEDGE

EDITORS:
The following selection is from *Der philosophische Glaube angesichts der Offenbarung*, pp. 147–51. The translation has been prepared by the editors. In E. B. Ashton's translation, *Philosophical Faith and Revelation*, the selection is found on pp. 87–91.

TEXT:

1. The Idea

We may each adhere to a different faith, yet we can understand each other as adhering to a faith; this is analogous to our asserting ourselves as existence, yet such that we are able to understand the other's self-assertion.

As we bring to mind the modes of the Encompassing we illuminate the space common to us as human beings; in this space we impart to each other what we mean and want and what exists for us.

According to its intention, such self-assurance is prior to any formulated philosophy that is substantive and historic. It aims at what is to be grasped in common and what is possible in common.

The aim of such fundamental knowledge is not necessarily to establish a new mode of configuration for our constantly expanding knowledge of the possibilities that have been actualized in history. The aim, rather, is to do, in conformance with the situation into which we are born today, what remains to be done by the one who is informed: Torn from all past unquestioned matters of faith, man can neither restore them nor establish new ones according to plan; an artificial restoration would vainly attempt to maintain a tradition that had become dishonest. However, something else can come into being: In dealing with the tradition—assimilated with understanding—of primal sources and spiritual actualizations, in possession of such knowledge based on understanding, and capable of infinite reflection, man must found his earnestness in a new configuration which searches for a formal fundamental knowledge which, as it is imparted, can become universally binding as its presupposition.

Up to now there has not been a single, universally acknowledged, fundamental structure of that as which and within which we find ourselves. Each one of the great historical configurations seems to have its own specific structure vis-à-vis which a different structure contains an incommensurable element.

As we observe them in a historico-analytical manner, we find that each of these structures has its own definite limitation, a blind spot to others, an absoluteness which transforms what is other into conformity rather than letting it be in its own right.

It may seem to be utopian to search for a fundamental structure in the manner in which we are sketching the modes of the Encompassing. The sense of such a sketch is neither the self-understanding of a faith, nor a description of what is historically given, nor the abstraction of the universal contained in the faith-content common to all actualities of faith, an abstraction which supposedly is a dilution that can be acknowledged by everyone: hence the tentative nature of the sketch, which jells into a fleeting solidarity for the moment of its being imparted. But hence also the assimilation of fundamental experiences uttered long ago.

The sketch is, therefore, not a plan of order for the historically given possibilities of faith, but a means of communication.

For sketching out such fundamental knowledge it is necessary to listen to the reports of believers amongst all of mankind. This is so not only because we are affected by every earnestness which we encounter. We also do not wish to lose any dimension of primal, common, formal possibilities. We wish to expand our ever insufficient openness.

It may be asked whether all men on this globe could finally found themselves in common on universal reason, which is here essentially sketched as the very form of their bond with each other. Is a common frame of greatest breadth possible within which communication of faith can take place, a communication of faith both in its heterogeneous historicity as well as its self-understanding? In such communication faith is not relinquished, but is transformed out of its profundity into the new configurations which form the foundation of man's earnestness under the conditions of the incipient global age.

The self-understanding of man's great configurations of faith has so far rested on metaphysical and ontological presuppositions that are based on revelation. These faiths have either tolerated each other, though they have by no means understood each other; or else they have, in their non-understanding, fought each other with passion. They could mutually be brought to an understanding of themselves and of the other only if they were related within a framework of communicability in which no historical, primal source of faith would be lost or would have to be relinquished.

2. Fundamental Knowledge and Science

Even though the development of fundamental knowledge does not lead to cogent, universally valid cognition, as is the case with science, it is not meant to express a faith. Its place is at the limit of scientific cognition and existential philosophy.

Like science, such fundamental knowledge is never complete; in articulating it, we test it.

With the fundamental knowledge, the forms are worked out in which we are for us in the world, comparable to the forms or categories by which all that can be thought appears to consciousness-as-such. Such categories, which determine the whole universe of what can be thought, are now reduced to a specific set within consciousness-as-such and are encompassed. The task of thinking objectivities is enclosed within the modes of the Encompassing; the ascertainment of these modes draws them within the realm of thought, though inadequately. In comparison with the objectivity of what can be known, such ascertainment moves, by means of objectivities, toward the non-objective of encompassing presence. Because it moves at the limits where all objective knowledge ceases, it can never become cogent science.

Thus, the elaboration of the modes of the Encompassing does not mean that by means of them we gain insight into the ground of things. They project a scheme whose nature must ever remain tentative, hence capable of modification, of broadening and deepening. The project does not arise from some principle; there is no guarantee of its completeness, it does not become a closed system even if, in being sketched, it it may temporarily assume such a form.

Insight into the modes of the Encompassing brings us into a state of suspension and is itself in suspension.

3. Fundamental Knowledge and Existenz

We do not become encompassing by means of ascertaining the Encompassing. The distinction between a thought-sketch and actuality shows that every utterance relativizes, and one's being within actuality is beyond cognitive grasp. The relativity of articulation in thinking the Encompassing does not correspond to the earnestness of existing.

Hence, there is no pronouncement regarding the Encompassing which could be accepted as the known truth. The idiom of knowledge must not be a substitute for the decisions of actuality.

However, by thinking the Encompassing our consciousness moves closer to what we authentically will without being able to say it directly.

For actuality is absolutely historic and not universal. Decision is not derivable from a universal, but there is the urge to clarify it in the light of the universal and to awaken it by means of the universal.

If one were to meet this sketch of the Encompassing with the criticism that it is indecisive, the response would be that decision does not consist in thought, which transforms everything into possibility. Decision is to be found solely in historic Existenz. Thought is merely orientation and illumination; it is a means. Hence, philosophy does not prove itself in the stringency with which thought is elaborated but in the practice of the thinker's life.

4. Objections to the Idea of a Fundamental Knowledge

The following objections may be voiced: Every fundamental knowledge, so also any that may be attempted today, is in fact one expression of faith among others, and not the only one.

Like every primal source of a faith, so the primal source of the present fundamental knowledge is regarded as the authentic one and the only true one.

It is a self-deception to regard oneself as capable of attaining a general fundamental knowledge prior to and beyond all faiths.

In such a philosophical attempt, which is meant to be neither science nor faith, and by means of which one wishes to go beyond the bond of faith in order to claim universal, binding truth, there lies hidden nothing other than an abstract faith.

Its nature as a faith is revealed by the fact that it is by no means universally accepted.

The response is as follows: The objection is itself abstract, for it is not responsive to the aim of the concrete presentation of this fundamental knowledge, nor to the attempt.

Yet the objection is not without basis, for we are not dealing with cogent science. Only the inference is not valid, according to which the standard here, as in all philosophy, is faith.

A faith is indeed fundamentally at work. But this faith does not intend a content of faith that is exclusive of others. It is merely the faith in the possibility of our understanding each other without restriction. It is the faith which says: truth is what ties us together.

It is by means of the modes of the Encompassing, therefore, that we can realize our situation with the aim of finding within the whole—even by means of clarifying what divides us and by means of knowing the sources of mortal struggles—ways of confining and transforming such struggles.

The aim requires a universally open realization in which everyone becomes aware of the scope of his possibilities. Yet it does not require a specific content of faith or a mode of absolute fundamental knowledge. Therefore, the sketch of the modern form of fundamental knowledge does not imply the proclamation of an insight which was finally attained, but only the extending of one's hands. It is hoped that this fundamental knowledge which is to be the condition of a universal unification becomes unfolded within this unification.

This cannot be accomplished merely by means of mental labor. What is presupposed is that which leads us, what we hearken to, without being able to bring it forth. In philosophizing, no less than in the practice of life, we presuppose the human being; not an intellectual apparatus, functionaries, exponents, robots.

The conceptual configurations of the Encompassing which one sketches do not gain their significance by virtue of an object to which they might refer, nor by virtue of a subjectivity which is expressed thereby.

Rather, there is a power at work in the thinker that is not identical with him, yet within him. It motivates self-understanding and communicability. One must name it, yet naming it is inadequate. If we name it "reason," then this is essential but insufficient. To the thinker that other power does not become transparent, yet he perceives its presence in his impulses. It will not let him rest. Reason as such is not as yet creative in the sense of the formation of spiritual works, yet it is mighty in the sense that it is the means through which everything attains meaning. Reason reacts to events and situations. It is to be experienced only in its movement through phenomena. It points to the permanent which is at a right angle to time, to the reference point with respect to which and out of which the substance of truth becomes manifest in concrete historic configurations.

III.

Philosophy and Its History

EDITORS:

In the previous subpart we have seen how, for Jaspers, philosophy, with perie-chontology as its main systematic task, bears an essential relation to its past. Selection 27 elaborated how this relation is not one of conclusion but of open-ing up the spaces of communication, guided by the "high expectations that have become articulated in history." Accordingly the periechontologic turn of philosophy impels an "authentic understanding" of its past and can be the "key" to such an understanding. At the same place Jaspers announces a work of his that is to be devoted to the understanding of the tradition of philosophy under the title "World History of Philosophy." Jaspers's labors on this project in fact occupied the major part of his energy during the last twenty-five years of his life. It outweighed even the preoccupation of his later years of relating philosophy to history, politics, religion, and education. Work on other pro-jected systematic books was abandoned.

Jaspers's projected "world history of philosophy" is vast. As can be seen from the first selection below (29), it was to have consisted of six distinct approaches to the history of philosophy, some of which are original with Jaspers. Certain book that Jaspers published fall under only one of the six approaches, the one that seeks out "the company of the philosophers," "the miraculous greatness of unforgettable human beings." The main publication of this approach is *The Great Philosophers*, which is actually the first of three projected volumes. Dr. Hans Saner, Jaspers's literary executor, published some of the more or less finished literary remains of the other two volumes in 1981.* To the project of *The Great Philosophers* belong publications on spe-cific philosophers: some are book-sized (on Nietzsche, Descartes, Nicholas of Cusa, Max Weber, Schelling, Leonardo da Vinci); some are articles (on Scho-penhauer, Goethe, *et al*). Most of these writings have appeared in English translation. An exception is Jaspers's essay on greatness, which is the second of the following selections. The political import of philosophy in the sense of promoting communication among disparate persuasions is no less evident in coming to terms with the great philosophers of the past as it was in the

---

*To be published in English translation as *The Great Philosophers*, Vol III.

periechontologic task of systematic philosophy. Jaspers argues for a recognition of human greatness that does away with the deification of man: "Every human being, even the greatest, the most rare, the most precious remains a human being."

Selection 29

THE IDEA OF A WORLD HISTORY OF PHILOSOPHY

EDITORS:
The original of the following selection is to be found in *Die Grossen Philosophen, Erster Band*, pp. 7–9. In English translation by Ralph Manheim the passage appears in *The Great Philosophers: The Foundations*, pp. vii ff. What follows is Manheim's translation emended by the editors.

TEXT:
Over the last half century the neglect of philosophy seems to have been accompanied by its liberation from the chains of academicism. In the struggle to gain the substance of our own times amid the storm of arbitrary, fortuitous, anarchic thinking, we gain an advantage if the historic substance can be made to break through the crusts of philosophical conventions and we are able to hear it speaking. . . . It is my intention to participate in this process of redirection.

Starting with Hegel the history of philosophy has become a deliberate element in contemporary philosophizing; today it is that in a quite different way than in Hegel's time.

On the one hand, philosophy needs its history. Present thinking finds itself in its past. Its own character is disclosed by its relation to the past. It may be merely an echo, but in that case it reveals itself as vacuous. Or it may arrange the history of thought into images, structures, or logical orders. Or it may assimilate truth by approaching history as the eternal presence; and thereby it fulfills its aim.

On the other hand, the pursuit of the history of philosophy is not possible without one's own philosophizing. Orientation with respect to facts and texts from a point outside is, after all, not as yet actual philosophy. The sense of penetrating the history of philosophy presupposes that we are under the guidance of philosophy. Only philosophy understands the philosophy that once was and that is today.

For us the philosophical tradition is like an ocean whose extent and depth

are unmeasured and unmeasurable. Never has there been so much encyclo-
pedic knowledge; never before were so many texts available in excellent editions; never before were there so many records of what men have thought, so
many indexes, bibliographies, reference works, in which one can quickly find
what one is looking for. These admirable achievements are indispensable for
any serious occupation with the history of philosophy. But in themselves they
do not bring philosophy to life in the present. Instead, they make for bewildering juxtapositions or sequences of disparate facts or misleading dogmatic
simplifications. In either case, the essential is lost amid a mass of information.
It is astonishing that despite the increase in our historical knowledge there
seldom seems to have been such a decline in the effective tradition of authentic philosophy.

We cannot remedy this sad state of affairs by condensing large encyclope-
dias into smaller ones. Nor can we bring the history of philosophy to life by a
continuous narrative of a single complete process, because for us there is no
such process. A total view of the history of philosophy is impossible. We are in
it. We see it from within, not from some point outside it. Yet, though we
cannot survey the history of philosophy, we can look into it, but always with
the presuppositions and aims of the moment. Accordingly, our view of it will
take on clarity only if we begin by methodically developing certain distinct
aspects of the history of philosophy on the basis of the actual material. They
are as follows:

First, the *historical* aspect: guided by chronology and geography, I formulate a representation of an epoch, of the mysterious modifications that take
place for reasons that are little understood; of the changing conditions of the
thinker's existence, the natural circumstances and social conditions which history has brought forth in so extraordinarily many forms. The assumptions
and modes of thought characteristic of the different epochs are the historical
cloak of the eternal questions.—Second the *thematic* aspect: I turn to the
problems and systems of thought, examine the history without concern for
the chronological sequence to see what questions it has asked, what answers it
has given. I acquire a systematic view of the various matters with which philosophy has concerned itself.—Third, the *genetic* aspect: I observe how philosophy has sprung, at the beginning and at all times, from myth, religion,
poetry, language. The independent origin of philosophy is hidden, as it were,
in something else, from which it draws its nourishment or which it
opposes.—Fourth, the *practical* aspect: I see the actualization of philosophy in
the practice of life, its consequences therein, and observe conversely how it is
subject to the conditions of practical life.—Fifth, the *dynamic* aspect: I perceive the "field of forces" where philosophizing gives rise to a battle of minds
which can never be concluded in time, which seems to culminate in great
comprehensive systems, only to break through them and appear in new

forms. Because I can gain no vantage point outside, I witness my self doing battle within this field of forces, even in the way in which I interpret the forces and fronts. . . .

Taken together, these different ways of approach provide a world history of philosophy. But it is not enough. None of these aspects will quite bring us to what really matters. Just as human beings form loving bonds when they do not merely meet in a common cause but through this cause seek their bond in the ground of Being, so we seek the company of the philosophers. . . . They should be regarded in their own right, in their singularity, tied to the universal yet going beyond it, as the miraculous greatness of unforgettable human beings who, through their existence and their deeds, actualized in thought the potentialities of knowledge. It is only through these men that we can enter the core of philosophy. They present more than the other five aspects. They reveal the essence of philosophy, which becomes original actuality only in the person of a philosopher.

Selection 30

GREATNESS IN PHILOSOPHY

EDITORS:
The following is excerpted from *Die grossen Philosophen, Erster Band*, pp. 29–31, 33–41, 44–48, 58–61. The material appears here for the first time in English in a translation provided by the editors.

TEXT:

Human Greatness in General

What Is Greatness?   The great man is like a reflection of the whole of Being, susceptible of infinite interpretation. He is the mirror or the deputy of Being. He stands within the Encompassing which guides him, and is not lost to surface manifestations. His appearing within the world is at the same time a breaking into the world of what becomes the language of transcendence, be it as the fair glow of perfection, be it as tragic foundering, be it as the strange tranquility within the incessant movement of his life whose animation arises from its ground.

The great man also achieves something useful. But greatness does not yet consist in performance or usefulness, no matter how considerable. For greatness is not measurable. Only that which refers to the whole of our existence, to the whole of the world, to transcendence, attains greatness. The utility of performance becomes great only when it derives its meaning from the Encompassing. Greatness obtains where reality—which constitutes, for our experience, the actuality within the world—becomes a symbol of the whole by virtue of that reflection. Where there is greatness, there is strength, but strength is not yet greatness. . . .

Greatness is universal in the irreplaceability of a historic, unique figure. All that is merely universal is as such finite because it is conceived and it is abstract because it is thought. The universal, which in historic form has become actual, retains the grounding in the ineffable infinity of actual Being. Greatness, therefore, carries within it universality and universal validity, but it is not reducible to the universal which had been brought by it into the world. It does not exist several times in the same way. What someone else could have achieved as well is not great. What can be taken over, learned, and repeated in an identical way does not make for greatness, even though someone must have done it for the first time. Irreplaceability alone marks greatness.

Irreplaceability does not make for greatness as this individual in the particularity of his suchness, nor as the uniqueness of each loving soul which is secretly visible only to the lover and the beloved. Greatness consists in such irreplaceability only when it gains an objective feature through performance, word, deed, or creation and, beyond these, becomes, by virtue of their uniqueness, a truth for all. Greatness presupposes that something universally valid assumes historic, personal form. Only the unity of the personal individual with the universality of a cause makes for greatness. . . .

Greatness, since it does not consist in performance alone, since it is not simply signified by deeds, inventions, results of research, beautiful paintings, fine verse and virtuosity; since, in short, is not possessed by what can be objectively grasped and pointed to, is, in the absence of cogent criteria, a manifest mystery.

How Do We Discern Greatness? In our urge to be free of narrowness we look for human beings who are more than we are, we look for the best. By becoming aware of our insignificance while at the same time experiencing the expectation posed by the great, we expand the limits of the being-human possible for us.

Greatness is present where we perceive with reverence and clarity that through which we become better. From great human beings there emanates the strength which lets us grow by means of our own freedom. They fulfill us with the invisible universe whose configurations, in their appearance, are discovered by them, whose language becomes audible through them.

What I am is revealed to me by him whom I recognize as great. I come to myself through the way I regard greatness and the way I deal with it. The more pure the will, the more truthful the thinking, the more clearly are we addressed by the will and the truth of the great. The possibilities of one's own essence are the means of perceiving greatness.

Reverence for the great includes respect for each human being. Only he who has respect for the human being is capable of perceiving greatness as it is granted to his own age, even in *his* contemporary world. . . .

Against the Deification of Man.   Reverence for greatness is not deification of man. Every human being, even the greatest, the most rare, the most precious, remains a human being. He is one of our own kind. What is proper to him is not a cult but our seeing unveiled his own actuality in which we become certain of his greatness. Greatness is to be preserved not in mythologizing, but in beholding the entire reality of the great person.

In early times the actual personality was not regarded. What one had in mind was not this real singular person, but the divine powers acting through him; not his inwardness and conviction, but his deed; not the singular person as such, but the community which he represented. And when one subordinated oneself to another individual as the authority, it was not with regard to his personal nature, but because one believed either divine will or demonic power to be incarnated in him.

Something of this original attitude has continued through subsequent history until today. The idea of the One, transferred from the idea of God to man, raises this one man, vastly different from the others, above all others. No matter whether the deification concerns the quick or the dead, he moves to another mode of Being. A far removed not-man-any-more, an overman, even god, a suitably positioned or veiled reality is then raised up against all the others who remain in their equality of non-greatness, differentiated only by whether they believe in him or not.

It is the great and particular task of philosophy to cancel out the deification of man in its light of reason in favor of a reverence for human greatness. The great have never tolerated deification with respect to themselves, so also not Jesus. . . .

It is noteworthy that Emerson, though a proponent of hero-worship, also saw the untruth of idolatry. He saw how, through this perversion, the teachers of mankind become its oppressors. His examples are Aristotelian philosophy, Ptolomaic astronomy, Luther, Bacon, Locke. It happens without the will of the great. Only small minds who desire to be great "delight . . . to dazzle and to blind the beholder. But true genius seeks to defend us from itself." The individual, said Emerson, even the greatest, is an exponent of a greater mind and will. No man, not even the greatest, is a whole. Hence we desist from our search for a completely perfect human being. Great men are here so that greater ones may arise. However, the greatest is, for Emerson, the one "who makes himself and all heroes redundant by introducing in our thoughts the element of reason which does not seek out persons, this mighty power which grows so great that its possessor is nothing."

Where the greatness of man as man is seen, there the singular individual is not seen in isolation. The great human being remains human. His greatness awakens what can be like him in everyone. Corresponding to the irreplaceability of what counts as great in the world is the irreplaceability of every human soul which, being hidden, remains invisible. Whoever beholds greatness experiences the call to be himself.

Philosophers in Distinction to Other Greats

We may regard philosophers to have the following in common with poets, artists, heroes, saints, and prophets; the relationships to the whole of the world, the illumination of the secrets of Being and existence, transtemporal truth in historic garb, freedom from particular interests in the world. Wherein, then, does the distinctness of philosophers consist? They are those thinkers who—in distinction to those using as their means deeds, creations, and literary works—arrive by means of concepts and the operation with concepts at what is appropriate to any greatness. With philosophers, thought attains dimensions where it also reflects upon itself and thereby means to experience Being in its entirety. What is otherwise present in symbols—be it in the intuitable grasp of the eye or the ear, be it in the sense of deeds—is here undertaken in the mode of thought which is called philosophic. . . .

Since, in philosophy, thought takes precedence over concrete configurations and images, the demands made upon thought are extraordinary. Philosophic reason believes that it reaches farthest through its insights. It assumes the position of examiner and judge over everything, even over what it itself can never create and which it longs for as the truth which is not mere thought. It attains a dimension which transcends all others. Hence, the identification of the philosopher with the great thinker begins where, by virtue of the distinction of thought, a tension arises between the demands of philosophy and those of myth, religion, and poetry.

This distinction of philosophy occurred when it claimed to be science in the broad sense of the sort of rational activity that is distinct from myth, imagelike configuration, prophecy, music, rhythm. It meant to offer proof through thought. Only in the consequence thereof—and then relatively late and only in the West—did the perception arise of the specific nature of authentic science, i.e., cognition which is not only methodical but cogent and universally valid, and which concretely proves its validity as identical for everyone. Philosophy has, in recent times, also become more clearly aware of its original, irreplaceable character of being more than science while remaining tied to it. It was only then that the question of its own thinking, in distinction from that of science, became fundamental.

Criteria of Greatness in Philosophy

External conditions without which greatness cannot be perceived as such are:

First, written works have to be extant, though there are exceptions. . . .

Second, greatness is recognizable in the philosophers' demonstrable influence on the thinking of later great men, on the thinking of wider circles, and in the way in which they became authorities. The lifetime of the great men is followed by a process in which they are both understood and misunderstood, a process that, in consideration of the inexhaustible nature of their works, has not been concluded to this day.

The criteria of the inner substance that becomes perceptible as we immerse ourselves in the philosophy of the great, are:

First: Within time they stand beyond time. Every man, so also the greatest, has his historic place and wears his historic garb. The mark of greatness, however, is not to be tied to it, but to become suprahistoric. . . . The great philosopher is not one who just articulates his times through his ideas, but one who in this way touches eternity. The transcendence in his life and work hence causes the great man to be a figure who, in principle, is able to speak to any time and to any one.

Second: A genuine thinker is, like everyone, authentic insofar as he is true and essential. Yet the great thinker is original in his authenticity, i.e., he brings a communicability into the world which was not there before. The originality consists in the work or in the creative achievement which cannot be repeated in an identical way by someone else and yet is capable of guiding those who come later to their own authenticity.

Originality constitutes a leap in history. It is the miracle of novelty which even retrospectively cannot be derived from what preceded it and from the conditions of the existence in which it arose. . . .

The insights gained by the original great expand mankind and the world itself. Emerson says, "What they know, they know for us. With each new mind, a new secret of nature transpires; nor can the Bible be closed until the last great man is born."

Third: The great philosopher has gained inner independence without rigidity. It is not the independence of capriciousness, of defiance, of a doctrine fanatically adhered to; rather, it is the independence which consists in risking constant restlessness in time and gaining absolute tranquility. The independence of the philosopher lies in his abiding openness. He can bear to be different from the others, without seeking to be so. He is able to rely on himself and to be for himself; he is able to bear solitude.

But what he is able to bear, he does not wish for. He knows the dependence of man in the mutuality of self to self. He desires relentlessly to hearken. He experiences the help of others who encounter him in earnestness. He does not refuse help but seeks it. He lacks pride of uniqueness but has the strength of independent self-correction. . . .

Finally, there are some criteria of greatness dealing with the substance of philosophic works:

First: Since the time of the ancient sophists, and especially in the last two centuries, the character of "science," i.e., the logical form and character of a system, has been regarded as the measure of membership. Essayists, aphorists, poets, writers of philosophic fiction have been excluded. However, in time this standard has become questionable. Today there are two extremes: On the one hand, there is a positivistic and formalistic attitude of scientism which rejects all metaphysics and what was formerly called philosophy. On the other hand, philosophy has turned into an anti-scientific manner of affective speech. Neither of these two mutually opposed possibilities is conducive to great philosophy. . . . Philosophy's relationship to the sciences has now become the decisive problem. But the way in which science affects philosophy has all along been a criterion of great philosophy.

Second: Philosophers have helped us to achieve an awareness of our existence, the world, Being, the divinity. They illuminate, beyond all particular purposes, our life's path as a whole; they are gripped by questions concerning the limits; they search for the ultimate.

Their essence is universality. They themselves actualize the idea of the whole, even if only in contemplation and in the symbolic historicity of their existence, as if they were its representatives. What is proper to a philosopher as philosopher gains greatness through the substance of this wholeness.

However, greatness can also appear where the content of the work seems to be particular if by means of this particularity the whole is actually at work. . . .

The universality of the philosopher may take many forms, but it is always there. Emerson speaks of it; he would like to live through the entire history in his own person, Greece, Palestine, Italy, and would like to rediscover the creative principle of all things within his own mind. . . .

Third: There is a touch of the normative in the great philosopher. Whether intentionally or not (usually the latter), he becomes in some sense a paradigm, not in the sense of an authority who is to be obeyed, but as a source of strength for him who questions ardently as well as critically. . . . The difference between the normative character of philosophy and religion is that the former is effective in complete freedom, always through individual philosophers; the latter, however, through the agency of ecclesiastical institutions, through posts with interchangeable incumbency, through direction and censorship, confession and obedience. The difference from the validity of the sciences is that philosophizing lays claim to the self-being of the entire person, the sciences merely to the understanding of consciousness-as-such.

Selection and Arrangement of the Great Philosophers

Above the changes of history there is the idea of the one eternal realm of the great. We enter it, hearkening and perceiving, even though we belong, ourselves, to the flow of history. The realm is there, though it has no determinable limits and no one is able to determine its scope and parts. It is open to us in the manner in which we are capable of seeing.

The structure of this realm is hidden from our view. When we believe we have discerned an ordered arrangement of philosophers we have merely found a reflection of this structure. . . . Our historical viewpoint sees groups of philosophers who, by virtue of belonging to one age, or influencing one another, or succeeding one another, or standing in polemical relation to each other, serve to further philosophy. . . . For those who are schooled in the traditional groupings it takes an effort to regard historical grouping as merely relative, even as comparatively superficial, and not to be bound by them. However, when we are affected by the great and ask what, for us, are the ultimate motives of philosophizing, entirely different relationships emerge. . . . Historical groupings are not the only ones, and not the best.

Correspondence in this formulation of problems and their contemporaneousness mean little when we are concerned with the center which nourished their power of thought. Groupings of another kind may juxtapose names which, according to the standard of the usual historical arrangements, have little to do with each other as regards chronology of the history of philosophic problems. Yet such a grouping may well reveal, by presenting them in their living appearance, the relationship, in the eternal realm of spirits, between such extraordinarily different modes of greatness. The attempt to express this relationship will succeed only with respect to their philosophical tasks, their modes of fundamental knowledge, the constitution of their lives and their basic mood, their mental activity and the social reality of their times.

My Arrangement of the Great Philosophers

The first main group consists of men who, through their existence and the nature of their humanity, have determined, like no others, the historicity of men. Theirs is the testimony of influence throughout millennia down to our own day: Socrates, the Buddha, Confucius, Jesus. A fifth, equal in historic power, can hardly be named, and none who still speaks to us today at the same level. One might hesitate calling them "philosophers." However, they have been extraordinarily significant for philosophy as well. With the exception of Confucius, they have not written anything. However, they have become the basis for mighty philosophic movements of thought. We call them the four *exemplary men*. Their position is prior to and outside of all the rest who, by common consent, are called "philosophers."

The second main group includes the *great thinkers* who commonly are called "philosophers." Four subgroups have to be distinguished:

The thinkers who, through their work, continue to be seminal form the first subgroup. More than any others, they are the ones who, when they are studied, impel a philosopher's own thinking. They do not bring thought to a conclusion but through their work they become the origin of inexhaustible possibilities of thought. They belong together solely by virtue of their work's effect of bringing other thinking to its self-realization. Their thinking does not admit of being taken over as something finished. Rather, it forces others to think on, yet without this onwardness implying a going beyond or surmounting of that source. I know only three thinkers whose work can, historically and for us, be characterizied in this manner, namely Plato, Augustine, and Kant.

The second subgroup is that of the visions of thought. It includes: first, the original metaphysicians who arrived at and lead to serenity (Parmenides, Heraclitus, Plotinus, Anselm, Nicholas of Cusa, Spinoza, Lao-tzu, Nagarjuna); then the secularly pious (Xenophanes, Empedocles, Anaxagoras, Democritus, Poseidonius, Bruno); then the gnostic dreamers of truth and verity (Origen, Boehme, Schelling); finally the constructive minds (Hobbes, Leibniz, Fichte).

The third subgroup are the great disturbers; namely, the probing negators (Abélard, Descartes, Hume) and the radical awakeners (Pascal, Lessing, Kierkegaard, Nietzsche).

Finally there is the fourth subgroup, the edifices of the creative orderers (Aristotle, Thomas, Hegel, Shankara, Chu-hsi). These great systems are the crowns of long developments.

The third main group includes philosophical thought within the realms of fiction writing, research, literature, practical life, and the teaching of philosophy. Great writers are not only in possession of philosophy which may be accessible to them, but they speak and function as philosophers. They may not present the original thoughts which mankind owes to the real thinkers, but they have an effect on thought by virtue of something that is more than philosophy.—Scholars and researchers are also philosophers insofar as they think philosophically in their respective sciences, and have philosophical effect through science.—Surrounding the realm of thinkers who are commonly acknowledged as philosophers there is a realm not sharply delineated, in which men speak who are either not regarded as philosophers, or, if so, then not highly or only exaggeratedly so. They are wise men who propose and enact ideals of life, or writers in a literary sense, or great critics and humanists.

Furthermore, there are rulers, statesmen, and saints, who testify to their deeds in written works, and theologians whose interest in philosophizing springs from the church and the religious community. Last are the professors of philosophy, who turn the great enterprise into a learned profession indispensable to tradition and education.

How to Deal with Philosophers

1. *Observing and Dealing with Philosophers.*   Should we edify ourselves or take pleasure in a gallery of great philosophers? Or look at them in such a way that all of them, each in his own way, is good, fair, and true? Or let them pass in review, without any commitment on our part? Or enrich our knowledge? All this may take place; however, philosophy begins when philosophers concern me in my own possibilities, when I hear their summons, where I assimilate and reject. . . .

2. *Distinction between the Quick and the Dead.*   There is a radical difference in our intercourse with the quick and the dead. Dialogue between the living involves questioning and answering, borne by the strength of mutually facilitated self-being. There is an analogous dialogue in the intercourse with the dead. In the dialogue I bring him to life, as it were. When I quicken him, I receive answers from his texts, which are revitalized by my question; someone who does not ask would simply read on. However, such answers are actual only if what I hear can be confirmed by the "intended meaning" of the text. When no such meaning responds in the text by the departed, he remains silent.

If I venture to understand what lies unspoken behind the text, beyond its expressly intended sense, then I have to know what I am about and must say so. This procedure belongs to the assimilation of the authentic substance, but it requires a confirmation through a combination of the explicitly expressed thoughts of the philosopher. . . .

What arises from dialogue with the dead becomes alive only in the exchange between the living. . . .

Intercourse with the dead is a source of the truth of our own essence; its purposes are: not to lose what has clearly been grasped and not to fall prey to illusions which have long ago been exposed; not to become impoverished by letting go of forces which, in temporal struggle, guide man to his highest possibilities; to discharge our responsibility with respect to the greats by giving them tongue anew, according to our capacity; to actualize ourselves in the clear space of what had already been thought, and to educate ourselves through the attainments of history.

3. *Temporal and Trans-temporal.*   Every thinker belongs to his time and world and must be seen as such. But this does not preclude that something speaks through him that can be heard by human beings at any time.

It is a mark of the greatness of a thinker that he can be potentially contemporaneous with all men; that he utters what, throughout the ages, awakens human possibilities, what can function as their mirror, what encourages and strengthens them; and whereby he is engaged in a struggle with them. A thinker who is merely time-bound and who is adequately and essentially discussed by means of our historical analysis does not belong to the circle of the great. However, insofar as no human being is time-bound only, even the most insignificant of us is able, by virtue of his independence, to enter that unique contemporaneousness with the great. In this he hears answers, experiences impulses, attractions, and repulsions. The great are his eternal contemporaries.

4. Modes of Dealing with Philosophers.   Intercourse with dead philosophers is based on the different ways of understanding the texts they left behind. First, we try to retrace what is meant, to think the philosopher's thoughts with him, to represent the whole by means of the intellectual operations which he himself presents. We practice his methods of construction, of dialectic, of penetrant probing, of analogizing given phenomena, etc. In this way we learn, and attain order.

But then, again, we do not merely read texts, for we are affected, awakened, liberated, are attracted and repelled. Thereby we arrive at the movement that listens and asks. Now genuine intercourse begins.

A space of metaphysical substance has opened up. We see visions in concepts and feel strangely at peace. We fulfill ourselves with ciphers of great intuitions in which Being imparts itself to us within the consciousness of the great thinkers. Through creative philosophers, the capacity for original thought that is proper to every human being is set in motion.

Philosophy is at one with the sort of humanity which sustains it. We become aware of the task of letting ourselves be addressed in our personal orientation within the realm of philosophy through dealing with the texts, and thereby criticizing the personality of the thinker. Greatness itself is questioned and then confirmed in an appropriate manner that is different from what had been presupposed. . . .

We do not permit ourselves to linger with those whom we prefer. Justice and the desire to know demand that we look around the entire space of possibilities. We observe such possibilities and approach them with sympathy or antipathy, though not as our own cause. In this way we are informed of the heterogeneity of what appears as philosophy. With a sense of philosophy we can have the will of arriving, through experience, where everything, even the mutually inimical, meets—providing it is not vacuous—within a circle of possible communication. But if we do all this in the sense of taking literary delight in variety, then we slip into curiosity about many things, into the distraction of an aesthetic playfulness devoid of obligation.

There is something within us that is ready to respond when the phenomenon of greatness, in whatever form, comes to meet us. Only as possible Existenz do we hear what speaks to us from the Existenz of the philosopher who
imparts his thoughts to us. . . . In this contact all intercourse attains its ultimate meaning. It is the philosopher himself whom we must hear if we are to
perceive his greatness; if we, as judges, want to grasp his truth. Such hearing
occurs through the cogitative work of understanding, individually undertaken.
How it takes place is, methodologically, simply inaccessible; it is, rather, the
sense-giving factor within the employment of any method.

IV.

Philosophy in its Everyday Mode

Selection 31

EDITORS:

In the Appendix to *Way to Wisdom* Jaspers says, "If it is true that philosophy concerns man as man, it must lie within our power to make it generally intelligible. . . . It has been my intention to give an intimation of those elements of philosophy which are the concern of every man." *Way to Wisdom* is a series of radio lectures, the first such series for a general public by any philosopher. The following selection is taken from a book containing the text of a series of television lectures. It shows that Jaspers was not only concerned to present the complexities of philosophy in an everyday idiom, but to identify the continuity between the concerns of the philosopher and those of the everyday man.

The selection is taken from *Philosophy is for Everyman,* translated by R. F. C. Hull and Grete Wels, pp. 119–25. Emendations have been provided by the editors. In the original the passage is found in *Kleine Schule des philosophischen Denkens*, pp. 168–175.

TEXT:

Does philosophy exist for man as man, or for an elite, secluded among themselves? Only a few, Plato taught, are capable of it, and this only after long schooling. There are two lives on earth, said Plotinus, one for the wise, one for the masses. Spinoza, too, expected philosophy only of rare souls. Kant alone thought that the path he struck could become the broad highway: Philosophy is there for all; it would be bad if it were otherwise; philosophers are, as it were, only the creators and keepers of the archives, and everything in them has to be most carefully laid down.

As against Plato and Plotinus and almost the whole tradition we follow Kant. This is a philosophical decision in itself, of the greatest import for the inner disposition of all who philosophize. It is a slap in the face of reality. It says: As it has been till now, so it is today. But it ought not and must not remain so. The demand of man as man, often hidden and obscured, brushed aside and neglected, shall be heard. The decision rests with every individual.

Are we, perhaps, making a virtue of the necessity that there is an absence of any philosophy of genius in our time? No, the experience of our own ordinariness, of man as he is, who yet can understand the great ones of the past, make them his own, approach them reverentially but without deifying them—this experience gives us courage: What is possible for us is possible for nearly all, if so they wish.

There is one great exception in history. The Church Fathers, conscious of the task of preaching salvation and the duty of love, addressed themselves to everybody. The fact that the Greek philosophers addressed themselves only to the elect was, for them, an argument against the truth of that philosophy. The policy of the Church became: No one who wants to believe is excluded. What is unfolded in fullest clarity in the sublime thoughts of the elect is contained in the simplest belief.

But this solicitude for the masses is ambivalent: it wants at the same time to rule them and, in the interests of ruling, tolerates untruth and superstition and engages in politics. So this great historical example can be no exemplar for us.

The other enemy of independent philosophizing and hence of man's freedom is supposedly democratic thinking. It is right to say: What is unsuitable for the masses must in the end disappear. What arouses no response was without actuality to begin with. But it is wrong to say: We know what this actuality is. What is now will always be. What does not work now will never work. Man does not change. —On the contrary: What is isolated now can spread. What arouses no response can still find it. But above all: What works in the smallest circles can become the supreme actuality of an epoch and prove itself such in the sequel. What has not yet reached the masses can permeate them in the future.

The way to the masses, amid the hubbub of publicity, is unavoidable for the freedom of truth. The alternative is rule over the masses, censorship, standardized education. Human beings become raw material for despots.

In our uncertainty only one thing remains: To believe in the possibility of man's freedom and, so believing, stand related to transcendence, without which that belief in its seriousness cannot prevail.

Yet it is right to say: In the world, philosophy becomes conscious of its impotence. It arouses little response, it is no world-shaping force, no factor in history. So it has seemed till now.

But it is by no means impotent in what it can become for the single individual. In this respect it is perhaps the greatest single force by which man finds his way to freedom. It alone makes inner independence possible.

I gain this independence precisely when and where I am completely dependent, that is, when I know that I have been given to myself—in my freedom, in my love, in my reason. None of them is given into my power, I cannot produce them. But whatever I produce will be created out of them.

If I arrive at the place where I am given to myself, I gain a distance from all things and from myself. As from a standpoint outside myself, which in fact I can never gain, I look upon what happens and what I myself do. It is as though I immerse myself in historical actuality only from there.

From there comes the light that makes my inner freedom grow. I become independent in the degree to which I see things in that light.

This independence is a stillness, without violence, without defiance. It is the less presumptuous the more certain it becomes of itself. It proves itself by standing firm in obscurity.

In independence my freedom does not remain empty. To limit oneself to oneself would not be independence. Independence calls for commitment in the world. It takes a hand. It follows the summons of opportunity and chance. It does not fail the demands of the day. When fate seems to beckon, it dares to become involved in perilous situations in the hope of mastering them.

But always it submits to the criteria it cannot betray because they come from the place of its origin. Betrayal would be self-annihilation.

The independence of the philosopher is falsified when he takes pride in it. In the authentic human being, the consciousness of his independence is always concomitant with the awareness of his impotence; the rapture of creativity is always accompanied by the resigned acceptance of failure, hope by a glimpse of the end. Philosophizing makes us fully aware of the various forms of our dependence, but in such a way that, instead of remaining crushed by our impotence, we find, from the vantage point of our independence, the road to recovery.

Here are two examples of the way this happens in our thinking:

a) The quantitative has predominance over the qualitative. The universe, in which the earth with all its inhabitants is less than a speck of dust, has preeminence over it. In the hierarchy matter, life, psyche, spirit, each preceding stage has this kind of predominance over the succeeding one. Finally the masses have predominance. Compared with them the individual is as nothing. What alone counts is the universe, matter, the masses, the quantitatively predominant.

But we reverse the scale of values: The most precious thing in the universe is man; in the hierarchy of realities, spirit; in the masses, the individual come to himself; in the products of nature, the work of art created by man. To judge otherwise is to succumb to the influence of the quantitative, renouncing the meaning of being human.

b) The totality of history, which nobody can know, which does not even need to be thought of as totality, overwhelms us. The individual feels defenseless. Everything that he is, is determined by this totality. He must submit.

But what happens to humanity happens because of the infinitesimal power of billions of individuals. Each of them bears a co-responsibility by what he does and how he lives. Though history seems meaningless, there is nevertheless reason in it. That reason depends on us.

But then: The little world around us is our immediate actuality. To meet its demands is our first task. If we despair of the future because we cannot guide events, or if we expend ourselves in empty demonstrations as though we were keeping the whole thing in motion, we miss the immediate actuality. We prove ourselves in the actuality of this world around us. It is the medium through which we do our share of work on the whole.

Our epoch has made us conscious of our impotence in a new way. We all know that democracy in its reality is corrupt, but it remains the only possible way to freedom. It is even more questioned among nations where it is not historically indigenous.

Satisfaction with the economic miracle is the opium of the free world. The others long for this miracle, but are not ready to meet its conditions, and blame the free world for their own misfortune.

In the West, economics has priority over politics. Consequently, the West is digging its own grave. Its political freedom constantly diminishes. Often it is no longer understood. Consciousness of freedom and the courage to make sacrifices are on the way out.

All over the world we see the trend to military dictatorship and totalitarian rule, because freedom has failed. Nations become the prey of men of violence.

The population explosion, if it continues, must lead to a catastrophe in which millions will be annihilated.

The colored races (more than two-thirds of humanity) are turning against the white man with increasing irritability and savagery.

The atomic bomb looms over all. For a while yet it will hold off the great war which, one knows not when, will let loose its total destruction if men remain as they are today.

Until now, when states, peoples, and cultures perished, others appeared on the scene. Humanity was permanent. The question today is whether humanity will annihilate itself.

We can enjoy the happiness of existence in the interim granted to us. But it is a last respite. Either we avert the deadly peril or prepare for the catastrophe.

The calm, prevailing air in the West, based on the assumption that this pleasurable existence will continue indefinitely, seems outrageous. The consequences of deluding ourselves before 1914 and ever afterwards have shown where this moral and political irresponsibility leads.

Today we stand poised on the razor's edge. We have to choose: to plunge into the abyss of the lostness of man and his world and the consequent extinction of all earthly life, or the leap to the authentic man and his boundless opportunities through self-transformation.

What rôle does philosophy play in this?

At least it teaches us not to let ourselves be deceived. It will not permit any fact or possibility to be brushed aside. It teaches us to look probable disaster in the face. It disturbs the tranquility of the world. But it also prevents us from taking the thoughtless attitude that disaster is inescapable. For what will be still depends on us.

If it were vigorous in its thinking, if it were made compelling in its arguments and trustworthy by the integrity of its spokesmen, philosophy could become a factor of salvation. It alone can change our way of thinking.

And in the face of possible and total shipwreck, philosophy would still preserve the dignity of man even in his perishing. In the companionship of sharers in the same fate that is grounded in truth man faces what may come.

For in perishing there is not Nothingness. The ultimate is man, preserving his love even the face of shipwreck and an incomprehensible trust in the ground of things.

To speak in ciphers: The origin from which emerged the universe, the earth, life, man, and history harbors potentialities inaccessible to us. In experiencing shipwreck open-eyed, we can assure ourselves of them.

It was an experiment, to be followed by other experiments without end. But love and truth, when present for a while in such an experiment, testify that it was more than that. A word of eternity was spoken.

No realizable thought, no knowledge, no tangible embodiment, no cipher can enter into eternity. But thought, transcending all ciphers, enters into the silence filled with the unfathomable ground.

Part Four

WHAT IS TRUTH?

EDITORS' INTRODUCTION TO PART IV:

Jaspers's treatment of the question of truth is presented here in two subparts. The selections of Subpart i, "Truth for Man in Time," address the nature of truth on the dual basis of the existential redirection and the periechontologic orientation of philosophy. The special problem of the truth of ultimate questions in metaphysics, religion, mythology, and art is the subject of Subpart ii, which is entitled "Metaphysical Truth: The Reading of Ciphers."

I.

Truth For Man in Time

EDITORS' INTRODUCTION TO SUBPART I:
Jaspers's broadly elaborated theory of truth is his response to the demands of the philosophical situation, specifically, the break-up of unity among human beings as to what animates them, what they value, what aims they pursue and carry out. For Jaspers, this dissolution of unity required that philosophical thinking be given a new direction; thus his focus on human existential actuality. Accordingly, the realization of truth is now seen as tied to Existenz in its singularity, i.e., to man's historicity, since only in lived time is man responsible for what he realizes, and only in his "absolute consciousness" is his risk of faith original. Potentially, then, what is true is to be found in each human being. But the unity of truth does not thereby become an unimportant question.

Jaspers thought that prevalent theories of truth do not address the need for grounding the multiplicity of human realizations in an open-ended unity; yet without such grounding all possibility for communication would be missing. With his theory of truth Jaspers hoped to offer an "ingenuous synthesis" which would be able "to admit all that is true in any sense whatever."

But how can the truth for man bounded by time have unity? For Jaspers the only unity of truth for Existenz is transcendent and not achieved in time. Hence the point of departure for the question of the unity of truth is: Truth in its wholeness is never present in time, and in time there is no one way of "being true."

Though our truths are at most particular truths, for Jaspers we are always within the "encompassing" truth which we can illumine with finite shafts of light. To do this is his program for dealing with the question of truth in its unity.

Three possible ways of illuminating truth are explored by Jaspers. The first is: Every human realization of truth has untruth as its inevitable fellow traveler. The second focuses on the fragmentation of truth for man. Truth in its unity is, as such, transcendent. Within time truth is fragmented. Thus truth in its unity manifests itself in time by breaking through the confines of time and by presenting itself in certain configurations which can be characterized by philosophy. The existentially effective ways in which truth may become complete for man is the focus of the third illumination. Rather than seeing truth in time as completely realized, it becomes our task through the activity of communicative reason.

In each of these illuminations, then, truth in its wholeness is seen as exceeding man's capacity, but thereby it is preserved as encompassing and as transcendent. At the same stroke, however, man is assigned the task of actualizing truth through the modes of the Encompassing that constitutes man, most fundamentally through communicative reason which is nothing less than the actualization of his freedom. The unity and completeness of truth which can have only a transcendent meaning thus become an "infinite" task for man, the only challenge that can fully actualize all man's resources.

Jaspers elaborated his theory of truth in *Von der Wahrheit*, pp. 453–1054. As this work has not been translated, the English reader heretofore had access to his theory only in two summary forms: *Reason and Existenz*, Chapter III; and *Philosophy of Existence*, Chapter II. The following subpart is structured as follows: The existential background to the reopened question of truth consists of two Selections, 32 and 33, from *Philosophy*. This is followed by the summary of the theory found in *Philosophy of Existence*, Selection 34. Discussions of some aspects of the theory are excerpted from *Von der Wahrheit* in Selections 35 to 42; these appear here in English for the first time. An elaboration of "Truth and Communication," excerpted from *Reason and Existenz*, is the final Selection, 43.

BACKGROUND

EDITORS:
Truths which are cognitively evident are intersubjectively valid and can claim universal assent. Where agreement cannot be justified by the appeal to such evidence, truth has no other than existential validity. Such truth is certain precisely to the extent that a person exists by his or her commitment and testimony to it. It is always someone's truth, and consequently there may be as many truths as there are Existenzen. In Selection 32, Jaspers develops the existential basis of the multiplicity of the truths by which human beings live. Is there then no truth in its unity? For Jaspers the matter of the unity of truth ends in paradox if pursued in its purely formal, theoretical mode. However, he sees an existential concern for unity, and it is this concern which provides the exigency for a renewed pursuit of the question of the unity of truth for man. This is developed in Selection 33.

Selection 32

BACKGROUND (1):
TRUTH IN RESPECT OF EACH OTHER

EDITORS:
The original of this selection appears in *Philosophie*, Vol. II, pp. 416–19. The
translation is provided by the editors. For E. B. Ashton's translation, see *Philosophy*, Vol. II, pp. 361–363.

TEXT:

Truth as One and as Many

Existenz differentiates between truths—the truth I know to be cogent, the
truth in which I participate (idea), the truth which I myself am; this makes
possible the actualization of Existenz. Only that truth is universally valid for
all which, being valid for consciousness-as-such, is a cogent truth based on
rationality and empirical findings. However, where the truth of the idea and
of the existing being-I expresses itself objectively and directly, I see, as I observe, that men have taken what is dissimilar and opposite to be true for them.
But in this way I do not comprehend any of these truths in their origin because
in their objective form, in the image of believed truths, it is merely their
appearance which is present for me as consciousness-as-such; and this consciousness orients itself in the world. Truths contradict each other; but the
person who participates in them is not the one who knows them all but the
one who himself is identical with one of them. *My* truth, which I am absolutely
as freedom insofar as I am Existenz, impinges upon another truth of Existenz;
through and with this other truth Existenz becomes itself. It is not unique and
alone but unique and irreplaceable in its relation to other truths.

I cannot step outside of this truth; I cannot observe it and cannot know it. If
I were to step out of it I would plunge into the void. To be sure, the objectivizing self-understanding that is the particular appearance of truth can be turned
into infinite reflection. Yet I can take truth, in its appearance, to be absolute in
the historic moment even if I relativize it again. However, I am able to do this
only out of the truth of the Existenz which, in its temporality, is always becoming; I do not do it on an intellectual level and without origin. Only in the
service of Existenz can the relativizing understanding have content through
the destruction of all objectivity; for existential thought, in overcoming, simultaneously brings forth new objectivity. As Existenz I am at home nowhere
else (unless it be in the transcendence which reveals itself to this Existenz); I

am at home in the existential identity with myself. This identity stands behind all apparent dissolution but does not succumb to it because only its particular appearances—not it itself—is accessible to questions. Only in communication do I see the truth of other Existenzen; as I turn away from the deceptive mirrors of those who merely acknowledge me or reject me I live in growing certainty only in this contiguity of truth with truth.

Objective truth is present for some standpoint either as the one truth for all or as a particular truth, which in each instance is based on some reason. But to existential truth the following applies: Because I cannot step outside of the truth that is the possibility of my Existenz in order to observe it, I cannot say "there are several truths"; for all multiplicity is valid only for the external appearance of visible configurations, of thoughts that can be expressed, and of dogmas. The truth of Existenz, however, is not manifold since it cannot be seen as manifold from the outside and cannot be established as permanent. Neither can I state "I am myself the one and only truth"; for I am not without the others to whom I stand in relation. The unconditionality of my Existenz lacks the validity of the universal; it is never an unconditionality that can be transferred in identical form.

The Choice of Truth

Truth is either cogent and hence is not chosen, or the truth becomes unconditional *through* choice.

If there were many unconditional truths so that I could confront them and choose one for myself, then the meaningfulness of truth would be suspended. Then I would be able to know truths which, in their unconditionality, exclude one another, as many truths. This is impossible. No matter whether I know truth, participate in it, or am this truth: in every case there can be only one truth which excludes untruth as an Other.

The proposition: what world-view a person chooses indicates what kind of a person he is, is countered by the question: what are the alternatives available to him? All alternatives of the objective sort obtain within the determinateness of something specific within a situation. But they are not valid for a number of world-views between which one could choose because when the whole is at stake, nothing determinate and specific can make the difference. To assign to all possibilities of thought a place within the idea of a totality is meaningful for orientation about thought transmitted through language. But taking an overview of world-views as cogitative configurations in effect cancels them as world-view and renders him who comprehends them in their cogitative nature capable of choice in the radically other sense: the choice from which I proceed as the primal source of truth is the choice of Existenz in which it *chooses itself.* Instead of my choosing one truth out of the multiplicity of

234 WHAT IS TRUTH?

types of truth offered to me, I arrive at my truth by way of a choice based on
freedom. Through it Existenz illuminates itself in the world-view that is true
for it *alone*.

Self-*understanding* commences with individual concrete acts of choosing
which, in an indeterminable sequence, construct our life. One can then ask:
why did I choose in this way? What are the meaning and the consequences of
this choice? What unconscious presuppositions or principles was it founded
on? In replying to such questions there develop rationally consequential coherences that seem to lead to fundamentally ultimate possibilities which,
functioning as presuppositions of rationally formulated world-views, present
themselves for choice. However, this method of searching for what is inferen-
tial, and for ultimate presuppositions which, though not themselves derivative, are not meant to be object-less, always leads to a relative conclusion; for I
am not satisfied and remain skeptical when it is maintained that the ultimate
alternatives of world-views are necessary.

The path of rational self-understanding out of ultimate principles—
starting with concrete acts of choosing—retains, on the contrary, Existenz as
ground and indissoluble end. This Existenz persists as the possibility which
supercedes all principles that function for cognition as supposedly ultimate
and mutually exclusive. On the path of an interpreting that is merely theoretical and thus does not aim at the choice of Existenz whereby it chooses itself,
there Existenz understands itself only relatively in its particular objectifications and not in the unconditionality of its own origin.

The choice of the truth of Existenz understands itself, after the infinite
reflection of its appearance, to be in the leap toward the truly *original* which
knows itself, at the same time, as vis-à-vis other origins.

Selection 33

BACKGROUND (2): THE RICHNESS OF DIVERSITY AND THE ONE

EDITORS:
The following selection is a translation by the editors of *Philosophie*, Vol. III,
pp. 116–118 and 120–23. E. B. Ashton's translation appears in *Philosophy*,
Vol. III, pp. 102–04, and 106–09.

TEXT:
The meaning of the One is manifold. In logic, it is the unity as thinkability. In

the world, it is the unity of what is actual in nature as well as in history. For Existenz, it is the One in which it has its being because the One is its all.

In metaphysics we search for the One, be it by transcending beyond unity in its thinkability, be it in taking hold of the unity in the world, be it in transcending *out* of the unity insofar as it is, as the existentially One, the unconditionality of historic self-being. The paths intersect: they may converge for a joint perspective; for the time being they remain apart.

The Existential Origin of the One

In the illumination of Existenz the unconditionality of action becomes palpable through the identity of self-being with the One which it grasps in existence. Only where there is one thing for me that matters am I truly myself. As, to a self consciousness, the formal unity of the object is the condition for its being thinkable so the substantial One is the appearance of unconditionality for a self-being. Whereas, however, thinkability is proper to the unitary coherence of the one universally valid truth, the existential One is the truth that has other truths beside it, truths which it is not. There is no knowable whole in which all would be sheltered; there is, instead, the boundless possible communication of these existing truths in a Being which never becomes whole and which, from the outside, is not even thinkable.

Existential unity is, first of all, limitation as historic determinacy in one's self-identification which, through its exclusiveness, manifests the depth of Being. To be sure, in existence, Existenz may want the One as well as the other. It vacillates and experiments. It founders and attempts anew. But all this is only right in existence as long as I am not in it myself but only make use of it. Where I am myself, I am myself only in the identity with what—seen from the outside—is a restricted actuality. I am only where, out of possible Existenz, I become historic, where I immerse myself in existence. A lapse leads to the dispersion of multiplicity. If everything could also be different I am not I myself. If I want everything I want nothing; if I experience everything I am dissipated in the infinite without reaching Being.

Secondly, unity is the whole as *idea.* Whatever stands in relation to the ideas as totalities has its unity in the relative whole of this idea; without it, it would be the mere manifold of the accidental. The lapse from unity therefore leads to particularity and its absolutization, hence to division into arbitrary battling opposites without path or goal.

Existential unity which prevents dispersion, and the unity of idea which, through its wholeness, prevents endless multiplicity, do not stand in a relationship of coincidence but of tension. Ideas are borne by Existenzen but the unity of Existenz breaks through an idea that has become rigid or exhausted. Ideas, conceived as the cosmos of the spirit, give us an image of the spiritual world; before their apparent totality the Existenzen disappear without which this world would have no actuality. I myself am not the image of the spiritual world once it has turned into the free flight of ideal entities. As possibility it is indeed more, as actuality, however, it is less than I.

Unity is, thirdly, the unity of existential origin as decision through choice. The lapse here lies in the direction of what remains undecided and of indecisiveness. I cannot reach either my being or the consciousness of my self by my staggering toward them and protecting only my existence, by having decisions made about me rather than being myself a factor in those decisions.

Thus the unity of the primal source signifies historic determinacy, ideal totality, decisiveness. The lapse points toward dispersion, isolating absolutization, indecisiveness.

If existence—with which, as historic determinacy and full of ideas, I became decisively identical—becomes absolute for me, it does not become absolute *as* existence. At the very instant of becoming existential we encounter its transcendence in historicity. As existence, the One becomes the way to transcendence, the secrecy of the One becomes the certainty of standing in relation to it. For the One cannot be substantiated nor can it be expressed; all statements apply only to an external unity; they are objectifications within finitude. As mere objectivity a statement can possess numerical unity without the One, i.e., as the fixation of a finitude onto which I fasten by force without transcendence. The One is the beating heart in the finitude of existence; it is the ray of the unknown one light. Each person has only his own ray of light which is illuminated for him in communication. Even if, speaking metaphorically, all the rays proceed from the one divinity, the one God still does not become the objective transcendence for all. In each instance he is merely the pulsation of the One for the Existenz that transcends in the One.

Only he who is never touched by the One, who considers the positivity of the manifold of existence to be absolute, who believes that it is possible to find a substitute for everything and hence forgets about death—only he would be able to say: There is no purpose in attaching, in life, one's heart too much to one human being or to one cause; instead one should distribute one's love among many people and many things and thus give oneself a broad basis. For, if the loss of one individual were right away to call the whole in question, then the death and destruction of the others would hit one's own existence too hard, would indeed deal it a destructive blow. We can prevent this by parcelling out our love and not loving any individual thing too much.

This way of thinking which, measuring everything against the criterion of its utility for existence, remains immanent, stands in the most decisive contrast to the experience of transcendence in the One which posits Existenz as existence reaching beyond itself as identical with itself.

Transcending to the One

As we look back at the configurations of unity accessible to us, we see that there was, in each of them, a possible relation to transcendence. Our metaphysical grasp of the One itself is rooted in the existential One. Our relation to transcendence has its existence in the realm of the One of world and of history. The logical configurations of the One are means of expression which possess their rational meaning even without transcendence.

The One is not one world, one truth for all, is not the unity of what binds all men to each other, not the one spirit in which we understand each other. The validity of the One in logic and in orientation within the world, and further the transcending within these unities, receives its metaphysical meaning only from the One of Existenz.

We ask ourselves: Why does the deity as the One have such fascination for men, and why is the One a matter of course such that it could not be different? Why would it be like an infringement and a lostness if transcendence, as divinity, would not be the One? It is because I find my authentic self-being in the One of transcendence and because this self-being vanishes only before the one transcendence and does not do so truly anywhere else.

If I, being possible Existenz in existence, have revealed to me the One with which I become identical and thus come to myself, then, out of its appearance, I come upon the unthinkable One of the one God. All unities proclaim their relativity; but the existential One in its unconditionality remains the origin out of which we see God as the one ground of the historicity of all Existenz. I can believe the one God to the extent to which I grasp unconditionally the One in my life. It is the condition of transcending to the one divinity that I transcend, as Existenz, to the One in the historic actuality of my life. And conversely: that I live, after this last leap, in the certainty of the one God, is the source out of which I also accept the One in my world unconditionally. For me there is only so much transcendence as there is the One in the continuity of my existence.

Thus the one God is, by means of the existential One, always *my* God. He is close to me only if he is exclusively One. He is not mine in the community of men. The closeness of the One is an aspect of my transcending; but the most certain presence is, objectively, merely a possibility, a reaching down to me; it is the only way in which he can be One for me. This proximity does not invalidate what approaches me out of the world as alien faith and other gods for others. But if I look at this world, then I find that the One is distant from me and totally inaccessible. When, in the One of Existenz, the one divinity becomes palpable, then it either enters into the untranslatable incommunicable proximity of the historicity of this moment, or it enters into the most abstract inaccessibility of distance. To be sure, it never becomes identical with me. Even in the closest proximity it keeps its absolute distance. And yet its proximity is like presentiality. The distance, on the other hand, is beyond the task, first to be carried out, of penetrating by transcending mundane existence in its unclosed state, its divisions, its multiplicity, its ungovernability. Only way beyond the aspects of the powers, whose configurations struggle against each other in mundane existence as transcendence, could the one God be found.

As the impulse toward wholeness in existence encounters the other, so does the impulse toward unity in transcendence encounter the divinity which does not show the same face to everyone. If I act against others, having mustered my strength by looking at the One, it is hubris to consider my God to be the only one. Truthful Existenz cannot lose sight of the distant God for the sake of the proximate God. Even in struggling against the other, Existenz wants to see that this other is also bound to God. God is my God as well as my enemy's. Tolerance becomes positive in the unbounded will to communication—and if this fails it is still there in the consciousness that the struggle is a fateful one: it must lead to a decision.

Proximate or distant, the one divinity simply defies cognition. It is absolute as the limit and then only as the One. If one takes the diverse configurations, the multifariousness of the cipher script to be the divinity, then one falls prey to arbitrariness; for the many gods somehow approve everything, no matter what I want. In my arbitrariness I go from One to the Other; but the one, broken up into the small change of the Many, is no longer unconditional. As I face the multiplicity of transcendence I still know that I bring it about myself. However the One as limit is the Being which in no way I myself am; rather, I stand in relation to it by relating to myself as genuine Being. If it were not different from me I would not stand in relation to transcendence but to myself, albeit without being myself. Solely by way of my being, which is the actuality of the One of Existenz and which is dependent on me, am I able to open up to the One that I am not myself.

In aesthetic multiplicity I lose the unity of unconditionality. Such multiplicity may, as in a beautiful picture, be objectively tamed into a palpable unity, yet I will find that there are other beautiful pictures also. As the One which, in Existenz, always becomes exclusive and is not objectively determinable for the understanding, so the one God is inaccessible as objectively one. In order to preserve the One and not betray it one must avoid precisely this objectification. For knowing and intuiting there is the richness of existence and of ciphers; but this richness remains façade and play if it does not become, in concrete presence, the historic configuration of the One.

I am certain of that which I experience and do: my factual community with people, my factual inner actions, i.e., my relationship to myself, those actions which are directed outward. I will never cognize what God is; but I can become certain of him through what I am.

The transcendence of the One is not universal transcendence for all, but neither does it remain the absolutely incommunicable transcendence of the isolated individual; rather it becomes that which is founded by the deepest— but not universal—communication. For Existenz it amounts to a banalization of transcendence if one declares the true divinity to be the one which is capable of universally uniting all men. The most penetrating communication is possible only in narrowly limited circles. Here transcendence reveals its depth in particular historic configurations. What binds all men together in our time is no longer the divinity but the concerns of existence and technology, or the intellectuality of the universally valid understanding, or a universally human, unbridled impulsiveness of the lowest order, or the forced utopias of a unity, or the negative unity of a ready tolerance toward the juxtaposition of those who have nothing in common and are essentially different from each other. To live in the utmost universality as if living in transcendence means losing the latter. For it is only by way of exclusion that the One becomes appearance within existence. Our visions of the one world and of a transcendence for all disappear before the actual power of Existenz in the limit situation of the struggle. Here Existenz first has to appropriate transcendence as its own; out of genuine communication it can then reach out into the historic breadth of possible union with all people.

Selection 34

TRUTH: SUMMARY OF THE THEORY—FIRST PART

EDITORS:
The following essay on truth presents some of the main features of Jasper's theory of truth. After identifying the many meanings of being-true, Jaspers shows that these many meanings can find order in a periechontological foundation. He thereby also reopens the question of the unity of truth. Two configurations are then discussed whereby truth in its transcendent unity can break into truth in its multiple and finite human realizations, namely, "authority" and "exception." (The concept of the exception is also discussed with reference to Kierkegaard and Nietzsche in selection 6.) The selection ends with the topic of communicative reason as man's ultimate way toward truth in its unity; this topic is more elaborately considered in selection 43.

The following is a slight emendation by the editors of Richard F. Grabau's translation, *Philosophy of Existence*, pp. 33–57. The original appears in *Existenzphilosophie*, pp. 26–50. Grabau's is one of the best translations of Jaspers into English, and he accompanies his translation with an excellent introduction to the little book from which this selection is excerpted. *Philosophy of Existence* is a title in the series *Works in Continental Philosophy*, General Editor, John R. Silber.

TEXT:
Truth—the word has an incomparable magic. It seems to promise what really matters to us. The violation of truth poisons everything gained by the violation.

Truth can cause pain, and can drive one to despair. But it is capable—merely in virtue of being truth, regardless of content—of giving deep satisfaction: there is truth after all.

Truth gives courage: if I have grasped it at any point, the urge grows to pursue it relentlessly.

Truth gives support: here *is* something indestructible, something linked to Being.

But what this truth might be that so powerfully attracts us—not particular determinate truths but truth itself—that is the question.

A. The Many Meanings of Truth

There is truth, we think, as if that were a matter of course. We hear and speak truths about things, events, and actualities that are questionable to us. We even are confident that truth will ultimately triumph in the world.

But here we stop short: Little can be seen of a reliable presence of truth. For example, common opinions are for the most part expressions of the need for some support: one would much rather hold to something firm in order to spare himself further thought than face the danger and trouble of incessantly thinking further. Moreover, most of what people say is imprecise, and in its apparent clarity is primarily the expression of hidden practical interests. In public affairs, there is so little reliance on truth among men that one cannot do without an attorney in order to make a truth prevail. The claim to truth is turned into a weapon even of falsehood. Whether truth will prevail seems to depend on favorable chance events, not on truth as such. And in the end, everything succumbs to the unexpected.

All such examples of the lack of truth in psychological and sociological situations need not affect truth itself if truth is self-subsistent and separable from its actualization. Yet even the existence of truth in itself can become doubtful. The experience of being unable to agree about truth—despite a relentless will to clarity and open readiness—especially where the content of this truth is so essential to us that everything seems to depend on it because it is the basis of our faith—can cause us to doubt truth in the familiar sense of something lasting. It could be that the truth that matters is by its very nature not amenable to univocal and unanimous statement.

The unquestioned truth that governs my life proves to be false for others. In our Western world we hear conflicting claims coming from essentially different sources, and the deafening noise that echoes through the centuries as they explode into mass phenomena.

In the face of this situation, one is inclined to accept the proposition that there is no truth. One does not allow truth to be self-sustaining; one derives it from something else as the condition on which alone truth is truth.

In consequence, thought has vacillated throughout its history: first the claim to absolute truth, then doubt about all truth, and along with both the sophistically arbitrary use of pseudo-truth.

The question of truth is one of the dizzying questions of philosophizing. As we think through this question, the magic gleam of truth is obscured.

Confronted by this confusion, we quickly imagine ourselves to have a secure foundation: We conceive unequivocal truth to lie in the *validity of statements* made on the ground of sensible givens and logical evidence. Despite all the skeptical subtleties, we nevertheless find the objects of the methodologically purified sciences. Through our understanding we discover cogent intelligibility and, corresponding to it, the in fact universal assent to its results on the part of every rational being who understands them. There is a realm of established correctness for consciousness-as-such, a narrow but vaguely limited realm of valid truth.

Our highly developed insight into the logical connections between the meanings of statements—a field of scientific investigation all the more intensive in proportion as it is more and more subjected to mathematical techniques (in logistics)—yet always finds that logical stringency stops when we come to the facts themselves. The truth lies in the *presuppositions* of this logical analysis; truth becomes essential only on the strength of their *content*.

This content is either empirical—evident as something perceivable, measurable, and so on—in which case it is logically something that we can only accept, or it lacks this compelling power to impress itself upon everybody, having instead grown from roots which are different in essence and are the sources of those absolute contents that sustain man's life—though not every life in the same way—and that are then also communicated in statements.

Although consciousness-as-such, this realm of the sciences, is also the realm where matters become clear for us because they can be stated, yet its compelling correctness is by no means ever in itself alone the absolute truth. Rather, truth emerges from *all* modes of the Encompassing.

Truth that is vitally important to us begins precisely where the cogency of consciousness-as-such ends. We encounter the limit where our existence and another's existence do not acknowledge a truth as being one and the same even though they are aiming at truth that is one and universally valid. At this limit we either come into conflict, where force and cunning decide matters, or else sources of faith are imparted which are related to each other yet can never become one and identical.

At these boundaries another truth speaks. A specific meaning of truth emerges from every mode of the Encompassing that we are, not only from consciousness-as-such, which is the locus of cogent insight, but from existence, spirit, and Existenz as well.

We shall present this multiplicity of truth: of existence, of spirit, of Existenz.

As knowledge and volition at the level of existence, truth has neither universal validity nor compelling certainty.

Existence seeks to preserve and extend itself as this particular existence; whatever furthers existence (life), whatever is useful, is true; whatever harms, limits, paralyzes it, is false.

Existence wills its own happiness: Truth is the satisfaction of existence resulting from its creative interaction with its environment.

Existence, as consciousness or soul, manifests and expresses itself. Truth is the adequacy with which the inwardness of existence is manifested, and the adequacy of consciousness with respect to the unconscious.

In sum: existence grasps truth as the behavior best suited to its purposes, useful first for the preservation and enhancement of existence, second for lasting satisfaction, and third for the adequacy to the unconscious of expression and of consciousness.

This is the pragmatic concept of truth. Everything that is, is in that it can be perceived and used, is raw material, is means and ends without a final end. Truth does not lie in something permanent and already known, or in something knowable, or in something unconditioned; it lies in whatever arises here and now in the immediate situation, and in what results. Just as existence itself changes in accordance with differences in its make-up and in the course of changing time, so there is only changing, relative truth.—

As spirit, truth is again not universally valid for the evidence of the understanding.

Truth of the spirit exists by virtue of membership in a self-illuminating and self-contained whole. This whole does not become objectively knowable; it can be grasped only in the action of the membership which endows it with existence and knowability.

In its understanding of being, spirit follows the ideas of wholeness which stand as analogies before it, serving as impulses to move it, and as methodical

system bringing coherence to its thought. Truth is what produces wholeness.—

Although we, being consciousness-as-such, think in terms of cogent correctness; being existence, in terms of what promotes and what threatens; and
being spirit, in terms of what produces wholeness—none of this occurs in us
with the certainty of a natural event. Rather, most of the time we end up in a
bewildering hodgepodge. Only to the extent that we are truly ourselves do we
actually grasp each given meaning of truth resolutely, and with an awareness
of the limits of every meaning of truth. In other words: truth that comes from
any other source derives purity only from the truth of Existenz.

Existenz appears to itself as consciousness-as-such, existence and spirit;
and it can assume a position with respect to these modes. But it can never take
a position outside itself, cannot know itself and at the same time be what is
known.

What I myself am, therefore, always remains a question, and yet is the
certainty that sustains and fulfills everything else. What I authentically am
never becomes my possession but ever remains my possibility of Being. If I
knew it, I would no longer be it, since I become aware of myself in temporal
existence only as a task. The truth of Existenz can therefore rest in simple
unconditionality on itself, without wanting to know itself. In the most powerful Existenzen one feels this parsimony and resignation—that attains no image, no visible representation of its own nature.

This short presentation points up the plurality of meanings of truth. We
shall now compare these meanings, each of which, seen in this light, has its
appropriate source in a particular mode of the Encompassing.

1. The truth of *existence* is a function of the preservation and extension of
existence. It proves itself by its usefulness in practice.

The truth of *consciousness-as-such* has validity as compelling correctness.
It is by virtue of itself, and is not valid out of another for which it would be a
means. It proves itself by evidence.

The truth of *spirit* is conviction. It proves itself in actuality through existence and thought, to the extent to which it submits to the wholeness of ideas,
thereby confirming their truth.

Existenz experiences truth in faith. Where I am no longer carried by a
pragmatic truth which has proved effective in existence, by a demonstrable
certainty of the understanding or by a protective totality of spirit, there I have
come upon a truth in which I break through all worldly immanence. Only
from this experience of transcendence do I return to the world, now living
both in it and beyond it, and only now for the first time myself. The truth of
Existenz proves itself as authentic consciousness of actuality.

2. Each mode of truth is characterized by him who speaks in it at any time.

The mode of truth is given along with the encompassing [mode of Being] as that by which we stand in communication.

In *existence* a purposefully and limitlessly self-interested life speaks. It subjects everything to the condition that it must enhance its own existence. It feels sympathy and antipathy in this sense only, and enters into community only on the basis of this interest.

Here conversation is either conflict or expression of an identity of interests. It is not unlimited, but breaks off to suit its own purposes and uses cunning against the enemy and against the possible enemy in the friend. It is constantly concerned with the practical effects of what is said. It wants to persuade and suggest, to strengthen or weaken.

In *consciousness-as-such* an interchangeable point of mere thought speaks. It is thought-as-such, not as this existence or as the self-being of Existenz.

Conversation, appealing to a universal, proceeds by giving reasons. It seeks the form of correct validity and of cogency.

Spirit expresses itself in an ambiance of concrete self-completing wholeness to which belong both the speaker and he who understands.

Such conversation takes place—constantly tied to a sense of totality— through guidance by the idea, in the selection, emphasis and context of what is said.

In *Existenz*, the man who is himself present speaks. He speaks to another Existenz as one irreplaceable to another.

Their communication takes place in a loving struggle—not for power but for openness—in which all weapons are surrendered but all modes of the Encompassing appear.

3. In each mode of the Encompassing that we are, truth confronts untruth, and in each a specific dissatisfaction finally arises that presses on to another, deeper truth:

In *existence*, there is the exultation of fulfilling life and the pain of being lost. Arising *in opposition to both*, however, is the dissatisfaction with mere existence, the boredom of repetition, and the fright in the limit situation of foundering: All existence contains its own destruction. Happiness of existence cannot be concretely imagined or even thought as a non-contradictory possibility. There is no happiness in duration and permanence, no happiness which, when it becomes clear to itself, is still sufficient unto itself.

In *consciousness-as-such* there is the compelling power of cogent correctness, the inability to tolerate, and hence the repudiation of incorrectness. *Opposed to both* is the barrenness of correctness, because it is endless and in itself unessential.

In *spirit*, there is the deep satisfaction in the whole and the torment of continual incompleteness. Arising *in opposition to both* is dissatisfaction with harmony and the perplexity that results when totalities are broken.

In *Existenz* there is faith and despair. *Opposed to both* stands the desire for the peace of eternity, where despair is impossible and faith becomes vision, that is to say the perfect presence of actuality itself.

B. *The Question of the One Truth*

Thus far in our discussion of the various modes of the meaning of truth, the different modes simply stand side by side, and nowhere do we find truth itself.

But the modes of the meaning of truth are in no sense an unrelated aggregate. They are in conflict: They may do violence to each other. Each truth falls into untruth when, violating the coherence of its own meaning, it comes to be dependent on other truth and suffers distortion from it.

One example must suffice: The question of the extent to which the truth of consciousness-as-such—the compelling certainty in knowledge of all that can be experienced—is useful, that is, true, for existence. If knowledge of this universally valid truth always also had beneficial consequences in existence, there would be no division, and thus no possible conflict, between the truth of existence and the truth of universally valid knowledge. But, in fact, existence constantly offends against universally valid truth by veiling, displacing, and suppressing it. It is by no means clear whether doing this in the long run serves the interests of existence or brings about its ultimate destruction. In any case, complete acceptance and conveying of the truth of universally valid knowledge is, at first, almost always also a threat to one's own existence. The truth of cogent correctness becomes untruth in existence. To a self-isolating will-to-existence, truth can appear as a misfortune to be rejected. Conversely, practical interests become a source of untruth in that in the medium of consciousness-as-such they deceive me into thinking that things are the way I would like them to be.

From these conflicts we acquire a feeling for the uniqueness of each individual meaning of truth—and in each conflict we apprehend a specific source of possible falsehood. If we now try to overcome these conflicts and seek for truth itself, we never find it by giving precedence to one mode of the Encompassing as the authentic truth. We alternately incline toward the prejudices that absolutize one Encompassing. Thus we absolutize existence as if furthering life were the last word and could be taken as absolutely unconditional; or we absolutize consciousness-as-such, the understanding, as if correct knowledge could put us into possession of Being and were not merely a cone of light in the darkness, a perspective we chance upon within the encompassing actuality; or we absolutize spirit, as if an idea were actual and self-sufficient; or we absolutize Existenz, as if self-being could suffice unto itself, whereas, to the extent that it is itself, it comes from an other, and sees itself as directed toward the other. Truth can no longer remain truth in the isolation of a single one of its meanings.

The fact that all modes of the meaning of truth come together in the actuality of our being human, and that man thus exists out of all the sources of all modes, urges us on to the one truth in which no mode of the Encompassing is lost. And only clarity about the multiplicity of meanings of truth brings the question of the one truth to that point where breadth of view becomes possible, and an easy answer—in the presence of an intensified urgency of the One—becomes impossible.

If the one truth were present to us, it would have to permeate all modes of the Encompassing and join them all together in a present unity.

It is a fundamental condition of our actuality that, for us, this unity is not attained by means of a conceivable harmony of the whole, in which every mode of the encompassing would have its sufficient as well as limited place. Instead, we remain in motion, we see every fixed harmonious form of truth once again destroyed, and we must therefore always continue to seek this unity. Our knowledge would sometimes mislead us into secluding ourselves within the consciousness of what we at any given time systematically hold to be actual and true. But in the course of time new experiences and facts befall us. Our knowing consciousness, too, must change in unforeseeable ways. For—as Hegel said—truth is in league with actuality against consciousness.

The one truth would be accessible only in conjunction with its content—not as one kind of formal truth—and consequently in a form that binds all the modes of the Encompassing together.

We cannot, therefore, directly grasp the *one* truth in a known whole. Grasped directly, truth is expressed formally, perhaps as the manifestness of the other that comes to meet us, then further as the being that is what it can be only through its becoming manifest; that is, as a manifestation that is simultaneously the actualization of that being: self-being.

But this formally expressed truth becomes the truth for us only along with the content of the actuality of Being. And because of the nature of our temporal existence this content becomes accessible to us as one and whole only in historic form. Perhaps we come closest to this form when, ruthless toward the inherited shells of our understanding, we come face to face with configurations of the ultimate limits where the unity of all modes of the Encompassing are actualized.

It is precisely these phenomena that, measured against the validity and freedom of cogently valid rational knowledge, seem to us a threat to all truth: *exception* and *authority*. The exception, by its actuality, destroys truth as permanent and universally valid. And authority, by its actuality, gags every particular truth claiming absolute autonomy.

The illumination of the modes of the Encompassing and the experience of conflicts and relentless movement have demonstrated, at the limit, that the whole truth is sufficiently and actually present neither as universally knowable nor in a single form.

This fundamental situation within temporal existence makes possible the actuality of the exception which, as primal truth, is contraposed to universality with its tendency to become fixed. And this situation demands authority as encompassing truth in historic form to counteract the arbitrary multiplicity of opinion and will. Exception and authority must now be clarified.

C. Configurations of the Breakthrough of Truth: The Exception and Authority

The man who is an *exception* is an exception first to universal existence, whether this appears in the form of the ethos, institutions and laws of the land, or the health of the body, or any other normalcy. Secondly, he is an exception to the universally valid, cogently certain thinking of consciousness-as-such. Finally, he is an exception to spirit, in belonging to which I am as a member of a whole. To be an exception is an actual breaking-through any kind of universality.

The exception experiences his exceptional status, and in the end his exclusion, as a destiny whose meaning remains for him insolubly ambiguous:

The exception seeks the universal that he is not. He does not want to be an exception, but rather submits to the universal. He takes upon himself his status of being an exception in his attempt to actualize the universal, an attempt that now takes place not with natural élan but in self-abasement, and thus it founders. The exception understands himself as exception only through the universal. Because he is an exception his understanding, in his foundering, grasps the positive universal all the more energetically. Through love for what the one who thinks from the depth of his source cannot himself be, what is understood is rendered all the clearer and brighter; so clear and so bright that even one who is successful and richly endowed with respect to what is thusly understood, could never himself transmit it.

But in spite of his submission to the universal, being an exception is in itself also the task of being the way to a unique actualization; it is necessary for him to be such a way leading—counter to his will—against the universal. He can lose the world in the service of transcendence, and can virtually disappear in consequence of negative resolutions (without a profession, without a family, without foundation). In so doing he can be the truth without being a model, without pointing a way for others by his own being. The exception is like a lighthouse where the roads end, illuminating the universal from the situation of the non-universal.

The exception can communicate himself: He thereby always returns to the universal. If he were certain of an absolutely incommunicable truth, it would be a truth in which no one could share. Then the exception would be as if he did not exist at all. For his communicability is a condition of his existence for us.

If, in summing up, we now express what the exception is whom we find philosophically so important, he eludes us. Exceptionality is not a generic category that can be used to define a person. The word aims at a concept of a possibility that is a source of truth, pervading all the modes of the Encompassing and absolutely evading all definition. It is like an encompassing of everything encompassing, yet not absolute in itself, but rather approaching us in historic concreteness and at the same time repelling us even as it illuminates, sending us back to ourselves. Therefore, as an [integral] whole, it can be neither surveyed as an object, nor objectively distinguished, nor used as the starting point of a justification. We can perceive the exception by feeling the impact of its truth on our truthfulness; but at the same time we can fail to see it if we attempt to rely on it as on something known. Everything in the exception that becomes objectified is ambiguous both to us and to the exception itself.

Finally, if we ask who is an exception and who is not, the answer must be: The exception is not merely a rare occurrence at the limit—as in the most extreme and deeply stirring figures such as Socrates—but is ever-present to every possible Existenz. By its very nature, historicity comprises the condition of being an exception that has become inseparably one with the universal. It is characteristic of the truth of Existenz that, permeating and going beyond the configuration of all modes of universality, it is also always an exception.

The genuine exception, therefore, is not an exception arbitrarily. This would constitute merely defection. Rather, in his temporal existence he is inseparably bound to the truth of the Encompassing. What was at first addressed in extreme situations as the most alien, and therefore as exception, is we ourselves—is every one in so far as he is a historic actuality, and no one in so far as every true exception stands in relation to the universal which he illuminates. Truth is always apprehended in openness to the exception and with a view to it, but in such a way that he who apprehends does not seek to be an exception. He acquiesces in being an exception, submitting to the universal; he acquiesces in being universal, knowing himself to be unimportant in the face of the sacrifice made by the exception.

As we penetrate to the ground of the truth which comes toward us out of concrete actuality, we meet exception and authority. Exception calls everything into question; it is startling and fascinating. Authority is the fullness that carries me; it is protective and reassuring.

We shall describe *authority*:

Authority is the unity of truth that binds all modes of the encompassing into one and appears to us in historic form as universal and whole. More precisely: Authority is the historic union of the power of existence, compelling certainty, and idea, with the source of Existenz which in this union knows itself to be related to transcendence.

Authority is therefore that form of truth in which truth is neither exclusively universal knowledge, nor exclusively external command and demand, nor exclusively idea of a whole, but all of these at once. Thus, although authority indeed comes as an external demand and compulsion, at the same time it also speaks from within. Authority is a claim based on transcendence which is obeyed even by the person who at any given time gives commands based on it.

The authority expressed in such formulae, however, cannot exist in time in a single and universal form for everyone without becoming superficial, without degenerating into mere power in the world, becoming violent and destructive. Rather, all authority has historic form. Thus, the truth of authority can never be made sufficiently transparent, nor can its content be stabilized, scientifically, by rational generalization. Rather, it encompasses all that is knowable without destroying it.

The unconditioned character of authority thus consists in its being a historic unity of truth for the person living by it. On the foundation laid at the beginning, it embraces us as the historic past in the present, speaking in images and symbols, in institutions, laws and systems of thought—all this by historic assimilation of the unique present that is identical with myself.

But that calm of true authority which may seem to be present in these abstract representations does not exist. Because authority is historic, and hence temporal, it is in constant tension, and in motion due to that tension.

First, there is tension between the authority that desires eternal stabilization (which, if it could reach its goal, would rob truth of all life) and the authority that *breaks through* every fixed form to create itself anew (which, if it were to move without direction, would turn everything into chaos). Order is rooted in what has once broken through order; the destructive exception becomes source of new authority.

Secondly, there is tension within the individual person between *authority* and *freedom*. At the roots of his own being, the individual wants to rediscover as his own truth what comes to him as external authority. We shall describe this process of liberation *in* authority.

At first, authority taken on faith is the only source of genuine education affecting man's nature itself. In his finitude each individual begins anew. For his development he depends upon authority in order to appropriate the content that can be handed on by tradition. As he grows up within authority, the space opens up to him in which he everywhere encounters Being. If he grows up without authority, he will indeed come to possess information, he will master speaking and thinking, but he will remain at the mercy of the empty possibilities of the realm where Nothingness stares him in the face.

As the individual matures, his own origin becomes present to him in his own thinking and his own experience. The contents of authority come alive to the extent that he makes them his own. If this does not happen, they remain alien; they are countered by freedom, which admits only what can be transformed into self-being. Freedom, which came to be by seizing on authority, can then resist authority (in determinate appearances). Having come into his own by means of authority, the individual outgrows it. A limit concept becomes possible, of a mature and autonomous man who continually recollects, who forgets nothing, who draws his life from the deepest sources; a man capable nonetheless, with the widest vision, of acting with decisive assurance; one who, on the basis of the authority that produced him, is true to himself. During his development he needed support; he lived by reverence and obligation; where he could not yet decide on the basis of his own origin, he relied upon decisions others made for him. In the gradual process of his liberation, an inner source grew to clarity and resolute power until he heard the truth in himself with full assurance. Now that he was liberated he seized upon this truth for himself, even in opposition to the demands of external authority. For him freedom has become the necessity of the truth that he has seized himself; arbitrariness has been overcome. Authority is the transcendence he inwardly experienced and which speaks through his selfhood.

But this limit of the absolutely free and autonomous man can never be reached once and for all. Every individual fails at some time; he never becomes the whole man. Therefore, no matter what level of mature freedom he has reached, the honest individual cannot do without the tension between his freedom and authority; without it his way would seem uncertain and unstable to him. The contents of his own freedom clamor for confirmation by authority; or they clamor for resistance to authority; to prove themselves in that resistance becomes a sign of their possible truth, without which sign they would not be different from arbitrary and chance impulses. Authority either gives a confirming strength, or by resistance gives form and support, and prevents arbitrariness. The individual who can help himself is precisely the one who wants authority to exist in the world.

Even if many individuals were able to acquire genuine freedom in community, there would still remain the vast majority that on this road to freedom would only fall victim to chaos and to the power of its existence-impulses. Therefore authority remains necessary in the reality of the community that embraces all men, as the form of truth claiming to support all truth; or, if it is lost, authority re-constitutes itself, out of the resultant chaos, in a fateful form.

As we bring to mind such movements arising from the ever-present tension we are led back to the encompassing authority. Authority is the enigma-become-form of the unity of truth in historic actuality. The essence of true authority prevails where truth from all the modes of the Encompassing concurs with mundane power as well as with a supreme human excellence carrying those truths and excercising that power.

I am familiar with authority inasmuch as I have grown up in it. I can live by it, but never deduce or classify it. I can penetrate it in my historicity, but never grasp it from outside.

I cannot gain an overview of this authority. I do not confront it as a whole confronting an other. An authority that I only view from the outside and in which I have never lived I never perceive in its substance—I never catch sight of it as authority.

To what authority I owe my maturing into self-being, what authority I have seized upon and devoted myself to (though perhaps only to its remnants) is a matter of my transcendentally grounded destiny. But it is not possible to compare authorities consciously, to test them, and subsequently to choose which I think is true or best. By seeing authority as authority, I have already chosen it. Nor is it possible—on the strength of philosophical insight—to seek the true authority in the continuity stretching from the origin to the present, to will and constitute it as a goal.

Yet in philosophizing I can explain the decline of authority through its failures. Authority becomes untrue when connections are sundered; when individual modes of truth—whether existence, cogency, or spirit—become autonomous and arrogate authority unto themselves; when it becomes a mere power in existence without the vitality of all the sources of truth; when it claims validity merely by virtue of the position of single individuals who have no power in the world, who do not make the sacrifices and do not take the risks needed to win and to maintain authority; when I relinquish the freedom of selfhood and on the strength of a supposed insight "freely surrender my freedom"; when I act in thoughtless obedience instead of yielding to the depths of authority.

In their historic actuality, *exception* and *authority* are the unfathomably Encompassing. What they reveal seems absurd and reprehensible to the mere understanding: The one truth and the one being-human do not exist; truth, for men, exists in time and is therefore historic, is therefore a task that is continually threatened.

Wherever they occur, truth based on authority and truth uttered by the exception are the most immediate and overwhelming truths—and when they are absent, men miss them most deeply and yearn for them with their whole being. Only where men conceal what is original and substantial by means of a spurious clarity of the merely correct truth of the understanding does this encompassing actuality of truth disappear. But it is only in this actuality that I know myself as Existenz.

Exception and authority lead to the ground of truth that no longer belongs to only one mode of the Encompassing but, penetrating through all of them and appearing to itself in all, may constitute a unity. In this unity, the conflicts arising from the struggle among the modes of the Encompassing seem momentarily to be resolved—not violently by a single Encompassing gaining preeminence, but through transcendence, which seems to speak as the One in all the modes of the Encompassing. This is not a harmony of the modes of the Encompassing, but a momentary fusion through the One that still in fact permits tension to persist and provides room for new break-throughs.

Though the most extreme opposites, exception and authority belong together as pointers to the ground of truth. Let us characterize the common element in their polarity once more:

1. They are grounded in transcendence. Where they appear, they are certain of transcendence. Without a relation to transcendence there is no existential exception and no genuine authority.

2. Both are incomplete. They are in motion, like in a constant self-sublation in which each, in its own moment, emerges from the tension as the one truth.

3. Both are historic, each is specific, there is not surrogate for either. The original truth they contain thus cannot be imitated or repeated. But encompassing and enclosing all that is historic, they are in their historic concentration open in all directions.

4. Both contain truth that eludes formation into an object to be grasped and known. If they are objectively construed, as a principle of rational deduction, exception and authority are constricted, robbed of their life and truth. I immediately lose them if I make them into objects of my purposeful planning and action. The words "exception" and "authority" seem to denote unambiguous phenomena. But the meaning of these words refers to a transcending in which the ground of truth becomes present as the union of all Encompassing. Neither poetry nor philosophy master this truth. Poetry touches the limit when what has taken shape in it is, as such, not the ultimate inwardness which is its real concern. Philosophy touches the limit where thought is never the being of truth itself which is the aim of all philosophizing.

When one has entrusted himself to rationally knowable truth in the form of concrete science—when one has further brought to mind the meaning of truth based on the modes of the Encompassing which he has already realized—and when one finally has come to see the configuration of truth in the exception and in authority, one is taking steps on the way back to actuality.

But philosophically one does not reach the ultimate either through being deeply stirred by the exception or through the tranquility gained in authority.

To live unquestioningly by authority is denied to anyone once philosophizing has become an actuality for him. It is one thing to live in authority, and quite another to conceive it and to think one's way to it. If I live in authority, truth lies in plain simplicity; if I conceive it, however, it is infinitely complex: If one tries to give rationally adequate expression to the historic actuality of authority, no rational analysis does it justice. Yet, as one matures in philosophizing, his thinking is inseparably bound to life within authority.

This philosophizing cannot deduce authority. *That* I believe this authority is an origin within the totality of the Encompassing; *whether* I should believe it, that can never be established. The illumination of authority can not as such serve as the justification for a concrete authority in its historic determinacy.

Philosophic thought *does not fall silent even in the face of exception and authority.* To be sure, the paradoxical situation, i.e., that authority requires justification, does not arise since every such justification would invalidate authority *qua* authority by the very act of justifying. But philosophic thought is not only able to criticize failures that turn into untruths but is likely to bring what emerges from the primal source into purest and clearest presentiality.

The road that does not stop even in the presence of exception and authority, but penetrates them—the road of philosophic truth—is called *Reason.* Instead of possessing truth with finality, in any of the configurations discussed so far, and instead of simply demonstrating truth in its content, we shall end up by speaking about reason.

What reason should be, to enact it and to know what it is about: This has always been and always will be the truly philosophic task.

D. Reason

The basic characteristic of *reason* is the *will to unity.* But everything turns on what this unity consists in. It is decisive for truth that the unity be grasped as actual, single, and only unity, and not as a unity that still has something outside it. For in every premature and partial grasp of unity, one either never reaches or has already lost truth.

It has become evident that truth is not one, because the exception breaks through it, and because authority actualizes it only in historic configuration. But as long as there is reason, the impulse to go beyond the multiplicity to truth in configurations of the One and universal remains undiminished, even in the face of the exception, and in spite of obedience to authority:

One cannot proceed by once again taking hold of truth in the world of consciousness-as-such, and by taking hold of its cogent intellectual knowledge adequately as correct cognition and correct behavior. But if I travel this road and confine myself to it I will lose the truth out of which I live.

Understanding is itself often called reason because reason cannot take a simple step without the understanding. But within the impulse of intellectual cognition—to the partial unities of the level on which cogent statements are valid—there is concealed the impulse of reason to that deeper unity to which the unity of the understanding is only a means. The thinking of the under-standing is in itself not yet by any means the thinking of reason.

Reason seeks unity, but not just any unity simply for the sake of unity. It seeks the One that contains all truth. This One is made present by reason as if from an unattainable distance; it is the force of attraction overcoming all division.

In our approach to this unity reason performs a unifying role in all situa-tions. Reason seeks to bring everything back out of the dispersion of mutual indifference to the dynamism of mutual relatedness. From the disintegration into elements alien to each other, reason seeks to have everything matter again to everything else. Every lack of relation is to be overcome. Nothing is to be lost.

The unifying power of reason is at work even now in the sciences as the drive to cross over every limit of any one science, as the seeking out of contra-dictions, relations, complementations, as the idea of the unity of all science.

Reason presses beyond this unity of scientific knowledge to an all-encompassing unity. It is reason that elucidates the modes of the encompass-ing, that then prevents their isolation, and presses on toward the union of all the modes of the encompassing.

Therefore, reason is concerned with what is alien by the standards of scien-tific thinking. It turns—expecting truth—toward the exception and authority. But reason does not stop even in them, as if it had reached its goal. Measured against the demands of the One, even exception and authority are provisional; they belong to temporal existence, and are forced into being by it. But reason cannot rest in anything provisional, no matter how great it may appear.

Reason is attracted even by what is most alien. It wants to bring into lucid being, to endow with language, and to keep from disappearing as if it were nothing, even that which, breaking the law of day, makes the passion for night a reality through self-destruction. Reason pushes on to wherever unity is frac-tured, in order within this breach still to grasp its truth and to prevent a meta-physical rupture, the disintegration of being itself, in this fragmentation. Reason, the source of order, accompanies everything that destroys order; it remains patient—incessant and infinite—in the face of everything alien, be-fore the irruption from without or the failure from within.

Reason is, therefore, the *total will to communication*. It wants to give heed to everything that can be expressed in language, to everything there is, in order to preserve it.

Reason seeks the One by way of honesty which, in contrast with fanaticism in the pursuit of truth, possesses an unlimited openness and availability for questioning; and by way of justice, which wants to let every originary thing count as itself, even while allowing it to founder on its limits.

ASPECTS OF THE THEORY (1): TRUTH AND UNTRUTH

EDITORS:
In selections 35, 36, and 37 the meaning of 'being true' is illuminated from the perspective of the circumstance that truth for man seems to be a criterion rather than an actuality. Measured against any such criterion, what man realizes in his directedness toward truth is not truth but untruth. The wholeness of truth in its encompassing transcendence is manifest, as it appears to man, as being less than truth. In one form or other, untruth is ultimately an indispensable mode of the very being of truth for man. It is in such light that Jaspers discusses the truth value of various phenomena, such as the use of fictions in science, of symbols in religion, and of compromises in politics. The phenomenon of shipwreck or the foundering of thought (discussed in selection 49) is, to Jaspers, a prime mode of exposing thought as being inadequate to the realization of transcendent truth, and thus as being dependent on the vehicle of untruth.

In selection 35, Jaspers traces the inevitability of untruth in man's pursuit of truth to man's finitude and to consciousness. Selection 36—with its reference to Benjamin Franklin's contribution to the U.S. Constitutional Convention, Philadelphia, 1787—shows how untruth can be the deliberate medium of truth for man. Selection 37 addresses the problems of distinguishing truth from the untruth to which it is tied.

All three selections appear in English translation for the first time.

Selection 35

THE SOURCE OF ALL UNTRUTH: FINITUDE AND CONSCIOUSNESS

EDITORS:
This selection is a translation, by the editors, of *Von der Wahrheit*, pp. 529–31.

TEXT:

Without consciousness there is neither thought nor action. Both take place in consciousness even though never through consciousness alone.

Whatever is consciousness for us is finite. We are also finite as existence and Existenz.

Hence the origin of the appearance of truth and falsity . . . can be grasped in the following formulations:

The Finitude of Man

We are dispersed, as individuals, in space and time: we did not create ourselves, we are bound to the conditions of life and live for a limited span.

As existence we are dependent because of our needs, are bound to nourishment, cooperation in our labors, community. We need the satisfaction of our drives by what comes to meet us or grows toward us.

As thinking beings we are dependent because the intentions of our thought rely on fulfillment through perception and experience, through something other than thought. Our discursive thinking is bound to detours, relies on givens.

As Existenzen we are dependent since we are in our freedom only as we are given to ourselves through transcendence.

The finitude of man is the source of untruth. But man can become aware of infinity. He becomes conscious of his finitude because the possibility of infinity is active in him; this is the source of authentic truth within him.

Consciousness

Consciousness brings us, on the one hand, the clarity, the objectivity of knowledge, the possible breadth; and on the other hand, the knowledge about darkness, the estrangement from Being, the possible narrowness. As soon as there is consciousness we cannot repeat existence identically in a tranquil circularity; instead, our motion must be a forward progression. Each place we occupy contains untruth which we sense in its narrowness and contradiction, and which does not let us come to rest: we must leave it, must continue our search in the direction of true actuality, of Being or of Nothingness.

Unconsciousness leaves us at peace. If, unaware, we make use of false representations which are, perhaps, to a limited extent, beneficial to life; or if we bring forth a certain piece of knowledge, or illuminate our Existenz, or, in reading ciphers, transmit an effective language: then we accomplish all this, we take hold of the successes brought about through these accomplishments, without rendering them transparent for us.

As soon as we take possession of these accomplishments by means of our consciousness and render them transparent in their untruth as well as their indispensability, then the question is: can we hold on to them? Are they still effective even though we recognize them as false at the same time? Can we carry through the "as if" in science, the "symbol" in the consciousness of transcendence, such that we see through their untruth and yet preserve the power of their effect in our being? Can we, through the way in which we use what is itself untrue—being undeceived and yet advanced by it—find our relationship to authentic truth and actuality?

It is, in fact, like an alternative: Either we relinquish ourselves, sink back into a lesser consciousness, into thoughtlessness, into a deception which has once again become unconscious, and live until we are unavoidably ruined but without understanding this ruin. Or we find, in consciousness, through our methodically intensified awareness, the way of progressing, and the strength of being true. This strength comes upon the deepest and most certain ground precisely in the most complete suspension of what is ultimately infirm—in movement as such—and is able to base its life on it.

With the movement of consciousness untruth unavoidably enters and returns in ever new configurations. This fact is borne out as well as overcome through awareness of the movement. Consciousness is the source of untruth—but this untruth must serve us to approach the depth of truth.

Selection 36

TRUTH EXPRESSED THROUGH UNTRUTH

EDITORS:
This selection from *Von der Wahrheit*, pp. 575–76 and 578–84, has been translated by the editors.

TEXT:
It would be a convenient alternative simply to do away with lies and sophistry according to the principle that he who has once been caught in a lie cannot expect to be believed even when he tells the truth. However, lies and sophistry belong to man *qua* man. One has to deal with them in reality and cannot get the better of them by eliminating them.

Man does not possess perfect truth but, as temporal existence, remains on the way. Individual man is no angel in the form of the pure presentiality of truth but always confronts the task of gaining control over the untruth in himself. We must recognize the sophist in ourselves who is always ready to get the better of us; only in illuminating and overcoming sophistry do we prepare for genuine communication. But even if individual men were able to come close to the ideal of pure truth, they could not just live with each other as select, unique individuals, but, living in the world of men in its totality, they would have to deal with lies and sophistry. We are, after all, engaged in the struggle for existence and stand in an order of existence which prevails through all of humanity or not at all.

One can put up with untruth, indeed one can actually desire it; and yet, by taking hold of it, we must also overcome it to an immeasurable extent. Let us see how this happens by taking a look at a number of situations that repeat themselves, of necessity, in men's dealings with one another.

The *ordering of our communal existence* is possible only through our putting up with untruth (a).

The limit of order is the *struggle of existence*. We cease speaking with another when we do battle, or: in battle, speaking is itself only a weapon, not a means of bringing together (b). But as long as the order remains incomplete because of the untruth present in it, the intercourse between people who preserve the order is either a matter of talking with one another for the purpose of mutual accommodation (c), or a relationship of commanding and obeying (d); i.e., truth is brought into being either by convincing each other and agreeing, or the truth lies in the command.

Corresponding to the possibilities of accommodation and of obedience there are two opposing impulses expressed in our favoring either an increase in free accommodation or a solidification of absolute authority. Either I believe that men, at bottom, are unified and that this unity can become manifest through freedom and can be actualized, or I despair of this possibility. This unity is then regarded as perhaps occurring in a religious cult, far removed from reality, but not in reality itself; together we can pray to God but cannot jointly rule over our world; rather, one person must command, the other obey.

The struggle of existence vs. ordered talking together and of accommodation vs. obedience toward authority are, however, not alternatives but polarities. For in the one the other yet remains present: in the struggle, the possibility of once again talking to each other; in accommodation, the possibility of struggle; in obedience, the desire to understand; in talking to each other, the unnoticed ascendancy of the commanding authority.

What, on a grand scale, constitutes—as struggle, talking to one another, obeying—the structure of the world of men is reflected, is supported, and has consequences in the personal relationships of individuals to one another, expressed as consensus, tension, antipathy in the professions and in public service (e). . . .

Talking to One Another to Arrive at Accommodation.   In talking to one another, truth is achieved through communication. It is in communication that truth is to become manifest. Communication itself is either true or untrue depending on whether it aims at truth or whether, pretending this to be its aim, it wants to deceive. But, since truth is not yet present, communication must risk untruth as its passageway, as temporary means and stage.

Either the one partner is in possession of a truth in which the other is to participate. In this case there are again two possibilities: Either the truth is proclaimed, revealed by the one side, is put into the world by prophets; in this case one has to put up with untruth that consists of the lack of insight [on the part of the one who does not share the truth]. Or the person possessing the truth—conscious that he must not place himself above the other—preserves the appearance of a shared standard and leads the other imperceptibly, seduces him, as it were, into truth. Whenever direct communication cannot be carried out because of the inequality of the presuppositions on each side, there the untruth of seeming equality is necessary in the service of truth.

Or, in *their joint search* for truth, *both parties are indeed on the same level.* Neither of them possesses the truth. They have to find it jointly. In this they can succeed only if neither of them claims possession of the truth. If it is the aim, in such communication, to arrive at consensus for the purpose of joint action, then again an untruth is necessary as a factor to be tolerated within the context of the whole.

Let us illustrate this with a single instance which is extremely important in life. Accommodation in existence, especially political accommodation, develops the art of talking to one another for the sake of finite goals even without the more profound existential communication of individuals. Here rules are arrived at which the Anglo-Saxon world has clearly expressed. Baumgarten has expounded this in his Franklinian principles (I shall quote him almost verbatim):

In the constitutional battles of the United States Franklin has discovered the formula: Joint action on the part of men demands a "working compromise" since absolute unity is impossible.

This demands first of all a certain method of discussion. Franklin had a high opinion of the Socratic method of seemingly humble, uncertain questioning. He wanted to develop this into a social method of imparting and accepting truths and hoped thus to make possible real personal influence. For this purpose it is necessary to hide one's own initiative and to coax forth the initiative of the others. The speaker must adhere to the Socratic illusion of uncertainty: he must not express an opinion as firm and categorical. The goal is that people become willing to listen to each other and to give all possible viewpoints a chance to be considered. All forthright maintaining of truth would destroy the effective imparting of truth. For, in the first place, the other resists the domination of what is maintained and listens poorly. In the second place, the person maintaining a certain position will receive no reply: "If I sound sure of myself, no man of experience and tact can reply, i.e., do something which he definitely was not asked to do." The manifest possession of truth excludes a joint grasping of truth. In this way the principle of imparting truth becomes more important than the truth itself. And the person who realizes the nature of his close connectedness with the other, gradually gives up all truth that is reasoned out only by oneself.

This is in line with the famous concluding speech (the compromise speech) of the Constitutional Convention in which Franklin demands of the warring parties the following:

1. Tolerance toward other opinion but not in the sense that I leave to the other his conviction as I hold on to mine, namely each as unalterable; rather, I must keep in mind the other man's conviction, considering that it may be even now, or perhaps later, destined to change my own.

2. Franklin demands the capacity to agree to a matter with all its faults (in this instance the Constitution). For every construction of a political instrument that is meant to create something perfect, he says, would have to end in confusion since it misunderstands its own proper possibilities. Only the prospect of a fundamentally vague area of utility could lead to the unanimous creation of a political instrument which would then enter the "sphere of action." In this sphere alone it could become evident, in the course of time, how one will have to, in the future, operate intelligently with this instrument *in concreto*. In other words, let us agree on this Constitution as the basis and, based on our unanimity, remain willing to talk to each other about the proper administration of this Constitution from case to case.

3. Franklin demanded that those who, on the basis of good reasons and convictions, saw themselves absolutely unable to participate in this unanimity, at the least cast their vote for this instrument of the Constitution. For this pretence is more than pretence; it is the reflection in actuality of a will that is held back and temporarily suspended in order to help make possible, in the best way, an action urgently needed at a particular time.

Here a fragmentary concept of truth is operative, i.e., one which is capable of absorbing untruth temporarily: truth does not lie behind me in what I have learned and now know; truth lies ahead of me in what originates, in what results, in what gradually comes into being through my rational action. There is only becoming truth, just as the world itself is in the state of becoming. This world-process may take such a course that the standpoint of an adversary—today unjustified—might tomorrow, in a different situation, acquire essential importance even for my purposes.

Hence compromise is the wisdom which tells itself that we must be prepared that every standpoint, no matter how apt for the business at hand, may one day be refuted after all. The Good needs to be complemented by the Less Good. For all of this to succeed we constantly have need of the art of talking with one another.

In the development of this art by Franklin two motifs manifest themselves which differ in their nature: first of all, the art of dealing with the sensitivity of the person asserting himself, through the rules of the urbanity of speaking and behaving; and secondly, the art of preserving the objective and historic possibility that truth may shift, and the possibility of proceeding in an appropriate manner even though situations, tasks, and men may change at some future time.

These motifs include acknowledging authorities and powers which lead without being rigid. They exclude uninhibited struggle by giving priority to human society as such.

Obeying and Commanding

Obeying and commanding take place in the realm of authority. Obedience in the sense of slavish obedience devoid of understanding would signify the end of being-human. Hence the one who obeys always has, in fact, an understanding, a way of believing in the meaning of authority. This authority must make itself understood. It does this in fundamentally different ways, according to the kind of authority which constitutes the background of its leadership, and according to its task, i.e., whether a certain action in a present situation or a whole of conditions and ideas is to become comprehensible.

The Demagogue

People who obey believe that in concrete situations, when they follow a leader who makes his point through demagoguery, they do so on the basis of their own insight. He exerts his leadership through his speech which is intended to convince. In no way is he able clearly to state the truth; for that would presuppose that he possesses it. One could expect, however, that he says what seems true to him. However, what is decisive is that he says what he says in such a manner that it passes for truth as far as the others are concerned because it acts on them as if it were true. Whether he wants to or not, the demagogue must let himself be led by this purpose in a given situation; at the least he must choose, accentuate, suppress; further, he can simulate, anticipate what has not yet come to be—always with the aim of gaining assent and commitment for what he wants.

Thus the demagogue—like the lawyer—has two possibilities at his disposal in regard to truth. He can represent either good or evil, and he can employ his efforts in behalf of either. The question is to what motivations and instincts he appeals, what human types are reached by his words, i.e., what efforts he uses to arrive at his goal. And this question is further, in what sense he is willing to tolerate untruth, for what purpose, within what limits, under what conditions.

The Idea of the Whole

Those who obey subordinate themselves to the representations of a whole, of an idea, whether traditional or revolutionary.

The great interpretations in the area of the philosophy of history—be these interpretations organic or revolutionary—create the medium in which the self-consciousness of the people who thrive under these systems becomes fixed as self-understanding. Out of this understanding arise the arguments which they consider a matter of course and within which they have knowledge about things that must not be touched, which it is heretical to deny; such a denial would testify to bad intentions or stupidity.

Such interpretations constantly absorb untruth as something unavoidable without which the faith of the masses would be subverted and the momentum of innovation be paralyzed.

The Authority of Traditional Systems

The interpretation of the existing authority with its organic systems and institutions elicits the edifice of ideas whose adoption brings about the education of those who live within these systems. The great interpretations of existing authority, which treat it as if it were the eternal one which alone is actual and unchangeable, become fixed by way of deceptions. Such deceptions are the suppression or playing down of the constantly necessary violence, the exclusion of the spontaneity of free creativity, of the exception, of the risk-taking that propels us forward. The interpreting individual who, basing himself on tradition, serves dominating, authoritative institutions, who feels protected in the solidarity of community, is forced, in his grandiose designs of the whole, to close his eyes, or to be silent, or to argue in an advocatory manner. Whoever has been given the official function, by such authority, to transmit these interpretations, to develop them further and to adapt them to new situations, subjects himself with each of his thoughts—unwittingly and unadmittedly—to the conditions of this authority. In the end he understands and gives reasons for the conscious lie in the service of authority even in the concrete individual case (Luther: "a strong lie," a "useful lie"), just as Plato justifies the lie of the philosophically superior authority for the purpose of benefitting the governed.

Thus these interpretations of the particular, dominant, comprehensive powers are always ambiguous. Their application proceeds in two opposing directions:

The impulse of interpretation may be, on the one hand, the will of the power of self-assertion. The interpretation as a whole is not really believed nor is it doubted; rather, it serves as the natural means of maintaining what is already existing. As such, it is advantageous for those who promote this interpretation by sustaining its representatives as well as for those who accomplish it in thought. But this, in fact, becomes the road toward the destruction of the authority and its institutions. For the lie acts slowly like a poison. It no longer serves the purpose of construction but is merely suited to preserve as fiction— in the manner of an advocate—what is no longer believed. Such interpretation holds on with nervous fanaticism, blinds itself with anxious passion. It is the spiritual perversion of which all great systems in history have perished in the end.

Or, there is in the interpretation a constant insufficiency, a readiness for sacrifice in order to actualize completely and genuinely what already is but has not as yet been carried out truly and actually. It is the road of strength because the systems are being built out of an unconditional commitment of existential conviction. In that case one remains alert to recognize harm, deception, and lies; does not justify these but stands up against them. It is the impulse out of which have arisen all the great systems in history.

The Authority of Revolutionary Movement

The interpretations of revolutionary movements are a different matter. What is desired is not yet present. What exists is wrong in its very roots and must therefore be destroyed. That which is desired has in reality always been true; it has existed once before and has only gone wrong. Now it is to be restored. Or, due to the necessary course of history, its time has come. The truth of the new system is a vision believed in during the unhesitating process of destruction. For the time being one only has to destroy. The whole impetus rests in the faith in the eternal, the necessary which is to follow, either in the form of mere restoration or in new and original creation.

But at every step expectation is contradicted by experience: all that clearly succeeds is the destruction. The reconstruction, however, merely restores what has just been destroyed, but in another form and with other people. The harm, the deceptions, the lies have not become less, they may even have increased.

Hence the ambiguities of revolutionary interpretation are different but are not less than those of traditionalistic interpretation:

It is either a question of a nihilism which doubts all truth and only admits what serves the power in which I myself participate.—Cynical teachings are developed that deal with the methods of lying and of brute force, doctrines that deal with religions and world-views as mere means of power, and with the contempt for men and the world. This is the final self-destruction of so many revolutionary movements in history.

Or it is a question of a future, firmly believed in, which speaks to us out of the deepest past. Differences are not denied but are faced. Obedience is given to those men who, through the example of their manifest, self-sacrificing commitment, guarantee the truth of the movement. The impetus of the will to reconstruction is untiring, risks itself in deception and lies, and becomes the basis of what is substantial, out of which a new order can develop. This is the origin of the positive effects of revolution.

Nowhere, however—neither in traditional nor in revolutionary conditions—do we find ultimate order and truth. Each absorbs insurmountable untruth. In all conditions, however, there is the radical difference: On the one side the resigned or defiant or infernal pact with untruth which only becomes greater and the source of the destruction of the whole; and on the other, the unceasing battle against untruth which is seen, admitted, unmasked, contained, borne with gnashing of teeth but which again and again is seized upon and destroyed even if it keeps on growing back as did the heads of the Hydra.

Selection 37

TRUTH AS TIED TO FALSEHOOD

EDITORS:
The selection to follow has been translated by the editors. The original is in *Von der Wahrheit*, pp. 590–94.

TEXT:
Inasmuch as truth exists within the world it must also bring falsehood with it. To be sure, through unceasing effort truth still is developed, but this truth still carries with it the false which continues somehow unconquered as it is overcome.

However, the falsehood that is carried along is not of a single kind. A new fundamental question grows out of the differentiation of the falsehood that is true, as it were, because it belongs to truth and remains even as it is overcome, from the falsehood that is untrue because it is to be abolished in principle. There is a falsehood which actualizes a truth and a falsehood that falls away from truth. We must ask whether such a differentiation can be carried out.

Falsehood that is Untrue because it must be Abolished

Eristics and sophistry, which the activity of struggle involves, suspend the meaning of communication. Overcoming this sophistry is the condition of possible communication.

There are dreams and illusions which merely divert from actuality but have become fixed as sterile illusions. These illusions may be animated by vital forces through which they are made fanatical, but at the root of such fanaticization they can, in principle, be overcome and cast off. As traditional ideologies, the illusions can still be valid in society without being animated by a creative life. They have then become nothing other than an appearance and, in spite of those who have an interest in them and who cling to them in fear, collapse at some point in time as nonentities.

There is the clear and manifest lie, the falsifying inherent in the particular, that which can be proven to be generally incorrect.

But all suspension of such unconquerable untruth demands prudence and goodwill. It sometimes astonishes and can drive one to despair if even what is provable is not acknowledged. Just because it is possible, in principle, to overcome falsehood it does not follow that such overcoming is easy and happens as if by itself.

Falsehood that is True because it cannot also be Suspended

To be sure, falsehood which belongs to truth is constantly overcome and allows the truth to become manifest ever more deeply; but this occurs in such a manner that falsehood reappears in new configurations.

The negativity in the origin of the world signifies: Untruth is the condition of truth just as nothingness is the condition of Being. This is the meaning of phrases such as: one must sacrifice one's life in order to gain it; or: to offer up Existenz in order to exist; "as long as you do not possess it, this: die and become! . . ." This negativity, which is present in the origin and thus unconquerable, can be characterized in the following ways, based on its appearances:

(i) The false within the true is unconquerable because each specific truth is *particular*. Hence it is correct, to be sure, but it is relative (the confusion of cogent validity and absolute truth). Thus, in order to remain true it must remain in its relativity; it becomes false if it is absolutized. A strength drawn from encompassing truth is needed so that the specific, finite, relative truth does not turn into the falsity of an absolute—which is the ever-present temptation for the thinking person.

(ii) If truth is *the whole* and each position, as such, remains untrue because it is singular and finite, then truth is never without some configuration of falsehood since, for us, it always assumes the finite configuration of a specific position, and since, for us, the whole is never present.

(iii) If truth is *the One* and the following statement is valid: "Truth is only one and error is manifold," then in the manifold as such—and with it, in all our Being and knowing—untruth lies hidden.

To counter the insuperable falsehood in order to penetrate with it into truth, the following paths are open to us:

1. I call to mind that there is *no objectivity-in-itself*. To be sure, objectivity is true in the sense of events occurring in existence that can be assessed as the

exploration of nature. Objectivity is true, furthermore, in the forms of propriety, of systems, and of the laws of justice; they are our protection and serve to contain arbitrariness and to preserve the space for the historic freedom of the individual. But every objectivity becomes untrue if it seeks to be the form in which absolute truth is expressed. Therefore I enter into objectivity as into a game plan or into a role; I am unconditionally only in my commitment to the rules of the game as well as the roles, i.e., to objectivity as such as the condition of meaningful existence.

2. In *methodical empirical research* I consciously put up with untruth in order to get ahead on my project. In models and work hypotheses contradictions must be tolerated at the beginning. For contradiction spurs on progress, not by our avoiding this contradiction as a matter of course but by taking hold of it in its fruitfulness and overcoming it there; we will then encounter it again as a new contradiction in a different form. The avoidance of contradiction, which is the presupposition of each step, paralyzes research.

3. In all *symbolism* I grasp truth in the form of *conscious deception*: what I mean is never the way it appears; I attain what I mean by letting the deceptive something disintegrate, and I touch it precisely in this disintegration.

For the person traveling these three roads, these roads signify the carrying out of attitudes of thought which do not need to be aware of themselves. Such attitudes seem to destroy themselves in the reflection which brings untruth to light. For to us, as finite beings, the following inclination is inescapable: We want to have truth and Being in some embodiment, in some configuration, in some definite, known form, in tenet and dogma, palpably and absolutely at the same time, as it were. Only in this way do we have firm support; only in this way can an unconditional energy be operative in us. Reflection, even if true, may seem to paralyze the energy which alone resides in the untruth which is unaware of itself.

If we assume those attitudes of reflection they protect us from confusing truth with falsehood. They teach us to glimpse, in carrying out the indissoluble untruth, truth in its purity after all. Thus, for example, we must not confuse the unconditionality of our historic involvements with the fluid fixation on some finitude fanatically adhered to. However, that unconditionality should not become weaker in the process but rather stronger because it is more wide-awake and brighter and more aware of itself. It does seem to the observer, however, that—compared to the deceptive effect of the fixation in objectivity, in what is incontrovertibly correct, in the embodied symbol, and in comparison with the essentially blind force of activity arising from it—there lies not only danger in reflection but also an inherent weakness. It seems that the self-illuminating, total openness for truth on the part of Existenz must, in the end, have a devastating effect. But what appears thus to the observer, and what is psychologically true where the primal source of being-human remains ineffectual, that cannot be true where man takes hold of his highest possibilities. The weakness referred to above is the consequence of new confusions, of ruinous untruths brought about by half-heartedness, of lack of courage, absence of self-being. To be sure, the more closely man approaches truth the greater the danger becomes. But here lies also the possibility of his encompassing energy of being-true which is completely rooted in his ground.

The Way in which Deception, in being Suspended, Turns into Truth

The significance of the overcoming of deception varies in accordance with the kind of truth. The deception itself is a fact; it is to be sublimated in the search for truth. It seems as if the deception is to disappear. However, without fixing one's glance on the deception one does not truly experience the corresponding truth nor does one know it decisively. Hence the deception is reestablished, not in order for us to succumb to it, but so that we may recognize it.

In the last levels of the truth of Being that are accessible to us the form of truth for knowledge is even such that the deception itself turns into truth and, as such, remains a necessary element of our existence; it is present, however, only in a movement in which deception is suspended alternatively by an opposite deception.

Thus, for example, Being as that which is thought objectively and determinately is universally valid; but we become entangled in it and the universal turns into a deception about Being. If, however, in committing this deception, we then retreat to the subjectivity of our experience as to the very presence of truth delighting in itself, we enter into the stream of dark subjectivity which is the deception out of which we again strive decisively toward the objectivity of the universal.

Another example is our life within temporality and finitude. For us this is the only form of what is authentic: each person arrives at the awareness that the decisions which have to be made are up to him. But as we ascend toward transcendence we take hold of the reverse idea, namely that in eternity everything is determined and everything, as it were, is orderly and attuned to everything else, and that, in time, we merely discover what eternally is.

Thus one thing becomes the deception of the other. We assure ourselves of the truth of one through overcoming the other, but in alternation, in a process whose goal we cannot see, in which each form of knowledge turns into a deception which is suspended only in ignorance.

Truth is Ultimately Ungrounded

If, out of the finitude of existence, out of all relativities of what can be thought, we gain firm ground in the possibility of our Existenz, then there is revealed to us the abidingly questionable nature of Existenz. Its unconditionality is given to itself in its depth, it is not through itself. In self-reflection it is not certain of itself as would be something known and taken into possession.

Hence there arises constantly, in the bottomlessness of Existenz, the question about transcendence through which Existenz knows itself to be posited (i.e., is given to itself). But transcendence, for its part, does not manifest itself as clear, unequivocal revelation, nor as a knowable on which I could rely as something not to be doubted. Among all other ambiguities I must also always hesitate even before the knowledge of what God wills and what God is. Indeed, to man in his faith, given to himself as a task within the earnestness of Existenz, the Cartesian notion of God who cannot deceive is not the self-evident expression of his experience. Rather, his experience is that of Pascal's notion of the deceiving God.

The manner in which one becomes aware of the deceptiveness is less decisive than that one becomes aware of it. The following interpretations are offered: God reveals himself in such a manner that man is bound to misunderstand him if he does not believe; but his lack of faith is a not-hearing of what is understandable and hence his fault. Or: God wills man to be free, in accordance with his image; hence man may take hold of what is true only out of himself and must not have it presented to him objectively or palpably, for this would make him unfree. Or: Ambiguity is the profoundity through which alone, within the realm of appearances, the truth can be found lying in the depths beyond all limits of finitude. Every interpretation presupposes that a radical untruth is the inescapable form of the appearance of truth itself.

ASPECTS OF THE THEORY (2): THE BREAKTHROUGH OF THE ONE TRUTH

EDITORS:
Our situation is such that when we turn to truth that is manifest to us, we discern a multiplicity of modes of truth. The very pursuit of the wholeness of truth brings the fragmentation of the truth that is ours into focus. Truth in its wholeness is—for man—the way to it through its fragmentation. Truth in time is the truth we attain through inquiry or enactment, the order we live in or try to establish, the guidance we receive which may pit us against others in their truth, etc. In any of these instances, truth in time is recognized as being limited and encompassed by truth in its transcendent unity. Truth in time, then, can not take the place of truth in its encompassing unity. What is unaccounted for, unexpected by us, not allowed for, beyond the knowledge or power of human realization—will burst into our lives and into human history, signaling a truth which encompasses man's truth. For Jaspers the main configurations by virtue of which truth in its unity functions in its breakthrough

for man in time are those of authority and the exception. Authority and exception are discussed above in Selection 34 and briefly considered below in Selection 40. However, they do not constitute the ultimate configurations of the directedness toward the one truth on the part of man in time. The possibilities here are reason and catholicity, which are discussed by Jaspers in Selection 41.

The first of the following three selections (38) introduces the concept of the breakthrough of truth in its unity with respect to the fragmentation of Being. In Selection 39 Jaspers presents the significance of the breakthrough for man's consciousness of truth. Finally, Selection 40 introduces the concept of "configurations of truth in the breakthrough." These selections are presented here in English translation for the first time.

Selection 38

BASIC SITUATION AND PHILOSOPHIC DECISION

EDITORS:
The following are excerpts from *Von der Wahrheit*, pp. 703–09 in a translation by the editors.

TEXT:

A. The Fragmentation of Being

As we progressed through the history of the manifestation of Being, our assurance of the meaning of truth indicated ever more clearly, ever more ineluctably: Being is fragmented, both within each mode of the Encompassing as well as in the multiplicity of modes of the Encompassing.

As cognizable world-being, the *world* is divided by fissures. Without any transition between them, the spheres of the lifeless (anorganic), of the living, of consciousness and of spirit stand together and are intertwined. One cannot cognize a world-being as a whole, based on one principle. Rather, precisely where cognition is clear and decisive do we always surrender the whole of world-being.

Transcendence is present for the many in a variety of configurations. One would think that all people could be brought into relation with the distant one God through the figure of the near God, the God who is specific to them. But the distant God turns out to be so distant and hidden that he disappears as such. One can find no identity for all men in his appearance and language. Historic actuality exhibits precisely this diversity in the language of transcendence. Hence religions battle with each other in the world as do philosophies. Transcendence is torn apart through the historicity of its language. This is symbolized by the confusion of languages at the tower of Babel.

In the infinite variety of its individualization, *existence* stands over against itself. Split up into many existences in constant life and death struggle, it can only actualize one specific existence. In its unending destruction and regeneration it is never existence as such.

Consciousness-as-such is split up into many consciousnesses, but they are replaceable and are one as far as their meaning is concerned. However, the fragmentation of Being manifests itself in this consciousness through unsolvable antinomies wherever infinity comes into play. Consciousness-as-such is unable to think of Being as One, as a closed whole.

Spirit, as totality, is in every instance something complete in itself. But it is actual as an incompletable plurality of totalities that do not coincide but are engaged in the movement of constant transformation and final destruction. The different spheres of spirit are not connected to each other, their stance toward each other is one of potential conflict.

Each *Existenz* is together with other Existenzen; each is unique and irreplaceable in its various possibilities, but is related to others who are also irreplaceable in their otherness. Existenz stands over against another Existenz in infinite, incompletable communication as well as in rejection, in loving struggle as well as in exclusionary denial of itself to the other.

Thus the division is contained in each mode of the Encompassing. However, the modes of the Encompassing are not bound to each other in one visible and knowable ground. Philosophically, the fragmentation of Being is demonstrated by the fact that we cannot carry out the most comprehensive illumination of Being through developing it from a principle but can do so ultimately only out of a manifold of origins.

B. The Unity of Being

Even if we ruthlessly bring to mind the fragmentation of Being in all its aspects, we still feel, with every fiber of our being, that this cannot be the last word. In spite of everything we remain conscious of the unity of Being and of being-true, even if only in a completely indefinite way. Every glance into the fragmentation is followed immediately by the question about unity because Being only remains Being, and being-true itself only remains true for us when they again become One for us.

We search for the unity of the *World*. We try to find connections across the chasms by investigating how, in fragmentation, one relates to the other. Even if these relations across the chasms are of a radically different nature than are the relations within the internally investigable individual world-spheres, they are—if comprehensible in any form at all—indicators of a unity of world-being. We presuppose the possibility of the question of how everything in the world can be related to everything else. And we assure ourselves that in this way the world is one for us. For there could not exist for us several worlds that would have no mutual relationship since they could not encounter each other in our one consciousness without immediately evincing their relationships.

We only acknowledge the *transcendence* that is One. Beyond all historicity of language, passing through all the different configurations and contents, we direct ourselves toward the distant God who is the One for all.

Existence seeks to heal its fragmentation by constructing comprehensive communities and by limiting and ultimately suspending the struggle for being and non-being.

Consciousness-as-such seeks the intellectual means to master the antinomies and to get in touch with the One as it can be thought, even if such thinking takes place in thoughts that somersault over themselves or move on the detours of indirectness.

To be sure, *spirit* in its historic actuality is self-contained, but it searches for the One Spirit which is the cosmos of all that is spiritual by remembering and understanding everything that is and was. Spirit absorbs, in the form of comprehending, what it itself is not; it seeks *ad infinitum* the One Universal Spirit to which everything belongs according to its meaning.

Existenzen are concerned with one another. They demonstrate their interconnectedness by not being able indifferently to pass by other Existenzen once they have encountered them. The One of each Existenz's historicity presses forward into the One of the invisible realm of Existenzen where all are together, all are One in infinite communication.

Thus all unity is not present in the individual modes of the Encompassing, for in each instance unity reaches its limit and its point of foundering. But for each mode of the Encompassing, unity constitutes a purpose of its search.

In this search the modes of the Encompassing mutually support each other. The unity in each Encompassing is tied to the meaning of unity of all Encompassings. To be sure, true unity, which is the pivot of all unity, is to be found solely in transcendence but it is accessible only by way of all the unities in all the modes of the Encompassing. And the way in which I experience and take hold of the unity of Being is indissolubly bound to the unity which I become and am.

C. The Decision: How to Grasp the One (either through solidification or in an open-ended movement)

As all Being searches for itself in the One it constantly finds itself getting sidetracked from its meaning. The One is grasped mistakenly in an objectified Being (in everything we call materialization and naturalization), in fixed antitheses (of the One over against the Not-One), in emptiness (in all that is merely abstract, incorporeal, other-worldly). We lose our openness for the

One when we either, erroneously, take in at a glance the One as a whole, as an enduring logical system, or we look at it as the one, familiar, necessary movement. In no way can we see it from the outside, nor can we grasp it as the whole based on its beginning and end.

Being is like something broken apart that cannot close. Out of the deepest ground of the whole it presses on toward the One which always is not yet and yet—in secret— always is as if completed, even though it immediately breaks apart again in every tangible completion.

Hence the manner in which the One is grasped constitutes the fundamental philosophic decision. I either grasp the One in any one of the knowing, fixating, constricting modes, or I grasp it on the road for which all philosophic thoughts are mere preparation and enablement: in an encompassing, traversing, losing, and again gaining movement out of the origin back into the origin. Since this authentic movement toward the One cannot be seen from the outside, it cannot be known as a whole and hence cannot be directly willed. For this reason no guidelines are possible as to how this road can be found on the basis of a road map and statement of aim, in an universally valid and identical way. Yet the movement out of the ground of Being, out of the One toward the One, must be able to guide all knowing and wanting. Then our knowing and willing remain open and, in being broken apart, remain aimed at the One without getting stuck in *culs-de-sac* or in fixities. . . .

Taking hold of Each Unity. In the course of the search for the One, each possible unity is taken hold of, not as the final unity but as step and condition. No possible unity may be passed over if one wants to avoid searching in vain for the One in the bottomless void.

Hence the road toward the One proceeds via the clarity of definite objective thought which encounters in each instance a specific One. This thought searches in everything investigable for the one world even if this world is never accessible as the closed cosmos of the one whole investigated and known world. It seeks to participate in the ideas of the spirit, designs its Being-constructs even if these are merely schemas of the ideas which, to be sure, are valid systematics but which, as systems of the known and ordered, are broken up at the same time. This thinking leads into the historicity of Existenz without fixating its objectivity as universally valid for all. It follows the impulse of reason toward establishing universal relations, toward universal remembrance, toward universal preservation (without forgetting or allowing anything to disappear). And it lets us experience the One of transcendence in eloquent ciphers right through everything without possessing it.

Operating with Philosophical Standpoints. The principles of expressed assertions that are beyond discussion are called standpoints or positions. Standpoints oppose other standpoints. No genuine philosophy can be grasped or comprehended as a standpoint because it moves, beyond all standpoints and without a standpoint, in the Encompassing.

However, the intellectually objective structures of philosophizing can appear as if developed out of standpoints from which one can see what is. An inclination to want to take philosophies in at a glance and to know them as wholes seduces us to simplify their objective formulations into standpoints.

If, in this manner, philosophies are grasped externally in their results, then a pseudo-philosophizing takes place, operates with those standpoints, formulas and thought techniques, but now detached from the origin out of which they grew and from the purpose which they should serve. Such philosophizing becomes dependent on the standpoints rather than dominating them. To be sure, these standpoints are useful as an external, rational means in the ordering of the skeletal remains of philosophizing. But in order to arrive at free philosophizing one must overcome this operating with standpoints. This is made possible by a rational treatment of the standpoints through a movement that carries us beyond them:

1. Contradictory standpoints are contrasted with each other based on the presupposition that either one or the other would have to be true. A supposed choice within rationality takes the place of the genuine decision which is grounded existentially within the Encompassing.

2. Contradictories are *taken together dialectically*. Opposites are united, an overview is gained, a reconciliation takes place. A supposedly comprehensive knowledge of the whole replaces the search for the One.

3. Each standpoint and each conciliation of standpoints is demonstrated in its inconsistencies and limitations. The place of conciliatory dialectic is taken by the dialectic of dissolution, and the way is opened for freedom within the realm of possibility. In this way the standpoints in their formulations are known, recognized, and overcome. The way is open toward the illumination of the origin out of which these standpoints had been thought in philosophical activity at one time before they fell prey to the rigidity of a logical objectivity.

The One as Breakthrough. The ways in which the modes of the Encompassing belong together has been discussed under the headings of Aggregate, Conflict, and Order. These three possibilities seem to exhaust the subject. A further possibility does not seem conceivable.

Those three possibilities of Aggregate, Conflict, and Order of the Encompassings were easy to comprehend, the overview of which according to schemata could satisfy an orderly mind. The whole remains on the level of mere observation and hence supplies useful tools for psychology and sociology. But it is only at the limits that the precipitousness, the absence of order in the depth, the desperate confusion which we want to escape become clear to us.

We seek the manifestation of the ground of truth which demands more profound organs for comprehending and gaining certitude than mere observation is capable of supplying. The realization of the possibilities of order on the level of observation, the experience of its consequences and its actualization, has the result that we are at a loss if we do not climb to a completely new level of the meaning of truth. Only in breaking through the protective coverings of these seemingly complete possibilities can truth be achieved.

If the unity is not present as true and universal, if it is not immanently at our disposal either as fixed or in known movement, then there is unity only in the breakthrough:

The experience of limits is everywhere the fundamental experience of Being. This depends on the disappearance of all absolutizing universality, on our remaining open to the always possible breakthrough, to the experience of the One in the actually occurred breakthrough.

The configurations of the One as they appear in immanence must be configurations of the breakthrough. They are the language of the One which never is the One itself; in them is manifest the unity of all Encompassing in its depth.

Selection 39

INTERPRETATION OF BREAKTHROUGH

EDITORS:
This selection is from *Von der Wahrheit*, pp. 719-23. It has been translated by the editors.

TEXT:
Breakthroughs, in their totality, leave man with the vague consciousness that all universal truths fail at some point and that all historic truths are in incessant motion.

Events, which we expect to be ordered under rules known to us, turn out, surprisingly, to have an entirely different character. The rules according to which we are to live, suddenly turn out, in an instant, to be fragile because they are not meant to be unconditional. In both instances man finds himself beyond all the rules recognized by him; he sees events and moral imperatives subject to a force which breaks through them, a force which he does not understand. This force is not simply the historicity of Existenz which, as such, can break through all universality. For this historicity itself is merely a particular unity which again is broken through, out of itself, in movement, or by another historicity, and which comes to an end in foundering.

If, out of all this, there grows the vague consciousness that universal and historic truth nowhere become absolute and nowhere become the whole and that an other is in control, then man is impelled out of this vagueness toward its interpretation. Where there is knowledge, anxiety is lessened. Therefore man wants to cognize that other which lies beyond all his cognition, this dark force that guides him and the world, destroys or saves it.

Whenever there is an irruption of the unexpected into the continuity of events, whenever that which until now has been considered impossible does happen, man wants to understand, for in understanding the event he appropriates it. What is understood is no longer frightening.

Whenever man breaks through his order he understands himself in some manner; what he does by breaking through he wants to do knowingly. He is justified through his interpretation.

Such understanding of that which, after all, breaks through understanding, this interpretation of the incurring darkness, always takes place in an all too brief anticipatory thinking. It becomes concrete in a tangible symbol or in a sham knowledge. . . .

Interpretations of breakthroughs can approximate truth only if, interpreting, they keep themselves open to breadth. Each specific interpretation (whether as a genuine symbol or the appropriate knowledge) must—if it is to remain true—be valid within the framework of the whole which is turned toward that breadth of Being. Keeping this framework in mind can help us to hold our interpretations in abeyance and to preserve them from becoming fixed. An indefinite interpretation originating in the Encompassing opens the door to all kinds of definite interpretations. This framework turns into criticism of the interpretations if they are ossified into absolutes, but it becomes their affirmation if they address us through their own substance.

The interpreter always responds to the questions: What is being broken through? What are the forces that are breaking through?

It is always something universal that is broken through: it is the universal as something very common and average; as the conventionally valid and that which makes life possible in a state; as the universally valid of consciousness-as-such; as the universally normative of morality. What is broken through is always a constructed unity; it is every configuration that is closed off in itself, it is the unity of the state, of social institutions, of occupation and marriage, of every historic ordered unit.

The forces that break through are either the specific Encompassing or another Encompassing or, if the unanimity among the Encompassings is lacking, a singular out of the depth of Being: the Encompassing of all Encompassing. Let us look at this more closely.

The specific Encompassing breaks through what it has itself brought forth. In this it has unfolded and illuminated itself but then has become narrow and fixed. The Encompassing loses itself in its creations. Hence, the force which breaks through is the Encompassing that destroys what it has brought forth when what has been brought forth threatens to enchain it. Further, every Encompassing has the tendency to confine itself to itself and to force everything else into its service. If this happens, then the Encompassing which arrogates control to itself is again broken through by another Encompassing.

Existence is solidified in the configurations of its permanence; as exuberant vitality it again melts these down to enable the emergence of new configurations. If existence relies on itself it is broken through by the correct truth of consciousness-as-such which not only serves existence but also disturbs it; and finally existence is broken through by the terror wrought by images which, as phenomena in the other modes of the Encompassing, have their origin in transcendence. Existence is helpless in limit situations when that which becomes manifest is no longer merely existence.

Consciousness-as-such becomes solidified in correctnesses which again are overcome by new correctnesses. When it attempts to become independent it experiences its incompleteness in the form of the unresolvable antinomies. Bound to the reality of existence it experiences the breakthrough through the purposes of existence which force it into their service, limit it, and lead it into absurdity.

Spirit is solidified as the world of culture. It moves by transforming this world through efficacious ideas which support it reliably until these ideas have experienced life to the fullest in the richness of such a world of culture. They are then again melted down by new ideas. If spirit posits itself as absolute it is shipwrecked, for its completeness is insufficient for the forces of Existenz and transcendence which destroy the forms of the spirit and stimulate them anew.

Being-world is objectified as matter, corporeality, as life, as an event subject to laws. All solidifications are dissolved in progressive cognition until every manner of an "ultimate" in being-world is made to disappear through cognition itself, and the richness of the—always relative—cognition unfolds itself in the fundamentally bottomless. The world itself is broken through by transcendence which becomes its ground.

Transcendence is solidified as sensuous object, as tangible event, as word, and as a known. Demons, gods, fetishes, rites, and magic—these force transcendence into a narrowness which it breaks through to form new shapes in which a new narrowness comes into being. Whenever transcendence occurs in the world as a particular in spatial and temporal isolation, it is most decisively and inviolably stable and unchangeable, which is indeed characteristic of all cults, rites, and dogmas. But even this experiences an imperceptible transformation through reinterpretation as long as cults, rites, and dogmas continue to harken to transcendence. Moreover, all of transcendence as a separate configuration in the world is put in question because the most profound transcendence speaks through all modes of the Encompassing; this transcendence breaks through not only every specific configuration of transcendence but the figurative character of transcendence as such. The dis-enchantment dissolves each particular sanctity, every remaining taboo, so that now—in imagelessness, beyond all speech, in all that is essential—transcendence can be heard to speak indirectly. The universality and closeness to actuality of transcendence is bound to the breakthrough of every specific transcendence.

There is sameness everywhere, in existence, consciousness-as-such, spirit, being-world, and transcendence. Our inclination to possess—in the sensuous, in the objective, in law, in obligation, in what is thought and in the content of knowledge, in every particular—Being itself, in order to have in it a reliable support, is the reason for the solidification as well as the suspension of movement. In this way we are stuck in a sandbank, as it were, and lose, together with the movement, the manifestation of Being itself. The Encompassing is lost to us; the ground of unity of all modes of the Encompassing has lost its effectiveness as the goal that impels us forward. The breakthrough is the road to truth.

The attempt at interpretation out of the multiplicity of the modes of the Encompassing teaches us to understand: first, how the Encompassing breaks through its own configurations, and, secondly, how each Encompassing is penetrated, broken through by other Encompassings. But this understanding itself teaches us that its thought construct is relative and can itself be broken through. For it contains the need to dissolve the solidifying schema of all the modes of the Encompassing:

(i) it teaches the multiplicity of Existenz, the conjunction of possible truth which is no longer one truth;

(ii) it teaches the historicity of transcendence for Existenz; i.e., there is no possibility of our getting an overview of the whole, no possibility of our letting it close upon itself. At best, we can remain open to it in our own historicity.

The scheme of the modes of the Encompassing and, with it, the understanding of the breakthroughs, contains within it the explosive that will make the scheme come apart. But it is precisely in this way that the explosive makes philosophically accessible what could never be comprehended in a direct manner, namely the One out of the depth of Being, the Encompassing of all Encompassing.

In all interpretations of the breakthrough, a categorial counter-position is evident, whether expressed as that of law and arbitrariness, truth and falsehood, universal validity and particularity, regularity and interruption, or order and chaos.

They seem to be two mutually exclusive possibilities. In the end the whole must be an ordered one; each breakthrough through an order is again comprehended in a more inclusive order. Or there is a bottomlessness in the end, in which all order ceases to be. This picture of an infinite, though far-off, harmony is contested by indignation and defiance, basing itself on the way things are, on all the horror and dread which are so easily overlooked by him who is not directly affected. Both are correct but both have their limitation. Each thought-out order, each intuited harmony, is premature, for each founders on ever new actualities. Every final bottomlessness is premature because it sweeps us along into a dead, permanent state of indignation through a knowledge which—for finite beings—always remains open.

The difference between the two counterposed possibilities is that all interpretation soon presupposes, unnoticed, some kind of order, whereas the expression of bottomlessness must exhaust itself in pure negations.

Selection 40

CONFIGURATIONS OF TRUTH IN THE BREAKTHROUGH

EDITORS:
The following selection, translated by the editors, appears in *Von der Wahrheit*, pp. 745–47.

TEXT:

The Empty Breakthrough: The Irrational

In no mode of the universal were we able to grasp adequately what the one truth is. To be sure, we always seek truth in the form of universal truth. But we can come to rest in one configuration of the universal only if we restrict our sense of truth and veil the Encompassing.

If we become aware of this, then we can be deceived by the simple counter-stroke against the universal: we take up the irrational as irrational as if it were a better truth and actuality. Adventure and the sensation of the extraordinary have the effect of similitude of truth, although, lacking necessity or constraint and thus also the substance of historicity, they dissipate into insignificance. There is an inkling of the depth which fascinates, though in the wrong way. One can find satisfaction in causing disturbance, in bringing about embarrassment in saying, in the midst of reasoned thinking: "For once I want to be inconsistent". . . .

The deception lies in our seeking, in this way, the irrational in a rational manner. However, the desired irrationality is itself negatively rational. The liberation of disruption or destruction is a content-less one. But there is still one truth in such deceptive impulses, namely, the experience of the insufficiency of solidified truth in its universality.

Whoever is no longer capable of such impulses and deceptions would most likely have sunk into the flat reasonableness of the Philistine, into the consciousness of security pacified by pedantry, of the man of order, into the moral self-satisfaction of the Pharisee, into the non-binding, aesthetically formed multiplicity of experiences of the man of culture. In him there would no longer be present a sense of the Encompassing.

Configurations in Breakthrough: Exception and Authority

Only in a space in which the opposition of universal and irrational loses its absolute necessity can we perceive what is the one truth. The one truth—if it were present for us—would, as form, only be simultaneously with its content; it would be universal as well as historic. Further, it would not be in one particular form but in a configuration embracing all the modes of the Encompassing.

This whole would have to fulfill demands that contradict each other. For us this is unthinkable and unimaginable. Therefore we can never grasp it directly. In our temporal existence, which we are incapable of leaving, this whole is never accessible to us other than in a particular historic configuration; and this configuration is not one, and is, moreover, in each of its appearances also in motion.

It would be the configuration of being-true which is actual, as existence spread through consciousness-as-such and spirit, grounded in Existenz, and—moved by reason—boundlessly open in the world to transcendence.

Perhaps we come closer to such truth if we face directly the most extreme configurations at the limit, an actualization of the unity of all modes of the Encompassing.

These are configurations which—measured against importance and freedom, cogent knowledge and each particular mode of being-true—appear as a downright threat against all truth: the exception and authority.

Selection 41

ASPECTS OF THE THEORY (3)
AT THE LIMIT: TWO POSSIBILITIES
REASON AND CATHOLICITY

EDITORS:
Authority and exception are historically the main configurations of the breakthrough of truth into the confines of human realizations, but reason and catholicity are the ultimate configurations of the directedness toward the one

truth on the part of man in time. Reason and catholicity can and will function within both authority and exception. Reason is, for Jaspers, the impulse toward the unity of truth. The quest for this unity is not fulfilled in time; in Jaspers's conception the fulfillment in time of this quest is at variance with reason because reason is essentially also the affirming of the historicity of the quest. A position which holds truth is fulfilled in time is, therefore, the ultimate and only rival of the rule of communicative reason. It is this that Jaspers calls—wherever in human affairs it may appear, whether in culture, politics, or religion—the position of catholicity. Though the impulse toward unity springs from reason in either case, there is an irreducible, ultimate difference in the mode of executing this impulse in the concreteness of human existence, according to whether oneness of truth is a matter of communicative openness or a matter of realizing a vision of truth that is deemed to be valid for all and binding on all.

A note on terminology: The reader should pay attention to Jaspers's footnote in this selection where he explains that "catholicity" is a concept more general than—and does not exclusively refer to—Christian "Catholicism".

The following are excerpts from Jaspers's essay on catholicity and reason in *Von der Wahrheit*, pp. 832–36, 840–41, 843–47, 857–58, 861–62. They appear here for the first time in English translation, which has been rendered by the editors.

TEXT:

The Antithesis of Reason and Catholicity

Philosophically, the ultimate is neither the upheaval caused by the exception nor the tranquility to be found in authority.

Following the exception is absurd; for the exception can merely awaken and orient.

Living within authority without questioning is forbidden: for philosophizing is the questioning about essentials which permits no limitation.

Philosophic thought does not fall silent before exception and authority. To be sure, the exception is not justified in such thought, for no justification can arrive at the meaning of exception; nor is a reason given for authority, for any such reason would suspend it through the very act of giving this reason. But philosophic thought does more than explode the deviations that become untrue: perhaps it can bring into the purest present that which emerges from the primal source both in exception and in authority.

The road which does not break off before exception and authority but leads right into them—the road of philosophic truth—is called reason. Reason—rather than possessing truth in any of the previously discussed configurations, and rather than showing truth clearly in its content—is the unlimited openness for truth.

The basic characteristic of reason is its will to unity. But it has become evident that from the multiplicity of the encompassing origins of truths there does not emerge one truth; for when these truths come together in the concrete situation the exception breaks them up again, and authority only actualizes each in historic form as one among many. But the impulse to go beyond the multiplicity toward the truth in the form of the one and universal remains unbroken, in spite of the exception and in spite of obedience toward authority, as long as there is reason.

However, I cannot travel the road of grasping this one truth once again in the world of consciousness-as-such, in cogent intellectual cognition as correct knowing and behaving. As long as I limit myself to this road, the truth out of which I actually live is lost. Yet in the impulse of intellectual cognition—toward the partial unity of what is valid in cogent statements—lies hidden the impulse of reason toward the deeper unity for which that intellectual unity is merely medium and symbol.

The truth of one's life is decided by the way in which this unity is grasped.

The historic unity in exception and authority is always in a state of flux and of foundering.

The unity which is thought shows itself to be untenable in every configuration; it is not possible as a subsisting unity, neither in constructive thought, nor in the ideal, nor in a knowable actuality.

If, however, the unity of the world can be grasped only in the appearance of historicity, only in the cipher of the One but not as the One itself, then the final opposition between men takes the following form:

Either the historic unity becomes unconditional not only for the historic human being living in it but becomes absolutely universally valid, i.e., the only true unity. For example: a revelation is exclusively the only true one, such as God incarnate who appeared only once.

Or there remains the knowledge about the multiplicity, the consequence of which is the unconditionality not only of one's own historicity but also of the recognition of the historicity of the other person.

The clearer one's thinking and the more honest one's attitude, the less reconcilable do these two possibilities become—at least so it seems. For the one excludes the other. We call the one the standpoint of catholicity, using the word "catholic" in its original meaning (not only the Catholic Church makes this claim)[*]; the other claim we call the claim of reason (reason understood here in its authentic philosophic meaning).

[*] In this chapter the word "catholic" should not automatically be applied to the Catholic Church. What we are talking about here can be seen everywhere in the world and thus also in the Catholic Church. However this church, taken as a whole, contains much more than this.

This antithesis is not that of authority and freedom, not that of religion and philosophy, not that of faith and knowledge. For these opposites are all polarities which are bound to each other even as they struggle with one another. But the antithesis of catholicity and reason, which cuts across the former ones, seems unbridgeable, not polar but exclusive. It exists only when it has become a conscious antithesis. But then each of the two camps is conscious of it in a way that is radically different from the other. No unanimity is possible—not even in the knowledge about this antithesis.

This antithesis appears not only in the great historical configurations but everywhere in one's inner attitude toward everyday things; toward one's conception of science, one's moral principles; in the relationship of man to man, in the manner of speaking, in communication. Usually veiled and hardly conscious, often existing side by side in the same person, the antithesis manifests itself suddenly in decisive situations. It seems as if two irreconcilable ways of life confronted each other, which come to light in the way in which one becomes aware of the totality of all the modes of the Encompassing.

We, for whom the road of reason is the true road, are left with the task of bringing the greatest clarity into this antithesis; most importantly, we must not mistake one for the other. We must, in the end, not break off contact but, questioning, continue to reach out. . . .

Discussion of the Antithesis

Original Historicity and Forced Historicity.   Existenz is historic. However, if a person becomes aware of historicity in an objective form, there arises a twofold danger:

On the one hand, what is known historically takes the place of historicity such that historical knowledge is grasped as that which is authentic. What I know about the past casts a veil—in the form of the myth of what has been—over the whole of my origin and path. Whatever could find no place for itself in what is known to me, I let drop; I enhance what may be alien to my nature: what I will does violence to my substance. What grew out of historicity and, as objective configuration, was particular and relative, mobile and changeable, then turns into the historic itself. However, forcibly holding on to the known and forcing this known onto myself robs me of my historicity. Thus subjugated to what is known and factitious, I am merely in seeming historicity, entrapped in a universal that has become constricting. In the process I become an ahistoric material, surrendered to nothingness in the transitory illusion of a historicity; this becomes obvious in the moment when this illusion collapses through the intervention from outside of the forces of existence.

On the other hand, the knowledge of historicity in its specific, objective incarnations robs our life of its unconditionality. The relativity of what is historically objective makes life itself relative. The non-universal undermines the unconditional validity for me in my historicity. I mistrust the historic and make the impossible, self-destructive attempt to live my life in the merely universal validity of consciousness-as-such. I become helpless in the bottomlessness in which I find myself.

Original historicity is able to maintain itself over against these two dangers—the forced historicity together with the authoritative coercion of the objectively known, as well as the bottomless historicity of historical relativity. The clear space of reflection must serve not only to preserve original historicity but to develop it. The difficulty is that in it one must hold fast to the unconditional which, however, must not assume universal validity. To become conscious of the authentic ground, and hence not to let myself be enmeshed in rigidified particularities but to live out of this ground in ever new particularities that arise from each other in a natural transformation: this is not a matter of the will which could actualize it immediately as a purpose; it is, rather, the result of the freedom of constantly illuminated inner action consequent on the situations arising in the world.

The whole clarity of humaneness, its nobility and power, is to be found only where one's own historicity is not turned into an absolute historicity for all but remains unconditional for itself. Only in this historicity is man open to the breadth of human possibilities, their hierarchy and value, and is also identical, as self-being, with his historicity in which he lives, unwavering, in readiness for death.

Catholicity leads to forced historicity—reason keeps alive the primal source of historicity. Catholicity demands absoluteness for its historicity—reason out of its grounds presents the claim of historicity on the part of men in their singularity. Both—catholicity and reason—reject the nihilism of historical relativity.

Catholicity and reason mutually exclude each other. Just as soon as they become articulated they are embroiled in battling each other.

The claim of absoluteness, e.g., on the part of Christianity, includes the demand that all men become Christians. To be sure, Christianity is ready to acknowledge the truth of all other religions but only as partial truths, in which capacity they are to incorporate themselves into Christianity and cast off the untruths attached to them. True, Christianity presents an attitude of openness toward what is alien to it which allows it merely to discover, in the other religion, the truth which is itself Christian. Man *qua* man is already a Christian—*anima naturaliter Christiana*—he merely must understand and acknowledge himself as such.

This is countered by the claim: I can live truly only in that historic ground out of which I have sprung, i.e., can follow only that authority into which I was born. A "Damascus-experience" can easily break a person, make him ugly and fanatical; conversion always brings with it the danger that the convert's existential ground will be extinguished. Faced with a person who has experienced such a break I am repelled by his lack of restraint and his instances of inhumanity (even if they are covert and remain unconscious), and am turned back toward my own ground all the more decisively. Hence we must not admit one authority for the whole world (i.e., a catholic authority); instead we must demand the preservation of the authority that has come down to us. Allegiance to the authority of our own ground goes hand in hand with our acknowledgement of a different authority for the other person. (The exception, however, constitutes a breakthrough within each authority and creates anew out of the change which he causes. This is the case for every authority insofar as it remains true, i.e., in motion.)

Catholic authority demands the obedience of everyone, basing itself on its own onsight into the nature of authority. The people who believe this authority expect—also as a sign of their own truth—that all men will subjugate themselves to this absolute authority in which they themselves believe.

Counterposed to catholic authority there is the rational knowledge about the historicity of all authority. It is the claim of finitude that there is not one authority for all, not the paralyzing permanence of the one authoritative world organization, nor the immuring of all motion and possibility in the mausoleum of the one universal authority which, now immobile, would also have to lose the attributes of genuine authorities. . . .

Assurance out of Knowledge of the Whole or Certainty out of the Primal Source.   Man can only live in certainty. If he finds himself in uncertainty he looks for assurance. He takes hold of this assurance in the form of objective guarantees on which he can depend—or certainty is given to him, incomprehensibly, out of his origin when he dares to live without assurance by objective guarantees.

The assurance of truth occurs through an objective knowledge of the whole. This assurance which, by virtue of the closed and final nature of knowledge assigns a place to all actuality and possibility, suspends all genuine risk. I know ahead of time what is and what happens; I know the meaning. I no longer really live in time but in eternity, but not in the concrete eternity which is identical with the fulfilled moment but in the abstract timelessness of the perduring being-in-order.

Such knowledge of the whole in systematic form is the aim of philosophy and theology. If I know the whole, I possess, as it were, a pre-knowledge that cancels out danger as long as I obey the laws imposed on me out of my knowledge of the whole. But the totality of truth in the form of a system does not in fact become accessible to man in time without deception. In time there is always a need for risk—and only that fulfillment is possible which is not the result of knowledge which gives guarantees, but arises, in all uncertainty, solely from tranquil trust in the inexplicable cipher.

To be sure—every philosophic thought, even the thought which, in attempting, illuminates—can be misunderstood in the sense of a reassuring pre-knowledge. If, countering the system, I carry out the illumination of risk and foundering as a thinking in which, through my insight, I assure myself in advance of the meaning of my foundering, then I have lost what is meant in the philosophic remembrance of this thinking. In that case I misunderstand the fundamental character of philosophizing. For philosophizing, if it is granted to me as a gift, is not the acquisition of guarantees but the awakening illumination of what I do in my innermost actions.

The truth contained in something definite is always a particular one and always merely a stepping stone. All definite truth, measured against truth as such, is merely an indication, is a specific fulfillment which again is called in question; it is a step forward, not completion.

Catholicity wants and asserts knowledge of the whole, guarantees of an objective nature, security. Reason risks the road that leads through definite knowledge into the indeterminate, knows no guarantees other than those specific and relative for each case which are given through finite knowledge and through contact between men. Reason is replete with certainty despite the uncertainty remaining in the whole. . . .

Catholic Methods and Communicative Methods.   The historicity of man lies in the communication from Existenz to Existenz in which that first comes into being which authentically is. Catholicity has established a community in which only that is imparted which exists in an objectively identical manner for all, and is believed, coupled with the impulse toward the functional recurrence of the same. Instead of the elevating struggle among the minds, there is command and obedience, the imparting of truths possessed which the other person merely need accept, there is the noncommittal exchange of conventional phrases which are the expression of a mood of tranquil community.

We call "catholic methods" those institutions, modes of behavior, practical rules which seek to bring about and to hold fast for an unlimited time to the universal oneness of human community based on a faith in catholic authority.

Historic Existenz is effective precisely in its non-universality. Complete universality would abolish communication. Since history would be at an end so also would communication. All that is left then is what is established for all time. To this corresponds the notion of total understanding in unity at the end of time. Counter to this, the seriousness of communication in time can be found only when truth is not complete and is not merely a possession, when history, rather, is undecided and open without bounds. Communicative methods search for the path of this truth.

Let us characterize the *catholic methods:*

(a) In a *rational system* a whole is thought in which everything that is possible has its place and through it its space, but also its extent and limit.

Nothing is left out, nothing opposed absolutely; rather, everything is tolerated but in such a manner that, instead of rupturing the whole, it serves it by becoming part of it.

Hence, in thought, the attempt is made to find the mean between the extremes, the "as-well-as" to counter the "either-or," conciliation instead of exclusive decisiveness. Exclusion is practiced only against that whose aim it is to destroy the principle of totality, against all radicalness which, rather than seeking membership, turns into a heresy. There is truth in everything if only it is understood properly. There is untruth in everything if, in its self-will, it wants to assert itself.

Thus in the world of thought everything that was ever thought must be brought together into a system but in such a way that each original thought is blunted, each impulse is, as it were, robbed of its soul. Hence the immense realm of thought does not consist in the contemplation of what was once actually thought; rather, in this way of appropriating, everything is turned into the corpse of something merely objectively rational. The whole has become a graveyard. This is true no matter how different a system looks, how original in its conception, how grandiose in its structures, or how profound it may appear in its contents, as in Thomas or Hegel.

In all of us, whether of a catholic mind or oriented toward reason, the power of unity has a fundamental effect on us that varies with the degree of clarity with which it penetrates us. It is the effect of taking hold of everything living as such, sharing its life and, in sharing it, to appropriate it, not to close ourselves off, not to offer blind resistance; for everything that is must relate to the One. However, a unity which pretends to be the only all-inclusive one is lost when there actually arises, *over* against it, another unitary power. Out of this experience grows the repudiation or assertion of the possibility of the one rational system of all Being:

Reason recognizes that Being cannot be comprehended within the system and that thinking, with all its systematic character, must remain open at the same time.

The catholic method, on the other hand, designs the system into which everything can be accepted. It proceeds by argumentation: by separating the true from the false, by conceding the partially and relatively true, by transforming substantial content into a mere product of thought. The price paid for this catholic-rationalistic unity is the loss of substance in everything that was assimilated, transformed, and accepted from the outside. In such a system one is unable to perceive anything as original if it is alien. One loses the authentic mystery of the transcendent One and its compelling attraction in worldly communication in favor of a rationalistic-systematic unity which is considered universally valid.

Through the design of the whole each form of life, each task, each way of being human is to have its place in the world of human institutions. In the organic social doctrine there is a place for everyone, the prostitute as well as the saint, the slave as well as the master, and each existence, as a member of the whole, has the dignity peculiar to it. No existence represents absolute lostness, none is a being-at-the-mercy-of-another. But all have been deprived of their boundlessness; they revolve, as it were, in eternal recurrence of the same, all is repeated in the enduring, immovable state of things.

This way of thinking, in which man wants to comprehend the whole and would like to establish it as that which has always been and—if it is wholly actual—will always remain. It seems as if man were able to survey the whole and to arrange it in a practicable manner as if he were a second creator of the world. Even if he believes that he is merely following, in his thinking, what God has already thought, he still confuses man and God.

(b) In *practical behavior* the following principle applies: under the condition that the center of catholic power and of decision—which, in the case of conflict, rests solely with the earthly representative of the apex of this truth—is acknowledged, the greatest latitude is granted to particular developments, even to arbitrariness, to superstition, to moral laxity.

It is not the splendor of a great destiny which may achieve validity, not the high stakes of risk and adventure, not the exception—for these could come to pose a danger to the permanency of the whole; rather it is the narrowness of the private sphere, the arbitrariness of the pitiful particular which is given freedom by being treated with benevolent tolerance.

Excuses are offered everywhere as long as the doer and the thinker obey the whole at least in principle and become part of it. However, there is pitiless rejection whenever a spark of inner rebellion can be felt, no matter whether it originates in lofty enthusiasm, devoted love, or ethically unconditonal substance.

No truly independent self-being can be permitted; however, the hierarchy of sociological possibilities does allow for perennially keeping one's distance, supra- and subordination, being-more or being-less.

For the sake of all that seems to be clear and comprehensible in the ordered realm of thought, the discordant element in the practical order is tolerated, even though this order is merely approximate and, in the final analysis, only superficially successful. It is a soothing, muffling pacification; it does not permeate or animate.

(c) In the *political behavior* of the leaders of catholicity an unrestricted empirical realism is operative. They do not interfere with the actual political forces, their sole criterion being how they can be made to serve as factors in the preservation and consolidation of catholic authority in existence.

What Machiavelli and Kantilya have expressed in ingenuous awareness is in fact practiced ingenuously by the forces of catholic authority but the reasons

given for it are always different. Catholic authority boasts of its true realism—
because it comes from God—over against the irrealism and illusionism of the
atheists, agnostics, and heretics. It invests itself with the self-righteousness of
legitimacy.

Both, catholicity and reason, are universal. But there lies a chasm between
the objective universality of leveling superficiality as it grows out of everything and the existential breadth of reason. In spite of all its richness, catholic
universality is closed and hence becomes narrow as well as bottomless; reason
remains boundlessly open and moves out of the primal source of each historic
Existenz, having achieved its certainty in its immediacy to trancendence.

Over against the catholic methods stands the *impulse toward unrestricted
communication*.

One condition of becoming oneself is the communication between those
who are different from each other in their origin; for this reason communication is actualized no matter what the inherent danger. Reason sustained by
Existenz is identical with the total will to communication. All order is to be
deepened and broadened by unlimited openness and bringing-into-relation.
Order is not absolute.

Here the multiplicity of convictions is no longer arbitrariness; for, in the
realm of minds, one conviction recognizes another. Communication brings
together what is essentially different in the solidarity of Existenzen against
being of no consequence. The unconditionality which recognizes and loves
itself in the other is distinguished from what is scattered, accidental, always
conditioned by something else, which is merely put into an order in
catholicity.

In time, the actuality of existence never coincides with reason; rather every
being of reason is, as existence, also constricted; it is limited in what comes
toward it from inside as well as the outside. Hence reason is present, to be
sure, as driving force but not as completely permeated actuality. In spite of the
will to communicate, those who are different in their origin become embroiled in the struggle of existence. The communicative attitude is actualized
even then, in the gallantry of the struggle: I am inwardly affected by what I
myself am not; I do battle with my equal who is also bound to me even as we
struggle.

The passion toward night is the limit at which, even in its absence, communication strives to remain actual in spite of everything. It is the place where
succumbing to anti-reason with reason—or redeeming anti-reason with
reason—may yet succeed. Here encompassing reason assumes the oddest
forms: there is truth in deception; knowledge that is greater than can be carried out remains in communication with anti-reason with the aim of redeeming it through interpretation but without being able to complete it. Reason's

entrance into absolute historicity becomes the radical polar opposite of catholic methods.

But no man can assist another in essence. All help between people is given either through practical-technical acts in the area of general correctness, which is an enclave of cognizable Being in the midst of unknown Being; or this assistance takes place in communication in which, in fact, each person helps himself as he is with the other being. For all that is possible is the community of those who are themselves. These touch each other as they become manifest, in the loving struggle, in making each other attentive; this touching produces impulses but not help. Each remains in doubt but is not in possession, raises himself higher but has not reached his goal. Since, however, man is so often helpless in the absence of his self-being, he strives to go beyond the limit of what is possible to man and receive help from the other even in his innermost self. And there were men who believed they could render this help. They did not awaken the other maieutically, as did Socrates, but transmitted the truth directly to the other as did Christ. Christ first grants the grace which transforms man so that he becomes capable of receiving the faith in the perfect truth that did not reside in him before.

But whoever philosophizes can neither give nor receive such truth. He can neither possess nor receive truth but can merely grow toward it in mutual communication.

Hence, philosophically, our strength grows whenever we encounter self-being and truth in struggle; and we are overcome by helplessness where we encounter helplessness. Where man stands existentially in communication with man, there real help in what is knowable and particular combines with the clarity of searching for the truth as a whole through the loving struggle.

Transcendence appears only in the existential truth, invisible from the outside in its multiplicity and searching for itself in communication.

To be sure, the ideal of reason, with its unlimited communication, is possible neither as an image nor in actuality. Yet this image-less ideal is the most profound impetus in man. . . .

The Choice between Catholicity and Reason

In existence it is impossible to avoid choosing. If we do not choose we become as nothing since decisions are then made for us. For us, choice is unavoidable. In the perception of possibilities and knowabilities we do not have the Encompassing, sheltered in which we would no longer need to choose. Rather, the whole of all the knowabilities is merely our means of arriving at the proper decision. Our neutrality with respect to the ultimate means the surrender of our selves; and that leads to the void.

However, everything depends on our grasping things in a way proper to their nature. We must not let them become unclear through confusing them; we must distinguish where choices need to be made and where they are unnecessary.

For example, we distinguish between choice in existence and choice in what is thinkable. In existence, in which each person has his own distinct origin, I belong some place even if external events have robbed me of my country and my people; by belonging there I choose myself in my origin, do not stand outside in neutrality; I suffer and hold on, am not merely interested but am bound to it and participate in it. I must choose my origin or, lacking this ground, I shall drown.

In thinkability, on the other hand, positions that can be formulated generally exclude each other as being rationally contradictory. But in acknowledging this contradiction—which I would have to do because of the evidence, even if I did not want to—there is no choice. Rather, it does not make sense to choose something knowable in the absolute meaning of existential choice. It is a matter of my breadth and freedom to determine where I—thinking, observing, appropriating—will arrive within the space of knowabilities and configurations. It does not make sense to swear by a formula or system as if each were a dogma unless it is a particular symbol in a situation that forces us into battle.

If one has to make a choice between catholicity and reason, then this is not a logical decision between general thought positions; for the opposition cannot be reduced to a logical contradiction but can only be illuminated in various directions, which is what we tried to do. Also, it is not a choice of historic origin versus another kind of origin for each of them is grounded in a particular origin that is historic. This kind of choice is all too easily taken care of in a narrow or crooked or superficial manner which produces a false clarity, or, remaining unclear, it avoids decision. But the main point is: through the false identification of catholicity with historic authority and of reason with intellect, all that is essential is concealed to the point of inversion.

For philosophizing, this choice is the decisive one, namely whether it should take place at all. . . .

Let us now discuss the *contradictions of catholicity and reason*: This contradiction lies, as such, not in Being itself but in our nature. It is the deepest tension of being-human. Within it, being-human forces itself upward.

It appears to us as an ultimate contradiction, one that we cannot adequately comprehend. For it is constituted in such a manner that the one side looks completely untrue to the other, and in such a manner that each side believes itself to be grasped wrongly, superficially, without understanding.

But the contradiction is also such that, from the vantage point of reason, the other, i.e., catholicity, must and shall remain in the world. Perhaps it *must* remain because the historicity of Being cannot be actualized in its concrete form in the majority of people without the illusion of universality. It *shall* remain so that the clarity of truth can reconstitute itself through reason in a constant struggle with this most dangerous—because most reductive—lapse. The fact that catholicity is the refuge of all men for whom reason in its open historicity is intolerable, forces reason itself to acknowledge, even participate in, the phenomenal world. This is especially true whenever catholicity becomes politically all-powerful, as was the Church in previous centuries, and as perhaps a new, unchristian catholicism will be in the future. In that case the question is only what, in the case of conflict, will have priority for the person who lives within reason. What is decisive is not the participation in forms, rites, language, but the choice made in a situation of concrete collision.

Since catholicity always has the greatest opportunity to assume world dominion while reason, on the other hand, is always threatened with extinction, indeed with being nipped in the bud, only the clearest consciousness which unfolds methodically can offer such an opportunity to the reason residing in the individual human being.

The fact, however, that catholicity and reason are irreconcilably opposed to each other is one of the phenomena which reveal the deepest contradictions within time.

In the court of reason, a contradiction must not be absolutized into one of irreconcilables. Therefore even the contradiction of catholicity and reason is to be grasped as a whole, with one side having preeminence and truth. Even though the contradiction is an irreconcilable one, reason puts up with catholicity as an existent; but it puts up resistance.

Selection 42

ASPECTS OF THE THEORY(4):
THE COMPLETION OF TRUTH IN TIME

EDITORS:
Radically speaking, the form in which truth is effectively complete is a matter of the singular Existenz. However, in philosophical abstraction we can only generalize about the forms which such completion tends to take. The two types of existentially effective completion which Jaspers characterizes are "original intuitions" and "philosophizing."

Religion, art, and poetry are the ordinary designations of what, for Jaspers, are the intuitions that afford visions of the ground of truth. They are thus the life-founding completion of truth for man in time; they accomplish this in a manner that is original, i.e., not primarily reflective, though their expressions and traditions can reach pinnacles of spiritual sophistication. The one form of "original intuition" which Jaspers elaborates in *Von der Wahrheit* is the phenomenon of the tragic world-view; this essay was translated into English under the title *Tragedy is Not Enough*.

Deliberate reflection is the mark of distinction of the philosophical concern over the completion of truth in time for man. But the stress is on philosophizing, which is an activity, not a doctrine or a distinctive way of crafting a doctrine. Here the completion of truth in its wholeness is seen by Jaspers as impossible in time, but completion of truth in time is ultimately a matter of communication. Selection 43 deals with this.

The inclusion of a set of selections which would constitute a topical treatment of the completion of truth in time exceeds the scope of this Reader. However, the topic is addressed in other parts of this book: Part Three, the tasks of philosophy; Subpart ii, below, reading of the cipher-script. In the brief selection to follow, Jaspers gives an overview of the topic. It appears in *Von der Wahrheit*, pp. 903–05; the translation has been provided by the editors.

TEXT:
If we look at the historical actuality of the completion which men have achieved, we see the same everywhere: greatness does not endure; one prepares for it, it unfolds with a sudden burst of speed and is already transformed into emptied configurations while one still believes that one is seeing its continuance.

One grand example is the transition from the world of myth to the world of reflection. In one historic moment the world of myth is dissolved through man's bold venture to think everything that is possible, to take hold of every experienceable actuality and again to confront critically what is thought as well as what is experienced. Myth is still alive at this point; it is just passing through a last transformation, raising itself to the language of immediacy of actuality in creative unfolding and deepening. At the same time a kind of knowledge has become actual which threatens to rob man of everything that has given him stability, meaning, and tranquility, as well as a kind of myth which, having reached its depth, immediately annuls itself. It is a tragic situation in which man now becomes fully aware of the tragedy. At this culminating point between two eras when the Greeks invented tragedy, two things are possible: the capacity, on the part of being-human that has become conscious, to endure the dreadful situation, as well as an all-encompassing humanity. In the very next instant we see enlightenment become any kind of reflection at all, experiential knowledge enter a new narrowness, and myth, for the educated person, de-actualized into a mood and a symbol understood aesthetically. We see the capacity to endure impoverished to become lamentation and passive imperturbability and humanity diluted into pallid humaneness.

It is, as it were, an explosion of man. He is actualized in his highest possibilities, the splendor of his nature radiates from there throughout the ages. But it goes no further. The apex is at the same time the end. For the tradition is not a holding fast of the heights that have been achieved but a distant admiration that does not come closer to a true understanding of something past. It is a transformation that is theatrically noisy, that makes harmless what no longer is and no longer can be.

Thus Greek tragedy stands between the myth that is still alive and the enlightenment that has been robbed of myth. In Meister Eckart there occurred a unique actualization of speculative mysticism at its height because he still believed totally in the doctrines of his church and yet already lived in them out of the primal source of reason, out of the whole breadth of man in his freedom. Even those figures who belong to a time of stability, such as Dante and Thomas, are unique in the origin of their truth and the meaning of their work and can never be duplicated, even though it seems as if the content of their teaching is transmitted unchanged; at the border between two eras they achieve the ultimate (Thomism is not Thomas). The philosophy of German idealism stands between Christianity and godlessness: out of the being-no-longer and the not-yet-being grows the situation in which this philosophy reaches its dizzying heights. Kierkegaard and Nietzsche are phenomena of a change that becomes conscious of itself in a unique manner at the moment when, in their clairvoyance, they see with dread the actualization of tremendous innovation.

No matter how we look at history in its changing aspects, we find that it is always the state of transition which serves as the matrix of greatness; greatness is being-transition. All of history up to now—this brief span of a few millennia—can appear to be one single transition; and we, too, are in this transition: the transition of a flash of light in the history of the earth, measured against whose duration this transition is perhaps an insignificant instant. In all of human history, the extraordinary high point of transition, the axis, as it were, of spiritual events, is to be found in the centuries around the middle of the last millennium before Christ (in China, India, and the West).

But the great transition phenomena are merely the most sublime configurations of what occurs all the time: All actuality is in the transition proper to it; everything, even what is less exalted, is, in its uniqueness and authenticity, always both end and completion. All enduring uniformity, all that has been handed down and that repeats itself: these are the medium in which the authentic occurs. What is handed down makes possible what is essential in each instance but does not remain the same as it was in its origin. It is knowable, intuitable, re-thinkable; but it is no longer present, as itself, in the observer or re-thinker.

Personal biographies also evince this characteristic. One's enduring substance is present at sublime moments and in a series of original steps out of which and toward which one lives this life. The illumined thought whose germinal appearance can be determined in time but which is immediately present in its full clarity (as in the case of Nicholas of Cusa, Kant, Descartes) is such a phenomenon. In borderline cases we speak of men who have written a single book (*homines unius libri*) and whose lives found their completion and their end in this work. Another borderline case is incipient mental illness which, in its transitional stage, reveals an extraordinary and unique depth of the soul. It is as if, in short-lived incandescence, man manifests himself in the manner of a meteor.

Selection 43

TRUTH AND COMMUNICATION:
SUMMARY OF THE THEORY—SECOND PART

EDITORS:
In the final selection dealing with Jaspers's theory of truth, the completion of truth in time is turned into the task of self-realization through exercising a will to total communication. And, the other way around, communication is seen as the ultimate vehicle of the concretion of truth in time. Truth in time is, then, not something we can realize in its completeness, but its completion is our task. In time, the completion is never-ending. But our existential actuality, being placed within truth, is of the essence of truth in its becoming. In the activity of communicative reason we testify to the circumstance that, in our finitude, we realize less than truth; at the same time we mitigate this finitude by being informed by and informing other finitudes and thereby enlarging the scope of realized unity. In Jaspers the problem of truth for man in time, even as it is informed by the testimony of man's experience with the question, is turned, for its realization, to the enactments of human life, the everyday life as well as the bigger scenes such as politics, religion, the life of the spirit.

The selection appears in *Vernunft und Existenz*, pp. 91–103; the translation has been prepared by the editors. In William Earle's translation it is found in *Reason and Existenz*, pp. 95–106.

TEXT:
From the situation of Existenz in time it follows, first of all, that, if truth is bound to communication, truth can only be in becoming; that, in its depth, it is not dogmatic but communicative. Only then, out of the consciousness of the becoming truth, does the possibility of a radical openness of the will to communication arise in actuality, yet without ever being able to fulfill itself except in the historic moment which, as such, again becomes incommunicable.

There follows, secondly—in the foundering before the manifold of truth—a self-recovery of the boundless will to communication which sees the failure of the whole as decisively as it holds fast to its path not knowing where it will lead.

It follows, thirdly, that, if the truth in communication cannot be won and established as the final one, truth as well as communication will see themselves disappear, as it were, before transcendence and its becoming before Being, and that its decisive actualization brings forth also the deepest openness for this transcendence.

A. The Twofold Meaning of Truth in Time: Dogmatic and Communicative Truth. To what extent is total communication itself the actuality of truth, i.e., is our truth in time? This question becomes clear as we discuss the twofold meaning of truth in time:

When the nature of truth seemed to be grasped both conclusively and in its historicity—as object, symbol, and statement—then the only question remaining was how this truth, attained and now present, is to be transmitted to all men. This truth was closed in itself, timeless in time, therefore complete by itself and not dependent on men; but men were considered dependent on it. Then began its dissemination from man to man which did not consist in mutually bringing forth truth in each but in giving, on the part of those possessing truth, to those not yet partaking of it. But herewith commenced the process of transformation of this truth; for those who absorbed it understood it out of themselves. It was, indeed, no simple act of acceptance. The truth, instead of remaining the same in its originality and being transmitted to men as such, was watered down and perverted, or transformed into something quite different out of another source. Its diffusion, in such configurations, among men went as far as the limits beyond which its further diffusion was, for all practical purposes, halted.

The truth which would bind itself primally to communication would be different. It would not be at all, apart from its actualization in communication. By itself it would neither be present nor complete. As its condition, truth would have the transformation not only of the man to whom it is imparted but also that of the man who does the imparting. This transformation would be the result of his readiness and capacity to communicate, his equally decisive ability to hear and express, and his conscious awareness of all modes and levels of communication. It would be the truth which is actual only as and through communication, and thus originates only in it. This truth is neither present prior to communication and then to be imparted, nor does it represent a goal attainable through a certain method, at which point it could then be valid without communication.

Historically, established truths have developed philosophic and religious techniques for the molding of men, i.e., all the spiritual exercises, yoga techniques, and mystical initiations that will transform the individual so that he may behold the truth, albeit not through communication but through a discipline which locks him up in it. But if one does not rest content with such a type of human being which, even though grandiose, is yet fixed in his form, is reduced to one level through the very process of formation, is firmly molded yet debasing, and if one does not consider this the perfection of man, then one needs the deeper discipline of the constantly enforced transparency of communication. That which has often been achieved by limitation to goals in the transparency of the intellect but what, beyond that, few have actualized in historic community, albeit in a questionable manner, that would have to become the beginning: it would become the challenge to bring forth human beings under the conditions of a communication which does not deceive, is not made easy, is not debased, but which illuminates without limit.

But in this communication untruth must also be present insofar as it contains movement; hence the truth is not complete but remains open even as it completes itself.

Here we find again the radical abyss between the dogmatic and the communicative modes of knowing the truth:

If we presuppose an established truth which is accessible to us as such, and if we consider this truth to be something solid standing outside of me which is already present and only has to be found; if, thus, our task is a discovering and not a creating, then there exists, in pure immanence, either the one correct world order, which it is our task to bring about, or the hereafter, which is merely like another world that has been firmly promised to us.

If, however, every configuration of truth remains limited for us through the actualization of communication, then the unresolvable incompleteness of the world and of all mundane cognizable truth is the ultimate within immanence. Every configuration must founder in the world, none can prevail as the absolute truth.

Thus, if truth takes this path, then it can be found only in that transcendence which is neither a world beyond that is merely a second world, nor this world once more but better. The notion which really takes hold of transcendence, basing itself on the incomplete nature of communication and on the foundering of every configuration of truth in the world, is like a proof of God's existence: from the incompletion of every sense of truth and under the presupposition that there must be truth, it encounters transcendence. Hence it is valid only for Existenz, which is absolutely concerned with truth, and for the honesty of Existenz, to which truth never manifests itself in the world as one and unique in the tranquil permanency of timelessness.

B. *The Openness of the Will-to-Communicate on Its Path Through Actuality.* In order to become aware of communicative truth, it is a matter, philosophically, of thinking through all the modes of the Encompassing in such a manner that the path of possible Existenz in the world is given the widest space. Existenz, as a movement in temporal existence that cannot be sublated, ought to maintain itself in the face of the total breadth of actualities and possibilities. Only then can the radical will to communication which springs from reason and Existenz be effective, whereas the possession of a truth regarded as being final, in fact, breaks off communication.

The openness of the will to communication is a twofold one:

It is open, first, to the knowability of what is not yet known. Since what cannot be communicated is as though it were not at all, openness impels toward bringing all that is merely possible into the medium of communicability so that it may attain Being for us. Second, openness is readiness for the substance of the being that unbosoms itself to me, thus it is readiness for an other who I am not but with whom I can be in solidarity as regards the boundless will to be oneself. Man's loving search is never concluded.

My consciousness always remains a narrows: in the first place with respect to any being which, lacking communicability, is not for me, yet imperceptibly affects me, my existence, and my world; and in the second place, by virtue of the existence and the Existenz of others who are not identical with me and do not think identical thoughts, yet also determine my existence by addressing me without my being aware of it and whose communication could bring me more profoundly to myself. Therefore, since my consciousness is never the whole, it is never absolutely true consciousness. I am always reminded through the unforeseen effect of communication that I must not cease moving toward truth, or I am bound to experience my own untruth through the fact that things pass me by. The truth, says Hegel, is in league with actuality against consciousness. This actuality is the effect of what is not communicated and what perhaps is not communicable in the world. It is that to which we listen without understanding it, that which intrudes and which we can merely suffer. In this case the boundless will to communication never means simply submitting to the other as such; rather, it means knowing it, hearing it, being willing to take it into account up to the point where its own transformation becomes necessary.

Thus life within the totality of the Encompassing in which I find myself comprises the necessity of risk: Illumination itself shows me to be in the situation of risk, not because I seek danger out of bravado but because I must risk. Only a life lived blindly can conceal the constant risk from itself and remain in the polarity of supposed safety and an anxiety that must be endured but is soon forgotten. It is a daring thing to envisage possibility even unto its highest degree, to attempt to entice it out by risking my own openness and yet bear responsibility for which people I trust and how I trust myself—knowing that at each level communication is possible only among equals. I must take upon myself as my guilt both failure and deception, perhaps as the crisis in which the communication that has been established can now grow, perhaps as the ruination whose meaning I do not comprehend.

   C. *The Radical Will-to-Communicate Faces the Multiplicity of Existential Truths.*   Where the Encompassing remains present in each configuration, where the will to communication can truly be total, there Existenz confronts the ultimate limit, namely that there are many truths in the sense of existential unconditionality.

One might seem lacking in character if, in philosophizing, one admits this multiplicity of truths. One can interject: Only *one* truth is *the* truth; it is unconditional, if not for God then for man; man cannot commit himself totally if he does not believe his truth to be the only one.

One can counter this by saying: Since it is impossible for man to possess transcendence in temporal existence as a cognizable object, identical for everyone like something in the world, each mode of the One Truth as absolute in the world can, in fact, be only historic: it is unconditional for this Existenz and precisely for this reason not universally valid. It may, psychologically, be extremely difficult, but it is not impossible for man to realize his own truth in total commitment—having regard, at the same time, for the truth of the other though it is not truth for him—and also to hold fast to the relativity and particularity of all truth that is universally valid. For this reason he must not evade the highest demand of truthfulness of carrying through simultaneously what is only seemingly irreconcilable. One can never project the idea of man to too high a level; all one has to do is to avoid the absolutely impossible that conflicts with the finitude of man's temporal existence. Empirical improbability,—i.e., what is improbable, given the data obtained by the usual observation of humankind—does not apply to the idea of the ever-ready communication that is possible in the primal source of human nature: before empirical actuality it is transformed into the infinite task whose limits of actualization are beyond all calculation.

However, the most radical breaking-off of communication is liable to occur where the multiplicity of truths is recognized existentially. But the total will to communication, once it has become aware of its path, cannot abandon itself. It places trust in itself and in possibility in the world, a trust that can be disappointed time and again and lead to doubt, not in its foundation but in its specific actualization. It also trusts the truth of the other, which is not his but which, as truth, must include some mode of the possibility of communication. Therefore this will cannot simply be extinguished under the burden of failure. Perhaps it possesses, where it is actual, a kind of spirited moderation in which it plans out a vision of its path as idea—to be sure, without an extended actuality but as the expression of his possibility which never betrays itself:

The utmost in clarity and truth can come into being even under conditions of battling enmity when Existenzen, originally different in nature, knowingly take hold, in the battle of existence, of a fate which they cannot escape. Out of their possible communication they will impose laws on the battle itself and thus cease to be disguised beasts; they will fight gallantly, i.e., subject to laws that presuppose mutually possible Existenz, and leave the way open for a later, genuine communication. But when this is achieved, then the leap to genuine communication would, in fact, have been made. The battle, subject to conditions in this manner, would no longer be the acting out of the necessities of existence but like a game, though a fateful one, one which threatens and perhaps even destroys life.

Only in this way could the unbounded will to communication be maintained in truthfulness. There would come into being a humaneness, not as a softness but as the immeasurable ability to grow through openness, as being deeply affected by each actual substance, as the unique consciousness of the limit at which transcendence—not a dogmatically rigid but a genuine transcendence—manifests itself to the actuality of action.

Only in this manner could the true strength of man be actualized. The force of the unconditional in him, having stood the test in each possibility of battle and of questioning, would no longer need suggestion, hatred, the pleasure of cruelty, in order to become active, nor the intoxication of big words and dogmas that are not understood, in order to believe in itself. Only in this way would man become truly strict, hard, and clear-headed. Only on this path can self-deceptions disappear and man himself not be destroyed together with the destruction of his life's illusions. Only thus would the genuine ground manifest itself, without a veil, out of its depths.

On the other hand, as soon as one maintains that there is one truth which is universally valid for all men, untruth comes into being at the same time, in spite of the past greatness of those who lived in that one truth, and of the magnificence of their history.

This is manifested in the most various contexts. No matter whether this one truth, in the shape of a comprehensive universal validity which is the form of all truth, is taken to be the achievement of reason, or whether, conversely, as the content of faith, it is above reason or counter to it: all must bow before this enforced truth even if they cannot share in it. Since consequent upon the false presupposition that there is basically only one form of the truth accessible to man, and consequent upon the related perversion of the multiplicity of the Encompassing where there always remains, at the limits, a lack of understanding of what is compatible with that which one believes to be truth, a fanaticism which breaks off all communication may suddenly appear. In the seemingly free medium of speaking, communicating, hearing, showing and giving reasons, decisions are made in secret by the brute force of what, in the context of existence, brings external power to bear at the time.

However, a *doctrine* of the many truths would have the same effect, i.e., to bring forth untruth if—instead of appearing as the attitude of an unbounded will to communication by virtue of one's own possible truth—it would come forth as a knowledge of the deplorable multiplicity of truth. The many truths become untrue at the very moment when they are seen, from the outside, as many, and become fixed as standpoints: For he who thinks them also can himself assume all these standpoints. Further, they become untrue when they are mutually indifferent and merely stand alongside of each other. These truths cannot and will not become the same truth; yet they are involved with each other through their relationship to transcendence which touches upon the One and which—even if our gods are different ones—senses the distant God above all proximate gods. This distant God demands that we do not become corrupt in the dissipation of our multifariousness in which we battle each other in mutual indifference and hostility toward each other's existence for the space in which to exist. It is the sophistry of comfortable tolerance to allow the other to be, but not to let itself be touched. By contrast, it is the truth of tolerance to listen and give and enter into the boundless process of the communication which restrains violence and in which man, out of his roots, achieves the heights possible to him. The very highest can be achieved only in transformation through appropriation, in a knowledge that penetrates— even if only to reject for oneself—all that one encounters in the world.

If one were to demand, in time, perfection and solution, or even the image of a solution: this would amount to the suspension of the task allotted to man, who can become himself only through communication. What matters is that one does not close off in advance the possibilities of genuinely becoming human.

Our horizon is not bounded by images replete with content. The forms of our attitude, our statements of a goal which is itself thought merely as form, the truths experienced only in their rudimentary beginnings: such are the philosophic ultimates for us. They are not alien impossibilities but possibilities on the verge of speaking, even though they constantly seem to fade away once more.

D. *Transcendence: Communication as the Appearance of Truth in Time.* The imperfection of communication and the gravity of foundering make manifest a depth which nothing other than transcendence can fill: If God eternally is, then for man truth is as becoming truth, indeed as truth becoming communication. Detached from communication it is, as permanent truth, immediately debased into a knowledge of something in remaining of itself, into a finished contentment instead of a demand that is all-consuming within temporal existence.

However, before transcendence the imperfection of communication disappears at the temporally existing appearance of truth. Our communication is animated, as it were, by something manifesting itself in metaphysically playful notions, i.e., of a pretemporal origin of the need to communicate in time, or of an ultimate perfection overcoming communication; as they disappear again, such notions cannot make clear and knowable, but can touch for an instant on what, as the actual force, is the overpowering motivation in genuine communication:

In the primal source there was the One, the truth as it is inaccessible to us. But it is as though this lost One is to be recovered from its dispersion through communication, as if the confusion of the many could dissolve into the calm found in congruence, as if a forgotten truth could never again be wholly recaptured.

Or, truth lies in the future. To be sure, the consciousness of limit remains in temporal existence. Whatever is not communicable is as though it were not because it is not present for any consciousness or knowledge; but it is precisely in communication that the motivation goes beyond this limit. It does not turn back into insensitivity but goes forward in unlimited manifestness so that it will point out to itself what is authentic by entering into communicability. But then the motivation proceeds beyond each clarity, even the most existentially lucid, because in it there always remains an unsatisfactory component. To be sure, the high moments of seemingly total harmony of communication in the pervasive presence of all the modes of the Encompassing—of the knowable and of transcendence—show themselves in time to be either as false or, again, as the germ of a new impetus toward its manifestness, i.e., toward continuity in time. They are like the anticipation of a possible, perfected communication which would mean, at the same time, perfect truth and timeless oneness of the souls and of the universe. However, thinking this irreality of a communication that reaches its goal means annulling this communication in a transcendent perfection in which there is no need for further communication. The question whether, in the boundless will to communication on the part of reason and Existenz, we do not, in actuality, already live out of this communication-less Being which guides us—cannot be answered. Either the question is directed toward something which, for us, is empty, or it is an unquestioned certainty which cannot be communicated and which, wrongly expressed, would only destroy communicability. It would thus paralyze the actualization of the unconditional readiness to communicate which propels us toward communication, by an illusory knowledge about perfect communication.

If, however, all communication—being a flaw of temporal existence—must be thought as suspended in transcendence, then all conceivability is also suspended.

If, for example, I think of the ancient proposition that God is truth, then this truth—compared with all truths seen as the modes of correspondence—would lack such correspondence since it is undivided and, lacking an antithesis, would merely be in itself. This is indeed an empty notion, to be filled by me only existentially in my historicity. Wherever I cannot penetrate, truth no longer has a thinkable meaning for me. The foundering of all thought about truth can plunge into its own abyss but no thought can maintain itself there.

The calm of Being of truth in transcendence—not in the abandonment of the modes of the Encompassing but in going beyond their worlds—this is the boundary where the undivided whole can be momentarily illuminated. However, this illumination is infinitesimal in the world even though it has a decisive effect on the essence of man, and it cannot be communicated because, in communication, it would be drawn into the modes of the Encompassing where it would always be misunderstood. One's experience of it is absolutely historic, it is in time yet reaches beyond time. One can speak out of it but not about it. The ultimate of thought as well as of communication is silence.

II.

Metaphysical Truth: The Reading of Ciphers

EDITORS' INTRODUCTION TO SUBPART II:

In Jaspers's philosophy the question of metaphysical truth is a special topic within his theory of truth. He considers it as such in connection with the cipher as a form of the completion of truth in time. (The chapter of *Von der Wahrheit* which treats this topic appeared in English under the title *Truth and Symbol*.) But the conception of metaphysics as the reading of the cipher-script of transcendence is also the culminating point of Volume III of his earlier main work, *Philosophy*. Moreover, a renewed preoccupation with the meaning of ciphers occurred in Jaspers's later philosophy, particularly in connection with his debate with revealed religion and in his political thinking.

In his conception of cipher, Jaspers is concerned with the meaning and possibility of metaphysics. From the perspective of Existenz, metaphysics is a matter of man's assurance of the transcendent ground of whatever he knows, and especially of his freedom. Since nothing is real for man unless it is thought, such assurance is itself a matter of thought. Yet thought, in its determinative character, is inappropriate for the assurance of the—as such indeterminate—ground of determinate Being. Hence the unavoidable determinacy of the expression of such assurance must be cancelled, lest it be confused with scientific thought which, in its determinacy, is a more proper employment of thought. This confusion can be avoided if expressions of transcendental grounding are understood as the cipher-script of transcendence, the key to whose decipherment is unknown to man, whose human decoding, therefore, is never achieved with finality and ever remains man's unfinished task and a challenge to his creativity. For Jaspers, expressions of such assurance, even if they are supported by established traditions (such as religions), are ciphers. These may be: myths; religious doctrines; general ideas such as nature, history, or evil; metaphysical ideas such as God and soul; speculative proofs, such as that of God; existence, man's freedom, the oneness of Being; or the experience of art.

The selections of this subpart begin with Jaspers's consideration of the dependence of transcendence on existence as the form of its appearance (44).

Three selections deal with aspects of the nature of ciphers: The reading of the cipher-script is true as existential assurance of the transcendental ground of Being (45). The different modalities of the expression of metaphysical truth derive their meaning and significance as expressions of existential assurance (46). Because ciphers function for historic Existenzen, their meanings are not unitary but many, not solid but fluid (47). A consequence of the nature of ciphers is considered in Selection 48, according to which the truth of ciphers does not lie in their content but in the struggle among ciphers, a struggle carried out in communication. Ciphers are read at the limits of thought and lead to the limits of thought. Under the title, "At the Limits of Ciphers," three aspects of reading ciphers are presented. The first deals with Jaspers's well-known conception of the shipwreck or foundering of thought as a function of metaphysical truth (49). Selection 50 presents a correlate appropriate to the cipher-philosophy of what, in Christian theology, is known as negative theology; in this connection Jaspers interprets a great monument of Buddhist art as well as Meister Eckhart's mysticism. Buddhism and a way of thinking that is meant to transcend absolutely both existence and the determinacy of thought are the topics of Selection 51. In Selection 52, Jaspers presents what, for him, is a final issue in the problem of metaphysical truth: "reason vs. mysticism."

Selection 44

BACKGROUND: THE APPEARANCE OF TRANSCENDENCE IN EXISTENCE

EDITORS:
The inevitability and indispensability of existence for the historic realization of metaphysical truth is the topic of this selection. It is theoretically connected to the distinction of existence-Existenz (see, e.g., Selection 8) and to the special function of "appearance" whose periechontologic version is presented in Selection 25.

This selection has been translated by the editors and is excerpted from *Philosophie*, Vol. III, pp. 24–28 and 29–30. E. B. Ashton's translation is found in *Philosophy*, Vol. III, pp. 24–26 and 27–28.

TEXT:
    1. *Community and Struggle in Transcendent Relation.*   Transcendence, as historic appearance in an objectified symbol, establishes a community that is unique in kind. Not only is my historicity a communicative one, but in extended historicity Existenz follows the substance of the tradition out of

which it arose. The fact that the metaphysical content is historic means that Existenz adheres to the revelation of transcendence it has received in the particular configuration it has encountered and in the language it has heard. This is so not because this revelation is one configuration among others, thus also a truth, but because it is, for Existenz, simply the truth on the basis of which its self-being will stand or fall.

Truth must assume this historic form because the truth of transcendence, for Existenz in existence, is not there as the atemporal enduring truth to be grasped in the same way as the insights of the intellect. However, as long as a community of free Existenzen is kept in motion by such historic form, Existenz will not confuse the meaning of universality and hence will remain open to the truth of other Existenzen. Adhering unconditionally to its own truth and conscious of its historicity, Existenz would avoid exclusivity vis-à-vis others as well as the claim to universality and would not assign to truths in their historic form the character of timelessly valid truths of the understanding. Existenz would, however, respond affirmatively to the question whether the being of the self in its transcendent relatedness could be grounded in an accident of history. Historicity becomes the source of the conviction of not being everything and of not considering oneself as that type of being which should be the *only* being.

Historical actuality shows us a different picture. Symbols become the forces bringing about community which, excluding or destroying the other, consider themselves to be the sole truth. The darkness of transcendence becomes intermingled with the darkness of the vital passions. Whoever resists clarity and, inviolable in his blind self-existence, wants to live in passionate intoxication, will travel this road. Here validity lies in that which is unquestioned. While the battle for transcendence lends the appearance of tremendous rightness one can abandon oneself to the wild instincts of violence. Here the symbol brings about community without communication.

This fanaticization is made possible through confusing the heterogeneous meanings of the universal and taking them to be one and the same. However, the authentic truth of transcendence grasps itself consciously as being historic and hence not universal, as unconditional and hence not universally valid.

However, the inescapable consequence of the historicity of the appearance of transcendence is the struggle that ensues when the *existence* of one *collides* with that of another because of the world situation in which both find themselves. Transcendence seems to refuse to relinquish without struggle its appearance in the form of each particular historicity. That men of this particular kind and with this particular substance of Being are to live on earth—this can be felt as if it were an unconditional commandment from a hidden source. The battle is fought not only by the will to self-preservation on the part of blind existence; rather, it is the aim that the future of human life be constituted in such a manner that this historicity of transcending consciousness be known and appropriated by men as their past. This aim can be achieved not only in victory but also in genuine foundering.

In existence this most profound battle among the contents that are existentially rooted cannot be suspended. Lessing's parable of the three rings* does not reflect our situation; for in the various aspects [of our situation] it is not the case that we know the one truth, only in different guises. Rather, the uniquely-universal of transcendence causes irreconcilable truths to do battle in mundane existence in the form of particular historic universality. The passions exhibited in this battle have been greater than those caused by the vital interests of existence. Here, in belief in transcendence, everything seems to be at stake, not only the believer but Being itself.

2. *The Tension between the Three Configurative Spheres of Metaphysical Objectivity.* Mythology, theology and philosophy seek to express and present the Being of transcendence explicitly and objectively: *mythology* does so as an overflowing, constantly changing plenitude of stories, figures, and interpretations, as the unfolding of a knowledge about transcendence that breaks through world-knowledge and accompanies it; *theology* does so on the foundation of a revelation fixed in history as the rationally grounded systematic completion that results in knowledge of truth; *philosophic metaphysics* does so by conceiving transcendence in existence through thoughts that press forward to ultimate sources and boundaries, vault over themselves and fulfill themselves only in the presence of a particular historic Existenz. It appropriates what is everywhere present as mythical actuality and seeks to understand what is strange to it in mythology and revelation.

The three spheres of configuration approach and penetrate each other and then repel each other all the more decisively. But they remain bound to each other even in their mutual hostility. The unhistoric ever-recurring type of their configurations allows no rest in their battle without clear battle lines being drawn; for the battle lies hidden in the individual soul as an unstoppable movement.

Philosophy casts off the myth from which it originated. Over against the narration of stories which it holds to be delusions and dreams it sets rational, reasoned insight. But one day, having become independent, it casts its glance backward and attempts to grasp myth as truth. It then grasps it in one of two ways. On the one hand, philosophy regards myth as the *masking* of philosophic insight for those who cannot as yet understand it in the form of thought, or else as philosophy proper in those moments when the philosophizing individual becomes aware of the certainty of Being, not through thought but through such intuited configuration. On the other hand philoso-

*cf. Gotthold Ephraim Lessing, *Nathan the Wise*, Act III, Scene 7.

phy sees in myth the very expression of a truth which remains inaccessible to all thinking; philosophic thinking is then merely capable of noticing that there is something which seems inaccessible to it and can be grasped in its purity only in the form of myth, which presupposes—as the way toward it—the way of thought. Where philosophic truth claims to comprehend the core of myth rationally, it becomes strangely empty or shows itself to be mere thinking about something without being in it. Philosophy, however, affected by this experience, returns to Being when it becomes true as a thinking *in* myth just as it is true as a thinking *in* life, or *in* world orientation.

Philosophy also casts off theology because of its dependence on revelation. But it again approaches theology where it sees revelation as transformed into the historic configuration of the appearance of transcendence. In this way theology becomes a truth addressing itself to philosophy even though this truth has lost its universality.

Because experience teaches philosophy that it evanesces when it seeks to solidify and close itself through the mere universality of the rational, it grasps consciously its particular historic substance even in theological tradition; it transforms this tradition but does not deny it.

Theology, on the other hand, rejects myth as paganism but adopts many myths, integrating and thus transforming them into parts of its wholeness. It rejects philosophy as an independent configuration of absolute truth but assimilates it, either as the preliminary stage of its own truth or as the means of expressing the content of its revelation.

The battle between the spheres of configuration of the truth of transcendence will continue in the temporal existence of the soul because this battle is the means of motion on the part of transcendent objectivity; this objectivity cannot, as object, achieve an ultimate stability any place where Existenz remains in its freedom. The battle ceases but leaves behind the sepulchral quiet of unfreedom where man sinks back into the heathendom of theosophic materialization now termed superstitious; or sinks into the dogmatically fixed theology of a church; or sinks into purely rational philosophy that alleges to bring about, through knowledge, an assurance of authentic Being. It is only in the numbness of the absence of struggle, in the immobility of one of the configurations, that myth can become, for philosophy, the poetic randomness of dreamlike entertainment and thelogy can turn into the errant delusion of fanatical priests that has been overcome; but in the judgment of theology myth can turn into heathen demonism and philosophy into the self-deification of man in his subjectivity and relativity.

3. The Language of Transcendence in the Stages of Metaphysical Consciousness

As we have seen, the historicity of metaphysics means, in the first place, its diversity which can only be observed from the outside and studied as a dead accumulation. And secondly, it means that the past of metaphysics is seen only by each Existenz in relationship to itself.

The second mode of historicity is the attachment of possible Existenz to the tradition of the three spheres of configuration of objective symbols. This attachment includes a movement between the metaphysical substance that is handed down and the freedom of its appropriation. The symbols that, throughout history, have become rigidified need—in order to speak once more out of their primal source—the animation through a particular individual in the historicity of his own destiny. To be sure, they can be preserved from oblivion only through being transmitted according to fixed rules and through the obedience of later generations. But the individual comes to himself only through his emancipation from the required obedience and can then take hold of his transcendence truly as himself without any mediator. There is existential commitment only if there is liberation from tradition. This occurs where its substance is translated into the presence of Being for me even if there is the danger that I may be able to chance it without the firm configuration of tradition. But the objectivity of tradition is the condition of freedom. For freedom as such cannot be transmitted as tradition; it can only be earned by the individual. Handed down, it is no longer freedom; as possession won without a struggle, it is lost. The tradition of freedom is handed down only indirectly; it is present as a summons, on the part of those individuals who have cared, to those later ones who hear their voice. It is the clandestine community of those who are themselves, a community which is excluded as much as possible by all those who serve objective tradition and which is sentenced to remain silent. It is excluded and silenced by the churches, the parties, the schools of rationally fixed philosophy, by the particular public opinion within which all men understand each other as a matter of course. . . .

The truth that metaphysical objectivity does not lie on one level is of decisive importance. My coming into possible communication with what is alien to me and my being able to understand what is proper to me depend on this insight.

From this insight there follows, further, an attitude toward the other that is aware of the possibility of making wrong demands. To be sure, the readiness to attack everything through questioning and to seek verbal expression for every openness is unlimited for possible Existenz. Nonetheless there is a certain hesitation at the point where thought seeks to penetrate into transcendence. It cannot cognize God but can merely bring to consciousness how, *in our situation*, transcendence enters our soul. To express, here, what I experience, not to hide abyss or antinomy, to see transcendence itself in the light of questionability: all this is demanded of me because the consciousness of my freedom demands truthfulness as the expression of the ground through which I am unknowingly. The deity itself seems to will that every mode of seeking for truth be attempted despite the danger of making an error. We need not fear that we may uncover what it wishes to hide, only that we may fall prey to untruth. Risking all and saying all find their limit at my stage of consciousness. Not everyone is ready to grasp each thought and to think it truthfully, to let himself be affected by every fact and to divine the cipher in it. In the case of children it is the task of the educator to decide responsibly what can be said to them in each instance; but there remains a risk in this. For adults even less information is possible regarding their stages of consciousness. It may be a matter of humaneness, and thus of veracity, to be silent and not let the other feel it; for in the final analysis it is up to each individual what he wants to ask himself. We can neither expect every thought from everyone nor can we prohibit anyone from thinking any thought at all. In books the speaker addresses his own stage of consciousness but sets himself no limits. However, knowing about the stages of consciousness without knowing them in particular, and without knowing one's own objectively, increases our hesitation in concrete situations. There is a right time for everything. The great crises and leaps transform the whole person. It is as if organs of sight were to develop and others to disappear. Even between men who truly belong together there may still be a discrepancy between their stages of consciousness. The one may have had a radical, fundamental experience not shared by the other. In its wake every metaphysical symbol is affected in its language. The symbol that gives me strength and clarity in its luminousness is itself so low in objective univocity that I see it through what I myself am at any given point; but I am conscious that, with this symbol, I cast my glance into the real substance of Being.

Selection 45

THE NATURE OF CIPHERS (1):
EXISTENZ: WHERE THE CIPHER SCRIPT IS READ

EDITORS:
This selection appears in *Philosophie*, Vol. III, pp. 150–52. The translation is by the editors. For E.B. Ashton's translation see *Philosophy*, Vol. III, pp. 131–33.

TEXT:

Reading Ciphers by Means of Self-Being

Being that is grasped in reading the cipher-script does not at all consist independently of me; rather, such reading is possible only together with my self-being. The Being of transcendence in itself is independent of me but as such not accessible. Only things in the world possess this kind of accessibility. Of transcendence I learn only as much as I become myself. If I flag, it is dimmed in its presentiality which is constant in itself. If I become extinguished to the point of being the existence of a mere consciousness-as-such, it disappears. If I grasp it, it is, for me, the one and only Being that, without me, remains what it is.

Just as my sense organs must be intact so that I can perceive the actuality of the world, the self-being of possible Existenz must be present in order that I be struck by transcendence. If I am existentially deaf, I cannot hear the language of transcendence in the object.

For this reason I do not yet penetrate cipher-script by insight gained through research, by collecting and rational appropriation; rather, I do so only with this material through the movement of existential life. The experience of the first language demands at the same time that possible Existenz commit itself. It is not an experience that can be brought in and demonstrated to everyone in an identical manner, for it is attained only through freedom. It is not just any immediacy of experiencing but is the echo of Being by way of the cipher.

If everything can become a cipher, then being a cipher seems to be something arbitrary. If it possesses truth and actuality it must be verifiable. In my orientation in the world I verify by making a thing perceivable or logically cogent, by producing and achieving something. In the illumination of Existenz I verify through the way in which I deal with myself and the other, through the way in which I am thereby certain of myself through the unconditionality of my actions, through the movement I experience inwardly in rising to the heights, in love and hatred, in closing myself off and in my failures. But I am unable to verify point-blank the truth of the cipher, for once it is expressed and hence objective, it becomes a game that does not lay claim to validity and therefore needs no justification. For me, however, it is no mere game.

When I read ciphers I am responsible because I read them only through my self-being whose possibility and veracity become evident to me in the way I read the ciphers. I verify through my self-being and have no yardstick for this, other than this self-being itself which recognizes itself by the transcendence of the cipher.

Thus the reading of the cipher-script takes place in inner action. I attempt to tear myself out of my constant backsliding, take myself in hand, and experience the decision that comes from me. This process of becoming myself, however, is at one with my harkening to transcendence without which it would not be at all. In my actions, in opposition, success, failure and loss, and finally in my thinking, which comprehends all this and in turn is its condition, I have the experience in which I perceive the cipher. What happens and what I do in this happening are like question and answer. I learn from what happens to me by my attitude toward it. My wrestling with myself and with things is a wrestling for transcendence which appears to me as cipher only in this immanence. I penetrate into the sensuous presence of the practical experience of the world, into actual doing in victory and defeat because here alone is the arena where I hear what is.

It is folly to believe that Being is something which everyone could know. What people were like, in what form they were certain of transcendence, in what way they were fulfilled by it, which actuality signified the authentic one to them, how they lived their inner lives based on it, what they loved—none of that can ever be comprehended by an individual in its presentness. There is no way in which Being is for everyone. All remains dark for him who is not himself.

Thus I grasp, in the reading of the cipher-script of transcendence, a Being which becomes audible to me by my struggling for it. To be sure, it is only in the Being of transcendence that I have the consciousness of genuine Being; only here do I find tranquility. But I always find myself again in the unrest of struggle; I am abandoned and as if lost; I lose myself if I no longer sense Being.

Philosophic Existenz can bear the burden of never approaching the hidden God. It is only the cipher-script which speaks to me, if I am ready for it. Philosophizing, I remain suspended between harnessing my possibility and being given my actuality as a gift. It is an associating with myself and with transcendence but it seems only rarely as if an eye looked at me out of the dark. Day in and day out it seems as if there were nothing. Out of the unease of his forsakenness man seeks a more direct access, he seeks objective guarantees and a firm hold, grasps the hand of God, as it were, in prayer, turns to authority and sees the godhead in a personal form; for it is only in this form that it is God, whereas the godhead remains at an indeterminate distance.

Selection 46

THE NATURE OF CIPHERS (2):
THE THREE LANGUAGES

EDITORS:
Jaspers argues here that since the significance of the reading of the cipher-script is fundamentally existential (*see* above, Selection 45), all modes of expressing metaphysical truth derive their meaningfulness from their being expressions of "the absolute consciousness of Existenz." The immediacy of such consciousness may be designated a "language." The imagery of myth

would then be a "second language," and articulate speculation a "third language."

This selection has been excerpted from *Philosophie*, Vol. III, pp. 129–36. It has been translated by the editors. E. B. Ashton's translation appears in *Philosophy*, Vol. III, pp. 113–19.

TEXT:
We refer to metaphysical objectivity as "cipher" because it is the language of transcendence but not transcendence. In its being language it is not understood or even perceived by consciousness-as-such; rather, this kind of language and its mode of address can be heard only by possible Existenz.

The Three Languages

True content that is *immediate language of transcendence* is present only to the absolute consciousness of Existenz; the language is heard by the individual at the moment of historic uniqueness. —The uttering of this language proceeds by way of a universalization by which alone it is understood even by the one who had originally heard it. This *second language* of an intuitable communicating among Existenzen breaks loose from that primacy and, in the form of a story, a picture, a shape, a gesture, turns what seemed to be incommunicable into a content that can be imparted. What was originally language of transcendence becomes common domain, but, by virtue of the heritage of the second language, it is able to fulfill itself again in renewed relation to the origin. —When thought turns to this—merely intuitive—language and penetrates it to its origin, then such thought comprehends in this form of metaphysical speculation what, to be sure, cannot be cognized but becomes, in this thinking, a *third language of philosophical communication*.

1. The Immediate Language of Transcendence (First Language)

In the ciphers of transcendence one finds out about Being. It is only in actuality that transcendence is revealed. One cannot know about it in general; one can only hear it historically from actuality. Experience is the source of empirical knowledge as well as of the assurance of transcendence.

As "sense perception" experience means knowing something present as a spatial-temporal object. It is in existence as "lived experience" that becomes aware of itself. As "cognition" it is methodically trained deductive-inductive research in its particular results; as such it is a trying-out of what I can make and what I can predict. As "thinking" it is my carrying-out of thought processes with its consequences for my consciousness. As "empathy" it is a sensing of the whole of a present actuality in its situation, its criterion being whether I am able to hit on what is decisive for others as well as for myself. Only on the basis of all these experiences does *metaphysical experience* come to be. In this experience I stand before the abyss; I experience a disconsolate lack if the experience remains mere experience of existence. There is fulfilling presence in it if it becomes transparent and hence a cipher.

This metaphysical experience is the reading of the first language. Reading it is not an act of understanding, is not an unlocking of what lies at the bottom, but an actual being-with-it oneself. It is not rational assurance but goes beyond it to a transparency of Being in existence which begins in the most primitive immediacy of Existenz and which, even in the greatest mediation by thinking, is never this thinking but is a new immediacy conveyed by it.

This metaphysical experience lacks all verifiability that could turn it into an experience valid for everyone. It becomes a delusion if I believe that I can bring it about at will and have it in consciousness-as-such if treated as knowledge, but it also becomes a delusion if I treat it frivolously as mere subjective feeling. I grasp in it a mode of Being other than mere positive existence. There is in it a translation of Being from mere existence into the eternity to which knowledge cannot penetrate.

In experiencing mundane things, in living experience and thinking, the negative boundary was set by ignorance. Now ignorance is fulfilled in the return to present sensuous actuality, not to actuality as a content of existence but as a cipher. If I seek the Being of transcendence then I want all possible concrete experience to be actualized by me in order for transcendence to become manifest in it. The thirst for knowledge, to see what there is to see, to do what can be done, is, to be sure, still existentially blind but it is the driving force of finding the way to Being. Beyond the diversity of what is accessible to knowledge, the entrance to the world leads through grasping of the task of actualization which is the bond to responsibility. This entrance, which can never be justified satisfactorily by reference to a demonstrable final goal, is powered by the deeper impulse to arrive at my own experience of authentic Being—be it in embracing or be it in abstaining and limiting. I want to come up against actuality while suspending possibility. Filled with possibilities I stride toward actuality and become myself singular and limited because I want to get to where there is no more possibility but only the decisively actual which only is because it is simply Being. I can never encounter this in temporal existence. But reading its ciphers becomes for me the meaning of all other action and experiencing.

Reading the first language demands experience. It is not abstract thought but the cipher in the historic particularity of the present that manifests Being. It is shown to me not by a metaphysical hypothesis in which I deduce and calculate what Being might be like but, instead, by the embodiment of the cipher beyond which I do not think because Being is radiant within it. But "experience" has many meanings. A priori, thought itself becomes an experience. The demand that there be an experience is directed only against empty

thought and not against the Being that I experience in the cipher of the factually carried out, substantial thinking.

The more universal the experience of transcendence becomes the more it
pales; however, the experience is all the more decisive as it ascends to the peak
of what can only be fulfilled here and now. Our experience of nature, for
example, becomes a reading of the cipher-script as the distinctions of the
wholly individual increases: where I gain the most concrete knowledge of the
most minute actuality in the presence of the totality of a world.

2. The Language that Becomes Universal in the Process of Communicating (Second Language)

In the reverberation of the language of transcendence—which can be heard
in the immediacy of the present moment—the languages in the form of images and thoughts are created which are to convey what has been heard. The
language of man comes to join the language of Being.

The objectified configurations of the language of metaphysical content
have three intuitable forms. They appear as "myth in a particular form," as
the "revelation of a world beyond," as "mythical actuality."

a. The Greek gods are not transcendent but are still within actuality. Philosophic transcending, from Xenophanes to Plotinus, first proceeds beyond the
world and these gods which—a myth within actuality—are different from the
other actuality. The gods can encounter man in the world for, as distinct figures, they are an actuality alongside empirical actuality. For us, the actual
ocean is a cipher of something unfathomable; in the figure of sea gods as
speaking symbols the ocean becomes a myth in a particular form.

Myths relate events that are said to have determined the ground and essence of existence. They lead to the solution of existential tensions not by way
of rational cognition but through the telling of a story. Myths unveil in veiling
anew and remain as effective configurations. They are the anonymous creations of millennia. In a superhuman world man sees what he himself is. He
intuits as the deed of divine beings what he does not as yet raise to the level of
reflection as his own being and doing but which he, in fact, places under the
determination of intuition. The meaning of the myth changes. It is no unequivocally logical structure and cannot be exhausted by interpretation. In
every case of historic myth there always remains the eternal truth even when
it is recognized and distinguished as myth. The meaning of the myths, however, reveals itself only to the person who still believes in the truth that assumed in them its particular and as such evanescent configuration. If one
interprets them, a spurious simplification always results; their historic content is lost. Interpreting becomes a shifting since it makes that seem necessary
which is not meant to be cognized as necessary.

b. The myth of a world beyond devalues empirical actuality into merely sensuous contents, into that which really is not. But in the myth the Beyond appears, gives signs, and performs wonders. A super-sensual whole opens up. Instead of feeling increasingly at home within actuality taken as divine, Existenz penetrates into an actuality beyond, an actuality that is another world and authentic Being, transmitted to Existenz by revelation. Either this revelation is historically fixated, does not repeat itself but takes place as a single comprehensive world-drama of unique acts succeeding each other whenever the particular time is fulfilled, until, with the completion of revelations consisting of divine word and deed, the world can cease to be; or repeated revelations take place, the world drama is not arranged in the economy of a whole. Infinite world periods succeed each other. To be sure, the way is clear for the final ascent out of existence but we are in the dark as to when this will succeed and whether it will be successful for all and everything.

c. If actuality itself is also mythical, then what is actual is neither devalued nor complemented by an objective particular form. Actuality, as actual, is seen at the same time as possessing the meaning bestowed on it by transcendence. It is neither the simple empirical actuality of what can be investigated (rather, as actuality, it surpasses everything investigable); nor is it transcendence without empirical actuality. Being totally of the present it is, to the very last, both actual and transcendent at the same time. For Van Gogh, landscape, things, and people are, in their factual presentiality, mythical at the same time; hence the unique force of his paintings.

If I live in my sensuous presence without existing in it as in transcendence, then my yearning is awakened, a yearning that is curious because it seeks what is, after all, right here and present. It does not urge me to go beyond things into another country; rather, it must consider such striving into a beyond as betrayal because I do not carry out what is existentially possible in the present. This yearning is not the pathological phenomenon where I am unable to comprehend things as actual or myself as in existence, or to experience the moment as real presence. The yearning which would find satisfaction in the presence that is mythical consists precisely in spite of complete sensuous presentness—as mere empirical actuality in a vitally fulfilled sense of existence. Its torment stems not from a lack of actuality but a lack of transcendence.

Through communication with the other, directed toward me and him as appearances of original self-being, I come closer and closer, and my yearning grows, to be fulfilled only in those moments for which death no longer exists. To be empirically close to a person and thereby to intensify one's longing and to be transcendentally united with him through this empirical proximity without an imaginary beyond, and only thus to quench one's longing—this is metaphysical love: it is for such love that there is mythical actuality.

3. *Speculative Language (Third Language)*

When thought interprets the cipher language for itself it obviously can neither cognize transcendence as the other nor broaden world-orientation about existence *qua* existence. However, faithful to its own formal law, it thinks of necessity in objectivities. It reads the original cipher-script by writing a new one: it thinks transcendence in analogy to worldly existence that is present to it logically and palpably. What is thought is itself merely symbol as a language that has now become communicable. This language can be spoken in various ways.

In one way I may keep my eye on actuality as such. Everywhere actuality is asked the question: why this? But this question is posed not as a rational question of world orientation, a question searching for causes; rather it is posed as the transcending question that wants no answer because it recognizes it is impossible; it seeks to bring what is actual into full existential presence, wants to penetrate it, as it were: existence is such that this is possible in it; such is Being that this existence is possible. We see in astonishment, in hatred, in dread and despair, in love and in soaring upward: this is the way it is. It is a way of grasping Being in existence which, differing in its essence from world orientation based on cognition through research, is yet possible only through the materiality of the latter. To be sure, imparting information, moving exclusively within the actual, can be understood even without transcendence; such is the case with the description of nature as representation of what occurs in space, the representation of history as a form of a summarizing which imparts empirical research into mankind's past. But when the language of transcending apperception speaks in them, then they function as the medium of metaphysical communication where the intellect is not in a position to decide whether they have this function. For it is audible only for Existenz which is itself transcending.

Or, in another way, I might speak explicitly about the authentic Being of transcendence and think what it might be in analogy to existing Being, to self-being, to being-historic. A whole is rounded off in a mental construct. But even as it is developed into a metaphysical system the thought is merely a thought symbol and not cognition of transcendence. It is itself a cipher, a possibility of being read, and hence not self-identical; i.e., it is not itself until it is in each particular appropriation.

Or, in still another way, I could hold fast to the existence that I am myself in my world in order to find the way to the Being of transcendence. In movements of thought that are taught under the name of "proofs for the existence of God" I assure myself of Being in factual correlation to my own substance. Through it my thoughts—in themselves indifferent as cognition and deteriorating easily into logical trifles—gain an existential power of persuasion which they lack completely as objective proofs.

Or I may puzzle out, in transcending remembrance and forethought, the origin and the end.

These and other modes of analogical thinking of transcendence in the cipher of thought symbols together constitute what is called speculation: this is neither the cognition of an object nor an address to man's freedom through reflection which illuminates his Existenz, nor a categorical transcending that does not take hold of anything but instead liberates, nor an interpretation of existential relations to the transcendent. It is, rather, a contemplative self-immersion for the purpose of coming into contact with transcendence in a self-apprehended, pondered, formed cipher-script which brings transcendence before the mind as metaphysical objectivity. . . .

Since speculation is always tied to a cipher no configuration of Being as such can become transcendence for it. In its symbol speculation is only closer to or farther away from transcendence. The world that speaks to it as cipher-script does not lie on level ground. The factuality of the positive which speculation accentuates is far from me, as the last vestige of Being in an existence alien to me; it is closer, as that which takes hold of me decisively from the outside; and it comes closest in what I myself do. The regions of Being of existence—becoming clearly surveyable in the categories—lack equal relevance in the analogical thinking of speculation. Each cipher hits Being in a different way; none hits it truly or totally.

Selection 47

THE NATURE OF CIPHERS (3):
THE MANY MEANINGS OF CIPHERS

EDITORS:
In this selection Jaspers considers some aspects of the many meanings of ciphers. Aside from the circumstance that the existential significance of cipher-reading results in a multivocity of meaning, the problem concerns the nature of symbolic expression and its interpretation.

This selection consists of excerpts from *Philosophie*, Vol. III, pp. 141–44; 146–50. Translation is by the editors. E. B. Ashton's translation is *Philosophy*, Vol III, pp. 123–26; 128–31.

TEXT:
A cipher is the particular unity of a world-being and transcendence. It ceases to be when it is thought of as signifying some other: In cipher-script it is impossible to separate the symbol from what is being symbolized. Cipher-

script brings transcendence into the present but it cannot be interpreted. If I were to interpret I would have to separate again what only is in togetherness: I would compare cipher-script with transcendence which, after all, only appears to me in it but is not cipher-script. Interpretation would constitute a lapse from the reading of the cipher-script to a comprehension of purely immanent symbolic relationships. Even though the reading of the cipher-script takes place in clear consciousness, doing so is a matter of my standing within unconscious symbolism: such symbolism is not additionally known to me *qua* symbolism. Conscious symbolism, in the manner of possessing things in the world through the relationship the one bears to the other as something which otherwise is also an existent in the sense of sign, metaphor, comparison, representation, model—this is not cipher-script. Whereas this conscious symbolism derives its clarity only in interpretation, the unconscious symbolism of the cipher-script is not touched at all by interpretation. What is grasped in it through interpretation is not this cipher-script but one that has been destroyed and denatured to become mere symbolism. As symbol it would become as clear as the symbol, whose significance can be shown to be tied to something that is present somewhere. But cipher-script exists as such and cannot be clarified through something other.

Symbolism as such is a relationship, through which and transcending which the nature of metaphysical cipher-script is expressed; yet the cipher-script is no longer a relation but a unity in the existence of transcendence. Hence clarity about symbolism as such is the condition for a decisive and illusion-free grasping of the cipher-script of transcendence.

Symbolism As Such (Expression of Being and Communicative Expression)

All of existence is permeated by possible symbolism: I encounter nothing and no one comes toward me who could not be such an expression. This expression is either a mute being-there as an expression of Being which, when asked, does not reply; or it is a communicative expression that addresses me and which, when questioned, gives an account of itself and replies to my question. The expression of Being is universal, the communicative expression is limited to persons.

I perceive the expression of Being in human physiognomy and in involuntary gestures. Between the perceiver and the perceived there is no mutual verbal exchange. It is merely an unconscious expression of one's own nature without either the will to open up to the other or to remain closed off from him. . . .

Yet even this existence, though empirical, is in no way identical at all times and for all men. The perception of an expression is not merely a perceiving on the part of consciousness-as-such but is a seeing of freedom by freedom. For what is visible here is dependent on one's own nature, is, in being expressed, still possibility (as a challenge to the other as well as to me, to look more deeply as I come to be myself). . . .

Communicative expression, in distinction to mere expression of Being, means to impart something. It alone is language in its authentic meaning, based on which all other expression can be called "language" only metaphorically. In it lies the intended meaning as impartable content; from it issue challenge and demand, question and answer.

In communicative expression we also seek to impart our own original perception of symbols. In communication with ourselves the second language brings us to understand what, in its immediacy, is, to be sure, actual yet indistinct. It is only the symbolism become communicative that is authentically present. In its reverberation within the perceiving person the symbolism of all existence becomes communicable in accordance with its facet of universality. What is originally merely immediate becomes conscious only as it is reproduced. The immediate symbolism remains the source; but it itself is perceived mostly only to the extent that it has already become language. It is the moments of creative vision of Being which alone broaden language by bringing it forth. . . .

Interpretable Symbolism and Envisageable Symbolism

As soon as we investigate, in our thinking, what meaning is by separating meaning from what is meant, we merely find ourselves in the endlessness of a universal symbolism. Everything can mean anything. It is a back-and-forth within a universal replaceability according to the point of view from which certain rules and schemata are valid. *Interpretable* symbolism is objective, its meaning can be solved. It consists of comparison and designation and derives its solidity solely from convention or through psychologically comprehensible customs.

But as soon as we approach the symbol as the cipher of transcendence it becomes *envisageable*. In envisageable symbolism we cannot separate signs and meanings but grasp both in one. To be sure, one makes a separation in order to clarify to oneself what has been comprehended. But this is done by means of a new symbolism and not by interpreting one by way of the other. What one already possesses merely becomes clearer. One returns and gazes into new depths. For an Existenz, envisageable symbolism as the language of cipher-script is accessible only through such deepening. Interpretable symbolism is there for consciousness-as-such.

If I ask what symbols ultimately mean, then interpreting symbolism does in fact tell me such ultimates: a theory of myths maintains, for instance, that natural processes and human activity in agriculture and crafts are what the myths are all about; psychoanalysis refers to the libido, and Hegelian metaphysics to the movement of dialectical logical concepts. Thus the ultimate may be plain reality as well as the logos. No matter what it is, it is unequivocally determined. However the symbols which have such univocal meanings at the end of this multifarious interpreting still remain ambiguous and indefinite since they mean anything.

Envisageable symbolism knows no ultimate. There is present in it an openness which knows a deeper fulfillment but does not know an other through which it comprehends itself. It is not centered, from the outset, on the Being which is already otherwise known and whose appearance it is; rather it remains in its manifestness, which opens itself to the present moment, and in its unfathomable depth, out of which indeterminate Being shines only through this very symbolism.

Since this envisageable symbolism lacks any true possibility of interpretation it can exist only as the cipher-script of transcendence. In it the thinking which presents itself as interpretation becomes itself a symbol. By seeing through the logos, the eye that reads the cipher-script penetrates to the very ground of the logos. All interpretation becomes the expression of a cipher that is legible for Existenz. In this cipher, Existenz perceives the Being which it believes to be its transcendence.

Arbitrary Multiplicity of Meaning vs. the Many Meanings of the Cipher

With interpretable symbolism each case becomes fraught with endlessly many meanings yet unequivocally vacuous as regards the excogitated ultimate which interpretation produces. The envisageable symbolism of the genuine cipher, on the other hand, possesses a different multiplicity of meaning.

If the cipher is interpreted and changed into a knowledge and is thus to become objective and valid, multiplicity of meaning in this existentially deracinated form remains the same as that of all interpreting symbolism. However it does not possess *this* multiplicity of meaning if it is not interpreted at all but is preserved in its origin.

If, however, an interpretation of an original cipher becomes, in turn, a cipher in the process of being thought, then its multivocalness is not lessened; it is, however, not an arbitrary multiplicity of meaning but lies in the diversity of possible existential appropriation. As the possibility of appropriation it becomes unequivocal for Existenz only at the moment of its historic presentiality in a non-transferable and—for Existenz—unknowable way. This unequivocalness lies in the irreplaceable nature of the transcendence that fulfills this particular Existenz.

In the arbitrary interpretation that is supposed to be knowledge each particular point of departure is determinate, the interpretation endless, the goal of the interpretation a finite being. In the interpretation of the cipher-script the point of departure is in itself the infinite self-presence of transcendence, the ciphers are finite and determinate, the goal of the interpretation indefinite yet already present infinity.

The finite stands at the beginning of interpretation seeking knowledge. Endless interpretation would not be a way leading out of the finite and toward mastery of infinity. This interpretation never takes place in actuality but only seems to happen through formulas which in no way master facticity but merely repeat themselves and accumulate. In interpreting symbolism as supposed cognition everything turns stale because it is merely finite. The infinite is lost while we succumb unwillingly to endlessness. In grasping the cipher-script, on the other hand, infinity stands at the beginning; out of that infinity; which is the presence of transcendence, the finite at last turns into cipher-script.

The unequivocal, infinite presence of transcendence itself would—within the temporality of Existenz—be a fulfilling culmination. However, if a cipher gains an aspect of universality whereby it encounters us in a communicable manner, moreover in a manner in which those culminations may subsequently address us, then a multiplicity of meanings prevails that is the result of the possibility of existential assimilation and actualization.

Hence, for the metaphysical stance of questioning there is nothing final in cipher-script. It is found wherever, in it, freedom brings transcendence into the present. The cipher can always be read differently. From it one can never draw a conclusion regarding transcendence that would be inferred on its basis. Seen from my own standpoint it retains a permanent multiplicity of meaning. But from the standpoint of transcendence we can say: it can communicate in yet other ways. Cipher-script could never become valid in any final sense within temporal existence for then there would be no possibility; univocal completion would take its place. Being at first the realm of what is still non-binding but possibly binding, but later the binding force for this Existenz, it would remain neither the one nor the other, would be cipher-script no longer but would become the sole Being of transcendence. Being at first a particular without the possibility of becoming a whole it would negate itself in the totality. At first evanescent and historic, it would become permanent and absolute.

The unending multiplicity of meaning of all ciphers shows itself, in temporal existence, to be its nature. The interpretation of a cipher by another cipher, of the intuitive cipher by the speculative one, of the actual by the factitious, is without end since it is the medium in which Existenz seeks to assure itself of its transcendence and, in preparation, to create possibilities for itself. A system of ciphers is impossible since they would fit into it only in their finiteness and not as the bearers of transcendence. The unending multiplicity of meaning excludes a system of possible ciphers. A system may itself be a cipher but can never embrace, as a schema, genuine ciphers in a meaningful way.

Selection 48

THE STRUGGLE IN THE REALM OF CIPHERS

EDITORS:
Since metaphysical truth appears to man in the form of ciphers, and since human beings are engaged in a communicative struggle for their truths, ciphers are conceived by Jaspers as a realm of the struggle for truth. This conception has certain implications for the relation among human beings of diverse ultimate commitments, thus also among religions, philosophies, civilizations, and nations.

The selection has been translated by the editors from *Der philosophische Glaube angesicht der Offenbarung*, pp. 201–11. For E. B. Ashton's translation see *Philosophical Faith and Revelation*, pp. 128–35.

TEXT:

1. The Situation:

The realm of ciphers is not a harmonious realm which makes known to us the abundance of Being in an unequivocal manner.

Even though some ciphers promise tranquility, knowledge of the whole of the world of ciphers does not by any means provide this tranquility. Ciphers speak out against other ciphers. Paying heed to these ciphers I deny those. Though we immerse ourselves in individual ciphers, their background remains this realm as a whole as a realm of struggle.

But what kind of a struggle is it? It is not the struggle of existence, not the struggle for power; rather, it is the struggle for truth at its primal source. This struggle may incarnate itself, as it were, in the struggle of existence, and struggles of existence can obtain their battle flags from the realm of ciphers. In this case the pure meaning of the ciphers, their movement toward the truth of transcendence and again back from this truth, are muddied or spoiled or have disappeared.

The struggle ceases only when we go beyond the world of cipher-language and thus the world-as-such, into the unutterable and unspeaking. But then the world is lost to us.

Or else the struggle ceases or has not yet begun when we do not take all ciphers seriously but see them all together on the level of the non-binding, the phantastic, the fascinating. But then we have lost the consciousness that inquires after the ground of things; then we have lost transcendence.

2. The Objectification of the Forces:

The struggle in the ciphers is related to transcendence. But the individual perceives that it is not transcendence itself which is immediately with him and that it is not only with him alone. For it is the ground of everything, his ground as well as that of his mortal enemy, of himself as Existenz and of himself as nature which sustains but also destroys him. By means of the ciphers there takes place a struggle of the will to truth that encounters a multiplicity of forces we vainly attempt to comprehend. For, standing in the midst of this multiplicity, we cannot take them in at a glance.

If we objectify them as a battle of the forces that collide in the ciphers, then this objectification is itself either a signum: it applies to the appearance of our Existenz in existence, as the latter becomes the arena where the battles take place; or it is itself a cipher of something that is rooted in transcendence. The battle takes place in such a manner that we ourselves—each Existenz—choose the ciphers which we heed, that we stand firm in our choice, that either we forfeit ourselves by depending on special ciphers as absolute or we move freely within them. This struggle is a movement of Existenz bringing itself back to itself or of Existenz propelled forward to itself.

3. Examples of the Objectifications of the Forces:

There has always been enacted, in polytheism, an objectification of the struggle among the forces; it is unreflected but magnificently present in its intuitability. The Greeks knew—and we believe we still know as they did—what it meant to serve Apollo, Hermes, Dionysius, Aphrodite, Artemis the enemy of Eros, Hera the guardian of marriage; and to serve Athena, this supra-sexual goddess, not born but sprung from the head of Zeus, wise, militant, rational, this perhaps most gripping, uniquely Greek figure of polytheism who cannot be compared with any other goddess in the world. She addresses the ingenuous pure nobility in man in a natural and measured way. One cannot reconcile the worship of these gods, yet they open up all human possibilities and provide their justification. The gods have different dominions; they make mutually exclusive demands, exist side by side, or engage in battle with one another. The person serving one of them may insult the other. Without reasoning logic, the Greeks imbued with the most wonderful clarity what, out of the forces, assumed form for them, and consecrated it as their personal gods.

Polytheism contains an abiding truth which even the monotheistic churches have not been able to evade in practice. This truth has endured until today but is not called by the name of polytheism.

Quite different are the modern attempts to conjure up, without reference to myths, in mental objectification, not authentic forces but to construct meaning-imagery. It is their purpose to comprehend the situation of the struggle of the forces in the form of concepts. They do not become ciphers. As thought-imagery they stand at the boundary of science and philosophy. Of these, too, I cite only a few examples.

A. I consider certain thoughts expressed by Max Weber in his *Sociology of Religion* to be the weightiest attempt of this kind. He speaks from the standpoint of scientific man. Hence he merely claims "to be a means of orienting oneself according to ideal types rather than to teach his own philosophy." His subject is the rejection of the world. He demonstrates the directions taken by the rejection of the world in regard to the economic, political, aesthetic, erotic, intellectual spheres. He wants it to be meaningfully clear how and where inner conflicts of ordered ways of living are possible and adequate. Yet he does not want to maintain "that there are no standpoints from which they could be considered as 'suspended.' " Max Weber carries through his constructs by constantly using illustrations from historical phenomena. In this way he shows, at the same time, the historic character of what he presents to us here as one aspect of the battle of the forces.

Through this construction of the meaning-imagery within the reality of human behavior, in each instance one encounters, as one follows up the meaning, the ultimate presuppositions. This construction teaches the antagonists to arrive at these presuppositions through thinking and to become conscious of them. It aims at determining whether or not these presuppositions have, in their historic actualization, proceeded consequentially.

B. The project of fundamental knowledge as the doctrine of the modes of the Encompassing manifests, in the first place, a struggle within the modes of the Encompassing, due to the multiplicity of the phenomena occurring in them and, secondly, a battle between the modes of the Encompassing. The doctrine establishes the idea of modes coexisting in an order and in subordination; but it also establishes the breach of this coexistence by individual modes (such as the intellect, existence, spirit) due to their absolutization based on the claim by each of them to be qualified to lead the others. . . .

C. In illuminating truth one may arrive, in a particular horizon of thought, at final alternatives which, at first, one cannot go beyond, such as the alternatives of communication that is unbounded or is limited by certain conditions, or the alternatives of openness and exclusivity, or of reason and catholicity. . . .

4. *Objectification of and Involvement in the Battles:*

As we conceive of the forces, we do not stand outside of their struggle but in it. Our attempting to objectivize the forces from some perspective and to schematize them does not mean that we can survey the whole from an Archimedian point outside, as if it were the arena of a battle in which we did not participate. In spite of all our energies, directed toward our aim of being purely spectators, we—as bearers of the forces—are also always involved. We cannot lead the forces through speculation, the way a conductor leads the members of his orchestra, without playing along with them.

Rather, the situation is as follows: if we endeavor to objectivize the struggle as though surveying it from afar, we simultaneously plunge right into the middle of it in order to participate in it. We must be outside and inside at the same time, we must comport ourselves as observers and simultaneously be Existenz. To be sure, we can strive for maximal distance in relationship to ourselves, and hence for freedom from ourselves. But as we think the forces and battlefields, we produce, every time, configurations which themselves become instruments of battle. Every image of forces also stands in the service of forces. We cannot escape this. Only when our freedom in distancing ourselves from the battle combines with our freedom of plunging into the battle do we gain the whole freedom that is possible for us.

The battle of the forces does not take place altogether on a single level between clearly differentiated forces. The front lines become entangled with each other. It is impossible to grasp even a single force definitely and substantially. The battle is such that the care of the forces, i.e., their substances or subjects, stay in the background. Thus the battle may appear to be as a happening in the foreground which can be objectivized in meaningful connections. Could there be, in the very ground of the battle of the forces, a unity combining them all?

5. Struggle and Communication in the Ciphers:

If philosophy is involved in the battle of forces which it cannot survey adequately from without, then there takes place in this battle not merely a mutual repelling but also communication.

Truth is not possible without struggle. Here it is a question of the most vehement battle, the battle for truth itself. This battle has a unique character. Where it has reached its purity and depth at the same time, it takes place without violence and coercion in existence. If it degenerates into a brutal struggle for existence it is no longer guided by the forces. Ciphers, as any mental imagery, are then merely made use of as the means of maintaining existence and broadening of power, interchangeable as slogans. The struggle for truth is over.

This battle takes place by guiding us to the limits, by our learning to see and to hear, in rational thought, in invocatory direction toward transcendence through ciphers, and in interpreting ciphers. It takes place in the challenge of imparting information. That which authentically is, is to be given tongue, until silence itself, as fulfilled language, becomes substantive. To speak straightforwardly, to say everything I am able to say to myself, not to hold back anything: these are the conditions of the struggle. But even when this is most successful there remains the indirectness in which self encounters self.

Wherever we hear ciphers, there we are involved already. And when we are involved we pursue thoughts not logically but with our very being.

The ciphers always battle among themselves, even if this battle does not become conscious or, like something of indifference, remains marginal. Sometimes the battle seems completely forgotten. Often it is constrained. Only our whole freedom—through distancing ourselves from the battle as we plunge into the battle of the ciphers—keeps us open, urges us toward communication, expands the space of understanding into infinity, and supplies the battle with its ground in the historic actuality of Existenz.

Mutual understanding through ciphers means communication that touches on the transcendent. There the most intimate union is possible as well as the strangest enmity. Wherever men are bound to each other there remains the struggle for the purity and the weightiness of the ciphers. Wherever men see themselves separated by an abyss because of ciphers, there something drives them on to understand the other even as his ciphers are rejected: It is the desire to become of one mind—not in this or that particular language but in the wholeness of movement within the world of ciphers. Behind the battle within the meaning-imagery there is hidden what perhaps joins carriers of the battling forces together in spite of appearances to the contrary. The ineradicable alternatives may appear as mere tentative, fateful play or even as something that belongs together within a comprehensive whole which is, in turn, thought in ciphers. But even such a cipher is itself always smashed in the phenomenality of time.

Great spiritual orders of ciphers have appeared in history, mostly in connection with sociological and political realities (as in the higher civilizations of antiquity, in China and India, in the Christian Middle Ages), sometimes in the form of purely intellectual formulations as in Hesiod; the polytheistic multiplicities are joined together in orders in which each god has his own domain and the battles among the gods are contained in the generational sequence of the gods. The later, all-inclusive systems, whose ultimate pinnacle was Hegel, seemed to turn into palpable form everything there is, converting it into a magnificent harmony which absorbed in orderly fashion even the most radical battles.

In such constructs one strives, objectively, factually, and impersonally for what is considered to be the one complete truth, in the belief that all men would come together in it. But such totalities of what is thought and observed by men always show themselves to be limited. They are breeched by experiences which, in never-ceasing, never-to-be-completed struggling communication, this dynamite of all systems, first opens us up to the whole extent of possibilities within the constraints of time. Here insight grows out of experience, and will out of insight; and out of this insight the will to be united in the ultimate motive of the struggle, and yet not to have the struggle contained and concluded within a harmony of ciphers no matter how magnificent.

One cannot find progress in the battle of the ciphers analogous to progress in the sciences. There are the great historic leaps when new ciphers appear on the scene. There are instances of the unfolding of particular spheres of ciphers. And there is, above all, the change in the strength and truthfulness of the unconditional.

Hence even though, for example, the struggles of the theologians are intended to facilitate the cognition, in progressive insight, of a single fundamental fact through a better understanding of faith ("no one can lay a ground work other than that which had been laid down from the beginning"), it is not a question of progress. There are only the unceasing struggles of religious cognition in which the forces which we cannot survey from the outside are ranged against each other. These forces clarify to themselves the understanding of their faith, providing that this is not merely an intellectual struggle. They establish their symbols and creeds.

6. Liberality and Dogmatism:

In the battle of the ciphers—whether they make their appearance as theology or philosophy—we speak about liberality and humanism in contradistinction to the dogmatic, orthodox, illiberal, unhumanistic. It is the difference between the open, loving struggle and the unopen, loveless struggle for what is true. In the loveless struggle this sole truth is already present through revelation, a master, a school, a system. The person engaged in the struggle has already surrendered to this authority as one that is powerful and acknowledged in the world or as an authority that is still powerless but which he believes in.

Liberality is tolerant. This tolerance is not one of indifference toward what is secretly despised, which simply is in the world and cannot be eradicated. Tolerance means, rather, taking seriously what is strange; it means listening closely and letting ourself be concerned. Tolerance resists the reduction to one unitary color of what is possible, in time, only in the movement of battle through boundless communication. But even this tolerance must submit itself to the question: Is not that which appears to it as authentic freedom merely the expression of one force among others? After all, the consciousness of being on the way and not in possession of the sole truth confronts irreconcilably the consciousness of obedience which has submitted itself, for all time, to the one objectively guaranteed truth allotted to it. In the end, tolerance and intolerance resist unification. Hence the saying: Tolerance itself becomes intolerant against intolerance. Here we must differentiate: Whenever intolerance makes use, in existence, of means of coercion and brute force, then tolerance must be—though unfortunately has not always been—utterly intolerant of this way of perverting the spiritual into the violent. Within the domain of spiritual struggle, however, tolerance will never abandon the hope of opening up the other communicatively through talking to each other, and of arriving at that accord which, though remaining on the level of questioning, allows for a relationship with that person who remains an antagonist not only in regard to specific ciphers but even in his fundamental attitude toward the world of ciphers.

This accord is present when the antagonists grant to each other the unrestricted right to have their own faith, insight, conviction. The accord is possible when each allows the other a frank exchange of views without holding anything back. For otherwise the veil remains in place which makes it possible everywhere in the world for people to live alongside each other and which, at the same time, undermines this communal life. Authentic communication is stifled by convention. In this accord the antagonists do not want to restrict, either directly or indirectly, their freedom of public dissemination of information, of announcing facts, of intellectual movements, and of promulgation. They grant each other the right—not only outwardly assured but also inwardly affirmed—to bear witness to their Existenz. However, such accord also means being affected by each other in one's innermost being.

We live together in the arena of the battle that is replete with ciphers. Within this spiritual living space there occur time and again the seemingly unbridgeable antitheses. No man is everything. No comprehensible truth is all the truth. Nothing tangible is absolute. Seen from the vantage point of this freedom all claims made by man—in firmly asserting, in confessing, in supposedly ultimately true ciphers—seem like the claims made by prisoners.

The illiberal person says: the fact that you do not assert or confess to anything fixed testifies to your lack of seriousness. With your attitude, given the multiplicity of what is possible, you can never and nowhere take hold of the truth. You are unable to differentiate true ciphers from false. There is no end to the struggle.

We answer: There can indeed be no end to the struggle within a lifetime. Why not? We must differentiate: unconditional truth, which has its being solely through the historic decision of Existenz—and universal truth, which is expressed in the tenets of faith.

The historic existential truth lies in the moment of decision and its repetition, which in each instance springs from the primal source. In its unconditionality this truth cannot be expressed in general terms. Ciphers and general explanation can illuminate it but cannot penetrate to its core. Neither the I as Existenz nor its love can be justified. In attempting such justification we lose sight of them. What is existentially actual cannot be substantiated and is yet the presupposition of all that is serious as we talk to one another.

General confession and firm assertion seem to give security, which makes me feel strong. Its content can be substantiated through tradition and is grounded either in revelation or in a dogmatic philosophy.

This differentiation results in two theses: the struggle has its end in each historic Existenz that has made the decision to come out of possibility and enter actuality and has found the grounding of his life.—The struggle has no end in propositions, judgments, ciphers.

At this point the discussion becomes entangled. One person says: your confession and firm assertion are an evasion of genuine seriousness, a liberation from your freedom. The other says: you avoid truth by laying claim to a subjective, non-objectivizable truth of your Existenz.

But is this antithesis which, when expressed, makes each side feel completely misunderstood by the other, superficial after all? Does it apply only to deviations? We are not able to penetrate it in a thought-configuration of faith on which we could agree. Hence there is, on both sides, a readiness to communicate coupled with wonderment.

The antithesis seems unbridgeable only when it is formulated in general terms. Human actuality, however, does not conform to any one schema of alternative concepts. The person who seems to commit himself unreservedly to a formulated principle is yet always more than what takes place in such an act.

7. *Lack of Commitment and Play:*

The ambiguity and mobility of the cipher lead to an aesthetic indifference devoid of a sense of obligation. It is serious only when the movement arises from the primal source of Existenz. One may remonstrate that the freedom of movement of the ciphers testifies—since an absolute, objective criterion of its truth is lacking—that it is itself such an aesthetic lack of commitment.

To this we may reply: although a purely aesthetic absence of a sense of obligation may be rejected as a way of life, this rejection does not apply to play, which is indispensable. If I do not venture into the infinite world of as yet non-obligatory experience, I also shall not reach the genuine earnestness of obligation.

The great poets and artists were gripped by earnestness which came toward them from transcendence. They translated it into this configuration of freedom and did away with dogmatics and coercion. They spoke to us indirectly in an immediacy that grips us. We understand them only where we understand their earnestness. Together with them we are directed toward the truth of transcendence. But they leave us free. They lead us to experience all possibilities in play. They enable us to experience together with them as if we, within ourselves, were acting out for ourselves a drama in infinite metamorphoses. We become in possibility what we in this way neither actually are nor want to be. We are filled by a whole world of perceptions which expand us as individuals into the boundless possibilities of being-human. Here lies an irreplaceable source of our liberality and humanity. For earnestness that lacks the space to breathe freely what is created by poets and artists turns into dull earnestness without breadth and humaneness.

8. *Beyond Ciphers:*

Ciphers point beyond themselves to the ground of things, to what is called "Being," "Nothingness," "Being-Nothing," "Above Being," "Before all Being," "Beyond all Being," and which, for millennia, has been touched upon by philosophy.

Does not the demand that transcendence be imageless destroy all ciphers? Is not that which lies beyond all ciphers alone the truth?

Each cipher is merely a signpost or a guiding light. No cipher is the ultimate one nor the one and only.

Each cipher is also appearance, foreground, a language. Each requires a consciousness of its limitation in order to sense what lies beyond it. The battle of the ciphers is necessary to prevent that any one of them make itself absolute.

Hence we would like to go beyond all ciphers to the point where they disappear. But to do even this we are again dependent on a cipher-language so constituted that it includes even this disappearance.

But though we believe to have gotten beyond the ciphers, we still always return, as long as we live, to the phenomenality of our temporal existence. If we are able, in existential thinking and with clear consciousness, to enter perhaps for one moment the inner sanctum of the unthinkable, inconceivable, inexpressible, we drop back immediately into the world in which the ciphers are our language.

There remains disquietude in the battle of the ciphers. No cipher is adequate but each may seduce us into premature tranquility.

Yet tranquility in a cipher becomes itself a cipher; it is not complete tranquility. We know the wondrous tranquility to be found in the moment. But as duration in time it is existentially impossible.

We yearn for tranquility, are always inclined to find it in thoughtlessness or oblivion or inertia. But the will to truth is more powerful. It shatters all sham tranquility. It realizes that, together with the abandonment of disquietude, the truth of Existenz is lost also.

The tranquility granted to man in truth must find its anchor in the beyond of all ciphers where, however, no human anchor seems to take hold. But from there our ciphers gain their light and their shadows.

Selection 49

AT THE LIMIT OF CIPHERS (1): FOUNDERING

EDITORS:

Shipwreck or foundering (in German: *Schiffbruch*) is a metaphor Jaspers uses to indicate a point in thought where the failure of thought becomes apparent, a failure of thought—which by its nature is determinative—in articulating the as such indeterminable transcendent ground of Being. Foundering, to Jaspers, need not be regarded as only negative; according to him foundering can be the opportunity of recovering thought from the restrictions of its determinacy and of releasing Being in its encompassing openness.

This selection is a translation by the editors of passages from *Philosophie*, Vol. III, pp. 218, 220–23, 225, 230–34. In E. B. Ashton's translation these appear in *Philosophy*, Vol. III, pp. 192–206, *passim*.

TEXT:

Ciphers can not become fixed for possible Existenz, and yet they do not need to be nothing. But no matter what they are, having become objective they are infinitely ambiguous and are true only if they are preserved in the cipher of *foundering*; this is seen only factually with a positivistic lack of restraint, but is taken with existential seriousness in the limit situations. . . .

The Many Meanings of Foundering

For mere existence there is only a passing-away of which it knows nothing. Only for knowledge is there foundering as well as my attitude toward it. An animal is subject only to objective transitoriness. Its existence is wholly of the present; it is the sureness of its instincts, the perfect adaptation of its actions to its proper conditions of life. But if these are denied the animal, its behavior will be ferocious or a brooding stillness, or will show dull fear without knowledge or will. Foundering is only for man and, in such a manner, that it is ambiguous for him; it challenges him to react to it. I can say: nothing founders and nothing remains in itself. But I allow it to founder in me through the way in which I cognize and recognize this foundering. If I let my knowledge about the end of all things go under in the undifferentiated unity of the wholly dark abyss before which I would like to close my eyes, then I can see the animal as the ideal of existence of pure present fulfillment and can, with love and longing, raise it above me. However, I cannot enter animal existence, I can only give myself up as a human being.

If I remain within the human situation I make distinctions. What founders is not only existence as transitoriness, not only cognition as self-destruction as

I attempt to comprehend absolute Being, not only acting where a final purpose capable of permanence remains lacking. The limit situation reveals that all which is positive for us is bound to its corresponding negative. There is no good without possible or actual evil, no truth without falsehood, no life without death. Happiness is bound to pain, actualization to risk and loss. The human depth which gives voice to its transcendence is in reality tied to what is destructive, sick, or extravagant, but this bond in its unbounded variety is not unequivocally present. In all existence its antinomial structure is visible.

Thus the modes of foundering exist as objective actuality or as the inescapability of what can be thought, and hence signify, in some sense, a foundering in existence and as existence. The foundering of Existenz, however, lies on a different plane. When I come, in freedom, from existence to the certainty of Being, then I must experience, precisely in the clearest decisiveness of self-being within my acting, its foundering as well. For the impossibility to stand absolutely on one's own feet does not grow out of my being bound to existence, which is in fact destructive, but out of freedom itself. Through freedom I become guilty in every instance; I cannot become whole. Truth as genuine truth which I grasp because I am and live it lacks the possibility of being knowable as absolutely valid. What is absolutely valid could persist, timeless, in ever-changing existence; but authentic truth is precisely the truth that perishes.

Authentic self-being cannot maintain itself through itself alone; it can miss being itself, and cannot be forced. The more it succeeds in being itself, the clearer becomes the limit at which it fails. It will be ready for its Other, for transcendence, when it founders in its desire to be sufficient unto itself. But that transcendence remains absent from me, that I can be deceived in my confidence of finally finding myself in transcendent relationship—in neither case do I know what my guilt was and what I must bear as having happened to me; it is possible that I founder as I myself without philosophic trust, without the aid of a divine word or a religious guarantee, although truthfulness and readiness all seemed to be present.

Contained in the multifariousness of foundering is the question whether foundering is destruction plain and simple because that which founders does, indeed, perish, or whether in foundering a Being becomes manifest; whether foundering can be not merely foundering but may be perpetuation. . . .

Foundering and Perpetuation

When, in the face of the transitoriness of all things—even if they pass away only after millennia—existence as possible Existenz ultimately sees authentic Being only in the concrete present actuality of its own self-being, even destruction and perishing become a Being if they are grasped freely. Foundering, suffered only as if accidentally as the foundering of my existence, can be grasped as authentic foundering. The will to perpetuation, rather than repudiating foundering, seems to finds its goal in foundering itself.

If, as a vital being, I possess the will to persist; if, in losing, I seek a new support in something enduring: then, as possible Existenz, I desire the Being that I am able to take hold of even as I perish although it does not last. Vis-à-vis the downfall I have suffered, when what is dearest to me eludes me uncompleted, I can take upon myself what has happened. In clear-eyed endurance I can yet find out that which, for a moment was fulfilled present, is not lost. If, however, through my transfiguring phantasy I then combine in my thoughts Being with perishing; if I believe that the gods take unto themselves only what is dear to them, or that whatever became form and configuration partakes in eternity, then Existenz will resist. If all that remains to it is to suffer in passivity, it will not resign itself to contemplation and pacification. For its consciousness of authentic Being cannot complete itself in the pure contemplation of not-being-lost. Rather, it must have injected itself into the foundering, at first in the activity of risking itself and then in allowing itself to founder. The cipher becomes decidely manifest not only for contemplation, which merely accepts, but for Existenz which, perishing as existence, brings forth the cipher out of freedom, which shatters as Existenz and, in this shattering, finds its ground in the Being of transcendence.

The contradictoriness of foundering remains as appearance. We do not know the solution, for it is within Being which remains hidden. Whoever, in his own particular fate, passed through the levels of Existenz comes up against this Being. This Being cannot be presupposed. No authority is able to administer or to mediate it. Its glance is turned toward the one who, in risking, approaches it.

To will foundering outright would be a perversion in which Being would again become wholly darkened to the point of nothingness. Genuine revelatory foundering does not lie in any perishing at all, not in every act of destruction, not in every act of giving oneself up, in every renunciation or failure. The cipher of perpetuation in foundering becomes clear only when I do not want to founder but dare to founder. I cannot plan the reading of the cipher; I can only plan what guarantees duration and continuation. The cipher does not disclose itself when I want it but when I do everything to avoid its actuality. It reveals itself in *amor fati*; yet a fatalism which would surrender prematurely and hence does not founder would be untrue. . . .

Actualizing and Not-Actualizing

From the consciousness of foundering does not necessarily follow the passivity of the trivial but the possibility of true activity: what perishes must have been. Perishing only becomes actual through the actuality of the world; otherwise it would be merely the disappearance of possibilities. Hence I place the weight of my Being completely into existence as actualization in order to create duration and believe in it as something to be done. I want permanence in order to experience the fulfilled foundering in which Being first dawns on me. I grasp the world and extend myself with all my strength within its richness in order to see, out of this origin, its fragmentation and its perishing, and not in order merely to know it in abstract thoughts. Only when I step into the world without reservation and suffer whatever its destruction brings with it can I actually experience foundering as cipher. Otherwise there would only be the groundless, indifferent downfall of all things.

For possible Existenz's consciousness of Being the world constitutes the realm in which it finds out what is authentic. I turn to the society in which I live and participate by taking hold of those spheres of activity available to me; to communicative duration in family and friendship; to the objectivity of nature in its laws and the possible mastery of it through technology. As existence, I breathe in a world; as a human being together with others I bring forth a fulfillment of existence. Even if all fulfillment is mere transitoriness there is yet in it, through it, the cipher script of Being. . . .

What is Excluded from Interpretation

Every interpreting thought that is held to be true and is actualized will allow the cipher of Being to be seen in foundering. It is an expression of the soaring upward of absolute consciousness. But the interpretation only includes what can be grasped in human thought as self-fulfilling content.

However what, in the first place, does not fit such interpretation is, first of all, senseless ending. Negativity, as it is overcome, can become the source of authentic actuality; it can awaken and bring forth. But the negativity that merely destroys, the fruitless suffering that does not awaken but merely constricts and paralyzes, the mental illness that, beyond any coherence, merely overpowers out of what is other: these *cannot* be interpreted. There is then not only productive destruction but also simply ruinous destruction.

What, secondly, does not fit interpretation is the failure of possibilities when that founders which has not even existed yet but has already announced the possibility of its existence. . . .

Thirdly, there is no interpretation of destruction in the form of an end point in history, where all record and trace is buried, thereby excluding any possible continuity of what is thusly human. Our passionate desire not to lose authentic Being in its appearance urges us to rescue its documents so that it may continue preserved in historic spirit. If what has once been is retained in memory, and if its demise produces its presence in the form of its effect in a being that preserves, then the annihilation of the possibility of remembrance would be its final destruction. Whatever was actual as human grandeur, existential unconditionality, creativity, is forever forgotten. What we remember in our historicity is like a random selection which has to stand for all that has been lost. The ruin of absolute oblivion has no interpretation.

The Cipher of Being in Foundering

Through non-interpretable annihilation all that is achieved in philoso-phizing is put in question time and again. It seems that the one who actually sees what is must behold the darkness of the void. Not only is he abandoned by all existence; foundering exists as merely the Being of nothingness and no longer as cipher. If foundering remains this *mene tekel* then everything is only impenetrable in empty night. The threatening extreme of non-interpretable foundering must shatter everything that had been envisioned, imagined, erected behind the blinders of illusory happiness. No life is possible based on this actuality. . . .

The Ultimate Cipher as Sounding Board for All Ciphers

The Being that, in actual fulfillment, became revealed by ciphers is put in question vis-à-vis the non-interpretable foundering and must live backwards out of the wellsprings of the Being experienced in silence, or else it must wither. For foundering is the all-embracing ground of all being-cipher. My seeing cipher as the actuality of Being only grows out of my experience of foundering. Out of this experience the ciphers that are not rejected receive their ultimate confirmation. What I allow to submerge in annihilation I am able to receive back as cipher. In my reading of ciphers I let them emerge in view of the ruin that, in the cipher of my foundering, first gives to each partic-ular cipher its resonance.

Passive ignorance remains merely the pain of possible nothingness or the critical reservation against false ontological knowledge. In the experience of the non-interpretable, on the other hand, not-knowing becomes active in the presence of Being as the source of all authentic consciousness of Being within the infinite richness of experience in the world and of the actualization of Existenz.

Non-interpretability as the ultimate cipher is, however, no longer a deter-minable cipher. It remains open, hence its silence. It can become the absolute void as well as final fulfillment.

Selection 50

AT THE LIMIT OF CIPHERS (2): TRANSCENDING ALL CIPHERS

EDITORS:
In this selection Jaspers interprets the Buddhist temple of Boro Buddor on

Java and the mysticism of Meister Eckhart as attempts of realizing the open fullness of Being at the limits of ciphers.

The selection appears on pp. 399–406 of *Der philosophische Glaube angesichts der Offenbarung*, a work of his later years in which Jaspers examines the confrontations of philosophy and Western revealed religion, and of Eastern and Western thought. The translation has been provided by the editors; for E. B. Ashton's translation see *Philosophical Faith and Revelation*, pp. 265–70.

TEXT:

Negative theology acts as a gentle shadow that merely enhances, in the West, the light of the glorious world of ciphers. In Asia, however, transcending occurred not through the energy generated by thought but through the attitude toward and the way of life actualized by means of it. This happened in such a thoroughgoing manner and to such depth as perhaps nowhere else among men. We cannot be sure how much of this we understand. But it is certain that we can be affected by it in a unique way, and that we are then more sensitive to its rudimentary forms in the West. We are to understand the astounding paradox of the suspension of speech by language.

The attempts that have been made of going beyond—not only all reality, but also the ciphers toward the unthinkable and hence inexpressible of that which yet sustains us and is the Encompassing of all Encompassing—are, wherever they have occurred, possessed of a wondrous power. To be sure, the attempt must always assume a form which enables it to enter our thinking. But this occurs counter to its meaning and counter to the intent of this thinking. That is why it is so strangely ambiguous: either it is, for the mere intellect that wants to cognize something objectively, an incomprehensible, invalid stammering; or it allows what is not and can never be expressed to become manifest through the transparency of these rationally meaningless thoughts.

We are deeply affected by these ideas insofar as we can hear in them at the same time a historic person in the actuality of his conduct of life and in his meditation. But since in the traditions such personalities come through and can be perceived only faintly, indeed sometimes not at all, these ideas, which, according to their meaning, have to be extremely abstract, may seem tenuous. But precisely in their abstractness they can grip us as no others can. As we assimilate them, they are most likely no longer that which was contained in them originally.

Boro Buddor

Buddhist thought, which transcends all ciphers, has been expressed in Boro Buddor (Java) in a gripping representation through an enormous edifice. In its space, pictures, spatial arrangements, allegories, and the movements of the pilgrim serve as visual aids.*

A terraced pyramid rises out of a broad plain under an open sky. The pilgrim climbs this pyramid over stairs and circular galleries. Down below, the mundane forms of life are brought before him in inexhaustible series of bas-reliefs: on his way up Buddha-statues are visible to him in many modifications of their poses fraught with meaning. At the top there are no more images. There are cupolas and geometric forms, until the very last cupola reaches into the empty heavens which alone remain for the wanderer.

Everything is a sign. The delightful images of the exuberant world below are seen by the pilgrim within the narrow confines of the corridor whose outer balustrades lead the eye toward walls that are themselves decorated with pictures but do not allow the pilgrim to gaze into the landscape. But if he looks up he will already glimpse the void of the blue sky.

Only on the topmost of the angled terraces is the amount of imagery reduced and the space opens up. The corridors, narrow up to this point, lose their exterior wall. The latter descends to form a fence crowned by a cupola which, imageless, allows the formless vault of the heavens to appear on one side of the pilgrim.

For the upper square galleries no longer partake of the world of the senses that is replete with forms but of plateaus of a vision filled with forms. The content of the chronicle told by its reliefs refers to the Buddha Maitrenja who is still to come and whose glory no sensuous eye has yet beheld but is seen only by an inner vision.

Finally, in the area of the upper circular terraces all forms of pictorial representation and continuous ornamentation have disappeared. Seventy-two smaller cupolas covered by stone lattice-work are situated around a large, closed cupola which, as the pinnacle of the edifice, rests on a raised center. All of the cupolas comprise a forest of symbols of Nirvana and reach into the pure void of the heavens. Their apexes are merely stereometric, pure forms of a mathematical nature.

The filigree cupolas are not yet signs of the highest state beyond all imagery, for they hide in their interior a Buddha-figure whose shape is almost removed from sight by stone lattice-work and is just barely visible. They are the signs of a higher, formless vision of the outer court of Nirvana. Finally the one massive cupola which contains the Buddha-figure towers over everything but withholds it from view by surrounding it with closed arches.

Zimmer understands the meaning of the ascent: the development of an

*Cf. Heinrich Zimmer, *Kunstform und Yoga*, Berlin 1926, pp. 94ff; O. Fischer, *Kunstwanderungen auf Java und Bali*, Stuttgart 1941, pp. 47ff; Karl Wirth, *Java*, Hagen i.w. 1920, plates 1–33.

intensive image by the pilgrim is brought about first by way of unfolding, followed by the fusion of what has unfolded. The development of the ciphers is followed by the transcending of all ciphers.

Being cipher, Buddha himself must disappear. Along the lower parapets he was visible to the eye in niches. In the latticed cupolas he begins to withdraw. In the massive central cupola he is invisible. This means: the symbols of the glimpsed forms of inner vision are followed by the representation of the transitory stages that are becoming formless (latticed cupolas) and, finally, by the signs of enraptured Being. Or: from the regions of an interior vision filled with forms the pilgrim proceeds to eternal Nirvana.

It is the purpose of the plastic-architectonic representation to be an allegory of the road to what cannot be represented. The goal is the pure void of eternity which, in human consciousness, has bifurcated into the I and the objects of the world of forms. This road ascends through the world of the figures of the senses and of vision, of the manifold field of joy and sorrow, of life in its richness; it crosses over the realm of formless vision on to the Nirvana that has no beginning. The pilgrim sees the fetters of ignorance, which hide his own nature from him, drop off him circle by circle which remain behind as traversed terraces.

The symbol of the Buddha-image occurs at all levels of the edifice, from the lowest to the highest: in the Buddha-legends represented here which show him enmeshed in human life and the continuity of nature; in the niches he appears solitary, no longer caught up in existence but still clearly visible; in the latticed cupolas he is found at the borderline of being beyond our ken, until the Buddha at the very top can no longer be comprehended visually.

No tradition bears witness to the identity of the patrons of the architects of this wondrous, powerful edifice, no document describes their intentions. It is only due to the durability of stone that these mighty remains have been preserved, though damaged and weather-beaten, neither living up to nor at variance with the wishes of the builders. They did not think about future, duration, or monument but only about the eternity of Nirvana. They did not think in historic terms about future generations but unhistorically about worldlessness. Zimmer's interpretation is possible only on the basis of his knowledge of the Buddhist texts of India. But these cannot inform us about details with respect to the infinite particularities of the images or as to the meaning of the individual terraces, stairs, and gates. Only their totality seems clear.

We must consider the following as we comprehend this Buddhist transcending of all ciphers:

Buddhist ascent simply cannot be achieved as speculative transcending by means of pure thought. It takes place, rather, through specific meditative exercises, through a transformation of the conscious state. The meditating person isolates himself within the world. When he returns to worldly communicability he will understand himself as the essence of the inexpressible eternal Being-Nothing which loses all illusory individuality and all illusory objectness in Nirvana.

By taking up and then discarding all ciphers (meanings), the meditating individual does not arrive at a place from which he still intends to participate in the world. He has left the world. Falling back into the world from beyond, he still experiences it but only as an indifferent series of happenings in existence. This has no further meaning for him except that it can become, as disguised signs, a pointer to that through which world and meaning disappear.

It is erroneous to believe that what is meant here could be reached purely speculatively in universal consciousness. What is essential is the actual experience, and this can be gained only through meditative exercises practiced for years of one's life in isolation from the world. It is very easy to overlook the fact that there is no way of avoiding this foundation in experience (just as, in a different way, the Jesuits cannot be understood without the power of the spiritual exercises which leave their specific imprint on them).

But we must ask ourselves whether the speculative thoughts of the Buddhists are significant also for us. We take them up as communicable thoughts in the world of universal consciousness, detach them from their roots that are planted in the meditation which alters the conscious state. What we lack are the specific fulfillments, inaccessible to us but experienced by those men. But we do carry out the thoughts which are transcending by virtue of their liberating operation. As such they become irreplaceable for us. We have the experience of being addressed, not by an oddity but by something that concerns us personally. The great distance that separates us from the original world of the Buddhists consists of the following: we use thoughts operatively in order to come to ourselves together with transcendence; the Buddhists, however, seek to lose their selves totally and in every sense.

Let us try to visualize the state of the perfected Buddhist. The Buddhas, those who appeared once upon a time and those who are still to come, are called the "universally benevolent." They are all-mercifulness in object-less love, the phenomenality of one who already is at home in Nirvana. This love is to be represented in gestures and to be actualized in life to which one has in all respects become indifferent; this is all that remains to him who has achieved knowledge about the undifferentiated void for as long as its bearer is still in the world. The Buddha does not force his knowledge or his practices on anyone; the Buddhists are the only ones who have never waged a religious war. He does not despise anyone, does not become angry, shows pity and compassion without himself suffering under this compassion. From the tranquility of the perfect void he is able to "let go" of all world-being, whose happiness and whose calamity—all the paths of the world from re-birth to the glories of paradise—still all confine man in chains and do not achieve Nirvana. He helps by pointing out the path to Nirvana through teaching and actual example and not by making demands. Everything is granted to him who does not desire. The Buddhist does not intervene, not by force, not by resistance. Being free of the world he knows neither emotion nor puposive will, neither pride nor resentment, neither longing nor deprivation, and least of all the everyday irritations and rages of men. Toward death he is indifferent. He neither fears nor welcomes it.

There is little doubt that this human- superhuman state has been attained now and again. Without this foundation in fact the texts we read would not have been written. But this complete freedom from the world exacts the price of giving up all meaning, all ways of possible fulfillment in the world; it means not only transcending the being-cipher of one's own way and experience of life, indeed all ciphers, but losing them entirely.

Meister Eckhart

The interpretations of Meister Eckhart remain within the imagery of Christian theology. When we are with him we breathe the air of the West. His points of departure and his formulas are not the Buddhist ones. Nonetheless he moves along the same limits, searches for that which one can attain only when all ciphers and even God, when absolutely everything, is transcended.

1. Eckhart differentiates between "deus" and "deitas," "God" and "Godhead." He says: "Godhead and God are as different from one another as heaven and earth; God, too, comes to be and passes away."

2. The Being of God occurs through effluence from the Godhead in an act in which there come to be, simultaneously, God (Father, Son and Spirit), the world, and time. This effluence is that through which occurred, in the "simple Now of eternity," what did not occur after all, "not in time but together with time." God, Trinity and world are co-eternal. "At the same time and all at once God, by himself coming to be, by begetting the Son as equally eternal and equal to Him in everything, has also created the world." That emanation of God from this Godhead is something quite different from the begetting of the Son, the inspiration of the Spirit, or the creation of the world. It is the primal source before all of this.

3. To be sure, for Eckhart God and Godhead are also identical. In this case the distinction becomes intra-divine: God has performed only one act in eternity and became God through this act. Prior to this act (that is, not in time but prior to time) He is Godhead without act or effect, without personhood, and without world. With the distinction of God from Godhead, Eckhart progresses beyond God. The differences between Godhead and God are expressed variously in his formulas.

The Godhead is Being, not acting. It is not the Godhead who acts but God. Only God created all things, only He is the father of the whole world. God has been only since there have been creatures. Not only has He created them but they also created Him. Therefore we can say: that God is—I am a cause of that; that there is the Godhead—that is out of itself. Vis-à-vis the Godhead, creator and creature belong to the same sphere.

4. How does thinking assure itself of the Godhead? By the suspension of all that is thinkable, every distinction, every determinacy.

For example: "Equality" cannot be predicated about the Godhead, for: "where there is equality there is no unity, since 'equal' is privative of unity; and where there is unity there is no equality, for equality remains within difference and multiplicity. Where there is a 'being-equal' there cannot be any 'being-one.' "

"In unity the Father never knew of a Son nor a Son of a Father: for here there is neither Son nor Father, nor Holy Spirit." Equality is only where there is differentiatedness. And where there is differentiatedness there is no unity that, transcending all determinability, is no longer "unity" in the categorial sense.

The Godhead is lost to thinking, because thinking demands that we think in terms of definition what lacks definition. Even Being, God, creator are thought in categories that are not proper for the Godhead. We must go beyond all determinations, including the notion of God.

In our thinking we posit "Beingness" (essentia) and "Being" (esse, existentia). We juxtapose them, and they are two; we think of them one inside the other, and they are one. But the Godhead can be grasped neither in its differentiation nor in its unity.

5. We are linked with God only as His creatures within the realm of our existence. But man is free to penetrate to where he once was and will be again or rather always is, namely not with God but with the Godhead. By penetrating through God man can find his way to that which God himself was before he came to be by setting about the work of creation.

We humans have both: our inmost, which is one with the Godhead, and our creatureliness, which God created (i.e., brought into existence) by himself coming into being. Hence we attain tranquility only in the Godhead rather than in God. We attain this tranquility when we become dead to being creatures and thus to creating and becoming, when we are no longer on the way, when we come to nothing, when we "unbecome." Then we no longer need to know anything of God and the three Divine Persons (for they are still in the sphere of the something, in otherness and manyness). We are in a state of bliss only where God is no longer the creator but where the Godhead (unity and nothingness) is, when we are there where, through all of Being, we encounter the place where God was identical with the Godhead, and I, in the sparks of my soul, was identical with the Godhead also and can be again—the place where God was not yet a Person just as I was not yet this I.

"God comes into being only where all creatures address him. When I still tarried in the wellspring of the Godhead, no one asked me where I wanted to go or what I was doing . . . But when I flowed out, all creatures said: God . . . Thus all creatures speak about God. And why do they not speak of the Godhead? —Everything that is in the Godhead is One, and one cannot speak about that."

"When I enter into the wellspring of the Godhead, no one asks me whence I come and where I have been. There no one misses me—for there even God un-becomes." From "created light" we shall be transformed into the "un-created radiance" of the divine essence and we "shall be what he is." It is "nobler" to "break through" toward the Godhead than to "flow out" of it. But this breaking through means experiencing what I myself am as uncreated, what I am from all eternity as this "spark of the soul."

Eckhart's thinking avoids letting the soul become equal to the Godhead. For "God" and "equal" and "become" are extinguished before the unity of spark of the soul and "Godhead." The caesura between world and transcendence is no longer that between world and God; for both of these belong to the Being that originates when God and the world are present at the same time, constituting a single realm to which belong things, men, and God, inseparable from one another. The caesura lies between this whole realm of Being and the Godhead.

This is the split between our creatureliness, what we are as God's creatures, and what we are, without God, before God, in the ground of the Godhead, namely the spark of the soul, the uncreated to which we belong.

Selection 51

AT THE LIMIT OF CIPHERS (3): THE OTHER WAY OF THINKING

EDITORS:
In this selection Jaspers is challenged by and attempts to penetrate a way of thinking which he regards as outside the Western tradition that is schooled by "antiquity and the Bible." He calls it "Asian philosophy," and it is the thinking which has its roots in Indian Hindu and Buddhist mysticism. Jaspers understands it as a way of fulfillment in the foundering of thought, beyond all ciphers.

The selection is to be found in *Der philosophische Glaube angesichts der Offenbarung*, pp. 416–21. It has been translated by the editors. For E. B. Ashton's translation, see *Philosophical Faith and Revelation*, pp. 276–79.

TEXT:
1. Let us once more call to mind the state of the world and of our knowledge in a cipher which was nowhere as decisively an experienced thought as in India: everything that is, is concealment. Knowledge in the world, of objects in the world, implicit in purposive acts—precisely that is ignorance, the veil of Maya. What, seen from our existence in the Maya is Nothing, that is itself the truth and plenitude.

All cognition, especially the scientific cognition of our age, is cognition of illusion, itself belonging to illusion and caught in the circle of illusion. The concealment is only reinforced through objective brightness and rational clarity. It is a tremendous knowledge which, measured against the truth of genuine knowledge of Being, is, rather, one single illusory knowledge, a nonknowing (*avidya*).

Where does it come from, this veil, this our reality of existence that is not out of itself, not authentic Being? Was it an original primal deception? a historic process in which what had once been clear has become obscured? an act of the magic of illusory world-creation? There is no answer. Or, it is given to us in ciphers which allow precisely that to get lost which is at stake here, i.e., the transcending of all ciphers.

Insight into the state of our world and our knowledge demands a different thinking, one that breaks through the concealment. It is as if the origin of the illusion derived from a turning, the turn of the turning, the return from the first return that had ended up in darkness.

But the image that all of this is the history of the Being of the world, of our selves, which came to be, as illusion, through an incomprehensible defection, and which maintained itself through the appearance of ignorance—all this is itself meant unhistorically: the turning and the turn of the turning are what happens at all times and not at a particular time. From the realm of truth there is defection at every moment, and to the realm of truth there is return at every moment also.

The return is accomplished through a different thinking, whether it be the meditative transformation of consciousness or whether it be through speculative thought—carried out, to be sure, by way of the intellect but inaccessible to the intellect as such.

2. Beyond all ciphers: Whoever has felt it, experiences from there a powerful, silent attraction. At first he is silent but he cannot remain so. For he wants to be clear in his own mind and also to clarify the silence even if it returns again after each clarification.

I think the beyond of all ciphers. But in the very moment when I think it, it is, in fact, no longer. It can only be thought by my paying the price of losing it precisely in my thinking it.

The thinking that loses it is objective thinking, the thinking guided by representations and images, the thinking in determinacies, that is, in concepts, the thinking in ciphers.

Is there a different way of thinking, one that does get there? This would be a thinking that suspends itself. In this thinking, thoughts and objects collapse. They come to naught but in such a manner that the thinker becomes aware of what is authentic and essential and through itself, what is not for something else and not for us as something thought. But even the words "authentic," "essential," "through itself," "beyond Being" say too much.

For they as well as all traditional metaphysical determinations—since they express and designate—are themselves again a veiling. To be sure, that which suspends the silence also clarifies it, but it also disturbs it. Silence, put into words, loses its depth. Therefore Asian philosophy used this whole thinking in the end only in order to destroy itself and has repeated it tirelessly in this process of self-destruction through thought.

But what comes to be in the thinking individual is this way, what becomes accessible to him, what reveals itself to him in the restored muteness of the silence—that does not arise together with the self-suspending thinking. This merely makes room for it. It pursues objective thinking into the very last corner in which it wants to take refuge and out of which it wants to come forth once more. For we surely wish to triumph, in the end, in this other thinking by taking hold of what is authentic. But then we betray it, and what we wanted to know hides from us now all the more. Again and again we want to possess it, if only by merely naming it; but since we have drawn it once more into the realm of the thinkable, we lose it in the same instant.

Hence, this thinking—driven by sublime dialectical means, to utter foundering—serves, in Asiatic philosophy, only for purposes of warding off and preparation and is not, itself, a way of fulfillment. Fulfillment is attained there by way of a meditation that is a transformation of consciousness. Speaking in respect to it and from its perspective—that is the purpose, in Asia, of conceptual speculation, of the thinking that is, in distinction to intellectual thought, the new thinking. Lifelong meditative exercises are the path toward, and bring fulfillment to, that truth before which all objectively thinking knowledge is merely ignorance.

Asian philosophy calls this truth "emptiness." For our thinking, too, as we transcend beyond all ciphers—however without any transformation of consciousness—that which we seek becomes, in fact, completely empty because our invariably objective thinking cannot reach it. Being cleansed of objectivity is nothingness for this thinking. Is it possible, then, to drop our anchor there where there is no bottom, no support, only nothingness? Obviously not, not the thinking consciousness which seeks to cognize something. We are not familiar with any other consciousness because we neither engage in nor give credence to those alterations of consciousness through meditation.

But are the following possible without our practicing meditation, namely that, in lucid consciousness and proceeding by way of and beyond thought, Being comes from where there is "nothingness"; that our existence is put into a different light; and that our freedom—within the space of the world and in the language of ciphers—is fulfilled beyond these? This question is answered by existential experience which is both active and passive. The answer manifests itself in the manner in which we deal with our real cognition, how we move around within cipher language, how our consciousness becomes aware that we are in the world, how we see criteria appear everywhere without knowing whence, and experience a guidance without knowing how.

This actuality is served by the other thinking, the thinking of philosophical speculation in which we and the Asians encounter each other. It is thinking that suspends itself. This thinking which, seen from our intellectual conception of things, actually seems to be no longer any thinking at all since it cognizes nothing—this thinking is itself a different kind of meditating without any alteration in the state of consciousness. Over the millennia it has become as richly developed as has music but is less accessible. Whoever does manage to penetrate it experiences speculative thought in a unique way. These experiences are, to all appearances, less powerful, weaker, paler than the massive experiences of the techniques and exercises of deep absorption; but appearance is deceptive. It is precisely because of its technical-psychological ineffectuality that the experience of speculation has an existential impact that is all the purer.

Such thinking may make us angry. It is then experienced—often unjustly—as ineffectual self-torment or—sometimes justly—as deceptive conceptual fraud lacking earnestness. But wherever this thinking lights a spark it can inflame enthusiasm because, as we think along with it, it takes us on the path to where thinking ceases through thinking itself and from whence comes guidance for the person liberated in his thinking. It is the thinking which ceases, at the level of highest abstraction, to be abstract because it becomes existential in the process of divesting itself of objectivities.

3. I repeat once again: Every cipher delimits, makes comprehensible, makes figurative in imagination and thought. Whatever is thought confronts the thinker as well as the other thoughts.

Ciphers that are thought are molded by categories. No matter if they are as comprehensive as Being, Nothingness, Substance, Meaning, etc.: they remain categories. Each comprehensibility restricts what is thought. Determinacy is limitedness.

Beyond all ciphers and categories lies transcendence—and this word "transcendence" is, as designation, itself again inappropriate. Transcendence means going beyond all objects and all ciphers, it means stepping beyond and climbing over; however, it does not mean the act but its destination and precisely that which can no longer be expressed. Hence statements here are neither appropriate nor inappropriate; rather they are a bridge in speculative thinking such as "God is Being," "God is Nothingness."

Insofar as we human beings are sensuous rational creatures, transcending, for us, does not mean that we give up ciphers and categories but that we do not let ourselves be caught up in them. For as, in using them, we go beyond them, so we immediately slip back into them.

Ludwig Curtius, a great modern humanist, has written: "I know nothing about God, indeed I cannot even say that he exists; and yet I constantly feel sheltered in him."

4. One may speak of the *self-suspension of metaphysics*. After metaphysics was developed into an objective craft, the first step taken was its suspension. This was done by Kant the "all-devourer," but done by him in order to preserve its character as cipher.

The second step—after the actualization of the meaning of ciphers and of their battle—was its transcending into the Beyond of all ciphers, a step that had been taken for thousands of years.

The suspension of the objective craft of metaphysics is brought about by showing up the unavoidably arising, unwanted and unrecognized contradictions, the endless argumentation leading to no result, the typical logical route taken by this erring, and the lack of existential commitment of such knowledge.

Going beyond the world of ciphers does not bring about our loss of this world but prohibits us from settling down in this world as if it were absolute.

The thinking of such going beyond is able to dissolve ciphers but not to produce them. Or it merely produces them in order to dissolve them. The game of dissolving then seems to be the truth itself.

Buddha and the Buddhists thought the self-suspension of metaphysics for the first time in its very radicalness. We right away experience the ambiguity. This thinking does not find a home in the real world nor in a world of thought. It finds a "home" in disappearing and letting disappear. This self-dissolution of the metaphysics of ciphers leads, in temporal existence, to nothingness.

5. But there is temporal existence. In complete self-dissolution man is unable to desire anything any more in the world, is unable to do or to build anything. He no longer knows anything but the indifference and arbitrariness and absurdity of nothingness. But this is not the last word for us. Indeed, it is the expression of a possibility which we resist with our existential energy.

For we are beings that are not merely left to chance and submissive to nature; we are not in the world in vain. The timeless "eternal realm" is a cipher, but one that speaks only in the world. This realm is not another world into which I could flee but is itself present in this world. If I ground my life in a future realm, in the wholly other, somewhere else, that awaits me; and if I ground it in the bodily resurrection so that I may live there forever—then my earnestness in the world and for the world will vanish and, with it, eternity itself. I am nothing if I do not actualize in the world what eternity can reveal to me here. For if I miss the world then I also lose eternity. To be sure, we measure our world-being by eternity. But I must not give up what is measured: Expressed paradoxically, I must decide, in the worldly realm and in time, what I am eternally and what eternally is.

Even in the Beyond of all ciphers, we of the West—educating ourselves through the traditions of antiquity and the Bible—still feel the challenge in our existence as it is given to us: to actualize ourselves as Existenz, fulfilled by our view of transcendence.

Selection 52

REASON VS. MYSTICISM

EDITORS:
Jaspers regards revelation and mysticism as being ways of fulfillment in man's quest for metaphysical truth for which there have been credible testimonies. For him the way of philosophical thought is different from either revelation or mysticism; it is the way of reason, of the communicative reading of the cipher-script.

This selection from *Von der Wahrheit*, pp. 659–701, in a translation by the editors, appears here in English for the first time.

TEXT:
We may seek unity in the depth of the Encompassing that we are. It may seem to us that there, in the depths, there is no longer any division or that there was none as yet in the immediacy. There is no division there between living existence, thought and idea, none between logos and ethos, between spirit and Existenz, none between feeling, will, purpose. Experiencing this One in immediacy should bring us to genuine Being; thinking this One clearly should lead us to the highest knowledge.

It would have to be that which passes through all the modes of the Encompassing which I am and keep them together as One. In the depth of the One which I am I would touch the One in which and out of which I am. This experience of unity would be the experience of the absolutely One through the One that I am.

But is it possible to experience this One when every temporal existence already constrains us within determinate finitudes? And is it possible to speak of the One when all clear speech must make distinctions? The unity of all—if there were such—would still be impossible to experience and to know. For in its very first clarification it would determine, divide, differentiate, in the division of subject and object, of the one thing from the other, of one existence from the other existence, of one Existenz from the other Existenz. In cognition, in relation, in struggle, in love, there the One would be no longer but it would be sought. . . .

We call the experience of the One most likely the *unio mystica*, or our fundamental certainty, our frame of mind (disposition, condition), the decision of our will which supports us, the moods, the absolute consciousness.

What is experienced there is irreplaceable. But it becomes questionable when one wants to refer to it. For then it needs to be developed by the roundabout route over divisions, distinctions, conflicts.

What one says about it is allusion and recollection. But this becomes empty when one attempts thereby to take hold of the One. Then there ensues a thoughtless speaking about a unity that is collapsing. One believes to be expressing the concrete concept of the One, such as "life," "experiencing," "Being," by simply joining together antitheses. But in this way one is left with meaningless turns of speech when one maintains, for example, the unity of intuition and thinking, body and soul, freedom and authority, theory and practice. Such paradoxes may be meaningful for an instant as an articulation in transcending but they become absurd as realities or as definite tasks to be performed. Such a bringing together of mutually exclusive words does not create a unity. The words serve to veil and stupefy. They prevent clear thought and decisive action which are the path to unity.

And yet there remains truth in the immediate experience of the One. We touch upon this experience in three ways: (1) as a transformation of consciousness in mysticism; (2) as absolute consciousness in the clear presence of the unconditional; (3) as the movement of consciousness in reason.

1. *Unio Mystica.* Man experiences this union by stepping out of his present consciousness into the clarity, as it were, of object-less light. There is no more division, neither into subject and object, nor of the objects among themselves. There is no more I and no more object and no differentiation of one object from another. Lacking image and mode there is only the One in *unio mystica.*

This unity is experienced in the separation from world and existence.

These are experiences of the transformation of consciousness into worldlessness. Its meaning manifests itself only in that which grows out of such experiences in the world for the one whom they befall. It is decisive whether
mystical experience and mundane life remain disconnected from one another
or whether they enter into a mutual relationship.

If *unio mystica* and real life remain unconnected, then the man who has
such experiences and this experience itself are merely in juxtaposition. The
experienced unity remains distant, alien, and uncommunicable. The experiences admit only of external psychological description but not of a meaning
construct that has consequences. The experience is the goal of a longed–for
enjoyment or is an indifferent accident; it awakens a wondrous amazement or
is put aside like a confused dream. It has no meaning on the level of vital
concerns. Nothing comes of it.

Things are quite different if the *unio mystica* functions as an experience
that through its deep significance affects life. In that case the mystical union
becomes the source of unity in the world. It then becomes communicable—not
directly, to be sure, but indirectly—through the way it informs the human
being and his actions in the world. From this union his knowledge, feelings,
and actions gain their impetus and contents in the world that is divided once
more. Then *unio mystica* transforms man, becomes the origin and goal of his
mundane existence; in it the *unio* becomes phenomenal and completes it. The
unio mystica no longer merely stands apart from the world but is the contact
with the One that endorses the world within it. From there it inspires man to
turn to the world. It enters into relationship with the unity of the historicity of
our Existenz and with the unity which opens up to reason.

The questions that are asked regarding the experience of a *unio mystica* are
intended to examine its genuineness and truth: In what way is a merely psychological state different from encompassing Being? What is lost of the Encompassing in the mystical union? Or: In what way is the Unity of the One in
fact not achieved in the mystical experience of the One? How can one preserve the depth of this experience of the One without becoming a failure in
the world? What—considering the fundamental incommunicability of the
experience—is communicable after all in the writings of the mystics and in
what form? How does the richness of imagery in speaking about the One go
together with its imagelessness?

2. *Absolute Consciousness.*   In the medium of all divisions, consciousness, rendered clear because of them, is capable of an experience of unity that
we call "absolute consciousness." We can be aware of the One in the unconditionality of our conscience, our love, our faith. An encompassing One may
precede in us all our specific knowing and acting. Absolute consciousness is
not a specific state of consciousness and not a special consciousness; rather it is
the background that supports our consciousness. We speak of this conscious-

ness in various ways. But as one speaks about it, it has already slipped through
our fingers. And especially if one appeals to it, then it is lost. . . .

We may speak about a fundamental certainty. This kind of certainty precedes all thinking as the encompassing immediacy. Yet it is not present like a
determinable fact but only becomes clear when we penetrate into the ground
out of which it comes. This happens only by means of trials in the reality of
our world. The basic certainty must first be awakened and in this way
earned—through constant questioning and testing. Its ultimate ground would
be where all modes of the Encompassing are held together, where nothing is
excluded because a joint knowledge with creation, as it were, becomes clear to
itself. . . .

Fundamental certainty becomes questionable whenever one bases himself
on it. As basic assurance it becomes the expression of a violent unconcern of
existence that wants to believe in itself. If utilized for the purpose of community in the world it turns into the violation of all. As mere immediacy it lacks
clarity, has not proved itself, is clouded by what is alien to it.

Fundamental certainty is task and question, is in the movement and in the
attempt. It is risked by the individual to whom this ground speaks even in his
solitude. But there always is the danger of premature sureness brought about
by the deceptive semblance of the ultimate ground.

3. *Mediated Immediacy of Reason.*   Countering the difficulties of the
immediate unity of the being of truth there is the alternative of seeking unity
in a mediated immediacy, by way of the mediation of a unity that is thought.
To be sure, this unity, sought by way of the intellect, withdraws into infinite
distance. But if all premature unity is breached, it acts out of this distance in its
truth. It is distant and yet it is present in the movement itself, in the mediated
immediacy of actual reason. . . .

Unity enters actuality by way of reason. Reason is not unity but the Encompassing which we are as the impulse to the One, the impulse to the actualization of oneness in the understanding of all Being. Reason is unity as task and
as way. Movement is the only presentiality of this unity which is always incomplete in temporal existence but is palpably present as origin and as goal of
reason in all activity.

Part Five

PHILOSOPHY: DISTINCTIONS AND RELATIONS

EDITORS' INTRODUCTION TO PART FIVE:

In the selections which follow, Jaspers treats questions of science, history, politics, and religion. Other topics taken up by Jaspers that, space permitting, might have been included here are education, art, technology and what he calls "unphilosophy," i.e., phenomena such as nihilism, demonology, and the deification of man.

Just as Jaspers has been criticized for having spent so much effort of his later years on areas that are not strictly philosophical, especially on politics, it might be asked whether such topics belong in a philosophical reader. However, the array of these topics is not a miscellany of occasional interests on the part of Jaspers. They are to be understood as integral to his philosophy. There are two reasons for this:

First, in Jaspers we are confronted with a philosophical mind that is consistent in its basic impulses and aims. For example, in his early work in psychopathology (*see* selections 1 and 2) Jaspers devised a methodological pluralism that developed, decades later, into the philosophy of the Encompassing. In Jaspers's entire body of writings it is safe to speak of all aspects of his production as the testament of a single mind, unfolding and articulating itself in response to the challenges it encounters.

Second, Jaspers's thinking, in its existential and periechontologic turn, conceives of the realization of Being and truth for man in time as being a task of communicative reason. But it is the nature of this task that it be assigned to each human being in his singularity, each searching, in confrontation with others, for the truth that he can freely accept as worthy of his risk. Hence, in its concern over truth philosophy will be directed to the concreteness of man's enterprises—be they day-to-day concerns or the larger ones of politics, history, or the struggle among contending beliefs. On the one hand, philosophy will be attentive to this concreteness as the testimony of man's success and failure at realizing truth. On the other hand, philosophy will guard the possibilities of truth for man, against whatever may threaten them, and will promote them within the arenas of their realization.

These reasons are at play in Jaspers's life-long effort to define the nature of philosophy and of the communicative truth of reason in its deliberate distinction from the truth of modern science, which is universally valid because of its methodological validation.

Furthermore, truths whose validation involves the commitment and risk of the singular Existenz must not be invested with universal validity of another kind, i.e., the one which consists in the exercise of power. Here it does not matter whether the power is the moral power of a community claiming to possess the truth that excludes all others, or the temporal power based on force. Hence Jaspers's concern over the communicative openness of institutional religions which base themselves on exclusive biblical revelation. Hence also his concern over the chances of political freedom in the face of the dual threat of totalitarian mass movements and nuclear annihilation.

The chances for the dignity of man, safeguarded by the commitment to communicative reason, require a reflection on the sources of reason in history and on the possibilities for the enactment of reason in the situation of the times and in the prospects for the future. Hence Jaspers's study of history.

Selected aspects of how Jaspers conceives the distinction of philosophy from and its relation to those areas of human endeavor will be presented in the following subparts: (i) Philosophy and Science; (ii) Philosophy and History; (iii) Philosophy and Politics; and (iv) Philosophy and Religion.

I.

Philosophy and Science

EDITORS' INTRODUCTION TO SUBPART I:

For Jaspers, the relationship between science and philosophy is of vital concern to mankind. Through its modern achievements of methodical research, science has preempted the realm of cognitive thought with its intersubjective evidential procedures and its claim to universal validity. Philosophical truth is now to be conceived in its distinctness, i.e., as involving the free risk of faith, commitment, choice and enactment. Such truth would be destroyed if it were bent to the pattern of universal scientific validity, and, with it, man himself would be destroyed—man who is the actuality of truth in time through the dignity of his singularity.

But according to Jaspers distinguishing philosophic truth from scientific cognition is not possible simply on the basis of theoretical reflection and definition. It is a task whose success depends on an assimilation of scientific knowledge, ultimately through participation in research. The more concrete the assimilation, the more clear will be the limits within which the cognitive certainty of science is gained; and also more clear becomes philosophy's open questions of ultimate concern which are untouched by cognitive resolution and require for their certainty the risk of choice.

What is at stake, then, for Jaspers, in establishing the purity of science and the distinctness of philosophy is the dignity of man. Early in his career Jaspers had engaged in scientific research which confronted him with problems arising at the limits of science, confrontations that initiated his own philosophizing. His many writings on "philosophy and science" thus reflect a central impulse of his thinking.

The following selections present four aspects of this topic. In Selection 53, "Characteristics of Modern Science," Jaspers consolidates his position regarding the distinctness of modern science, which requires a re-thinking of the nature of philosophy and its truth. Selection 54, "Ordering the Sciences of Actuality," addresses the specificity of scientific cognition and the resulting multiplicity of scientific actuality. One aspect of this problem is the distinction between natural sciences and human studies (*Geisteswissenschaften*). Selection 55, "Limits of World-Orientation," deals with some of the limits. The

problems involved in distinguishing and relating philosophy and science are
the subject of Selection 56.

A Note on Terminology: The word "science" is used to translate *Wissenschaft*, which Jaspers uses in accordance with general German usage. In Jaspers's definition (*see* Selection 53) it means any methodical inquiry that results in an intersubjectively (i.e., "universally") valid knowledge whose mode
and degree of certainty can be clearly determined. Accordingly, Jaspers includes under this term a wider range of disciplines than does the English and
American usage of "science." The latter usage tends to restrict "science" to the
exact sciences, especially the natural sciences, in which explanatory theories
can be couched in mathematical models. Areas of study which cannot conform
to such models, such as the "humanities" and aspects of the "social" or "behav-
ioral" sciences are usually excluded from this designation, "science." However, this distinction does not accord with Jaspers's meaning of science, i.e.,
Wissenschaft. In his sense the inquiries into both natural and human phenomena are scientific if they proceed by means of methods that are appropriate as
well as open to public criticism. Hence *Wissenschaft* includes history and
literary criticism no less than physics and economics.

Selection 53

CHARACTERISTICS OF MODERN SCIENCE

EDITORS:
In this selection Jaspers takes account of some phenomena whereby the ancient idea of scientific cognition achieved distinctive fulfillment in modern
science. By means of this account Jaspers also provides a basis for redefining
the nature of philosophy and the problems connected with it. The passages
below are excerpted from *The Origin and Goal of History*, pp. 83–88. The
translation is by M. Bullock and has been emended by the editors. In the
original the passages are found in *Vom Ursprung und Ziel der Geschichte*,
pp. 109–15.

TEXT:
Science possesses three indispensable traits: It is methodical cognition, cogently certain and universally valid.

I know scientifically only if I am also cognizant of *the method* by which I
gained my knowledge, and can therefore substantiate it and demonstrate its
limits.

I know scientifically only what I know with *cogent certainty*. In this way I also know uncertainty, probability or improbability.

I know scientifically only what is *universally valid*. Because the insight can be cogently experienced by every intelligence, scientific knowledge is spread abroad and yet retains the same meaning. Unanimity is a characteristic of universal validity. Where the unanimity of all thinkers throughout the ages has not been achieved, universal validity is doubtful.

By these criteria, however, science was already present in the Greek sciences, even though the task of achieving its full articulation remains an ongoing process even today. Keeping these three factors in mind, what else characterizes modern science?

1. In its spirit, modern science is *universal*. In the long run nothing can elude it. Whatever takes place in the world is subjected to observation, inquiry and investigation, no matter whether it involves the facts of nature, the actions and statements of men, or their creations and destinies. Religion, too, as every kind of authority, is investigated. And not only every reality, but also every intellectual possibility becomes an object of investigation. There are no limits to inquiry and research.

2. Modern science is in principle *incomplete* . . . Modern science is motivated by the ardent desire to reach the limits, to break through all definite forms of knowledge, ever and again to revise all knowledge from its very foundations. Hence the sudden reversals that take place at every breakthrough, accompanied by the preservation of factual acquisitions as an element in the new postulation. There is a constant awareness of the underlying hypotheses, that is, of the presuppositions that constitute the point of departure for research at any given time. Everything is there to be overcome (for the presuppositions are explained in terms of more comprehensive presuppositions and so relativized); when it is facts that are involved, they are used as a means to further advances in the continuity of increasing and more penetrating knowledge . . .

Because the content of knowledge is basically unclosed and unclosable (contrary to the Greek cosmos), this science thinks in terms of unlimited advance and in its self-consciousness lies the idea of progress . . .

3. *Nothing is indifferent* to modern science: it considers everything worth knowing and directs its attention to the smallest and most individual phenomenon, to every fact as such . . .

This self-surrender to every object, to chance, to the misshapen equally with the well-shapen, has its roots in an all-embracing self-consciousness that is both restless and sure of itself. Everything that is must and shall be known. Nothing may be left out of consideration.

Thus the breadth of attention to everything capable of being experienced, the multi-dimensionality of being affected by everything that occurs in the world, is essentially modern.

4. Modern science, attentive to the most individual phenomenon, looks for its *universal interconnections*. It is not able to apprehend the cosmos of Being, but it is able to apprehend the cosmos of the sciences. The idea of the coherence of all the sciences brings about dissatisfaction with every isolated cognition. Modern science is not only universal but lives with the unity of the sciences as its goal, which, however, it never attains.

Each science is determined by its method and its object. Each science is a vista into the world, no science comprehends the world, each science lights upon one sector of actuality, not actuality itself—one facet of all actuality perhaps, but not actuality in its entirety. There are distinct sciences, not the one science as the science of the actual. Thus every science is particular and specialized, but each one belongs to a world that is without confines and yet is held together.

What connects the sciences and in what sense do they form a cosmos?

This is more easily recognized *negatively* than positively. The unity of the sciences does not consist in the unity of the actuality about which they give knowledge. The sum-total of the sciences does not give us actuality in its entirety. They do not constitute a hierarchy through increasing approximation to actuality. They do not constitute a unitary system that becomes master of all actuality . . .

Postively it can be said:

The interconnection of the sciences consists in the *form of cognition*. They are all of them methodical, they all think in categories, are cogent in their particular cognition, but at the same time restricted by their respective presuppositions and by the delimitation of the object.

Then there are the interconnections that arise from the *relation* between the sciences, which render one another mutual assistance through their findings and methods. They become auxiliary sciences to one another. One science becomes the material of another.

They have a common fundament in the subjective impulse of the *universal* desire to know.

Through the guiding idea of the particular fields of cognition there speaks an idea of indeterminable unity, as a *demand* for the openness of everything real and thinkable. All science is a *path*. The paths cross, separate, combine again, and do not show the destination. But all of them are to be followed.

The sciences are organized within themselves—into categories and methods—and related to one another. Endless multiplicity in research and the idea of unity set up a tension and drive science from the one to the other.

In modern cognition, the *systematic* character of knowledge, instead of leading to a world view, leads to the problem of the system of the sciences. The system of the sciences is mobile, manifold in its possible classifications, open. But it is characteristic of it that it constantly remains also a problem, and that no mode of knowledge and no knowledge is to be left out of consideration . . .

5. The *radicality of inquiry* carried to the extreme—but with the proviso that it be accomplished in *concrete cognition*, and does not operate by jumping directly to ultimate universals—has been intensified to its highest point in modern science. Thought that contradicts visible appearances (which began in antiquity in astronomy), not in order to submerge itself in the void, but precisely for the purpose of comprehending visible appearances in a better and unexpected fashion, dares everything. The manner in which physics deals with that which is beyond imagination, through non-perceptual mathematics, is an example.

The capacity for repeatedly breaking away from the rounding-off and totalization of a knowledge makes it possible to experiment with new hypotheses that at first seem highly paradoxical, as in modern physics. An unparalleled freedom of experiment has become possible at certain high-points. Every question is asked afresh. There is always one more inquiry into the possibility of presupposition that have been overlooked. And in the play of preparatory cognition, the most audacious presuppositions are tried out.

6. One might be tempted to regard *certain categories* and their effects as being typical of modern science. . . .

But what is characteristic of modern science is neither a category nor an object, but *universality in the articulation of categories and methods*. Every form is tried out and every object dealt with that appears mathematically, physically, biologically, hermeneutically or speculatively possible. The results are a world of categories capable of limitless expansion and a correspondingly unclosed theory of categories.

The problem becomes that of the appropriateness of categories and methods and not the superiority of any one of them. Where actuality is involved experience itself is reliably defined. Where speculation is called for this is carried out as a sovereign act with full knowledge of its meaning. The crucial problem is to avoid confusing the one with the other.

7. In the modern world a *scientific attitude* has become possible that is able to question, investigate, test and reflect upon everything that happens from the viewpoint of all-inclusive reason. This attitude does not become one of scientific dogmatism, it does not swear by results and principles, it stands aloof from all sects and all communities of creed and conviction, in order to keep free in science the realm of the knowable.

The scientific attitude differentiates between that which is cogently known and that which is not cogently known; it desires its cognition to be accompanied by knowledge of method, and hence by knowledge of the meaning and limits of knowledge; it seeks unrestricted criticism. It urges us on toward the clarity of the definite, as opposed to the approximations of every day speech; it demands concreteness in substantiating.

Man's veracity is determined by his scientific attitude, once science has become actualized. Hence it is an element in the dignity of man, and possesses the enchantment that comes from illumination of the world. Hence, too, however, it knows the anguish caused in spiritual commerce by the unscientific nature of blind assertion that is unaware of itself and therefore impassioned and uncritical. It renders the lies of life transparent. *Sapere aude* is the motto of its courageousness.

Any man who is scientific through his own research-work will be capable of understanding everywhere what is authentically scientific. To be sure, specialist routine and *de facto* achievements can exist without a scientific attitude *in toto*. But no one's scientific stance can be relied upon who has not himself taken part in science at some point.

Selection 54

ORDERING THE SCIENCES OF ACTUALITY

EDITORS:
In distinction to philosophical truth, scientific cognition is determined by a realm of objectivity—an object, principles of research, methods employed, and evidence gained. The realm of science comprises many sciences which, however, do not fall into place to form a coherent whole. How the sciences are distinguished and related is a philosophical problem Jaspers addresses in this selection. One of his major contributions to psychiatric research is reflected here, namely, the methodological distinction between the natural sciences and the human studies or mind sciences (*Geisteswissenschaften*). The methodology which fundamentally distinguishes the latter is that of *Verstehen*. (About both concepts see the notes on terminology.) The issue of value-freedom of the sciences, touched on in this selection, is more thoroughly discussed in Selection 68.

Notes on Terminology: Geisteswissenschaft is translated here as "mind science" in order to counterpose it to "natural science" (*Naturwissenschaft*), as required by the context. In other sections, such as those on Max Weber (68, 69), *Geisteswissenschaft* is translated by the more usual "human studies."
—The German word *Verstehen* is usually retained in the English text when it refers to the basic methodology of the human studies. The reason is that the literal translations of *Verstehen*, i.e., "understanding" or "comprehension"

connote, in normal English usage, meanings beyond the methodological one. Where functional variants of *Verstehen* are used in the German, these are translated literally into English, followed, in parenthesis, by the German word to indicate that the meaning is related to the methodology of *Verstehen*. For example: understandable (*verstehbar*); comprehensibility (*Verstehbarkeit*).

The following is a translation by the editors of *Philosophie*, Vol. I, pp. 185–95. For E. B. Ashton's translation see *Philosophy*, Vol. I, pp. 204–13.

TEXT:

1. General Divisions

After dividing actuality into matter, life, soul, and mind it might seem plausible also to juxtapose four types of science—the physical, biological, psychological, and mind sciences—as exhausting the content of all existents. Two things, however, preclude a mere side-by-side arrangement: in each of the four realms, actuality has a different mode of objectiveness; and the actualities mesh. *Physics* (together with chemistry) is a relatively internally coherent field of study. So is *biology*, although there the coherence is due to its relation to the exact natural sciences, on which it draws at each step while its own roots remain obscure. *Psychology* is far more questionable; in fact, it strays into the realms of life and the mind, or else it poses as a universal science. *Mind science*, finally, is actual only as a multiplicity resulting from research into the documents, works, deeds, or institutions of man; by no means has it produced the kind of unity we see in physics and biology. It is the arena for the battles of differing world views, battles which decide, radically and without appeal, about the meaning and value of proposed inquiries and modes of research, indeed about the very objects of research. Joint and continuous efforts in any field come about only on the basis of a common, shared way of thinking, not as overall objectifications for everybody.

The changing mode of objectiveness permits *no common yardstick that would fit the substance of those four types of science*. All that they have in common is what makes them science: the cogency of empirical cognition by means of a method for the purpose of objective determinations. . . .

And yet the empirical sciences are neither a unit nor a distinct series. In fact, their life occurs in the polarity of *natural and mind sciences*. Time and again their practical research activities seem to reconstitute them as these two entireties alien to one another. The scientists in either of the two realms share an atmosphere of questioning and thinking. They understand each other— the natural scientists clearly and unequivocally, the mind scientists within historic limits. But between the two groups there usually yawns an abyss, and very few will even glance across it at the other side. . . .

This prevailing dichotomy is not absolutely valid, however. It fails to see what is specific to the true biologist and the true psychologist. The questionable nature of the limits remains hidden. This division tends to estrange scientists from each other, thus dimming the truth of a world orientation that understands and defines itself only in its many-sidedness, and it tends to gloss over the diversity of distinctions for the sake of seeming entireties which are in fact incomplete.

The classification of the sciences of actuality remains open. It will always remain open, because of the incompletability of cognitive world orientations as such.

2. Natural Sciences

Motivation for research in the mind sciences comes from interest in partaking of ideas and in the dialogue from Existenz to Existenz. Motivation for non-*verstehen* research in the natural sciences comes from interest in knowing things in their externality, in the transparency of this externality as an event proceeding necessarily under cognizable laws as well as in the capacity to control what is transparent within limits due to this cognition. But then, at the limits, my interest spurs me on to bring existence as such into contact with incomprehensible Being. Even though the path of the cognition of nature leads first to the disenchantment of the world, there becomes palpable, at this limit of the particular knowledge arrived at, the impact of the Other and Alien as the reconstitution, in always different configuration and immediacy, of what has not been cognized. This impact, my being moved by the totally Other, does not, to be sure, carry the same meaning as the contact of Existenz with Existenz at the limits of the mind sciences. Nature does not respond; it does not speak to me as Existenz; it is not mind. True, in its uncanny impenetrability it may mean more to me than mind. This "more," however, does not become clear and is itself open only to possible Existenz and becomes for it the cipher of Being. The mind holds me in the world of men, it enables me, as possible faith, to enter into communication with another faith. Nature leads me into the fundamentals of all existence which I, as I orient myself in the world, cannot even question meaningfully. For Existenz, however, these become, through their factual nature, the springboard of my soaring upward in transcending.

It is peculiar to the natural sciences that they can effect, in their research, a radical separation from this possibly underlying transcending interest. They are pure world-orientation. In them, Existenz and research do not penetrate each other such that there is no need for any unclarity to arise. Absolute freedom from valuation—in the mind sciences merely a limited possibility in reference to what is cogent, which in those sciences remains, to be sure, one aspect of insight but is not everything—is possible, in the natural sciences, in principle and on the whole. This is so because they can limit themselves to the cogent knowledge of what is factual and to the methodical knowledge of their particular presuppositions and theories without becoming thereby the rubbish heap of endless facts. For they derive their meaning through the research ideas that are objectivized in theories and systematizations through which the facts are sought out or assigned their proper place. The strength of the natural sciences lies in cognition of universal laws whereas natural history, i.e., the diversity of forms in nature in their spatial and temporal distribution, is also apt to become an endless aggregation of material. Finally, these sciences can be justified pragmatically by their technical achievements which by their very nature cannot be achieved even in principle by the mind sciences. Political and economic action, invention, organization can perhaps be compared to medical therapy but not to acts that are completely rooted in natural science. In spite of all knowledge and in spite of the technical elements, such action, distinct from technology though controlling it, has as its center of gravity competence and responsibility which are rooted in the situation-consciousness on the part of a historic being.

The following questions must always be asked with respect to research in the natural sciences: What theoretical idea forms the horizon? How is this idea constructed rationally as a theory? How about its fertility, i.e., its capacity for discovering facts and relating them to each other, a capacity that is to be measured by its success? What is the boundary where theory leads to disagreement with fact? On the other hand, the pragmatic point of view of technical utility is not the source nor the measure of the truth of cognition in natural science; rather, it is the success appropriate to it which, reflexively, gives it its impulses.

3. Mind Sciences

Since they belong together and are complete in themselves, one would expect the mind sciences to be the members of a whole, i.e., of the one science of mind. Let us see why this is not the case.

Mind as ultimate actuality is dependent in its existence on prior actualities that encompass it and on which it is conditional. Mind as existence is causally determined, and in the course of time, inanimate matter grinds down—in our world-orienting view—what it has allowed for a certain time, as it were, to be vitally active existence; and yet mind, like every actuality, arises at the same time out of its own origin. As such, mind is simply incomprehensible out of its preceding actuality. It contains the freedom that is carried out in knowledge as self-consciousness and in the participation in ideas. Such freedom, for its part, is the presupposition and medium of existential freedom. In this respect mind remains open since it is carried by possible Existenz which is actualized in it.

It is the task of the mind sciences to investigate empirically what is understandable as meaning. Mind is accessible for orientation in the world through its products and documents, its communications, actions, works. Understanding these is already a matter of daily life; it is the task of mind science to make this understanding methodical, systematic, and universal. What is gained in this manner can again be brought into actual life. This task of mind science leads to two boundaries of understanding (*Verstehen*). It comes up against the merely existent which can be investigated only as an actuality of nature, and against Existenz which remains invisible to world orientation. Mind is embedded in what cannot be understood and which is explained in the context of the actualities of nature but, in the end, always reappears as incomprehensible in a different way. And it can be understood in such a manner that *Verstehen* goes as far as that boundary where *Verstehen* is replaced by communication, where Existenz becomes palpable for Existenz. Mind, taken by itself, keeps its flanks open toward two sides, toward the incomprehensibility external of actuality and the universally not-understandable inwardness of Existenz.

A. Verstehen *and Existenz.* Research in the mind sciences must be questioned as to the points of view which orient themselves by these limits of *Verstehen.*

We must ask, first of all, to what extent empirical determinations are made that can stand up as such. This is accomplished by reconstituting the testimonies accessible to *Verstehen.* Excavations, reconstructions, editions, archival and documentary research make factualities into possessions available at any time.

Then we must ask about the success of a rationally determined *Verstehen* of the meaning-content of our heritage of literature and monuments, of opinions and purposes that had actually once been put into practice; further, we must ask about the probable understanding of events and actions based on situations, premises, motives. Here we inquire about the success of such specific and particular representations that are comprehensible to the intellect as such, and to what extent such verifiable restorations have succeeded.

The third question asks about the understanding (*verstehend*) participation of the scholar in the actualized mental ideas. For a focus on the endless realm of particulars can be achieved only by a selection of essentials according to a criterion that can never be defined objectively, a selection based on ideas which, originating from the mind of the scholar, accords with the spirit of something that is past. But this process already lies beyond what is cogently provable.

And finally there remains the question to what extent the mental entity is merely the image and configuration of something that was, which I am observing—or to what extent there is created, together with it, a foundation for communication and existential appropriation. Only in this way does the dialogue of Existenz with Existenz become palpable in the research of the mind sciences. This "personal touch" is not an untrue subjectivity but the indirect expression of an Existenz having come to itself through communicating, with an alien mind, by way of the mind disciplines. Beyond all imagery of wholeness and all particularity—even if such media are its sole meaning of expression—mind science as world orientation comes from Existenz and, turning to Existenz, it addresses him who understands, urging him to come to himself.

Each of these four questions refers to a different kind of *Verstehen*: the first, a factual objectivity as the possibility of being understood; the second, what is validly understandable (*verstehbar*) and how it becomes evident to consciousness-as-such; the third, the possibility of participation, through *Verstehen*, in the particular wholeness of a mind; and the fourth, the really non-understandable of self-being that can be attained only through understanding (*Verstehen*). The first two questions refer to what can still be grasped by means of cogent science, the last two to what is more than science without whose specific nature mind science has no meaning.

The two substantial steps taken by research in the mind sciences are the participation in the ideas of the spirit and communication with Existenz as individual.

The first capacity proper to mind sciences that are a form of world-orientation—a capacity that transcends what is cogently knowable—is that of achieving an adequate re-presentation of ideas in the mode of objectivity appropriate to them. Spirit attains objectivity only indirectly and always—historically—as a function of itself; it thus becomes, in its self-illumination, also the co-creative factor of its own actuality. What is decisive for spirit—with respect to man's will to orient himself in the world—is neither what has most recently been valid or what has in fact been effective and acknowledged, nor, conversely, what has not been valid now or ever and not been acknowledged. Rather, the original greatness of research in the mode of mind sciences consists in eliciting spirit in its authenticity where it had been forgotten, and then to resurrect it for all to see. Such research becomes the co-creator of historic consciousness since it determines its content. Thus it gains conditions for possible self-being.

The second step taken by the substantial mind sciences is to hear, in the world which is subject to ideas, Existenz in its singularity and to be addressed by it. To be sure, this is a task that is always merely particular and never universal; yet its fulfillment is the most gripping task. For the will, on the part of Existenz, to communicate with all Existenz that approaches it is the most profound meaning of mind science. It is that which draws the whole personality into the true research of the mind sciences. Even when its investigations are the most far-reaching and its efforts are directed toward utmost precision it leaves the space open to what cannot be known but is present in Existenz.

However, the endless material of the mind sciences becomes meaningless if it does not have the possibility of becoming the element of such an idea and, furthermore, of such existential addressing. Mind science, which lives through its participation in ideas that are manifest or will again become manifest to it, does not merely establish facts. It separates them and perceives their rank and origin. For it, things are divided into those of the mind and those alien to the mind, into what has been from the very beginning and what has been derived. It passes over what is trivial. Evidential *Verstehen* takes place on but one plane, in its endless particularities; only through the idea and existential rooting does it rise to rank and substance.

The fact that mind can withdraw from itself, that it can become detached from Existenz and thus become uncommitted, concerns a specifically mental actuality.

To be sure, the detachment from Existenz does not occur in a world-orienting knowledge, but the possibility of mental formalization as a mode of defection belongs to the principle of investigation in the mind sciences. For Existenz, all that can be grasped in particulars and is crudely empirical, is always, as such, either a defection or a possibility. Hence actual spirit, as the object of mind science, is in suspension: it is to be actual and free at the same time. For this reason all essential insights in the mind sciences are not compelling; rather, their truth lies only in the idea. What is cogent is the particular, the materiality, and not what, in the end, constitutes "science" here. Mind, where it understands without ideas, is emptied and formalized; it is then endless [determined solely by the distinction] correct/incorrect, or by [considerations of] purposes and their pragmatic formulation. This—and never the idea—can be considered the mere means of the intellect for the vital purposes of life. If the impulse of the idea and of possible Existenz is absent then that— which could become the material of the mind sciences—becomes just a collection of trivia, the debris of a few millennia of human existence.

If mind science, as the re-presentation of ideas, can thus rank highly it may still run great risk through becoming detached from Existenz. Mind science, directed at ideas as if they were objects, teaches us to see them as images, to enjoy them removed from Existenz without appropriating what has been understood (*Verstehen*) as a commitment into one's own life. Participation in the ideas active in what can be understood (*verstehbar*) gives a satisfaction that is achieved in this very *Verstehen*; but it does not prevail as such if the demand on Existenz does not become palpable at the same time.

Hence, in *Verstehen*, I can be at home in the world of the spirit without being Existenz if, merely as observing consciousness, I allow that specifically representational function of *Verstehen* to be active which is analagous to perception. Although this is necessary as a part of my world-orienting activity, such behavior paralyzes Existenz if the deception is created that mind and idea exhaust what is essential. Since, as a matter of fact, Existenz has no sphere in the world that is specifically its own, spiritual actuality appears to an eye that merely scans the surface as rounded and resting in itself. Hence the separation of spirit and Existenz is not manifested in world orientation either. But this separation is the condition and expression of the salvation of the "I myself" as existing soul from the enchantment of spiritual culture which allows me to gain alluring riches in the enjoyment of worlds spread panoramically before me, at the cost of Existenz becoming empty or, since it is merely private, becoming inconsequential. Transcending to Existenz in original absolute consciousness is neither founded nor possible in world orientation; this positiveness comes from another source. To be sure, it can be replaced, deceptively, by artifical and untrue, pathetic or sentimental obligations which may be derived from an elucidation in history. But since such obligations have been won in *Verstehen* without consciousness of limits, they immediately fail in a concrete situation, where, at the decisive moment, they are betrayed to plain positivism and to universally human self-concern.

We have found that: the cognition of mind science is cogent only where it determines, in the particular, a comprehensibility (*Verstehbarkeit*) and factuality without ideas. As it participates in ideas its understanding becomes an ordering according to rank. It becomes a possible path to existential self-understanding but, at the same time, lures us into a satisfaction with an erudition sufficient unto itself. On its way toward Existenz and already affected by it, mind science, as it comprehends the actual, creates—by participating in ideas—new actuality. As the path to the illumination of Existenz it is always unique, indirect, and objectively incomprehensible.

B. Verstehen *and Actuality.*   The comprehensibility (*Verstehbarkeit*) of the mind founders, on the one hand, on Existenz, out of which, in the last analysis, grows all impulse toward world-orientation in the mode of comprehending (*Verstehen*) and, on the other hand, it founders on the alien actuality of nature which remains opaque, without which mind has no existence. In the comprehensibility (*Verstehbarkeit*) of the mind Existenz seeks to create the space to come to itself, and urges forward no less toward what cannot be grasped, to the very limits of *Verstehen*, so that it may become aware of itself at the abyss of existence.

To be sure, the clarity of orientation in the mind sciences demands that we think of spirit as pure. But then it is a matter either of objective isolation of the contents of mind in the direction of their timeless validity (e.g., of the meaning of valid judgments); in this mode they are merely the condition of the life of mind, never its substance. Or it is a matter of constructs that transform, such as the change of a living idea into a concrete ideal which was actual at one time, of the historic process into a necessary development of mind; these are spiritualistic constructs, as if the mind were by itself without any other actuality and trod its own historic path, following its own laws which can be cognized by us. It is permissible to think of spirit in such—always merely supposed—purity if I use such constructs merely as heuristic means and know at the same time that these ideal-typical configurations do not exist at all without the real body of causal actuality and its strictures.

In its world-orientation mind science probes all the more deeply the more sharply and relentlessly spirit is cognized and re-cognized in the actual. Here there are two opposite temptations: As spirit is [as such] unactual, there is the temptation to spiritualistic dilution into a bloodness being. On the other hand, by applying the modes of observation proper to the earlier realms of actuality [matter, life, psyche] to mental structures, there is the other temptation of losing sight of the realm of spirit. In these ways, however, we deprive research of its proper subject.

If I ask, for example, what factual events were decisive for the cause of society and the states, what brutal facts and coincidences; what natural givens and what insights and purposes of will determined the course of history in its material, economic and political actuality, in the rise and fall of nations—then this question has meaning only as it refers to the actualities of the mind. For otherwise research, directed only at random actuality, would become an inquiry into a hodgepodge, and history would not only be not different from natural phenomena but would not even be subject to research as these are. To comprehend the role even of what is alien to mind, of all that is nature and, analagous to nature, can be embracing and determinative of mind: that is merely the condition for the cognition of the mind in its actuality which—though, as existence, is totally dependent on other existence—nonetheless remains original in its specificity. . . .

The circumstance that mind sciences understand their comprehensible (*verstehbar*) contents to lie in the middle between mere existence and Existenz brings into them, from these boundaries, forms of cognition that would have to be regarded as alien to a pure mind science if such a science were possible. On the one side, actual spirit always possesses an aspect of nature, and mind science has points of view in its cognition that are proper to nature. On the other side, the originality of spirit is anchored in Existenz which either expresses itself dogmatically or sheds light in free, always original, philosophizing. Dogmatics are not only a subject matter of historical mind science but are themselves, as well as their analogue of a philosophy that overcomes dogmas, a root and, further, a predominant but inexpressible goal on the part of the scholar in the mind sciences. For this reason mind science is always exposed to the twofold danger: the danger of naturalization and that of dogmatic passion. The first can be critically limited by an awareness of the relativity of its point of view, the latter only through the relentless separation of what is objectively cogent in facts from the participatory experience of ideas and from existential appropriation. In that realm of objective cogency unity can be achieved even from among the most heterogeneous Existenzen and ideas, and discussion is possible about the correctness of statements but not about the meaning of research.

Selection 55

LIMITS OF WORLD ORIENTATION

EDITORS:

To Jaspers, establishing the purity of science and the distinction between science and philosophy is an urgent task for modern man. It requires a clarification of the limits within which the movement of scientific cognition takes place and of the boundaries which it reaches at these limits. Some aspects of Jaspers's thinking on this matter are presented in this selection.

The following is an emended translation, by E. B. Ashton, of *Philosophie*, Vol. I, pp. 85–88; in English: *Philosophy*, Vol. I, pp. 120–23. The emendation is provided by the editors.

TEXT:

World orientation in the form of science means to conquer an existence *independent of the knowing subject*. It is motivated by the urge to know what applies always and everywhere, regardless of changes in time and in historic individuality—to know what will be valid even beyond man, for any possible rational being.

Not independent, of course, is the knowledge we possess in fact. Whether and how this is acquired and understood depends upon historical, psychological, and sociological conditions. Its validity, however, is independent. It is like the existence to which it applies even if nobody knows of it. Laws of nature and norms of logic are valid and meaningful before they are discovered. What exists need never enter the realm of any conscious being; it still exists unknown, although for no one.

What no one knows about might seem to be nonexistent. It may seem senseless to speak of the Pythagorean theorem as something that applied before its discovery, or of the existence of a flora which no eye has ever seen. But what was before it was discovered is the very target of scientific research; this is exactly what we mean by an object of cognition. It is true that what can never be known in principle does not exist for science, but everything that is not yet known does. Thus scientists can explore as empirical existence that which was or is beyond the directly perceptible but which is linked with the perceptible in ways that can be made accessible. They unlock an endless past with the aid of clues left, not by any human being, but by other actualities. They establish valid meanings in the consciousness—not of bringing them forth but of discovering them by their scientific investigations.

There is something uniquely enthralling about the world of science. Having abandoned his self-enclosed, merely vital existence and become an aware, thinking being, man is uncertain what to expect in existence, alarmed by every surprise, fearful in his ignorance; but science, as far as it goes, gives him the solid support of cogent, universally valid knowledge. He can rely on it. In existence he is consigned to endlessness; with nothing to stand on, he cannot cope with anything. But science teaches him how to bring the endlessness under control, how to survey and anticipate it in each possible instance. In existence all things crumble into diversity, but science points out the unity of what can be known. It comprises a systematic whole in which everything is connected with everything else.

Neither cogency nor unity nor the control of endlessness is an acquisition immediately accessible to him who reaches for it. The historic development of our human cognition is the path leading to it, a path to which self-criticism and lucky ideas bring us and which is jeopardized time and again; we climb its steps but cannot see its goal. When we distinguish science—as the universally valid knowledge of consciousness-as-such—from existence in its subjectivity and diversity, we are not distinguishing a realm conquered once and for all but the path of true world orientation.

With this distinction we have drawn two boundary lines. One of them delimits the path in relation to what we distinguish it from, while the other turns up as an unexpected limit to the path itself.

The first boundary appeared because in taking up the pure object we would always *abstract from something* which, as an other, we had to eliminate so as to arrive at universally valid truth. We designated the other as subjectivity, as the distortion of a perspective, as arbitrary appraisal, as a mere standpoint; we wanted to get beyond all this in order to reach that which is objectively to which the knowing individual subject is merely added. What we eliminated turned into an object of its own, then, an object of psychological and historical study—for the subjective did exist, after all, though as a delusion. Faith and subjectively experienced absoluteness are psychological experiences whose expression does make them empirical objects in the world. They have, of course, the qualities of change and historic evolution, but this does not stop them from having at some time been actual and belonging to mythological, religious, and philosophical history. As an object of empirical research, however, the eliminated element does not remain what it was. Objectified, it has been deprived of its soul. Even in the most splendidly understanding (*verstehende*) representation it will be seen only from the outside whereas it had originally been believed and taken for the truth. As possible Existenz, therefore, I realize that in my scientific being, as consciousness-as-such, I have eliminated what can itself never again be accessible to me in this consciousness, be forever closed to me—hence, that the world as it is in consciousness-as-such is not all there is. It is at this boundary—where science no longer knows what it has eliminated as it is itself and cannot even feel it any longer—that we let ourselves be addressed in the illumination of Existenz and in metaphysics.

However, in philosophical world orientation we come up against the other boundary. This is experienced in pure objectivity as such in that its meaning remains incomplete. I acquire cogent insight, but the cogency does not become absolute. I prevail over endlessness, but it also remains unconquered. I attain unities, but not the unity of the world.

As consciousness-as-such I allow these limits to concern me only in the sense of my working at their conquest. I can realize, then, finality but this is not relevant since I am advancing in fact; I note the additions which my research makes to knowledge, without taking fright at the limitlessness of the path.

But if I become fully conscious of the path itself, I may lose heart and be paralyzed—but only if, misunderstanding the way of world orientation, . . . I have gotten ahead of myself and thought I was possessing what really only shows me the direction to take in my investigative orientation: the world's unity as an infinity ruled by a cogent and therefore reliable knowledge. I had held the existence of the world taken as the object of research to be the Being-as-such which satisfied me. This tranquility, engendered by knowledge, could not endure because once I found myself in it, I forgot the limits. This tranquility must be disturbed so that the interest in knowledge not also be paralyzed when it is not even intended as knowledge but as the means of my self-pacification. Disturbing this tranquility means destroying a delusion; for that which cannot be achieved in the world of knowledge, i.e., tranquility out of unrest, is possible only existentially: instead of achieving it in the objectively cogent we reach it in the reliability of self-being; instead of in the world-unity, in the cipher of the One; instead of in controlled endlessness, in the infinity of the present, given to us as a gift. If the meaning of world-orienting knowledge is confused with that which enters existence solely through the actualization of possible Existenz, then all of science may appear to be a matter of indifference because one did not take hold of it out of the impulse inherent in it but out of a deceptive satisfaction whose untrue tranquility could not last. Then one will lament that there is nothing solid, that everything is questionable, that the profusion cannot be mastered and everything is merely possibility, that many kinds of principles are at odds so that people can no longer understand each other; in short, that science is meaningless. These complaints express the nature of science in its objectivity, what happens when research has lost the existential impetus that guides it and belongs to it: its arbitrary relativity, its endlessness and randomness. For the meaning of science which is the ground of research, is not an object of evidential knowledge but its limit.

These limits of world orientation are relevant for possible Existenz. They demonstrate two things at once: that the world cannot be rounded into being-in-itself—i.e., that cognition is not exhausted with cognition of the world; and that world orientation derives its meaning as science from a different source that cannot be cognized through science itself. An awareness of these limits is what we pursue in philosophical world orientation.

Selection 56

PHILOSOPHY AND SCIENCE

EDITORS:
In this selection the distinction that Jaspers draws between philosophy and science is tied to the relation he discerns between the two. The focus is on the will-to-know, on the one hand as it is grounded in Existenz, on the other hand as it is fulfilled in scientific cognition.

The selection is in part an emendation of E. B. Ashton's translation, in part a retranslation of *Philosophie*, Vol. I, pp. 318–328; in English: *Philosophy*, Vol. I, pp. 316–25. Emendation and retranslation by the editors.

TEXT:
What we call science is not only cogent knowledge in the world, it is also the rational form of methodical communication. Philosophy seeks such a form. We may call it scientific, therefore, not only because the sciences are its own way to itself but because it develops these methodical forms of thought and communication—although in the sense of useful or valid discovery in the world, these forms do not involve any cognition at all.

First, however, philosophy *is* not science. We clarify it in distinction from science, rather, for it is both more and less than science. Second, philosophy itself is a *fundamental will to know*, with scientific knowledge one of the directions in which we actualize it. And third, it is engaged in a *struggle* for knowledge on behalf of science, against false science.

1. Philosophy as Distinct from Science

Every science has an object. A philosophy posing as science has no object to prove the legitimacy of its claim.

It may perhaps describe its object as "the whole." Unfolding from this whole as a strict science, it will know the object of its researches at a distance, as will any other theoretical activity that stands apart from its object. This cognitive technique makes sense for the cognition of things in world orientation, but not for philosophy. We cannot grasp "the whole" in this fashion. No matter what I call it, as an object it eludes me. In a pure science of theoretical philosophy I have to look for a fixed point on which to rest the objective edifice of its supposed cognition; I would like to know objectively, as a principle, what all things hang upon—whether I call this principle matter, I, spirit, or God. No matter what I think along this line, however, before my eyes there will be nothing but relative constructions of mundane particulars.

Hence, as philosophizing differentiates itself from science it becomes aware that it does not have an object as do the sciences which cease at the point where there is no longer an object. The object of philosophy—instead of being the whole as an object—would be the ground of all objectivity, and "every object" insofar as it can be related to that ground. Measured by science, philosophical thinking remains as though suspended in thin air. To give philosophy an object in a not merely metaphorical sense is to invest it wrongly with the form of scientific cognition.

And yet, without an object we cannot take even one philosophizing step. Though not one object is specifically its own, philosophy moves in all objects without meaning them strictly as such. Objects are transmuted in philosophizing; moving in them, we transcend them. The object is not transformed by construction, as in the methodical insight of a special science. In philosophizing it becomes transparent, rather, because it is phenomenal: instead of being known, it acquires a voice. When I mean the object itself, I am scientific; but I philosophize when I use the object to envision Being.

If I identify cogent insight with science, philosophy is less than science, from which it differs precisely by giving up the claim of cogent validity for what really counts in it. But philosophy means the pursuit of unconditional truth, and in this respect it is more than science. Philosophizing is the thought whereby, in possession of cogent insight, I assure myself of the insight that is not cogent, the insight that is an explication of faith. But without the untouchable fundament of scientific insight, the other kind cannot attain its own truth.

Philosophical thoughts are compelling only when they are negative. But once these negative insights are no longer cogent they will form the way of transcending, and not until then are they properly philosophical.

In its positive statements, philosophy expresses thoughts that have the character of possibilities. Its positivity is true only as detachment, as appeal, as adjuration. It has many meanings and is necessarily open to misunderstanding. Having arisen from freedom, as an expression of unconditionality, it will be understood in freedom only. Philosophy cannot say . . . what it means, in the direct form that possesses and bestows. Nor, being never really scientific, is philosophy accorded the universal factual recognition of science. It becomes self-destructive when a desire for such recognition makes it don the disguise of an existentially noncommittal, valid science—which, after all, it can only seem to be.

The crucial difference between philosophy and science lies in the kind of communication. Scientific results and methods are communicated from person to person as interchangeable consciousness-as-such. In philosophizing this becomes a mere medium in which not everybody will communicate at random but *one individual with another individual,* in a communication that involves commitment because it is historic. Philosophy as a linguistic structure is a means of communication with the unknown possible individual.

For the same reason there are essential differences between scientific and philosophical discussion. In the sciences we argue impersonally about a matter that is particular and definite, and we continue to mean this matter. There are reasons and facts and circumstances and experiences that we summon up and bring to bear until we can settle the issue in an objectively cogent manner. In philosophizing, scientific discussion remains our basis and our medium; but at the same time we mean something else in it. Philosophical speech is not exhausted with the objectively expressed content.

The object of philosophizing is *not separated* from what it is really all about. In the sciences, to know something does not identify me with the thing I know. An insight into a chemical process is not itself a chemical process. But when I philosophize, I commit my self-being to be present in the object. This is why philosophical discussions can only be relative, carried on in a communication which by way of dealing with things is meant to be personal as well. My philosophizing ceases to be philosophizing to the extent to which I want to be nothing but objective. Letting things speak for themselves, a course that can be meaningful and productive in science, becomes, in philosophy, a deception. If I want only reasoned explanations in philosophizing without committing myself, I fall prey to sophistry; it is the vengeance exacted by the mere intellect for a betrayal of philosophizing. Even in science, insight will fade more and more as visuality yields to an empty permutation of logical forms and endless empirical facts; and so it does in philosophizing when there is no longer a possible Existenz to speak and to be spoken to.

Yet the self-differentiation of philosophy from the sciences presupposes the latter as its condition and, further, absorbs science in the sense of the methodical form of its own communication. In these two respects philosophy can be regarded as a "scientific world-view." Yet while such a philosophy is *grounded* upon scientific world-orientation and expressed *in the configuration* of articulated thought, it is not a world-view that is *proven* by science. Philosophy does not differentiate itself from the sciences in order to surrender to a dream but in order truly to incorporate them. It is not by coincidence that almost all great philosophers were masters of a particular science. The sciences serve philosophy, not the other way round, because as the meaning of all knowledge it is more than science. The goal of any special science is objective cognition in world orientation; the goal of philosophizing is the self-understanding of Existenz as individual in the appearance of worldly existence.

The question arises what still remains for philosophy once it has been so distinguished. If it cannot be a directly communicated statement of essential truth as objective and exclusive, and if it cannot be the contemplation of possible standpoints and forms of *weltanschauung* either, offering them to the intellect for choice—for in the first case it would have become a message of salvation, and in the second case a science—what is left?

The commitment involved in philosophy must appear as a *summons*. When it speaks in propositions that say what, from its standpoint, is and ought to be, it becomes *prophetic philosophy*. When it drafts possibilities—not several for choice, however, but the unconditional ones which it holds to be true and which concern the listener as himself—it is *awakening philosophy*. It cannot be one without the other. In naive consciousness the prophetic side comes to the fore; and in critical consciousness, the appealing side, itself still covertly prophetic. For in philosophizing, freedom turns to freedom; it is my unconditionality that would like to join the unconditionality of another but can find it only if the other comes to meet me originally, out of his own self-being, not if he goes along with the objectivity of what I say. In philosophizing, I do feel impelled to speak urgently, to approach the other tempestuously; but if this makes him follow me, I lose. Self-restraint and thinking of *objectivities as possibilities* are the conditions on which another will grow close to me, until in a concrete historic situation the philosophical word, the expressed decision, may unite two selves. Philosophic thinking, spread out before us and presented to us in works, wants to awaken us to this possibility; it does not want submission or imitation.

2. *Polarities in the Movement of the Will to Know*

Since philosophizing is an original will to know, it seems bound to take the form of a science. But while scientific knowledge is determined by the specifics of method and result, philosophy as the will to know manifests itself only vaguely and antithetically if we want to catch it in a definition. It wants to know about *unconditionality* as genuine Being, and it always finds only a *particular* it has to grasp it in. It aims to *possess* knowledge, and its radical *questioning* overrides every possession it has won. It aims at *objectivity*, yet it is meaningless without the reality of an *Existenz* that will use objectivities as its guidelines in existence. Whenever our search for a definition of philosophy stresses one side of such antitheses, we are left with the one-sided dogmatics of a dead philosophy. It is only as movement in those polarities that philosophy is true.

   a. Particularity and Entirety. Expertise is the knowledge and skill in a specialty that has been acquired in world orientation. But the knowable is endless, and to know everything is not philosophy; those possessing broad but superficial knowledge have been repudiated by it from the outset. Only the will to know that does not aim at some particular but at the whole—in other words, at being-in-itself rather than at the endless multiplicity of what is, at the origins rather than at what has become scattered—only that will is philosophy. But though philosophy, as knowledge, aims at entirety, it will always be real only in an individual. Though not a science, it is in all sciences. Every particular realm of objectivity will at some time be dealt with in a specific discipline; there is no object that is not individual and particular. Only as an idea is entirety a philosophical impulse of the specific discipline, and in the entirety of sciences as well. The endlessness of scientific cognitions and methods makes it impossible to master knowledge to the point of omniscience; what is possible, however, is to master knowledge as a function of thought by taking part in every essential perspective, by grasping the principles, by an erudition that makes possible, in each particular instance, the acquisition and understanding of what has been cognized up to now. And yet, philosophically the whole subsists as the will to limitless world orientation along all possible paths; it is the readiness to follow these paths individually without simply accepting results.

   Philosophizing, as it arises from the will to know, affects specific cognitions; yet the disciplines that stand in the very closest relationship to the philosophy animating them keep changing. Thus at one time it was theology, at another time mathematics and mathematical natural science, or philology and history, or psychology, or sociology. To be sure, objectively valid insights are always only the ones obtained in the specific disciplines; but just as these were gained through the motive power of philosophy, so they remain relevant to philosophy and thus are more than a random specialized knowledge.

   b. Possession of and Striving for Knowledge. Philosophy turns us against its supposed possession, against what can be learned in a philosophical scholasticism and would either aim to comprise, encyclopedically, all the knowledge there is or appear as a special philosophical knowledge. The very name of philosophy came from the idea that it is a striving, not a having. Insofar as he is a philosopher man is cognizant of his ignorance and strives for knowledge.

   This striving is not possible if I am untouched by knowledge, nor is it possible unless I keep knowledge transparent in a conceptuality that does become my possession; the final possession of knowledge would put an end to striving. Thus Kant knew: one cannot learn philosophy, only philosophizing. Both—philosophy as a doctrine as well as the denial of philosophy—lack genuine knowledge. The first manipulates concepts that owe their merely artificial validity to a school; the second cannot get anywhere on the basis of its negation.

Philosophy, not knowing and yet moving toward knowledge, can be characterized as this striving: since it aims at the whole, philosophy will strive toward the outermost limits. When it reaches a limit, it will not stop but will find the question that urges it to go farther. Calling itself radical, it will go to the roots of whatever poses as being. There is nothing it will not question once again; it endangers every possession. To comprehend being, it searches for the point outside of all being. It knows that this search is an antinomy: realizing that it seeks the impossible, and refusing nonetheless to give it up.

What this original philosophical will to know seeks by way of all particular knowledge is the clarity of consciousness that culminates in self-consciousness. A philosopher does not want merely to live; he wants to live consciously. To him, being is authentically what he has grown aware of—not in the external reflection of the mere intellect, but in the specific clarities that may result from daily philosophizing. These are not communicable like cognitions of things; only one who knows can awaken them in one who is prepared. To find oneself in knowledge, out of the dark of mere instincts, is philosophical. But since the possession of knowledge would be a matter for the deity, the philosopher never achieves definitive clarity, but feels the urge to entrust himself to the dark. For his clarity does not emerge from the void; it is not self-sustaining. As the clarity of water it would be an indifferent clarity. This is why the self-understanding involved in the philosophical quest serves equally to reveal what will lastingly, and thus genuinely, defy understanding. The peculiarity of knowledge in philosophizing is that at the crucial point we know by not knowing.

   c. Knowledge and Existenz.   Science explores an existence that is what it is *independently of the scientist's being.*Philosophizing inquires into the Being that is experienced by virtue of the fact that I myself am; I can know about Being only in the way in which I am through myself. Hence philosophical knowledge depends upon my being. It is my self-assurance.

It is not the intention of philosophy, forgetful of itself, to identify itself with the knowledge of world-orientation as if the concern of philosophy were the same again as that of the sciences, or if there were an object of knowledge which they had overlooked. Whenever philosophy means to examine and solve problems individually and then to possess the results, it assumes the stand of being within the continuity of a science, of going one more step beyond traditional philosophy and of holding out the prospect of further results to be expected shortly. But philosophy is truth only as the process of appropriation of possibilities of Being and not as mere appropriation of the results of knowledge.

To the extent that the sciences find their meaning in philosophizing, from which first comes the impetus to take hold of these sciences, they serve philosophy as its substance. But its total content does not as yet fulfill Being. True, as consciousness-as-such in scientific world-orientation, I believe I can say, What I know is what I am—I am as knowledge in which everything comes together. Being is comprehended within the known. Yet it is only as possible Existenz, that is, in the leap of philosophizing, that I can say, What I know is merely the condition for the way in which I become certain of my Being.

Hence, if one clings to science as the only way of taking hold of the truth, and disavows everything else, then one rejects philosophizing. If, however, one gives up science as the world of cogent universal validity, one tumbles into the void and is unable to philosophize in this manner. However no synthesis of science and philosophy is possible such that they were to become a whole of knowledge. Their dichotomy and dialectical tension belong to our appearance as temporal existence in which we can transcend only when we recognize in the sciences the world beyond which we transcend.

Neither is philosophy the theory by which one is guided as in technical operations we are guided by a scientific theory. The coincidence of thought and life does not signify the possibility of subsuming the concrete individual under the law or image of a theory. What, as a thought, was not already a function within life, is thought untruthfully. The originality of philosophy consists in thinking each day in its concreteness, as the inner action of thought. Hence, the underlying criterion of what is conceived and represented in a philosophic work is the rootedness of thought and life in the One or the illumination of present self-being; it merely brings order into what has arisen from it and can be expressed and reproduces it methodically. I am only as thinking, and philosophizing is thinking within existence, insofar as possible Existenz in its freedom comprehends itself, as being unconditional; hence philosophy, as that which is expressed, is indeed theory for one moment, but not as mere objective intelligibility, and only as possible translation into self-being.

In philosophizing we cannot avoid using some kind of conceptualizations when we express ourselves, but these are not the essence of philosophic thought in the same sense as they are the essence of scientific cognition. Scientific conceptualization marks the end of philosophizing as does the stammering of conceptless speech. Just as philosophizing becomes untrue in a philosophic conceptuality that is merely terminology, it sinks into turbidity in conceptless speech.

Although philosophy reaches beyond science and is itself not science, it always seeks, in its language, also to express a knowledge. Instead of the differentiation between philosophy and science, we pursue, in philosophy, the tension of knowledge and Existenz. To be sure, knowledge is that which achieves its methodically clear form and unfolding solely in the sciences; but it is present also in philosophy in some concretion of its substance and form. It is the nature of this presence—that knowledge has a meaning and hears an obligation that is still lacking in mere knowledge—which constitutes philosophizing. In it, knowledge remains in the tension of having to contain contemplation on the one side and action on the other, neither one without the other.

Philosophy as knowledge is contemplation. The Greeks compared life with a festival: some attend in order to exhibit their artistry, others in order to make a profit off the festival crowd, and others in order to look. The latter, claimed the Greeks, are the philosophers. But they did not consider philosophizing to be contemplation without involvement; rather, in contemplating the divine they wanted to become god-like. For them, philosophy is not merely knowledge but practice, the study of true life. It proves itself in the face of death; philosophizing means learning to die.

If the antithesis of life and knowledge were established in such a manner that a merely contemplative knowledge were to confront a merely acting Existenz, then each side, in losing the other, would also lose itself. If one limits oneself to knowledge, demands objectivity in which the self is no longer involved, then one sees a magnificent picture of the world and believes that one knows; but one does not allow oneself to be affected, neither by the other nor by one's own thoughts. If, however, one scorns knowledge, calls it a mere matter of indifference, and retreats, instead, to feeling, instinct, intuition, then one permits all communication, in which one participates as a rational being, to come to an end; for by rationalizing this attitude, one then means to furnish proof for its truth by the life that one lives, by the experiencing that one exhibits, as an obtrusive paragon of virtue. As psychological attitudes, these opposites each turn into the other; and since each, by itself, is dead, each creates its own boredom and causes one to make a new attempt with the opposite.

Philosophizing stands between these poles, fulfilling both. Philosophy is the becoming aware of truth by way of science in one's own life. It demands that research be conducted in the world. Without science our desire for knowledge would remain empty; it wishes that everything, without limits, be illuminated rationally. But it demands that what is known be taken up into Existenz, that it not be left standing by itself, indifferent, as its own end; rather, we are to move within the known as the way to true consciousness of Being. Not to lose oneself neither in the endlessness of objective knowledge nor in the chaos of emotions—this is possible only through a movement between the two in which Existenz is actualized as a Third, never merely objective and never merely subjective, which is to be illuminated philosophically.

Clarity cannot be the clarity of nothing. A philosopher who proceeded like a mathematician, who thought up a particular object which it would be possible for him to possess as the mere object of reason and which would have no destiny of its own—this philosopher would remain within the clarity of formality but without true illumination. The impetus toward clarity is philosophical in nature only when it is directed at the dark ground of the appearance of Existenz, rich in content. The philosopher, ready for and open to his destiny, hungers for world; he seeks to know it as nature and in the breadth of historic objectivity, to experience it in the factual historic concreteness of his own existence. Philosophy cannot remain aloof. Only he could practice it by himself in solitude who would take along into his solitude a life and a world which he has gained.

But Existenz is not given complete as a Being which would then be illuminated; rather it is still to be actualized through the particular clarity I have gained. Philosophy grows not only out of existence and the sciences but, penetrating both, brings about Being in its appearance. Philosophizing out of my primal source I am like the fabled Baron von Münchhausen who pulls himself out of the swamp by his own shock of hair.

Hence a dogmatic philosophy that presents itself as only knowing is different in essence from the philosophy of freedom which, *in* knowledge, soars upward. In the former there occurs a bonding to a content-filled statement about Being; here, in the latter, however, the bonding is one to existential decision. In the former we find a passionate struggle for cogent validity, its acceptance as objective truth, and the need for disciples and dissemination. In the latter, the passion is directed toward the purity of soul, toward openness and communication, the love of historic unconditionality. Growing out of these, in mutual illumination by objectivities which, as such, remain always mere questions and possibilities, is a tolerance that will cease only before the intolerance of dogmatics; hiding behind it, man, in effect, breaks off communication. In the former instance, philosophy becomes a rounded objective whole. In the latter it is the vehicle of communication in the service of Existenz. There it is faith in an objectivity having universal character. Here it is a self-penetration of the individual in regard to his Existenz in an unending progression.

Hence philosophizing is neither merely science nor merely Existenz. It is methodical illumination that thinks scientifically; its result lies solely in the transformation into consciousness of Existenz which it makes possible.

As *scholar* I withdraw from life, take hold of objects as objects in themselves, seek universally valid criteria and verifications. Here *life* is private; in it I take a different stance than in research. As one who *philosophizes*, however, I return to both of them. To be sure, I have to deal with myself as possible Existenz; I do my thinking based on this life and verify or disappoint what I think in it; but now I am no longer able to draw a line between life as private and thought as objective, for one turns into the other. If I do not philosophize daily in my existence then I do not philosophize at all. Philosophy is a factor of life which, as appearance of Existenz, knowingly creates itself and urges on beyond itself. But philosophy is clear not through its mere relationship to life but through itself. Philosophizing thought is life, and life is only as thinking life.

II.

Philosophy and History

EDITORS' INTRODUCTION TO SUBPART II:
Jaspers's need to gain a perspective on history arose from his concern to arrive at an effective critique of the times and its problems. Jaspers published two general works in this area: *Man in the Modern Age* (see Selection 7), and *The Origin and Goal of History*. The two following selections are taken from the latter work, which was written after the Second World War. The main theme of the book is as follows: Mankind is now irreversibly one and stands at the threshold of world history. The main tendencies of the age are socialism, world government, and a sense of faith. Upholding the cause of personal freedom, Jaspers tries to disclose in these tendencies the dangers to and the chances for political freedom as the basis for personal freedom. The great challenge of the age to the realization of freedom is to find a *modus vivendi* with science and its technological use so that they serve man's liberation and not the forces of enslavement. In this situation Jaspers sees in the renewal of the unfinished task of reason mankind's vast and only chance of stemming the forces of totalitarianism that threaten to gain the upper hand and to destroy freedom.

The following selections are taken from the beginning and the end of *The Origin and Goal of History*. In Selection 57, "The Axial Period," Jaspers develops the theory of the axial times when the impulse of reason first arose in mankind. Selection 58, "Overcoming History," indicates the limitation of history as man's only point of reference.

Selection 57

THE AXIAL PERIOD

EDITORS:
Jaspers regards the first millennium B.C. as the watershed of history when—in a diversity of civilizations, and apparently independently of each other, in China, in India, in Persia, in Israel and in Greece—man woke from a way of

thinking that was primarily pragmatic and explanatory of things at hand; in its larger concerns it was tied to imagery, concrete representation, and myth. Man awoke to a way of thinking that is more sweeping, open and free in its vision; that is able to rise above restrictive differences by searching for reconciling ideas and unities; that is not content with knowledge of the world as it is found but questions whatever is less than the one and ultimate truth and restlessly pursues this truth. Jaspers calls this "reason" in distinction from the "understanding" or "intellect" (*see* Selection 24). It is this intellect, however, that, through the achievements of modern science, is now the most effective means of domination of masses of mankind, and thus is a threat to freedom. To Jaspers the sense of the study of history lies in recalling the ancient power of reason and enacting it in its communicative mode.

The following selection is an emendation by the editors of M. Bullock's translation of *Vom Ursprung und Ziel der Geschichte*, pp. 18–25, 40–43, 102–06; in English: *The Origin and Goal of History*, pp. 1–6, 18–21, 74–77.

TEXT:

In the Western World the philosophy of history was founded in the Christian faith. In imposing works, ranging from St. Augustine to Hegel, this faith saw the movement of God through history. God's acts of revelation represent the decisive turning points. Thus Hegel could still say: All of history goes toward and comes from Christ. The appearance of the Son of God is the axis of world history. Our chronology bears daily witness to this Christian structure of world history.

But the Christian faith is only one faith, not the faith of mankind. This view of universal history therefore suffers from the defect that it can only be valid for believing Christians. But even in the West, Christians have not tied their empirical conceptions of history to this faith. For them an article of faith is not a statement of empirical insight into the real course of history. For Christians sacred history was separated from profane history, as being different in its meaning. Even the believing Christian was able to examine the Christian tradition itself in the same way as other empirical objects of research.

An axis of world history, if such exists, would have to be arrived at *empirically*, as a factual situation that as such can be valid for all men, Christians included. This axis would be at the point where there came into being what man can be from that time on, where the most overwhelming fruitfulness occurred in the shaping of being-human; this would happen in a way that, for the occident and Asia and all men, without the criterion of specific religious content—even if it is not empirically compelling and comprehensible—could yet be convincing on the basis of empirical judgment. There would then come into being a framework of historic self-understanding common to all peoples. It would seem that this axis of history is to be found in the period around 500

B.C., in the spiritual process that occurred between 800 and 200 B.C. It is there that we meet with the most deep–cut dividing line in history. Man, as we know him today, came into being. For short we may style this the "Axial Period."

Characterization of the Axial Period

The most extraordinary events are concentrated in this period. Confucius and Lao-tse were living in China, all the directions of Chinese philosophy came into being, including those of Mo-ti, Chuang-tse, Lieh-tsu, and a host of others; India produced the Upanishads and Buddha, and, like China, ran the whole gamut of philosophical possibilities down to skepticism, to materialism, sophism and nihilism; in Iran Zarathustra taught the challenging view of the world as a struggle between good and evil; in Palestine the prophets made their appearance, from Elijah, by way of Isaiah and Jeremiah, to Deutero-Isaiah; Greece witnessed the appearance of Homer, of the philosophers—Parmenides, Heraclitus, and Plato—of the tragedians, of Thucydides, and of Archimedes. Everything that is merely intimated by these names developed during these few centuries almost simultaneously in China, India, and the Occident without any one of these knowing of the others.

What is new about this age, in all three of these worlds, is that man becomes aware of Being as a whole, of himself and his limitations. He experiences the terrible nature of the world and his own impotence. He asks radical questions. Face to face with the void he strives for liberation and redemption. By consciously recognizing his limits he sets himself the highest goals. He experiences unconditionality in the depth of selfhood and in the clarity of transcendence.

This took place in reflection. Such awareness led to consciousness becoming conscious of itself; thought directed itself to thought itself. Intellectual battles arose, accompanied by attempts to convince others through the imparting of thoughts, reasons and experiences. Contradictory possibilities were essayed. Discussion, the formation of parties, and the division of the intellectual realm, even in opposition, remained related to one another, created unrest and movement to the very brink of spiritual chaos.

In this age were born the fundamental categories within which we still think today, and the beginnings of the world religions, by which human beings still live, were created. The step into universality was taken in every sense.

As a result of this process, hitherto unconsciously accepted ideas, customs, and conditions were subjected to examination, questioned, and liquidated. Everything was swept into the vortex. Insofar as the traditional substance still possessed vitality and actuality, its manifestations were illuminated and thereby transmuted.

The *Mythical Age*, with its tranquility and self-evidence, was at an end. The

Greek, Indian, and Chinese philosophers and Buddha were unmythical in their decisive insights, as were the prophets in their ideas of God. Rationality and rationally clarified experience launched a struggle against the myth (*logos* against *mythos*); a further struggle developed for the transcendence of the One God against non-existent demons as well as against the untrue figures of the gods out of moral indignation toward them. Religion was rendered ethical, and the status of the deity thereby increased. The myth, on the other hand, became the material of a language which expressed by it something very different from what it had originally contained: it was turned into metaphor. Myths were remolded, were understood at a new depth during this transition, which was myth-creating after a new fashion, at the very moment when the myth as a whole was destroyed. The old mythical world slowly sank into oblivion, but remained as a background to the whole through the continued belief of the mass of the people (and was subsequently able to gain the upper hand over wide areas).

This whole change in being-human may be termed *intellectualism*: Out of the unquestioned involvement in life there occurs a loosening, the calm of polarities becomes the disquiet of opposites and antinomies. Man is no longer enclosed within himself. He becomes uncertain of himself and thereby open to new and boundless possibilities. He can hear and understand what no one had hitherto asked or proclaimed. The unheard-of becomes manifest. Together with his world and his own self, Being becomes palpable to man, but not with finality: the question remains.

For the first time *philosophers* appeared. Human beings dared to rely on themselves as individuals. Hermits and wandering thinkers in China, ascetics in India, philosophers in Greece, and prophets in Israel all belong together, however much they may differ from each other in their beliefs, the contents of their thought, and their inner dispositions. Man proved capable of confronting inwardly the entire universe. He discovered within himself the origin from which to raise himself above his own self and the world.

In *speculative thought* he lifts himself up toward Being itself, which is apprehended without duality in the disappearance of subject and object, in the coincidence of opposites. That which is experienced in the loftiest flights of the spirit as a coming-to-oneself within Being, or as *unio mystica*, as becoming one with the Godhead, or as becoming a tool for the will of God, is expressed in an ambiguous and easily misunderstood form in objectifying speculative thought.

It is the authentic human being which, bound to and concealed within the body, fettered by drives and only dimly aware of himself, longs for liberation and redemption and is able to attain to them already in this world—in soaring toward the idea, in the calmness of stoic imperturbability, in the absorption of meditation, in the knowledge of himself and the world as *atman*, in the experience of *nirvana*, in concord with the *tao*, or in surrender to the will of God. There are surely extreme differences in meanings, in attitudes, and the contents of faith; but what they have in common is that man reached beyond himself by becoming aware of himself in the whole of Being and that he enters upon paths which each man must walk individually. He may renounce all wordly goods, may withdraw into the desert, into the forest or the mountains, may discover as a hermit the creative power of solitude, and may then return into the world as the possessor of knowledge, as a sage or as a prophet. What was later called reason and personality was revealed for the first time during the Axial Period.

What the individual achieves is by no means passed on to all. The gap between the peaks of human potentiality and the crowd became exceptionally great at that time. Nonetheless, what the individual becomes indirectly changes all. Being-human as a whole took a forward leap.

Corresponding to ths new intellectual world, we find a *sociological* situation showing analogies in all three regions. There were a multitude of small states and cities, a struggle of all against all, which at first nevertheless permitted an astonishing prosperity, an unfolding of vigor and wealth. In China the small states and cities had achieved sovereign life under the powerless imperial rulers of the Chou dynasty; the political process consisted of the enlargement of small units through the subjection of other small units. In Hellas and the Near East small territorial units—even, to some extent, those subjected by Persia—enjoyed an independent existence. In India there were many states and independent cities.

Mutual contacts served to spread the intellectual movement within each of the three worlds. The Chinese philosophers—Confucius, Mo-ti and others—wandered about the country and met in places of renown favorable to the spiritual life, founding schools which are termed academies by sinologists; the sophists and the philosophers of Hellas travelled about in similar fashion, and Buddha passed his entire life in wandering from place to place.

In the past, spiritual conditions had been comparatively enduring; despite catastrophes everything had repeated itself, confined within the horizons of a still, very slow spiritual movement that did not enter consciousness and was therefore not apprehended. Now, on the contrary, tension increases and becomes a basis of the torrentially swift movement.

This movement reaches consciousness. Human existence becomes, as *history*, the object of thought. Men feel and know that something extraordinary is beginning in their own present. But this very realization also makes men aware of the fact that this present was preceded by an infinite past. At the very commencement of this awakening of the specifically human spirit, man is sustained by memory and is conscious of belonging to a late or even decadent age.

Men see themselves faced by *catastrophe* and feel the *desire to help* through insight, education, and reform. The endeavor is made to dominate the course of events by planning, right conditions are to be re-established or brought about for the first time. History as a whole is seen as a sequence of configurations of the world, either as a process of continual decline, or as a circular motion, or as an ascent. Thought is devoted to the manner in which human beings may best live together, may best be governed and administered. Practical activity is dominated by ideas of reform. Philosophers travel from state to state, become advisers and teachers, are scorned or sought after, enter into discussion and compete with one another. A sociological parallel can be drawn between Confucius' failure at the court of Wei and Plato's failure at Syracuse, between the school of Confucius, which trained future statesmen, and the academy of Plato, which served the same purpose.

The age that saw all these developments, which spanned several centuries, cannot be regarded as a simple upward movement. It was an age of simultaneous destruction and creation. Completion was not achieved by any means. The highest potentialities of thought and practical expression actualized in individuals did not become common property, because the majority of men were unable to follow. What began as freedom of motion finally became anarchy. When the age lost its creativeness, a process of dogmatic fixation and leveling-down took place in all three cultural realms. Out of a disorder that was growing intolerable arose a striving after new ties, through the re-establishment of enduring conditions.

The *conclusion* is at first of a political character. Mighty universal empires, the result of conquest by force, arose almost simultaneously in China (Tsin Shi Hwang-ti), in India (Maurya dynasty) and in the West (the Hellenistic empires and the *Imperium Romanum*). Everywhere the first outcome of the collapse was an order of technological and organizational planning.

But the *relation to the spirit of what had gone before* remained everywhere. It became a model and an object of veneration. Its achievements and great personalities stood clearly in view and provided the content of schooling and education (Confucianism was evolved under the Han dynasty, Buddhism by Asoka, and the age of Augustus consciously established Graeco-Roman cultural education).

The universal empires which came into being at the end of the Axial Period considered themselves founded for eternity. But their stability was deceptive. Even though these empires lasted for a long time by comparison with the state-formations of the Axial Period, in the end they all decayed and fell to pieces. Subsequent millennia produced an extraordinary amount of change. From one point of view the disintegration and re-establishment of great empires has constituted history ever since the end of the Axial Period, as it had constituted it through the millennia during which the ancient civilizations were flourishing. But these more recent changes possessed a different significance; there was added the tension to the spirit which arose in the Axial Period and from then on was constantly operative by conferring on all human activity a new questionable character and a new meaning.

The Significance of the Axial Period

The problem of the meaning of the Axial Period is something quite different from that of its cause.

The fact of the threefold manifestation of the Axial Period is in the nature of a miracle, insofar as no really adequate explanation is possible within the limits of our present knowledge. The hidden meaning of this fact, however, cannot be discovered empirically at all, as a meaning somewhere intended by someone. Rather, asking about the meaning merely indicates what we make of the fact, i.e., what grows out of it and comes toward us. If, in the process, terms creep in which seem to indicate that we have in mind some plan of providence, these are only metaphors.

A. Really to see the facts of the Axial Period and to make them the basis of our universal conception of history is to gain possession of something *common to all mankind,* beyond all differences of creed. It is one thing to see the unity of history merely from one's own ground and in the light of one's own faith, another to think of it in communication with every other human ground, linking one's own consciousness to the alien consciousness. In this sense, it can be said of the centuries between 800 and 200 B.C. that they are the empirically evident axis of world history for all men.

The transcendental history of the revealed Christian faith is made up out of the creation, the fall, stages of revelation, prophecies, the appearance of the Son of God, redemption and the last judgment. As the contents of the faith of an historical human group it remains untouched. That which binds all men together, however, cannot be revelation but must be experience. Revelation is the form taken by particular historical creeds, experience is accessible to man as man. We—all men—can share the knowledge of the reality of this universal transformation of mankind during the Axial Period. Although confined to China, India, and the Occident, and though there was to begin with no contact between these three worlds, the Axial Period nonetheless founded universal history and, spiritually, drew all men into itself.

B. The fact of the threefold historical modification effected by the step we call the Axial Period acts as a *summons to boundless communication.* To see and understand the others helps in the achievement of clarity about oneself, in overcoming the potential narrowness of all self-enclosed historicity, and in casting off toward far horizons. This risking of boundless communication is once again the secret of becoming-human, not as it occurred in the inaccessible prehistoric past, but as it takes place within ourselves.

The task of such communication—posed by the historical fact of the three-fold origin—is the best remedy against the erroneous claim to exclusive possession of truth by any one creed. For a creed can only be absolute in historic Existenz, not universally valid for all in its predications, like scientific truth. The claim to exclusive possession of truth, this tool of fanaticism, of human arrogance and self-deception through the will to power, this calamity for the West—most intensely so in all its secularized forms, such as the dogmatic philosophies and the so-called scientific ideologies—can be overcome by considering that God has manifested himself historically in various ways and has opened up many paths toward Himself. It is as though the deity were issuing a warning, through the language of universal history, against the claim to exclusiveness in the possession of truth.

C. If the Axial Period gains in importance with the degree to which we immerse ourselves in it, the question arises: *Is this period, are its creations, the yardstick* for all that follows? If we do not consider the quantitative aspect of its effect, nor the extent of the areas involved in its political processes, nor the pre-eminence accorded to spiritual phenomena throughout the centuries, is it still true that the austere grandeur, the creative lucidity, the depth of meaning and the extent of the leap toward new spiritual worlds contained in the phenomena of the Axial Period are to be regarded as the spiritual peak of all history up to the present? Do later manifestations, in spite of the heights to which they attained and in spite of having become irreplaceable in their turn, pale before the earlier—Virgil before Homer, Augustus before Solon, Jesus before Jeremiah?

It would certainly be wrong to answer this question with a mechanical affirmative. The later manifestation invariably possesses a value of its own, which was not present in the earlier one: a maturity of its own, a sublime preciousness, a depth of soul, especially in the case of the "exception." It is quite impossible to arrange history in a hierarchy following automatically from one universally applicable conception. But the manner in which this question is formulated—and also, perhaps, a prejudice against the later ones—does result from the comprehension of the Axial Period. This in turn illumines what is authentically new and great after a different fashion and does not belong to the Axial Period. For example: Anyone who philosophizes is likely to find that after months with the Greek philosophers, St. Augustine affects him like a liberation from coldness and impersonality into questions of conscience, which have remained with us ever since the time of St. Augustine but were alien to the Greeks. Conversely, however, after spending some time on St. Augustine, he will experience an increasing desire to return to the Greeks and cleanse himself of the impurity that seems to grow with his participation in this thinking and thus to regain his health. Nowhere on earth is there truth or authentic salvation.

The Axial Period too suffered shipwreck. History went on.

Only this much seems certain to me: Our present-day historical conscious-ness, as well as our consciousness of our present situation, is determined, down to consequences I have only been able to hint at, by the conception of the Axial Period, irrespective of whether this thesis is accepted or rejected. It is a question of the manner in which the unity of mankind becomes concrete for us.

Once More: A Schema of World History

The present situation has been created by *Europe*. How did it come about?

The great divisions and leaps that charaterize occidental history lend it the appearance of being fragmented and of continually giving birth to itself afresh in radical metamorphoses. By comparison, India and China, notwithstanding the movement that took place there, too, give an impression of uniformity.

There have been times when the West has sunk so deep into its substratum as to look as though it were almost extinguished. A visitor from some other planet who had travelled around the earth in about A.D. 700 would perhaps have found in Tshangan (then the capital of China), the highest seat of the spiritual life of the earth, and in Constantinople a strange residue; the north-ern districts of Europe would have appeared to him merely realms of barba-rism. Around the year 1400 the overall life of Europe, India, and China was most likely on a comparable level of civilization. However, the events that occurred beginning with the fifteenth century, i.e., the discovery of the world by Europe and Europe's giving its imprint to this world, give rise to the ques-tion as to what caused what was new and peculiar in Europe which made this development possible, and what were the stages that led to it. This becomes the fundamental question of universal history. For a break took place in the Occident that was unique in its importance and, in its consequences, for the whole world; a break whose results make up our own situation and whose ultimate significance is still open.

The major steps leading up to it were: The prophetic religion of the Jews set men free from magic and the transcendence of objects with a radicality such as had not occurred anywhere else on earth; although it did so only for a historically limited moment and for a small number of men, it left its message in the Book for all who came after and who were capable of hearing it. The Greeks created a clarity of distinctions, a plasticity of forms, and a consistency in the operations of reason never before attained anywhere in the world. Christianity actualized awareness of the most extreme transcendence—as In-dia and China also succeeded in doing—but with the difference that Christian-ity fettered this actualization to the world of immanence, and thereby brought about the perpetual unrest involved in the task of giving a Christian confor-mation to the world.

But the great break really took place only after the late Middle Ages. These steps and the memory of them may have been its preconditions. The break itself is the great new enigma. It is by no means a transparent, rectilinear evolution. Development of the preliminary stages of modern science in late medieval nominalism was accompanied and immediately followed by the orgies of witchcraft. The changes that, in the sequel, occurred in the actuality of man while he was creating science and technology and winning mastery over the forces of nature and over the whole surface of the globe, are in horrifying contrast to these palpable achievements.

The steps that separate the whole historical past from the still veiled future were definitively taken only during the nineteenth century. Again and again the question arises: what is it that constitutes—perhaps palpable from the very beginning, coming to the fore time and again, then at times seemingly flagging—Europe's character as informer of the earth? What is it that develops after the nominalists as science, spreads across the planet since the seventeenth century, and becomes definitive during the nineteenth century?

Europe's exceptional spiritual achievements from 1500 and 1800, that outshine science and technology—Michelangelo, Raphael, Leonardo, Shakespeare, Rembrandt, Goethe, Spinoza, Kant, Bach, Mozart—challenge comparison with the Axial Period of two and a half millennia earlier. Is a second Axial Period to be discerned in these later centuries?

The difference is considerable. The purity and clarity, the ingenuousness and freshness of the worlds of the first axis are not repeated. Everything stands too much in the shadow of exacting traditions and takes the wrong step at every turn. However, from these wrong paths a redirection toward the most miraculous successes occurs in those great and solitary figures—in spite of everything, as it were. On the other hand, however, possibilities are open to the second axis that were unknown to the first. Because it was able to take over experiences and appropriate ideas, it possessed from the outset both more variety of meaning and greater richness. In its very fragmentation it allowed depths of being-human to become manifest that had not previously been visible. For this reason preeminence might be given to the second axis, because, while making an original contribution to the continuity of Western culture and at the same time enjoying a more sweeping view through its position on the shoulders of its predecessor, it achieved the greater breadth and the greater depth. But it must be relegated to second place because it did not live entirely on its own resources and because it suffered and permitted extraordinary distortions and aberrations. It is our own immediate historical matrix. We are alternately at war and on intimate terms with it; we are unable to look at it in the same calm of distance as that in which we see the first axis. Above all, however, it is a purely European phenomenon and for that reason alone has no claim to the title of second axis.

Most likely, these centuries are the most fruitful period for us Europeans; they constitute the indispensable fundament of our culture and the richest source of our intuitions and insights. But they do not represent a universally human, world-embracing axis, and it is improbable that they might become such in the future. A quite different axis was established by the activities of the Europeans, with their consequences of science and technology, which first made their appearance when the West, whose spirit and soul were already in decline, impinged upon an India and China whose spirit and soul had reached their nadir.

At the end of the nineteenth century, Europe seemed to dominate the world. The situation was thought to be final. Hegel's words seemed to be confirmed: "The Europeans have sailed round the world and for them it is a sphere. Whatever has not yet fallen under their sway is either not worth the trouble, or it is destined to fall under it."

What a transformation since then! The world has become European through the adoption of European technology and the demands of European nationalism, and it is successfully turning both against Europe. Europe, as the old Europe, is no longer the dominant factor in the world. It has abdicated, outstripped by America and Russia, upon whose policies the fate of Europe hangs. . . .

It is true that America and Russia are also permeated by the spirit of Europe; but they are not Europe. The Americans (even though of European provenance) may not yet have found a new autonomous consciousness and a new origin in their own soil, but have at least the claim to them. The Russians have a historical matrix of their own in the East and in the mingled European and Asiatic origin of their peoples; spiritually their matrix is Byzantium.

China and India, however, who do not wield any decisive power today, will increase in importance. Their vast populations, possessed of a profound and irreplaceable cultural heritage, are becoming an element of mankind—in common with all other peoples which are seeking their way in the present great metamorphosis of being-human into which all are being pressed.

Selection 58

OVERCOMING HISTORY

EDITORS:
In elaborating a philosophy of history Jaspers pays due attention to the importance that is attached to the idea of history. In his own philosophy of history Jaspers is able to direct mankind to the resources of communicative reason by

means of which the possibilities of freedom are to be enhanced in an age of refined techniques of domination. Yet he sees a danger in the absolutization of history whereby a knowledge of its origin and goal is claimed and whereby through such knowledge man is assigned his place in the scheme of things and his freedom abrogated. Against this danger Jaspers shows, in the following selection, in what way history recedes within various perspectives. The most decisive of these is the historicity of Existenz.

This is a selection from *Vom Ursprung und Ziel der Geschichte*, pp. 341-46; in English: *The Origin and Goal of History*, pp. 272-76. M. Bullock's translation has been emended by the editors.

TEXT:

We have called to mind: History is not completed—happening conceals in itself infinite possibilities—whenever history takes shape as a known whole this shape is broken through, that which is remembered discloses, through fresh data, hitherto unobserved truth; that which was discarded as inessential acquires overriding essentiality. The conclusion of history seems impossible; it proceeds from the endless into the endless, and only an external disaster can senselessly break off the whole process.

We are seized by a feeling of dissatisfaction with history. We should like to penetrate history to a point before and above all history, to the ground of Being, before which the whole of history becomes a phenomenon that can never be "right" in itself, to the point at which, sharing knowledge with creation, so to speak, we are no longer entirely at the mercy of history.

But for us there can never be a known Archimedian point outside history. We are always within history. In penetrating through to that which lies before, or athwart, or after all history, into the Encompassing of everything, into Being itself, we are seeking in our Existenz and in transcendence, what this Archimedian point would be if it were capable of assuming the configuration of objective knowledge.

1. We go beyond history by addressing ourselves to nature. Face to face with the ocean, in the mountains, in the tempest, in the radiance of sunrise, in the iridescence of the elements, in the lifeless polar world of snow and ice, in the primeval forest, wherever nature devoid of man speaks to us, it may happen that we feel as if liberated. A homecoming into unconscious life, a homecoming still more deeply into the clarity of the inanimate elements, can sweep us along into stillness, into exultation, into painless unity. But all this is deception if it is more than the mystery of totally silent natural Being, which can be experienced in taking this step, of this Being beyond everything that we call good and evil, beautiful and ugly, true and false, of this Being that leaves us in the lurch without heart and without compassion. If we really find sanctuary there, we have run away from men and from ourselves. But if we take these

momentarily overwhelming experiences of nature as mute signs, pointing to that which is above all history but which they do not make manifest, then they remain true in that they impel us forward and do not hold us fast.

2. We go beyond history into that which is timelessly valid, into the truth that is independent of all history, into mathemathics and into all cogent knowledge, into every form of the universal and universally valid, which, unaffected by all change, always is, whether recognized or unrecognized. We may be carried along as we apprehend this clarity of the valid. We have a fixed point, a Being which persists. Again, however, we are misled if we remain at this point. This validity, too, is a sign but it does not sustain the substance of Being. It leaves us singularly unaffected; it is disclosed in the continuous progress of its being discovered. It is essentially the form of validity, whereas its content touches upon infinitely much of what is, never on Being itself. Only our understanding is at rest here in something that persists. We are not. That this validity exists, however, independently and detached from all history, once again points to the supra-temporal.

3. We go beyond history into the ground of historicity, that is, into historicity in the whole of world-being. From the history of mankind a road leads into the ground out of which the whole of nature—unhistorical in itself—moves into the light of a historicity. But this is so only for a speculation for which it becomes like a language that something seems to come forward out of nature toward man's historicity which lies in his own biological makeup, in landscapes and in natural events. At first these are only meaningless and weak; they are catastrophes and indifferent presence; and yet they are, as it were, animated by history as if they were correspondencies springing from a common root.

4. It is the historicity of our own Existenz that leads us into this ground of historicity. For there is a point at which we, as historicity—i.e., in the unconditionality of our adoption and choice of the way we find ourselves in the world, of our decisions, of our being given to ourselves in our very love—become Being athwart time. It is from this point that light falls upon the historicity of history through the agency of our communication, which, passing through what is knowable of history, comes upon Existenz. Here we go beyond history to the everlasting present; as historic Existenz in history we are above and beyond history.

5. We ovecome history in the direction toward the unconscious. The mind of man is conscious. Consciousness is the medium without which there is for us neither knowledge nor experience, neither being-human nor relationship to transcendence. That which is not conscious is called unconscious. "Unconscious" is a negative concept, endlessly ambiguous as to its content.

Our consciousness is directed toward that which is unconscious, that is, toward everything we come upon in the world from which nothing inward communicates itself to us. And our consciousness is supported by the unconscious, it is a continual emerging out of the unconscious and sliding back into the unconscious. But we can gain experience of the unconscious only through consciousness. In every conscious step of our lives, especially in every creative act of the spirit, we are aided by an unconscious within us. Pure consciousness is incapable of doing anything. Consciousness is like the crest of a wave, a peak rising from a broad and deep substratum.

This unconscious that supports us has a dual meaning: the unconscious that is nature, *per se* and for ever obscure; and the unconscious that is the germ of the spirit which strives to become manifest.

If we overcome history in the direction of the unconscious as the Being which becomes manifest in the appearance of consciousness, this unconscious is never nature, but that which is revealed in the outcrop of symbols, in language, literature, representation and self-representation, in reflection. We live not only out of it, but also toward it. The more clearly consciousness renders it manifest, the more substantially, profoundly, and comprehensively it becomes present itself. For within consciousness that germ is awakened whose wakefulness heightens and widens itself. The passage of the spirit through history not only consumes a given unconscious, but also produces a new unconscious. Both modes of expression are fallacious, however, in relation to the one unconscious, the penetration of which is not only the process of the history of the spirit, but which is Being, above, before, and after all history.

But the designation "unconscious" is merely negative. No cipher of Being is to be gained with this concept, as Eduard von Hartmann vainly sought to do in a world of positivist thinking. The unconscious is of value only to the extent to which it assumes a form in consciousness, and thereby ceases to be unconscious. Consciousness is the actual and true. Heightened consciousness, not the unconscious, is our goal. Rather, we overcome history in the direction of the unconscious in order to attain heightened consciousness.

The longing for unconsciousness, which takes hold of us humans at all times in adversity, is deceptive. Whether a Babylonian god seeks to undo the uproar of the world with the words "I want to sleep," or whether Western man longs to be back in the Garden of Eden before he ate of the Tree of Knowledge, whether he considers it best never to have been born, whether he strives to find his way back to a state of nature prior to all culture, whether he conceives of consciousness as ill fate and looks upon the whole of history as a false trail and desires to bring it to an end—it is forever the same thing in manifold configurations. It is not an overcoming of history, but an evasion of history and one's own existence in it.

6. We go beyond history when man becomes present to us in his most exalted works, through which he has been able, as it were, to catch hold of Being and has rendered it communicable. What was done here by men who let

themselves be consumed by the eternal truth that came to be through language, that is—though in historic garb—beyond history. It leads us, by way of the historic world, into what is prior to all history and is given tongue by means of it. Here there is no longer any question of whence and whither, of future and progress, but in time there is something which is no longer solely time and which comes to us, above all time, as Being itself.

History itself becomes the road to the supra-historical. In the contemplation of the great—in creation, action and thought—history shines forth like an everlasting present. It no longer satisfies curiosity, but becomes an invigorating force. The greatness of history, as object of veneration, binds us to the ground above all history.

7. The conception of history as a whole leads beyond history. The unity of history is itself no longer history. To grasp this unity means to soar above and beyond history into the source of this unity, through which that unity enables history to become a whole. But this ascent above history to the unity of history remains itself a task within history. We do not live in the knowledge of the unity; insofar, however, as we live by this unity we live supra-historically in history.

Every ascent above history becomes deception if we abandon history. The fundamental paradox of our Existenz, i.e., that it is only within the world that we can live above and beyond the world, is repeated in the historic consciousness that rises above history. There is no way around the world, only a way through the world; no way around history, only a way through history.

8. A look at the long ages of prehistory and the short span of history gives rise to the question: Is history not a transitory phenomenon, in view of the hundreds of thousands of years of prehistory? At bottom, there is no other answer save the general proposition: that which has a beginning also has an end—even if it were to last for millions or billions of years.

But the answer—which is impossible to our empirical knowledge—is superfluous to our consciousness of Being. For even if our image of history may be considerably modified according to whether we see unending progress, or the shadow of the end, the essential thing is that knowledge of history as a whole is not the ultimate knowledge. What matters is the demand made on presentiality as eternity in time. History is encompassed by the broader horizon, in which what is present derives its validity in functioning as stage, attestation, decision, fulfillment. That which is eternal appears as decision in time. To the transcendent consciousness of Existenz, history vanishes in the everlasting present.

Within history itself, however, there remains the perspective of time: perhaps the history of mankind will continue for a long, a very long time on the earth that has now become unitary. Within this perspective then, the question for everyone is: where he will stand, for what he will work.

III.

Philosophy and Politics

EDITORS:
For Jaspers, philosophy and politics are intimately related. He writes

> Philosophy has political consequences. . . . There is no great philosophy
> without political thought, not even that of the great metaphysicians, certainly not
> that of Spinoza, who even progressed to active, spiritually effective participation.
> . . . What a philosophy is, manifests itself in its political appearance, which is not
> a by-product but of central significance. It is not a coincidence that National Social-
> ism and Bolshevism recognized in philosophy their mortal enemy.
>
> It became apparent to me that not until I was gripped by politics did my philos-
> ophy attain its full clarity down to the very ground of metaphysics.
>
> From that time on I examine every philosopher as to his political thinking and
> doing and am able to recognize the grand, venerable and effective line of such
> thinking throughout the history of the philosophic spirit.[1]

The relationship between philosophy and politics should be apparent in
many segments of this book. For example, in Jaspers's tying the conception of
man to the freedom of his historic singularity, in the contraposition of reason
and catholicity, and in having the theory of truth culminate in communicative
reason. It is also apparent in his own relation to other philosophers, e.g.,
Heidegger.

Jaspers's preoccupation with political realities antedates his philosophizing. His father and uncle were prominently involved in regional politics, and
Jaspers was imbued with the liberalism of his age. Throughout his life he was
in close association with political thinkers of the first rank, especially Max
Weber and Hannah Arendt. The overwhelming events of the two world wars,
the Nazi regime, West Germany's desultory progress on the path toward
democracy—all this elicited Jaspers's attention. While, to Jaspers, the main
promise of the age lay in mankind's yearning for freedom, the overriding
concerns were the two dangers consisting in the potential for totalitarian
power and the threat of annihilation in a nuclear war. The aim of politics, says
Jaspers, is peace, not peace at any price, but peace in freedom grounded on
open and uncompromising integrity. In Jaspers's words: "No peace without

freedom, no freedom without truth." But truth for man in time requires the enactment of communicative reason in politics no less than elsewhere.

These main motives behind Jaspers's views on the relation of philosophy and politics are reflected in the following selections. Selection 59, "The Question of German Guilt," examines the meanings of guilt and liability and develops the idea of individual inner purification in its political significance. In Selections 60, "When Politics Fails: The Power of the Moral Idea," and 61, "The Supra-Political Power of Sacrifice," Jaspers identifies the supra-political horizon within which politics are directed. Reason in politics—especially in the face of the threats of totalitarianism and nuclear war—is the explicit topic in Selections 62 and 63. The former, "Reason and Democracy," examines democracy as the embodiment of reason in collective life, and as the source from which a new way of political thinking can arise. If, in the face of those terrible dangers to mankind, traditional political thinking were to prevail, mankind's continued existence seems questionable, according to Jaspers. His call for a new way of thinking about things political is the topic of "In What Can We Trust?"

Selection 59

THE QUESTION OF GERMAN GUILT

EDITORS:

The Question of German Guilt was written in the months following the defeat of Nazi Germany. *Prima facie* it provides the topic of its title with a sober analysis. Yet it thereby presented a challenge to the Germans to found their political consciousness and their new state that was to arise from it upon a redirection impelled by honesty about the crimes perpetrated in their name by the Nazi regime. Beyond that, it proved to be fundamental for Jaspers as a political philosopher: It defines the political responsibility of the citizen and the political leader and delineates the dimension of political life within the wider context of human reality.

The following excerpts are editors' emendations of E. B. Ashton's translation of the work, pp. 61–64, 71–81, 118–23. In the original, *Die Schuldfrage*, the passages are to be found on pp. 39–42, 48–58, 92–96.

TEXT:

Political Guilt

For crimes the criminal is punished. The restriction of the Nuremberg trial

to the criminals relieves the guilt of the German people. Not, however, so as
to free them of all guilt—on the contrary. The nature of our real guilt only
appears the more clearly.

We were German nationals at the time when the crimes were committed
by the regime which called itself German, which claimed to be Germany and
seemed to have the right to do so, since the power of the state was in its hands,
and until 1943 it found no dangerous opposition.

The destruction of any decent, truthful German polity must have its roots
also in modes of conduct of the majority of the German population. A people
answers for its polity.

Every German is made to share the blame for the crimes committed in the
name of the Reich. We are collectively liable. The question is in what sense
each of us must feel co-responsible. Certainly in the political sense of the joint
liability of all citizens for acts committed by their state—but for that reason
not necessarily also in the moral sense of actual or intellectual participation in
crime. Are we Germans to be held liable for outrages which Germans inflicted
on us, or from which we were saved as by a miracle? Yes—inasmuch as we let
such a regime rise among us. No—insofar as many of us in our deepest hearts
opposed all this evil and have no morally guilty acts or inner motivations to
admit. To hold liable does not mean to hold morally guilty.

Guilt, therefore, is necessarily collective as the political liability of nationals, but not in the same sense as moral and metaphysical, and never as
criminal guilt. True, the acceptance of political liability with its fearful consequences is hard on every individual. What it means to us is political impotence
and a poverty which will compel us for long times to live in or on the fringes of
hunger and cold and to struggle vainly. Yet this liability as such leaves the soul
untouched.

In the modern state, everyone performs political acts, at least by voting, or
failing to vote, in elections. The sense of political liability lets no man dodge.

If things go wrong the politically active subsequently tend to justify themselves; but such defenses carry no weight in politics. For instance, they meant
well and had the best intentions—Hindenburg, for one, did surely not mean to
ruin Germany or hand it over to Hitler. That does not help him; he did—and
that is what counts in politics. Or they foresaw the disaster, said so, and
warned; but that does not count politically, either, if no action followed or if it
had no effect.

One could think: there might, after all, be wholly non-political persons
who live aloof of all politics, like monks, hermits, scholars, artists—if they are
truly non-political, they would not share the burden of guilt. Yet they, too, are
included among the politically liable, because they, too, live by the order of the
state. There is no "being outside" the modern states.

One may wish to make such aloofness possible, yet one cannot help admit to this limitation. We should like to respect and love an apolitical life, but the end of political participation would also end the right of the apolitical ones to judge concrete political acts of the day and thus to play riskless politics. An apolitical realm demands self-withdrawal from any kind of political activity—and still does not exempt from joint political liability in every sense.

Moral Guilt

Every German asks himself: how am I guilty?

The question of the guilt of the individual, insofar as he looks into himself, is what we call the moral one. Here we Germans are divided by the greatest differences.

While the decision in self-judgment is up to the individual alone, we are free to talk with one another, insofar as we communicate with one another, and morally to help each other achieve clarity. But it is the moral judgment of the other that is suspended and not the criminal or the political one.

There is a line at which even the possibility of moral judgment ceases. It can be drawn where we feel the other not even trying for a moral self-illumination—where we perceive mere sophistry in his argument, where he seems not to hear at all. Hitler and his accomplices, that small minority of tens of thousands, are beyond moral guilt so long as they do not feel it. They seem incapable of repentance and change. They are what they are. Force alone can deal with such men who live by brute force alone.

But the moral guilt exists for all those who yield to conscience and repentance. The morally guilty are those who are capable of penance, the ones who knew, or could know, and yet walked in ways which self-illumination revealed to them as culpable error—whether conveniently closing their eyes to events, or permitting themselves to be intoxicated, seduced or bought with personal advantages, or obeying from fear. . . .

Metaphysical Guilt

Morality is always circumscribed also by concrete worldly purposes. Morally I may be obliged to risk my life in cases where some actualization is at stake; but morally we cannot be expected to risk our lives in the sure knowledge that nothing will have been gained. Morally we may be expected to undertake risks, not a duty to choose certain doom. In both instances it is more likely that morally the opposite is expected, namely not to do what for the sake of concrete purposes is senseless, but to preserve ourselves for actualizations within the world.

But there is within us a consciousness of guilt which springs from another source. Metaphysical guilt is the lack of absolute solidarity with man as man. It remains as an ineluctable summons beyond morally meaningful demands. This solidarity is violated by my presence at an injustice or a crime. It is not enough that I cautiously risk my life to prevent it; if it happens, and if I was there, and if I survive where the other is killed, I know from a voice within myself: I am guilty of being still alive.

I quote from an address I gave in August 1945: "We ourselves have changed since 1933. It was possible for us to seek death in the face of the indignity of our situation—in 1933 when the Constitution was torn up, the dictatorship established in sham legality and all resistance swept away in the intoxication of a large part of our people. We could seek death when the crimes of the regime became publicly apparent on June 30, 1934, or with the lootings, deportations and murders of our Jewish friends and fellow-citizens in 1938, when to our ineradicable shame and disgrace the synagogues, houses of God, went up in flames throughout Germany. We could seek death when from the start of the war the regime acted against the tenet of Kant, our greatest philosopher, who called it a condition of international law that nothing must occur in war which would make a later reconcilement of the belligerents impossible. Thousands in Germany sought, or at least found death, in resisting the regime, most of them anonymously. We survivors did not seek death. We did not go into the streets when our Jewish friends were led away; we did not scream until we, too, were destroyed. We preferred to stay alive, on the feeble, though correct, ground that our death could not have helped anyone. That we are alive—that is our guilt. We know before God what it is that deeply humiliates us. Something happened to us in the course of these twelve years which is like a transmutation of our very essence."

In November 1938, when the synagogues were burning and Jews were deported for the first time, the guilt incurred was chiefly moral and political. Both kinds of guilt rested with those who still had power. The generals stood by. In every town the commander could take action against crime, for the soldier is there to protect all, if crime occurs on such a scale that the police cannot prevent it or fails to do so. They did nothing. At that moment they abandoned the once glorious ethical tradition of the German Army. It was not their business. They had dissociated themselves from the soul of the German people, in favor of a military command system that was a law unto itself.

True, among our people many were outraged and many deeply moved by a horror containing a presentiment of coming calamity. But even more went right on with their activities, undisturbed in their social life and amusements, as if nothing had happened. That is moral guilt.

But the ones who, in utter impotence, outraged and despairing, were unable to prevent the crimes took yet another step in their metamorphosis by a growing consciousness of metaphysical guilt.

Consequences of Guilt

If what we said above was not wholly unfounded, there can be no doubt that we Germans, every one of us, is guilty in some way. Hence there occur the consequences of our guilt.

1. All Germans without exception share in the political liability. All must cooperate in making amends to be brought into legal form. All must jointly suffer the effects of the acts of the victors, of their decisions, of their disunity. We are unable here to exert any influence as a factor of power.

Only by striving constantly for a reasonable presentation of the facts, opportunities and dangers can we—unless everyone already knows what we say—collaborate on the presuppositions of the decisions. In the proper form and with reasons we may appeal to the victors.

2. Not every German—indeed only a very small minority of Germans—has to be punished for crimes. Another minority has to atone for National-Socialist activities. All may defend themselves. They will be judged by the courts of the victors, or by German courts established by the victors.

3. Probably every German—though in greatly diverse ways—has reasons for self-examination based on moral introspection. Here, however, he need not recognize any authority other than his own conscience.

4. And probably every German who understands, transforms in the metaphysical experiences of such a disaster his consciousness of Being and his consciousness of Self. How that happens no one can prescribe, and no one anticipate. It is a matter of individual solitude. What grows out of it has to create the essential basis of what will in future be the German soul.

Such distinctions can be used sophistically to free oneself from the whole question of guilt, for instance like this:

Political liability—all right, but it curtails only my material possibilities; I myself in my inner self am not affected by that at all.

Criminal guilt—that affects just a few, not me; it does not concern me.

Moral guilt—I hear that only my own conscience has jurisdiction, others have no right to reproach me. Well, my conscience is not going to be too hard on me. It isn't all that bad; let's forget about it, and make a fresh start.

Metaphysical guilt—of that, finally, I was expressly told that no one can assert it of another. One is supposed to perceive that as an inner change. That's a crazy idea of some philosopher. There is no such thing. And if there were, I wouldn't notice it. That I needn't bother with.

Our dissection of the concepts of guilt can be turned into a trick for freeing oneself of guilt. The distinctions are in the foreground. They can hide the source and the One. Distinctions enable us to conjure away, as it were, what does not suit us.

Collective Guilt

Having separated the elements of guilt, we return in the end to the question of collective guilt.

Though correct and meaningful everywhere, the separation carries with it the indicated temptation—as though by such distinctions we had evaded the charges and eased our burden. Something has been lost in the process—something which in collective guilt is always audible in spite of everything. For all the crudeness of collective thinking and collective condemnation we feel that we belong together.

In the end, of course, the true collective is the solidarity of all men before God. Somewhere, everyone may free himself from the bonds of state or people or group and break through to the invisible solidarity of men—as men of goodwill and as men sharing the common guilt of being human.

But historically we remain bound to the closer, narrower communities, and we should lose the ground under our feet without them.

Political Liability and Collective Guilt

First to restate the fact that all over the world collective concepts largely guide the judgment and feelings of men. This is undeniable. In the world today the German—whatever the German may be—is regarded as something one would rather not have anything to do with. German Jews abroad are undesirable as Germans; they are essentially deemed Germans, not Jews. In this collective way of thought political liability is simultaneously justified as punishment of moral guilt. Historically such collective thought is not infrequent; the barbarism of war has seized whole populations and delivered them to pillage, rape and sale into slavery. And on top of it comes moral annihilation of the unfortunates in the judgment of the victor. They shall not only submit but confess and do penance. Whoever is German, whether Christian or Jew, is evil in spirit.

In the face of this fact of a widespread, though not universal, world opinion we are challenged time and again not only to defend ourselves with our simple distinction of political liability and moral guilt but to examine what truth may possibly lie in collective thinking. We do not drop the distinction, but we have to narrow it by saying that the conduct which made us liable rests on a sum total of political conditions whose nature is moral, as it were, because they help to determine individual morality. The individual cannot wholly detach himself from these conditions, for—consciously or unconsciously—he lives as a link in their chain and cannot escape from their influence even if he was in opposition. There is a sort of collective moral guilt in a people's way of life which I share as an individual, and from which grow political realities.

For political conditions are inseparable from a people's whole way of life. There is no absolute division of politics and being-human as long as man is still actualizing an existence rather than perishing in eremitical seclusion.

The Swiss, the Dutch have been formed by political conditions, and all of us in Germany have been educated for ages—we to obey, to a dynastical attitude, to be indifferent and irresponsible toward political reality—and we have ingested something of these attitudes, even if we oppose them.

The mode of life brings about political events, and the resulting political conditions in turn place their imprint on the mode of life. This is why there can be no radical separation of moral and political guilt. This is why every enlightenment of our political consciousness proportionately burdens our conscience. Political liberty has its moral aspects.

Thus, actual political liability is augmented by a knowledge and through it a different self-consciousness. That in fact all the people bear the consequences of all the acts of their government—*quidquid delirant reges plectunter Achivi*—is merely an empirical fact; that they know themselves liable is the first indication of their dawning political liberty. Freedom is actually present and not merely a claim directed toward the outside on the part of unfree men, only to the extent to which this knowledge exists and is recognized.

Inner political unfreedom senses the opposite. It obeys on the one hand, and feels not guilty on the other. Feeling guilty and hence knowing oneself to be liable is the beginning of the inner upheaval which seeks to actualize political freedom.

The contrast of the free and the unfree disposition of mind appears, for instance, in the way the leader of the state is conceived of. The question has been raised whether nations are to blame for the leaders they put up with—for example, France for Napoleon. The idea is that the vast majority did go along and desired the power and the glory which Napoleon procured. In this view Napoleon was possible only because the French would have him; his greatness was the certitude with which he understood what the mass of the people expected, what they wanted to hear, what illusions they wanted, what material realities they wanted. Could Lenz have been right in saying, "The state was born which conformed to the genius of France"? To a part, to a situation, yes—but not to the genius of a nation as such! Who can determine the genius of a nation that precisely? The same genius has spawned very different realities.

One might think that, as a man must answer for his choice of the beloved to whom marriage binds him in a lifelong community of fate, a people answers for whomever it obediently surrenders to. Error is culpable; there is no escape from its consequences.

Precisely this, however, would be the wrong approach. The unconditional attachment to one person which is possible and proper in a marriage is pernicious on principle in a state. The loyalty of followers is an apolitical relationship limited to narrow circles and primitive circumstances. In a free state all men are subject to control and change.

Hence there is twofold guilt—first, in the unconditional political surrender as such to a leader, and second, in the nature of the leader submitted to. The atmosphere of submission is a sort of collective guilt.

All the restrictions concerning our liberation from moral guilt—in favor of a merely political liability—do not invalidate what we established at the beginning and shall now restate:

We are politically responsible for our regime, for the acts of the regime, for our starting the war in this world-historical situation, and for the kind of leaders we allowed to rise to the top among us. For this reason we answer to the victors, with our labor and with our productive power, and must make such restitution as is exacted from the vanquished.

In addition there is our moral guilt. Although this always lies only in the individual who must come to terms with himself, there still is, in collectivity, something moral, as it were, that is the mode of life and of feeling, from which no individual can altogether escape and which has political significance as well. Here lies the start of self-improvement; it is up to us to take hold of it.

Individual Awareness of Collective Guilt

We feel something like a co-responsibility for the acts of members of our families. This co-responsibility cannot be objectivized. We would reject any manner of tribal liability. And yet, because of our consanguinity we are inclined to feel involved whenever wrong is done by someone in the family— and also inclined, therefore, depending on the type and circumstances of the wrong and its victims, to make it up to them even if we are neither morally nor legally accountable.

Thus the German—that is, the German-speaking individual—feels involved in everything growing from German roots. It is not the liability of a national but the involvement of one who shares the life of the German spirit and soul—who is of one tongue, one stock, one fate with all the others—which here becomes the ground, not of a tangible guilt, but of an analogue of co-responsibility.

We further feel that we share not only in what is done at present—thus being co-responsible for the deeds of our contemporaries—but in the continuity of tradition. We have to take on ourselves the guilt of our fathers. That the spiritual conditions of German life contained the possibility for such a regime is a fact for which all of us are co-responsible. Of course this does not mean that we must acknowledge "the world of German ideas" or "German thought of the past" in general as the sources of the National-Socialist misdeeds. But it does mean that our national tradition contains something, mighty and threatening, which is our moral ruin.

We know ourselves not only as individuals but as Germans. Every one, in his authentic being, is the German people. Who does not remember moments in his life when he said to himself, in opposition and in despair of his nation, "I am Germany"—or, in jubilant harmony with it, "I, too, am Germany!" The German character has no other form than these individuals. Hence the demands of transmutation, of rebirth, of rejection of evil are made of the nations in the form of a task for each individual.

Because in my innermost soul I cannot help feeling collectively, being German is to me—is to everyone—not a state of being but a task. This is altogether different from making the nation absolute. I am a human being first of all; in particular I am a Frisian, a professor, a German, linked closely enough for a fusion of souls with other collective groups, and more or less closely with all groups that have become palpable for me. For moments this proximity enables me to feel almost like a Jew or Dutchman or Englishman. Throughout it, however, the given of my being German—that is, essentially, of life in the mother tongue—is so pervasive that in a way which is rationally not conceivable, which is even rationally refutable, I feel co-responsible for what Germans do and have done.

I feel closer to those Germans who also feel this way—without becoming melodramatic about it—and farther from the ones whose soul seems to deny this link. And this proximity means, above all, a common inspiring task—of not being German as we happen to be, but becoming German as we are not yet but ought to be, and as we hear ourselves challenged by our great ancestors rather than by the history of our national idols. Because of our feeling of collective guilt we feel the entire task of the renewal of being-human from its origin—the task which is given to all men on earth but which appears more urgently, more perceptibly, as decisively as all existence, wherever its own guilt brings a people face to face with nothingness.

As a philosopher I now seem to have strayed completely into the realm of feeling and to have abandoned conception. Indeed language fails at this point, and we may recall only negatively that all our differentiations—notwithstanding the fact that we hold them to be true and are by no means rescinding them—must not become resting places. We must not use them to let matters drop and free ourselves from the pressure under which we continue on our path through life and which is to bring to maturity what we hold most precious, the eternal essence of our soul. . . .

The Way of Purification

Purification in action means, first of all, restitution.

On a political level it means to fulfill, in inner affirmation, those legalized commitments which—though it means tightening our belts—provide for the restoration of a part of what was destroyed to the nations attacked by Hitler Germany.

Besides the legal form assuring a just distribution of the burden, such restorations presuppose life, the ability as well as opportunity to work. The political will to make reparation must inevitably flag if the political acts of the victors destroy these presuppositions. For then we should not have a peace aimed at reparation but continued war aiming at further destruction.

There is more to reparation, however. Everyone who is deeply affected by the guilt he shares will wish to help anyone wronged by the arbitrary despotism of the lawless regime.

There are two different motivations which must not be confused. The first calls on us to help wherever there is distress, no matter what the cause—simply because the need is there and calls for help. The second requires us to grant a special right to those deported, robbed, pillaged, tortured, and exiled by the Hitler regime.

Both demands are fully justified, but there is a difference in motivation. Where guilt is not felt, all distress is immediately reduced to the same plane. If I want to make up for the guilt in which I share, I must differentiate the victims of distress.

This way of purification by reparation is one we cannot escape. Yet there is much more to purification. Even reparation is not earnestly willed and does not fulfill its moral purpose except as it ensues from our cleansing transmutation. The clarification of our guilt is at the same time the clarification of our new life and its possibilities. From it spring seriousness and resolution.

Once that happens, life is no longer simply there to be naively, gaily enjoyed. We may seize the happiness of existence, where it is granted to us, in intermediate moments, in breathing spells—but it does not fill our existence; we accept it as the pleasing enchantment before a background of melancholy. Essentially, our life is permitted only to be consumed by a task.

The result is modest resignation. In inner action before transcendence we become aware of our human finitude and imperfectability. Humility comes to be our nature.

Then, without seeking power, are we able to effect, in loving struggle, the clarification of what is true and to unite with each other within this struggle.

Then we are capable of unaggressive silence—it is from the simplicity of silence that the clarity of the communicable will emerge.

Then nothing counts any longer but truth and activity. Without guile we are ready to bear what fate has in store for us. Whatever happens will, while we live, remain the human task that cannot be completed in the world.

Purification is the way of man as man. There, purification by way of unfolding the notion of guilt is just one moment. Purification is not primarily achieved by outward actions—not by an outward finishing, not by magic. Rather, purification is an inner process which is never ended but in which we continually become ourselves. Purification is a matter of our freedom. Everyone comes to stand again and again before the fork in the road, before the choice between purification and the murky.

Purification is not the same for all. Each goes his personal way. This way can not be anticipated nor pointed out by anyone else. General ideas can do no more than make aware, perhaps awaken.

If at this close of our discussions of guilt we ask what purification consists in, no concrete reply is possible beyond what has been said. If something cannot be realized as an end of rational will but occurs as a metamorphosis through inner action, one can only repeat the indefinite, comprehensive phrases: illumination and growing transparency as we are uplifted—love for man.

As for guilt, one way [of purification] is to think through the thoughts here expounded. They must not only be abstractly thought by means of the intellect, but visibly carried out; they must be brought to mind, appropriated or rejected with one's own being. Carrying this out and its consequence—that is purification. It is not something new, tacked on at the end.

Purification is the condition of our political freedom, too; for only consciousness of guilt leads to the consciousness of solidarity and co-responsibility without which there can be no liberty.

Political liberty begins when, within the majority of a people, the individual feels co-responsible for the politics of his community. It begins when the individual not merely covets and chides, when he demands of himself, rather, to see reality and not to act upon the faith—misplaced in politics—in an earthly paradise failing of actualization only because of the others' stupidity and ill will. It begins when he knows, rather, that politics looks in the concrete world for the negotiable path in each situation, guided by the ideal of being-human as freedom.

In short: without purification of the soul there is no political freedom.

How we progress with our inner purification based on our consciousness that we are guilty can be measured by our reaction to attack.

Without consciousness of guilt our reaction to every attack remains a counterattack. Once we have been deeply shaken in our innermost being, however, the external attack will merely brush lightly over the surface. It may still offend and hurt us, but it does not penetrate to the interior of the soul.

Where we have made the consciousness of guilt our own, we bear false and unjust accusations with tranquility. For pride and defiance have melted away.

To him who truly feels guilt, so that his consciousness of being is in transformation, reproach from others seems like harmless child's play, unable to hurt where the actual consciousness of guilt is an unavoidable goad that has forced self-consciousness to take on a new form. Reproached like this, one rather feels uneasiness at the other's unconcern and unawareness. If an atmosphere of trust prevails, one may remind him of the potential for guilt in every human being. But one can no longer get angry.

Without the enlightenment and transformation of our soul, sensitivity would only increase in helpless impotence. The poison of psychological transformations would ruin us internally. We must be ready to put up with reproaches, must listen to and then examine them. We must seek out rather than shun attacks on us, because they enable us to examine our own thinking. Our inner attitude will stand the test.

Such purification makes us free. The course of events does not lie in the hand of any man though man may go incalculably far in guiding his existence. Because there remains uncertainty and the possibility of new and greater disasters; because the natural consequence of the transformation in man's consciousness of guilt is by no means a reward in the form of a new happiness of existence: therefore purification alone can free us so as to be ready for whatever comes. The pure soul can truly live in this tension: to be tirelessly active in the world on behalf of what is possible in the face of total destruction.

In regarding world events we do well to think of Jeremiah. When Jerusalem had been destroyed, state and country lost, the prophet forcibly taken along by the last few Jews who were fleeing to Egypt—when he had to see those sacrificing to Isis in the hope that she would do more for them than Jehovah, his disciple Baruch despaired. And Jeremiah answered, "The Lord saith thus: Behold; that which I have built will I break down, and that which I have planted I will pluck up, and seekest thou great things for thyself? Seek them not." What does that mean? That God is, is enough. When all things fade away, God is—that is the only fixed point.

But what is true in the face of death, in extremity, turns into a dangerous temptation if fatigue, impatience, despair drive man to plunge into it prematurely. For this stance at the limits is true only if borne by the unswerving deliberation always to seize what remains possible while life endures. Our share is humility and moderation.

Selection 60

WHEN POLITICS FAILS:
THE POWER OF THE ETHICAL IDEA

EDITORS:
The previous selection ends with Jaspers's idea that purification must be the basis of a redirection in the political life of Germany. This idea is developed by him in the present selection in a more general sense. In face of the dangers threatening mankind a new kind of politics is needed, an innovation that does not simply consist of a change in political institutions but is grounded in a redirection in ethical convictions. Since it is the foundation of politics, the ethical cannot be intrinsic to politics, else it would be definable by what is politcally

expedient. The ethical has to be recognized as being beyond the political; thus it indicates a limit of politics.

The selection is a translation by the editors of *Die Atombombe und die Zukunft des Menschen*, pp. 49–53. For E. B. Ashton's translation see *The Future of Mankind*, pp. 24–27.

TEXT:

The Supra-Political Ethos without which Humanity is Lost

In the past, folly and wickedness had limited consequences; today they draw all mankind to perdition. Now, unless all of us live with and for one another, we shall all be destroyed together. This new situation demands an answer appropriate to it.

The answer to the human situation which has always been calamitous was given long ago and has been repeated often. The *prophets* of the Old Testament dared to give this answer and taught it to mankind for all time. But in the course of time—whether meant earnestly or not—this answer was given in vain time and again, and many have become sick and tired of it. Nonetheless, let us recall the ancient and ever new and always valid demand which is made by our situation today with the utmost urgency: It is not enough to find new institutions; we must change ourselves, our characters, our moral-political wills. What has been present in the individual person for a long time already, what was effective in small groups but remained powerless in society as a whole, has now become the condition for the continued existence of mankind. I do not believe that I am exaggerating. Whoever continues to live in the manner in which he has lived up to now has not grasped the menace. Merely thinking this intellectually does not yet mean absorbing it into the actuality of one's life. Men must turn their lives around, if they do not want to lose them. If they want to continue living, they must change. If they think only of today, then the day will come on which the atomic war begins through which most likely everything will come to an end.

The Way Things are Today

But what is today's factual situation? On the one hand, the politically effective forces do not reach far enough, and on the other, we can see nothing of a change in moral motivations. Man remains what he has always been: the same brutality, ruthlessness, belligerent recklessness, over against the same indolence, unwillingness to see, need for quiet and the lack of provident concern among those who happen to be well off at the moment (a condition in which bold adventurers have always found them easy prey). We see the same brazen blackmail and the same yielding to it, the same general hiding behind the legal argumentation of a merely fictional authority that is secretly despised by some and seen by others as the guarantee of their comfort and which can be abandoned by all at the decisive moment.

The change can come about only through the way in which each person lives his life. It depends, above all, on him alone. Each small act, each word, the conduct of each among the millions and billions—all are significant. What happens on a large scale is merely a symptom of what is being done in the privacy of the many. Whoever cannot live in peace with his neighbor, who, through his malicious behavior, makes life difficult for the other, who secretly wishes him ill, who slanders, lies, commits adultery, does not honor his parents, takes no responsibility for the education of his children, whoever breaks the laws—he prevents, through his acts (which are never merely private, not even behind locked doors) peace in the world. He does, on a small scale, what, on a larger scale, brings about the self-destruction of humanity. There is nothing in human life and action which does not also have political significance.

Thus the actions of the statesmen also stand in need of illumination out of the ethos which is the presupposition for the survival of humanity. No matter if, at the conference table, a man has delivered the most impassioned moral-political speeches; if at home he behaves perfidiously he shares in the culpability for the continuing calamity. If, with his tolerant attitude toward the human, all-too-human, he tolerates within his jurisdiction men who lead lives of depravity, he undermines the spirit of trustworthiness in the whole. If someone desires the miracle of change on the part of moral man and yet, in spite of all his intelligence, participates in the world, thoughtlessly going on as before, then he misuses a formulation that has lost its binding character as a smokescreen and makes morality itself suspect. Thus it goes on: in talk, negotiation, enterprise, organization—until the day when everything is wiped out.

To be sure, we may ask how "private" conduct can affect political action, when obviously one has nothing to do with the other. The question rightly points to the absence of a direct causal link, but it fails to recognize that man's private sphere is a symptom of his personality: he remains the same in whatever sphere he may move. It is only opportunism which, in one sphere, lets him obey rules he may flout in others. A stockbroker keeps his word because one failure to do so would finish him in his profession. The politician follows the rules of a community of nations because their violation would, under normal circumstances, have consequences that are too unpleasant. But in politics, in distinction to particular professions, the normal is itself the exception which has the appearance of permanence. It always rests either on a foundation which is the strength derived from the most recent decisions remembered as effective; or it stands poised on the slippery sands of oblivion. What a politican does—not in obedience to an ethos but prompted by the opportuneness of a certain sphere and the conventions of a social group—this he cannot continue to do when it is a matter of "to be or not to be." At that point motives come into play that are different from such as may pertain to a determinate realm and which are held in reserve until applied to a specific case. The motives that are to prevail here can be effective only under certain conditions. One condition is that they have in fact been at work perennially under politically indifferent circumstances and throughout an individual's life. Another, that in politics itself the consciousness of the ultimate "to be or not to be" always demands to be heard out of the dim background, and that it is not forgotten in the cozyness of pacific amity and cunning. The ethos is one and indivisible.

The Independence of the Supra-Political

Though the political is dependent on the supra-political, the supra-political must itself remain independent from politics. Though politics has value only in the service of the supra-political, it kills the supra-political through politicization. The absolutization of politics leads to failure even vis-à-vis the political tasks. If politics does not remain dependent on the supra-political it may rush blindly into ruin. . . .

The Unplannable

In contrast to all things political, the ethos cannot be planned. The wrong purpose would be operative if moral earnestness were to be intended not for its own sake but as a means of preserving human life. The reverse is true. The unconditionality in supra-political ethos may have the saving of human life as its consequence but not as its goal. To posit ethos as a means of saving nothing but one's life is self-defeating because in such goal-directedness ethos itself is abandoned.

As everything that can be planned shifts to the political realm one would think that something unplannable has to take place. Here the question as to what we are to do no longer finds an answer that tells us how to go about it; instead we hearken to the invocation, by the prophets of old, of dormant possibilities. Today, face to face with the ultimate threat, more is needed than merely a better insight: a turning on the part of man. But this turnabout cannot be brought about forcibly.

We can point to the realities and give voice to the millennial challenge. Both would have to penetrate all the way into our schools: what men can know about future possibilities, and what is demanded by that voice of the prophets. Whether, in this way, something happens in the individual person, that is up to the freedom of each individual, even the youngster. If the fundamental facts of our political existence are laid bare today and the consequences of the different modes of behavior are developed, then the answer resides in the individual and is expressed not through an opinion but through his life.

Can Man Change Himself?

Is it possible for man to change? Can he turn himself around? Was he not always the same in the thirty or fifty centuries of his known history and, by inference, in those that went before? History teaches that anything great made by men was soon destroyed by men. It is said that man cannot change. History is a field of rubble. On grounds of experience we can expect no change.

What is correct in this thesis refers to the natural given of man as one living creature among others. But it does not apply to what makes man genuinely human and not merely one zoological species among others. Although his psychophysical constitution remains the same, man turns himself around time and again and thus changes his historic appearance. All that is great, luminous and inspiring arose—contrary to all possible expectation and in spite of all that constantly drags him down—out of a different primal source. In spite of what is comprehended by biology and psychology, historically man can change. This is what happened with the ancient prophets in Israel, with the thinkers and poets of Greece, with the innovations of late antiquity and the first Christian centuries, with the biblically grounded ethos of the Protestant world. To be sure, each of these changes soon withered away; but their memory challenges us.

The Dilution of Ethos into Morality

Ethos becomes morality when it exhausts itself in commandments and prohibitions. This morality still has its own truth but only as the moment of something that goes beyond it. To be sure, it is unconditionally valid and cannot be passed over insofar as it is what is called "form" in Kant's Categorical Imperative. But one cannot calculate how it is to be fulfilled concretely by the material of the temporal situation. The content cannot be deduced from the form of the unconditional. . . .

Ethos is diluted into mere morality when it is detached from the courage to sacrifice which is the ground of our actuality, and from reason that is more than mere intellect. It is reason which guides ethos as well as the courage to sacrifice, although both of these, together with reason, come out of the unconditional. What is hidden in the ethical is more than merely ethical.

Selection 61

THE SUPRA-POLITICAL POWER OF SACRIFICE

EDITORS:
The background to this selection is as follows: The search for a new politics in which the modern tendencies of freedom and liberation can be realized and in

which the novel situation of the threat of nuclear war can be faced, leads to a disclosure of the limits imposed on political reality by supra-political dimensions of human significance. One such dimension is that of ethical redirection (Selection 60); another is the human capacity and readiness for sacrificing oneself and others. This is pertinent to the politics of fear to which the practitioner of nuclear politics may tend to take recourse. But the political import of the supra-political power of sacrifice is of wider interest and is explored by Jaspers in this selection.

In connection with a discussion of the responsibility of the statesman, Jaspers considers Max Weber's distinction between *Gesinnungsethik* and *Verantwortungsethik*. This section is omitted in the English version of the book. *Gesinnungsethik* is translated by "ethics of [moral] conviction," and *Verantwortungsethik* by "ethics of [social] responsibility."

The following is a translation by the editors of *Die Atombombe und die Zukunft des Menschen*, pp. 70–77, 92. Parts of this may be found in the English version prepared by E. B. Ashton under the title *The Future of Mankind*, pp. 41–43, 55–56.

TEXT:

Pacifism and the Atom Bomb

The correct insight is abroad today that the atom bomb cannot be abolished without abolishing war altogether. But many still believe they can render the atom bomb alone ineffectual. Their passions are directed not against war but against the atom bomb. They protest only against the bomb in the way in which pacifists protest against all war. But just as pacifistic organizations have contributed absolutely nothing to the prevention of wars, all present endeavors which merely repudiate the atom bomb without seeing it within the whole context of the real acts of nations and of the manifest motives of most people, are in vain. For they do not come close to the root of the human calamity but stick to the symptoms. Because they divert us from what is essential, they contribute to the obfuscation; as if they could achieve something with their indignation. For whether they are pacifists or not they continue, behind a façade of opinion and emotion, in their daily actions and judgments, in that way of living and thinking which—as the rotten ground of human actuality— has those horrors as its consequence. Their fearful adjurations are, as such, just as untrue as their glossing over the facts of their own lives. But actuality disregards such empty opinions. For over against self-satisfied consciousness "truth is in league with actuality" (Hegel). That is: Truth, to be effective, demands that we do not fool around with symptoms but see the fundamental process at work in the source of the calamity.

Actuality, however, is, on the one hand, the atom bomb and on the other the present-day ethical-political condition of mankind. What truth is "in league" with these actualities?. . . .

The Nature of Sacrifice

In the situation of brute force there may become actual out of the ground of things something that is incomprehensible to our rationalistic thinking, limited as it is to purposes in the world. Moreover, it quashes our absolute will to live and therefore tends to be talked away. . . .

The self-affirmation of a people in its will to freedom manifests itself in sacrifice. But sacrifice for what? For a life worth living? For the preservation of this people and its traditions? Certainly; but this is not enough. There is more contained in the sacrifice: something that cannot be expressed at all as a purpose in the world, and only inadequately as a meaning which goes beyond this purpose: It is the sacrifice for the sake of the deity whose unfathomable paths have led to where the possibility of risking this sacrifice becomes unavoidable for him who wants to salvage for himself the consciousness of his eternal being and hence of his transcendence. Whoever feels that his submission, his refusal to take the sacrifice upon himself, would have as its consequence his corruption as a soul in the world and his descent into absolute indignity, realizes at the same time that, together with his denial of sacrifice, there would be a betrayal of something in the ground of things. Together with his surrender of his being-human just in order to stay alive he would achieve merely the nullity of nothingness in an illusion of life.

The remembrance of the survivors is not the purpose of the sacrifice but its possible consequence in the world (whose absence does not, however, negate the meaning of this sacrifice). These survivors will someday attempt once more what has failed in the past. Martyrs enhance the powers of those whose example they become.

But in reality there remains the inflexible boundary line: it is only by leadership and organization that anything political can achieve permanence and become actualized. The subtle terror of a superior power can cause all freedom to wither away. The battle of the free can but exacerbate their misery; the end is the liquidation of some and the starvation and freezing to death of the others. Perhaps they experience in this their death their dignity of which the world knows nothing.

There is no limit to naked force for it can destroy everything as existence. But there in *one* limit: namely, that in destruction can become manifest what is more actual than existence and all brute force.

Force and Sacrifice.   It is true of human existence that the possibility of a final rational order in human relationships founders in the face of brute force. Where there is such force—killing and being-killed—there is the battle that demands the sacrifice of existence.

Where this extreme does not take place, where, rather, life is lived under an order still secured by force, a "peaceful" battle is fought for the material conditions of life. This battle is as pitiless as that fought by physical force. Sacrifice belongs to existence, be it either as the momentary risk of one's life or as a permanent attrition due to the loss of life's possibilities.

But this is not merely a fact of life for as such it would be common to all living things. What is essential for man is the *conscious* sacrifice which, as conscious risk in the world, cannot be comprehended adequately out of the world. At the foundation of all that is exalted in man lies a sacrifice, and even in foundering this sacrifice is still a fulfillment in which infinite substance is made manifest.

Man knows himself as he himself only when he proves himself through his courage and contempt of death. These have a different grounding than mere life. There is more for man than life.

To be sure, self-denial—should we remain alive—is merely partial sacrifice. But we can experience it as if it were the destruction out of which another life comes to be.

Veiling the Sacrifice.   We seek to hide from view the sacrifice and its meaning because we cannot bear it. Or we try to invalidate it, as it were, by renunciation meant to take its place. We do not come face to face with it because we do not want to make the sacrifice. We would like to be happy without sacrifice. But in vain do we wrest our happiness from the sacrifice which we have evaded. Without sacrifice a rift cuts through our existence which becomes muddied in self-deception.

Beyond the World or in the World.   Sacrifice assumes two distinct aspects: withdrawal from the world and action in the world.

The sacrifice is world-less if a life is wasted in a wild, arbitrary battle, a battle that merely makes the fighter proudly conscious of his own contempt for death; it is world-less also if it consists in blind submissive obedience out of obscure expectations.

Even ascetics and saints who are prepared to die at all times, without will to partake of the world and without responsibility for anything in the world, make a world-less sacrifice.

This is also the case with conscientious objectors who do not want to save their life but are ready to bear all suffering and all humiliation, who would rather be killed by their state than participate in killing; in short, those who make it harder for themselves than for the others rather than easier. For they shift the sacrifice to where they will be despised as well, while the others make that sacrifice in which they are supported and commended by the community of all.

But the risk of death that wants life *in the world* is quite another matter. Through this risk there first arises genuine earnestness. Only he is grounded in life who is prepared to give up this life and who sacrifices it as he lets himself be constantly consumed by his task. Such sacrifice—unless it comes to an end in sacrificial death—acts constructively, becoming-world, fulfillingly. If, however, dying is called for, than this man—after having thought out and done what caution demanded and having considered the hierarchy of what is essential—becomes credible in his own eyes by being able to die in tranquility and to bear the shipwreck of his cause.

Sacrifice For Something and Sacrifice in Itself. We asked: If life is sacrificed for the sake of life, then for which life? For what purpose the self-affirmation which offers the sacrifice? What is worthy of this sacrifice?

Here lies the insuperable paradox: the sacrifice is made for something in the world, a sacrifice which retains its meaning even if everything in the world for which it occurred miscarries. This means: that for which the sacrifice is made does not make this sacrifice adequately comprehensible if this "for" is merely a purpose in the world.

To understand a soldier's death as a means to an end demeans the soldier. To say that he has died in vain if the objective is not attained robs his sacrifice of its substance. The eternal meaning of the sacrifice is independent of the success of that for which it was brought into the world. And yet it has substance only in unity with the will toward an actualization in the world.

The "what-for" is something for which one fights in the sense that life would not be worth living if one did not risk the sacrifice. But bound up with the sacrifice is something supra-temporal and supra-sensory and unconditional. The sacrifice, even if "in vain," is not "senseless."

Sacrifice reveals the secret at the limits of all matters human. Man's awareness of this fact reaches back to primordial times when it was expressed in the myth of the god who sacrificed himself. . . .

The Situation of Brute Force in the Political Struggle

Politics is based on the possibility of the use of physical force. The application of this physical force is the task of the soldier.

There are two extremes: Politics as such which wants nothing but power, and the supra-political which lives in a different world for the sake of the purity of soul. The supra-political no longer gives meaning to pure politics. What counts is the will to power of this existence; but because it lacks content, it is nothing. The supra-political turns away from this world and brings politics to an end; the relation to politics is lost; politics is left to its own devices. In fact, the extremes can bring each other forth; indeed, they can find themselves together in one and the same person but they cannot combine in him (for his soul is now divided, he is no longer he himself).

Grand Politics, on the other hand, is guided by the supra-political. This consisted at first of the ethical demand to eliminate war, in accordance with the commandment: Thou shalt not kill. It was the basis which gave meaning to the regulation of force on the part of the constitutional state. But then the supra-political became the meaning of sacrifice when a life was risked for the sake of a life worth living. But this risking of one's life must not be bereft of meaning even if its purpose fails and everything suffers shipwreck. The way in which the supra-political comes into play in politics—that is the grounding force in politics itself.

The problem is discussed as the question about the relationship of politics and morality. It is argued that morality is a private matter. Politics is a matter of more than morality. Transferring private morality to politics means a violation of the duty which a statesman takes upon himself vis-à-vis the existence and the interests of his nation, people, country. Response: The splitting of the ethos into private and political morality annuls them both.

It is argued: In politics the statesman bears the responsibility for others, for a people. What he is permitted to risk and sacrifice for himself as an individual he may not carry out as the risk and sacrifice of the others. Response: In politics, responsibility for others inevitably leads the statesman to draw the people into the risk he has himself taken on, as a common risk. If he thinks responsibly, the will to sacrifice must be shared. The ethical question is: do the politician and the military leader identify themselves, in the long run, with the whole which they represent as they lead it, and do so to such an extent that they risk their own persons more than others do, that the question of life and death is faced by them first?

It is argued: In morality moral conviction is decisive, in politics it is success. Something done out of conviction may have ruinous consequences. This concerns only the person who took them upon himself. But what is done in politics may not have ruinous consequences and cannot be justified by good intentions since it affects the whole people. Response: In the actions of the individual the question of success or failure is also not a matter of indifference. The individual is not alone and hence may not sacrifice himself without regard for others, his neighbors and friends. And conversely, there is also in politics a moral disposition, namely, that of the people whom the statesman represents. Evil action on behalf of the people, which thus becomes the beneficiary of evil, is calamitous for them in the long run.

In every instance, whether of a private or political nature, mere "good will" or mere "opinion" with no thought behind it and without a clear picture of the total reality are irresponsible. Lack of responsibility, whether individual or political, is always immoral.

But the questions that lead us into the depths of decision on the part of man about himself and for which a rationally comprehensible, unequivocal solution cannot be found in these depths, cannot be answered as simply as the ones above. Max Weber treated them when he formulated the concepts "ethics of [moral] conviction" and "ethics of [social] responsibility" that have become famous.

He formulated first of all the "irreconcilably contradictory maxims": The practitioner of the ethics of moral conviction "acts rightly and leaves the success to God. . . . If the consequences of his acts which flow from his moral conviction are bad, then he holds responsible not the acting individual but the world, the stupidity of the others or the will of God who created them." The practitioner of the ethics of responsibility, on the other hand, demands "that one has to accept responsibility for the (foreseeable) consequences of one's actions." He reckons with the usual human defects, has "no right at all to presuppose man's goodness and perfection." He does not shift the blame for the consequences of his own acts onto the shoulders of others.

There are no universal ethics that could establish commandments whose contents are the same for all material spheres, for relationships in business, officialdom, family, between the sexes, etc. But the question as to what is the all-embracing One that manifests itself in this diversity is as inescapable as it is rationally insoluble.

As regards the ethical demands of politics the following is of fundamental importance: Politics operates with the specific means of power behind which stands violent force. This specific means brings about the special nature of all ethical problems in politics.

Brute force is a morally dangerous means. The achievement of "good" purposes is, in politics, bound in numerous instances to putting up with morally suspect means. "No ethics in the world can tell us when and how and to what extent the morally good end hallows the morally dangerous means. . . . It is impossible to decree morally which end is to hallow which means, if one is to make any concession to this principle." Ethics of moral concern and of social responsibility cannot be subsumed under a common principle in this way.

But these statements are merely Max Weber's point of departure, not the conclusions of his ethical deliberations. First he thinks through the consequences of the ethics of moral conviction on the one side and the ethics of social responsibility on the other.

When the practitioner of the ethics of moral conviction wants to act, he founders because he must disavow altogether the justification of the means by the end. Since political action is bound to the specific means of force, he must be consistent and reject all action that makes use of this morally dangerous means.

But the practitioners of the ethics of moral conviction are not wont to proceed in this manner. Even if they have just finished preaching at us to respond with love to violence, they exhort us, in the next moment, to use violence ourselves, deceiving themselves and others into believing that this would be "the final" violence which would bring about the annihilation of all violence.

The practitioner of the ethics of social responsibility derives his sense of responsibility from something supra-political. For the cause in whose service he seeks political power, or that for which his self-affirmation comes into play, cannot be found by way of a political thought but must be given to him instead. Thus, for example, it is his faith in the national or the universally human, the social-ethical or the religious meaning of the existence he wants to maintain or attain which gives substance to his politics. "Otherwise the curse of the insignificance of all creatures lies heavily even on the superficially greatest political successes." The practitioner of the ethics of social responsibility is dependent on something that is not politics in order to engage in politics. He does not wish for power for its own sake since he does not want his efforts to lead "into the void and the meaningless."

The person acting politically is able to take responsibility upon himself to the extent to which he can foresee the consequences. But this foresight is always limited. Deeds have consequences different from what was intended. "It is a fundamental fact of history that the eventual result of political action often, no, just about regularly, stands in a totally inadequate and often down-right paradoxical relationship to its original meaning." The practitioner of the ethics of social responsibility is dependent on the cohesion of consequences within which he acts but which he can never survey at a glance. His "service to the cause" gives substance to his actions, a substance which is taken up by something else which he does not know to begin with and which, in retrospect, he does not comprehend as being necessary.

The fact that political responsibility enters a relationship with brute force, means that it deals with the suspect and the dangerous, i.e., with the "dangerous forces." Intimacy with "diabolical powers" has consequences as regards the motives of political action. The practitioner of the ethics of social responsibility must dare to lie, break contracts, kill. In principle, he cannot want to do this and yet must carry it out in actuality and hence even want to do it if, conscious of his responsibility for the cause, he does battle for its sake, for a cause whose self-affirmation he has made his political task. He is enmeshed in the evil with which he deals. If physical force is being used already and he must respond in kind, then trickery, deception, and lying are unavoidable. Were these unavoidable already where politics were practiced previously (albeit necessarily with an eye to possible force)? And are they all the more inescapable, the closer one gets to possible physical force?

The practitioner of the ethics of social responsibility is not the unscrupulous practitioner of *Realpolitik*. He does not crave power as such but the power for a cause. If this cause is destroyed through the application of the means, this politics has lost its meaning. Where is the borderline between the evil that is impossible because of the encompassing ethos and the evil which is called for out of responsibility? This question cannot be answered save through reference to decision:

This *political decision* is neither a calculable consequence in the service of an arbitrary self-affirmation, nor is it the unequivocal consequence of a dogmatically formulated ethics of moral conviction. Rather, it is something to which one cannot appeal and on the basis of which no one may justify himself. However the concrete decision is not allowable because of its arbitrary character. Whatever cannot be adequately justified manifests itself to responsibility through an inner voice, as it were, which, when expressed, is capable of convincing a community and of leaving its moral-political imprint. It leads to actualization in a course of action that is constructive in the world because it stands within a continuity and has coherence.

The practitioners of the ethics of social responsibility stand within a tremendous tension. This tension cannot be borne by those who—collapsing— live with the rationally comfortable extreme consequences either of the *Realpolitik* of the bare pragmatics of power or in the apolitical, politically non-responsible ethics of moral conviction; nor can those bear the tension who, letting go completely, prefer thoughtless confusion to such consequences. This is no place for children and boys. Hence Max Weber asks "what kind of person one has to be in order to be allowed to stick his hand into the spokes of the wheel of history." And to him it is "immeasurably moving" when "a person who perceives his responsibility for the consequences as real and, with his whole soul, says at one point: I can do no other, here I stand. For this situation, to be sure, is bound to occur at one time or other for each of us who is not inwardly dead."

To that extent, Max Weber says explicitly, the ethics of moral conviction and of social responsibility are not absolute opposites but complement each other; only together do they constitute the person who can have a vocation for politics.

Hence what was at first—and remains—an "unresolvable" opposition now becomes "complement." The ethics of social responsibility is not identical with an absence of conviction. Rather, it turns out that: relative to the unequivocal ethics of moral conviction that does not take consequences into account and the *Realpolitik* of bare pragmatics of power which lacks conviction, the ethics of social responsibility is preeminent, i.e., the antithesis of the ethics of moral conviction and that of social responsibility becomes misleading.

Max Weber sees the image of the statesman as the union of three factors: passion, feeling of responsibility, a sure eye. *Passion* in the sense of passionate devotion to a "cause," to "the god or demon who governs it"; a *feeling of responsibility* toward this very cause as the guiding star of his actions: and *a sure eye* as the ability "to let the realities affect one without losing one's inner concentration and calm," to preserve "a distance toward things and men." The problem is how to "draw together, in the same soul, hot passion and cool judgment". . . .

Conclusion

The supra-political nature of sacrifice, if it is to be generally substantiated, leads only to dead ends. Thought in general terms, it has no meaning that would justify it. It is concrete and historic. There is no sacrifice as such (except in an inaccessible metaphysical sense) that would be true and great. For example, a sacrifice as a proof which a person gives to himself about himself to the effect that he is superior to his life, hence risks it and dares everything, being indifferent to purpose and time; this appears as the irreverent revolt against transcendence which demands life in this world of us. If, however, the purpose gives decisive meaning to the sacrifice, then this is always insufficient. The notion of sacrifice, being universal, can only point to what is not universal, to the unique in the transcendent grounding of an actuality that is impervious to knowledge.

But sacrifice is the ineluctable ground of being-human. If it can be found no longer in its soldierly embodiment, it will take on other forms. The renunciations, self-denials, risks which in the ongoing itinerary are aspects of a new reason, cannot be specified in advance. Only this is certain: without sacrifice there is no being-human. Great renunciations are not only necessary for the salvation of a free world but are necessary also in order to recover man from the lostness of a life that, after a circumscribed period of work perceived as a burden, is used up in a consumer's existence devoid of substance. Sacrifice would not only make possible the state of peace but would give it content.

If a lasting state of peace is to be achieved, then only if the greatness and the strength and the courage of sacrifice, hitherto known to history through the life of the soldier, were to be actualized today no less than before.

Selection 62

REASON AND DEMOCRACY

EDITORS:
The new politics—the politics that would promote freedom in the face of the danger of totalitarianism and nuclear war—would, according to Jaspers, have to bring communicative reason into play. But the idea of reason in politics

seems to be utopian. Jaspers faces this problem in several ways. One is to make manifest that the concept and practices of democracy are the "ineluctable" way for reason "to become effective and durable," not only among political leaders but among the very peoples of the body politic. The following is an excerpt from that discussion. It is an emendation by the editors of E. B. Ashton's translation of *Die Atombombe und die Zukunft des Menschen*, pp. 419–24; in English, *The Future of Mankind*, pp. 291–99.

TEXT:
It would be folly to expect the world to be put right by a few reasonable men. To become effective and durable, reason must pervade the nations. This is why "democracy" is ineluctable. It is its purpose to bring forth reason in the collective thinking and acting of a people as well as among peoples.

What we hear today about democracy is paradoxical. All governments, whether totalitarian or free, claim to be based on the will of the people and call themselves democratic. All of them present the people as their sovereign, at least in mass meetings, national celebrations, and festive orations. As a word, "democracy" has become publicly sacrosanct, an idol of our time.

In print, however, democracy is rejected by a large body of opinion. It is described as unable to put reason into practice and thus, in fact, resulting in the worst tyranny, either by the majority or by total rule. It is said that human-ity by its nature lacks reason and hence makes democracy madness.

Against this antithesis of idolizing and demonizing democracy, its real meaning can be established only by reason itself. Then, instead of glorifying or damning it, we shall examine its factuality in all its ramifications and see it as our hard, stony, but only possible road. All the basic ideas about the risks of democracy have been with us since De Tocqueville and Max Weber, but in these men we find a pained, indeed a shocked awareness of its possibilities combined with an ineradicable faith in man and his freedom. The ruthlessly critical view of these political thinkers is not directed against democracy but toward its self-improvement; for they realize that the actual course of social history and the necessity of reason itself make democracy indispensable. The human task is to surmount its risks in the unforeseeable course of history by intense, patient effort and practical, effective self-criticism.

Churchill is said to have called democracy the worst form of government, except for all others. His sense of humor found a word for the fundamental disorder of human affairs, in which democracy seems the least noxious form of government, being the only visible or conceivable way to provide opportu-nities for incalculable improvement by the growth of reason in the peoples themselves.

Only in small states, under favorable circumstances, can the love of home and country become one with democratic thinking. In large nations, the human ruthlessness in politics and the terrors and dangers of democracy are felt more strongly than the beauty of its challenge. Shortly before the First World War, I was present at a conversation between a Swiss jurist and Max Weber, the great German political thinker. Both men were profoundly democratic. "We must love the state," said the Swiss. "What?" replied Weber, "On top of it all one should love the monster?" But what is democracy? The notions regarding it are manifold and contradictory. But its idea is unitary. Let us try to state it in a few theses.

1. Reason can prevail reliably only if it guides the people along with their leaders, not just a few lone, aloof individuals. This is impossible unless every individual has a chance to participate in thinking and acting. Democracy, therefore, requires the whole people to be educated so as to develop everyone's thought and judgment to the limits of his natural capacity. It calls for publicity of thought, especially of news, discussions, propositions, and plans.

2. Reason does not mean possession but being on the way. Only by way of universal education can it lead to democracy as common thought and action. It follows that democracy is never in its final form but keeps changing as it is shaped. From this, in turn, follows the requirement of self-criticism. Democracy will endure only by continuing to improve.

3. In principle, reason belongs to every human being. Hence, every individual has absolute value and must never be a mere means. Each individual is irreplaceable. The objective is that everyone, according to his abilities, should be able to actualize man's innate essence, his freedom. Hence, democracy aims at equality; it seeks to give everyone equal rights, in the sense of equal opportunities. This goal, insofar as it is possible at all, including the heads of the government, must be tied to laws that have been legally enacted and can be legally amended. New conditions call for new laws; the injustice that always remains requires constant improvement in the laws.

4. Reason works by persuasion, not by force. But as force is actually present in human action, rational self-preservation must meet force with force. Democracy, therefore, employs police powers against lawbreakers, but only as authorized by law or in judicial proceedings. Thus everyone is protected from arbitrary and illegal violence by the state, secure in life and limb.

5. As a state of mind, reason is prior to all specific laws and institutions. Recognized above any laws and not subject to legislation are human rights that both bind and free all men. These human rights are not subject to legislation which, by its very nature, can be changed. Before any judgment, evaluation, and regulation of the manifold actions and qualities of men comes a liberality in the recognition of all human potentialities; before the conception, adoption, and enforcement of any law comes sensitivity to injustice and to wrong as such. Democracy defines the rights of man and tries to safeguard them against future encroachments. It protects individuals and minorities

from majority coercion. It lives by the active solicitude that makes a wrong
done to one a matter of concern to all.

6. In its political actualization, reason never forgets that it is men who
govern. Like the governed, they are creatures with human failings and prone
to error. At some time, government even by the best of men needs checking
up on. But this control, carried out by human beings, must be mutual: in the
intellectual battle of opinions, in the distribution of offices, in the accounting
rendered to the voters.

Democracy aims at a government of reason, through government by the
people. Yet how can the people govern before they are rational?

This is a question of the means of making the popular will clear, public, and
a fact. These means are the press, the assembly of all the people—in very
small democracies an actual meeting of all citizens, in large ones a popular
vote on previously published and extensively debated issues—and the representation of the people in elected parliamentary bodies. But what if these tools
of the democratic idea turn against the idea of democracy itself? If, for instance, a parliamentary majority violates its own principles, as in the German
Reichstag's suicidal enabling act of 1933? And if a plebiscite decides, by majority vote, to do away with the government of laws—as happened also in the
Germany of 1933, when National Socialists, German Nationalists, and Communists agreed on this objective? What if the people freely resolve to have no
more freedom? Has the majority the right to say that it will not carry any
weight in the future? Has it the right to abolish democracy, to wipe out human
rights, to do violence to minorities? Can it be just and lawful for a majority
decision to destroy all justice and legality?

Here lies the Gordian knot that can become inextricable for democracies at
some time, in some crisis. No democratic form of government can guarantee
the democratic idea. And where is the authority that can cut this knot?

The trouble is that democracy, which is to evoke reason in the people,
already presupposes this reason. Irrational force will not vanish until all are
rational. But what if reason deserts the people?

We can distinguish between the will of a temporary majority and the people's basic, permanently ingrained, rational will. The temporary will may go
astray, and a minority, perhaps only a few, may be representing the true, basic
will. But in reality there is no organ of government to speak for that basic will;
every institution—the head of the state and its smallest governing body, the
legislature, the judiciary, the plebiscite—can fail and succumb to irrationality.
We depend upon real authorities. In a democracy we depend upon majorities,
on the assumption that their decisions, if proved wrong, can be corrected later.
But what if the decision abolishes correction and effects destruction?

No political apparatus is capable of preventing, reliably, the use of the
institutions of democracy to counter the idea of democracy. Only the enduring

attitude of reason on the part of those who use these institutions can do so. The limit lies where reason itself, in the minority and in opposition to the brute force of a majority that would destroy all reason, submits and allows itself to be overwhelmed by violence. By such submission the minority opens the floodgates to the deluge of force as such (until, in the Second World War, it surpassed all previous dimensions and, by happenstance, led at the end to at least a partial restitution of the opportunities for freedom; next time the atomic war could bring about the destruction of all). Or reason, now embodied in great statesmen allied perhaps with tiny minorities would, for its part, resort to a maximum of skillful maneuvers within the framework of legality and, at the decisive moments, to brute force in order to counter its violation by the majority and by terror. This act is counter to law since it is carried out against the law-destroying actions of the formally legal majority; it cannot be justified by any institution.

Democracy, in short, can sustain itself as an actuality only if it masters in its institutions the purely rational consequences of its laws guaranteeing freedom; or, expressed differently: if it can overcome, based on the strength of its ideas, those votes that would lead to its suicide. But this is possible only through acts of those who, at critical moments, either are at the helm or reach for it. The same form of legal institutions can be used in order to save or to destroy democracy. No law and no order can anticipate what will happen at such moments. Straightforward rational consistency, jurisprudence, the different spheres of influence, the bureaucracy—all of these fail. The great statesman who, at such moments, either reveals himself as such or fails to be such, proves himself by his capacity of also winning his allies for his sense of reason at decisive instances and by the significance of the action with which he successfully brings about lasting effects.

Democracy is tolerant of all possibilities but must be able to become intolerant of intolerance itself. It is against force but must maintain itself by pitting force against force. It permits all intellectual, social, political movements but where these, through their organization and through their actions turn against the cause of democratic reason itself, there the power of the state must, for its part, be in a position to act against them. All too often, politicians and officials unworthy of democracy are tied into legal knots by the shrewd men who do away with all legality. Unable to disentangle themselves, they conceal their failure by talking, negotiating in all directions, and doing nothing. The democratic idea is lost in the hands of mere politicians who will let it die in pseudo-democratic emotionalism.

Yet all this goes to show only that democracy is built on volcanic soil and cannot be maintained by legal guarantees alone.

Democracy is dangerous as is all of human existence. The moments of great crisis in the super-powers of a particular age are decisive for world history, and at such moments democracy cannot survive just by patient bargaining, making sensible compromises, and splitting the difference. It may do so in periods of calm, but even then the breath of evil must be felt and kept in mind—even then, vigilance must be at a constant alert if the men of democracy, instead of being paralyzed with fright in times of peril, find, in their broad horizons, their daring decisions and stick to them, moving and convincing others.

Democracy is an idea. This means that it cannot be perfect anywhere, that indeed it is beyond visualization even as an ideal. Man's reason tells him that no right, perfectible order exists in the world. The awareness of human imperfectibility is a corollary of the democratic idea.

As an idea, however, it is not weak or skeptical. It has the thoughtfulness of reason, its powerful impulse, its inspiring enthusiasm. The idea is before our eyes—never grasped, ever present yet ever elusive, and always guiding. To the realist it seems fantastic, and if we were to take its mere outline for a program of actualization, and our awareness of the impulse for real achievement, he would be right. He is wrong if he fails to perceive that any real, more than fleetingly successful achievement is bound up with the idea. But it takes broad horizons, extensive knowledge, and competent action to make the idea strong.

The word "democracy" is used today in self-justification by all states, yet the concept defies any simple definition. We must distinguish, first, between the idea of democracy and its institutions of the moment—which are almost endlessly variable, filled with the idea only to a degree, and apt to turn into configurations destructive of the idea. The idea of democracy lives out of the substance of a historic tradition extending to the everyday ethos of a people. Democracy, turned into a palpable idol in the form of a written constitution, is either adopted cut and dried as a panacea or a charm, or else foisted on peoples, supposedly in their own best interest. Hence the idea has had a long history, from its manifestations in Antiquity by way of the guild systems and Mediterranean city-states to its modern forms, which have achieved a relative measure of historically grounded stability only in countries that have long known freedom, such as Britain, the United States, the Netherlands, and Switzerland. Since the French Revolution, it has had another modern history which perverted the idea into abstract principles, with the merely rational consequence of institutions and actions that have over and again destroyed the idea of democracy as well as freedom.

Second, we must distinguish between a form of government and a way of governing. Democracy may mean one of the several forms that a state can assume, such as democracy, aristocracy, monarchy, as taught in Antiquity. Or it may mean a way of governing—what Kant calls the "republican manner of government," which has only one antithesis, i.e., despotism. Both, the democratic and despotic way of ruling, may occur in all three forms of government.

Third, we must distinguish the idea of democracy from the notion of popular sovereignty. Identical at first, the two diverge and become opposites if the path toward reason is given up for the postulation of an absolute wisdom already in place in the actuality of the people. Now the objects of idolatry are not only specific institutions but the people themselves, by means of their institutions. The sovereign people are imbued with the character of sanctity, as it were, as absolute princes used to be: "The people's voice is God's voice."

The true, wise, popular sovereign demands obedience, and there is no more appeal from the people's will than there ever was from that of a sovereign prince in the age of absolutism. The presupposition that there is a will as such of the people demands that it be determined what it is. It often seems to deceive itself where it expresses itself. Where is it free of deception? The answer is: either in the majority that emerges in elections, or in the minority of a vanguard which, in contrast to the confused, vacillating and manipulable multitudes, claims to know the genuine will of the people. It is men, always, who claim to rule in the name of the sovereign people, and since the sovereign people's will is absolute, the result is either a brutal assault on minorities by rulers chosen by the people to be the representative of the majority, or violation of all by a minority. From the supposed existence of a popular will, which the rulers claim to represent, they further deduce the right to exterminate their opponents as rebels against the sovereign people. Such an absolute, institutionalized popular sovereignty will reject all deviation as falsehood and ill will. Rule by absolute sovereignty of the people incarnate in organizations and leaders puts an end to all discussion.

The democratic idea is the way to counter the idolization of the existing sovereignty of the people. It knows no reigning and governing sovereign, but it knows a will that must constantly evolve anew among the people in a process of self-education, in institutions which, for all their firmness and despite all checks and safeguards, remain modifiable. This way requires solidarity of the most diverse members of the community oriented toward and guided by reason. It requires, on the one hand, a liberal approach, and on the other, the inviolability of existing law. The ruling individuals who are on the way of the democratic idea are always bound by the law, while the individuals embodying popular sovereignty can, in extreme situations, rule by decree which they may breach once more since they are sovereign over law and decree.

The way of the democratic idea is an incessant struggle as a community to find truth. Everything is subject to unlimited public debate, though not based upon debate but on decisions. Whatever truth is found at any time must be decided under the pressure of the situation. In case of disagreement, provisional agreement on actions that are deemed necessary is achieved by majority vote, with the minority suspending its divergent views, knowing that in the future, in new situations, it will have another chance to put them to the test and make them prevail. Complying loyally with what are now common decisions, the minority in turn enjoys the protection of the laws and of a solidarity resting upon the common ground of the democratic idea.

The idea of democracy is sober, clear, and inspiring; the claim of absolute popular sovereignty is wild, murky, and fanaticized.

Should we avoid the word "democracy" because it invites so many interpretations and is open to so much abuse? Would not its abolition be all the more justified since the doctrine of Antiquity coined the concept as that of a form of government, alongside monarchy and aristocracy? But the abolition would be in vain and inappropriate, for the word does mean the people—all the people of a state. All of them shall get to exercise their right of thinking and acting in concert.

The only stark contrast is between democratic and despotic ways of ruling. When we speak of the idea of democracy, we mean Kant's "republican manner of government." For this, there is no better name than democracy.

Wherever a government lays claim to democracy—as all of them do nowadays—there we find the question of the alternative: of that which is not democratic. Everything "undemocratic" is rejected and each accuses the other of being ruled by a minority rather than by the people. Here, we hear, monopoly capital is in the saddle, there a party clique. Here men are subject to capitalistic exploitation, there to despotic exploitation.

Yet these alternatives are propagandistic arguments that take the particular for the whole. They refer to tangible, specific aspects. Against them, there is one sole and radical alternative that determines the totality of what we want and do, and this can only be circumscribed *ad infinitum* but not itself determined. For its primary characteristic is that it is not an alternative of antithetical doctrines. It is an alternative of the basic direction of our lives. The way of reason knows doctrines as particular means to particular ends, but it never turns into a doctrine itself and thus cannot have a doctrine for its antithesis. It resists any doctrinization—any type of confinement in definitive rigidities, in the embodiment of an absolute, or in the acrobatics of a dialectical movement.

As a way of reason, democracy refuses to be absolutized. If it is based on reason, it cannot help realizing that, while reason ought to prevail, it is actually neither all-pervasive nor certain that it can continue on its way without being limited (although it hopes to do so). Yet democracy refuses to conclude from this experience that the rule of irrationality is unchangeable, that unreasonable mankind must be forever ruled by equally unreasonable force.

Democracy does not permit us to assume that rulers are, or could or should be, superhuman. It insists that, in the nature of things, all challenges are directed at human beings, and it rejects any other legitimization, such as a certain post being a direct mandate from God, or the charisma of a person to indicate that he is a divinely instituted leader. It knows the seriousness of the responsibility connected with an office and the gifts of great men, and it respects both without idolizing them. Democracy knows that both of these must be actual if it is to thrive.

The alternative to the democratic idea is whatever seeks to shirk the task of being-human. This happened and happens in grandiose-appearing forms, in actualities making claims of divinity or of absolute knowledge. All alternatives to the way of democracy may be described, in Kant's term, as states of despotism. Even at best, they block the path of rational man; today they block the path to the rescue of mankind. In fortunate moments despots are said to have governed well, but such moments were mere accidents in the course of destruction. For it is not thus that the nations awaken: the mass of individuals achieve neither insight nor responsibility; they stay imprisoned in their particular environments—whether wretched or beautiful—under authoritarian direction; they are technically drilled, made into useful, skillful, knowledgeable tools of labor, but removed in all instances from the great, infinite process of human development.

The way of democracy, for all its errors and seeming dead ends, provides the opportunities for a majority of men to grow into thinking, responsible creatures; it does so even though its first result is a leveling that entails the risk of democracy's being perverted into one of the worst dictatorships ever known. The democratic idea has its ground in man's task of self-actualization in reason, and in the unique, irreplaceable character of every individual, and in his dignity based on his participation in reason. The failings in democratic actualization are not justified, of course, but put into perspective by the far greater failings of all other present systems. To despair of the democratic idea is to despair of man . . .

Selection 63

IN WHAT CAN WE TRUST?

EDITORS:
The following selection is excerpted from Jaspers's most elaborate book in political philosophy, "The Atom Bomb and the Future of Mankind," published in English under the title *The Future of Mankind.* Exploring here the possibilities of a new politics beyond fear, beyond optimism and pessimism, he discusses the need for all people and all peoples to be involved. Empowered by "the courage of reason," they are the necessary vehicles of the new politics.

The selection is excerpted from *Die Atombombe und die Zunkunft des Menschen,* pp. 458–59, 468, 473–76, 478–93; in English: *The Future of Man-*

kind, pp. 318–19, 324, 327–29, 331–39. E. B. Ashton's translation has been emended by the editors.

TEXT:

Let us recapitulate the situation once again. In the past, the worst disasters could not kill mankind. Multitudes, whole nations, guilty or not guilty, perished; others survived and forgot. But now our intellect tells us with inescapable logic that soon there will be no more oblivious survivors. No one will be alive. There could be confidence, in the past, because in every disaster some were spared. Life went on. Remnants led to new beginnings. Now, however, man can no longer afford disaster without the consequence of universal doom—an idea so novel, as a real probability, that we hesitate to think it through. It takes an effort just to put it into words. . . .

We should like to know for certain what will happen, but such knowledge is denied to man. Nothing is sure but the *threat* of total destruction. The situations embodying the threat change rapidly, and the causalities are so involved that any calculation is misleading—as indeed it always was. The conceivable combinations are endless, the possibilities inconceivable. Since there is no generally valid view of history, there is no knowledge of certain perdition either.

The result, on our part, should not be calm but intensified activity. What this can be and do is the great question; the answer is that no plan, no action can succeed without a change in our common will, based on a change in individual thinking. We cannot tell what men will freely do, which aspect of freedom will be actualized, by which decisions, in which situations. But what we cannot know is up to us to bring about, and everybody must begin with himself.

Thoughts of the future are bound to be discouraging if we forget freedom and transcendence. Mere intellectual thinking removes responsibility along with confidence; it weakens us and leads us to succumb passively to disaster. Or it makes us active only in clutching at straws, in vain comprehensive planning, in nihilistic thoughts and actions, in savage accord with total destruction that occurs, in false hopes or in the gratification of defiance.

He who will base his life on rationalistic certainties—who wants to be sure of the future—cannot help despairing. But he who experiences the human tasks out of the roots of his freedom in the face of transcendence will be inspired to do what he can. Once our minds are opened to the depths of transcendence, we stop asking for certainties. . . .

The Task Beyond Pessimism and Optimism

Neither hopelessness nor confidence can be proved adequately by rational knowledge. The arguments for despair, deducing inevitabilities from total knowledge, are as inadequate as the arguments that trust in the victory of common sense. Despair and confidence are moods, not insights. We call them pessimism and optimism. Neither one is open to persuasion; each finds infinite arguments and overlooks the counterarguments.

The pessimist today sees only total doom. He used to expect an endless, inhuman, ant-like existence, but this is old-fashioned now that all life threatens to end. Triumphantly and stoically he sees his worst predictions surpassed. He remains passive, leaving the course of events to chance and mankind a prey to the violent. He regards times of freedom as brief interruptions of despotism.

The optimist resents all calamitous forecasts. But it always remains to be seen whether his positive outlook can cope with the realities of the future, whether he will even see them or simply evade them. What will happen once his delusions are no longer borne out by a seemingly impregnable political position and prosperity? He will keep fooling himself, since in all events he will see that which will save him.

Optimism and pessimism are equally unfounded and inadequate. As knowledge they are delusive; in practice they distract from the task of man. They do not lead to the high road of humanity. Do not calamity and opportunity both lie in the course of events? Is it not only when man does his best and is ready for whatever happens, beyond optimism and pessimism, that he is rational and truly human? . . .

The Presupposition of Political Action: That All Know what Is Going on.

What matters is where the fear takes us, whether we repress it in blind obliviousness or let it sink in to clear our rational vision. Fear may cause us to recall the roots of being-human and to grow aware of our task: to prepare the ground, by changing the individual and thus the general political ethos, for dissolving the state of fear into a state of honesty upheld by self-sacrifice and reason. Yet this task can be fulfilled only together with our other task: to make life worthy to be lived, by the same self-sacrifice and reason. Fear for life, and for the foundation of all life, need not pass everywhere into the the blind fear that simply wants to prevent war at any cost—that will not arm when others arm, will not prepare for defense when others prepare for attack—a fear that vaguely tends to submit to the violent acts of the antagonist peacefully, step by step, without bloodshed, and to endure slavery if only life remains.

The first step today is to increase the fear—though perhaps not among the political leaders who know it, and live in it, if they are responsible. What needs increasing is the fear of the people; this should grow to overpowering force, not of blind submissiveness, but of a bright, transforming ethos that will bring forth appropriate statesmen and sustain their actions.

For fear is ambiguous. As sheer fear it merely cries for help at any cost and is in vain. It must turn into a power that compels men to save themselves in the sphere of reason; then it can evoke the will that grasps its meaning before transcendence, transforms man, and makes him true. The great fear of mankind can be a creative fear, and then it will work like a catalyst for the emergence of freedom.

To this end, all must know and be affected—not a few individuals, but the people of the nations. They must be reminded constantly, publicly, of our situation, of the facts and possibilities; from distraction they must be brought to attention by ceaseless repetition of the crucial point in new wordings and convincing mental pictures. Only thus can the point be brought home to all men. It must be said, argued, shouted daily. The matter must not be allowed to rest, neither in public nor in the mind and heart of any individual.

This demand is resisted by our desire to come to rest in a conventional order. We want to forget. We make moral taboos of our illusions; whoever disturbs them is rebuked for undermining our morale, for cutting the ground from under us, or for spreading panic. Panic, we hear, is always bad. But the cry, "Above all, no panic!" is misleading. We are not talking of the moment of crisis, when disaster is upon us and panic adds to the confusion. We are talking of the lasting, urging fear that may make us save ourselves.

The warning, "Above all, no panic," corresponds to the German slogan of 1933, "Above all, no civil war!" It voices the self-deceiving will to avoid one evil at the cost of getting into the worst of evils. You wait for a solution, for things to take a better turn "by themselves." A desire for quiet that ventures nothing is mere blind fear disguised as pseudo-reason.

Others object to alarming the people as futile, since a vast majority would react quite differently from our expectations. They would be too dull to hear the facts and too unimaginative to envision them; repetition would only deafen them further; at bottom, they would not believe us. Or they would refuse to give any thought to mankind's doom, fearing only their death, and that only when it is imminent. Or they would react passively, because "there is nothing to be done about it, anyway." They would live blithely from day to day: "We're here now, and the morrow will take care of itself—it won't be so bad." Or they might comfort themselves with international agreements, call for negotiations, and believe in the effectiveness of any accord, on the theory that things will get well "step by step."

A final objection points out that fear will cause panic wherever and whenever things are to be done that make the danger immediately sensible. People dread the construction of nuclear power plants, for instance. Or, if an army is to be equipped with atomic weapons, there is a frightened reaction: "We'll be safer if this hellish thing is elsewhere but not right here; let's renounce it, so we'll be spared." The consequence is a tendency to yield to the blackmail of one of the great atomic powers. This sort of panic shuts our eyes to the over-all world situation, to world strategy, to the possibilities of atom bomb use, and to the conditions of world peace. It paralyzes any comprehensive reflection on the true preconditions of security.

All these objections show the perils of half-knowledge and the possible results of fear. Are we to conclude that it is better to keep silent, to conceal things, and to calm people? No—for as human beings we have no way but that of knowledge and fear. It is too little knowledge that comes to the fore in the panicky fear; we must see to it that the relevant facts are known in their entirety. Senseless fear falls prey to abstract, inadequate, purely intellectual reactions, illusory hopes, silly blunders which lead to disaster. Such fear should be clarified so as to lead to rational vision rather than blind panic. If panicky fear drives us into irrationality, enlightened fear frees us for reason. We must take the unlimited risks of knowledge and fear if we want to remain truly human.

The dangers of a false reaction based on fear do not mean that all opportunities are lost. We may reason this way: it is in talking of the terrible threat that the challenge posed by man's true nature is illuminated. About the existence of this challenge there can be no doubt; and if it exists, we may hope that it can be heard and heeded. Not to share this hope means to have lost all confidence in man. Though shaken by no matter how many facts, this confidence can be restored from the depths from which every honest, thinking individual hears the challenge. If I have no confidence in man, I have no confidence in the source through which man is.

How can one live at all without any confidence? There seems to be such a living pattern—which may be cited as a final objection to confidence itself. In the last analysis, confidence must prevail without the support of any rational proof . . .

The Basic Question: What Makes Life Worth Living?

To achieve a life that is worthy of him, man must survive—but he will survive only if he achieves that life. This is a circle that we cannot break out of merely to stay alive. Now, at the brink, mere life depends on worthy living. This alone leads to the actions that would bar atomic doom. The life through which man comes to himself has now become itself the condition for the preservation of mere life.

For such a life it cannot suffice to be safe, peaceful, and prosperous. There are ambiguities in praising, revering life as such, and considering it holy. All this holds true for the exploration of the mystery of living; it is truthful for the protection of the human body—even a legally imprisoned criminal's—from physical violation by the state; it is still truthful when it shudders to kill in war.

But reverence for life is not the ultimate. It becomes untruthful, untrue, and ruinous when life as such is made the sole, the absolutely highest good. Then man takes the place of Transcendence, expressing an actual lack of faith.

Besides, it is a vain endeavor to stem the march to the abyss by proclaiming the sanctity of life, for this kindles only inconsequential emotions, not a revival of the ethos itself.

Reverence for life becomes untrue wherever it forgets that man is superior to his life. He can sanctify it only by fulfilling his task. The conditions of a life worthy of man, and for finding the road to salvation, are the risk and the sacrifice of life—not in themselves, but as moments of human reason and love.

The questions are always the same. What makes life worth living? What do I want in the face of extremity? What will I do, what will I be, how will I live in awareness of my being-human and our common peril? Is there a truth that makes the ultimate effort and, if it fails, lets us meet the end without fear?

This is where ends and means and plans and achievements cease. What makes life worth living has consequences in action and in the conduct of life, but it cannot be willed—for it is the source of our will. Man's present reality must show what is, and what he is. But the way I live is the preparation as well as the fulfillment that are necessary to show what is and what man is. My life is directed toward this manifestation; yet such a life already is the manifestation.

From the Old to the New Politics

The threat of doom will not be banished by measures confined to the atom bomb, nor by measures designed merely to prevent a new war; what is required is that all particular actions, purposes, plans, agreements, or institutions issue from the entirety of human life. What is done in any of these directions will be lastingly, constructively successful only if all of them, without exception, work together. The result would be a new politics.

At first, the new politics would have to move in the tracks of the old politics that is still with us but must be overcome. What the change in individuals can sometimes accomplish cannot be done at once in the community of all. Attempts at instant reformation would quickly produce total anarchy and despotism. The political change must let the new grow in the framework of the old; it must fill the old track with new meanings, until it can be left for a new track. Individual decisions make this a common process, with large areas still in darkness as the light starts shining here and there.

The old politics acts on the principles of present enmity and future war; the new politics will act on the principle that there can be honest, rational communication and ensuing peace. What matters in the old politics is neither to be deceived by your opponent nor to deceive yourself; each jeopardizes self-preservation. But what matters further, to make the new politics possible, is to impress the reality and the meaning of all those activities upon the general consciousness, to strip the camouflage from what goes on not only among our enemies but among ourselves—for it is only then that man can come out of his drifting; that ethos, reason, and self-sacrifice can awaken and find both the valor of self-preservation and the turn to a true will to peace in a new politics. The old politics sees everything in the reality of friend and foe, with reference to war. The new politics will search in this reality for the presuppositions of peace.

To the old politics, which ultimately relates all things to the Cold War and the impending hot one, all spheres of life turn into "theaters of war." In present world strategy we find not only a military theater, but economic, cultural, ideological, religious theaters of war—effects upon all of which are carefully considered and psychologically calculated in the propaganda effort to sway opinions, motives, ways of action. Our time will make the choice between this refinement of the old politics and its transformation. If the change occurs, the question will be not only where violent struggle shall cease, but where and how struggles that are not naturally violent shall be divorced from violence and retained. Every step toward pure, non-violent struggle is a step in the conquest of war.

While the threat of war exists, reason would be weakened if a statesman, or a nation, abolished all indirect, war-related methods at one stroke. But everyone today can know about these methods and be aware of the unnatural, poisonous, ruinous abuse they constitute. The question now is when it will be politically possible to venture into the new politics—to stop the abuse of economics as a political weapon, for instance, because the inner self-preservation of the Western world has developed far enough to permit it.

The old politics does not recognize any act that does not benefit the power of its own state. Even "cultural policy" is part of power politics. When it transmits its own national spirit, its language, its works, its way of life, it is thinking of national prestige, not of humanity—except, perhaps, when it fancies its nation as humanity's perfect embodiment, a model of human excellence which all the rest should join for their own salvation.

The new politics will be able to proceed with candor, because its self-preservation is strictly defensive and without expansionist aims. It gives up any claims to totality; it grants freedom; it allows ideas to be promulgated regardless of their political consequences. It dares to promote its own way as a common way for all, by relinquishing the power potentials of the old politics. It frankly shows both its self-interest, if any, and its disinterestedness. Thus it can awaken forces that agree with it.

The passage from the old politics to the new would be the passage from falsehood to truth. Today, the old "sophistical maxims" are still as effective as when Kant exposed them. *Fac et excusa*—do it when you have the chance, and explain later; the very brazenness of the deed lends it a certain glow of inner conviction, because success is the best advocate. *Si fecisti, nega*—if you did it, deny that you are to blame; blame others or human nature. *Divide et impera*—set the rulers against the people or against each other; side with the people as you pretend to grant them greater freedom; thus everything will depend on your will. By seeming to aid the weak you will subject them all, one by one. Kant says that these maxims, being generally known, do not fool anyone, and that no one is ashamed of being found out, only of having failed—for aggrandizement of power, however accomplished, is the only honor in politics.

The new politics would make men ashamed of following these maxims. They would no longer win appreciative smiles from the knowing and unironical applause of masses that do not believe in man because they do not believe in themselves. Not until men are changed can they resolve openly to discard the sophistical maxims, the principle of falsehood in politics, in word and deed.

The old politics culminates, on the one hand, in the frankly ruthless will to power that exterminates the enemy who does not submit and, on the other hand, in the disingenuous, deceiving and self-deceiving vindication of war by the sole guilt of the enemy, whom the victor calls to account. In the case of overt force there is the chance of mercy; in the case of hypocritical self-justification, there is merciless exploitation of victory by imposing intolerable burdens upon the vanquished.

The new politics, resting on the political ethos that regards peace as the now definitive condition of human existence as such, will press for the most decisive moral judgments, but the essence of evil, in its eyes, is the lie—above all, the hypocritical lie—including the gain of falsehood in a true accusation. It will end the most diabolical, though seemingly unbloody, type of combat: the tallying-up of one another's guilt by every means at hand. Instead, like a rational individual, it seeks to preserve itself by finding its own faults first. Where the fault lies with the other side, where a principle (and not, therefore, its every human representative!) seems morally and politically evil, the new politics will show concretely what is going on, will analyze, illuminate, expose the noxious principle—but it will do so, first, without abandoning its own truthfulness at any point of the exposure, and second, without censoriousness, intending, rather, to convince.

This struggle never ceases. To let it go on in the light of full publicity is the beginning of peace. In this true battle of minds—which today, in the framework of the old politics, is often so obscured as to be imperceptible—the point is to know the facts and to impart ideas. It is to cut to the root of the matter, to find the simplest forms in which men can absorb ideas and be convinced—not to falsify truth and conviction with suggestive slogans that will substitute for understanding. We cannot elaborate here, but ahead of us lies a great new world of intellectual struggle, distinguished by breadth, abundance, and precision, and inspired by the ethos of a true polemics that no longer wants to hoodwink men with sophisms but will seek truth together.

Violent war will cease once the battle of minds has shown it up, with all its presuppositions, as a thing we cannot want any more. War will cease when men no longer let themselves be deceived, when they sense the power of conviction in thinking for themselves, and when they understand that they themselves are responsible for the evil if they promote it by their untruthfulness.

In foolishly idealistic politics we act as if the condition we want had been attained already. In foolishly realistic politics we act as if that better condition of the new politics were unattainable. Both ways are irresponsible. The responsible way is to foster each rudiment, to nurture each germ, to make each good impulse our own, to see the possibilities of the future in the facts of the present and to think and act with these possibilities in mind. This is not a middle way between extremes; it is the high road above the two abysmal benightments that we call idealism and realism.

What we are asking here may seem too much. It is possible, but dishearteningly unlikely. Yet hopelessness is the anticipation of defeat; man is not entitled to it as long as he can act—and this appears to be his only way of acting so as to come to himself and at the same time save his temporal existence.

What Is Needed Today: The Courage of Reason

The course of human events has not been purely calamitous: there was, and is, the actuality of reason. The development of reason is the history of philosophy which is proper to man as man, which runs through mankind but has never ruled it yet. Now, our salvation hangs upon the rule of reason. If reason as a whole is ineffective, if its power fails, doom seems bound to follow—and yet, to the very moment of doom, it is not certain. Until that moment, the possibility of rational action leaves room for hope. If our faith in reason is shaken by the experience of many irrational moments in ourselves, and by the rule of unreason and anti-reason in the world of men, experience still tells us also how reason has been awakened and how it may grow. If we cannot count on meeting reason, we still see that everything good is done in the confidence of meeting reasonable men.

If I grow despondent in view of extremity, reason teaches me that it is not an act of bravery to draw conclusions about the end, about inevitable doom. The man of courage, no matter how much he knows, does what he can and keeps hoping as long as he lives.

Further, it is not a brave but a paralyzing philosophy that leads us to observe, unmoved, the catastrophe we presume to recognize until, finally, we are swept away by it. We are brave, however, when we let ourselves be stirred in our innermost depth and we experience what is revealed in the limit situation.

There remains to us our seeing the glory of the world and being lovingly bound to others for as long as this is granted to us. There remains our assuring ourselves in the historicity of our love, of our origin and of eternity. Based on this foundation, the meaning remains: To live in our world out of reason—not only out of finite intelligence but out of the great reason that unlocks everything to us, and to use this reason to direct our thoughts, impulses, efforts, beginning with our everyday activities, toward overcoming the threatening final catastrophe.

When we, when all come to reason—when some come to it, not only here and there, but in their entire lives, when this reason, once kindled among a few, spreads like a purifying flame—then only may we hope confidently that the total catastrophe will be overcome.

That which seems utopian is possible, this is told to us by a trust that is not grounded in this world but is given to us out of the Encompassing when we fulfill it by that which we are able to do. Yet if the moment of total perdition should come, there would be shown in the horizon of our knowledge that our reason, too, has been a temporal, transient phenomenon. We do not know its purpose; we are conscious only that there ought to be reason, conscious that it would be better to perish knowingly, in possession of reason, than to live blindly through the years and to plunge to our doom bereft of reason, first helping to bring it about ourselves, then overwhelmed by fear.

Reason gives us lasting confidence even if it should vanish in time, along with human existence. What sort of confidence? In the world, reason is the ultimate of our possible foundations. But it is not the ultimate itself.

At the Limit: The Possibility of Global Catastrophe

Temporal existence is not ultimate actuality. In fact, we cannot speak of ultimate actuality as we do of things in the world, of objects, of what is tangible or conceivable, to which, after all, all speech is bound. And yet, even if all temporal existence comes to an end, we still ask in our human categories: Whither? It is not nothing, if reason was heeded in freedom.

If we halt at the limits of the world and judge from its perspective, we are taking what is called the modern point of view. From this viewpoint, the present vista of doom—man's, not the world's—has not arisen from religious motives; it is the reality of the technological situation alone that compels us to recognize the total menace. It becomes the pivot of our lives. And in all honesty, our confidence in the world cannot be absolute: the peril remains; we can only trust that what ought to come to be is what is dictated by man's reason. But this trust, which allows us to live and act in the face of uncertainty, is grounded in a more profound confidence that is not of this world, nor born of reason alone. . . .

Indeed, if man is not driven by thoughtless vitality, nothing short of *transcendent actuality* will encourage him, as he continues, in an increasingly menacing world, to risk himself in his children. Nowhere else can he look for guidance that may show them the way to belong to those who will, perhaps, avert disaster.

Would the doom of reason be the revelation of nothingness? No, for where there is reason it is certain of not being nothing. To have striven for it is worthy of man—and possible for man, because his own self was given to him in the gift of reason, he knows not whence. Because it is certain of itself only if it is conscious of being a demand from elsewhere, reason has an unknown, unknowable actuality in the eternal.

In eternity, our notion of God is the only fixed point for us. What particular form it assumes is secondary, for any form is inadequate. To the Westerner, the notion of God in the limit situation of foundering is historically founded on the Bible: the ancient prophets spoke of total doom, of the "Day of Yahweh" when everything would be destroyed; the early Christians spoke of the imminent end of the world. When state and nation and even the faith of the Jews broke down and the remnants were sacrificing to Isis, Jeremiah replied to Baruch, his despairing disciple, "The Lord saith thus: Behold, that which I have built will I break down, and that which I have planted I will pluck up, even this whole land. And seekest thou great things for thyself? Seek them not; for behold I will bring evil upon all flesh." Suffice it that God is, is Jeremiah's meaning.

This is the final horizon, from which all things are seen in the proper perspective. In this horizon, courage grows from a trust in the ground that no foundering in the world can quench, not even that of reason. This confidence gives us the will to actualize reason as long as men exist, to dare and to see the purpose in building even if we cannot know how long our building will stand.

The actuality of God's existence is not anti-reason which triumphs as nothingness; it is suprarational and includes and encompasses reason. It is this actuality which demands reason from us. Reason is its gift to man, to be used for free, original unfolding and for holding fast. The ground of all things is not reason but the actuality above us, incomprehensible, is called by the cipher "God."

God is unthinkable. Thoughts and conceptions of God are ciphers, misleading if taken by themselves. We may call God "almighty," transcending all reason but encompassing reason—yet if this cipher is conceived after the fashion of temporal power, it becomes sacrilegious nonsense. The suprarational deity becomes irrational and arbitrary; the Almighty turns into a

440 DISTINCTIONS AND RELATIONS

tyrant. Or we may call God a "person." This notion, too, is a cipher, expressing my relationship to my ground, trusting in spite of all, as we trust a person. But "person" is an inappropriate word for the deity, which is more than a person—being, rather, the "ground" of personality as it appears in man. Thus the deity is being thought and represented in manifold, ever inadequate ciphers—most adequately, perhaps, where the idea has no worldly content any more and seems to vanish as a mere form in the void. Yet it is still from that void that we are upheld by the full force of the true actuality.

Trust is placed in the hidden deity. The sullying of the notion of God by Gnostic legends, by speculations and images entangled with gods and demons, turns our free trust into an unfree certainty. If the deity is present, immutable, and actual, the mists and will-o'-the-wisps and sorceries of thought and conception disappear. Before the deity, all worldly things become trivial and yet infinitely significant to finite rational creatures, as manifestations of that wherein they assure themselves of eternity. Here alone is true trust . . .

IV.

Philosophy and Religion

EDITORS' INTRODUCTION TO SUBPART IV:
Jaspers saw it as a vital task of contemporary philosophy to arrive at a clear
and valid distinction of philosophy vis-à-vis science and religion (see Selection 15). The task of distinguishing between philosophy and science falls
properly within philosophy. It is different in the case of religion, and, in particular, Western revealed religions. Both philosophy and religion are concerned with faith, i.e., the truth out of which we live. Yet in each case the
source of truth is different. As Jaspers sees it, the source of truth of the Western revealed religions such as Christianity is the unique revelation; for philosophy the status of revelation is that of a symbol among others. The source of
truth according to philosophy is man's risk of faith out of a freedom that is
grounded in an ineffable transcendence; this source is disavowed by revealed
religion. Neither philosophy nor revealed religion is of a higher order than
the other; nor is there a supernal third position. When speaking of the distinction between philosophy and revealed religion we have to ask therefore from
which of the two positions this distinction is being defined. Hence, for
Jaspers, what is primarily at play in the distinction of the two is the self-
clarification of philosophy in its confrontation with revelational faith. (Such
self-clarification on the part of philosophy is, in principle if not always in
practice, a matter of indifference to revealed religion.) Yet for Jaspers more is
involved in the confrontation with revealed religion than the distinctness of
philosophy:

First, inasmuch as the truth of philosophy is, according to him, to be understood as the impulse of reason toward the communicative unification of mankind, revelational religion cannot be a matter of indifference to philosophy
and must be challenged into dialogue. Second, revelational religion shares
with philosophy its grounding on the Bible and has, in the past, been its
indispensable vehicle of transmission; hence Jaspers's concern for safeguarding the heritage of the Bible in an age when the appeal of the religions based
on the Bible seems to be weakening. Third, the Christian churches, as the
main institutional manifestations of revealed religion, have been and may
continue to be decisive for the growth and continuance of the Western spirit;
hence, for Jaspers it is of vital concern for philosophy to spark, within revealed

religion, the human capacities for philosophic faith which actualizes truth through communication. Finally, a philosophical concern over the truth of faith, without which the human being would lose his humanity, will inevitably raise the question as to whether the inestimable truth of which revelational religion is the carrier must be accompanied by religious phenomena that, from a philosophical view, seem at odds with the truth of faith. Examples of these phenomena are the authoritarian mode of the Church's magisterial function, the claim to the exclusiveness of its truth, the dogmatic interpretation of the scriptures, the belief in the divinity of the man Jesus.

In his early work *Psychologie der Weltanschauungen* Jaspers already recognized the significance of faith as irreducible to cognitive thought. A matured treatment of faith as a fundamental feature of the absolute consciousness of Existenz appeared in *Philosophie*, Vol. I, "Illumination of Existenz" (Selection 13). He credits his wife with his insight into the phenomenon of faith:

> I gained a powerful impetus toward the question of faith from my wife. Early on, without a real break and in essential loyalty to her heritage, she inwardly transformed the orthodox Jewish faith into a biblically founded philosophizing. Her life was permeated by religious reverence. She respected the religious wherever she encountered it. . . . Her life—without dogma and without Law, touched from childhood on by the breath of the Jewish prophets—was guided by an unflinching, unconditional morality. I felt a kinship with her, and encouraged to bring to light what was surely effective yet hidden behind the veil of intellectuality.[1]

Before *Philosophie* was published Jaspers presented his research in his lectures. In the late 1920s a Catholic priest who was an auditor pointed out to him that he regards what Jaspers had presented to belong to theology. Jaspers recalls: "These words . . . took me aback. Clearly I am speaking of matters which others consider to be theological; yet I do not speak as a theologian but as a philosopher. This had to be clarified."[2] In consequence Jaspers worked out the concept of philosophic faith as distinct from revelational faith; the first published result was *Der philosophische Glaube* (1947), i.e., "Philosophical Faith," entitled in English translation *The Perennial Scope of Philosophy*. In 1953 there occurred the well-known controversy between Rudolph Bultmann and Jaspers on the question of Bultmann's program of demythologizing the biblical scriptures. The challenge which Jaspers's distinction of philosophic faith from revelational faith presented to theology was widely debated and

NOTES

1. *Philosophische Autobiographie*, p. 115ff. Translated by the editors.
2. *Ibid.*, p. 114.

continued to engage him in his later years. His final elaboration of this problem was also his last main work in philosophy, *Der philosophische Glaube angesichts der Offenbarung*; in English: *Philosophic Faith and Revelation*. All the selections in this subpart are taken from this work.

Selection 64

HOW PHILOSOPHICAL FAITH AND REVELATIONAL FAITH SEE EACH OTHER

EDITORS:

In this selection Jaspers observes that "what will become of the churches may decide the fate of the West." This is the key to the challenging concern with which Jaspers turns his attention to the revelational faith of the Christian churches. What motivates his concern is the need, as he sees it, for the perpetuation of the Bible as a source of faith; to him the Bible, like Greek philosophy, is one of the pillars of the Western spirit. Jaspers recognizes the Christian churches as irreplaceable proponents and carriers of biblical faith. The danger to the churches, which consists in their waning appeal, in their progressive failure to be convincing, in the "fragility" of their theology, especially in Protestantism, is therefore a danger to the perpetuation of biblical faith. The renewal of Christian theology as a vital spiritual force of the West—at a time when the West has ceased to be normative for what it means to be human and must take its place in a larger world that is now one world—is therefore of basic concern to a philosophy sensitive to the historicity of faith and to the role of tradition as a source of faith.

In this selection Jaspers spells out the problem of the philosophical concern over the revelational faith of the Christian churches, and proceeds to examine the different ways philosophic faith and revelational faith regard and appraise each other. The original of the selection appears in *Der philosophische Glaube angesichts der Offenbarung*, pp. 477–83; the translation is provided by the editors. For E. B. Ashton's translation see *Philosophical Faith and Revelation*, pp. 321–25.

TEXT:

The churches are the organizations that transmit faith from generation to generation. What takes place within them, what their message is and how it is promulgated, how they formulate their thinking and shape their symbols, how they perform their rites—this is of the utmost importance for the whole Western world. There the truthfulness and earnestness of individuals could find the ground of a great community. There, congregated around the rite, believers, priests, and theologians could testify to the way in which they exist in the presentness of the eternal.

Quite possibly the fate of the Western world will be decided by what will become of the churches. To the extent to which church-related matters become mere trappings of life, are leveled, as conventions and habits, to mere outward repetition, their power wanes even if most people remain church members. If, together with this, untruthfulness also grows, then, indeed, the groundwork is laid for any kind of disaster. Hence the great concern among the churches for the strength and truthfulness of the faith.

Philosophy, in distinction to faith in revelation, lacks organization; it is an actuality diffused among individuals, without the power emanating from the backing of a church, a state, a party, a structured mass movement; hence what philosophers think is considered "private." They may claim to stand within the *philosophia perennis*. But this claim is not recognized.

Whoever philosophizes cannot do so on the basis of an authority vested in him by some power in the world. He does it on his own authority before a power which he posits for himself by finding it present in the philosophizing of the millennia.

When such a person speaks about the possibilities inherent in the churches he must know that he is not invested with any kind of authority. But the inherent nature of this matter causes him, in his participation in the serious things that do—or do not—take place in the churches and by means of them, to direct his thoughts toward these possibilities. For it is there that the factors determining future being-human can be brought into play.

Perhaps he can glimpse a realm of the possible or even see farther, for one moment, than the customary playing-along with what already exists would allow. Perhaps his thinking might even help where individuals, being deeply affected out of their primal source, seek clarity in the church. Perhaps he can give encouragement where a life, out of a *pneuma* that is still obscure to itself, strives toward the light. Perhaps he places conceptual means at someone's disposal that are essential for practical thought. Perhaps he can confirm, in what exists at present, a presentiment of what may come to be, the very earliest signs of which are just beginning to be observable.

I am convinced that the substance of liberal faith will experience, in this at present so threatening situation, a radical transformation of its appearance as regards its language, message, practical living. This transformation in its radicalness may look to those who are bound by transmitted forms like the destruction of the faith promulgated by the churches. For the churches remain convincing only when they achieve this transformation out of the depth of their biblical earnestness and when this earnestness breaks down the shells of their institutions and dogmas and finds in them a contemporary language.

When I believe I see the fragility of modern Protestant theology then this very fragility seems to me to offer an opportunity. The fragility, together with the fundamental religious freedom of Protestantism, could arrive at a new form precisely at this juncture in this world where Christianity is weakest both in its ecclesiastical manifestation as well as in the practice of faith.

Everything I am saying here is merely thought without action. It is in the churches themselves that it would have to be carried out and, at the same time, be thought through better than I am able to. Only in practice, through actualization in community, can that take place in spiritual counseling, in sermons, and in ritual acts which is the goal of philosophical thinking.

How strangely disproportionate is the relationship when an individual writes about such great things! How minute is the thought of the individual before the overwhelming current of human history and its spiritual forces! In this thinking he may range far and speculate deep but his expression makes him humble. Perhaps he hopes, here and there, to expand a glimmer of light into a greater clarity or to bring back to this age an old forgotten truth.

It has always been a precarious enterprise for philosophers to interfere in the theologians' business and to tell them what they ought to do—as if philosophy, philosophical faith, were the court of last appeal of all faith. I merely wish to pose questions, indicate possibilities, try out schemes, remind.

Among those who believe in revelation and those who philosophize there are individuals who can be close to each other. The practical aspects of their lives and their judgments may in fact coincide. What may alienate them from each other are the tone of their statements of faith, their different hierarchical order of things, the exclusivity, the hidden breaking-off of communication. The believers on both sides hear the ciphers, and with the earnestness which, as such, is what is truly human, what binds together in truth. The believer, whether grounded philosophically or in revelation, does not want to quarrel but to tell about himself.

Let us summarize once more how philosophical faith and faith in revelation speak to each other across an abyss.

The Conception of Revelational Faith as Seen from Philosophy.

In our historical presentation we made the following distinctions: Prophets proclaimed what God said to them.—Churches and priests declared the texts to be holy and inspired and claimed to be the ones to interpret these texts correctly.—Apostles testified that God had appeared on earth in Christ.

All three modes of revelation require, in addition, an authority that will decide who was a genuine prophet, what texts are inspired, the testimony of which apostle is valid. Revelational faith must abide by this authority, otherwise it has nothing to hold on to. Ultimately it is the churches that are this authority. St. Augustine has expressed this . . . with magnificent clarity: I would not give credence to the Gospels if the authority of the Catholic Church did not prompt me to do so.

But if this authority is not believed, then this spells the end of the separation of the Holy Scriptures from the rest of literature. Then they are just like other writings of high caliber. Nothing can alter this even if this special status was a matter of course for thousands of years (what a brief span!). That certain texts were selected as being canonical is then merely a historical fact whose origin can be discovered and which has parallels in China and India. But these texts attain a higher rank by being selected as canonical only for those who believe in revelation and not for the rest of mankind.

However, in their substance they are by no means unimportant for the person who does not have faith in revelation. Only his relationship to them is a different, freer one. For now the prophets, inspiration, apostles are modes of appearance of the entry of truth into the world. These modes of appearance are comprehended in the ciphers "prophet," "inspiration," "apostle." This has two consequences:

First: The cipher can find its resonance in the self-understanding of the individual person. Thus, for example, my consciousness of being the instrument of an Encompassing, of doing and thinking what transcendence demands, of, to be sure, not knowing that I am in its service but feeling it to be a possibility—such consciousness can become a cipher that makes me humble. This cipher can be true only if it appears as a demand made by man on himself and not if it appears as the justification of a demand made on others. For I have to authenticate that it can be true and what its content is, not by considering myself an instrument but through what I do, what I realize and say.

Secondly: Whatever makes its appearance as revelation, whoever preaches as prophet or apostle, cannot as yet be valid as such. Cipher is possibility, not actuality. Hence everything that lays claim to holy absoluteness and unconditional authority is subject to criticism. Each of us has to put to the test, through his own possible Existenz, what the prophet claims, what enters the world by way of inspiration, what is testified to by the apostle.

This criticism is not—contrary to what theologians want to make us believe—a criticism of God; it is not a foolish instruction to God, prescribing what he can or cannot do. Rather, it is a criticism aimed at the authorities in the world who lay claim to being the ones empowered to speak in the name of God. Human beings, no matter what their position, no matter what their creed, remain human beings. And as far as we, who are not able to believe in revelation, are concerned, they wrongly demand as obedience toward God what is merely obedience toward their positions, their church, toward what has been wrought by human beings.

This is no judgment about God but about human pretensions. What is manifested in revelational faith exists, according to religious statistics, only for a minority of men and is, within this minority, in fact only for a second minority the word of God itself. For us it is a world of ciphers and not of divine realities—it is the floating idiom of transcendence and not a real act on the part of God—it is the interpretability of possible meaning and not the object of obedience.

What is actuality for the believer in revelation is not actuality as such. We do not speak against God but against the human claim to be God's representative. We must state the position valid for us. Negatively, there is no direct reality of God in the world, that is, no God who would speak in the world through an authority, representing him, residing in an office, word, or sacrament, a God to whom we would show obedience through our obedience toward these offices. Positively, God has created us for freedom and reason in which we are given to ourselves as a gift; in both we are responsible to an authority which we find in ourselves, that which is infinitely more than we are ourselves, and speaks only indirectly. We follow Kant's interpretation: divine wisdom is no less admirable in what it bestows upon us than in what it denies to us; for if God were to stand before us in his majesty we would become puppets in our obedience and would not remain free as the kind of being God willed us to be.

We find that, for us, the God who manifests himself in the reality of revelation, as measured against the hidden God, cannot be God himself. This is not the denial of God turning against faith in God but the hidden as against the revealed God. The philosophic consciousness of the actuality of transcendence turns against the reality of revelation.

The Conception of Philosophic Faith as Seen from Revelational Faith

1. The charge: Seen from the vantage point of revelational faith, a philosophical faith cannot be a faith in God. Bultmann writes: "Indeed, God can be correctly understood either here or there; and from the standpoint of Christian faith, humanistic faith in God must be designated as error, as delusion—insofar as it means to be a faith in God." (*Studium Generale*, Vol. I, p. 74) I quote this theologian, one of the personally most tolerant ones, to whom one can least ascribe the arrogance that occurs among theologians, in order to show that it lies in the nature of things, i.e., in revelational faith itself, to think along these lines. Thus, even a man such as Bultmann is forced to think along these lines.

Thence comes the constantly repeated charge: The notion of transcendence is a merely speculative experience. It remains pale in its abstractness. It is impotent in mere meditation. For it lacks actuality because it is aimed at what is not actual.—We are told further: For revelational faith is personal. He confronts us as the Thou with whom, in prayer, communication is possible from person to person (whereas philosophic faith knows God as person only as the cipher of what is the source of personality in man but is itself infinitely more than personality, whose form would limit him).—The revealed God helps in the world; he effects change through intervention; he is the cause of salutary worked-for events and is the guarantor that what looks to me like disaster is all to the good. I experience his mercy in his acts, which become palpable to me internally as real (whereas philosophic faith thinks of providence as a cipher the interpretation of which in the individual historic process seems to it to be rationally absurd and refutable; yet it is to illuminate as cipher the mystery intruding itself upon us without being knowable or realizable).— For revelational faith God's act of revealing himself comes first. It is not we who seek God. For revelational faith the proposition dealing with the prior action of God applies to concrete actions and happenings (for philosophic faith such a proposition applies only to being given to oneself as a gift in a world which is itself not the ultimate but is appearance or transition). The God of the revelational believer is concrete, proximate, he is the living God of the Bible; the divinity of philosophy is abstract, remote, merely thought.

2. Our answer: The proximate God is indispensable for finite beings but is present only in ciphers. These are manifold in their nature; hence the proximate God comes to be in a manner consistent with polytheism. This polytheism is present in veiled form in factual revelational faith even though the one God is preserved in dogma. For revelational faith the one God, when he is near, assumes—unnoticed—a particular form. The One remains the distant God whose oneness is itself a cipher.

The ciphers, having become the concrete reality of God, soon become many gods, hence untrue and the object of superstition. They remain possible truth in the ciphers only as the historic language of the distant God.

The distant God, even if only thought of, keeps the horizon open. He liberates us from the concrete gods and revelations if they become fixed in superstition; he liberates us from all exclusivities, fanaticisms, acts of force which lie hidden in the faith in the God who manifests himself in time and space.

Philosophic faith does not ever want to lose in the proximate gods as ciphers the distant, solely actual God, but it does want to experience the distant God in the proximate ciphers as living. Hence all that is proximate remains in suspension. But it is only through the proximate that there occurs the historic immersion of faith here and now.

Philosophic faith denies for itself a revelation that excludes and translates it and its contents into ciphers; a secondary reason for this is the enlightenment that knows, as it proceeds, what it does and does not know. But what is essential is the actuality of transcendence itself in its hiddenness as it is experienced by philosophic faith. Measured against the notion of God appropriate to it—as it is present in the high points of biblical scriptures and in philosophy—the assertion that God became man (if a mode of expression used by the believers in revelation could, and would, be permitted to be used by philosophy) would have to appear as blasphemy; this is how it would have appeared to the man Jesus according to what we know about him.

The actuality of God is most palpable where it is not veiled by any embodiment or human approximation, rather, where the words of the Bible are taken quite seriously: Thou shalt not make an image or likeness—your thoughts are not God's thoughts—and where these words at the limits are valid for believing Existenz in shipwreck. For, to be sure, Existenz reads the floating and ambiguous ciphers but does not create itself an image of God.

Selection 65

A CHANGE IN THE APPEARANCE OF BIBLICAL RELIGION?

EDITORS:

The following selection displays some of the central issues on which Jaspers challenges the Christian churches to move toward the kind of renewal whereby they can again be the primary carriers of the biblical tradition. Jaspers is quite clear about the fact that such a renewal would, in effect, be nothing less than a transformation of the biblical religion that is Christianity. He presses on to show that such a transformation would have to activate possibilities which run counter to established traditions of the Church regarded as an institution. Yet he also shows that such possibilities reside within the Church regarded as the embodiment of biblical religion.

The selection is divided into two sections. The first discusses various ways and aspects of "dealing with the Bible." Taking up the hermeneutical question which has been of such great interest to both theologians and philosophers, Jaspers shows that what is regarded as revelation is itself the result of interpretation, and thus not the source of faith any more than it is the result of faith. Jaspers develops the related point that the Bible has been the source of a great wealth of faith-content, including conflicting beliefs, and that the churches themselves have been the arena where such conflicts have been carried out. For Jaspers the validity of faith lies in its historicity. Thus it does not gain its validity by prevailing in a conflict of institutional forces nor does it lose its validity by succumbing in such a conflict. It is on the basis of such analyses that Jaspers upholds what he calls the principle of Protestantism in distinction to the Protestant creed; and he questions the creedal approach to

biblical faith and the concomitant phenomena of dogma, magisterial and min-
isterial authoritarianism, and the rejection of the continuous validity of
Judaism.

The second section discusses some provocative examples of how the faith
of the Christian churches is in need of transformation if they are to regain
their importance. The principle operative here is that interpretation involves
both appropriation and rejection; no creedal propositions can enclose the
truth of the Bible. The Bible so viewed is not the testimony of one specific
faith, but "the space in which different possibilities of faith—each related to
the depth of the divine—are locked in mutual struggle," for the Bible is as rich
as life itself. Accordingly Jaspers takes up certain features of the faith of the
Christian Church which he suggests as being inessential to its truth and obsta-
cles to its viability: the divinity of Jesus; the function of revelation as a foundational fact (rather than as a cipher); the claim that the truth of a dogmatic
creed excludes all other truth.

The selection has been translated by the editors from *Der philosophische
Glaube angesichts der Offenbarung*, pp. 489–508. E. B. Ashton's translation
may be found in *Philosophical Faith and Revelation*, pp. 329–43.

TEXT:

Is it possible for biblical revelational faith to change in its appearance? Can
this occur through recapturing its original earnestness? Can its vigor, which is
steadily declining today, be revived?

One can contest the fact of its weakness, and rightly so, insofar as it is not
possible to know faith as it is preserved within each individual in his suffering
and his dying. One can merely observe his behavior, his decisions, judgments,
and actions in the world.

We saw the resistance fighters in all European countries, their courage
unto death. Their resolution to fight grew out of their own freedom and not
out of obedience toward an authority in the world. We read their words expressive of their self-understanding. Independent of all classes and groups not
only Christians but liberals, socialists, skeptics, and people who considered
themselves to be communists manifested the same self-sacrificing courage,
with the same calm in the face of death, with the same strength of faith, with
the illumination of having to act in this way as the expression of their authentic freedom.

The way people express their self-understanding may be out of keeping
with what they experienced and did. What was the actuality of faith in the
resistance fighters nobody knows because of the totally different way in which
they expressed the content of their faith. The credibility and aptness of the
documents comes through for us only as we look at the individual human

being. Then we hear the tone, the utterly simple as well as strangely convoluted thinking, judging, and justifying.

Neither can anyone know—besides they themselves—what was the source of the earnest commitment on the part of those resistance fighters who believed in the Bible. Jews and Christians testified to their faith in biblical revelation to the point of death—a deeply stirring experience for the survivors. What is certain is that among our contemporaries there is proof of a high level of earnest faith and that biblical revelatory faith did not outrank the other faiths.

But our present question does not concern itself with this earnestness which may be inherent in all men out of every spiritual or historic source. It concerns, rather, the special world of biblical faith as the continuity of tradition in which men partake of the earnestness of their ancestors.

Is it possible for biblical faith to reconstitute itself out of its source and arrive at the pure earnestness that lies not in the confession of a creed but in the state of soul, in action and in practical decisions? To these may belong, in situations of the highest peril, the confession of a "martyr" but not the safe, tranquilizing, general confession felt to be a meritorious act and often combined with a dangerous aggressivity.

Can the *pneuma* once again become a force, can men experience it in community as a source in the present? Can it take hold of them in clarity, in measuredness and prudence to such an extent that man as individual knows himself to be one with the Encompassing that unites him with the others as if the fullness of Being were to infuse them?

The task is not the transformation of the substance of biblical faith but the transformation of its appearance in the form of statements of faith. To be sure, only through such statements can the substance be imparted. But where the statement is detached from the substance the believer does not recognize his primal faith in the statement. Modes of representation, thought formulations, ciphers which, under different spiritual presuppositions, were once appropriate to the historical situation, are so no longer. What is necessary if substance is to preserve itself is not its progress but a change in its garb.

1. What to make of the Bible?

There exists a theological expertise, first of all in the tremendous dogmatic labors of millennia, secondly in the historical knowledge of biblical texts (initiated by Spinoza and then further developed since the eighteenth century). It seems presumptuous to want to participate in the discussion in this world of expertise if one is a "layman" and "not an expert."

But what has happened and is happening here concerns all of us. Hence we do not need to respect an esoteric theological science that wants to dictate to us as our authority, except in what we realize ourselves. Since what is essential is simple, it is a matter of aiming directly at it and not drowning it in the mass of nonessential information.

a. The Bible is the depository of the religious, mythic, historical, existential experiences of a millennium. Its texts, which differ exceedingly in their literary form, have been selected in the course of time from a much more voluminous literature and were finally considered a completed whole and declared canonical. One can no longer divest the Bible of this canonical character, valid for thousands of years, since it is the expression of historic ties; this is true also of the corresponding Indian and Chinese texts.

The origin of the canon of the Old and New Testament, which came to be through selecting from among the texts available at the time (and now preserved only in part) is nonetheless an incidental historical result. It is not essential for the appropriation of the content. The motifs of this historical process are manifold and can hardly be disentangled; but this is a subject of historical rather than factual interest.

b. Like any other text, the Bible needs to be understood. This is conveyed through exegesis, but the text itself already conveys understanding; it refers to an underlying basic text, so to speak, which the spoken and written ones are already interpreting. Where is the line between basic and interpretive text, and between the interpretive text and our own interpretation?

Theologians have made a distinction between the substance of revelation—which comes from God and is eternally the same—and our exegesis, which is accomplished by theological effort and has no claim to absolute truth for its particular interpretations. These are subject to change.

Yet where is the thing itself, the revelation, and where does exegesis begin? After all, there is no sentence in the Bible that is not already exegesis. At the very least, it is translation into human language, into human ways of thought. We have the thing itself only in its exegesis. We can never encounter it pure or uninterpreted.

This view is opposed, first by Luther: *"Das Wort sie sollen's lassen stahn"*—the Word should be allowed to stand. But Luther himself made distinctions in the Bible; he even rejects the whole Epistle of St. James, for instance. Who can tell the Word that ought to be allowed to stand from the one that is questionable or even to be rejected?

Opposed, moreover, is any creed in the form of propositions. But what is a creed if not exegesis? The speculative-dogmatic interpretation effected by this confession and aided by gnostic and philosophic thinking had its beginning already in the New Testament, and this collection of texts contains altogether multiple interpretive theologies that defy reduction to a common denominator.

Once more: what is interpreted is present to us only in these interpretations. What we encounter in texts is such interpretation and interpretation of such interpretation. Correspondingly, even the historical investigation of the New Testament can at no place find that which is being interpreted without interpretation having taken place. These interpretations are developed, unfolded, proceed in different directions and receive quick divergent accents.[1]

If the unity, the substance, the unchangeable element of God's revelation is, in fact, not present as itself in any message or theology; if, rather, all language remains a cipher; if God's words, God's deeds, God's will, as expressed, are interpretations in the form of ciphers: cannot, then, philosophic interpretation and theological interpretation—which, from the very first, draw on one another—come together in the end?

c. Thoughtful use of the Bible and of what it speaks is a bringing before-the-mind's eye of what was seen, experienced, and thought, from the wondrous ancient Bible stories and the historical variations by way of the prophets' messages and the pious songs and writings to the propositions intended to be dogmatical.

The interpretation that has an existential concern and does not merely observe historically raises the import of the one who speaks from that position above the randomness of merely historical data. The vigor and essentiality of the interpretation arises from its earnestness and is manifested in its practical consequences.

Interpretation that is substantive is both appropriation and rejection.

Study teaches us the fundament of historical knowledge. We acquire information, images, thoughts. Historical understanding [*Verstehen*] is a means to the pure visualization of documentary evidence, to the seeing, from a distance, what does or does not concern us.

Appropriation, however, is more than historical understanding. Appropriation means allowing—in the battle of the cipher—these ciphers to become the language of an actuality. We are the target of this language insofar as we are existentially open. We reject it if we experience it as the language of non-actuality or of an alien power, or as enticement into darkness, untruthfulness, or evil. Appropriation is a matter for each individual, for each unique, irreplaceable Existenz that has come upon, in the Bible, the language that carries the greatest earnestness for it.

Whereas we study the texts in their historical connections, we hear truth in its timelessness. We arrive at the existential meaning in our historical studies the more we appropriate the unhistorical and supra-historical by means of what is in reality and in its intended meaning is historically factual. Those are not universal concepts and do not become adequately present in any universal thinking. This supra-historical is the eternal which knows no progress, which appears in time and renews itself in unlimited, always original, repetition.

We must beware of thinking that the eternal—which has spoken to men all through the ages—is now being expressed, in the language of our times, in its ultimate truth. We can never get a complete overview of ourselves in our appearance. And yet we know that we are historic as such appearance, even in our conceptions and forms of thought, even on the basis of a great tradition of thought which we can never sufficiently appropriate.

Hence even if, by virtue of our insight, we resist the fixation of dogmas and confessions, we do so conscious of that which endures in change, which speaks to us always but is not present, in its speaking, in its final form, which is eternally present in every authentic appearance but is absolute as such in none.

Historical investigation as such does not, by any means, lead to faith. To be sure, it shows, with understanding, the phenomena of faith, but from the outside, as it were. But it brings before our mind's eye a knowledge in which the self-illumination of faith can take place.

The purpose of historical cognition of the Bible is not critical destruction through relativizing and unmasking; rather, it is the road to historically accurate and true representation of those religious experiences which assume their true meaning for us only where we feel addressed by them, appropriate or reject them.

We owe it to the extraordinarily thorough work of theological historians that we are able to know the appearances and transformations of faith and its heterogeneous motives. When the historical facts are uncovered in honesty we find the ground that is indispensable for the truthfulness of faith.

But if, in our historical investigation, we search for the beginning and source of New Testament revelation itself, it cannot be found. Where lies this source? In Jesus as historic actuality? In the faith of the apostles? In the early church which, according to Overbeck, is, by the very nature of the thing, a place that is forever inaccessible to us? What we find in history is not yet the revelation but the reality of the living and the executed Jesus. But the revelation that follows is no longer just that but is already interpretation of revelation.

For the historic source of our common thinking the story exists in the first instance not as historical knowledge but as appropriation, always repeated and yet always new. We feel it and affirm it as the ground of our own being. Historical knowledge may entail the destruction of this historic fulfillment (through the relativizing of everything) as well as its enhancement (through our consciousness of eternal presentness). What is authentically historic is the infinite ground which cannot be diluted in a doctrine and become universal. This ground, in keeping with its substantial nature, can be changed in its appearance but it cannot be reconstituted as something historically knowable.

d. In our free appropriation of the Bible there takes place the awakening and enhancement of impulses different in their origins. There we find validated the joy of battle as well as the nonresisting humility of suffering, the idea of nationhood and the notion of humanity, polytheism and monotheism, priesthood and prophetic religion. There we hear about knowledge of the law and of God, about justice and love. There pure transcendence speaks and the immanence of man-become-God is preached. There is fanaticism there as well as free resignation, we encounter God as the guarantor of worldly ends and as the pure cipher of faith unencumbered by purpose. There are in it denial of the world as well as its affirmation, mystical obscurity and clear faith, an apocalyptic vision of history and an eternal present, the transfiguration of vulgar passions and the purity of life, rejoicing in nature and asceticism.

The Bible is as rich as life itself. It is not the testimony of one single specific faith; rather, it is the space in which different possibilities of faith—each related to the depth of the divine—are locked in mutual struggle. In doing so, they gain the higher level on which they can be taken altogether seriously. They lead to the highest summits of faith and speak in irreplaceable ciphers.

e. The Bible is full of contradictions. In this book of books irreconcilable spiritual forces, views of life, modes of practical living encounter each other. The way we treat the Bible is like the way we treat life: we must move within these contradictions in order to partake in the truth, which becomes clearer only through them.

These contradictions have challenged the power of thought, through the ages, to overcome them through interpretation—e.g., the multiple meanings to statements in accommodation and combination. What was sought was the unity of faith without opposition; this was maintained prematurely in theologies and sketched out rationally. Through its dogmatics the Christian Church made Christ the God-man into the unity to which everything was related and to which violence was done in its understanding. Yet this faith in Christ did itself not become unitary but suffered dogmatic schisms. One can neither determine historically nor fix conceptually a center of biblical experiencing and thinking. And therein lies a characteristic of the tremendous, life-giving power of the Bible which wakens our existential earnestness and fills us with ciphers that stay with us always.

Neither can we determine historically the unity of the Christian faith of the New Testament that is particular within the Bible. We have only the fact that men believed in it and that this faith fixed its object together with its inherent contradictions through the canonization of the chosen texts. We see the unity in fact only in the Church, in its will to unity, in its reality. The Church became the crystallizing center through whose decisions gnostic ideas, stoic ethics, Greek speculation came together, permeated, and surrounded the Biblical substance.

But is this will to unity which prevailed in the course of time—though accompanied by ever new divisions and schisms—the sign of the unity of this truth of faith and of its one unique truth? By no means! To be sure, in a sociological sense the unity made possible by the Church is what is most durable in the world. But in this way the original nature of the faith was made subject to the condition of ecclesiastical faith (i.e., the belief in the Church as the mystical body of Christ) and thus was changed or forgotten. However, the truth does not rest primarily in the sociological reality of the Church and the belief in it but in the multiplicity of ways of reading the ciphers on the part of Existenzen differing in their origins.

f. The bisection of the Bible into a Jewish and a Christian part—whereby the Christian elements are extracted from the Old Testament, while the rest is discarded, and the residual influences of what is Jewish are eliminated through criticism from the New Testament—is an outrageous act of Christian orthodoxy. Through this act even sober and objective scholars were motivated to operate with ideal-typical entities of Judaism and Christianity in such a manner that—rather than throwing a specific light on the earlier phenomena on the basis of certain points of view of later times—they constructed two mutually exclusive religious forces. In this process the best that belongs to the Jewish heritage is denied to the Jews. This bisecting act of spiritual violence prevents not only free appropriation in dealing openly with the Bible but, on the basis of prejudice, a historically and objectively, equally untrue separation is achieved. The Old as well as the New Testament both derive equally from the Jews. Within the pious wrestling of the Jewish soul arise all the mutually contradictory possibilities. The faith of the New Testament grew out of Judaism no less than did the Old Testament. Jesus was a Jew. The apostles, too, were all Jews. The establishment of synagogue and church is a historical phenomenon of secondary importance. It has no more impact on an individual's being deeply affected by the truth of faith—whether it be called philosophical or theological—than any worldly institution can have which arrogates unto itself the power of sanctity. Under the guidance [of organized religion] one is speedily led astray whereas the life of faith on the part of individuals, families, communities is the immediate actuality to which we are bound, into which we are born; this is a gift given to us by fate. Dealing with the Bible does not yet mean participation in a specific religious group; rather it means participation in appropriating interpretation out of each individual freedom.

As we ponder the sublime experiences which speak to us out of the Bible we come to know more readily how we live and what we do. Through the Bible depths are uncovered within us which allow us to gaze into the ground of things, for it leads to experiencing the ultimate. The Bible shows us the unconditionality of acting, in the consciousness of a convenant with God, in an obedience that understands itself in effective ciphers, yet in freedom that neither closes its eyes before the diversity of what is possible nor in any way anticipates completion.

g. The return, beyond traditional forms, to the primal source is not the Protestant Creed but is the principle of Protestantism. It finds this source in the Biblical texts. Here, within the changes occurring in tradition, lies the broad enduring ground. But this ground is here only in the way in which it is understood in each instance.

For the Protestant principle a scholarly acquaintance with the texts, their study, and historical knowledge are a presupposition for appropriating, with understanding [verstehend], the faith at its source. Hence we read the Bible together with learned commentaries; but we do not do this in order to be content with the historical knowledge and Verstehen gained in this manner. We expect, rather, to gain in this way in truth the real historical ground from which we are addressed through the texts, which is a matter quite different from historical significance and reality. The authority resides not in the word but in the "spirit." It speaks in the Bible only to him whose spirit comes to encounter this spirit. It is not learned knowledge and not some kind of cognition, it is only our appropriation in interpreting which awakens us to the present actuality of original faith.

h. There is a difference between the philosophic and theological interpretation and appropriation of the Bible. Theology knows "scriptural evidence," philosophy does not. Both interpret, but philosophy does so such that the Bible does not, on principle, possess priority over other texts.

Whoever is familiar with the "proof text" reserves for himself, for all intents and purposes, the correct interpretation, whether on his own authority (like Luther) or through the catholic authority of the Church. Other interpretations are considered as false. Experience teaches us that there is no end to the disputes between theological interpretations. The real battle is fought over who is the authority empowered to determine which interpretation is the right one. The self-certainty of the new interpretation, manifested by a reformer who claims this authority for himself, spells unrest for his contemporaries if they pay attention to him. But the silent power of ecclesiastical authority brings tranquility. It is irritating to follow the method used to do battle by means of proof-texts, for clear-eyed believers in revelation just as much as for people who philosophize. It is a battlefield on which comes to light what lies at the bottom of this kind of a faith whose proof rests on dogma: the persecution of heretics, Luther's "firm assertion," a sterile labor for cognition through faith, sophistical attempts at reconciling contradictions in the Bible.

Historically, the consequence of their contradictions has been their contradictory ways of believing that almost every way of living one's life, almost every concrete decision may claim to be based on the Bible. So much can be justified by reference to the Bible that one may be inclined to state that everything in it is contradictory. This is understandable considering that the Bible is a collection of texts whose origin spans a thousand years.

The person who rejects textual evidence on the grounds that a process by means of which one can prove everything in fact proves nothing, and that in the sphere of illumination through faith proofs are altogether meaningless, is able to accept as valid for himself what he receives through his appropriation. In the face of another actuality of faith he is modest, he is never absolutely certain of himself as regards statements [of faith]. For him, all essential resolve rests in his life's decisions, in the continuity of his Existenz, in his appearance within existence and not in acts of confession and tenets of faith. In the Bible he finds the ground of this freedom as well as of this earnestness.

Authority does not rest in the Word nor in the text nor in the Bible but in the Encompassing, in that which, in original appropriation, in free converse with the Bible, is subjective and objective at the same time.

i. Can we hear revelation? We can, in any case, hear its content expressed in human language but we cannot hear that it is revelation.

We must differentiate between revelation and revelatory faith. Revelation—if it were actual—knows no conditions; when God himself speaks then there is no authority that could impose conditions on him. There remains only obedience. Revelatory faith, on the other hand, is a reality that pertains to men, hence it is subject to conditions.

If the philosophic experience of transcendence appropriates contents of biblical faith it must relinquish the form of being-revealed. Can biblical faith be appropriated at all in philosophizing?

The person whose faith is grounded philosophically can agree with the following passage by Heinrich Barth which the latter means to direct against him: "What commandment of science or any obligation of truth demands of someone thinking critically that he set limits to the discovery of truth in such a way that he confine the possibilities of cognition and the 'illumination' of our Existenz to philosophy, literature, wisdom-doctrines of all sorts and that he exclude that unique possibility which, as 'revelation', has experienced epistemological distinction? What reason, what cognitive stringency forbids the philosopher to draw his instruction not only from the documents of the history of philosophy, of world literature, of mysticism, of far Eastern religions but also from Biblical tradition, especially since he observes that in it the central problems of Existenz are touched upon with incomparable forcefulness? It is up to a free and open spirit not to set arbitrary limits to the possibilities of the logos and consequently to remain open and ready to hear the 'Word' no matter to which order or provenance it may pertain."[2]

We only have to add: Keeping oneself open does not yet mean hearing and obeying. It means hearing in the sense of listening with one's own whole being. But the manner of hearing which believes to hear God himself in a revelation may remain absent. The hearing of revelation *qua* revelation cannot, as such, be proved. Within the framework of epistemological clarification it cannot be founded absolutely, for it proves only itself. It does not stand within the line of possibilities of experiencing truth. Hence it is not distinguished epistemologically, and does not fall within the scope of epistemological clarification. Where revelation is heard as revelation something entirely different comes to be.

However this other is not "forbidden." What is forbidden is to ground it through some kind of logos or to turn it into a universally valid cognition. Wherever this is attempted the meaning of revelation is violated, which, as revelation, can be heard only by him who is granted that grace. And at the same time the possibility of logos becomes unclear. Philosophically our thinking takes place within the truthfulness which does not intend to rob the monstrous, the inconceivable, the alogical and antilogical of its due.

It is possible that we appropriate the Bible without arriving at revelatory faith. An open philosophy demands of the thinker that this absence of faith not turn into self-satisfaction. However we cannot acknowledge the counterdemand according to which, in true openness, revelation must be heard as revelation.

The philosopher, who does not hear revelation as revelation, cannot submit to the believer in revelation, just as he cannot yield to a false enlightenment that wants to base itself on science alone. If science reproaches philosophy by claiming that it is a secularized theology, a surreptitious theology, our answer is: Philosophy is temporally prior to biblical revelation; it is existentially more original because accessible to each human being *qua* human being; it is capable of hearing truth even in the Bible and to appropriate this truth.

2. Some Main Aspects of Possible Change

It is impossible to predict what contents of faith will be operative among men in the future. If one could truly tell it would already constitute its actualization. The individual can only express the manner of thought of his faith, as I have attempted to do. At this point I would like to speak of three acts of renunciation which seem to me to be the condition for the future earnestness of a life in the communality of faith. We have in mind people who are born into our era and hence live with its knowledge, its realities and its unprecedented experiences.

a. Jesus is no longer Christ the God-man for all believers.

(1) Let us summarize once more: The historical situation at the beginning of Christianity, when it was one of the forms of biblical faith, was the following:

Jews laid the foundation in their experience of God. Their Bible is our Bible. It has been enlarged through an appendix, the New Testament, by Jews who, after the execution of Jesus, believed him to be the Christ. This appendix also contains the tradition handed down about Jesus the man.

Jesus and his original message can be apprehended as historical reality. As is all historical reality, this one, too, is uncertain in its limits. Up to a certain point it is accessible to historical research by using the means proper to it. But in these data Jesus stands before him who is able to look and be addressed, as a unique, unmistakable actuality and is seen with a subjective certainty that goes beyond what can be proven objectively by rational means.

But what is negatively certain, by way of historical analysis, is that: Jesus did not declare himself to be the Messiah, to be the Christ (the "Messiah-secret" is an untenable interpretation).

Jesus did not establish himself as a Sacrament. The Last Supper as a ritual act was instituted by the Apostles.

Jesus did not found a church; rather, the presupposition of his life and message was the imminent end of the world, to occur in his generation. Slowly, beginning with the community of the Apostles and the establishment of congregations, did the Church develop. Jesus is not its founder. The Church has to do with Jesus insofar as he was believed in as the Christ. This belief first appeared after his execution.

The churches carried with them the fire which, time and time again, broke through their incrustations and adaptations to the world. Through Jesus there comes into play what the churches conceal while basing themselves on him: the question directed to the fate and possibility of man. Through the Existenz of Jesus the man this question was posed, out of his closeness to God, with a depth never before achieved. Question and answer together both lay in the actualization of a human being who was able to say what he saw, believed, and demanded, what he lived and suffered.

The probity of the man Jesus measures all reality against the genuine being-human in the kingdom of God. Knowing himself as living immediately before the end of the world, Jesus is himself already a sign of the actuality of this kingdom.

For Jesus, the last of the Jewish prophets and bound to them, the idea of nationhood, the notion of law, the organization of priests and rites all faded away; theologies became a matter of indifference.

The Jews—suffering endlessly from injustice and lovelessness, persecuted, tortured, tormented, slain time and again—the Jews who, covenanted with God, still managed to maintain themselves as a remnant solely on the strength of their faith—a miracle of history—have brought forth in Jesus this great, humane figure as their representative, as it were. This figure represents human fate and Jewish fate in one.

Jesus as man is a cipher of being-human that says: Whoever lives and thinks like Jesus and is true without limitation must die by man since the reality of untruthful being-human cannot endure him.

(2) But this cipher is appropriated and interpreted further:

The cipher of the shipwreck of true man becomes the ancient cipher of the God who sacrifices himself.

Jesus is the Son of God, Christ, God Himself who, out of his love, wants to rescue man from being lost in sin, sacrificing himself in human form.

The cipher becomes an example to be followed. Man achieves eternal salvation by sacrificing himself like Christ-Jesus or by being sacrificed. Both— active seeking of martyrdom and passive having-to-suffer the ultimate—find tranquility in their approximation of the act of God.

However, every man who wants to build or be active within the world withdraws thereby from the imitation of Christ. But he, too, can be helped. For, without sacrificing himself or being sacrificed, he finds salvation through his faith that God the Christ sacrificed himself and was crucified in his place. He finds his justification solely through his faith in this act of Christ. It is astonishing: It is not I who make the sacrifice but the other does so for me. He has liberated me from the ultimate and allows me to live within the peace of such a faith.

Our perception of the man Jesus turns against this evaluation of the cipher.

(3) It is decisive for the future of biblical faith to assign central importance to the man Jesus and his faith. We are able to do this with our whole strength only when we give up the Christ as one of the particular biblical configurations insofar as the Christ-cipher intends to posit itself as absolute.

But the imitation of Jesus is not the only task demanded of man. Whoever denies himself this imitation is not at all dependent on that "justification solely through faith." Not only is it obvious that we—as well as the faithful of all the denominations—do not live according to the Sermon on the Mount but rather that we admit, with the honesty demanded by Jesus, that we do not want to. Our unwillingness to do so is based on our positive will to live, be active, plant and build in the world. We desire the way that leads through the world. Since no other path to eternity is granted to us than Existenz in the phenomenal world, we are—with respect to possibility beyond this world— left solely with truthfulness without reservation: we must not confuse, do things by halves, but must respect him who travels the other path, such as Francis of Assisi and many another.

And still more: we are bid to orient ourselves by Jesus in order to arrive at the truthfulness possible to us. For through the actuality of our world we pay an ineluctable price. As we orient ourselves by Jesus we become clearer in our mind as to what we do and want. The cipher of his being-human directs us toward becoming conscious of our fundamental limits and imperfections. We are not liberated from them by our desire for martyrdom no matter in what form. Neither are we liberated by justification save the one that is present in the good will, in probity, in the unconditional decision to truthfulness, but primarily in the power of love in which we are given to ourselves as a gift in the world.

(4) The question as to what role is played, in biblical faith, by the man Jesus and Christ-God is a particular and, as a whole, not a decisive question. God can be reached not only by way of Christ (as the Apostles teach). We are "Christians" even without believing in Christ as God become man. Christians? This appellation is to be understood historically. A complex situation caused biblical faith to be clothed in this name. Under the name of "Christianity," biblical religion became the fundament of the West. It seems correct historically as well as objectively to give today to Christian religion also the more comprehensive appellation of "biblical religion." The historical name "Christian religion" is, though ancient, restricting and hence misleading. In accordance with the texts which this Christian religion considers holy and on which it founds itself, it is a biblical religion.

Perhaps the greatest of the achievements credited to the founders of Christianity of the first centuries is their impressing the Bible, the whole Bible of the Old and New Testaments, on the faith and thought and interpretation of the West. The attempts to eliminate the biblical religion, to reject totally the Old Testament, to keep out of the New Testament a whole group of texts that now are part of it, with the intention of achieving a supposedly pure Christianity, all failed at that time. But these attempts have occasionally found approbation up to the present time and captured the sympathies even of Adolf Harnack. Whoever takes seriously the substance of biblical faith in God confronts with surprise and shock this phenomenon in which heterogeneous motives come together, ranging from a liberalistic easygoing attitude by way of abstract asceticism to the madness of racism, to form a poisonous mix.

b. Revelation Becomes the Cipher of Revelation

From the standpoint of philosophy we can ask: Is it possible that not only the content of revelation but the reality of revelation itself, which is maintained by faith, become a cipher? As far as our insight goes, the philosophizing person will never encounter revelation as reality unless he forgoes philosophizing. But is it a hopeless attempt to try to understand the very reality of revelation which exists for revelatory faith as cipher? Revelation seems to us to be either reality, in which case it must itself exist and needs no sign; or it is not reality at all; then the believer finds signs for it. Even for him the reality would not itself exist but be present in signs and ciphers. And further: he would not mean the reality in its true sense but as cipher.

What does it mean when we say that revelation becomes a cipher? Can a cipher of transcendence achieve its import by being experienced bodily as a reality in the world accompanied by the knowledge that it is not a reality in this sense?

Take the image of Moses on Mount Sinai. This event, including its details, has a power in its language that makes palpable that there is more involved in the Ten Commandments than law-like precepts that could be changed. Whence the unique power of the moral demand in its unconditionality which goes beyond its formulation in general terms? The cipher of the reality of an action by God gives us an answer.

Children are deeply moved by and accept such ciphers as if they were fairy tales about which the question of reality or unreality is not yet asked clearly. The ciphers do not lose their efficacy on adults when they lose their validity as unequivocal reality. But the reality of a tale told of the acts of God, of a divine event, of a human being that is more than human—this remains as cipher. Its reality is suspended and yet, as cipher, it is a language still. What is the nature of ciphers, namely to divest themselves of embodied reality, that becomes—in reality as cipher—something that can be expressed only as a paradox: a reality divesting itself of reality.

But does such a conception not weaken revelation? It is, in any case, a transformation of the meaning of revelation. Revelation as cipher is no longer what the believer in revelation meant by it. The theologian would in any case be distinguished from the philosopher in that he would unfold the cipher of revelation in all of its might.

We cannot do away with the paradox inherent in utterance, i.e., that what is contained in the substance of revelations would become purer and truer through divesting itself of the reality of revelation. The reality of revelation as such become a cipher of God's presence and would lend extraordinary might to its substance.

If it were possible to allow revelation as such to become a cipher, a change would take place in revealed faith. Perhaps this change has occurred at all times. It seems necessary for the general consciousness of our age. Then dogmas, sacraments, cults would find themselves in a crucible, as it were, one that does not destroy them but would change them into other forms of their conscious actualization. This actualization would become the medium in which biblical faith—out of its full seriousness and not only in cultic, meditative satisfactions and not in the shelteredness of the churches, and not at all in conventional acts—would find once more its inspiring, portentous, and credible appearance. The transformation would take place under the conditions of our age, its new knowledge and new world situation, in a manner which is in accord with the nature of the thing. It is not substance that changes but its appearance in consciousness. Philosophy and theology would enter upon the road to reunification.

Such a goal, so easily expressed, is not the object of a plan. The philosophizing indiviudal can look in that direction with uncertain hopes only. But he must remain aware that embodied revelation, whose embodiment is for him merely a cipher, may contain, for many a believer in revelation, a different secret of which he, the philosophizer, does not even have an inkling.

When the reality of revelation is considered a cipher it no longer stands out from the world of ciphers as a whole. It would then be the cipher that would allow the boundless yearning of man—that God himself be really present—to be viewed for a moment as fulfilled, as it were. But then man would immediately have to revert to the severity and greatness of his being-free as which man is created and for which God remains implacably hidden.

I am told that no theologian can join [the philosopher] in effecting the transformation of revelation into cipher, for doing so would destroy the foundation of his believing and thinking. My response: Perhaps the theologians who are influential today cannot do so; many of these are exceptional historical scholars but as theologians they are latter-day epigones. In believing they hold fast but feel no longer the *pneuma* in the strength of their faith. But perhaps modern men are capable of this transformation; men who, unwilling to subjugate themselves to the dogmas of faith that, for them, are questionable, or to the current enlightened nihilism, grasp the ciphers out of their actual present situation.

If the theologians do not join those of us who philosophize in effecting the transformation of revelatory realities into ciphers it seems to us as an act of violence, unintended and not conscious of itself. But the philosophizing individual must be on guard against maintaining here as true something that, in spite of his certitude, merely seems to him to be so. This certitude makes the situation so disturbing for him, for he would respond to the reproach of obduracy by the believers in revelation by using the same reproach against them. But the philosophizing individual yet means to respect what, to him, seems like failing oneself since he cannot be certain that he, in his thinking, is representative of everyone. He cannot other than say to himself: That rejection of the transformation into ciphers is directed not only against reason in philosophy but against the very thought of God and against the possibility of free Existenz. The philosophizing person would give up embodiment because he must, in favor of what has been efficacious in the believer from the very beginning and at all times even without embodiment. He would impart the philosophic way of thinking to modern man and to the nations in such a manner that they not merely surrender to the rationalistic intellect and to psychological affects but so that they grasp the meaning of the ciphers and, by way of the thought of God, open themselves to transcendence, with all the consequences such a turning would have.

Is it not possible for philosophy and theology to meet in the idea, across the abyss of their consciousness of actuality, in these interpretations of philosophizing out of the primal source and of revealed faith?

The presupposition is that clarity is gained on both sides regarding what is meant by the actuality of God's words and deeds, and that the power of faith prevail in clarity and honesty, without internal or external violence.

It is surely wrong for revealed faith to give the lie to the reality of what is cogently known and knowable. It is also false to maintain any knowledge as a whole to be rationally final.

Philosophic faith and revealed faith could meet in their consciousness of standing together in the unfathomable course of things that, for the latter, is canopied, as it were, by an embodiment of what is revealed and that, for the former, is accepted in fulfilling ignorance (as Plato, Nicholas of Cusa, Kant conceived of it across all differences between them).

The two modes of faith could be linked in the consciousness of each individual that he can become himself in what we—going beyond categories by means of categories—address inadequately as "meaning," "salvation," as "the enduring in the evanescence of everything," as that which is neither temporal nor atemporal but eternal.

It is that which, whether as revelation or as ignorance, brings about unease in time and, with it, earnestness.

It is that which, when questioned, does not respond, or, through its silence, seems itself to pose the question; it is that which makes us tremble through questions to which no intellect, no confession of faith, no cipher gives us an adequate answer; or that to which the answer springs from the earnestness of the practical life of Existenz, an answer that cannot be divorced from ciphers and embodiments in which the actuality of the silence of transcendence is never captured satisfactorily or adequately.

This earnestness would have to testify to itself and prove itself today in our sinking world; this is a world that drowns itself out, thus man has such difficulty finding himself because he seems to be capable of hearing less and less—in the din of the tremendous bustle of production and the emptiness of his leisure time—the actuality of transcendence.

c. The Fall of the Exclusiveness of Dogmatically Determined Truth of Faith.

We call "claim of exclusiveness" the claim of being or of expressing the only truth, absolutely valid for all men. This claim is not contained in the words said by Jesus: "I am the way, the truth and the life: no man cometh unto the Father, but by me." It lies in the sentence: "Outside of the Church there can be no salvation (*extra ecclesiam nulla salus*)."

The claim of exclusiveness on the part of a faith (whether revealed faith or philosophical faith gone astray) has always been the source of discord and of a life-or-death struggle.

We demand of the believers in revelation that they give up the idea of exclusivity and, concurrently, sheathe their swords (once meant literally, to-day figuratively). No longer valid are the words perhaps unjustly ascribed to

Jesus: I have not come to bring peace but the sword (dissension). Only when the poison of the claim to exclusivity has been removed can biblical faith truly become earnest and thus communicative and peaceful, can its essence be actualized in its purity.

In order that this be done in full consciousness, we need this simple insight, important in its consequences: The truth that is universally valid in its correctness is relative to presuppositions and methods of cognition yet cogent for every intellect. Existentially historic truth is absolute in practical life but when expressed is not universally valid for everyone.

Only when exclusivity falls can faith itself become true in its appearance. Only then is purity possible in the battle of ciphers, i.e., their liberation from the interference of mundane interests. Only then do lack of bias, and tolerance become actual in it.

The uniqueness of revelation would lose, together with its massive embodiment, also its historic exclusiveness. The one, the only embracing historicity of all that we are and know is not founded on revelation but on what is common to all men. It is within this communality that the ciphers of revelations of historically diverse origin have a variety of shapes.

NOTES

1. Cf. Rudolf Bultmann, *Theologie des Neuen Testaments*, Tübingen, 1953. An extremely instructive book, as scholarly as it is simple, clear and reliable. But the author hardly conceives of the meaning of the book in the way in which I, learning from it, permit myself to do.

2. Heinrich Barth, *Theologische Zeitschrift*, Vol. IX (1953), p. 114.

Selection 66

CAN THE TWO FAITHS MEET?

EDITORS:
A dialogue with philosophy may further the kind of transformation of Christian faith as a prime carrier of biblical religion—the subject matter of the previous selection (65). But if it is to take place it must be an inner transformation of the Christian faith itself. Hence the problem remains, i.e., the problem of whether revelational faith is able to safeguard its viability by affirming the truth of its believers without gainsaying the truth of those who believe differently. It is against this background that Jaspers here faces the question as to whether it is possible for philosophic faith and revelational faith to meet or

whether they are irreconcilable. The enormous difficulties that lie in the way of this meeting are duly identified by Jaspers, yet he also recalls that the division of the two had not been normative for all of Western history. In the existential earnestness of both kinds of believers, however, resides the possibility of mutual recognition without either believer betraying his own faith-commitment. For in existential earnestness each is bound to what is overarching: the one source, as Jaspers sees it, that could make love of the other possible with whom one is locked in communicative struggle.

The selection, which has been translated by the editors, has been taken from *Der philosophische Glaube angesichts der Offenbarung*, pp. 527–36. In E. B. Ashton's translation: *Philosophical Faith and Revelation*, pp. 356–63.

TEXT:

If these two origins of faith cannot achieve communication though remaining separate entities, theology and philosophy would also remain divided and each exclude the other.

The original unity of Greek religion and philosophy was not abolished when individual thinkers lived out of the very wellspring which first began to flow independently because of them. This unity came to an end only in the West—a decisive though not planned-for end—that began approximately in the thirteenth century. This occurred on the one hand through the priestly arrogations of power on the part of ecclesiastical authority when it claimed the right to control thinking itself, and on the other hand through the power of truth in the Existenz of individuals responsible for themselves. Today our goal could not be unification, not authoritarian control by one side or by a higher authority but solely the regaining of the unity that once was unquestioned but now would be the deliberate unity of separate entities in the communication of poles that also continue to repel each other.

A. Let Us Recall what Divides Revealed Faith from Philosophical Faith:

They are divided by the way each founds itself out of its origin: either out of revelation or out of the individual's being given to himself as a gift, in the medium of reason. This being-given-to-himself becomes clear for him through his participation in the philosophic tradition.

They are divided by the way in which they serve God; there, this service takes the form of communal liturgy expressing the certainty of salvation made present in the sacrament; and here it takes the form of philosophic reflection.

They are divided by the sense in which they speak of transcendence: For revealed faith, it is the other that approaches from outside and which is guaranteed by its embodiment in the world in sacred churches, objects, acts, persons, canonical writings. For philosophic faith there is no security in the world

of an objective or universal nature; instead, the believer is dependent on his
innermost inwardness where transcendence either makes itself felt as actuality or eludes him.

B. *The Difference Between Invoking Transcendence in Philosophy and
Preaching the Gospel:*

Philosophic invocation of transcendence and preaching have a like focus.
The difference is that invocation is free critical movement in ciphers while
preaching is constrained by the revelation it proclaims. In the first instance
there is authority conferred solely by the responsibility of the individual who
is able to be himself; in the latter, authority is founded in the Church and the
office conferred by it.

The person of philosophic faith cannot preach for he has nothing to proclaim. Hence he is rightly prevented from preaching in church. Only the man
who is ordained is granted ecclesiastical authority to preach.

Only when, in the churches, *kerygma* sheds its character of revelatory reality, dogma and confession, that is, if it were itself to become an invocation of
ciphers, would the conflict between theology and philosophy disappear. But
this is a transformation which today seems utopian in all churches and which
might, in fact, do away with that without which a church cannot exist: its
historic authority itself as an element of faith. The question would be whether
the language of ciphers could enhance rather than weaken the earnestness of
Existenz, and whether authority, as itself a historic cipher and not as the claim
of universal validity for all men, could maintain its influence. If, in the Existenz of the priest, the rationally indeterminable unity of authority and a state
of suspension becomes actual, it would then be a matter of freedom how the
individual experiences authority and *kerygma*.

Will the churches bring about this transformation from within? Perhaps
this is the only way in which they could ally themselves with the truthful, still
hidden forces in the modern masses. With the rigor of the language of reality,
with the power of love, and guided by reason, they would awaken the practical
earnestness that could move the world in the face of the most extreme threats
of our time. They would liberate Existenz in individuals whose faith can
"move mountains." They would not permit the world to sleep but would,
through truth, give to freedom the greatest impetus to actualize justice and
peace.

But if the earnestness of the churches can be achieved today only in the
personal freedom of the individual, then it is condemned—even today, and in
spite of its power for the individual—to be ineffectual in the great community
of all. Its appearance in the world is blown away like chaff. So far philosophic
faith has not become a visible, powerful, public appearance. Until now it has
remained in the concealment of personal communication.

The course of events is still co-determined, even today, by the shaping of the forces of faith on the part of the churches and their dogmatics. If these fail—and today it looks as if they do—then the world would fall prey to the false faith of science, thus to general unfaith and unfreedom. Hence philosophy should do what it can so that its reason penetrates the thinking about faith in the churches so that it can itself become believable for all in order for it to become the place where the knowledgeable masses—and each individual among them—may find an inner assent based on their human nature as well as the impulses for their way of life and their decisions.

Why then our disquiet in the face of philosophical invocation and theological preaching? Because the ciphers speak to us but may also remain silent so that we are terrified by the emptiness outside of and within us—or because certain ciphers become overpowering and obscure all others—but primarily because it is only in the struggle of the ciphers that the depths of the ground become manifest in which Existenz is related to transcendence and the guidance is found for our life.

C. The Different Meanings of Freedom and Authority

I proceed from an extreme interpretation: All existence and each Existenz is dangerous. Is the danger perhaps greater on the path of philosophizing than on the path of revealed faith? Yes, says Dostoevsky's Grand Inquisitor: men cannot be free. Jesus, who brought freedom then and appears again now, is arrested by him. Against Jesus, he argues: Men—these poor creatures, hounded by passions, subject to their own whims, and self-destructive—cannot help themselves. They need to be led by the nose. Whoever subjects them to total rule brings them happiness by the only route possible. They are freed from their freedom, from responsibility, from doubt, from thought.

This principle of domination as the condition of human happiness has a universal meaning. From this point of view it is a matter of indifference whether it is a revealed faith that has assumed the form of a dogma, or an ideology such as that of Marxism. If Marx were to appear today in Russia he, too, would be arrested.

Only the subjects need to believe in the truth, not the masters. The latter exercise their control, denying themselves in the name of God or of historical or natural necessity.

But wherever such control for the purpose of producing the happiness of all (with the exception of the knowing rulers who must forgo happiness and faith) would occur, this happiness could not at all be achieved in reality. Presupposing the necessity of such control, given the nature of man, justifies, without being expressed publicly, the regime of those despots in their own eyes. But on the path of such a manner of ruling neither human happiness nor any free steps of faith nor an enduring order of existence is possible.

The theory of the Grand Inquisitor can be countered decisively with the fact that it is always human beings who rule. And the rulers themselves are beings of the kind who, according to their own presupposition, are in need of domination because they are unable to be free.

The actualization corresponding to the ideal type of this theory looks something like this: The demand that one ought to live in the world in obedience to a ruler as in obedience to God or to history emanates not from God or history but from man. In the reality of their rule they do not need to believe either in God or in history, or else they can forget their faith in the practice of their control. They examine the particular realities as to their utility in achieving, extending, stabilizing their power, and which of them are dangerous to this power. They formulate in each instance the application of their faith as party line or infallible ecclesiastical decision. Many actually believe them when they appeal to a total authority having been conferred on them. This faith is intensified by the certainty of being a participant in the practical power and might which is or is to come. The tremendous rush to join the Church after Constantine had proclaimed Christianity as the state religion is just as characteristic for it as is the fact that almost all turn into communists (in Germany, into National Socialists) at the very instant when total rule is victorious. The demand of exclusive faith coupled with the certainty of being associated with power is a horrifying state of things that, at certain periods of history and as a result of the confluence of folly, cowardice before truth, injustice and arbitrariness, appears like a tidal wave inundating everything. Out of the despair over the self-inflicted spiritual and political anarchy comes the plunge into blind, total obedience. It is the mortal enemy of man which, together with the totalitarian order, insofar as it is achieved (with the coming of the age of technology its success seemed possible) deprives man also of the chance of freedom, truth, justice.

In fact, all our actions are based on what we expect of men—and that means of ourselves. Whoever despairs of man despairs of himself. Contempt of man is self-contempt.

If we do not fall prey to this despair or this contempt we live by hope, this gift—insidious, according to the Greeks—out of Pandora's box.

Hope is without deception insofar as it proves itself through its insight into realities, does not hide anything from itself, does not admit any utopia. Only the breadth of our consciousness lets us become clear as to where we stand and for what end we want to live and work and die. Our practical life with its decisions made in concrete situations testifies to the truth of this hope.

There is hope without deception only when we do not hold it to be a certainty, not even a probability, but dare to live by it because such a life can be worthy of us and founded in transcendence.

The greatest of the hopes, in historic-political conduct and thought, is that man can be free.

But the idea of freedom is the foundation of hope only when the ambiguous nature of freedom is present in clear knowledge, when the confusions of freedom can be recognized at any moment, when the mutual tie of freedom and authority is actualized.

What is the role of revealed faith in freedom? Does the secular claim to authority, hence, factually, also might, coercion, violence belong to revealed faith? By no means. There is no doubt that revealed faith had at one time allied itself with power. Perhaps during times where political power degenerated (on the one hand into anarchy, on the other into despotism), the relatively best way, in a hopeless situation, of letting spirit prevail was the attempt to found the order of political power on the revealed faith of the Bible. For in organizing religious power there was carried along, through the Bible as the Holy Writ, also its content which time and again has become the source of freedom. If such content is lacking, as in the writings of Marx and Engels, then the meaning of obedience to faith (in Marxism) is understood erroneously as obedience to science. Terrorist rule and, further, the organized coercion functioning under its threat, are actualized on the basis of the false faith of science and not on the basis of a faith on the part of man who experiences his freedom himself in the origin of transcendence and can only thus be truly free.

But it is not necessary to reject revealed faith because its representatives have used it—for a long time in the past, and do so in part even today—as a means of political power. Revealed faith as such is apolitical. It bears within itself the possibility of human freedom.

But a very different distinction remains between revealed faith and philosophic faith, namely in the ways in which they hope. Hope based, for instance, on the resurrection of the revealed actuality of Jesus or on revealed promises is something radically different from hope based on truth manifesting itself to philosophic reason.

D. Is the Final Mutual Rejection of Revelatory Faith and Philosophic Faith Inherently Necessary?

1. Schopenhauer wrote: "No one who is religious comes to philosophy; he does not need it. No one who truly philosophizes is religious. He walks without leash, in danger but free." Moreover: "Religion is the metaphysics for the people." Conversely, we hear from the protestant theological side: Philosophy cannot be taken seriously. It is superfluous and basically a nuisance. We can hear the tone of contempt for the adversary in each of these positions. This mutual rejection is most violent.

One could say ambiguously: "If I believed I would not philosophize." Is this supposed to mean it would be better if I would believe? Or does it mean: It is a good thing that I philosophize, otherwise I would go under in faith, which is intrinsically unphilosophic? Or is it merely being said from an external standpoint, that faith and philosophy are mutually incompatible? In no sense could I make that statement my own.

Often a way out is found that would weaken both revelation and reason. One can obey all ecclesiastical ordinances, partake of the sacraments, and still reserve for oneself one's philosophic freedom in a silent skepticism that binds all men together. But in this way one could also deceive oneself all too easily, the believer in revelation about his preserved freedom, the supposedly free individual about the leash that guides him.

This whole level at which there is mutual rejection in coexistence and mutual union without decisiveness is inappropriate to the seriousness of this matter. Neither the harsh alternative, conceived under the unlucky star of a philosophic or theological fanaticism, nor the conciliatory skeptical or amicable-inimical compromise is convincing.

We pose the questions once more:

Is it at all possible for the believer in revelation—if revelation is true for him since it is, for him, actually present—to acknowledge a different truth of the same rank and coming to meet him on the same level? This is of course impossible since God himself speaks for him.

Must the philosophical believer not arrive at the insight that divine revelation is impossible, and must he not therefore reject revelation on principle, since it is illusion?

What are the common presuppositions for mutual acknowledgement? The believer in revelation would have to infer the possibility, from the fact that the majority of people does not follow him, that what is absolute for him because it is divine revelation itself is not binding on all men. He may proclaim his message but must not expect others to follow his faith.

The philosophic believer, however, would have to acknowledge the faith that is alien to him as a possible truth emerging from a different source, even if he is unable to understand it. He would have to resist the temptation that wants to carry him—by way of his ability to think when this ability loses the consciousness of its limits—to the supposed insight that revelation is absolutely impossible because it is impossible for him.

For each of them his own presuppositions have something irresistible. He needs the whole critical energy of reason in order, in his own unconditionality, to see and hold on to the boundaries.

2. It is a sign of this possibility that, on both sides, the contempt may turn around into a consciousness of lack over against the other: How nice it would be to believe in such a manner that God is present in the world, that he helps me in person (but—says the philosophizing person—I cannot believe that and am now suffering from homesickness, as it were). How nice it would be to

think of my primal source like the philosopher and to find, in this way, tranquility in transcendence (but—says the believer in revelation—I do not succeed in this thinking, and when I reach certain boundaries I forbid myself to go on since it could disturb that out of which I live my life of faith). Thus it becomes evident that man as individual experiences within himself the possibility of either mode of faith.

It may happen that someone standing on the one side finds his own faith questionable in the light of the other faith. This is an event which the believer in revelation calls "temptation." It is no less dangerous to the philosophic believer, though in a different sense. It is unknown only to thoughtless "enlighteners" and positivists, to those who live conventionally, whether within or without the Church, in their dull self-certainty.

Temptation takes hold of the believer in revelation when he can no longer truly believe in revelation in its concrete form because of the cogently painful power of philosophizing: not in divine promises, not in the incarnation of God, nor in the resurrection of Christ, not in the Church as the mystical body of Christ, nor in the sacraments. The believer overcomes this temptation by the factually present actuality of God which he has experienced and which has impressed itself upon him from the very beginning of his own awareness in the divine service, in prayer, in the sanctity of ecclesiastic phenomena encountered day by day. God himself seems to overcome temptation.

The philosophic believer is no less familiar with temptation. It is infinitely difficult to live in uncertainty before hidden transcendence, to bear being absent from oneself, being able not to love, the emptiness of unbelief, when these overcome him. How liberating it would be then if God were to show himself, were to offer absolute assurance and would lead me by the hand! How attractive are the embodiments of the divine service, the sanctification of life, the penetration of the cosmos, of the landscape, of the environment, of human action by ecclesiastically attested sanctity! Honesty requires us not to enjoy it aesthetically but modestly to turn away, to give it up. But the enchantment is so great that it can be recognized and overcome as temptation only by the unconditional truthfulness enjoined on us by transcendence.

In overcoming the temptations, both sides—if they are honest—are brought around to acknowledge the other's faith.

If the temptation of the believer in revelation is overcome through the clarity vis-à-vis the revelation that is actual for him and turns into tranquility before this truth, the consequence will be an open and deep humanity. Then the believer will not expect from others as an act of their will what to him is a gift of grace. No longer does he accuse them of the obduracy of evil intent, nor does he demand any longer that all believe the same. But if, in overcoming temptation, the believer committed an act of violence against himself through his desire to believe and thus committed a dishonest act, then the consequence is a violence against others, no telling whence or where. Even the will to believe, the readiness to blind obedience toward the present holy church, to *fides implicita*, already constitute violence. From now on his life becomes closed off. This closed-off person coerces himself in the very ground of his own being without being transparent to himself as he does so. He does not wish to think or ask further. He has placed a boulder there that cannot be moved, can hardly be touched. There communication with man is broken off by the totally other. The man for whom it is sufficient, and to whom it gives the deepest satisfaction to be open to his God in his way, that man can no longer be unconditionally open to communication with other men. It seems that such an overcoming of temptation removes him from the risk of existing with other men.

If the temptation of the philosophical believer is overcome through the presence of reason which unites all modes of the Encompassing, then the consequence is not a passively tolerant but a deeply concerned inclination toward the person believing actually and earnestly in revelation. But if there lay, in this overcoming, a rationalistic violence of the intellect, then the consequence is a violence of this intellect in all things. Intolerant contempt in the guise of indifferent tolerance is an inhuman lack of deep concern before the earnestness of man. This is itself the untruthfulness that allows reason to submerge in the rationalistic intellect.

Hence the decisive question for our communicative togetherness remains: Is mutual acknowledgment possible? Is it possible for the believer in revelation to come to meet the one who, by his definition, is an unbeliever—to be sure, feeling pain for the other because of the absence of grace, yet with unlimited respect for him and his path? Is it possible that the philosophic believer—to be sure, feeling pain because he has not gained, in the believer in revelation, the true companion in fate in the impenetrable situation of man—comes to meet him with the same respect and ready to listen over again and anew to his experiences and to unite with him for all human tasks in this world?

Can the two act together in existence without becoming untruthful, without mental reservations?

Originally differing ways of conducting practical life and of the faith that goes with it are indeed mutually exclusive: they cannot be actualized in the same person. However they do not exclude each other if they encounter each other in different people in the world. Each historicity can love the other in its existential earnestness and can know itself to be bound to it in what is overarching.

Part Six

TESTIMONY OF COMMUNICATION

EDITORS' INTRODUCTION TO PART SIX:

Of his many partners in potential or actualized communication and about whom there is some written testimony by Jaspers, four are included here: Max Weber, Martin Heidegger, Hannah Arendt, and Gertrud Jaspers. Unlike the other three, where communication achieved fulfillment of truth and self-actualization, the one with Heidegger was frustrated. Moreover, the form in which Jaspers expressed his testimony differs in each case. The one on Max Weber is in the finished form of a publication. With the view of preparing a critique of Heidegger, Jaspers wrote, over a period of time, a great number of notes, some of which are well thought through, some are mere phrases, some drafts of letters never sent. The book, however, was never written. The testimony on Arendt consists of excerpts from a radio interview. The memoir of his wife and the drafted eulogy are personal, though intended for public utterance.

It is apt that these testimonies are so different because there is no general form of communication. Each instance of communication is singular—as singular as are the partners engaged in it, the historic situation in which it arises, and the truth whose realization is at stake in it.

These testimonies are, in fact, meant to show how Jaspers's philosophy of communication reflects the essence of the person Jaspers, and in turn how intent this person was on enacting the philosophy of communication in all the aspects displayed in this Reader: communication as the actualization of Existenz with other Existenzen, truth as communicability, and communicative reason. The correlation of philosophy and life as a test of truth is an explicit theme in Jaspers's thinking; it thus invites measuring his philosophy of communication against his own search for communicative realization. Jaspers himself encourages this, as can be seen in the following passages. They are from his "Philosophical Autobiography" where he presents a summary appraisal of his writings as a whole:

> Two main concerns of my writings should be indicated.
> First, it is only in limit situations that man becomes aware of what he is. . . .
> And secondly, as far as I can think back, I would be moved by the experience of mutual comprehension and incomprehension with others. Even as a schoolboy I suffered when after a quarrel good feelings could be restored only by conventional amenities. I was considered the hot-head, the battler, because I pressed for clarity. If an authority—a teacher, for instance—forbade the clarification, if an end was put to the matter by a word from above, I felt hurt. But I wanted still more: in spite of parents, brother and sister, in spite of friends, I was consumed by the yearning for a kind of communication beyond any chance of misunderstanding, beyond everything merely provisional, beyond all limits of the all too self-evident. Man can only come to himself when he is with his fellow man, never by knowledge alone. We become ourselves only to the extent of another's becoming himself; we become free

only insofar as the other becomes free. . . . Eventually all thoughts could be put to this test, whether they would help or hinder communication; truth itself could be gauged by the yardstick that truth is what unites us. . . . It was only with my wife that I entered on the road of loving struggle, the road of lifelong, never-completed, unreserved, and therefore inexhaustible communication. . . .

What I had in mind in my own philosophical work was to go along the road which the few great ones had taken . . . —the road of a fundamental human knowledge that makes room for all possibilities and can unite men despite the multiplicity of their faiths and lives.

My aim was the kind of philosophizing that can be accessible and convincing to man as man. . . . I would rather like, so to say, to talk as a man in the street with the man of the street. . . . Everyone has a chance to come to himself, in reverent regard of the great human beings and under the absolute guidance of love and reason in the framework of eternal order.

Desirable, to my mind, was a general thinking that is not the one universally valid knowledge, but which makes possible communication, a κοινή which is not dilution but consciousness of a realm in which all of us can meet.[1]

NOTES

1. *Philosophy and the World*, pp. 299–301. Transl. E. B. Ashton.

I.

Max Weber

EDITORS:
The selections below express the high regard Jaspers had for Weber. What Weber thought of Jaspers may be seen in an observation by Karl Loewenstein who was a witness to their relationship. Referring to Weber's Sunday-at-homes, Loewenstein reports:

> Among the regular visitors . . . were some of the foremost men in German intellectual life. But there were three who were Max Weber's real interlocutors, to whom he listened and with whom he had a genuine exchange of ideas. These were Karl Jaspers, Georg von Lukàcs, and Friedrich Gundolf. In the ritual that gradually developed on these Sunday afternoons, these three in particular played the part of Weber's friendly antagonists.[1]

For Jaspers, Weber was the "Galileo of the human studies." Beyond that he was the exemplary figure for the time because Weber lived at the limits of scientific cognition and thus manifested the existential authenticity possible in an age dominated by scientific reasoning. From Weber's own experience of shipwreck Jaspers drew the lesson that such shipwreck can make man aware of the origins that afford guidance in an age which tends to confuse matters of right and wrong with matters of science. And as the demystification of the world which Weber found in modernization did not prevent him from affirming the freedom and reason of Existenz in his day, so Jaspers thought that Weber might serve as a guide to those who seek their way of freedom today where the processes of bureaucratization and technical rationalization of society advance with inexorable intensity.

NOTES

1. Karl Loewenstein, *Max Weber's Political Idea in the Perspective of Our Time* (Amherst: University of Massachusetts Press, 1966), p. 95.

Selection 67

A MEMOIR

EDITORS:
The following excerpts, translated by the editors, may be found in *Schicksal und Wille*, p. 32f.

TEXT:
Max Weber I did not encounter as a friend, for to friendship belongs equality. To be sure, he behaved toward me entirely as if I were his equal and would not have done otherwise. But my respect before the greatness of this man was such that I felt shy before him. There were some exceptions. . . . It happened that, in conversation, we did battle with each other on the level of equals. These were very serious questions. In such conversations there was perhaps a slight hint of beginning friendship. Even today I would be too indiscreet if I were to talk about it.

I believe I am not wrong to have seen in Max Weber the intellectually greatest man of our era; great, to be sure, only in one area but possessing a universal character. I have gained my concept of greatness from the actuality that was Max Weber. When I speak of him as the greatest man of the age, I am not thinking of writers or artists or of statesmen. There is no point in measuring him and them against each other. In Max Weber there is philosophic actuality.

His achievements in research are already highly impressive. In addition there is his creation of a world of categories in sociology, then the clarification of methods that he carried out individually in specific treatises. But above all it was he who introduced the tension into the well-known and seemingly simple differentiation of value judgment and determination which aroused the passions of historians and sociologists. For it became evident to everyone who grasped this that there was a problem here that could not be solved rationally. For, though rational discussion was important, it was superseded in the most violent battles arising out of the fundamental attitudes of the scholars.

I see in Max Weber the Galileo of the Human Studies [*Geisteswissenschaften*] who had the will to actualize, to its maximum, what is possible as science in this area, and to develop at the same time its principles and methods.

But this would not be enough. Behind it stands a man for whom this whole scientific business is merely foreground and for whom it is not enough. He has a sense for all that is great, he loves greatness, yet because of his truthfulness he is so constituted that he can never forget how things have always been and how they are today and how things are in actuality.

Selection 68

THE SCIENTIST—THE MAN

EDITORS:
The following selection is a translation, by the editors, of excerpts from *Max Weber: Politiker, Forscher, Philosoph*, pp. 50–64, 70–75, 81–89. For Ralph Manheim's translation see *Three Essays: Leonardo, Descartes, Max Weber*, pp. 237–45; 247–48; 257–58; 260–61; 266–74.

TEXT:

Max Weber the Scientist

Max Weber, as universal historian, is not a narrator like Ranke, nor a philosopher of history like Hegel, nor a collector of data like Schmoller, nor a contemplator of great figures like Burckhardt, but a sociologist. Narrative, construction, collection, vision serve him as means of limited significance. Only by not letting himself be confined by any one of these as his goal is the world of human affairs fully opened to his inquiry into the causes. His sociology is universal history through his always incompletable ascent to the radical questions in order that he arrive, comprehending, at the great decisions, the ultimate sources of change in human affairs. He seeks to comprehend how human existence has come to be from factors which are determinable. He seeks to know, but at the same time to make clear, the limits of this knowledge. Hence, in spite of his knowledge which, to others, must have seemed to be a complete penetration of things, he continues to stand in awe before actuality which is never cognized in itself but only in certain aspects.

The Method (Possibility, Comparison, Ideal Type)

Just as, for Max Weber, history becomes a means of finding the clarity of present-day consciousness of actuality and of volition, he seeks to apprehend the past as that particular present. His consciousness of the present was important because he did not look at the present as if it were already history and events occurred necessarily. The one who observes thusly is not present at all but is an imaginary observer of something that is always only past. But his consciousness of the past became for him another present and only in this way truly actual. He who looks at the historical only as past involuntarily makes it falsely similar to his own present. Only thusly could Weber achieve the great-est clarity—historically and as present—about what really was decided.

He himself defined the method that is essential to such an approach: in order to grasp what is actual we must see the *possibilities*. In the present, a rough idea of the possibilities is the area in which I gain certainty concerning what I decide; without possibility, I have no freedom; without seeing the pos-sibilities, I act blindly; only a knowledge of the possibilities enables me to know what I am actually doing. Analogously, he employs the category of "ob-jective possibility" in his historical understanding of *past situations*. The historian pictures to himself a certain situation. The extent of his knowledge determines various constructions of what was possible at that time in the past. Against these constructions he measures first of all the possibilities which the persons whose actions were decisive at that time were aware of. And then he measures against the possible what actually did take place in order to pose the question: what was the unique cause for this particular actuality to emerge from among several possibilities? The historian turns once more into possi-bility what has in actuality already taken place in order to find the critical point in the decision which brought it about. Drawing on the logical investigations of others, Max Weber called the cause he found for the event which actually took place the adequate cause. This does not mean that what happened is regarded as an absolutely necessary consequence following from strict laws, but rather that, on the basis of certain regularities we have observed, we can understand why it happened as it did, because, if we ourselves had been in-volved, we should have expected it to happen.

One of the ways of discovering possibilities is *comparison*. As a universal historian, Max Weber constantly brings quite disparate events into relation with each other. When he compares developments in China, India, and the West, it is not in order to find historical laws or sociological types as abstract identities or similarities. Rather, he takes similarities as a means of arriving at an all the more decisive comprehension of what truly constitutes the differen-tiating factor. In similar historical situations, similar developments are possi-ble. But in the course of time events occur that are contrary or deviate com-pletely. By progressing through the similarities, in contrast with them, we can find the source of what is distinct in each situation which, for its part, is conceived as possibility. In this way Max Weber arrives at the clearest knowl-edge of what has occurred in each instance. He arrives at this knowledge of necessity only by way of universal history. This, and the decisive comprehen-sion of concrete connections, stand in correlation with each other. For this reason Max Weber's sociological analyses are cast in an ever-recurring form: by means of comparisons and limitations of what is possible he separates out what, in any sense at all, was decisive for the course of events. No matter whether he speaks about the development of Jewish prophecy and the world-historical importance of Judaism, of the circumstance that there is no progress in India, about the significance of the battles of Marathon and Salamis; in every instance it is the pivotal point on which Weber focuses with the breadth of his all-round empirical research. And it is on the basis of these that what, in the last analysis, is simple, also makes sense.

In order to compare matters dealing with human beings I must comprehend the facts through concepts expressing the meaning of these facts—whether as the meaning intended by the agents, or as possible meaning through their significance for something else, or as the objective meaning in the sense of a correctness. Actuality is an endless web of what is true or alien to meaning. In order to grasp actuality we need conceptual constructs, developed according to their intrinsic meaning; they merely serve as criteria for this actuality in order to see to what extent it corresponds to these concepts. These conceptual constructs Weber calls *ideal types*. They are, for him, cognitive instruments of approaching actuality, and not actuality itself. They are not generic concepts under which actuality is subsumed; rather, they are meaning concepts against which it is measured. Insofar as actuality conforms to these types it can then be grasped in its full meaning; and that which does not conform to them can, through them, be brought before us clearly as to its factual content. They are not the goal of cognition, nor the laws governing events, but the means to bring to the clearest consciousness the specific nature of each particular human actuality. The wealth of Weber's insights rests upon the construction of such ideal types which prove to be fruitful for the concrete cognition of actuality. For example: the types of governing authority as traditional, charismatic, bureaucratic; the types of church and sect; the types of cities, etc. The concepts of ideal types must be developed in sharp outline; there are gaps between them. Actuality, however, is fluid; in its transitions all becomes blurred.

The Divisions

An uncritical desire to know possesses the ineradicable urge to take hold of the truth that can be cognized as universally valid as the one which is whole and conclusive, by means of which one may know what is good, what one ought to do, and what constitutes Being itself. Max Weber's critical cognition goes counter to this monistic impulse. He demands cogently valid experiential knowledge; as a scientist, he is adamant about divisions which he demands in the service of true cognition as well as authentic philosophizing. Thus he fights for the actual carrying-out of the division: between experiential knowledge and value judgment; between cognition that is always one-sided and particular, and all modes of grasping totality; between empirical actuality, and the nature of Being.

A. Max Weber was relentless in reiterating: no empirical investigation may provide the foundation for determining what has value and what I ought to do. To be sure, once a purpose is presupposed, experiential knowledge may indicate the means which serve to promote or hinder it. It may also indicate the secondary effects of an activity through which other values are infringed upon. But it can never prove the value or purpose itself to be universally binding. Rather, the clarity of empirical cognition as well as that of decisive valuation and choice rests on the clear-cut division between the two. The fact that science is independent of value means that we must hold back our own valuations in order to come to see a state of affairs—even in the face of irksome facts—clearly and from all sides. The scientific duty to see the truth of facts and the practical duty to stand up for one's own ideals are two kinds of duties. This does not mean that the fulfilling of the one is possible without the fulfillment of the other. Weber merely comes out against their commingling; only their separation permits each of them to be actualized. Scientific objectivity is not akin to a lack of value conviction. The commingling, however, destroys objectivity as well as conviction. The method of speaking with apparent objectivity and supposedly extracting from the material a value judgment in a universally valid manner is rejected by Max Weber as a half way measure which, on the one hand, cannot stop the making of value judgments and, on the other, seeks to disclaim responsibility for these judgments. Only my distance from the object as well as from myself makes it possible for me calmly to ask questions of actuality. But the decisive valuations, which must be suspended in cognition, are themselves again essential conditions of cognition because they educate us to be sensitive to every possible valuation.

Hence the independence from value inherent in science does not mean, for Weber, that one is not to make value judgments in existence. Rather, the opposite is at play: the passion of valuation and volition first brings forth, as its own illumination and self-education, the authentic objectivity in the capacity of inquiry. Furthermore, independence from value does not mean, for him, that valuations—actually carried out or potential—are not to be the object of research. Instead, they are the essential objects for the exploration of things human; it is only through independence from value that that dispassionateness comes to be in the investigation of each valuation, of its meaning, its origin, its consequences, which actually brings it before our eyes and our consciousness. And finally, independence from values does not mean, for him, that the choice of the problems which are to be investigated rests on valuation. Rather, it is the value decision about what concerns me which is the presupposition for authentic passion in research.

B. Max Weber recognized that all research is particular and that the whole is inaccessible. If I could know what is universal in human affairs—be it in the form of the universal, unchangeably identical laws of nature; or as the totality; or as an unequivocal developmental principle—I could derive from them the particular event as necessary. But, cognitively operating under relative points of view, I recognize rules and laws which affect merely certain facets of actuality, and I recognize only relative wholenesses and never the whole. In each of its configurations actuality is individual, infinite, inexhaustible. The laws which apply to it are not such that we may derive actuality from them. Also, there is no universal, primordial, temporal state, neither a cosmic nor a human one, out of which there would develop—as a universal state not muddied by any historical accident—individuation in history. At all times actuality is equally individual in its historical, endless diversity. Hence there does not exist any universal, neither conceptually nor temporally; there is no principle, no substance, no human primal situation or primal essentiality, no existence that is still individually indeterminate, from which we could deduce what is actual. That was Max Weber's perspective when he said: "Endlessly the river of boundless happening rolls toward eternity." This is why man can only enter into actuality by means of experiential science but cannot derive it nor grasp it as a totality. The consequence of this insight is, on the one hand, the decisive grasp of the empirically actual, and on the other the rejection of all metaphysical insinuations into experiential knowledge.

Empirical actuality must be definitively demonstrable: in human action it is only the meaning *intended* by men (in distinction from an imputed objective meaning of history of which the agent is not aware); further it is the meaning intended by *individuals* and many individual people (whereas totalities cannot be empirically determined as such by groups of men acting unawares); only the actions of individuals are empirically actual. The task of empirical sociology is not the creation of conceptions of totality. Sociology examines them as conceptions operative in men in accordance with their functional significance; it finds them present. It neither absolutizes them nor denies their actuality, which has a different foundation and hence is not universally valid; nor does sociology decide that they may not be made use of in action. Its individualistic method does not imply individualistic valuation, just as the rationalistic character of its concept formation does not imply faith in the predominance of rational motives in human action. Empirical research inevitably does away, for itself, with the conception that the state, church, marriage, etc., are substances, yet without disputing their role as configurations of faith. As such configuration, empiric research examines them in their objectivity as conceptions intended by men and effective for them as motives. Hence for sociology itself the substance that is a matter of faith is transformed into the object of rational cognition of a meaning-content intended and wanted by actual people; thus, for example, the state is "merely chance that certain actions took place or will take place that are in conformance with each other according to their meaning-content in a demonstrable way. . . . A different clear meaning cannot be connected with the statement that the state still exists."

This is why Max Weber, as empirical sociologist, is against metaphysical concepts such as "spirit of the people," idea as a present force, against the notion of necessary development, against the materialistic conception of history as the clear-cut destiny of the course of world history. He does not permit himself any vision of the whole of human history nor any construction of world history. He remains limited to a methodical penetration of events by means of empirical research. For him there is no rounded-off whole. If he did possess a system, it could only be a system of the particular methods and basic concepts. But even this closed conceptual system is not a meaningful goal.

The relativity of all concepts that are suited for the cognition of empirical actuality combines the breadth of the possibility of cognition with the one-sidedness of a particular cognition; the significance of what is meant in each instance combines its palpability with its abstractness. Weber admits alleged insights of totality as being the development of world history in its entirety, as being the true actuality on which all else depends; but he admits them only as constructs of ideal types which are possible and which are to be examined as to their fruitfulness for the concrete cognition of matters of fact. Thus he took hold of Marxist constructs by rejecting their absolutization and their claim to being the sum total of all world-views. Thus he attempted, on the same level, to show the original nature of religious factors in their—again limited—efficacy for the history of economic systems and of society; and he tried to make clear to what extent in an empirical investigation that, which to other scholars appeared to be merely a dependent superstructure, could, for its part, have primary causal significance.

Weber examined all concepts and constructs by means of the criterion as to what extent they approach the questions which lead to substantive results by way of empirical research. In this way Weber created for himself the possibility of appropriating them, an appropriation which made all viewpoints accessible and allowed him to regard every factuality. Precisely because he did not allow any completion of knowledge, did not admit of any total picture as scientific, did not acknowledge any knowledge of the "real" factors of events, he gained for himself the unbounded perspectives and orientations which are the essence of disinterested cognition. To be sure, as far as he is concerned, no human world can be completely explained but remains an infinite problem. But because of this he gains knowledge reliable in its exactness and is able to avoid the deceptions spread about everywhere through looking at the whole, at the forces and all the absolutizations based on one-sided observations. By taking up the instances of radical one-sidedness, all of which represent cognitions, he overcame, through his knowledge of their one-sidedness, being dominated by them; instead, he dominated them.

C. As an empiric scientist Max Weber was against totality and for particular cognition; against universals and for specificity; against merely theo-

retical speculation and for concrete research; against overviews and label-
ling and for penetrating cognition; against imagery and for causal analysis;
against mere description and for mental constructs; against substance and for
resolution into empirically comprehensible factors. Hence, in grasping empirical actuality, he kept his distance from the core of things (this purity of the
knowable world becomes, in another context, the condition of love for authentic Being). His extraordinary closeness to actuality does not at all mean that he
cognizes the essence of things. In no instance does Max Weber believe that he
has grasped actuality itself in its ultimate ground. In the one instance which he
examined most thoroughly by means of its empirical material, namely the
derivation of modern capitalism from Protestant ethics, he brought out a
causal factor but said decisively: we have proven here that there is *one* causal
factor present; it has not been proven whether its quantitative significance is
great or small; I believe it to be great. Because Being cannot directly become
the object of empirical research, Weber reaches for every manner of empirical
being; he loses himself in none, questions each as to its causal significance.
The natural conditions, the technical means, the interconnection of situations
as well as the ideas and purposes intended by men, the religious conceptions in
their consequences as well as the pragmatics of power in political relationships—all these become, for him, empirical objects in their relative significance. Here, in his empirical investigations, Max Weber comes up all the
more decisively against the primal sources from which—as not comprehended presuppositions—he has to proceed. . . .

Ignorance in Knowledge

Max Weber's science is two-sided. One does not understand the one if one
forgets the other. Universal empiricism strives to know everything that is at
all knowable. It directs itself to whatever is demonstrable. For it, everything
happens in accordance with laws of causality that are comprehensible and in
accordance with rational connections that are determinable. Everything?

Only what is knowable and everything insofar as everything and the knowable are identical. For the capacity of knowledge nothing exists that is not
subject to its relativizing. Yet knowledge hits upon limits. Max Weber's
"science" is tied closely to the consciousness of that which is not known. First,
the endlessness of all individuality is inexhaustible. Then, this endlessness,
possessing a historic uniqueness, has under certain circumstances a meaning
the interpretation of which cannot be completed. And finally, the primal
source is always presupposed in some manner: the first conceptions of a religion cannot be grasped genetically even if we determine the constellations
and situations without which they would not have come to be.

This duality of knowledge and ignorance—of which empirical knowledge, as the "demystification* of the world," seems to dominate almost exclusively Max Weber's work—gives rise to misunderstandings. This tremendous knowledge, turned into research, is falsely understood as knowledge of human existence as such, one is foolishly satisfied with it or struggles against it.

Thus he is accused, for example, of having no understanding of religion, of Indian philosophy, of the world of the farmer and landed proprietor, of the wholeness and substantiality of the state. But all these reproaches are based on a confusion of universally valid knowledge *about* something, with being *in* something—a being-in that expresses itself through reflection on meaning. Anything that is primally original ceases to be such insofar as it is known; it then assumes the form of something relative, of some cognitive referent. Max Weber purifies knowledge into empirical knowledge but does so not in order to limit thinking to it but in order to make possible, clearly and decisively, the other modes of thinking with their different meanings and their always historic and not universally valid fundamental import. Because he is truthful he does not want to make any concessions to the manner of vested interests which, unwilling to know the facts, pass off their cause as being of knowable, universal interest; neither does he make concessions to the negativity of yearning on the part of non-believers who seek to possess in knowledge what they have lost in faith. It is characteristic that authentic believers are not offended by Max Weber's religious-sociological analyses, that those who are genuinely grounded in the political power pragmatics of the state have no objections to his dispassionate empirical statements. Grasping the knowable in its relativity only allows faith to shine forth in even greater purity.

Another criticism is that knowledge in the form of Weber's research leads too far afield; for living human beings can no longer master this grand mass of material. It is said that this knowledge becomes meaningless as it serves no purpose since, lacking substance, it is dissipated into endlessness. Max Weber's achievement is the final one and this road has now come to an end. However, this criticism confuses the endlessness of empty intellectuality with the infinity of the substantive process of investigation.

And, finally, these criticisms maintain that Max Weber foundered as a scientist. He did, indeed, founder, but he did so in the true foundering which belongs to the meanings of authentic science. Foundering is untrue in the intellectuality of random thoughts and clearly surveyable schemata which, being intellectual, seem to satisfy for a while but then leave behind that void of

NOTES

* "Disenchantment" is the term frequently found in sociological literature, cf., *From Max Weber: Essays in Sociology*, eds. H. H. Gerth and C. Wright Mills (New York: Oxford University Press, 1958), p. 139. Max Weber's word is "*Entzauberung*."

meaninglessness which is secretly inherent in them. That foundering is untrue which gives up, in resignation, the path of knowability merely because it cannot overcome endlessness. That foundering is untrue which, disappointed, abandons knowledge as such because it erroneously attempted to take hold, in knowledge, of Being itself. Untrue foundering pretends not to know and gives up trying. Max Weber's foundering consists in grasping positively—in limitless, definite, empirical knowledge that is close to the object and material—genuine ignorance and opening up for himself the possibility of a being as authentic Being rather than as known Being. The more comprehensive this knowledge becomes the more deeply does the foundering lead into Being; it is for this reason that Max Weber's research projects were so gigantic that he could never complete them, and his works, in spite of their breadth, are tremendous fragments, are the uncompleted edifices of a titan. That Max Weber rejected, in sociology, metaphysics in every form, no matter how disguised; that he turned the scientific attitude ascetic, as it were, means: He kept open the possibility of true foundering and prevented the untrue satisfaction with an adulterated science. Supposed knowledge is not to facilitate that which succeeds only if it is genuinely believed. The relative nature of knowledge seems to bring about our plunge into the bottomlessness; but it is precisely out of this plunge, in authentic originality arising from the historic present of wanting and believing, that we become aware of the ground that is purified only when it is hardened, in the furnace of our unbounded desire to know, into truthfulness and rationality. It is the broadest horizon that makes our own roots grow most freely.

Even though Max Weber's science, in its development, surpasses what human strength is able to accomplish, it is not complete in itself. It is the function of an Existenz which it serves. Sociology is merely one branch of his more profound being, which he kept hidden and which becomes visible only indirectly: Max Weber the philosopher. . . .

Max Weber the Man

To be sure, the dichotomy of world and Existenz [in Max Weber] made him in fact into an actuality of the time which was an expression of this dichotomy; but his era did not recognize itself in him. Unaware of its own divided nature, devoted to desire, wealth, and success, it suffered only in a few individuals what Max Weber actualized in his depth. He lived in the only way in which a man of eternity could live in such a time: in breaking through all illusory form, revealing the origin of being-human! The destiny of his time, the destiny of Germany were actualized in a man who did not stand on the sidelines and observed but who himself was this destiny and took part in enacting it. In his hope and torment he was like the beating heart of Europe which was on the point of losing its spiritual and humane life. . . .

[Man's] ascent [of reason] takes place in a desire to know expressed in his unreserved grasping of cogent knowability and orientation in the possible. But this does not happen in such a way that the mere intellect determines, subordinates, draws conclusions; rather, reason guides the intellect in the limit situations of existence out of its impulse toward what is essential. Hence the infinite outward reach of Max Weber's researches and their being held together by the essential which concerns man *qua* man. His openness toward things—even toward unreason and anti–reason—for the purpose of either accepting it as something mastered or of recognizing it as the other—created for him the wide spaces as well as the proximity to even the strangest human being that he encountered. His thrusting forward everywhere to the limits and seeking clarity for actions based on good will grew out of his reason. Reason, however, is freedom.

The way in which Max Weber sought freedom in himself and around himself as the condition of all that was essential to him was elusive, silently touching in always changing contexts of communication, of the questioning struggle, of unquestioned agreement; it was that which was the basis of the deepest trust in him. Freedom in the world cannot be defined as a mode of spirit, as idealism, as liberalism, as Germanism; it is absolute being-human which so often atrophies, is betrayed or not even risked. Therefore, where it does actually come to meet us it is like man himself becoming revealed, even though it is proper and possible to each man *qua* man.

If we look closely at [Max Weber's] and our own era, we find that—in its process of general illusion and fanatization, in which irrationality is given its blessing by false prophets, deceived deceivers, despots ruling by force—he is the ineradicable presence of reason.

And in an age of the process of the intellectualization and cheapening of reason into mere intellect, into ungrounded knowledge and sophistry which can only negate and destroy, Max Weber was the human being incarnate whose very humanity is the historic appearance of reason. . . .

Faith and Truth

Max Weber never wanted to make common cause with the militant adherents of any faith for, he maintained, one cannot talk with them. Their fanaticism depends on immovable contents. He, on the other hand, campaigned for unlimited rationality which, in its infinite movement, arrives at the very boundary where decisions have in truth to be arrived at through battle. Seen from this standpoint, those who do battle for faith hold fast to illusions. They manifest themselves in modes of thinking that pretend to a knowledge of the whole. Wholeness and totality—relatively justified as are all categories—belong, as dominant, as much to the idol of reactionary thought as well as to the utopia of revolutionary thinking. Fanatical faith—in its immanent intuition of the absolute image of Being, in trusting consciousness of harmony, in the certitude that, in the last analysis, things run properly by themselves according to necessity and human will, in its unquestioning certitude of its own rightness—has lost its original relationship to transcendence as well as the ability to communicate with others.

Max Weber stood his ground against these floods of illusions, perversions, suggestions, against the intellectual absolutisms, and no less against the lack of faith displayed by nihilism. He could have lost heart and, isolated as he was, become a misanthrope. But his faith sustained him, this simple, unknowing faith which, out of the deepest wellsprings, expressed its affirmation time and again, which sought and found what, in all the ruin, was still worthy of love, and which even acknowledged what is absolutely alien. He never wearied of life, nor was life as such the ultimate for him. He felt deep awe and respect before death in battle because through it, man can give meaning to what we must otherwise all suffer only passively. . . .

Nothing can be said with finality about what remained of the content of his faith, a faith which yet remained unshakably present as substance in all he experienced and thought.

If we want to express this faith in spite of everything, then by means of the words he spoke when he was dying as if he were telling a secret: "The true is the truth." It strikes us not as a tautology but like a magical formula expressive of an Existenz whose truth knows even the modes of knowledge as well as empirical knowledge only as functions in a responsible process whose origin and goal remain unknown but are affirmed.

The quest for truth in Max Weber manifested itself originally in struggle. As a young man he learned, in the climate of the age of Treitschke and Bismarck, "that earnest, conscientious work that does not concern itself with results and is performed solely in the interest of truth, is held in low esteem." From then on his battle for truth was waged against those who wish for content and conviction in knowledge *qua* knowledge but who confound, in an untruthful manner, precisely in this way valuation and knowledge, decision and insight. Further, he did battle against those who want knowledge to be absolute and who thereby become untrue because all knowledge is valid only from one standpoint and in certain respects. The battle is joined against the rationalists, because they do not observe critically the laws of knowledge, as well as against the irrationalists, because they misunderstand the meaning of knowledge and its irreplaceable manner of mastering the truth. He battled against philosophic untruthfulness which, for the sake of harmony, covers over the divisions by means of conceptual schemata: his most elemental anger was directed against the "Ladies Home Journal Style," as he called it. Weber, for his part, was attacked for his relativism, for his cold objectivity, because of the putative impossibility of independence from valuation, because of the lack of satisfaction from a science free of valuation. But behind Weber's demands stood his passion for truth which, through the clarity of every mode of knowledge, wanted to arrive all the more decisively at the point where cognition is achieved not through research but through acting and producing in the world. This freedom from valuation is related to the purity of research as well as to the originality of action. His sense of truth was far removed from satisfied this-worldliness as well as from the optimistic faith in research on the part of liberalism. For him, the self-responsibility of the free individual was inviolable as the precondition of all value in the world; and he rejected constraint upon conscience in any and all form.

The effectiveness of an absolute will to truth is manifested in a unique way in Max Weber's research. He gives us neither a picture of himself within history nor is history remote from him as a mere Other. He enters into it with eyes educated by the actuality of his own present, but he sees it as the other world, as if he were present both here and there at the same time. Hence comes the objectivity of his historical analyses as well as our being deeply affected because they concern us directly. And hence also our being shaken up by the thought that all possibilities of valuation are ambivalent. It has been thought that his investigations of Calvinism contain a secret glorification of the asceticism of which he himself approved. Others believed that in these investigations Max Weber, who was horrified by modern mechanization, pursued the unmasking of its nature to its very origins; both views can seemingly be justified, both are erroneous. . . .

It seems that the essence of human activity is given force through the unbounded justice and openness of this investigator who does not balance the scales, does not present us with half right and half wrong, but, without general valuation, shows us past events in their phenomenal origin, in their possibilities and actual consequences as a historical misfortune. There is contained, in these investigations, the indirect communication of the deeply hidden valuation of Existenz itself which, were it to manifest itself in rationally evaluating statements, would always do so in an untrue manner.

Shipwreck

Max Weber was, to be sure, a great political writer, the founder of contemporary sociology, a recognized scientist and the creator of exceptional works, the companion of his wife, friend of his friends, a man who knew happiness. Yet political action was denied to him, his works remained gigantic fragments; for many years his existence was threatened by illness and narrowly limited in its influence.

If we look at Max Weber's foundering in the externals of existence, on this level, which deals with it as a mere matter of fact, we miss what he really signified as a human being. There was around him an atmosphere of foundering in a deeper sense. His foundering does not conincide with what he was not able to do, his achievement was not congruent with what he was capable of achieving. His foundering was something he suffered but which is akin to an active willing; it was the true foundering of man in the historicity which is entrusted to him:

In the political sphere a simply incomplete determination of his being was submerged in pure possibility. His political insights were those of a Cassandra who cannot convince anyone and thus cannot change anything and can only suffer. He was like Machiavelli or Mirabeau who, possessed of the same relentless realism as he, perfected the political insights of their age yet were robbed of any great influence; but he also possessed integrity, which they lacked and consequently failed as human beings. He sought the highest: To act politically, based on a call to do so but yet without any real desire for power. His foundering was essential because he wanted what is true on human terms yet is impossible in practice.

In his research he produced a work that remained a fragment, not because he lacked strength but because of the truth contained in the task he set himself: he felt himself foundering in his quest for limitless knowledge precisely because it is the purpose of knowledge to founder at its limits in order to make room, in doing and in being, for more profound truth. He searched for the point where foundering becomes what is true. The essence of science is its incompletability; in it, however, the extraordinary fragment counts for more than any—merely apparent—completion.

In his philosophizing being-human, he suffered the limits of finitude; in spite of all the actuality of his actions he foundered outwardly on the lack of adequate scope and the lack of historical relevance of what he did succeed in. He searched for objectivity, for the whole and for validity in the world to which he wanted to give himself up in order to be genuinely himself—and must have felt himself thrown back upon himself from the far-ranging present to find himself standing alone like someone deprived of world and space. But as he regards himself, this foundering was not a foundering at all. He never gave up but took hold of his task no matter where he stood, totally committing his Existenz to it. That even this action—no matter whether it involves small or large parameters of actuality—manifests its relativity at the limits and shows its nature to be symbolic, and becomes quasi indifferent precisely where one totally commits one's Existenz: that was his true foundering, his return to his primal source.

Insofar as Max Weber experienced shipwreck according to every objective standard of meaning which disintegrated before his own criterion, this foundering is to be regarded as the very call to truth. When shipwreck is experienced—according to man's last innermost meaning—in realms that lie beyond the intimacy of a pleasant hour with those closest to us and beyond reliable loyalty, then Max Weber, the human being, is like the radiance of the ever present primal source, like perfection in the most minute, for here lies the possibility of everything. . . .

[The usual universal concepts of psychology, sociology or history] can be applied least of all to Weber himself. Those who do so believe they can see and understand all of him and thus rob themselves of seeing into his ground. It is essential to look through this man into the source of what is possible for man, to become aware, in its temporal manifestation, of what man is.

But those err just as much who accept him as their leader and model, something he refused to be in such a radical manner as hardly any other great man. It is a matter of becoming oneself together with him. He represents the ineluctable demand to search and to find for oneself, in one's progress through time, truth in communication, and not to read off what is true as if it were there in finished form and to accept it admiringly. Foundering, he passes the torch on to us, freedom to freedom.

The race of men born into the world of Homer and the Jewish prophets was not lost in Nietzsche. Its last great figure, for the time being, was Max Weber; he was a figure of our world which changes at such a mad pace that particular contents of Weber's world have already passed away in spite of the brevity of the time that has gone by. But what has not passed away are the fundamental questions of being-human, of being-able-to-know, of the decisive tasks. We no longer have a great man who could bring us to ourselves in this manner. He was the last. Hence even today our lives are still oriented by keeping him in mind even though he is slowly receding into history, a presence only for those who knew him while he lived, yet a possibility of appropriation for future generations seeking the German man in his authentic freedom.

In late antiquity, with its levelling and lack of faith, the individual derived support from Stoic philosophy. For philosophy Socrates represented the way because he had existed, acted, and suffered as an actual human being what philosophy now sought to comprehend throughout the centuries which followed. In the world which we are now entering, in the era of the aggregation of masses and of mass domination, of the exploitation of everything, of crushing misery and banal happiness, the task will be once again for the individual to seek his truth through philosophy. No objectivity will teach it to him. Feeling addressed by the open secret of a person such as Max Weber a flame may be kindled in him. But if this occurs then we may say: Whoever understands shipwreck and death draws close to Max Weber. But he remains incomprehensible to him who, in contemplating the beautiful world—which Max Weber, too, enjoyed in serene joyousness—forgets about death.

II.

Martin Heidegger

Selection 69

EDITORS:
In the 1950s Jaspers wrote a memoir of his relationship with Heidegger as part of the "Philosophical Autobiography" which he was requested to contribute to the Schilpp-volume on Jaspers. However, this memoir was held back from publication until after the death of both Jaspers and Heidegger. In a passage of the memoir Jaspers mentions that his and Heidegger's philosophy had been linked in the public mind, and he points out that both thought this was erroneous. In reference to this linking, he continues as follows:

> When I speak of Heidegger, I have to ignore this. My relationship to him [from 1920 to 1933] was of a personal, philosophical nature which had little to do with disquisitions that compare us and our writings.
>
> Only a friendship devoid of reticence and of tacit reservations, in which dependability prevails in regard to the simple things of right and wrong, in which loyalty is the carrier of word and thought and deed—only such a friendship attains a solidarity able to withstand the perturbations caused by publicity. The fact that such a friendship did not develop between us, neither of us can hold against the other. But the result was the indecisiveness and ambiguity of what was possible.
>
> However, the fact that what happened with Heidegger in 1933 could happen, raised new questions. We had become opponents, not through our books but through deeds. The philosophical thoughts had to be grasped in connection with the deeds of the thinker.
>
> Now the question pressed upon me, which I had never asked heretofore, whether something is at work in Heidegger's thinking which had to appear to me as the enemy of the truth that became accessible to me. . . . The question became a burning one but remained unanswered: Can there be a philosophy which is true as a written work while functioning as untrue in the factual [life of the] thinker? What is the relation of thinking and practice? Authentically, what is Heidegger and what is he doing?[1]

The question preoccupied Jaspers in his later years. As can be seen from the notes, the preoccupation impelled him to develop an early idea of his, namely, that as "forces" (*Mächte*) can be seen to join in battle within the palpable encounters of mankind, so also in the encounters between one Existenz and another. Jaspers had planned to write a critical book on Heidegger and had collected his jottings, sketches, and fragmentary drafts dealing with Heidegger. But the project never developed, probably because Jaspers did not reach a sufficiently satisfactory solution to the question. What, to him, was an indispensable condition for its solution was not fulfilled, namely a communicative confrontation, by letter or face to face, with an openness to challenge and response that is candid, mutual and unsparing of self and other. In accordance with Jaspers's view of the preeminence of communication as the way of truth in time, he sought such communication with Heidegger. What was at stake for Heidegger never became known to Jaspers since the encounter never took place.

We cannot expect to find in these notes a definitive analysis or criticism of Heidegger's writings because, as Jaspers admits, he never read more than parts of them. These parts apparently gave him enough information and a feel for what Heidegger was trying to do for him to discern the distance between them. Yet even within these limitations, Jaspers considers Heidegger the one and only fellow-sojourner within the lofty and rarefied realm of philosophy who can arouse his interest. Despite their different approaches and main concerns—Being in Heidegger's case, Existenz in Jaspers's—which prevent them from communicating within the realm of philosophy, they at least exist next to each other, not with each other, in a philosophical space where Jaspers apparently found no one else.

In accordance with the above comments the selected notes on Heidegger deal with three main topics concerning Jaspers's reception of Heidegger's thinking and doing: First, their personal relationship as defined by their differing approaches to life and philosophy, i.e., Heidegger's philosophizing at a distance from life vis-à-vis Jaspers who regarded philosophy and life as two aspects of the same actuality. Second, Heidegger's personal and sometime conscious involvement with the Nazi movement, inexplicable to Jaspers on one level and yet understandable—but not excusable—to him on another, viz., as an outgrowth of his cerebral approach to philosophizing where a chasm exists between thinking and doing. And finally, the appreciation and criticism of what Jaspers identifies as the pivotal ideas of Heidegger's philosophy and his mode of philosophical thought.

The following notes have been excerpted from a volume which Hans Saner, Jaspers's literary executor, compiled, arranged and published under the title, *Notizen zu Heidegger*. They appear here for the first time in English translation prepared by the editors. The excerpts appear in the original on pp.

111–12, 115–21, 137–38, 141–43, 145–47, 151–52, 163–64, 169–70, 183–85, 221–23, 229–30, 234–35, 255, 263–64. The numbering and the identification of the period in which these notes had been drafted were provided by Saner.

TEXT:

Note 93 (1954/55)

Dear Heidegger!
I have bought your latest publication, *Introduction to Metaphysics*, and have read large sections of it. I was again deeply struck by two facts: First by my agreement. —you are perhaps the only one among the professors of philosophy in whose writings I read sentences which reach that hidden place about which you wrote me recently; then I might feel all strange, as if we were in league with each other. None of the other living ones can interest me (even though this sounds rather arrogant, yet it is not meant that way but is merely a fact). But then I was no less taken aback by my shock about the other thing that strikes as folly. So far I have not succeeded in reconciling them. I would like to separate the two, but in this I am also unsuccessful.

I would follow the impulse to write you, to attempt judgments that are intended as questions, and to pose questions outright, if I knew you were disposed to respond. My letter would not show any consideration but be frank, otherwise it would be meaningless. Please send me word whether you desire this letter, not in order to hear something about which you may indeed want to be informed, but rather to take hold of the letter as an opportunity desired by you yourself to reply to me with equal frankness, no matter how it turns out. If there is any doubt about that, it would be better to leave things alone.

1. Discussion as "scientific" argumentation is not possible according to the way both of us conceive of it, —here no proof is furnished, there is only seeing and showing.
2. How, then, is community possible? Or are we merely reduced to mutually incomprehensible monologues, reproaches, absurdities?
3. The form information takes in language is that things must be asserted and substantiated. The meaning of both can be realized only when the field of scientific theses, proofs, and argumentation is acknowledged, presupposed and referred to—not as something alien, not as something secondary, but as a desire to know; and the recognition of both is not founded in anything beyond themselves. Only on this foundation is it possible to liberate logical thought, as authentic philosophizing, from arbitrary power play, and to let it be methodical.
4. One must attempt, each for the other, to hear right through the clumsiness of the sentences—and if the other does not hear, to give him a wink—in

this, one succeeds by sheer luck, as one hits on the right expression in a situation in which only this one word, and no long explanation, is helpful and clears the vision.

5. The fact that philosophy is not a science, but uses science as an aid, means at the same time that it cannot be pursued like a scientific matter. It is nothing other than deception [for philosophy] to assume the form of specific information within the framework of progressive knowledge. Rather, philosophizing must, at the same time, be represented through one's person. For this reason practice is not an argument but is itself a means of information, a means of making plausible and vivid. Therefore: philosophy is indivisible from politics,—a position testified to and expressed by you in 1933, and basically true, but one that must be questioned regarding its content, the actions themselves, and the consequences.

Note 96 (1955)

Plan

My Heidegger criticism including [that of] my autobiographical memoir must assume the form of an address to Heidegger, of a single long letter divided into individual letters.
An objectivizing presentation would be inappropriate vis-à-vis a living person.
The [form of] address must be revised as to its meaning: as shared memory or as a reminder coupled with the demand to think about it—as a question about actions—
as a question about matters, methods—
In these questions, extended development of thoughts is possible in the form of exposition, but it must always be kept in the back of the mind that they are addressed to Heidegger, and will be submitted to him—objectivization as such has a distancing effect.
The address, not followed by an answer in the text itself, must be allowed to proceed as the natural result of the biographical situation.
That this address takes place in public means that a distancing has occurred that could be revoked only by way of an answer to my address,—not by private, conventional civilities.
However, the relationship itself has become a public one because we are mentioned together, are played off one against the other. Because, furthermore, the political reality that divided us has itself public character since we both have gone public within it. . . .

Note 98 (1954/55)

Heidegger's absurdities have in part the power to startle, and then, per-

haps, the power to stimulate the thoughtless to make them more clearly aware
of the rational.

What is Thinking? Merkur 604

Authentic thought distances itself from the sciences.

"The reason for this state of affairs consists in the fact that science does not
think. It does not think because, according to the manner in which it proceeds
and according to its resources, it can never think; think, that is, in the manner
of thinkers. It is no lack but an advantage that science cannot *think*. This alone
guarantees science the possibility, in accordance with its ways of research, to
enter into and then settle down in any subject area in question."

About this: 1. The word "thinking" is obviously meant to convey something entirely other than what has been understood by it in speech throughout
the ages,—something that is almost the opposite but cannot be grasped even
as this opposite—

and yet it is talked about, thus made the subject, the "state of affairs" are
spoken of—

2. It is understood that the meaning out of which science, research, and
methodical thinking are pursued, cannot itself be given a foundation through
science. That the sciences in their actuality have still another foundation
beyond science—which is correct and points to *the* exciting philosophical
question—is confused with the foundation of the correctness of scientific cognition. The satisfaction with scientific cognition is a twofold one: with correctness, and with the significance of this correctness! (Max Weber: "What I
can tolerate").

3. The specific methodological difficulty of "*Verstehen*" in the *Geisteswissenschaften* is erroneously absolutized into a problem of all science. The
[hermeneutic] "circle" is first of all imputed to all learning, secondly it is
imputed to *Verstehen* itself erroneously even where a straightforward
grounding of the material is possible: for example, the correct reading of
editions—

4. [Heidegger's] formulations have an effect only on those who are vaguely conscious of their scientific doings (as regards the correctness of their results) as well as of the meaning of their doings (why they engage in science at
all, and why in this particular science), and are also vaguely conscious of this as
existentially fragile for their whole existence.

5. Heidegger wants to go back into the Before, into the ground: out of
metaphysics into the ground from which it arises as the fate of Being—out of
science (which itself is considered, erroneously, to agree with metaphysics
because both are: objective, representational)—this going back is, in its meaning, formally, nothing other than all philosophy, the overcoming of the

subject-object dichotomy,—touching Being itself, transcendence, the absolute —the presentiment of the eternal.

And this [going back] is further discussed, extremely different in content and meaning, in the following manner:
intellectual intuition,—thinking out of a knowledge that is privy to creation— anticipatory—dialectics—speculation—
Doctrinaire metaphysics, from the very beginning, has been a breaking away from these notions—but it is precisely the great philosophers who did not carry this out—

6. The astonishing, the provocatoriness [in H's works]:
—as such considered to be deep
—experienced as pleasing by many thoughtless people and those who live without grounding.

In fact, philosophic depth is touched upon. For this reason, Heidegger today— in the world of opportunistic rationalism—is an effective philosopher. He flogs and jolts. But then: he says nothing, teaches no technique,—creates no vision,—he leads into the chaos but in forms of an ordered, carefully constructed language—that, as language, is alone the ultimate support and guide—But what is meant in this language does not exist or does not let [anything] become existential.

"Scientific proof carries for too short a stretch." (*Holzwege* 343) True, if this is meant to penetrate to the ground of Being: if scientists absolutize their subject matter (which is a typical way that is unphilosophic and alien to science, but one that has remained the companion of modern science).
False, because it achieves its aim.

Phrased differently: A proof never carries further, never carries into the ground of Being.

When Heidegger differentiates between philosophy and science in the following: Science arrives at correctness of statements while philosophy is where the truth of Being is at stake—
this statement is itself "correct," but now the question of thinking concerns that which lets the truth of Being be revealed—such thinking itself can take place only within the subject-object dichotomy (or it is transformed into the *unio mystica* that itself is no longer thinking in the sense of differentiating, speaking, imparting,—even if out of the experience of this union, but leaving it behind, one speaks again within the subject-object dichotomy). For this reason methodical consciousness and methodical control of thought are indispensable; they are present in the subject-object dichotomy (there is, after all, speaking, imparting, meaning). It is not a question of trickery in thinking, not of a technique that can be stated and then applied and repeated on the basis of new specific insights: What is involved is the methodical philosophical self-

awareness of one's own doing; without it, total confusion reigns within the
form of the seeming order provided by speech: It is always possible that everything be turned and twisted into something else,—there are no absolute
statements,—one cannot demonstrate operatively in what way they have the
appropriate intended meaning,—when comprehended, they can be fundamentally misunderstood, since they are merely misunderstandings of oneself.

The extraordinary pains taken by philosophers to comprehend and overcome
the subject-object dichotomy since Kant,—and before that since Plato, but
always subsiding again—, in order to escape from natural naïvete, contained
in the view that truth is the *adequatio rei et intellectus,*—these pains can only
be comprehended if the philosophers themselves are methodical, i.e., if they
know that in all their speaking about the subject-object dichotomy and its
origin and meaning they themselves are already entering into this dichotomy:
that one cannot escape this dichotomy by thinking except through a thinking
that consciously carries out its communicating in the dichotomy, with the
meaning leading toward the Encompassing: —here, however, every position,
everything that is meant immediately, assumes an appearance within the
dichotomy.

Only within the illumination of the presentiality of thinking can the nature of
this subject-object dichotomy become clear and clarified through itself; and
even this clarification is itself never complete. This is not a presupposition we
make (that happens only in inadequate formulations of the presence of the
dichotomy); rather, it is the presupposition that we ourselves are as thinking
beings. (Cf. *Unecht sehen*: "*Sein und Zeit,*" p. 59ff.)

What does Heidegger want?

To escape from the sciences? To abandon the sciences? To find his way
back into a truth, the truth prior to all sciences?
—or to pass through the sciences to arrive at something that is more than
science, philosophy, or thought?
—or to make ready the thinking with which the sciences can finally be
overcome?
—or does he want this kind of thinking to take the place of the sciences and
make them superfluous?
—or to educate thinking by means of the sciences themselves?: (*Holzwege*
195) "To the preparatory thinking and to its execution there belongs an education in thinking in the midst of the sciences. The difficulty consists in finding the suitable form for this, so that an education in thinking does not fall
prey to confusion with research and scholarship. . . . Thinking in the midst
of the sciences means: to pass them by without despising them."

Heidegger's *Holzwege* 197 about understanding of texts, understanding of art: "A proper elucidation, however, never understands the text better than its author understood it, but does indeed understand it differently."

Holzwege 195: " . . . Intertwining of metaphysics with the sciences, which belong to the offspring of metaphysics itself . . ." this is only half true,—historical-genetical,—giving piety (?), giving impetus—
what is decisive is the special origin of science in distinction to and in contrast with metaphysics—and its pure unfolding without any metaphysics.

Is there a gulf between science and thinking? According to Heidegger, yes, so much so that: science is not thinking.

Note 117 (1954-55)

If I were to bring into relief in a few words some surface features of Heidegger's thinking through which one can glimpse our essential opposition, I would use the following as examples.

His exclusion of modern science in his philosophizing, this passing it by, his conceiving of science as a cognition that is not universally valid but founded in historic processes that themselves are not only factually historical but temporal in their meaning.

His use of the idiom of a cognition that claims for itself the same objectivity as the sciences, borrows from it its basic attitude, namely that what really matters is the thing and not the person.

The fact that he presents transcending thought in the form of a doctrine. Knowing about man is dogmatized in an objective construct. Illumination of Existenz is turned around by him into a knowledge of Existenz, i.e., into "Existentiales." It thus becomes applicable to psychology and anthropology—despite Heidegger's later warning to psychiatrists not to philosophize.

His presentation of illumination of Being, to be sure on the basis of the illumination of Existenz, but in the form of gnostic knowledge that does restrain itself in objectivizing but yet appears decisively in objectivizing concepts.

This is so especially in his total conception of history and his total judgements about the Presocratics, Plato and up to the modern philosophers,—then in the interpretation of the Being (*Sein*) above all beings (*Seiendes*) as a "fating" being, of the process that is itself historic.

His demand for a total renewal, transformation, and new founding of philosophy in the perspective of world history,—instead of a modest renewal in the form of a return to authentic philosophy vis-à-vis its professional academic representatives in the nineteenth and twentieth centuries.

The intimations in the history of Being with respect to him as the only one
who renews, the only voice, the time that is now timely; coupled with this the
provocative nature of his thinking and the toleration of the way his thinking is
received, which are reminiscent of the treatment accorded to magicians and
idolized prophets.

His conception of linguality as linguality, concealing within itself the
primal meaning of the true, and as such is capable of being disclosed: the
transformation of language into magic.

Heidegger's sundering of philosophy and life,—his inclination to the aesthetic gesture in transcending,—his detachment from possible Existenz in
favor of knowledge about Existenz and Being, or at least in favor of detached
questioning about both.

Note 122 (1954/55)

I honor whom I attack.

I attack Heidegger as my contemporary, as a phenomenon in my proximity, as a person, as the appearance of a hidden antagonist. I am not
"objective",—do not have an overview,—
I lack a great number of facts and documents that others might be familiar
with.
I am also not "subjective" in that I do not speak out of whim, inclination,
disinclination; but I am not unjust, not a stranger to the "cause."

Rather, I find myself in a struggle with a potential adversary,—who has
expressed several times his antagonism without mentioning me by name,—
and against whom I have occasionally—but mentioning his name—used criticizing and characterizing phrases that, however, do not touch the depth
where the authentic antagonism of essentialities and actualities is expressed.

I did not want to read *Being and Time* because it did not engage my
interest,—and to this day have read only very small parts of it. H. expresses
something that can be taken as an accusation of plagiarism against me, in
which his students obviously support him; but something like that is basically
impossible in philosophy, except if one copies and reports without any thinking of one's own.

If, however, he means that he influenced the content of my thinking, then
it must be said that during his visits such influence emanated to an incomparably greater degree from me, while H. was silent a great deal of the time. I
thought that I had been permitted the pleasure of having him understand me.

The fact that my *Philosophy* appeared toward the end of 1931 while his
main work was published in 1927 could indicate the dependence of the later

work on the earlier one. However, the point of departure for my book was my "Psychol. d. Weltansch," of 1919.

At the time when Heidegger's work appeared, large sections of mine were already worked out; it was not at all influenced by *Sein und Zeit*—, I still believed there might be analogies there but I did not look for them since I only read what was of benefit to me and nourished me—Heidegger nor his work gave me such benefit nor nourishment. Apart from the analogies, which are based on our common ground in Kierkegaard, I consider his work so heterogeneous from mine in motivation, content, and philosophical intent that—considering the measure and the manner of his objectifications that can so easily become dogma because they can be learned—I always have to deplore the circumstance that Heidegger is considered immediately and readily in accord with my philosophy, and my philosophy is misunderstood accordingly. This is due to the tendency, present in those readers who merely absorb and give back, to objectivize and doctrinalize all philosophies, and whom Heidegger meets half way—not I, at least not when it comes to the crucial element of philosophy itself.

Note 127 (154/55)

Heidegger's insights are mystical insights that find their expression speculatively in allegories, in images and poetry. He knows about that which man can experience in profound stillness, in solitude. In this breaking-open of mere existence he is given as a gift what has its ground and echo in his being.

But as all speculative mysticism in history teaches and demands, such insights in their purity are granted only to him who actively works toward the readiness for these insights by the way he lives his life and by his attitude of honesty toward all that can be thought and cognized. The impurity, indeed the magic, with which the manifest truth of Heidegger's statements is clothed, obscured, and smothered, yet which sometimes shines forth brightly for one moment in a rare and wondrous way, lets us ask in turn about the untruth exhibited in the totality of this thinking and lets us sense the fragility, untruthfulness, and morass-like nature of its ground.

Note 129 (1954/55)

Heidegger

There is in his life a disposition that expresses itself indirectly,—darkly and not clear to itself,—
with the philosophical impulse to gain presentiality in thought—
and with the desire for the power to achieve effect and recognition from it—
A profound despair:

No faith in communication,—awareness of total aloneness,—without actively suffering from it,—but in passive defiance—
An awareness of the decline,—the end of human history—and the artificial, non-credible invoking of primitive possibilities—a contempt for man,—desire for the recognition he does not want to do without,—and yet a growing contempt against all who follow him—

A modern phenomenon—many recognize themselves in it:
Romantic sentimentalities at the periphery—
Lack of obligation as a whole—
Content with vague, non-binding symbols lacking consequence, by means of which the self-illumination of the consciousness of one's own value within the negative is possible.
"Place-Holder of Nothingness", "Guardian of Being."

How is discussion possible with an existential-Existenz-opposed power that makes its appearance with great talent and in some profound depth of an ancient suffering—and yet always seems to betray itself in this deep ground—

Note 130 (1956/60)

Heidegger's "Turning" (Kehre)

To what extent it is actually present and wherein it consists—or whether that which remains the same is the decisive element after all, is that which does not change except in certain aspects.

Interpretation
1. from development of the "subject matter" ("*Sache*")—perhaps Nothing to Being (which, however, is present in the first thought and does not signify a "development"—the ancient idea of Plotinus, Meister Eckhart—expressed in 1929 with approval by Heidegger after the lecture about the Ground).
2. from the situation and how it is experienced
(a) "Sein and Zeit"—revolutionary openness
Exhibiting, but only within a formal framework—"decisiveness", not decision. Decisive to what end?

Then fulfillment by N.S. [National Socialism]. The latter as content to fill the experienced and passionately taken up form of this interpretation of existence—with all the defiance and fury and claim to power and with all that is dictatorial that spoke in it from the beginning.

(b) The disappointment with N.S. [National Socialism]. His own impotence. Not given any recognition by N.S., later regarded with suspicion—he held on to his own N.S. (the *late* Hitler-greeting),—and the experience of the consequences in 1945 (boys who stick their finger into the spokes of the wheel of world history), the defamation contained therein (the impossibility to retreat into the heroic pride of shipwrecked truth). Out of this experience, the other aspect: Being in Nothingness, the event of Being, the passivity of opening oneself up, of acceptance (no more talk about decisiveness and Being towards death)

These two aspects of the same "matter" [H's relationship with N.S.]— emphasized according to the particular situation.

Both equally untrue in their existential character.

Both founded in a common untruth:

(a) a philosophy yet withal the obscuring of questions, in fact dictatorial, prophetic

(b) without responsibility

(c) without the existential power of the authentic demand, aesthetic, existentially soft, untruthful.

Note 147 (1956/60)

Most likely I would have read him more thoroughly if I had not known him personally.

The "facts of the case" were repugnant to me.

I always measured what he had written against the man I knew so well. His writings made an exceedingly artful impression—but were not at all inspiring to philsophical thought.

Almost always I felt a frame of mind in all of them that was wrong for me. There was no objective knowledge. I learned nothing. There were no philosophical impulses that would move or advance me.

I knew the sources better and the truth in them, that here seemed attenuated and turned around and concretized: Kierkegaard, Schelling, Luther, Augustine.

H's stressing his relationship to Dilthey, Husserl, Cassirer, and other professors—his quoting them and then drawing attention to his quoting— flatly contradicted, it seemed to me, what had seemed real between us in our conversations.

I admired the work, the workmanship, the discipline and the construction— but none of that interested me, addressed me. Thus I always got bogged down very soon in his books. Wherever it got difficult it was not worth the effort— quite different than with Hegel or Schelling or Kant, where the difficulties, when I made the effort, dissolved fruitfully into new insights.

Note 155 (1959)

Perhaps on the Occasion of Heidegger's Seventieth Birthday

This is a welcome opportunity to extend to you, together with my good wishes, also my homage. To be sure, I have known only one among my contemporaries who appeared to me to be a truly great philospher, Max Weber. Apart from him I see no one besides you among my "colleagues in the field" who could move me—not through his practical achievements but by the kind of person he is, i.e., by being a philosopher. Early on already I considered you a man who is acquainted with what philosophy is. Long ago you encouraged me by your very presence within the academic world. I owe to you the thoughts I can express in detail. But contrary to my early expectations you have become, it seems to me, the representative of a force against which I do battle by means of my own [philosophical] efforts, albeit hesitantly and never in complete certainty about where you stand. If fate grants me the opportunity, I shall attempt to develop further my criticism of you, in accordance with Nietzsche's words: What I attack, I honor. This is difficult because no model exists for such polemics. I have often considered what these polemics could be like. But the execution is different from the knowledge of the principles that would have to be followed. I would have to read all your writings, which I always read in part only and soon put down again because they did not nourish me. What you intimated in our conversations does not show up in your printed works.

It is perhaps proper that we did not meet again after 1945. I did not purposely avoid a meeting, neither did I seek one. What I have since heard and read has intensified for me what I had to see in you as a National Socialist— alas, what kind of a National Socialist who was none at the same time!—and has clarified the inevitable, publicly still anonymous, antagonism. To bring this to discussion in a philosophic manner, i.e., in a manner uniting the so-called subject matter and personal Existenz, is a task perhaps too difficult for my abilities.

If I were to attempt this, then in conjunction with my personal aim of making possible between us a connection after all, one that had not existed heretofore or had been merely a sham. After I had written about this in my autobiography for the Schilpp-volume, I saw that it could not work the way I had written it. I then removed that section and did not mention your name at all. This silence had to be obvious and palpable even to the reader who knows very little about this matter.

Since we are well-known persons, I believe it possible that such polemics would serve the cause of philosophy, especially if you were to reply and an agreement between us were to result from this, as we had envisaged as a possibility about 1949.

Note 166 (1961/64)

To show how the basic disposition of this [Heidegger's] philosophizing has to lead to totalitarian government in practice. Where the impetus lay in 1933 to participate [in N.S.] (not as a fellow traveller, not opportunistical-ly)—and wherein lay the difference that made this participation impossible.

1. At that time, H. went further in some of his demands than the Party.

2. H. believed he could, on his own, decide for himself—he declined chairs in Berlin and Munich and thus demonstrated to the Party that he could de-cline, that he is not like them, is not obedient.

3. As philosopher he really wanted to educate the Führer.

4. He possessed no trace of that shrewd political sense that progressed along its path step by step, guided by the will-o-the-wisp of power, deceiving itself and the others, stage by stage to the destruction of Germany; that led first to the increase of the power of the state and the military, then to war and unconditional capitulation;—this path was not in accord with H's thinking. He stood on it like a stupid child who sticks his arms into the gears of history and is lucky enough not to be crushed by the wheel of history but comes away with merely a few scratches.

5. He has not even the slightest idea of genuine politics, no trace of a sense of responsibility. What he does and what he experiences strike us like an operetta in which he acts for a moment with an enthusiasm that seems igno-ble to us, and commits acts that are symbols of misdeeds; he does not notice the murderous character of the affair; he talks in the clichés of military hero-ism and deification of Hitler, Schlageter and others. He is eliminated before this murderous character becomes evident even to the blindest and, in practi-cal, matters, most stupid,—and even then he remains obstinate, distances him-self and yet participates, advocates as late as 1937 the Hitler-greeting, which the then officiating rector had abolished as the salutation in the lectures;—he remained a "philosophic" national socialist.

How this whole course of events is connected with his philosophy—i.e., how his practice and his thought are mutually illuminating;—how, as it ap-pears, even today he has not fundamentally comprehended what has hap-pened and what he has done.

This incapacity to learn from experience testifies to the granite-like foun-dation of his philosophical thought. He is always the same. What appears to be development and is taken very seriously by him as progression (the dating, the [chronological] arrangement of his writings), is non-essential in charac-ter; in these appearances, however, there are the modifications, the series of symptoms, or of objectifications, or of the clarification of that which is ex-pressed through him. This is something, it is not theater, it proceeds through decades, interrupted only briefly through disturbances of life and anxieties, dependent on states of mind. This is what he himself says (following Schopenhauer): every great philosopher has only one thought. But the greatness is dependent on the greatness of this thought and the nature of this thought.

Note 167 (1961/64)

What is Man,—Who is Man . . . ?

What H. did in 1933 were the "inhuman" consequences of a philosophy from which man in his freedom, his responsibility, his self-being has been lost:
in favor of an existential apparatus of functions whose forms, from the very beginning, are—as consequence of their ontologization and objectivization— not even forms but empty shells:
that appeal to conceptions pervasive among the moderns who tend toward radicalism as such, toward revolt, toward the functional, but which in turn is suffused into that which resists all that is functional, [and who are] stimulated by formalism without knowing for what purpose—Metaphysics of one's own Nothingness, set free from freedom;—that dupes the theologian because he believes that he can fill the void with Christian faith—
This savagery against *humanitas* (the humane as well as humanity), against "culture," against "education"—(Johst: when I hear the word *Kultur,* I cock my pistol);
this affirmation of barbarism
in the forms of linguistic discipline, in the work of the goldsmith (often with imitation gold).

All this is in Heidegger but is not he himself—he becomes its creature,— something quite different is involved here—not only an unusual measure of understanding of poetry and music,—but a metaphysical engagement.

Note 206 (1961/64)

This book is meant to do battle. It would like to destroy what is untrue for the author, i.e., rob the untrue of its persuasive power. This can succeed only if, though not in possession of the truth, it proceeds truthfully.
It is a spiritual battle that can unite the persons of the combatants even where—or especially where—they oppose each other most vehemently. In such a polemic one has to ask himself the critical question whether anger, whether indignation, can seduce him to use improper means to make the other appear contemptible, or resort to the tricks of rational analysis, or to overemphasize the opponent's incidental weaknesses. The main thing is: to let the spiritual force operative in the antagonist, perceived as inimical and untrue, appear in its essence as purely as possible.

I do not love this force: I hate it while I feel an inclination for the person of the antagonist. Persons, through whom the forces do battle with each other, can, through ideas, be personally united in the chivalrous obligation of carrying out the ineluctable destiny of this battle.

They are themselves yet not only themselves.

Forces also put their imprint on the persons, put distance between them. But both are human beings and partners in fate even where they have to do battle,—partners in fate, not in alliance, but in suffering and executing the calamity of battle between the forces, a necessity quintessentially imposed on man. No man can attain a commanding overview of the forces; if he could, the battle would be over.

An end to the battle would presuppose a revolution of the mode of thought, a conversion of one or both of the antagonists; such an end is highly improbable.

What is possible is the much more modest aim of contributing to the clarity regarding what it is all about.

Note 208 (1961/64)

H.'s own delimitation over against "Existenz-philosophy," "Existentialia." His main concern is "Being."

He believes he is asking a question that has never been asked before—which for him exposes a single pervasive error of Western metaphysics,—that, as it were, gives him a handle on all this thinking,—in order to posit the new in which the history of metaphysics will have its place as something that has been overcome (but that which is to be overcome, i.e., the modern age, will last for a long time yet).

What is this fundamental thought, this "one thought"?—We say it is a cipher—

Therefore, it is to be questioned not as to its correctness and truth—these are included in what is to be overcome—truth, now, is something else,—but what?

One cannot give a reason for the thought, it cannot be proven, it has no method that can be stated. As history of Being it overtakes the thinker, who catches it.

From now on it is presupposed; it bases itself on the fatedness of Being. Does it also base itself on the "destruction" of Western metaphysics? The thinker surrenders to it.

To inquire after its existential meaning, this is to be shown
1. by meaning relationships
2. by practical consequences in the disposition, the behavior, the actions, the judgments, and the power of judgment of the thinker.

Note 216 (1961/64)

Ontologization and Aesthetization of "Existenz" Philosophy

In reference to Heidegger:

The transformation of Existenz-philosophical thinking into doctrine, of thinking that is in motion and impels movement which needs the "other wing," into a thinking of existentialia that destroys its indirectedness, that loses its content and communication, that remains within the categorial and the analogous,—the transformation of Existenz-philosophy into ontology and gnosis,—of "decision" into the existential "decisiveness". The establishment of existentialia as the pseudo-science of a philosophy whose meaning loses its obligatoriness and makes irresponsibility possible,—the transformation of thought that is a call to a turning into aesthetic figurations, of the actuality created through words into the cult of the word itself.

Note 221 (1961/64)

In earlier times it was said: A philosophical system is not refuted by reasons but by another philosophical system.

I would not speak here of refutation. Rather,—I am speaking in the idiom of ciphers—spiritual forces through the agency of men catch sight of each other and battle each other without having any arbiter in the world besides individual men who feel themselves pledged to one or the other force.

The battle is fought by means of spiritual acts that characterize the antagonist as they catch sight of him. Polemics as argumentation refers to elements that are symptoms and not relevant in their own right.

The battle—if it is chivalrously fought—presupposes that human beings are human beings. They are not identical with the forces that we battle in each other and that each person perhaps battles in himself as well; rather, human beings are the battle ground and, as human, are still united by something that reaches beyond them; therefore, in the midst of battle, they will still feed on the possibility of meeting again when it is over, of being able to meet.

Note 239 (1961/64)

Those who philosophize today have in common that they live in a world in which no one hears them.

I am drawn to Heidegger, my worst antagonist among my contemporaries, because I sense that he knows in a certain way, though perhaps backwards, what philosophy is, and does philosophy just as I do but who, seen from his vantage point, travels backwards on his philosophic path. It is, after all, as if we—as antagonists—at least encounter each other in this realm that today is neither known nor regarded by the world at large.

The literary fact that our books are selling does not deceive us, neither does the fact that there are literary circles that occupy themselves with them; nor are we deceived because the "quiet minority" writes letters to us that testify to an understanding that moves us deeply. We are not quite alone.

The fact that we encounter each other in a realm, and again do not genuinely encounter each other, but at least pass by each other in this realm, a realm that very few enter today, has a curious result: The numerous criticisms of Heidegger, as far as I am familiar with them, force me, paradoxically for the most part, ever to Heidegger's side, not because I agree with him but because the nature of these criticisms does not concern that which to me is philosophically essential. There are exceptions in the form of simple, clear judgments that in turn are also not satisfactory only because they do not enter into his philosophical thoughts.

Note 241 (1961/64)

There are no antisemitic remarks in Heidegger's public, printed statements.

He possessed, as I know from my twelve years' association with him, no antisemitic instincts.

When instructed, as Rector, to put up a poster, saying: "The Jew who speaks German, is lying," he refused.

But in his actions as Rector he carried out the antisemitically based measures. In a letter to an administrative office of the [Nazi] party he could get himself to write about the "Jew Frankel".

In the last conversations that I had with him in 1933 he could get himself to speak about the danger of international Jewry.

Note 252 (1964)

High in the mountains on a vast rocky table-land the philosophers of each generation have been meeting since time immemorial. From there one can gaze down onto the snow-capped mountains and, still deeper, into the valleys inhabited by man, and into all directions under the heavenly canopy toward the far horizon. Sun and stars are brighter there than elsewhere. The air is so pure that it consumes all gloominess, so cool that it keeps the smoke from rising, so bright that it causes thought to soar into unfathomable spaces. It is not hard to gain access. Those who ascend by many different paths must only be determined to leave their dwellings time and again for a while in order to learn on these heights what authentically is. There the philosophers take part in an amazing non-violent struggle. They are gripped by forces that do battle with each other through their ideas, human ideas. They speak with one another, listen, question, communicate within a space that unites them in spite of the battles. For their main concern is the great seriousness of the essential subjects that man can touch upon. They share this relationship to them. But their differences also go deeper than any finite ends in the material struggles of the world. Yet even this high plateau is still in this world, is the miracle in this world: Men think beyond every limit and still do not fall into the void.

It seems that no one can be encountered there today. But it seemed to me as if I, seeking in vain among the eternal speculations for men who would find them important, as if I had encountered one man, no one else. This one however was my polite enemy. For the forces we served were irreconcilable. Soon it seemed that we could not speak to each other at all. Joy turned into pain, a strangely inconsolable pain, as if we were missing an opportunity that was palpably close.

This is the way it was with Heidegger. Thus I find the criticisms he has received intolerable throughout since they do not inhabit that high plateau. Therefore I search for the criticism that becomes actual in the substance of thought itself, for the struggle that breaks through the barrier of the lack of communication that prevails among irreconcilables; I search for the solidarity among those who are most strange to each other. Where that is possible it is a matter of philosophy.

Perhaps such criticism and such struggle are impossible. Yet I want to try to catch at least their adumbrations.

NOTE

1. Karl Jaspers, "Heidegger," *Philosophische Autobiographie*, R. Piper & Co. Verlag, Munich 1977, p. 103f.

III.

Hannah Arendt

Selection 70

EDITORS:

Hannah Arendt was a student whose work in turn influenced Jaspers's thinking. Their intellectual bond was also complemented by one of mutual friendship, and this enabled Jaspers to have a deeper appreciation of Arendt's complex mind than others had, especially those who were quick to pass harsh judgment on her. For example: Arendt would not exclude her fellow Jews from her forceful condemnation of what she discerned to be the moral collapse of Europe under the shattering onslaught of Nazi totalitarianism. But where some found in this an intellectual aloofness lacking moral balance, Jaspers understood her as an eminently humane intellect unsparingly engaged, with sovereign independence, in the penetration of truth.

The storm which raged over Arendt's book, *Eichmann in Jerusalem: A Report on the Banality of Evil*, aroused Jaspers to reflect on the risks of independent thought in confrontation with the politics of interests. Jaspers had planned to write a book on this issue under the title, "On the Independence of Thought"; only some notes, however, and a few developed sections were completed. The following selection is excerpted from an interview of Jaspers on the topic of Arendt's book, conducted by Peter Wyss on February 14, 1965, over the Swiss radio network. It was published in *Provokationen*; the excerpts are to be found on pp. 108–21. They appear here for the first time in translation provided by the editors.

TEXT:

Hannah Arendt emphasizes that her book is meant to be reportage and not a discussion of fundamental questions. In the case of this reportage she maintains she cannot avoid making use of general viewpoints in order to arrive at her conception and presentation; these, however, do not at all constitute her subject matter. She is not writing history. She does not wish to instruct the reader in the theory of evil or the structure of totalitarianism or such, but wants to present reportage. Shortly after the publication of the book, an

American, a German emigrant, replied to my question as to whether he had read it: "Yes—too good for a reportage—for a book . . . I am not sure what she is really trying to say." I thought this was not a bad reply. . . .

With her remarks about the German resistance Hannah Arendt merely wants to state facts and not really make judgments; it is a fact, however, that one cannot clearly differentiate the two in matters such as these. She states: active German resistance did not come into being until 1938 when war threatened and some generals thought that since they could not win the war they would have to prevent it. And the large-scale resistance and the large-scale conspiracies did not take place before 1942 when the fact of eventual German defeat became obvious and an attempt had to be made to save, from national points of view, all that could still be saved. To be sure, Hannah Arendt adds but does not elaborate further, that there had been exceptions. She mentions the Scholls. She speaks of the great courage of someone like Stauffenberg who had risked his life. She speaks of the quiet resistance that occurred in Germany but which never became active. Her most important point, however, is what she has to say about the resistance that culminated on July 20 [1944]. Here is what she maintains: This resistance took place—not because of the horror of the mass murder of the Jewish people, not because of other crimes, but for the sake of the German state and in order to bring the war to an end as favorably as possible to orchestrate the defeat,—as the expression went in those days,—for this reason and only for this reason.

The almost unanimous response to this, taken from the little that has so far been said on this point, is that Hannah Arendt is wrong. They are thinking here of Goerdeler and others who have spoken of these horrors and have said that the army is disgraced, that the German Reich, the German nation have been soiled by history, and that they can be rebuilt only through an act such as this.

In 1942, Stauffenberg had a picture of Hitler in his room. Asked how this is possible, he replied: so that everyone can see the disproportions of this face that one has to reject as soon as one looks at it. The question arises: why did he not see that in 1933? Why did he, in 1933, march as an officer at the head of a parade, full of enthusiasm for this great popular movement? Why did the generals, from 1933 on, accept rearmament, step by step, from Hitler's hands in the conviction of acting in the national interest? They identify the interest of their army, of Germany, with National Socialism. This is what Hannah Arendt wants to bring out. Why? Because she speaks in her reportage about Eichmann's conscience—one main topic of the trial. In order to comprehend this conscience of Eichmann's she has to refer to the world around him and asks about conscience in Germany. And here she is indeed provocatively radical. She wants to demonstrate the following: in the world around Eichmann conscience had become uncertain; indeed in many respects it is open to doubt whether conscience in this Germany had not generally been lost—at least that which the world had called conscience up to then. This is a very provocative statement in light of the fact that there were some magnificent and in their way admirable individuals such as Ludwig Beck, Julius Leber and others! But it is her basic thesis that is decisive here. And here she goes so far as to state: this other Germany was also drawn into the uncertainty of conscience; for up to the very end this other Germany did not consider as absolute the demand for unconditional surrender but had continued to hope—indeed had originally demanded—that unconditional surrender would no longer be necessary once another state had arisen out of the freedom of the German conspiracy and Hitler had been destroyed. They did not understand that at that time the Allies saw Germany necessarily as a whole because the German people devoted their whole strength and all their skill [to the war effort] so that Hitler almost conquered Europe and the rest of the world, and tremendous efforts were necessary on the part of the rest of the world, and great sacrifices by the Anglo-Saxons, French and others, in order to destroy in its very core what had become a danger for all of humanity, and in any case meant the end for Germany. It simply never occurred to these conspirators that the Allies could not but identify this collaboration of the power and of the fighting capacity on the part of this huge [German] army with Hitler. They believed they could dissociate themselves from him simply by going their own way. For Hannah Arendt this was, as she remarks in an aside, a totally unclear standpoint, i.e., one where conscience did not even come close to the simple, definite fundamentals of human conscience as such.

When I consider what Hannah Arendt has said on this issue over the course of years, then I find all her passions involved in the question: How was it possible and what does it mean that a state could carry out bureaucratic mass murder? The British formulated this concept and have rejected it explicitly as a means of domination. This bureaucratic mass murder was carried out, however. How is that possible, what does it mean?

What I am telling you here is not enough. For Hannah Arendt did not elaborate on the other side of the coin, the side evident in the case of the Scholls. If she had done so, instead of devoting merely one page to it, things would sound quite different. We don't want to make up for it here; that would be, in a certain sense, a supplement to her book. But what remains above all are the probing, decisive things she says about German resistance, the fact that she radically calls it in question as an ethical phenomenon. . . .

On the question of Jewish cooperation in the mass murder, Hannah Arendt takes her facts from available publications, the books of Hilberg, Adler, and others. In all things that do not concern the trial immediately she bases herself on the research of others. Here she asked quite correctly. She states their findings in a curt, challenging manner, in such a way that suddenly something enters the world that has been here all along. This happens in such a manner, to be sure, that misunderstanding can arise but only if one does not read very carefully. For example, her critics maintain that this cooperation was extremely important and expedient after 1933, which Hannah Arendt does not deny, however. She carefully distinguishes the Jewish councils during the war from all that amounted to Jewish cooperation previously. Further, it is not true that she states that all the Jewish elders were guilty. She merely clarifies: if one ever cooperated at all with the Nazis, gave them a little finger, so to speak, one became an accomplice in this cooperation. . . .

Now to Hannah Arendt's position, if you want to call it that, or her hypothesis: If the Jewish councils had not cooperated, then "to be sure there would have been the chaos and the terrible misery but hardly as many as six million Jews would have perished." Of course a hypothesis such as this cannot be proven. However, one can discuss possibilities, and one can cite examples—as she does in part—for the fact that indeed rescue through chaos was possible, as well as for the opposite, i.e., that the Jewish councils could not essentially change anything, neither for the better nor for the worse. But the question always remains: To what extent does this cooperation mean more than mere saving in personnel for the Germans; to what extent is it a causal factor for the number of murders committed? I repeat, this cannot be proven. This is, if you want to phrase it that way, a methodological question of presentation.

In every clear historical representation one needs—using Max Weber's term—ideal types, i.e., meaning constructs to which reality always corresponds to a greater or lesser extent only. Ideal types are a means of clarification without which we would have a diffuse muddle of infinite, infinitely varied things; they are a means to extract from reality certain meaning connections and then to be able to say: Something is wrong there, here reality does not correspond to the ideal type. There simply is no actuality that can be represented exhaustively by an ideal type.—Let us take an example out of Hannah Arendt: total domination. Its structure was studied very early on by Hannah Arendt: all the means used by terror, the two-track method, the method of mutual controls, etc. She claims—rightly, I believe—to have discovered a new type of domination that had not occurred previously. Now one can say: true, but it does not fit the Russians, or the National Socialists, or whomever. This construct is an abstraction, a generalization; in the concrete situation one can always see the other that breaks through this abstraction, of course. Total domination is never absolutely real. It fluctuates, as we have seen it do in Russia and Germany. There always remains the difference between the ideal-typical meaning construct which one understands completely, and the reality that contradicts it.

This is the method Hannah Arendt uses in her book about Eichmann but does not discuss explicitly. In our case she has emphasized one causal factor: The cooperation of the Jews facilitated the process of liquidation. One can use examples to prove that through this facilitation certain Jews were caught in the net who otherwise would have had the opportunity to escape. One can present examples to show how certain Jews were saved by opposing the Jewish councils and getting away from them. But one can never prove the quantitative or the causative factor, i.e., whether instead of six million only five, or only 100,000 fewer Jews would have lost their lives. Hannah Arendt does not carry this through methodologically; instead, we find the cited sentence that is qualified only by: "hardly would so many have perished." However, she maintained that this causal factor did exist; and, I believe that based on the facts available, she substantiated it sufficiently. . . .

Now, however, Hannah Arendt goes further and tries to understand Eichmann as much as possible with the means at her disposal, i.e., his own testimony and the rather sparse reports from earlier days. While the people in Jerusalem expect an evil demon, she liberates herself completely from all such preconceptions and realistically poses herself the following task: He is a human being, I must try to see to what extent I can understand him. She finds out in the process that originally Eichmann did not in his own mind subscribe to the mass murder, indeed such a violent solution was, as he says, alien to him. She now proceeds to show—and this was criticized as an error on her part—how Eichmann's conscience changed in the course of four weeks. His obedience toward the greatest man of his time who had proved himself to be just that by emerging from the lower strata of society to become the leader of a gigantic empire, necessitated Eichmann's realignment of his conscience. For Hannah Arendt, the ultimate decisive factor in Eichmann's turnabout of conscience was his participation in the Wannsee Conference. There he saw to his great astonishment—as he said in Jerusalem—that all these respectable personages (he had the greatest respect for bourgeois society) not only agreed as a matter of course but followed his remarks eagerly and enthusiastically. Therefore he was convinced he must be doing the right thing. He emphasized (in Jerusalem) that no one contradicted him, neither priest nor politician nor one of the bureaucrats—no one. This confirmed Eichmann in the turnabout of his conscience. Hannah Arendt believes she proved this turnabout because of the fact that Eichmann had rerouted the first deportation to the East, which was scheduled to go to Riga, to Minsk instead. He knew that in Riga all deportees would be killed immediately. Because he ordered this rerouting on his own initiative, he had great trouble with the people in Minsk. Himmler himself had to square matters. Here Hannah Arendt sees the last slight stirrings of his conscience. As far as he was able he tried not to send the people to their death.—The matter sounds dubious, not sufficiently plausible really to prove this turnabout of conscience. The proof lies in fact only in Eichmann's testimony in Jerusalem. He had forgotten what really occurred at that time and it was proved only in retrospect, albeit through documents.

Hannah Arendt proceeds step by step in this matter, intending to understand Eichmann: how does he get to be that way? Thus there comes into being a picture of Eichmann with which Hannah Arendt obviously is dissatisfied: a man who, being thoughtless, does not realize what he is in fact doing. Eichmann stands revealed as a banal figure. This self-denouement of banality defies the expectation of an evil demon to such an extent that it was an offense to all who believed that only a devil could have murdered the Jews. Hannah Arendt sees the horror in just this fact. It is much easier to fall victim to a devil or to a sinister historical law than to such banality on the part of a human being whom, in the final analysis, I must consider to be a clown and who can gain control under such circumstances. She states that, after all, the whole phenomenon of National Socialism was not demonic in character, that there could rise up from the totally commonplace, undemonic, quasi out of the gutter what then was to dominate all Germans and beyond that an infinity of people. The totally unremarkable nature of those who exercised this power, from Hitler downward, is something so frightening that one resists strongly having to deny all demonism. But it is just this banality that can rule the world. This is what one refuses to accept. Hannah Arendt judges according to this point of view the *niveau*, i.e., the spiritual level of the person. To maintain the total lack of *niveau* of this phenomenon, this is an insult to the Jews, to the Germans, indeed beyond them to many others.

Is this an excuse for Eichmann?—by no means! Hannah Arendt's method in these matters of considering not merely causal connections but also *niveau*, corresponds to her whole mentality with which we are—or could be—familiar from her important writings, among which the Eichmann book is merely an occasional piece of work. It is the basic attitude of understanding an individual realistically and then finally to use language devoid of hope such as clown and buffoon, with which no more is expressed than: true, I understand all that I present here, as individual traits; but the whole remains inaccessible for me; there remains a further something to be explored ad infinitum. Hannah Arendt assumes a psychiatric stance without being aware of doing so. She wants to understand; she disregards completely what other people imagine in their need for the legendary, the mythical, the grand. This is the reason for her complete rejection of this legendary, mythical element in our time, which she considers destructive because it muddled the minds and led the people to National Socialism and still muddles minds today. One simply has to bear the fact that Eichmann comes out of the gutter, is not a devil but a totally banal creature. Hannah Arendt does not at all mean to excuse him. Such an assertion is invidious. You yourself know that she endorses the conviction and his execution. . . .

[The question of punishing a crime such as this.] On this point, too, Hannah Arendt is ruthlessly provoking. Basically her point is that none of the penal codes extant are able to encompass this crime. Here such a deep incision has opened up in world history such as never before as regards the threats and dangers of the future: a criminal state with criminal organizations. One can no longer argue using such terms as "act of state," "duty to obey." The crimes can no longer be subsumed under the legal categories valid up to now: therefore, as Hannah Arendt points out, the constant references to the Nuremberg Trials as precedent. However, the Nuremberg Trials demonstrated the very same fact: a law had to be created and concepts had to be posited that actually did not fit. Thus, a grotesque situation arises: We are faced with a crime that is infinitely more than all the crimes known to man up to the present. And on the other hand, it is not a crime within the meaning of current criminal codes. According to the meaning of the penal code, Eichmann is not a murderer; he did not murder before, he did not murder afterwards, he lacks all the motives of a murderer. This then is the dilemma: According to the criminal code he would have to be acquitted.—*Nulla poena sine lege* (no punishment without a law covering the particular offense).

The law that was created in Nuremberg is inadequate. It does not possess the necessary clear categories in accordance with which judgment is to be passed. Hannah Arendt expresses this—after the many discussions in various contexts—by finally giving her own opinion in support of the verdict. She bases herself on the idea—an idea we actually abandoned long ago—that a horrible event must have an equally terrible response as punishment on a metaphysical level. The conclusion she arrives at is that something like that must be involved here after all; for justice must be done to both—to the victim as well as the perpetrator. But who brings about this justice? Who created the concepts? What about the criminal state? With her book Hannah Arendt has demonstrated the complete openness and lack of solution of the legal problem by letting all the different legal arguments pass in review before us. A monstrous danger to our future becomes evident: what has happened in our time with six million could be a trifle vis-à-vis that which is possible. She imagines the possibilities. One day one could kill the people whose IQ falls below a certain level because they have become useless in the increasingly automated industries and the population growth has become so great that a stop has to be put to it somehow. Or there is another war and after that a world government; it would then be quite thinkable, from the standpoint of this world empire, to keep the population within bounds by systematic, bureaucratically administered mass murder. Further, according to who governs the world, the idea would gain acceptance of eradicating either the Blacks or the Whites, in the following way: having one race migrate from a continent or vast territory and then destroying the remaining population with atom bombs. These are phantasies that point to one fact: Administrative mass murder can occur again and again. What can be done? The situation cannot be mastered through reason. Hannah Arendt does not discuss it. She merely wants to comprehend what has happened and see what it means. The decisive point is: No juridical basis has been found so far for judging this kind of crime. Hannah Arendt posits this and says it out loud; and a shadow falls on all courts of law, on Nuremberg as well as on Jerusalem, yet she cannot tell us how it can be done better. . . .

[Question of organized opposition to Hannah Arendt's book in USA] . . . . But where it is a matter of the spirit the fundamental question is, how this spirit—which is independent—acts in public. And an organized spirit is no longer spirit, no matter whether it has collected 2,000 or 18 or 5 signatures for some declaration. A collective of the spirit diminishes the independence of the individual, the very own, the sole responsibility of a person who speaks his piece in public, it diminshes his courage to answer for his stand; for he feels much safer within the collective. I believe that the collective as such is counter to the meaning of the public nature of the spirit. To that extent I reject in this polemic all that which assumes a collective character. But I must add immediately: There is much in this public polemic that has nothing to do with organization; and the most vehement polemics against Hannah Arendt were written by people of whom it cannot be assumed that they belong to the organized or manipulated. It is noteworthy that Hannah Arendt has experienced enthusiastic assent in America from some important writers such as Dwight MacDonald and Mary McCarthy. But all in all she has been manipulated and rejected by the literary world.

Who has vindicated her? The universities. I cannot deny that I was proud of that. The universities still have the idea that they uphold the truth itself, and in spite of all their dependence there are to be found, time and again, those in the universities who are independent. Their reaction to the treatment of the book in America was: several offers, several honorary doctorates, acceptance of her manuscripts and other items in the Library of Congress, one of the greatest honors. . . .

[What does Jaspers think of the book as a whole?] For me the book as a whole represents a marvellous testimony to the independence of thought. Hannah Arendt cannot be categorized as to her area of competence. One cannot say she is a writer. One cannot say she is a scholar. In order to clarify this I must say something about her personally.

When she finished her doctorate, with a brilliant dissertation—a thorough piece of work philosophically as well as speculatively—about the concept of love in St. Augustine, . . . she was still very young, I believe twenty-two; she was offered the opportunity to lecture at the university. She refused. Her instincts resisted the university, she wanted to be free. What did she do then?

First of all, before 1933, she wrote a book about Rahel Varnhagen that was as good as finished at that time but was not published until the fifties. This book, too, cannot be classified; in any case it was based on the most exact knowledge of the sources (in this process she managed to preserve material that was later lost). This book already bears the same characteristics as the later ones: dispassionate, but passionate in the cause of truth.

After 1933 she gave up all writing. All culture is a fraud, she said. One cannot depend on anything. She went into practical activities to further Jewish causes, joined the Zionist organization because it was the only one where one could act. During the war she began to write articles, mostly of a political nature. After the war she wrote one book after another. Whenever she had completed a book, she usually said: Well, this is my last book. But always there were new things to write about.

Hannah Arendt is not the kind of writer who seeks out her material; rather, when something comes her way, she takes up her pen. She is not a philosopher, she maintains. She gave that up a long time ago. Then what is she? She cannot be categorized. It is impossible to subsume her under any one area. She belongs to no organization, no club. She is completely she herself and dares to be who she is. And this total independence, it seems to me, makes her appear sinister in the eyes of many writers. She does not really belong to them. After all, she is not the type who keeps coming up with ideas and who must keep on coming up with new ideas in order to exist. She lives out of that independence which is not simply a freely soaring intelligence. This is the origin, I suspect, of an inner opposition to her felt by some writers. She does not belong to the closed circle that exists sometimes among writers, secret, unmentioned, without organization; even in this respect she is not typical. This independence is not the emptiness that lacks a foundation. There is an independence, which I would hardly call that, that manifests itself in a universal aggressiveness that says no and has the courage to keep on saying no and to keep on uncovering things. This is not at all the case with Hannah Arendt. The fundament out of which she lives is a fundament of the will to truth, of being human in its real sense, of infinite faith going back into her childhood but also the experience of ultimate abandonment when she was arrested (1933) and when she emigrated without a passport.

And finally perhaps this: one has so often heard it said about Hannah Arendt: her tone, the irony, this cold soul, this laughter, all this is like an insult to the dead, to the six million, an insult to all those who have suffered and are still alive. One has to respect that. This feeling has truth, but is not a truth that is universally valid. I feel differently. I like this tone of Hannah Arendt's. Since I have known her for many decades, I see in it again her independence. When Eichmann reveals himself as this nullity, then she laughs, because this denouement is like a joke. She amuses us that when she read the transcripts of the Eichmann-interrogations, she laughed—not once but often—loudly to herself. What does this mean? One can discuss back and forth how, in life itself, laughter and irony can be founded in an extraordinary seriousness. Plato says: Only a great writer of comedies can be a great writer of tragedies. There is some connection there. But this would lead too far.

IV.

Gertrud Jaspers

EDITORS:

In the preface to *Philosophy*, Jaspers gives an account of his antecedents. He begins as follows:

Our philosophizing is rooted in the tradition of the free thought of past millennia. As the Greek philosopher's clarity, as the bearing of the Nordic heroic mind, as the profundity of the Jewish soul, it has always, yet ever anew, pointed our existence in its direction![1]

The "clarity of the Greek philosopher" Jaspers received from his humanistic education. By the "bearing of the Nordic mind" Jaspers means the Friesian nation's fierce sense of independence, a legacy from his family. The "profundity of the Jewish soul" was the gift which Jaspers's wife brought to him throughout their fifty-eight years of marriage, as the following selections show. They also show that, for Jaspers, communication as the preeminent actualization of truth for man in time is no less a relentless though loving struggle where the partners are joined in marriage.

Selection 71

A MEMOIR

The following memoir is part of an autobiographical sketch which Jaspers presented on NDR, a German television network, in 1966–1967. A record of this presentation, revised by Jaspers, appears in *Schicksal und Wille*. The passages have been translated by the editors; in the original they are found on pp.31–32.

TEXT:

I got to know Gertrud through her brother, Ernst Meyer. At that time (1907) they were living in Heidelberg. Her brother had said to her: "I have

---

1. *Philosophie,* vol. I, p. viii.; editors; translation. For Ashton's translation cf. *Philosophy,* Vol. I, p. 2.

just met a student who is quite different; you must meet him!" He also told her that I am ill. Gertrud, who had experienced much sorrow (her sister had become deranged, a friend had committed suicide, and much more) had, through the fateful experiences of her youth, been torn out of ordinary life, as it were. Her nature had been transformed, her evaluation of things was no longer an ingenuously natural one. But she wanted to live. She met her suffering head-on. It seemed to her that the only new way open to her in renouncing a life filled with suffering was to apply herself to a task. She wanted to make up her comprehensive preparatory examination and then attend university. She studied Latin and Greek and did not want to divert her attention away from her studies. She was glad that her brother had found a friend but had no desire to meet him, especially since he was ill. Only at the end of the semester and to do her brother a favor did she consent to my visit.

During this visit something like a bolt of lightning struck us both. This occurred in the very first moment when Gertrud, still with her back toward me, got up and turned to face me. It was as if in this moment two people met who had been bound to each other since time immemorial. What really happened I cannot know and hence cannot report.

I have often written about love. Many consider what I have written on this topic as artificial and utopian. And yet it is for me an inadequate mirror of an actuality.

However, I can report the relatively external events. Since Gertrud has entered my life, since 1907, I have become a different person. Until then I was—in spite of my feeling of inadequacy and yearning—a man who desires to know, struggling for truth, cooly objective. Now I became a human being who is reminded daily of his humanity. Not through words but through the actuality of the partner who silently demands: You must not believe that your intellectual achievements mean that you have done enough. Gertrud sees to it that I do not miss too much, she reminds me of my personal obligations, about which I am so forgetful. She reads and scrutinizes everything I write. Her presence awakens those impulses in me which keep me from becoming totally immersed in the world of the intellect and in mere thought. And much more: I am convinced that if there is any depth to my philosophy I have achieved it because of Gertrud.

Selection 72

IF GERTRUD WERE TO DIE BEFORE ME. . . .

EDITORS:
Jaspers died five years before his wife. His draft of a eulogy for Gertrud Jaspers

was found among his papers. It was read at her funeral and printed privately by Jaspers's family. The translation is provided by the editors.

TEXT:

The corpse is not the human being. When Socrates's friends asked how they should bury him, he answered: If only I could convince you that it is not me whom you are burying!

And it is the human being whom we honor when the body that is left behind is not simply, unceremoniously interred like the remains of an animal, for we take the burial as a solemn occasion at which this human being is remembered.

No church could ever perform a solemn rite for my wife and me. Even our marriage had to be performed in heaven, on earth it was merely an act of legality. Because of the freedom of speech granted to ministers I could not expect my wife to go through a Lutheran ceremony; and she could not expect a Jewish one of me. At death there are rabbinical strictures that make it impossible for a rabbi to bury my wife's body in a general cemetery. A Lutheran minister would not suit my wife even though he would be prepared to bury her. As was the case at our wedding, we must again do without the church. We have lived and thought and chosen together; and now we want the solemn rite of the funeral even without the church. But not without the Bible.

I would like to speak some words that were dear to her:

The Lord has given it, the Lord has taken it, praised be the name of the Lord.

Yahweh plants and Yahweh uproots, and you desire great things for yourself? Desire not.

God was for her a cipher—yet more than a cipher: He was the actuality from which she did not sever herself whenever she doubted. She wrestled with God. I remember, once when she was still young we spent a whole day at the monastery ruin, Paulinzella, a twelfth century edifice in which Grecian beauty seemed to combine with biblical piety in a wondrous, stern discipline. In the evening when, taking leave, we looked back once more, she suddenly clenched her fist and said: And yet I do not forgive Him for letting Ida (her sister) go insane. My wife understood Job.

But on such occasions she stood at the outer limit. Her center and actuality was love, love on the part of the human being who, through this love, becomes more than mere changeable transient existence.

Her love was all devotion, capable of any sacrifice—yet it was also a stern love, bringing the beloved into a light and pure atmosphere; a struggling love which did not accept the beloved as he happens to be, but subjected him, together with herself, to a law that is neither written nor formalized, the law of unrelenting truthfulness. Whoever was loved by her could rely on her. But

the beloved person could not simply put up amiably with her tough and probing challenges; he had to prove himself vis-à-vis these challenges. Whoever
had the capacity to experience her love became a better person because of it.

There was an energy in this love akin to a consuming fire that leaves in
itself and in the other a purified residue.

A friend of hers used to call her "little flame" because her physical appearance seemed so frail and fragile. But when faced with serious matters this little
flame turned into a blaze, wholly invincible. She was herself affected by it,
subjecting herself to limitless criticism, conscious of the debt that is not settled
by means of conciliatory interpretations. In this way it happened that she
sought support from what—loving—she had done right; yet she dared not
regard herself as good.

In loving struggle we wandered through this wondrous, magnificent and
terrible life, bound to one another within this world from the first moment of
our meeting, entirely different from each other in the basic tenor of life, in
feelings, in our psychology, and yet united even to the point of mutual contradiction within that transcendent of which it is not possible to speak in an
appropriate manner.

Again and again she had occasion to say, along with Sophocles: better not
to have been born at all—while I said "yea" to life so very much, that thanks to
her I dared to say: I would live this life again.

We have lived this life philosophizing. If there is any substance in what I
have presented to the world as philosophy, then it is her I have to thank for it.

This philosophy knows no other ground than the actuality of love tran-
scendently given. It is not a confession. It is not a possessing of something that
might exist objectively.

If anything at all was the great truth for her, then—in the ephemerality of a
cipher—it was contained in the cry: Hear, O Israel, the Lord our God is One.

Part Seven

ENCOUNTERS WITH LIMIT SITUATIONS

EDITORS' INTRODUCTION TO PART SEVEN:
In an earlier introduction Jaspers is quoted as saying that two main motives impelled his philosophy: One is the search for communication; the other is the realization that limit situations awaken man to his task of becoming himself. This realization was gained not only through his study of history and of fellow man, and not only in his psychiatric research. It was gained through his own encounters with limit situations. Though Jaspers did not usually identify his life-long illness as a decisive limit situation, it did have this impact on him; Selection 73 should bear this out.

Jaspers is less reticent about acknowledging the incisive event of the Nazi regime as having the impact of redirection and of taking one's measure; this should become evident in reading Selection 74. Yet even here Jaspers is cautious as to what difference that experience made in his self-appraisal. He writes:

> In our lifetime the sense of existence was changed by the constant threat of the criminal National Socialist state, under which our personal future could look hopeless. If the course of one's life seems forfeit and as good as lost, one feels as if one had received a new gift of life when one has survived the danger. Yet my innermost being could not be touched or recast by any world catastrophe. Its shocks brought new probations and new examples clarifying what was already there.[1]

NOTES

1. "Philosophical Autobiography," *Philosophy and the World*, p. 298–299.

Selection 73

JASPERS ON HIS ILLNESS

EDITORS:
The following passages are from "Krankheitsgeschichte" (A History of My Illness), *Schicksal und Wille*, pp. 110–12; 118; 134–40; 142. The translation is by the editors.

TEXT:
Before I tell about myself I would like to recall for the reader two mutually contradicting value judgments that are made by healthy people about being ill.

Plato praises the wisdom of Asclepius who, he says, "exhibited the power of his art only to persons who, being generally of healthy constitution and habits of life, had a definite ailment; such as these he cured by purges and operations, and bade them live as usual, herein consulting the interests of the State; but bodies which disease had penetrated through and through he would not have attempted to cure by gradual processes of evacuation and infusion: he did not want to lengthen out good-for-nothing lives, or to have weak fathers begetting weaker sons;—if a man was not able to live in the ordinary way he had no business to cure him; for such a cure would have been of no use either to himself, or to the State." (*Republic* III, 407; Jowett transl.)

Macaulay, in praising Bacon, opposes Plato's views: "To make men perfect was no part of Bacon's plan. His humble aim was to make imperfect men comfortable. . . . In Plato's opinion man was made for philosophy; in Bacon's opinion philosophy was made for man. . . . A valetudinarian . . . took great pleasure in being wheeled along his terrace, who relished his boiled chicken and his weak wine and water. . . . Bacon would not have thought it beneath the dignity of a philosopher to contrive an improved garden chair for such a valetudinarian, to devise some way of rendering his medicines more palatable, to invent repasts which he might enjoy, and pillows on which he might sleep soundly; and this though there might not be the smallest hope that the mind of the poor invalid would ever rise to the contemplation of the ideal beautiful and the ideal good." (*Essays*, Vol. III; New York, 1860, p. 455 ff.)

Whoever is himself ill and does not merely observe the illness of others will read these lines of Plato and Macaulay with repugnance.

In Plato's words is expressed not only the cold haughtiness of the Greek. One can also feel in them the repugnance experienced by all healthy beings toward the sick members of their species which is found in all its pitilessness in the animal kingdom. Today the superior attitude expressed by Plato is not acceptable; instead, the barbaric demand is made to eliminate all that is uncomfortable. This instructive rejection of sickness continues to exist even today in the radically differing evaluations placed on the patient suffering from an acute but treatable illness and the chronically ill.

In Macaulay, however, we find an ultimate perversion of Christian *caritas*, above all an empty affirmation of mere happiness no matter of what kind. In actual fact it is a thoughtless *caritas* in which he does not believe himself.

What is true in Plato is the fundamental judgment that no life is worth living which is lived for the sake of the illness. The life of the patient—as the life of every person—is subject to the evaluation as to what extent objective content is realized in it and to what heights its spirit can ascend.

Macaulay is right when he says that the attempt to provide relief to the sick by means of technology should not be scorned. However, the purpose of such relief should be the creation of the best possible conditions to provide for the human being in his irreplaceable uniqueness the most favorable opportunities for the achievements still possible to him and to provide the strength for his inner acts.

Both Plato and Macaulay err in posing both the question and its answer in general terms. It is true that all healthy beings share among themselves a certain congruency, a something that can be subsumed in common categories, ranging from basic physical existence to sublimated spirituality. But one sufferer cannot establish a shared existence with another sufferer. In no way do they understand each other better because of their illness. Each patient as patient exists for himself, isolated, placed beyond the usual order. When the patient enters into some orders, accomplishes something, improves himself, then he belongs to the healthy. Every patient must find out for himself what he can achieve as a healthy person within his situation of illness. Each illness is specific and each instance of this illness has its own peculiarity impressed upon it by the nature and freedom of the unique individual. Man in his situation as unique individual is always faced with the task of finding in this world a modus vivendi with his illness. The modus can only be an individual one that cannot be repeated identically for other invalids.

The sufferer can assume this task only in a world that does not simply destroy him. In a world into which man is admitted only if he possesses general and typical abilities and fits smoothly into mechanized categories there is no room for the sick. It is, after all, impossible to offer to the sufferer rigid life categories within which he would have to realize his existence. He must be able to earn a place for himself within the sphere of the healthy as someone who is still partially healthy and has within himself some of the possibilities open to the healthy. This can only be realized if there exists free space for individual ways of life. The world can open possibilities to the patient but it can hardly lead him to a meaningfully fulfilled existence if it keeps him in a community of the sick and cared for by the healthy.

The demand of the sufferer voluntarily to renounce life and to die heroically if he is chronically ill denies him all possibility of life. Such denial does not perceive the real possibilities. It only eliminates that which is uncomfortable from the standpoint of the healthy.

However, permitting each and every vegetative existence devoid of content, merely as supposed happiness in comfort and pleasures, is destructive for the patient and is an offense against human dignity. Demands must be made even on the sick.

The way in which the sufferer finds his way is tied to the possibilities inherent in each age and the social situation in which he finds himself. It has been proven, I believe, through many cases, and among them my own existence, that if one limits one's expectations the possibility for relative success does exist in spite of failures. . . .

The Symptoms

Rarely do I feel really healthy. But even when this is the case for once, my condition does not remain the same no matter how careful I am. There are always ups and downs, sometimes because I did the wrong thing, sometimes spontaneously.

The majority of my days is clouded by physical discomfort. Back to my earliest youth I recall certain events as linked to my bodily failure. I think of places and situations without being able to prevent the association with the pain of this failure, the bodily sensations, the incapacity, the vain efforts. . . .

The Incorporation of Illness into Life

. . . June 9, 1903 (Diary): "Often I tend to moods in which I would like to . . . dream for the sake of becoming one with nature while my emotions gradually weaken, and finally to die . . . From such states of feeling I return eventually to work, deciding I must try once more . . . but secretly I believe that I am returning to a lost cause; for even if my vegtative existence were to continue for some time, this frequent poor condition of mine would prevent me from any proper intellectual progress. . . . Tired days, conditions . . . always have a melancholy, resigning character that inclines toward death. . . . I try to fight against it and to make myself understand that the will to active life is necessary for all Being and is therefore . . . indispensable in the world; its opposite . . . however is something evil because it negates change and Being. Of course most of the time I succeed in this fight on the intellectual level only. My feelings remain unchanged, and, abandoning myself to them even for a moment, I lie in the grass, fly up to the stars and want to sink into the earth."

As the motto for one of my notebooks I chose a quotation by Jean Paul: "Don't say: we want to suffer, for you must suffer. Say: we want to act, for you don't have to act." . . .

Aug. 11, 1905 (Diary): "It is easy to affect an attitude of irony vis-à-vis one's illness and impoverished existence. It is difficult to grasp clearly the seriousness of one's situation and the truth of one's prospects, and to strain all available capacities in order to achieve the achievable.—I am not gifted enough to perform intellectual feats of importance; too talented to be content to join the ranks of the average scientists. My whole being urges me to be active in the practical sphere by applying what I have learned to the material benefit of man and through affecting pedagogically the intellectually gifted young. Both of these are denied to me because of my body. Is there a way out? 'As long as one doubts one does not despair' (Jacobsen)." [In German, a play on words: *Solange man zweifelt, verzweifelt man nicht.*]

. . . . in all my activities inheres a vicious cycle. In order to be healthy I must really live; but this real life, in most of its forms, makes me ill. Any strong emotion—whether pleasure or pain—brings about the bad attacks that do not permit the natural development of the experiences I have had. Almost all the acts demanding my presence in the world are doomed to failure. I cannot fight without my vital forces weakening; then, having sunk below my level, I continue to fight but without being myself any longer. For this reason I was unable to function in faculty meetings if they lasted longer than an hour. I disappear, so to say, in every situation that stretches over an extended period of time. . . .

A life such as this was possible only under the specific circumstances of my life during that era [i.e., in Jasper's early twenties, at the beginning of the twentieth century]: sufficient means on the part of the parents, the comforts of life developed during the last century, lucky coincidences, friendly assistance by many people.

My life under such favorable conditions took place in my room; I worked in my room, lay down a lot—occasionally, on good days, during good hours, I made an excursion into the outside world. Everything I planned and undertook and what others desired, hoped, expected of me, had as its precondition my physical weakness.

In connection with my situation I always had worries and concerns which a healthy person simply does not know and which—if he hears about them—he considers strange or contemptible, thus my fear that I could be left without help in my apartment even temporarily, that I would be unable to find an apartment in the immediate vicinity of my place of work. A basic tendency goes through my whole life, a tendency toward discouragement of all projects in the outside world that have a physical component, be it travel, lectures, visits. I am paralyzed by the threat inherent in situations which disrupt the basis of my ability to function. My employment as University Professor depended on my finding an apartment near the University.

Because my condition was so unreliable I developed an aversion to deadlines: Yet I had to risk committing myself and had to take the chance of having to cancel at the last moment or to be inadequately prepared. Much too often did I hold poor lectures.

In public I could appear only for an hour at a time. Working at home I managed of course to achieve something by working in a series of short bursts of effort.

Because of this, an ambiguous element enters my life. In the same way in which I experience the feelings of capacity and of weakness simultaneously as I work does contrast imbue all [that I do and am].

The healthy can hardly comprehend my worries about my intellectual abilities. They see me—seated, to be sure—speaking from the rostrum, hear my voice and believe me to be healthy and do not know with what great care the physical conditions have to be prepared so that I am able to [lecture].

The contrast between my appearance, which seemed that of a healthy man, and my actual physical ability made me lose credibility, especially with strangers. I had a façade of strength, at least on good days: tall, a certain energy in my bearing, a voice that, though not loud, sounded strong from the rostrum. It happened often that my illness was not believed. On the other hand, I often felt like an impostor when I felt ill: I acted as if I were well and yet the whole day had been lived toward this one lecture hour. Returned home, I immediately had to lie down again on the couch and continue my expectorations. . . .

The Choice: . . .

If I want to live the life of an invalid, I can either retreat to my parents' house, live my life inside, desire nothing and achieve nothing in the world, pursue my intellectual hobby horses in uncommitted busyness. Or I can enter the world and move among men, illness and all. But then I have to be prepared for bad times and take their humiliating effects on myself. . . . Because of the unevenness of my behavior people did not really know what to do with me. I could be considered a nervous psychopath and weak in the head as well as an energetic, imperturbably quiet man. Even those who wished me well inevitably experienced a mixture of antipathy and sympathy toward me.

I wanted to take up a profession, i.e., I wanted under all circumstances to achieve something that would make me a member of human society. In the face of the seductiveness of invalidism I always chose again, after periods of incapacity, the path of work. Sometimes I became conscious of the hopelessness of my attempt. But I did not want to acknowledge it. . . .

Feb. 15, 1907 (Diary): "The future confronts me like a mountain which I cannot climb over. I have little hope of ever accomplishing anything. It seems to me that I have stumbled into the wrong profession after all. Wrong, because I am physically not up to it. I should have a profession that would allow me to work quietly in my room with books and paper. Unfortunately my system, apart from my illness, is not suited to this kind of life. . . . My desires tend so strongly toward real life, my aptitude for theoretical studies is so slight, that I would hardly accomplish anything in a field other than medicine, and specifically practical medicine. All my interests converge on practical medicine but I am as good as certain that I will never be active even in this field.—Thus my future is bleak, steadily I drift toward illness. My talent for literary production is so slight that here, too, I will not be able to complete anything.—It hurts to feel sterile. Frequently I feel as if I had to despise my existence. It would be good if I did not live any more, but I do not seriously consider taking my life". . . .

The Isolating Effects of Illness: "As a youth I was unable to hike, to dance, to ride, could not participate in the pleasures of youth. I could do no military service.

The isolating effect of illness is inexorable though silent. One is excluded without anyone saying so directly. One is treated with pity, surrounded with silence and secrecy. . . .

Often one is the object of dislike. One has no rights, is a bother, should be satisfied with little, should disappear."

From my diary: . . .

Dec. 31, 1904: "For a normal soul, the largest part of its capacities to be active and develop rests on physical characteristics. . . . The use of its body is the basis of its *joie de vivre*. If such a normal soul finds itself in a sick body, it must atrophy because its conditions for development have been taken from it. I am like that! Dreary prospects for the future, only to be able to decrease further! . . . People always demand from me what I am unable to give. Yet I have something to give, but which no one demands from me; what if some one, some time, were to ask me for it!?" . . .

The Acceptance of One's Illness. . . . If the illness is a chronic one and thus an irreducible fact of one's own existence, then one's attitude to illness oscillates between two extremes:

I can deny the illness, confront it as something wholly other: That is not I, that does not belong to me. It is a tendency to eliminate the illness although this is impossible. I try to live as if the illness did not exist. Or, I can identify the illness in its inescapable factuality with me as its temporal manifestation: I am ill. Being ill is a characteristic of my nature. My experiences are inseparable from my being ill. Through my illness I have experiences that I would not want to miss. Defiantly I posit myself as identical with my being ill. I want to be ill; it is my nature which I want in this way.

Both are wrong in their straightforwardness. But at some time both extremes are touched without fail in the struggle for the acceptance of one's illness. In the final analysis this acceptance is an insoluble task. No pure state is possible, something always goes wrong. Not only is the invalid more conscious of man's finiteness and his radical dependence, in his case it is something qualitatively different. Not even for a day can he depend on himself as existence.

Help: Throughout his long life my father constantly and without any conditions made available to me the necessary material help. I am indebted to my mother's love, and especially to my wife for her power of understanding which kept a step ahead of me so that I gladly lived. Through her I found the courage and desire for activity. The description of my illness must not give a wrong impression. I am not forgetting that all my suffering was truly alleviated. All the complaining and desperate phrases that I have reported here must be understood against the background of the fundamental situation: the certainty of being loved and of love itself.

Selection 74

JOURNAL ENTRIES 1939–1942

EDITORS:
Jaspers kept diaries at certain difficult times of his life. The following passages are from one such diary which he sporadically kept from 1939 to 1942. It concerned Jaspers's chances of emigration and is a grim account of his and his wife's life in great danger. The passages appear in *Schicksal und Wille*, pp. 143–62, translated by the editors.

TEXT:

1939

Feb. 6. It is possible that we may find shelter abroad, even if only a very humble one. The point in time when we shall have to decide can hardly be far off any more. The tremendous decision must now develop to leave Germany, probably forever, leave our whole existence, our people, friends, my parents and siblings. I shall keep a diary in order to ascertain what I really want.

I can only emigrate physically but not in my soul. The same is true for Gertrud. If our fatherland is to be taken from us by force: Every place else is exile for us. Only compelling necessity can furnish sufficient reason. This reason exists if we are threatened with loss of life, if our marriage is to be forceably broken up, if we are to be deprived of our means of subsistence, if our apartment is to be taken away (without our getting another one for ourselves). If we knew—with certainty or with probability bordering on certainty—about only one of these points that this was to happen, our decision would not be in doubt. But we are disquieted by the question: are we fleeing before phantasms? Are the current rumors actually baseless?. . . .

The world situation, with its danger of war, new crises, revolutions is similar everywhere: If a catastrophe were really to break out our situation would be hopeless wherever we might be.

If we were to be in trouble abroad, our situation would lack dignity: we cannot make any demands there.—Here in Germany we suffer though innocent. The injustice done to us cries out to heaven. If we were to die abroad it would be as if we forced ourselves on others and became burdensome for them. To die here means suffering the ultimate injustice but does not touch our dignity.

Going abroad means action, means interference with fate. To stay here would never mean guilt, is no interference, is retention of what belongs to us and our rights as long as possible, is holding fast to the soil and all wellsprings of our strength, remains familiarity with the *genius loci*.

Gertrud does not want to cause me to emigrate for her sake. She is thinking about my illness; she is tormented by the thought that a strange world would neither understand nor accept my physical disability. . . .

Feb. 9. The one notion that is really frightening and makes me want to leave is: They could try here, through certain measures, to separate Gertrud and me. Compared to this, everything else is less important. Besides these dangers similar threats exist abroad, maybe even more serious ones. But this separation would be improbable there.

Feb. 10. From now on, more than ever before, life stands in the shadow of death. Either here or there we would find ourselves in a situation—indeed we see this situation before us as a threatening possibility: a situation in which nothing is left for one to do but to take one's own life in order to prevent death under greater suffering and indignities. . . . Life enters a tension that does away with all comfortable, cozy atmosphere. More than ever everything is subjected to ultimate criteria. Remaining here, one is passive, sees the dangers. But they have come over us, we have not reached out for them; they must merely be suffered and affect us, whenever they are felt, as paralyzing. . . .

We have to put up with being quietly dropped. This is inherent in our situation. My being dismissed from office was a sensation. They sympathized with me, they sympathized with the University. I should be encouraged to hold private lectures. But now when things get serious, threaten body and soul, they withdraw silently, don't speak, do not stretch out a helping hand.

One cannot blame the individual person for this. It is a basic component of our existence that can only be broken through by exceptional people.

How so much, how everything that was said once turns out false as we think back on it!

Feb. 11. This new life is possible only if we are prepared to commit suicide. No one any more has the right to make us remain in the world because no one helps us any more unconditionally. Only my mother—but she knows about fate and misfortune and will forgive us if it were to become necessary someday. . . .

The philosophical reasons against suicide become invalid where destruction is certain anyway, is immediately impending, and leaves no space for a productive life—and where the proximity of people who unconditionally want our existence is lacking.

May our inner will speak clearly—for one cannot give a reason for it or generalize it—when the time is here! The deity will then resist no longer. I shall hope for the clarity of this moment and trust that the will of God will be evident in it. . . .

March 7. Philipp of Commines once explained very impressively how many great lords had perished because they had not fled on time. Today this question does not affect great lords but whole groups of people. However, this standpoint could be deceptive in its very ambiguity. Whoever chooses flight may very well plunge into misery and abyss.—There might be a time and a world situation when one perishes in any case. Then it is a matter of remaining faithful to oneself and not bringing about the end sooner or helping it along; rather, one must suffer it in purity and innocence.

I often have faith that the German spirit would not destroy me—but my reason tells me that when some injustice has occurred, any and all injustice is possible in principle. . . .

Gertrud and I—together we are wholly German—and my task lies in my work alone; my contribution—to complete this work. It alone justifies me in the world. It is a German work. But it seems that it is regarded with complete indifference. Would it be mere coincidence if it were to succeed? Reason must not fool itself.

March 14. . . . In the final analysis it is a matter of material things: the dangers for Gertrud and myself that could actually—as rumor has it—destroy our lives. I believe it proper to avoid this, it is not merely permissible to do so. I consider it a challenge. However, if our lives and our joint way of life, which itself is the condition of my productivity, remain possible, then not only can I work here in Germany, but my work will receive its greatest impetus right here. There remains a strong bond to the German spirit, even though it has become invisible, that demands that I suffer all the pain and that permits me to emigrate only in conditions of dire necessity. . . .

It is an astonishing magnanimity that seems almost like a miracle in today's world that France is willing to sustain my life without any demand on me other than that I complete my work in solitude. This mere fact as such is most extraordinary. But it is all the more frightening because, on a practical plane, it is combined with a meanness of spirit of which I have only now become aware:

1. that they are not willing to do just a little more to provide me and my wife with a modest resting place—

2. that, in the manner of a rich donor toward the beggar, they have excluded all possibility of negotiation, any question or remark on my part, and that I

must believe in accordance with the proverb: Don't look a gift horse in the mouth—

3. that it is accordingly impossible for me to travel to Paris, to show myself to see what impression I make there, to orient myself about the atmosphere and spirit there, before I accept—that they would even be put out if, once there, I were to go back once more to arrange things for my move.

4. that it is considered an annoying request and an impossibility to keep such an offer open for me in case of pressing need or at least to consider it renewable; rather just the opposite, a repeat offer is out of the question if I do not come now; one cannot even try for this because my sponsor would put himself in a bad light. The offer of a friend: You can come to me whenever the absolute need arises—cannot be realized here.

"Reality" for institutional men is that they are put out and negative, indeed have moral scruples about me if I hesitate or refuse. They simply do not put themselves in my place, do not consider the actuality of my illness and its consequences, the demands on me arising out of this actuality. They want something for themselves at the same time. It is not complete selflessness but the unconscious desire to use me to strengthen their standing in the world. But I want to make my stand solely through the content of my philosophical work, not through gestures and acts. What I do within the world for my existence shall be dependent only on material conditions, i.e., to secure the conditions necessary for my life together with Gertrud, for our work. My existence is "private"; it is public only through my work, through nothing else. . . .

Only in Germany can I live with love for the country and the ground of its history, even if I would gladly leave at this time. But only for the price that I gain the peace of mind to do my work so that I can complete my philosophy. Only in this way can I thank my benefactors; not through my politics, nor through my convictions, nor through my confession of faith.

It is clear: the present offer is the only real one, while the promising efforts of others have failed. It is most unlikely that we shall get another offer. If we refuse, we refuse for ever. Hopes for other possibilities must not be the motive that would make it easier to refuse.—On the other hand it is also unlikely that we would ever leave Paris again. We must not entertain the hope that this is merely a transition. We must go there with the feeling of finality. . . .

In this situation any decision is possible only in the face of death: Every decision risks the attendant dangers which are extreme in each case. For this very reason it is false and abstract to say: After all, death is the end in any case. Rather, the question is, in what situations, for what reasons death becomes preferable. Least of all one wants to have brought it about through one's own actions. . . .

Am I only deceiving myself if I believe that I remain attached there where I have become what I am, together with Gertrud? That my worries about the concrete changes of all conditions of existence are inspired by my love for remaining itself, for continuity almost at any price?. . . .

Pollnow said, once I have said No, the French would not even read my letter to the end, that is how little interested they are in reasons which they do not understand anyway. P. could hardly have found a more pointed expression for the cool indifference these men feel toward me, in the last analysis. . . .

It runs counter to reason and can in no way be justified, yet present within me is an indefinable faith in the spirit of my fatherland: that it could not rage too fiercely against us nor would we become its victims if we remain at our posts; perishing abroad would be quite different. Even as victims we are at home, innocently at their mercy but cradled and cushioned in the deeply suffering spirit itself that dies with us and is yet eternal. Here there is the secret bond of a fulfilled atmosphere that can become unnoticeable, is covered up all too often by foreground of events and experiences, by the disappointing behavior of many people but which becomes evident again for moments at a time. Out there is no air that belongs to us, that carries and quickens us inwardly in joy and sorrow.

March 17: We must be clearly aware of the menace. Even now it is difficult for us to find hotels that will take us. If they take away our apartment we are homeless,—if all mixed marriages are annulled we are powerless—then all that is left to us is death. If they take away our pension, our chances for survival are slim.—Whatever happens to us, it happens to us as Germans in Germany where we have certain rights, where we belong to our language and to ourselves. Death abroad is death away from one's base. In either case one is abandoned.—Abroad, with no one to depend on except ourselves, death is perhaps even truer in its dreadfulness: nothing remains to man but his God. This is a world-nihilism based on which life is hardly possible but if it is real and true, it may yet take the greatest step toward transcendence. But so difficult and questionable!

I may remain here only if I am prepared, at a given moment, to die with Gertrud. From now on life must be lived under this dimension and this danger.

If we leave, the same thing can happen to us in terrible misery and in strange surroundings; here it would occur out of the situation of the clear and dreadful injustice that is done to us. . . .

Even though I think of Gertrud and myself as one, as *one* fate indissoluble, I can still ask myself at certain times: what do I owe *her*, whether unconsciously I do not think too much of myself only. Whether I—since her life in this world is so totally curtailed—wanted to emigrate, simply for her sake, because of the situation. She does not demand this. But in a certain fundamental way her desire to leave is necessarily greater than mine, because of her experiences from day to day.

Should we risk it in spite of all the special, increasing difficulties? In spite of sickness, age, the legally uncertain basis of our existence, language difficulties, in spite of Gertrud's denial that she could learn the language and speak it, the questions regarding my work, in spite of my worries, all the strangeness of the world we would encounter?

This risk would be worth it in the extreme case of compelling necessity. The question is whether this compelling necessity is not actually here already—or whether it might not occur at all. No one can know. . . .

. . . Our staying together must remain the basis of all our actions; the world that wants to separate us through classification by race, must not intrude between us; we must remain *absolutely* united, not conditionally united. . . .

March 27: In the final analysis the meaning and purpose can only be to have room for the objectification of the philosophizing which has become completely clear to me only in these last years;—there is nothing else we can still do in this world.—The only task that remains is to make this truth an immediate one; this task is not life as existence at any cost but as existence becoming fruitful; under the presupposition, the only presupposition, that Gertrud and I remain faithful, close, intimate. We can produce this work together—or not at all.

March 30: If we die here—and if it is said: They could have saved themselves, they must have regretted having done so—, then we shall be considered—and lamented—as passive, stupid, unrealistic. But those who choose life on any terms forget that a life on any terms, a misery of one's choosing, are not the one and only truth. . . .

April 1: Our attitude toward life must change: we must reassure ourselves daily of our readiness to die.—We must bear in mind the radical uncertainty.—In this way we must advance the essential task that still remains to be done, without having any guarantee of success.

We are given a reprieve, so to say—the world looks more alien to us if we are not part of it—and yet closer, more related to us in its essential character in which alone we may be at home because no one can take it away from us.—Our path toward the ground of things—always ambiguous and yet, perhaps, revealing itself to us.—Life is possible only if it is grounded in transcendence.

April 7: Should we be victims?—I often get the feeling that we should. I would rather die where I am, where I have earned just treatment and a livelihood through my efforts, than—seduced by benevolent, reliable humane and noble persons—to put my trust, in the end, not in them but in strangers, that is in people who make the actual decisions but are unreliable; those people hide—in the magnitude of their politics of state as well as in the lesser sphere of practical actions—selfishness and mean spirit under the cloak of humane-sounding phrases and lawyer-like ways of speaking. . . .

1940

March 11: It cannot be God's will to have to endure *all*, if this enduring is a slow tormenting annihilation in total helplessness and indignity. Man *may* put an end to himself if he cannot be effective any more, if no one needs him, if he is abandoned, betrayed, shunned (he may do it together with someone if both are affected together in this manner)— but he *does not have* to put an end to himself. It is not a law but his free will, his consent. . . .

An actuality becomes evident to which one cannot be open if one wants to remain true. There are times when all people stand more or less on the side of powerlessness. It is then as if the soul were asleep, all creativity lamed, God absolutely hidden, transcendence without speech: Fear, like a blight, covers the soul. The strength to be able to die is then the negative attitude—the ultimate out of which new soul can grow.

Nov. 16: Gertrud keeps coming back to the idea: she wants to die by herself, she does not want to destroy me, too—my death tortures her, not hers. She wants my permission to leave this world.

But I cannot allow that she die without me. The powers that force her to die also destroy me. This solidarity is absolute.

It seems to me that everything would lose its substance if a separation such as what Gertrud proposes were to be ascertained by me as reasonable, permissible, possible. Then, indeed, there would be nothing serious left in the world. A person is human only if he, at some point, stands up for something at the risk of his whole life. Should I survive Gertrud if she is destroyed by the state, I would be as nothing. That I am responsible for Gertrud and she is responsible for me, that is our only protection in this world. If the state wants me to live, it must let Gertrud live, too. The responsibility for the destruction of one of us is always responsibility for the destruction of us both.

They say I must complete my work. Indeed, this is of very great concern to Gertrud and me. It is still in its nascent stage, it opens up for me the broadest vistas. Its completion might yet be an essential contribution to German philosophy. But this work is nothing absolute, nothing that can be done automatically. If human will destroys Gertrud without my dying with her—a forced separation would also be like death, a voluntary separation impossible—then my work is also gone: It lives and thrives only out of the substance of our fidelity. A perfidious act would destroy our existence and the substance of the work. . . .

Nov. 21. . . . Is there a situation where, if the one is forced to die, the other is also forced to die because, in such a situation, to die alone would be the most absolute abandonment? Indeed: If, measured against the criterion of human dignity, it is impossible to continue living under the prevailing conditions, then the destruction strikes jointly all those who truly stick together because their union . . . knows no inner reservation.

One cannot demand to go on living under *any* condition: To accept deportation . . . no one can ask that. . . .

We can live only where we are—or we must die. My illness and her age and frail health are barriers.

So much that was noble has been erased, so much soul trampled underfoot. Perhaps the time will come when the suicides of those who do not at all tend toward it ordinarily will increase because people are expected to bear the unbearable. It is impossible for people who value their dignity to want life at any price. . . . We who do not fight with weapons, who cannot give battle, we the powerless, live through conditions which we neither created nor would perpetuate ourselves. We cannot change what happens and what is done by others, but we can die. There is a considerable pathos in being scandalized, in talking big, in demanding, in judging. It is something else again to touch the limits where not-wanting-to-go-on-anymore quietly chooses death.

1942

May 2: If I cannot protect Gertrud against brute force, I, too, have to die—this is simple human dignity.—But that is not decisive and not enough.

My heart speaks quietly and reliably from its depths: I belong to her. It is God's will that if the will of man (and not nature) strikes one of the two of us with destructive force, both are struck together. One cannot separate in life by force those who are bound together for eternity, who are born for each other from one source. . . .

To become one in death is the fulfillment of love—it is like a kindly fate that permits us to die together, while mere nature, when it causes death, forces the survivor to go on living.

My philosophy would be nothing if it were to fail at this decisive point. Somewhere, fidelity is absolute or it is not at all.

Gertrud wants to die a martyr's death for me and for the completion of my philosophy as an accomplishment within the world. But then it would be no longer my, no longer our, philosophy but merely some thought-out stuff. I understand her unspeakable agony if she knows that I am dying with her without any external exigency. Each of us will always want to protect the other's life until the moment when—so I hope—worthy of each other and fundamentally at one—wedded to each other for eternity—we shall die calmly. . . .

August 28: Some people speak about Theresienstadt. They say one can live there, after all. There is something seductive in this talk: namely to remain in the world after all. However, deportation is as good as execution: The life there is life in the imprisonment of a concentration camp. But above all: who can put his trust in such an "old age home"? No messages come from there. Mail is forbidden "for the time being." One is completely at their mercy. Therefore, it is permitted and only worthy of one's humanity in such a hopeless situation to anticipate the death sentence. God does not want every kind of misery: he places man in situations where man is to make an end through his own efforts so that he does not have to sink—in a life of absolute powerlessness—to the point of losing his dignity in his agony. There is such a borderline when suicide is not really suicide any more. The important thing is not to deceive oneself about this borderline out of depression or a death wish. Wherever this border is clearly delineated, man departs this life very reluctantly; for he wants to live and to complete what he is able to, he would like to leave death to fate and not interfere himself. . . .

October 3: . . . The Christian demand, that one may not take one's life under any circumstances, is seductive. This is a thought that permits even the cowardice that wants to stay alive even if the beloved person is ruined by other persons. As if one could then continue, in good conscience, to be in the world and philosophize. God's demand, the prohibition of suicide, is played off against the genuine, historically concrete demand which is really felt to be God's demand and not an abstract law: not to deny oneself, to stand by the most beloved person without reservation.

Suicide, however, committed in order to escape agony and a drawn-out execution, is hardly real suicide but a deed that is forced on one, when the choice is between the courage to suffer death and the courage to endure the most extreme suffering. It cannot be denied that there is an accompanying desire for peace, and even less that there is an accompanying feeling of dignity: namely, not to abandon one's body to any and all torture if one can prevent it. . . .

Bibliography

1. JASPERS'S BOOKS AND MONOGRAPHS

Note: Where there have been several editions of a work, the latest is cited at the end of the entry.

A. IN GERMAN

1. *Allgemeine Psychopathologie: Ein Leifaden fur Studierende, Ärzte und Psychologen.* Berlin: Springer Verlag, 1913.

2. *Allgemeine Psychopathologie.* 2nd rev. ed. Berlin: Springer Verlag, 1920.

3. *Allgemeine Psychopathologie.* 3rd augmented and improved ed. Berlin: Springer Verlag, 1923.

4. *Allgemeine Psychopatholgie.* 4th completely rev. ed. Berlin, Göttingen, Heidelberg: Springer Verlag, 1946. 8th ed., 1965.

5. "Zur Analyse der Trugwahrnehmungen (Leibhaftigkeit und Realitätsurteil)." *Zeitschrift für die gesammte Neurologie und Psychiatrie, Originalien* 6:460–535. (Also published in item 17.)

6. *Aneignung und Polemik: Gesammelte Reden und Aufsätze zur Geschichte der Philosophie.* Edited by Hans Saner. Munich: R. Piper & Co., 1968.

7. *Antwort: Zur Kritik meiner Schrift "Wohin treibt die Bundesrepublik?"* Munich: R. Piper & Co., 1967.

8. *Die Atombombe und die Zukunft des Menschen: Politisches Bewusst sein unserer Zeit.* Munich: R. Piper & Co., 1958. 5th ed., 1962.

9. *Chiffren der Transzendenz.* Edited by Hans Saner. Munich: R. Piper & Co., 1970. 3rd ed., 1977.

10. *Descartes und die Philosophie.* Berlin: W. de Gruyter & Co., 1937. 4th ed., 1966.

11. "Eifersuchtswahn: Ein Beitrag zur Frage: 'Entwicklung einer Persönlichkeit' oder 'Prozess'?" *Zeitschrift für die gesammte Neurologie und Psychiatrie, Originalien* 1:567–637. (Also published in item 17.)

12. *Einführung in die Philosophie: Zwölf Radiovorträge.* Zurich: Artemis Verlag, 1950 and Munich, R. Piper & Co., 1953. 10th ed., Munich, 1965.

13. *Existenzphilosophie: Drei Vorlesungen.* Berlin: W. de Gruyter & Co., 1938. 3rd ed., 1964.

14. *Die Frage der Entmythologisierung* (with contributions by Karl Jaspers and Rudolf Bultmann). Munich: R. Piper & Co., 1954.

15. *Freiheit und Wiedervereinigung.* Munich: R. Piper & Co., 1960. (Also

published in item 22).

16. *Die geistige Situation der Zeit.* Berlin: W. de Gruyter & Co., 1931. 11th ed. 1965.

17. *Gesammelte Schriften zur Psychopathologie.* Berlin, Göttingen, Heidelberg: Springer Verlag, 1963.

18. *Die grossen Philosophen: Erster Band, Die massgebenden Menschen: Sokrates, Buddha, Konfuzius, Jesus; Die fortzeugenden Gründer des Philosophierens: Plato, Augustin, Kant; Aus dem Ursprung denkende Metaphysiker: Anaximander, Heraklit, Parmenides, Plotin, Anselm, Spinoza, Laotse, Nagarjuna.* Munich: R. Piper & Co., 1957. 3rd ed., 1981.

19. *Die grossen Philosophen, Nachlass 1: Darstellungen und Fragmente; Entwerfende Metaphysiker/Weltfromme: Xenophanes, Empedokles, Anaxagoras, Demokrit, Epikur, Lukrez, Poseidonius, Bruno;—/Gnostische Wahrträumer: Origenes, Boehme;—/Konstruktive Köpfe: Hobbes, Leibniz; Die Auflockernden/Bohrende Negative: Descartes;—/Die grossen Erwecker: Pascal, Lessing, Kierkegaard, Nietzsche; Schöpferische Ordner: Aristoteles, Thomas, Hegel; Philosophen in der Dichtung: Dante, Shakespeare; Philosophen in der Forschung: Einstein, Max Weber; Philosophen im politischen Denken: Marx; Philosophen im Bildungswillen: Voltaire, Cicero.* Edited by Hans Saner. Munich, Zurich: R. Piper & Co., 1981.

20. *Die grossen Philosophen, Nachlass 2: Fragmente Anmerkungen Inventar.* Edited by Hans Saner. Munich, Zurich: R. Piper & Co., 1981.

21. "Heimweh und Verbrechen." *Gross' Archiv für krim. Anthropol.* 35, no. 1:1 ff. (Also published in item 17.)

22. *Hoffnung und Sorge: Schriften zur deutschen Politik, 1945–1965.* Munich: R. Piper & Co., 1965.

23. *Die Idee der Universität.* Berlin: Springer Verlag, 1923.

24. *Die Idee der Universität.* (Not the same as item 23) Berlin, Heidelberg: Springer Verlag, 1946.

25. *Die Idee der Universität.* (Not the same as items 23 or 24; written in conjunction with K. Rossmann) Berlin, Göttingen, Heidelberg: Springer Verlag, 1961.

26. *Karl Jaspers K.H. Bauer: Briefwechsel 1945–1968.* Edited by Renato de Rosa. Berlin, Heidelberg, New York: Springer Verlag, 1983.

27. "Kausale und 'verständliche' Zusammenhänge zwischen Schicksal und Psychose bei der Dementia praecox (Schizophrenie)." *Zeitschrift für die gesammte Neurologie und Psychiatrie, Originalien* 14:158–263. (Also published in item 17.)

28. *Kleine Schule des philosophischen Denkens.* Munich: R. Piper & Co., 1965. 3rd ed., 1969.

29. *Lionardo als Philosoph.* Bern: A. Francke A. G., 1953. (Also published in items 6 and 37.)

30. *Max Weber: Politiker-Forscher-Philosoph.* Oldenburg: Stolling, 1932. 3rd ed., Munich: R. Piper & Co., 1958. (Also published in item 6.)

31. "Die Methoden der Intelligenzprüfung und der Begriff der Demenz: Kritisches Referat." *Zeitschrift für die gesammte Neurologie und Psychiatrie, Referate und Ergebnisse* 1:402–52. (Also published in item 17.)

32. *Nietzsche: Einführung in das Verständnis seines Philosophierens.* Berlin: W. de Gruyter & Co., 1936. 3rd ed., 1950.

33. *Nietzsche und das Christentum.* Hameln: Bücherstube Seifert [1946] and Munich: R. Piper & Co., 1952. (Also published in item 6.)

34. *Nikolaus Cusanus.* Munich: R. Piper & Co., 1964.

35. *Notizen zu Martin Heidegger,* Edited by Hans Saner. Munich, Zurich: R. Piper & Co. 1977.

36. *a. Philosophie.* Vol. I, *Philosophische Weltorientierung.*

b. Philosophie. Vol. II, *Existenzerhellung.*

c. Philosophie. Vol. III, *Metaphysik.*

Berlin: Springer Verlag, 1932.

37. *Philosophie.* 3 vols. 3rd ed. with a "Nachwort" in vol. I. Berlin, Göttingen, Heidelberg: Springer Verlag, 1956.

38. *Philosophie und Welt: Reden und Aufsätze.* Munich: R. Piper & Co., 1958. 2nd ed., 1963.

39. "Philosophische Autobiographie." In *Karl Jaspers,* edited by P. A. Schilpp. Stuttgart: Kohlhammer, 1957. (Also published in item 38.)

40. *Philosophische Autobiographie.* augmented ed. [including chapter: "Heidegger"] Munich: R. Piper & Co., 1977.

41. "Der philosophische Glaube angesichts der christlichen Offenbarung." In *Philosophie und christliche Existenz: Festschrift für Heinrich Barth,* ed. G. Huber. Basel, Stuttgart: Verlag Helbing & Lichtenhahn, 1960.

42. *Der philosophische Glaube angesichts der Offenbarung.* Munich: R. Piper & Co., 1962. 3rd ed., 1980.

43. *Der philosophische Glaube: Gastvorlesungen.* Zurich: Artemis Verlag, 1948 and Munich: R. Piper & Co., 1948. 7th ed., Munich: R. Piper & Co., 1981.

44. *Provokationen: Gespräche und Interviews.* Edited by Hans Saner. Munich: R. Piper & Co., 1969.

45. *Psychologie der Weltanschauungen.* Berlin: Springer Verlag, 1919. 5th ed., Berlin, Göttingen, Heidelberg: Springer Verlag, 1960.

46. *Rechenschaft und Ausblick: Reden und Aufsätze.* Munich: R. Piper & Co., 1951. 2nd ed. 1958.

47. *Schelling: Grösse und Verhängnis.* Munich: R. Piper & Co., 1955.

48. *Schicksal und Wille: Autobiographische Schriften.* Edited by Hans Saner. Munich: R. Piper & Co., 1967.

49. *Die Schuldfrage.* Heidelberg: L. Schneider Verlag, 1946 and Zurich:

Artemis Verlag, 1946. (Also published in item 22.)

50. *Strindberg und van Gogh: Versuch einer pathographischen Analyse unter vergleichender Heranziehung von Swedenborg und Hölderlin.* Bern: Bincher, 1922. 3rd ed., Munich: R. Piper & Co., 1951.

51. "Die Trugwahrnehmungen." *Zeitschrift für die gesammte Neurologie und Psychologie, Referate und Ergebnisse* 4:289–354. (Also published in item 17.)

52. *Vernunft und Existenz: Fünf Vorlesungen.* Groningen: J. B. Wolters, 1935. 4th ed., Munich: R. Piper & Co., 1960.

53. *Vernunft und Widervernunft in unserer Zeit: Drei Gastvorlesungen.* Munich: R. Piper & Co., 1950. 2nd ed., 1952.

54. *Vom europäischem Geist.* Munich: R. Piper & Co., 1947. Appeared originally in French translation by J. Hersch. *L'Espirit européen.* Paris: La presse française et. étrangère, O. Zeluck, 1946.

55. *Vom Ursprung und Ziel der Geschichte.* Zurich: Artemis Verlag, 1949 and Munich: R. Piper & Co., 1949. 4th ed., Munich, 1963.

56. *Von der Wahrheit: Philosophische Logik, Erster Band.* Munich: R. Piper & Co., 1947. 3rd ed., 1980.

57. *Weltgeschichte der Philosophie: Einleitung.* Edited by Hans Saner. Munich, Zurich: R. Piper & Co., 1982.

58. *Wohin treibt die Bundesrepublik? Tatsachen-Gefahren-Chancen.* Munich: R. Piper & Co., 1966.

B. IN ENGLISH TRANSLATION

Anaximander, Heraclitus, Parmenides, Plotinus, Lao-tzu, Nagarjuna. New York: Harcourt Brace Jovanovich, n.d. (Excerpt from *The Great Philosophers: The Original Thinkers.*

Anselm and Nicholas of Cusa. New York: Harcourt Brace Jovanovich. n.d. (Excerpt from *The Great Philosophers: The Original Thinkers.*)

The European Spirit. Translated by R. G. Smith. London: SCM Press, 1948 and New York, 1949. (Translation of item 54.)

The Future of Germany. Translated by E. B. Ashton. Chicago, London: University of Chicago Press, 1967. (Translation of parts of items 7 and 58.)

The Future of Mankind. Translated by E. B. Ashton. Chicago: University of Chicago Press, 1961. (Translation of item 8.)

General Psychopathology. Translated by J. Hoening and M. W. Hamilton. Chicago: University of Chicago Press, 1963. (Translation of item 4.)

The Great Philosophers: The Foundations, The Paradigmatic Individuals: Socrates, Buddha, Confucius, Jesus; The Seminal Founders of Philosophical Thought: Plato, Augustine, Kant. Edited by H. Arendt. Translated by R. Manheim. New York: Harcourt, Brace & World, 1962. (Translation of part of item 18.)

The Great Philosophers: The Original Thinkers: Anaximander, Heraclitus. Parmenides, Plotinus, Anselm, Nicholas of Cusa, Spinoza, Lao-Tzu, Nagarjuna. Edited by H. Arendt. Translated by R. Manheim. New York: Harcourt, Brace & World, 1966. (Translation of part of item 18 and of item 34.)

The Idea of the University. Edited by K. W. Deutsch. Translated by H. A. T. Reiche and H. F. Vanderschmidt. Boston: Beacon Press, 1959 and London: P. Owen, 1960. (Translation of item 24.)

Kant. New York: Harcourt, Brace and World, n.d. (Excerpt from *The Great Philosphers: The Foundations.*)

Man in the Modern Age. Translated by E. Paul and C. Paul. London: Routledge & Kegan Paul, 1953; New York: Henry Holt & Co., 1933; and New York: Doubleday & Co., 1957. (Translation of item 16, 5th ed.)

Myth and Christianity. New York: Noonday Press, 1958. (Translation of item 14.)

Nietzsche and Christianity. Translated by E. B. Ashton. Chicago: Henry Regnery Co., 1961. (Translation of item 33.)

Nietzsche: An Introduction to the Understanding of His Philosophical Activity. Translated by C. F. Wallraff and F. J. Schmitz. Tucson: University of Arizona Press, 1965. (Translation of item 32.)

The Origin and Goal of History. Translated by M. Bullock. New Haven: Yale University Press, and London: Routledge and Kegan Paul, 1953. (Translation of item 55.)

The Perennial Scope of Philosophy. Translated by R. Manheim. New York: Philosophical Library, 1949 and London: Routledge & Kegan Paul, 1950. (Translation of item 43.)

Philosophical Faith and Revelation. Translated by E. B. Ashton. Chicago: University of Chicago Press, 1967. (Translation of item 42.)

Philosophy. 3 vols. Translated by E. B. Ashton. Chicago and London: University of Chicago Press, 1969–71. (Translation of item 37.)

Philosophy and The World: Selected Essays and Lectures. Translated by E. B. Ashton. Chicago: Henry Regnery Co., 1963. (Translation of item 38.)

Philosophy is for Everyman: A Short Course in Philosophical Thinking. Translated by R. F. C. Hull and G. Wels. New York: Harcourt, Brace & World, 1967. (Translation of item 28.)

Philosophy of Existence. Translated by R. F. Grabau. Philadelphia: University of Pennsylvania Press, 1971. (Translation of item 13, 3rd ed.)

Plato and Augustine. New York: Harcourt, Brace & World, n.d. (Excerpt from *The Great Philosophers: The Foundations.*)

The Question of German Guilt. Translated by E. B. Ashton. New York: Dial Press, 1947. (Translation of item 49.)

Reason and Anti-Reason in our Time. Translated by S. Goodman. New

Haven: Yale University Press, and London: SCM Press, 1952. (Translation of item 53.)

Reason and Existenz. Translated by W. Earle. London, Toronto, and New York, 1955. (Translation of item 52, 3rd ed.)

Socrates, Buddha, Confucius, Jesus. New York: Harcourt, Brace & World, n.d. (Excerpt from *The Great Philosophers: The Foundations.*)

Spinoza. New York: Harcourt Brace Jovanovich. n.d. (Excerpt from *The Great Philosophers: The Original Thinkers.*)

Strindberg and Van Gogh. Translated by O. Grunow and D. Woloshin Tucson: Univ. of Arizona Press 1977. (Translation of item 50.)

Three Essays: Leonardo, Descartes, Max Weber. Translated by R. Manheim. New York: Harcourt, Brace & World, 1964. (Translation of items 29, 10, and 30, 3rd ed.)

Tragedy is not Enough. Translated by H. A. T. Reiche, H. T. Moore, and K. W. Deutsch. Boston: Beacon Press, 1952 and London: V. Gollancz, 1953. (Translation of excerpt from item 56.)

Truth and Symbol. Translated by J. T. Wilde, W. Kluback, W. Kimmel. New York: Twayne Publishers, and London: Vision Press, 1959. (Translation of excerpt from item 56.)

Way to Wisdom. Translated by R. Manheim. London, Toronto, and New Haven, 1951. (Translation of item 12).

C. CHRONOLOGICAL LIST

1909   "Heimweh und Verbrechen"
1910   "Eifersuchtswahn"
1910   "Die Methoden der Intelligenzprüfung und der Begriff der Demenz"
1911   "Zur Analyse der Trugwahrnehmungen"
1912   "Die Trugwahrnehmungen"
1913   "Kausale und 'verständliche' Zusammenhänge zwischen Schicksal und Psychose bei der Dementia praecox (Schizophrenie)"
1913   *Allgemeine Psychopathologie*
1919   *Psychologie der Weltanschauungen*
1922   *Strindberg und van Gogh*
1923   *Die Idee der Universität*
1931   *Die geistige Situation der Zeit*
1932   *Philosophie* (3 vols.)
1933   *Max Weber: Politiker-Forscher-Philosoph*
1935   *Vernunft und Existenz*
1936   *Nietzsche: Einführung in das Verständnis seines Philosophierens*
1937   *Descartes und die Philosophie*
1938   *Existenzphilosophie*

1946   *Allgemeine Psychopathologie* (4th ed.)
1946   *Die Idee der Universität* (2nd version)
1946   *Nietzsche und das Christentum*
1946   *Die Schuldfrage*
1947   *Vom europäischen Geist*
1947   *Von der Wahrheit*
1948   *Der philosophische Glaube*
1949   *Vom Ursprung und Ziel der Geschichte*
1950   *Einführung in die Philosophie*
1950   *Vernunft und Widervernunft in unserer Zeit*
1951   *Rechenschaft und Ausblick*
1953   *Lionardo als Philosoph*
1954   *Die Frage der Entmythologisierung*
1955   *Schelling: Grösse und Verhängnis*
1957   *Die grossen Philosophen: Erster Band*
1957   "Philosophische Autobiographie"
1958   *Die Atombombe und die Zukunft*
1960   *Freiheit und Wiedervereinigung*
1960   "Der philosophische Glaube angesichts der christlichen Offenbarung"
1961   *Die Idee der Universität* (3rd version; together with K. Rossmann)
1962   *Der philosophische Glaube angesichts der Offenbarung*
1963   *Gesammelte Schriften zur Psychopathologie*
1964   *Nikolaus Cusanus*
1965   *Kleine Schule des philosophischen Denkens*
1965   *Hoffnung und Sorge*
1966   *Wohin treibt die Bundesrepublik?*
1967   *Antwort: Zur Kritik meiner Schrift "Wohin treibt die Bundesrepublik?"*
1967   *Schicksal und Wille*
1968   *Aneignung und Polemik.*
1969   *Provokationen*

Posthumous Publications:

1970   *Chiffren der Transzendenz*
1977   *Philosophische Autobiographie* [with chapter: "Heidegger"]
1978   *Notizen zu Martin Heidegger*
1981   *Die grossen Philosophen, Nachlass 1: Darstellungen und Fragmente*
1981   *Die grossen Philosophen, Nachlass 2: Fragmente Anmerkungen Inventar*
1982   *Weltgeschichte der Philosophie: Einleitung*
1983   *Karl Jaspers K.H. Bauer: Briefwechsel 1945–1968*

2. WRITINGS ABOUT JASPERS

A. MAJOR STUDIES

Allen, Edgar Leonard, *The Self and Its Hazards: A Guide to the Thought of Karl Jaspers.* New York: Philosophical Library, 1951.

Armbruster, Ludwig, *Objekt und Transzendenz bei Jaspers.* Innsbruck: Felizian Rauch, 1957.

Basta, Danilo, *Karl Jaspers, Delo,* xxx/1–2. Belgrade 1984. Special issue on Jaspers with contributions by 12 authors.

Brecht, Franz Joseph, *Heidegger und Jaspers.* Wuppertal: Marées-Verlag, 1948.

Buri, Fritz, *Albert Schweitzer und Karl Jaspers.* Zurich: Artemis-Verlag, 1950.

Caracciolo, Alberto, *Studi Jaspersiani,* Milano: Marzorati 1958.

Collins, James, *The Existentialists. A Critical Study.* Chicago: Regnery, 1952.

Dufrenne, Mikel et Ricoeur, Paul, *Karl Jaspers et la philosophie de l'existence.* Paris: Éditions du Seuil, 1947.

Ehrlich, Leonard H., *Karl Jaspers: Philosophy as Faith.* Amherst: University of Massachusetts Press, 1975.

Feith, Ernst R., *Psychologismus und Transzendentalismus bei Karl Jaspers.* Berne: Buckdruckerei K. Baumann, 1945.

Fischer, Hanns, *Karl Jaspers Trilogy.* New York: Russel F. Moore, 1951.

Gefken, Gisela and Kunert, Karl, *Karl Jaspers: Die Primarbibliographie.* Oldenburg, 1978.

Hersch, Jeanne, *Karl Jaspers: Eine Einführung in sein Werk.* Munich: R. Piper & Co., 1980.

Horn, Hermann, *Philosophischer und Christlicher Glaube erläutert an dem Verständnis Jesu in der Philosophie von Karl Jaspers.* Essen: Neue Deutsche Schule Verlagsgesellschaft, 1961.

Howey, Richard Lowell, *Heidegger and Jaspers on Nietzsche.* The Hague: Nijhoff, 1973.

Jaspers, Ludger, *Der Begriff der menschlichen Situation in der Existenzphilosophie von Karl Jaspers.* Würzburg: Becker, 1936.

Kane, John F., *Pluralism and Truth in Religion: Karl Jaspers on Existentialist Truth.* Chico, CA: Scholars Press, 1981.

Lengert, Rudolf, ed., *Philosophie der Freiheit: Karl Jaspers 1883–1969.* Oldenburg: Heinz Holzberg, 1983. Contributions by 8 authors.

Leonhard, Joachim-Felix, *Karl Jaspers in seiner Heidelberger Zeit.* Heidelberg: Heidelberger Verlagsanstalt, 1983.

Lichtigfeld, Adolph, *Jaspers' Metaphysics.* London: Colibri Press, 1954.

Lohff, Wenzel, *Glaube und Freiheit. Das theologische Problem der Religionskritik von Karl Jaspers*. Gütersloh: C. Bertelsmann-Verlag, 1957.

Long, Eugene Thomas, *Jaspers and Bultmann: A Dialogue Between Philosophy and Theology in the Existentialist Tradition*. Durham, N.C.: Duke University Press, 1968.

Lotz, Johannes B., *Sein und Existenz*. Freiburg, Basel, Vienna: Herder, 1965. (pp. 243–298.)

Mader, Hans, *Problemgeschichtliche Studie zur Periechontologie Karl Jaspers*. Vienna: 1952.

Masi, Giuseppe, *La ricerca della verità in Karl Jaspers*. Bologna: C. Zuffi, 1953.

Olson, Alan M., *Transcendence and Hermeneutics: An Interpretation of Karl Jaspers*. The Hague: Nijhoff, 1979.

Pareyson, Luigi, *Karl Jaspers*, 2nd, augmented ed., Casale Monferrato: Marietti, 1983.

Paumen, Jean, *Raison et existence chez Karl Jaspers*. Brussels: Ed. Parthenon, 1958.

Paumen, Jean and Meyer, Michel, eds., *Karl Jaspers 1883–1983*, special issue of *Revue Internationale de Philosophie*, no. 147. Brussels, 1983. Contains articles by 5 authors and a posthumous article by Jaspers.

Penzo, Giorgio, *Essere e Dio in Karl Jaspers*. Florence, 1972.

Penzo, Giorgio, ed., *Karl Jaspers: Filosofia—Scienza—Teologia*. Brescia: Morcelliana, 1983. Contributions by 18 authors.

Pfeiffer, Johannes, *Existenzphilosophie. Eine Einführung in Heidegger und Jaspers*. Hamburg: Meiner-Verlag, 3rd ed., 1952.

Piper, Klaus, ed., *Karl Jaspers: Werk und Wirkung, Zum 80. Geburtstag von Jaspers*. Munich: Piper-Verlag, 1963.

Piper, Klaus and Saner, Hans, eds., *Erinnerungen an Karl Jaspers*. Munich: R. Piper & Co. 1974. (Contains 34 memoirs of Jaspers.)

Räber, Thomas, *Das Dasein in der 'Philosophie' von Karl Jaspers*. Berne: Francke-Verlag, 1955.

Ramming, G., *Karl Jaspers und Heinrich Rickert: Existentialismus und Wertphilosophie*. Berne: Francke-Verlag, 1948.

Ricci Sindoni, Paola, *I confini del conoscere*. Messina: Giannini 1980.

Ricoeur, Paul, *Gabriel Marcel et Karl Jaspers*. Paris: Éditions du Temps Présent, 1948.

Salamun, Kurt, *Karl Jaspers*. Munich: C. H. Beck, 1985.

Samay, Sebastian, *Reason Revisited*. Notre Dame, Ind.: University of Notre Dame Press, 1971.

Saner, Hans, *Karl Jaspers in Selbstzeugnissen und Bilddokumenten*. Reinbek: Rowohlt, 1970.

Saner, Hans, ed. *Karl Jaspers in der Diskussion*. Munich: R. Piper & Co.,

1973. (Contains reprints of major critical articles about Jaspers from 1914 to 1966 by 26 authors. Also included: a report on Jaspers's literary remains by the editor.)

Schilpp, Paul A., ed., *The Philosophy of Karl Jaspers*, 2nd ed., Lasalle: Open Court, 1981. Contains Jaspers's "Philosophical Autobiography" (including chapter: "Heidegger"), critical contributions by 24 authors, and Jaspers's "Reply to His Critics."

Schrag, Oswald O., *Existence, Existenz, and Transcendence*. Pittsburgh: Duquesne University Press, 1971.

Sperna, Weiland J., *Humanitas Christianitas. A Critical Survey of Kierkegaard's and Jaspers' Thoughts in Connection with Christianity*. Groningen, 1951.

Tilliette, Xavier, *Karl Jaspers. Théorie de la vérité, Métaphysique des chiffres, Foi philosophique*. Paris: Coll. 'Théologie', vol. 44, Aubier, 1959.

Tonquédec (de), Joseph, *L'existence d'après Karl Jaspers*. Paris: Beauchesne, 1945.

Wahl, Jean, *La pensée de l'existence. Kierkegaard-Jaspers*. Paris: Flammarion, 1951.

_____, *La théorie de la verité dans la philosophie de Jaspers* Paris: 'Les Cours de Sorbonne', Tournier et Constans, 1953.

Wallraff, Charles F., *Karl Jaspers: An Introduction to His Philosophy* Princeton: Princeton University Press, 1970.

Welte, Bernhard, "Der philosophische Glaube bei Karl Jaspers und die Möglichkeit seiner Deutung durch die thomistische Philosophie," *Symposion II*, Freiburg: Karl Alber, 1949, pp. 1–190.

Wisser, Richard, *Verantwortung im Wandel der Zeit*. Mainz: v. Hase & Koehler, 1967. (pp. 15–140.)

Young-Bruehl, Elisabeth, *Freedom and Karl Jaspers's Philosophy*. New Haven: Yale University Press, 1981.

B. ARTICLES IN ENGLISH

Arendt, Hannah, "What Is Existenz Philosophy?" *The Partisan Review*, XIII/1, 1946, pp. 34–56. Reprinted in *Men in Dark Times*. New York: Harcourt Brace & World, 1968.

_____, "Karl Jaspers, A Philosopher of Humanity," *Times Literary Supplement*, 3189, April 12, 1963, pp. 241–242.

Beatty, Joseph, "The Scope of Philosophizing in Jaspers," *Journal of the British Society for Phenomenology*, 8, May 1977, pp. 110–118.

Coffin, Peter R., "Philosophical Method and the Existenz Philosophy of Karl Jaspers," *Personalist*, 53, 1972, pp. 141–149.

Collins, James, "An Approach to Karl Jaspers," *Thought* 20, (Dec. 1945), pp. 657–691.

————, "Karl Jaspers' Philosophic Logic," *New Scholasticism*, 23, Oct. 1949, pp. 414–420.

Curran, J.N., "Karl Jaspers (1883–1969): Philosopher and Humanist," *Journal of the British Society for Phenomenology*, 1, Jan. 1970, pp. 81–83.

Dupre, Louis, "Themes in Contemporary Philosophy of Religion," *New Scholasticism*, Fall 1969, pp. 577–601.

Durfee, Harold, "Karl Jaspers' Christology," *Journal of Religion*, 44, April 1964, pp. 133–148.

————, "Karl Jaspers as the Metaphysician of Tolerance," *International Journal for Philosophy of Religion*, 1, Winter 1970, pp. 201–210.

Earle, William, "Jaspers and Existential Analysis," *Journal of Existentialism*, 1, Summer 1960, pp. 166–175.

Ehrlich, Leonard H., "Philosophical Faith and Mysticism," *Bucknell Review*, XVII, 1969, pp. 1–21.

————, "Jaspers and the Great Philosophers," *The Massachusetts Review*," X, 1969, pp. 383–393.

————, "Tillich's 'Symbol' vis-à-vis Jaspers's 'Cipher'," *Harvard Theological Review*, 66, 1973, pp. 153–156.

————, "Truth and Its Unity in Jaspers," *Revue Internationale de Philosophie*, 147, 1983, pp. 423–439.

————, "Jaspers Scholarship in 1983," *Jaspers Society Proceedings*, 6, pp. 1–5.

Gerber. Rudolph J., "Karl Jaspers and Kantian Reason," *New Scholasticism*, 43, Summer 1969, pp. 400–424.

Habermas, Jürgen, "Review of Jaspers' WOHIN TREIBT DIE BUNDESREPUBLIK?" *Atlas*, 12, Summer 1966, pp. 59–62. "Karl Jaspers: The Figures of Truth," in *Philosophical-Political Profiles*, trans. Frederick G. Lawrence, Cambridge: MIT Press, 1983, pp. 45–52.

Hartt, J.H., "God, Transcendence and Freedom in the Philosophy of Karl Jaspers," *Review of Metaphysics*, 4, Dec. 1950, pp. 247–258.

Hossfeld, Paul, "Karl Jaspers and Religion," *Philosophy Today*, 3, Winter 1959, pp. 277–280.

Howe, Leroy T., "Karl Jaspers on History: An Appreciation," *Personalist*, 52, Autumn 1971, pp. 691–716.

Junghy, Carl, "Confucianism and Existentialism: Intersubjectivity as the Way of Man," *Philosophy and Phenomenological Research*, 30, Dec. 1969, pp. 186–202.

Knudsen, Robert D., "Transcendental Motives in Karl Jaspers' Philosophy," *Philosophia Reformata*, 34, 1969, pp. 122–133.

Koenker, Ernest, "God and the Ambiguities of Freedom in the Thought of Karl Jaspers." *Proceedings of the American Catholic Philosophical Association*, 50, 1976, pp. 90–98.

Kornmüller, Hellmuth, "Karl Jaspers' Philosophy of History," *Modern Schoolman*, 42, Jan. 1965, pp. 129–152.

Krell, David Farrell, "Toward SEIN UND ZEIT," *Journal of the British Society for Phenomenology*, 6, Oct. 1975, pp. 147–156.

———, "The Heidegger-Jaspers Relationship," *Journal of the British Society for Phenomenology*, 9, May 1978, pp. 126–129.

Long Eugene T., "Jaspers' Philosophy of Existence as a Model For Theological Reflection," *International Journal for Philosophy of Religion*, 3, Spring 1972, pp. 35–43.

Majors, Troy E., "The Existence-Thought Disjunction," *The Southern Journal of Philosophy*, 8, Spring 1970, pp. 15–23.

Malhotra, M.K., "Karl Jaspers and Indian Philosophy," *Philosophy Today*, 6, Spring 1962, pp. 52–59.

Manasse, Ernst Moritz, "Jaspers' Philosophy of Existence and His Attitude Toward Psychoanalysis," *Journal of Existentialism*, 6, Fall 1965, pp. 59–68.

McInerney, Ralph M., "Metaphysics and Subjectivity: An Approach to Karl Jaspers," *Proceedings of the American Catholic Philosophical Association*, 32, 1958, pp. 172–183.

Michaelides, Constantine, "Plotinus and Jaspers: Their Conception and Contemplation of the Supreme One," *Diotima*, 4, 1976, pp. 37–46.

Olson, A.M., "Jaspers, Heidegger, and 'The Phantom of Existentialism'," *Human Studies*, 7, 1984, pp. 387–395.

Ricci Sindoni, Paola, "Teleology and Philosophical Historiography: Husserl and Jaspers," *Analecta Husserliana*, x., Dortrecht 1979.

Rigali, N.J., "New Axis: Karl Jaspers' Philosophy of History," *International Philosophical Quarterly*, 10, Summer 1970, pp. 441–457.

Riordan, Timothy M., "Karl Jaspers: An Existentialist Looks at University Education," *Educational Theory*, 26, Winter 1976, pp. 113–120.

Sablone, Gentile Maria, "Man Before God in the Philosophy of Karl Jaspers," *Philosophy Today*, 11, Fall 1967, pp. 155–165.

Schacht, Richard L., "On Existentialism, EXISTENZ-Philosophy and Philosophical Anthropology," *American Philosophical Quarterly*, 11, Oct. 1974, pp. 291–305.

Schrag, Oswald O., "Jaspers: Beyond Traditional Metaphysics and Ontology," *International Philosophical Quarterly*, 5, May 1965, pp. 163–182.

Stewart, David, "Paul Ricoeur and the Phenomenological Movement," *Philosophy Today*, 12, Winter 1968, pp. 227–235.

Wallraff, Charles F., "Jaspers in English: A Failure in Communication," *Philosophy and Phenomenological Research* 37 (1977), pp. 537–548.

Weldhen, Margeret, "The Existentialists and Problems of Moral and Religious Education: 2, Tillich and Jaspers," *Journal of Moral Education* 1 (Feb. 1972), pp. 97–101.

Wisser, Richard, "Jaspers, Heidegger, and the Struggle of EXISTENZ-Philosophy for the Existence of Philosophy," *International Philosophical Quarterly* 24 (June 1984), pp. 143–155.

Young-Bruehl, Elizabeth, " 'Cosmopolitan History'," *Revue Internationale de Philosophie*, 147, 1983, pp. 440–459.